Data Modeling
Essentials

Data Modeling Essentials

Third Edition

Graeme C. Simsion and Graham C. Witt

MORGAN KAUFMANN PUBLISHERS

AN IMPRINT OF ELSEVIER

AMSTERDAM   BOSTON   LONDON   NEW YORK
OXFORD   PARIS   SAN DIEGO   SAN FRANCISCO
SINGAPORE   SYDNEY   TOKYO

Publishing Director	Diane Cerra
Senior Editor	Lothlórien Homet
Publishing Services Manager	Simon Crump
Project Manager	Kyle Sarofeen
Editorial Coordinator	Corina Derman
Cover Design	Dick Hannus, Hannus Design Associates
Cover Image	Creatas
Composition	Cepha Imaging Pvt. Ltd.
Copyeditor	Broccoli Information Management
Proofreader	Jacqui Brownstein
Indexer	Broccoli Information Management
Interior printer	Maple-Vail Book Manufacturing Group
Cover printer	Phoenix Color Corp.

Morgan Kaufmann Publishers is an imprint of Elsevier.
500 Sansome Street, Suite 400, San Francisco, CA 94111

This book is printed on acid-free paper.

Library of Congress Cataloging-in-Publication Data
Application submitted.

ISBN-13: 978-0-12-644551-0
ISBN-10: 0-12-644551-6

For information on all Morgan Kaufmann publications,
visit our Web site at www.mkp.com or www.books.elsevier.com

Printed in the United States of America

07 08 09   5 4

*This new edition of Data Modeling Essentials is dedicated
to the memory of our friend and colleague, Robin Wade,
who put the first words on paper for the original edition, and
whose cartoons have illustrated many of our presentations.*

Contents

■ ■ ■ Chapter 2
Basics of Sound Structure **33**

■ ■ ■ Chapter 5
Attributes and Columns 145

■ ■ ■ Chapter 6
Primary Keys and Identity 183

Preface

Early in the first edition of this book, I wrote "*data modeling is not optional*; no database was ever built without at least an implicit model, just as no house was ever built without a plan." This would seem to be a self-evident truth, but I spelled it out explicitly because I had so often been asked by systems developers "what is the value of data modeling?" or "why should we do data modeling at all?".

From time to time, I see that a researcher or practitioner has referenced *Data Modeling Essentials*, and more often than not it is this phrase that they have quoted. In writing the book, I took strong positions on a number of controversial issues, and at the time would probably have preferred that attention was focused on these. But ten years later, the biggest issue in data modeling remains the basic one of recognizing it as a fundamental activity— arguably the single most important activity — in information systems design, and a basic competency for all information systems professionals.

The goal of this book, then, is to help information systems professionals (and for that matter, casual builders of information systems) to acquire that competency in data modeling. It differs from others on the topic in several ways.

First, it is written by and for *practitioners*: it is intended as a practical guide for both specialist data modelers and generalists involved in the design of commercial information systems. The language and diagramming conventions reflect industry practice, as supported by leading modeling tools and database management systems, and the advice takes into account the realities of developing systems in a business setting. It is gratifying to see that this practical focus has not stopped a number of universities and colleges from adopting the book as an undergraduate and postgraduate text: a teaching pack for this edition is available from Morgan Kaufmann at www.mkp.com/companions/0126445516.

Second, it recognizes that data modeling is a *design* activity, with opportunities for choice and creativity. For a given problem there will usually be many possible models that satisfy the business requirements and conform to the rules of sound design. To select the best model, we need to consider a variety of criteria, which will vary in importance from case to case. Throughout the book, the emphasis is on understanding the merits of different solutions, rather than prescribing a single "correct" answer.

Third, it examines the *process* by which data models are developed. Too often, authors assume that once we know the language and basic rules of data modeling, producing a data model will be straightforward. This is like suggesting that if we understand architectural drawing conventions, we can design buildings. In practice, data modelers draw on past experience, adapting models from other applications. They also use rules of thumb, standard patterns, and creative techniques to propose candidate models. These are the skills that distinguish the expert from the novice.

This is the third edition of *Data Modeling Essentials*. Much has changed since the first edition was published: the Internet, object-oriented techniques, data warehouses, business process reengineering, knowledge management, extended relational database management systems, XML, business rules, data quality — all of these were unknown or of little interest to most practitioners in 1992. We have also seen a strong shift toward buying rather than building large applications, and devolution of much of the systems development which remains.

Some of the ideas that were controversial when the first edition was published are now widely accepted, in particular the importance of patterns in data modeling. Others have continued to be contentious: an article in *Database Programming and Design*[1] in which I restated a central premise of this book — that data modeling is a design discipline — attracted record correspondence.

In 1999, I asked my then colleague Graham Witt to work with me on a second edition. Together we reviewed the book, made a number of changes, and developed some new material. We both had a sense, however, that the book really deserved a total reorganization and revision and a change of publisher has provided us with an opportunity to do that. This third edition, then, incorporates a substantial amount of new material, particularly in Part II where the stages of data model development from project planning through requirements analysis to conceptual, logical and physical modeling are addressed in detail.

Moreover, it is a genuine joint effort in which Graham and I have debated every topic — sometimes at great length. Our backgrounds, experiences, and personalities are quite different, so what appears in print has done so only after close scrutiny and vigorous challenges.

Organization

The book is in three parts.
Part I covers the basics of data modeling. It introduces the concepts of data modeling in a sequence that Graham and I have found effective in teaching data modeling to practitioners and students over many years.

---

[1]Simsion, G.C.: "Data Modeling — Testing the Foundations," *Database Programming and Design*, (February 1996.)

Part II is new to this edition. It covers the key steps in developing a complete data model, in the sequence in which they would normally be performed.

Part III covers some more advanced topics. The sequence is designed to minimize the need for "forward references." If you decide to read it out of sequence, you may need to refer to earlier chapters from time to time. We conclude with some suggestions for further reading.

We know that earlier editions have been used by a range of practitioners, teachers, and students with diverse backgrounds. The revised organization should make it easier for these different audiences to locate the material they need.

Every information systems professional — analyst, programmer, technical specialist — should be familiar with the material in Part I. Data is the raw material of information systems and anyone working in the field needs to understand the basic rules for representing and organizing it. Similarly, these early chapters can be used as the basis of an undergraduate course in data modeling or to support a broader course in database design. In fact, we have found that there is sufficient material in Part I to support a postgraduate course in data modeling, particularly if the aim is for the students to develop some facility in the techniques rather than merely learn the rules. Selected chapters from Part II (in particular Chapter 10 on Conceptual Modeling and Chapter 12 on Physical Design) and from Part III can serve as the basis of additional lectures or exercises.

Business analysts and systems analysts actually involved in a data modeling exercise will find most of what they need in Part I, but may wish to delve into Part II to gain a deeper appreciation of the process.

Specialist data modelers, database designers, and database administrators will want to read Parts I and II in their entirety, and at least refer to Part III as necessary. Nonspecialists who find themselves in charge of the data modeling component of a project will need to do the same; even "simple" data models for commercial applications need to be developed in a disciplined way, and can be expected to generate their share of tricky problems.

Finally, the nonprofessional systems developer — the businessperson or private individual developing a spreadsheet or personal database — will benefit from reading at least the first three chapters. Poor representation (coding) and organization of data is probably the single most common and expensive mistake in such systems. Our advice to the "accidental" systems developer would be: "Once you have a basic understanding of your tool, learn the principles of data modeling."

Acknowledgements

Once Graham and I had agreed on the content and shape of the draft manuscript, it received further scrutiny from six reviewers, all recognized authorities in their own right. We are very grateful for the general and specialist input provided by Peter Aiken, James Bean, Chris Date, Rhonda Delmater, Karen Lopez, and Simon Milton. Corine Jansonius and Hu Schroor provided valuable comments on the final manuscript and Dagna Gaythorpe brought her extensive data modeling experience and eye for detail to a full proofread. These criticisms and suggestions made a substantial difference to the final product. Of course, we did not accept every suggestion (indeed, as we would expect, the reviewers did not agree on every point), and accordingly the final responsibility for any errors, omissions or just plain contentious views is ours.

Over the past twelve years, a very large number of other people have contributed to the content and survival of *Data Modeling Essentials*. Changes in the publishing industry have seen the book pass from Van Nostrand Reinhold to International Thompson to Coriolis (who published the second edition) to the present publishers, Morgan Kaufmann. This edition would not have been written without the support and encouragement of Lothlórien Homet and her colleagues at Morgan Kaufmann — in particular Corina Derman, Rick Adams and Kyle Sarofeen.

Despite the substantial changes which we have made, the influence of those who contributed to the first and second editions is still apparent. Chief among these was our colleague Hu Schroor, who reviewed each chapter as it was produced. We also received valuable input from a number of experienced academics and practitioners, in particular Clare Atkins, Geoff Bowles, Mike Barrett, Glenn Cogar, John Giles, Bill Haebich, Sue Huckstepp, Daryl Joyce, Mark Kortink, David Lawson, Daniel Moody, Steve Naughton, Jon Patrick, Geoff Rasmussen, Graeme Shanks, Edward Stow, Paul Taylor, Chris Waddell, and Hugh Williams.

Others contributed in an indirect but equally important way. Peter Fancke introduced me to formal data modeling in the late 1970s, when I was employed as a database administrator at Colonial Mutual Insurance, and provided an environment in which formal methods and innovation were valued. In 1984, I was fortunate enough to work in London with Richard Barker, later author of the excellent *CASE Method Entity-Relationship Modelling* (Addison Wesley). His extensive practical knowledge highlighted to me the missing element in most books on data modeling, and encouraged me to write my own. Graham's most significant mentor, apart from many of those already mentioned, was Harry Ellis, who designed the first CASE tool that Graham used in the mid 1980s (ICL's Analyst Workbench), and who continues to be an innovator in the information modeling world.

Our clients have been a constant source of stimulation, experience, and hard questions; without them we could not have written a genuinely practical book. DAMA (The international Data Management Association) has provided us with many opportunities to discuss data modeling with other practitioners through presentations and workshops at conferences and for individual chapters. We would particularly acknowledge the support of Davida Berger, Deborah Henderson, Tony Shaw of Wilshire Conferences, and Jeremy Hall of IRM UK.

Fiona Tomlinson produced diagrams and camera-ready copy and Sue Coburn organized the text for the first edition. Cathie Lange performed both jobs for the second edition. Ted Gannan and Rochelle Ratnayake of Thomas Nelson Australia, Dianne Littwin, Chris Grisonich, and Risa Cohen of Van Nostrand Reinhold, and Charlotte Carpentier of Coriolis provided encouragement and advice with earlier editions.

Graeme Simsion, May 2004

Part I
The Basics

Chapter 1
What Is Data Modeling?

"Ask not what you do, but what you do it to."
–Bertrand Meyer

1.1 Introduction

This book is about one of the most critical stages in the development of a computerized information system—the design of the data structures and the documentation of that design in a set of *data models*.

In this chapter, we address some fundamental questions:

- What is a data model?
- Why is data modeling so important?
- What makes a good data model?
- Where does data modeling fit in systems development?
- What are the key design stages and deliverables?
- How does data modeling relate to database performance design?
- Who is involved in data modeling?
- What is the impact of new technologies and techniques on data modeling?

This chapter is the first of seven covering the basics of data modeling and forming Part I of the book. After introducing the key concepts and terminology of data modeling, we conclude with an overview of the remaining six chapters.

1.2 A Data-Centered Perspective

We can usefully think of an information system as consisting of a database (containing stored data) together with programs that capture, store, manipulate, and retrieve the data (Figure 1.1).

These programs are designed to implement a **process model (or functional specification)**, specifying the business processes that the system is

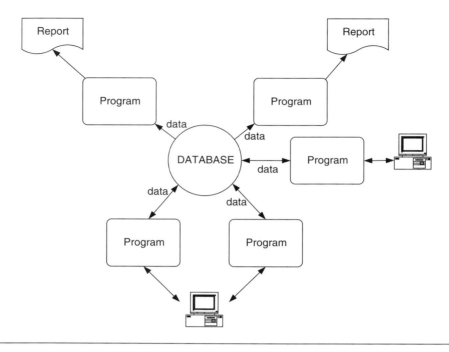

Figure 1.1 An information system.

to perform. In the same way, the database is specified by a **data model,** describing what sort of data will be held and how it will be organized.

1.3 **A Simple Example**

Before going any further, let's look at a simple data model.[1] Figure 1.2 shows some of the data needed to support an insurance system.

We can see a few things straightaway:

- The data is organized into simple **tables.** This is exactly how data is organized in a relational database, and we could give this model to a database administrator as a specification of what to build, just as an architect gives a plan to a builder. We have shown a few rows of data for illustration; in practice the database might contain thousands or millions of rows in the same format.

---

[1]Data models can be presented in many different ways. In this case we have taken the unusual step of including some sample data to illustrate how the resulting database would look. In fact, you can think of this model as a small part of a database.

POLICY TABLE

Policy Number	Date Issued	Policy Type	Customer Number	Commission Rate	Maturity Date
V213748	02/29/1989	E20	HAYES01	12%	02/29/2009
N065987	04/04/1984	E20	WALSH01	12%	04/04/2004
W345798	12/18/1987	WOL	ODEAJ13	8%	06/12/2047
W678649	09/12/1967	WOL	RICHB76	8%	09/12/2006
V986377	11/07/1977	SUI	RICHB76	14%	09/12/2006

CUSTOMER TABLE

Customer Number	Name	Address	Postal Code	Gender	Age	Birth Date
HAYES01	S Hayes	3/1 Collins St	3000	F	25	06/23/1975
WALSH01	H Walsh	2 Allen Road	3065	M	53	04/16/1947
ODEAJ13	J O'Dea	69 Black Street	3145	M	33	06/12/1967
RICHB76	B Rich	181 Kemp Rd	3507	M	59	09/12/1941

Figure 1.2 A simple data model.

■ The data is divided into two tables: one for policy data and one for customer data. Typical data models may specify anything from one to several hundred tables. (Our "simple" method of presentation will quickly become overwhelmingly complex and will need to be supported by a graphical representation that enables readers to find their way around.)

■ There is nothing technical about the model. You do not need to be a database expert or programmer to understand or contribute to the design.

A closer look at the model might suggest some questions:

■ What exactly is a "customer"? Is a customer the person insured or the beneficiary of the policy—or, perhaps, the person who pays the premiums? Could a customer be more than one person, for example, a couple? If so, how would we interpret Age, Gender, and Birth Date?

■ Do we really need to record customers' ages? Would it not be easier to calculate them from Birth Date whenever we needed them?

■ Is the Commission Rate always the same for a given Policy Type? For example, do policies of type E20 always earn 12% commission? If so, we will end up recording the same rate many times. And how would we record the Commission Rate for a new type of policy if we have not yet sold any policies of that type?

■ Customer Number appears to consist of an abbreviated surname, initial, and a two-digit "tie-breaker" to distinguish customers who would otherwise have the same numbers. Is this a good choice?

■ Would it be better to hold customers' initials in a separate column from their family names?

■ "Road" and "Street" have not been abbreviated consistently in the Address column. Should we impose a standard?

Answering questions of this kind is what data modeling is about. In some cases, there is a single, correct approach. Far more often, there will be several options. Asking the right questions (and coming up with the best answers) requires a detailed understanding of the relevant business area, as well as knowledge of data modeling principles and techniques. Professional data modelers therefore work closely with business stakeholders, including the prospective users of the information system, in much the same way that architects work with the owners and prospective inhabitants of the buildings they are designing.

1.4 Design, Choice, and Creativity

The analogy with architecture is particularly appropriate because architects are *designers* and data modeling is also a design activity. In design, we do not expect to find a single correct answer, although we will certainly be able to identify many that are patently incorrect. Two data modelers (or architects) given the same set of requirements may produce quite different solutions.

Data modeling is not just a simple process of "documenting requirements" though it is sometimes portrayed as such. Several factors contribute to the possibility of there being more than one workable model for most practical situations.

First, we have a choice of what symbols or codes we use to represent real-world facts in the database. A person's age could be represented by **Birth Date, Age at Date of Policy Issue,** or even by a code corresponding to a range ("H" could mean "born between 1961 and 1970").

Second, there is usually more than one way to organize (classify) data into tables and columns. In our insurance model, we might, for example, specify separate tables for personal customers and corporate customers, or for accident insurance policies and life insurance policies.

Third, the requirements from which we work in practice are usually incomplete, or at least loose enough to accommodate a variety of different solutions. Again, we have the analogy with architecture. Rather than the client specifying the exact size of each room, which would give the architect little choice, the client provides some broad objectives, and then evaluates the architect's suggestions in terms of how well those suggestions meet the objectives, and in terms of what else they offer.

Fourth, in designing an information system, we have some choice as to which part of the system will handle each business requirement. For example, we might decide to write the rule that policies of type E20 have a commission rate of 12% into the relevant programs rather than holding it as data in the database. Another option is to leave such a rule out of the computerized component of the system altogether and require the user to determine the appropriate value according to some externally specified (manual) procedure. Either of these decisions would affect the data model by altering what data needed to be included in the database.

Finally, and perhaps most importantly, new information systems seldom deliver value simply by automating the current way of doing things. For most organizations, the days of such "easy wins" have long passed. To exploit information technology fully, we generally need to change our business processes and the data required to support them. (There is no evidence to support the oft-stated view that data structures are intrinsically stable in the face of business change).[2] The data modeler becomes a player in helping to design the new way of doing business, rather than merely reflecting the old.

Unfortunately, data modeling is not always recognized as being a design activity. The widespread use of the term "data analysis" as a synonym for data modeling has perhaps contributed to the confusion. The difference between analysis and design is sometimes characterized as one of *description versus prescription*.[3] We tend to think of analysts as being engaged in a search for truth rather than in the generation and evaluation of alternatives. No matter how inventive or creative they may need to be in carrying out the search, the ultimate aim is to arrive at the single correct answer. A classic example is the chemical analyst using a variety of techniques to determine the make-up of a compound.

In simple textbook examples of data modeling, it may well seem that there is only one workable answer (although the experienced modeler will find it an interesting exercise to look for alternatives). In practice, data modelers have a wealth of options available to them and, like architects, cannot rely on simple recipes to produce the best design.

While data modeling is a design discipline, a data model must meet a set of business requirements. Simplistically, we could think of the overall data modeling task as consisting of analysis (of business requirements) followed by design (in response to those requirements). In reality, design usually starts well before we have a complete understanding of requirements, and the evolving data model becomes the focus of the dialogue between business specialist and modeler.

The distinction between analysis and design is particularly pertinent when we discuss creativity. In analysis, creativity suggests interference with the facts. No honest accountant wants to be called "creative." On the other hand, creativity in design is valued highly. In this book, we try to emphasize the choices available at each stage of the data modeling process.

---

[2]Marche, S. (1993): Measuring the stability of data models, *European Journal of Information Systems, 2*(1) 37–47.

[3]Olle, Hagelstein, MacDonald, Rolland, Sol, Van Assche, and Verrijn-Stuart, *Information Systems Methodologies—A Framework for Understanding,* Addison Wesley (1991). This is a rather idealized view; the terms "analysis" and "design" are used inconsistently and sometimes interchangeably in the information systems literature and in practice, and in job titles. "Analysis" is often used to characterize the earlier stages of systems development while "design" refers to the later technology-focused stages. This distinction probably originated in the days in which the objective was to understand and then automate an existing business process rather than to redesign the business process to exploit the technology.

We want you to learn not only to produce sound, workable models (buildings that will not fall down) but to be able to develop and compare different options, and occasionally experience the "aha!" feeling as a flash of insight produces an innovative solution to a problem.

In recognizing the importance of choice and creativity in data modeling, we are not "throwing away the rule book" or suggesting that "anything goes," any more than we would suggest that architects or engineers work without rules or ignore their clients' requirements. On the contrary, creativity in data modeling requires a deep understanding of the client's business, familiarity with a full range of modeling techniques, and rigorous evaluation of candidate models against a variety of criteria.

1.5 Why Is the Data Model Important?

At this point, you may be wondering about the wisdom of devoting a lot of effort to developing the best possible data model. Why should the data model deserve more attention than other system components? When designing programs or report layouts (for example), we generally settle for a design that "does the job" even though we recognize that with more time and effort we might be able to develop a more elegant solution.

There are several reasons for devoting additional effort to data modeling. Together, they constitute a strong argument for treating the data model as the single most important component of an information systems design.

1.5.1 Leverage

The key reason for giving special attention to data organization is *leverage* in the sense that a small change to a data model may have a major impact on the system as a whole. For most commercial information systems, the programs are far more complex and take much longer to specify and construct than the database. But their content and structure are heavily influenced by the database design. Look at Figure 1.1 again. Most of the programs will be dealing with data in the database—storing, updating, deleting, manipulating, printing, and displaying it. Their structure will therefore need to reflect the way the data is organized . . . in other words, the data model.

The impact of data organization on program design has important practical consequences.

First, a well-designed data model can make programming simpler and cheaper. Even a small change to the model may lead to significant savings in total programming cost.

Second, poor data organization can be expensive—sometimes prohibitively expensive—to fix. In the insurance example, imagine that we need to change the rule that each customer can have only one address. The change to the data model may well be reasonably straightforward. Perhaps we will need to add a further two or three address columns to the **Policy** table. With modern database management software, the database can probably be reorganized to reflect the new model without much difficulty. But the real impact is on the rest of the system. Report formats will need to be redesigned to allow for the extra addresses; screens will need to allow input and display of more than one address per customer; programs will need loops to handle a variable number of addresses; and so on. Changing the shape of the database may in itself be straightforward, but the costs come from altering each program that uses the affected part. In contrast, fixing a single incorrect program, even to the point of a complete rewrite, is a (relatively) simple, contained exercise.

Problems with data organization arise not only from failing to meet the initial business requirements but also from changes to the business after the database has been built. A telephone billing database that allows only one customer to be recorded against each call may be correct initially, but be rendered unworkable by changes in billing policy, product range, or telecommunications technology.

The cost of making changes of this kind has often resulted in an entire system being scrapped, or in the business being unable to adopt a planned product or strategy. In other cases, attempts to "work around" the problem have rendered the system clumsy and difficult to maintain, and hastened its obsolescence.

1.5.2 **Conciseness**

A data model is a very powerful tool for expressing information systems requirements and capabilities. Its value lies partly in its *conciseness*. It implicitly defines a whole set of screens, reports, and processes needed to capture, update, retrieve, and delete the specified data. The time required to review a data model is considerably less than that needed to wade through a functional specification amounting to many hundreds of pages. The data modeling process can similarly take us more directly to the heart of the business requirements. In their book *Object Oriented Analysis*,[4] Coad and Yourdon describe the analysis phase of a typical project:

> Over time, the DFD (data flow diagramming or process modeling) team continued to struggle with basic problem domain understanding. In contrast, the Data Base Team gained a strong, in-depth understanding.

---

[4]Coad, P., and Yourdon, E., *Object Oriented Analysis,* Second Edition, Prentice-Hall (1990).

1.5.3 **Data Quality**

The data held in a database is usually a valuable business asset built up over a long period. Inaccurate data (poor **data quality**) reduces the value of the asset and can be expensive or impossible to correct.

Frequently, problems with data quality can be traced to a lack of consistency in (a) defining and interpreting data, and (b) implementing mechanisms to enforce the definitions. In our insurance example, is Birth Date in U.S. or European date format (mm/dd/yyyy or dd/mm/yyyy)? Inconsistent assumptions here by people involved in data capture and retrieval could render a large proportion of the data unreliable. More broadly, we could define **integrity constraints** on Birth Date. For example, it must be a date in a certain format and within a particular range.

The data model thus plays a key role in achieving good data quality by establishing a common understanding of what is to be held in each table and column, and how it is to be interpreted.

1.5.4 **Summary**

The data model is a relatively small part of the total systems specification but has a high impact on the quality and useful life of the system. Time spent producing the best possible design is very likely to be repaid many times over in the future.

1.6 **What Makes a Good Data Model?**

If we are to evaluate alternative data models for the same business scenario, we will need some measures of quality. In the broadest sense, we are asking the question: "How well does this model support a sound overall system design that meets the business requirements?" But we can be a bit more precise than this and identify some general criteria for evaluating and comparing models. We will come back to these again and again as we look at data models and data modeling techniques, and at their suitability in a variety of situations.

1.6.1 **Completeness**

Does the model support all the necessary data? Our insurance model lacks, for example, a column to record a customer's occupation and a table to record premium payments. If such data is required by the system, then these are serious omissions. More subtly, we have noted that we might be unable to register a commission rate if no policies had been sold at that rate.

1.6.2   **Nonredundancy**

Does the model specify a database in which the same fact could be recorded more than once? In the example, we saw that the same commission rate could be held in many rows of the **Policy** table. The Age column would seem to record essentially the same fact as Birth Date, albeit in a different form. If we added another table to record insurance agents, we could end up holding data about people who happened to be both customers and agents in two places. Recording the same data more than once increases the amount of space needed to store the database, requires extra processes (and processing) to keep the various copies in step, and leads to consistency problems if the copies get out of step.

1.6.3   **Enforcement of Business Rules**

How accurately does the model reflect and enforce the rules that apply to the business' data? It may not be obvious at first glance, but our insurance model enforces the rule that each policy can be owned by only one customer, as there is provision for only one Customer Number in each row of the **Policy** table. No user or even programmer of the system will be able to break this rule: there is simply nowhere to record more than one customer against a policy (short of such extreme measures as holding a separate row of data in the **Policy** table for each customer associated with a policy). If this rule correctly reflects the business requirement, the resulting database will be a powerful tool in enforcing correct practice, and in maintaining data quality as discussed in Section 1.5.3. On the other hand, any misrepresentation of business rules in the model may be very difficult to correct later (or to code around).

1.6.4   **Data Reusability**

Will the data stored in the database be reuseable for purposes beyond those anticipated in the process model? Once an organization has captured data to serve a particular requirement, other potential uses and users almost invariably emerge. An insurance company might initially record data about policies to support the billing function. The sales department then wants to use the data to calculate commissions; the marketing department wants demographic information; regulators require statistical summaries. Seldom can all of these needs be predicted in advance.

If data has been organized with one particular application in mind, it is often difficult to use for other purposes. There are few greater frustrations for system users than to have paid for the capture and storage of data, only to be told that it cannot be made available to suit a new information requirement without extensive and costly reorganization.

This requirement is often expressed in terms of its solution: as far as possible, data should be organized independently of any specific application.

1.6.5 **Stability and Flexibility**

How well will the model cope with possible changes to the business requirements? Can any new data required to support such changes be accommodated in existing tables? Alternatively, will simple extensions suffice? Or will we be forced to make major structural changes, with corresponding impact on the rest of the system?

The answers to these questions largely determine how quickly the system can respond to business change, which, in many cases, determines how quickly the business as a whole can respond. The critical factor in getting a new product on the market or responding to a new regulation may well be how quickly the information systems can be adapted. Frequently the reason for redeveloping a system is that the underlying database either no longer accurately represents the business rules or requires costly ongoing maintenance to keep pace with change.

A data model is **stable** in the face of a change to requirements if we do not need to modify it at all. We can sensibly talk of models being more or less stable, depending on the level of change required. A data model is **flexible** if it can be readily extended to accommodate likely new requirements with only minimal impact on the existing structure.

Our insurance model is likely to be more stable in the event of changes to the product range if it uses a generic **Policy** table rather than separate tables (and associated processing, screens, reports, etc.) for each type of policy. New types of policies may then be able to be accommodated in the existing **Policy** table and take advantage of existing programming logic common to all types of policies.

Flexibility depends on the type of change proposed. The insurance model would appear relatively easy to extend if we needed to include details of the agent who sold each policy. We could add an **Agent Number** column to the **Policy** table and set up a new table containing details of all agents, including their Agent Numbers. However, if we wanted to change the database to be able to support up to three customers for each policy, the extension would be less straightforward. We could add columns called Customer Number 2 and Customer Number 3 to the **Policy** table, but, as we shall see in Chapter 2, this is a less than satisfactory solution. Even intuitively, most information systems professionals would find it untidy and likely to disrupt existing program logic. A tidier solution would involve moving the original Customer Number from the **Policy** table and setting up an entirely new table of Policy Numbers and associated Customer Numbers. Doing this would likely require significant changes to the programming logic, screens, and report formats for handling the customers associated with a policy. So our model is flexible in terms of adding agents, but it is less flexible in handling multiple customers for a policy.

1.6.6   **Elegance**

Does the data model provide a reasonably neat and simple classification of the data? If our **Customer** table were to include only insured persons and not beneficiaries, we might need a separate **Beneficiary** table. To avoid recording facts about the same person in both tables, we would need to exclude beneficiaries who were already recorded as customers. Our **Beneficiary** table would then contain "beneficiaries who are not otherwise customers," an inelegant classification that would very likely lead to a clumsy system.

Elegance can be a difficult concept to pin down. But elegant models are typically simple, consistent, and easily described and summarized, for example "This model recognizes that our basic business is purchasing ingredients and transforming them into beer through a number of brewing stages: the major tables hold data about the various raw, intermediate, and final products." Processes and queries that are central to the business can be met in a simple, reasonably obvious way by accessing relatively few tables.

The difference in development cost between systems based on simple, elegant data models and those based on highly complex ones can be considerable indeed. The latter are often the result of incremental business changes over a long period without any rethinking of processes and supporting data. Instead, each change is accompanied by requirements for new data and a corresponding increase in the complexity of the model. In our insurance model, we could imagine a proliferation of tables to accommodate new products and associated persons as the business expanded. Some rethinking might suggest that all of our products fall into a few broad categories, each of which could be supported by a single table. Thus, a simple **Person** table could accommodate all of the beneficiaries, policy-holders, guarantors, assignees, etc.

The huge variation in the development costs for systems to support common applications, such as retail banking or asset management, can often be traced to the presence or absence of this sort of thinking during the data modeling phase of systems design.

1.6.7 **Communication**

How effective is the model in supporting communication among the various stakeholders in the design of a system? Do the tables and columns represent business concepts that the users and business specialists are familiar with and can easily verify? Will programmers interpret the model correctly?

The quality of the final model will depend very much on informed feedback from business people. Programmers, in turn, need to understand the model if they are to use it as intended.

The most common communication problems arise from high levels of complexity, new concepts, and unfamiliar terminology.

A model of twenty or thirty tables will be overwhelmingly complex for most nonspecialists, unless presented in a summary form, preferably using graphics. Larger models may need to be presented at different levels of detail to allow the reader to take a "divide and conquer" approach to understanding.

New concepts—in particular highly generic tables intended to accommodate a wide range of data—may bring stability and elegance to the model, but may be difficult for business specialists and programmers to grasp.

Unfamiliar terminology is frequently the result of the data modeler striving to be rigorous and consistent in constructing table and column names, rather than using terms that are familiar to the business but ambiguous or dependent on context.

1.6.8 **Integration**

How will the proposed database fit with the organization's existing and future databases? Even when individual databases are well designed, it is common for the same data to appear in more than one database and for problems to arise in drawing together data from multiple databases. How many other databases hold similar data about our customers or insurance agents? Are the coding schemes and definitions consistent? How easy is it to keep the different versions in step, or to assemble a complete picture?

Many organizations address problems of this kind by establishing an organization-wide architecture specifying how individual information systems should work together to achieve the best overall result. Developing a data model in the context of such an architecture may involve building onto existing data structures, accepting a common view on how data should be organized, and complying with organizational standards for data definitions, formats, and names.

1.6.9 **Conflicting Objectives**

In many cases, the above aims will conflict with one another. An elegant but radical solution may be difficult to communicate to conservative users. We may be so attracted to an elegant model that we exclude requirements that do not fit. A model that accurately enforces a large number of business rules will be unstable if some of those rules change. And a model that is easy to understand because it reflects the perspectives of the immediate system users may not support reusability or integrate well with other databases.

Our overall goal is to develop a model that provides the best balance among these possibly conflicting objectives. As in other design disciplines, achieving this is a process of proposal and evaluation, rather than a step-by-step progression to the ideal solution. We may not realize that a better solution or trade-off is possible until we see it.

1.7 **Performance**

You may have noticed an important omission from our list of quality criteria in the previous section: performance. Certainly, the system user will not be satisfied if our complete, nonredundant, flexible, and elegant database cannot meet throughput and response-time requirements. However, performance differs from our other criteria because it depends heavily on the software and hardware platforms on which the database will run. Exploiting their capabilities is a technical task, quite different from the more business-focused modeling activities that we have discussed so far. The usual (and recommended) procedure is to develop the data model without considering performance, then to attempt to implement it with the available hardware and software. Only if it is not possible to achieve adequate performance in this way do we consider modifying the model itself.

In effect, performance requirements are usually "added to the mix" at a later stage than the other criteria, and then only when necessary. The next section provides an overview of how this is done.

1.8 **Database Design Stages and Deliverables**

Figure 1.3 shows the key tasks and deliverables in the overall task of database design, of which data modeling is a part. Note that this diagram is a deliberate over-simplification of what is involved; each task shown is inevitably iterative, involving at least one cycle of review and modification.

1.8.1 **Conceptual, Logical, and Physical Data Models**

From Figure 1.3, you can see that there are three different data models produced as we progress from business requirements to a complete database

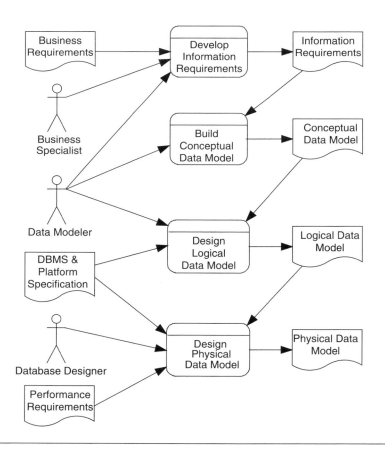

Figure 1.3 Overview of database design tasks and deliverables.

specification. The **conceptual data model** is a (relatively)[5] technology-independent specification of the data to be held in the database. It is the focus of communication between the data modeler and business stakeholders, and it is usually presented as a diagram with supporting documentation. The **logical data model** is a translation of the conceptual model into structures that can be implemented using a **database management system (DBMS).** Today, that usually means that this model specifies tables and columns, as we saw in our first example. These are the basic building blocks of relational databases, which are implemented using a **relational database management system (RDBMS).** The **physical data model** incorporates any changes necessary to achieve adequate performance and is also presented in terms of tables and columns, together with a specification of physical storage (which may include data distribution) and access mechanisms.

Different methodologies differ on the exact level of detail that should be included in each model and at what point certain decisions should be taken. In some methodologies, the translation from conceptual to logical is completely mechanical; in others, including our recommended approach, there are some decisions to be made. The step from logical to physical may be straightforward with no changes to tables and columns, if performance is not a problem, or it may be highly complex and time-consuming, if it becomes necessary to trade performance against other data model quality criteria.

Part 2 of this book is largely about how to produce these three models.

1.8.2 The Three-Schema Architecture and Terminology

Figure 1.4 shows an important feature of the organization of a modern relational database. The three-layer (or **three-schema**) architecture supported by popular DBMSs achieves two important things:

1. It insulates programmers and end-users of the database from the way that data is physically stored in the computer(s).
2. It enables different users of the data to see only the subset of data relevant to them, organized to suit their particular needs.

The three-schema architecture was formally defined by the ANSI/SPARC standards group in the mid-1970s.[6]

---

[5]We say "relatively" because the language that we use for the conceptual model has grown from the common structures and capabilities supported by past and present database technology. However, the conceptual model should certainly not reflect the capabilities of individual products within that very broad class.

[6]Brodie and Schmidt (1982): Final Report of the ANSI/X3/SPARC Study Group on Database Management Systems, *ACM SIGMOD Record* 12(4) and Interim Report (1975), ACM *SIGMOD Bulletin*: 7(2).

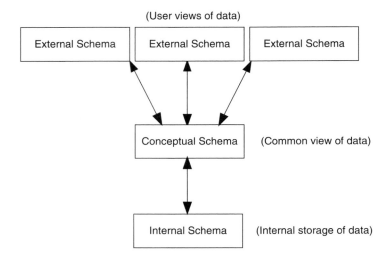

Figure 1.4 Three-schema architecture.

The **conceptual schema** describes the organization of the data into tables and columns, as in our insurance example.

The **internal schema** describes how the data will be physically stored and accessed, using the facilities provided by a particular DBMS. For example, the data might be organized so that all the insurance policies belonging to a given customer were stored close together, allowing them all to be retrieved into the computer's memory in a single operation. An index might be provided to enable rapid location of customers by name. We can think of the physical database design as the inside of a black box, or the engine under the hood. (To pursue the architecture analogy, it represents the foundations, electrical wiring, and hidden plumbing; the owner will want only to know that the house will be sound and that the lights and faucets will work.)

The **external schemas** specify **views** that enable different users of the data to see it in different ways. As a simple example, some users of policy data might not require details of the commission paid. By providing them with a view that excludes the **Commission Rate** column, we would not only shield them from unwanted (and perhaps unauthorized) information, but also insulate them from changes that might be made to the format of that data. We can also combine tables in various ways. For example, we could add data from the relevant customer to each row of the **Policy** table.[7] It is usual to provide one external schema that covers the entire conceptual

---

[7]The ways in which views can be constructed and the associated constraints (e.g., whether data in a view constructed using particular operators can be updated) are beyond the scope of this book. Some suitable references are suggested at the end of this book under "Further Reading."

schema, and then to provide a number of external schemas that meet specific user requirements.

It is worth reemphasizing the role of the three-schema architecture in insulating users from change that is not relevant to them. The separation of the conceptual schema from the internal schema insulates users from a range of changes to the physical organization of data. The separation of the external schema from the full conceptual schema can insulate users from changes to tables and columns not relevant to them. Insulation of this kind is a key feature of DBMSs and is called **data independence.**

The formal terminology of conceptual, external, and internal schemas is not widely used in practice, particularly by database designers and administrators, who tend to think of the database in terms of the way it is described in the **data definition language (DDL)**[8] of the particular DBMS:

1. The total database design (all three schemas) is usually referred to as the **database design** (reasonably enough) or sometimes the **physical database design,** the latter term emphasizing that it is the actual implemented design, rather than some earlier version, that is being described. It is more common to use this collective term than to single out the individual schemas.

2. Each external schema is generally referred to in terms of the views it contains. Hence the term "view" is more widely used than the collective term "external schema."

3. The conceptual schema is sometimes referred to as the **logical schema** or **logical database design.** There is room for confusion here since, as we saw in Section 1.8.1, the terms "conceptual" and "logical" are used to describe different data models. To distinguish the conceptual schema from the views constituting an external schema the term **base tables** can be used to describe the tables that make up the conceptual schema.

4. There is no widely used alternative term for the internal schema. This is perhaps because, in the data definition language used by relational DBMSs, the details of storage and access mechanisms are typically specified on a table-by-table basis rather than being grouped together in a single place. If the need to refer to the internal schema does arise (typically in the context of defining the respective roles of the data modeler and database designer), most practitioners would use the terms "indexing and storage structures" (or something similar) and generally convey the message successfully.

The practitioner terminology presents plenty of opportunity for confusion with the names for the various stages of data model development discussed in the previous section. It may assist to remember that the different data

---

[8]In the relational database world, DDL is the subset of SQL (the standard relational database language) used to define the data structures and constraints and Data Manipulation Language (DML) is the subset used to retrieve and update data.

models are the outputs of various stages in the overall data modeling task, while the three-schema architecture describes the various layers of a particular database.

In our experience, the most serious problem with terminology is that its ambiguity frequently reflects a lack of clarity in methodology, roles, and deliverables. In particular, it may effectively license a database technician to make changes to tables and columns without the involvement of the data modeler. We cannot emphasize too strongly that the conceptual schema should be a direct implementation of the tables specified in the physical data model—a final, negotiated, deliverable of the data modeling process.

1.9 Where Do Data Models Fit In?

It should be fairly clear by now that data modeling is an essential task in developing a database. Any sound methodology for developing information systems that require stored data will therefore include a data-modeling phase. The main difference between the various mainstream methodologies is whether the data model is produced before, after, or in parallel with the process model.

1.9.1 Process-Driven Approaches

Traditional "process-driven" or "data-flow-driven" approaches focus on the process model.[9] This is hardly surprising. We naturally tend to think of systems in terms of what they *do*. We first identify all of the processes and the data that each requires. The data modeler then designs a data model to support this fairly precise set of data requirements, typically using "mechanical" techniques such as normalization (the subject of Chapter 2). Some methodologies say no more about data modeling. If you are using a process-driven approach, we strongly advise treating the initial data model as a "first cut" only, and reviewing it in the light of the evaluation criteria outlined in Section 1.6. This may result in alterations to the model and subsequent amendments to the process model to bring it into line.

1.9.2 Data-Driven Approaches

"Data-driven" approaches—most notably Information Engineering (IE)[10]— appeared in the late 1970s; they have since generally evolved into parallel or "blended" methodologies, as described in the following section.

---

[9]See, for example, De Marco, T., *Structured Analysis and Systems Specification*, Yourdon Inc. (1978).
[10]Usually associated with Clive Finkelstein and James Martin.

The emphasis was on developing the data model *before* the detailed process model in order to achieve the following:

- Promote reusability of data. We aim to organize the data independently of the process model on the basis that the processes it describes are merely the *initial* set that will access the data. The process model then becomes the first test of the data model's ability to support a variety of processes.
- Establish a consistent set of names and definitions for data. If we develop the process model prior to the data model, we will end up *implicitly* defining the data concepts. A process called "Assign salesperson to customer" implies that we will hold data about salespersons and customers. But a second process "Record details of new client" raises the question (if we are alert): "What is the difference between a client and a customer?" Designing the data model prior to the detailed process model establishes a language for classifying data and largely eliminates problems of this kind.
- "Mechanically" generate a significant part of the process model. Just by looking at the insurance data model, we can anticipate that we will need programs to (for example):

  - Store details of a new policy
  - Update policy details
  - Delete policy details
  - Report on selected policy details
  - List all policies belonging to a nominated customer
  - Store details of a new customer.

We do not need to know anything about insurance to at least suggest these processes. In defining the data we intend to store, we have implicitly (and very concisely) identified a whole set of processes to capture, display, update, and delete that data. Some **Computer Aided Software Engineering** (**CASE**) tools make heavy use of the data model to generate programs, screens, and reports.

- Provide a very concise overview of the system's scope. As discussed above, we can infer a substantial set of processes just by looking at the data structures. Not all of these will necessarily be implemented, but we can at least envision specifying them and having them built without too much fuss. Conversely, we can readily see that certain processes will *not* be supportable for the simple reason that the necessary data has not been specified. More subtly, we can see what business rules are supported by the model, and we can assess whether these will unduly constrain the system. The data model is thus an excellent vehicle for describing the boundaries of the system, far more so than the often overwhelmingly large process model.

1.9.3 **Parallel (Blended) Approaches**

Having grasped this theoretical distinction between process-driven and data-driven approaches, do not expect to encounter a pure version of either in practice. It is virtually impossible to do data modeling without some investigation of processes or to develop a process model without considering data. At the very least, this means that process modelers and data modelers need to communicate regularly. Indeed, they may well be the same person or multiskilled members of a team charged with both tasks.

The interdependence of data and process modeling is now recognized by many of the most popular methodologies and CASE products, which require that the models are developed in parallel. For example, an early set of deliverables might include high-level process and data models to specify the scope of the computerized application; while further along in the life-cycle, we might produce logical models specifying process and data requirements without taking into account performance issues.

1.9.4 **Object-Oriented Approaches**

Since the mid-1990s, we have seen increasing use of object-oriented approaches to system specification and development, and, for a while, it seemed (at least to some) that these would largely displace conventional "data-centric" development.

It is beyond the scope of this book to discuss object-oriented approaches in detail, or to compare them with conventional approaches. From the perspective of the data modeler, the key points are:

■ Many information systems remain intrinsically "data-centric"—containing large volumes of consistently structured data. Experience has shown that the basic principles of good data modeling remain relevant, regardless of whether an object-oriented or conventional approach is taken to their development. In short, if you are an object modeler working on a data-centric business application, you should still read this book!

■ True object-oriented DBMSs are not widely used. In the overwhelming majority of cases, data associated with object-oriented applications is stored in a conventional or extended relational database, which should be specified by a conventional data model.

■ Unified Modeling Language[11] (UML) has become popular as a diagramming standard for both conventional models and object models. The UML option is discussed as an alternative to the more traditional standards in Chapter 7.

---

[11]Rumbaugh, Jacobson, and Booch (1998): *The Unified Modeling Language Reference Manual,* Addison Wesley.

1.9.5 **Prototyping Approaches**

Rapid Applications Development (RAD) approaches have, in many quarters, displaced the traditional **waterfall**[12] approaches to systems development. Rather than spend a long time developing a detailed paper specification, the designer adopts a "cut and try" approach: quickly build a prototype, show it to the client, modify it in the light of comments, show it to the client again, and so forth. Our experiences with prototyping have been mixed, but they bear out what other experienced designers have observed: *even when prototyping you need to design a good data model early in the project*. It comes back to the very high impact of a change to the data model in comparison with the relatively low cost of changing a program. Once prototyping is under way, nobody wants to change the model. So designers using a prototyping approach need to adopt what is effectively a data-driven approach.

1.9.6 **Agile Methods**

Agile methods can be seen as a backlash against "heavy" methodologies, which are characterized as bureaucratic, unresponsive to change, and generating large quantities of documentation of dubious value.[13]

In valuing working software over documentation, they owe something to prototyping approaches, and the same caution applies: a good data model developed early in the project can save much pain later. However the data model is communicated—as formal documentation, by word of mouth, or through working software—a shared understanding of data structures, meaning, and coding remains vital. We suggest that if you only document one aspect of the design, you document the data model.

1.10 **Who Should Be Involved in Data Modeling?**

In Part 2, we look more closely at the *process* of developing a data model within the context of the various approaches outlined in the previous section.

---

[12]So-called because there is no going back. Once a step is completed, we move on to the next, with no intention of doing that step again. In contrast, an *iterative* approach allows for several passes through the cycle, refining the deliverables each time.

[13]See, for example, Ambler, S. and Jeffries, R (2002): *Agile Modeling: Effective Practices for Extreme Programming and the Unified Process,* John Wiley & Sons; and The Agile Manifesto, 2001 at www.agilemanifesto.org.

At this stage, let us just note that at least the following people have a stake in the model and should expect to be involved in its development or review:

The **system users, owners,** and/or **sponsors** will need to verify that the model meets their requirements. Our ultimate aim is to produce a model that contributes to the most cost-effective solution for the business, and the users' *informed* agreement is an important part of ensuring that this is achieved.

Business specialists (sometimes called **subject matter experts** or **SMEs**) may be called upon to verify the accuracy and stability of business rules incorporated in the model, even though they themselves may not have any immediate interest in the system. For example, we might involve strategic planners to assess the likelihood of various changes to the organization's product range.

The **data modeler** has overall responsibility for developing the model and ensuring that other stakeholders are fully aware of its implications for them: "Do you realize that any change to your rule that each policy is associated with only one customer will be very expensive to implement later?"

Process modelers and program designers will need to specify programs to run against the database. They will want to verify that the data model supports all the required processes without requiring unnecessarily complex or sophisticated programming. In doing so, they will need to gain an understanding of the model to ensure that they use it correctly.

The **physical database designer** (often an additional role given to the **database administrator**) will need to assess whether the physical data model needs to differ substantially from the logical data model to achieve adequate performance, and, if so, propose and negotiate such changes. This person (or persons) will need to have an in-depth knowledge of the capabilities of the chosen DBMS.

The **systems integration manager** (or other person with that responsibility, possibly an enterprise architect, data administrator, information systems planner, or chief information officer) will be interested in how the new database will fit into the bigger picture: are there overlaps with other databases; does the coding of data follow organizational or external standards; have other users of the data been considered; are names and documentation in line with standards? In encouraging consistency, sharing, and reuse of data, the integration manager represents business needs beyond the immediate project.

Organizing the modeling task to ensure that the necessary expertise is available, and that the views of all stakeholders are properly taken into account, is one of the major challenges of data modeling.

1.11 Is Data Modeling Still Relevant?

Data modeling emerged in the late 1960s, in line with the commercial use of DBMSs, and the basic concepts as used in practice have changed remarkably little since then. However, we have seen major changes in information technology and in the way that organizations use it. In the face of such changes, is data modeling still relevant?

Whether as a result of asking this question or not, many organizations have reduced their commitment to data modeling, most visibly through providing fewer jobs for professional data modelers. Before proceeding, then, we look at the challenges to the relevance of data modeling (and data modelers).

1.11.1   **Costs and Benefits of Data Modeling**

We are frequently asked by project leaders and managers: "What are the benefits of data modeling?" or, conversely, "How much does data modeling add to the cost of a system?"

The simple answer is that *data modeling is not optional*; no database was ever built without a model, just as no house was ever built without a plan. In some cases the plan or model is not documented; but just as an architect can draw the plan of a building already constructed, a data modeler can examine an existing database and derive the underlying data model. The choice is not whether or not to model, but (a) whether to do it formally, (b) whom to involve, and (c) how much effort to devote to producing a good design. If these issues are not explicitly addressed, the decisions are likely to be, respectively, "no," "a database technician," and "not enough."

A formal data-modeling phase, undertaken by skilled modelers, should reduce the costs of database development (through the greater efficiency of competent people), and of the overall system (through the leverage effect of a good quality model). Unfortunately the question about cost is sometimes prompted by past problems with data modeling. In our experience, the two most common complaints are excessive, unproductive time spent in modeling, and clashes between data modelers and physical database designers. Overly long exercises are sometimes due to lack of familiarity with data modeling principles and standard approaches to problems. Surprisingly often, modeling is brought to a standstill by arguments as to which of two or more candidate models is correct—the "one-right-answer" syndrome. Arguments between data modelers and physical database designers often reflect misunderstandings about roles and a lack of hard data about the extent to which the logical data model needs to be changed to achieve performance goals. Finally, some data modeling problems are just plain difficult and may take some time to sort out. But we will not solve them any more easily by leaving them to the database technicians.

It is certainly possible for data modeling to cost too much, just as any activity that is performed incorrectly or not properly managed can cost too much. The solution, however, is to address the causes of the problem, rather than abdicating the job to people whose expertise is in other fields.

1.11.2 **Data Modeling and Packaged Software**

In the early days of information technology, information systems—even for such common applications as payroll and accounting—were generally developed in-house, and most large organizations employed teams of systems developers. As DBMSs became more prevalent, development teams would often include or call upon specialist data modelers. Good data modeling was essential, even if its importance was not always recognized.

That picture has changed substantially, with many organizations adopting a policy of "buy not build" as packaged software is now available for a wide range of applications. Packaged software arrives with its data structures largely predefined, and the information systems practitioner focuses largely on tailoring functionality and helping the organization to adopt the new ways of working.

What is the role of data modeling in a world increasingly dominated by packaged software?

Obviously, the original development of packaged software requires data modeling of a very high standard. Such software needs to be comprehensive and adaptable to suit the differing needs of the vendors' clients. As we have discussed, flexibility starts with the data model.

In organizations using packaged software, rather than producing their own, there is still important work for data modelers, beginning at the selection phase.

The selection of a suitable package needs to be based on an understanding of the organization's requirements. These will need to be formally documented to ensure that they are agreed and can be supported, and possibly to enable alternative candidate solutions to be compared. A data model is an essential component of such a statement of requirements, and the data modeler faces the challenge of being comprehensive without restricting creativity or innovation on the part of the vendor or vendors. This is an important example of the importance of recognizing choice in data modeling. Too often, we have seen data modelers develop the "one right model" for an application and look for the product that most closely matches it, overlooking the fact that a vendor may have come up with a different but no less effective solution.

Once we are in a position to look at candidate packages, one of the most useful ways of getting a quick, yet quite deep understanding of their designs and capabilities is to examine the underlying data models. An experienced data modeler should be able to ascertain fairly rapidly the most important data structures and business rules supported by each model, and whether the business can work effectively within them. This does presuppose that vendors are able and willing to provide models. The situation seems to have improved in recent years, perhaps because vendors now more frequently have a properly documented model to show.

After the package is purchased, we may still have considerable say as to how individual tables and attributes are defined and used. In particular, some of the Enterprise Resource Planning (ERP) packages, which aim to cover a substantial proportion of an organization's information processing, deliberately offer a wealth of options for configuration. There is plenty of room for expensive errors here and thus plenty of room for data modelers to ensure that good practices are followed.

If modifications and extensions are to be made to the functionality of the package, the data modeler will be concerned to ensure that the database is used as intended.

1.11.3   **Data Integration**

Poor data integration remains a major issue for most organizations. The use of packages often exacerbates the problem, as different vendors organize and define data in different ways. Even ERP packages, which may be internally well integrated, will usually need to share data with or pass data to peripheral applications. Uncontrolled data duplication will incur storage and update costs. To address these issues, data models for each application may need to be maintained, and a large-scale enterprise data model may be developed to provide an overall picture or plan for integration. It needs to be said that, despite many attempts, few organizations have succeeded in using enterprise data models to achieve a good level of data integration, and, as a result, enterprise data modeling is not as widely practiced as it once was. We look at this issue in more depth in Chapter 17.

1.11.4   **Data Warehouses**

A **data warehouse** is a specialized database that draws together data from a variety of existing databases to support management information needs. Since the early 1990s, data warehouses have been widely implemented. They generally need to be purpose-built to accommodate each organization's particular set of "legacy" databases.

The data model for a warehouse will usually need to support high volumes of data subject to complex ad hoc queries, and accommodate data formats and definitions inherited from independently designed packages and legacy systems. This is challenging work for any data modeler and merits a full chapter in this book (Chapter 16).

1.11.5 **Personal Computing and User-Developed Systems**

Today's professionals or knowledge workers use PCs as essential "tools of trade" and frequently have access to a DBMS such as Microsoft Access™. Though an organization's core systems may be supported by packaged software, substantial resources may still be devoted to systems development by such individuals. Owning a sophisticated tool is not the same thing as being able to use it effectively, and much time and effort is wasted by amateurs attempting to build applications without an understanding of basic design principles.

The discussion about the importance of data models earlier in this chapter should have convinced you that the single most important thing for an application designer to get right is the data model. A basic understanding of data modeling makes an enormous difference to the quality of the results that an inexperienced designer can achieve. Alternatively, the most critical place to get help from a professional is in the data-modeling phase of the project. Organizations that encourage (or allow) end-user development of applications would do well to provide specialist data modeling training and/or consultancy as a relatively inexpensive and nonintrusive way of improving the quality of those applications.

1.11.6 **Data Modeling and XML**

XML (Extensible Markup Language) was developed as a format for *presenting* data, particularly in web pages, its principal value being that it provided information about the meaning of the data in the same way that HTML provides information about presentation format. The same benefits have led to its wide adoption as a format for the *transfer* of data between applications and enterprises, and to the development of a variety of tools to generate XML and process data in XML format.

XML's success in these roles has led to its use as a format for data *storage* as an alternative to the relational model of storage used in RDBMSs and, by extension, as a modeling language. At this stage, the key message is that, whatever its other strengths and weaknesses, XML does not remove the need to properly understand data requirements and to design sound, well-documented data structures to support them. As with object-oriented approaches, the format and language may differ, but the essentials of data modeling remain the same.

1.11.7 **Summary**

The role of the data modeler in many organizations has changed. But as long as we need to deal with substantial volumes of structured data, we need to know how to organize it and need to understand the implications of the choices that we make in doing so. That is essentially what data modeling is about.

1.12 **Alternative Approaches to Data Modeling**

One of the challenges of writing a book on data modeling is to decide which of the published data modeling "languages" and associated conventions to use, in particular for diagrammatic representation of conceptual models.

There are many options and continued debate about their relative merits. Indeed, much of the academic literature on data modeling is devoted to exploring different languages and conventions and proposing DBMS architectures to support them. We have our own views, but in writing for practitioners who need to be familiar with the most common conventions, our choice is narrowed to two options:

1. One core set of conventions, generally referred to as the **Entity Relationship**[14] (E-R) approach, with ancestry going back to the late 1960s,[15] was overwhelmingly dominant until the late 1990s. Not everyone uses the same "dialect," but the differences between practitioners are relatively minor.

2. Since the late 1990s, an alternative set of conventions—the **Unified Modeling Language** (UML), which we noted in Section 1.9.4—has gained in popularity.

The overwhelming majority of practicing modelers know and use one or both of these languages. Similarly, tools to support data modeling almost invariably use E-R or UML conventions.

UML is the "richer" language. It provides conventions for recording a wide range of conventional and object-oriented analysis and design deliverables, including data models represented by **class diagrams.** Class diagrams are able to capture a greater variety of data structures and rules than E-R diagrams.

However, this complexity incurs a substantial penalty in difficulty of use and understanding, and we have seen even very experienced practitioners misusing the additional language constructs. Also some of the rules and structures that UML is able to capture are not readily implemented with current relational DBMSs.

---

[14]Chen, P, P (1976): The Entity-Relationship Model—Towards a Unified View of Data, ACM Transactions on Database Systems (1,1) March, pp. 9–36.
[15]Bachman, C (1969): Data Structure Diagrams, Bulletin of ACM SIGFIDET 1(2).

We discuss the relative merits of UML and E-R in more detail in Chapter 7. Our decision to use (primarily) the E-R conventions in this book was the result of considerable discussion, which took into account the growing popularity of UML. Our key consideration was the desire to focus on what we believe are the most challenging parts of data modeling: understanding user requirements and designing appropriate data structures to meet them. As we reviewed the material that we wanted to cover, we noted that the use of a more sophisticated language would make a difference in only a very few cases and could well distract those readers who needed to devote a substantial part of their efforts to learning it.

However, if you are using UML, you should have little difficulty adapting the principles and techniques that we describe. In a few cases where the translation is not straightforward—usually because UML offers a feature not provided by E-R—we have highlighted the difference.

At the time of writing, we are planning to publish all of the diagrams in this book in UML format on the Morgan Kaufmann website at www.mkp.com/?isbn=0126445516.

As practicing data modelers, we are sometimes frustrated by the shortcomings of the relatively simple E-R conventions (for which UML does not always provide a solution). In Chapter 7, we look at some of the more interesting alternatives, first because you may encounter them in practice (or more likely in reading more widely about data modeling), and second because they will give you a better appreciation of the strengths and weaknesses of the more conventional methods. However, our principal aim in this book is to help you to get the best results from the tools that you are most likely to have available.

1.13 Terminology

In data modeling, as in all too many other fields, academics and practitioners have developed their own terminologies and do not always employ them consistently.

We have already seen an example in the names for the different components of a database specification. The terminology that we use for the data models produced at different stages of the design process—*viz* conceptual, logical, and physical models—is widely used by practitioners, but, as noted earlier, there is some variation in how each is defined. In some contexts (though not in this book), no distinction may be made between the conceptual and logical models, and the terms may be used interchangeably.

Finally, you should be aware of two quite different uses of the term **data model** itself. Practitioners use it, as we have in this chapter, to refer to a representation of the data required to support a particular process or set of processes. Some academics use "data model" to describe a particular way of representing data: for example, in tables, hierarchically, or as a network. Hence, they talk of the "Relational Model" (tables), the "Object-Role Model," or the "Network Model."[16] Be aware of this as you read texts aimed at the academic community or in discussing the subject with them. And encourage some awareness and tolerance of practitioner terminology in return.

1.14   Where to from Here?—An Overview of Part I

Now that we have an understanding of the basic goals, context, and terminology of data modeling, we can take a look at how the rest of this first part of the book is organized.

In Chapter 2 we cover **normalization,** a formal technique for organizing data into tables. Normalization enables us to deal with certain common problems of redundancy and incompleteness according to straightforward and quite rigorous rules. In practice, normalization is one of the later steps in the overall data modeling process. We introduce it early in the book to give you a feeling for what a sound data model looks like and, hence, what you should be working towards.

In Chapter 3, we introduce a method for presenting models in a diagrammatic form. In working with the insurance model, you may have found that some of the more important business rules (such as only one customer being allowed for each policy) were far from obvious. As we move to more complex models, it becomes increasingly difficult to see the key concepts and rules among all the detail. A typical model of 100 tables with five to ten columns each will appear overwhelmingly complicated. We need the equivalent of an architect's sketch plan to present the main points, and we need the ability to work "top down" to develop it.

In Chapter 4, we look at **subtyping** and **supertyping** and their role in exploring alternative designs and handling complex models. We touched on the underlying idea when we discussed the possible division of the **Customer** table into separate tables for personal and corporate customers (we would say that this division was based on **Personal Customer** and **Corporate Customer** being subtypes of **Customer**, or, equivalently, **Customer** being a supertype of **Corporate Customer** and **Personal Customer**).

In Chapter 5 we look more closely at columns (and their conceptual model ancestors, which we call **attributes**). We explore issues of definition, coding, and naming.

---

[16]On the (rare) occasions that we employ this usage (primarily in Chapter 7), we use capitals to distinguish; *the* Relational Model of data versus *a* relational model for a particular database.

In Chapter 6 we cover the specification of **primary keys**—columns such as Policy Number, which enable us to identify individual rows of data.

In Chapter 7 we look at some extensions to the basic conventions and some alternative modeling languages.

1.15 **Summary**

Data and databases are central to information systems. Every database is specified by a data model, even if only an implicit one. The data model is an important determinant of the design of the associated information systems. Changes in the structure of a database can have a radical and expensive impact on the programs that access it. It is therefore essential that the data model for an information system be an accurate, stable reflection of the business it supports.

Data modeling is a *design* process. The data model cannot be produced by a mechanical transformation from hard business facts to a unique solution. Rather, the modeler generates one or more candidate models, using analysis, abstraction, past experience, heuristics, and creativity. Quality is assessed according to a number of factors including completeness, non-redundancy, faithfulness to business rules, reusability, stability, elegance, integration, and communication effectiveness. There are often trade-offs involved in satisfying these criteria.

Performance of the resulting database is an important issue, but it is primarily the responsibility of the database administrator/database technician. The data modeler will need to be involved if changes to the logical data model are contemplated.

In developing a system, data modeling and process modeling usually proceed broadly in parallel. Data modeling principles remain important for object-oriented development, particularly where large volumes of structured data are involved. Prototyping and agile approaches benefit from a stable data model being developed and communicated at an early stage.

Despite the wider use of packaged software and end-user development, data modeling remains a key technique for information systems professionals.

Chapter 2
Basics of Sound Structure

"A place for everything and everything in its place."
– Samuel Smiles, Thrift, 1875

"Begin with the end in mind."
– Stephen R. Covey, The 7 Habits of Highly Effective People

2.1 Introduction

In this chapter, we look at some fundamental techniques for organizing data.

Our principal tool is **normalization**, a set of rules for allocating data to tables in such a way as to eliminate certain types of redundancy and incompleteness.

In practice, normalization is usually one of the later activities in a data modeling project, as we cannot start normalizing until we have established what columns (data items) are required. In the approach described in Part 2, normalization is used in the logical database design stage, following requirements analysis and conceptual modeling.

We have chosen to introduce normalization at this early stage of the book[1] so that you can get a feeling for what a well-designed logical data model looks like. You will find it much easier to understand (and undertake) the earlier stages of analysis and design if you know what you are working toward.

Normalization is one of the most thoroughly researched areas of data modeling, and you will have little trouble finding other texts and papers on the subject. Many take a fairly formal, mathematical approach. Here, we focus more on the steps in the process, what they achieve, and the practical problems you are likely to encounter. We have also highlighted areas of ambiguity and opportunities for choice and creativity.

The majority of the chapter is devoted to a rather long example. We encourage you to work through it. By the time you have finished, you will

---

[1]Most texts follow the sequence in which activities are performed in practice (as we do in Part 2). However, over many years of teaching data modeling to practitioners and college students, we have found that both groups find it easier to learn the top-down techniques if they have a concrete idea of what a well-structured logical model will look like. See also comments in Chapter 3, Section 3.3.1.

Employee Number:	01267	Employee Name:	Clark		
Department Number:	05	Department Name:	Auditing	Department Location:	HO
Qualification			**Year**		
Bachelor of Arts			1970		
Master of Arts			1973		
Doctor of Philosophy			1976		

Figure 2.1 Employee qualifications form.

have covered virtually all of the issues involved in basic normalization[2] and encountered many of the most important data modeling concepts and terms.

2.2 An Informal Example of Normalization

Normalization is essentially a two-step[3] process:

1. Put the data into tabular form (by removing repeating groups).
2. Remove duplicated data to separate tables.

A simple example will give you some feeling for what we are trying to achieve. Figure 2.1 shows a paper form (it could equally be a computer input screen) used for recording data about employees and their qualifications.

If we want to store this data in a database, our first task is to put it into tabular form. But we immediately strike a problem: because an employee can have more than one qualification, it's awkward to fit the qualification data into one row of a table (Figure 2.2). How many qualifications do we allow for? Murphy's law tells us that there will always be an employee who has one more qualification than the table will handle.

We can solve this problem by splitting the data into two tables. The first holds the basic employee data, and the second holds the qualification data, one row per qualification (Figure 2.3). In effect, we have removed the "repeating group" of qualification data (consisting of qualification descriptions and years) to its own table. We hold employee numbers in the second table to serve as a cross-reference back to the first, because we need to know to whom each qualification belongs. Now the only limit on the

---

[2]Advanced normalization is covered in Chapter 13.

[3]This is a simplification. Every time we create a table, we need to identify its primary key. This task is absolutely critical to normalization; the only reason that we have not nominated it as a "step" in its own right is that it is performed within each of the two steps which we have listed.

Employee Number	Employee Name	Dept. Number	Dept. Name	Dept. Location	Qualification 1	
					Description	**Year**
01267	Clark	05	Auditing	HO	Bachelor of Arts	1970
70964	Smith	12	Legal	MS	Bachelor of Arts	1969
22617	Walsh	05	Auditing	HO	Bachelor of Arts	1972
50607	Black	05	Auditing	HO		

Qualification 2		Qualification 3		Qualification 4	
Description	**Year**	**Description**	**Year**	**Description**	**Year**
Master of Arts	1973	Doctor of Philosophy	1976		
Master of Arts	1977				

Figure 2.2 Employee qualifications table.

number of qualifications we can record for each employee is the maximum number of rows in the table—in practical terms, as many as we will ever need.

Our second task is to eliminate duplicated data. For example, the fact that department number "05" is "Auditing" and is located at "HO" is repeated for every employee in that department. Updating data is therefore complicated. If we wanted to record that the Auditing department had moved to

Employee Table

Employee Number	Employee Name	Dept. Number	Dept. Name	Dept. Location
01267	Clark	05	Auditing	HO
70964	Smith	12	Legal	MS
22617	Walsh	05	Auditing	HO
50607	Black	05	Auditing	HO

Qualification Table

Employee Number	Qualification Description	Qualification Year
01267	Bachelor of Arts	1970
01267	Master of Arts	1973
01267	Doctor of Philosophy	1976
70964	Bachelor of Arts	1969
22617	Bachelor of Arts	1972
22617	Master of Arts	1977

Figure 2.3 Separation of qualification data.

another location, we would need to update several rows in the **Employee** table. Recall that two of our quality criteria introduced in Chapter 1 were "non-redundancy" and "elegance"; here we have redundant data and a model that requires inelegant programming.

The basic problem is that department names and addresses are really data about *departments* rather than employees, and belong in a separate **Department** table. We therefore establish a third table for department data, resulting in the three-table model of Figure 2.4 (see page 37). We leave Department Number in the **Employee** table to serve as a cross-reference, in the same way that we retained Employee Number in the **Qualification** table. Our data is now normalized.

This is a very informal example of what normalization is about. The rules of normalization have their foundation in mathematics and have been very closely studied by researchers. On the one hand, this means that we can have confidence in normalization as a technique; on the other, it is very easy to become lost in mathematical terminology and proofs and miss the essential simplicity of the technique. The apparent rigor can also give us a false sense of security, by hiding some of the assumptions that have to be made before the rules are applied.

You should also be aware that many data modelers profess not to use normalization, in a formal sense, at all. They would argue that they reach the same answer by common sense and intuition. Certainly, most practitioners would have had little difficulty solving the employee qualification example in this way.

However, common sense and intuition come from experience, and these experienced modelers have a good idea of what sound, normalized data models look like. Think of this chapter, therefore, as a way of gaining familiarity with some sound models and, conversely, with some important and easily classified design faults. As you gain experience, you will find that you arrive at properly normalized structures as a matter of habit.

Nevertheless, even the most experienced professionals make mistakes or encounter difficulties with sophisticated models. At these times, it is helpful to get back onto firm ground by returning to first principles such as normalization. And when you encounter someone else's model that has not been properly normalized (a common experience for data modeling consultants), it is useful to be able to demonstrate that some generally accepted rules have been violated.

2.3 **Relational Notation**

Before tackling a more complex example, we need to learn a more concise notation. The sample data in the tables takes up a lot of space and is not required to document the design (although it can be a great help in

Employee Table

Employee Number	Employee Name	Dept. Number
01267	Clark	05
22617	Walsh	05
70964	Smith	12
50607	Black	05

Department Table

Dept. Number	Dept. Name	Dept. Location
05	Auditing	HO
12	Legal	MS

Qualification Table

Employee Number	Qualification Description	Qualification Year
01267	Bachelor of Arts	1970
01267	Master of Arts	1973
01267	Doctor of Philosophy	1976
70964	Bachelor of Arts	1969
22617	Bachelor of Arts	1972
22617	Master of Arts	1977

Figure 2.4 Separation of department data.

communicating it). If we eliminate the sample rows, we are left with just the table names and columns.

Figure 2.5 shows the normalized model of employees and qualifications using the **relational** notation of table name followed by column names in parentheses. (The full notation requires that the primary key of the table be marked—discussed in Section 2.5.4.) This convention is widely used in textbooks, and it is convenient for presenting the minimum amount of information needed for most worked examples. In practice, however, we usually want to record more information about each column: format, optionality, and perhaps a brief note or description. Practitioners therefore usually use lists as in Figure 2.6, on the next page.

EMPLOYEE (Employee Number, Employee Name, Department Number)
DEPARTMENT (Department Number, Department Name, Department Location)
QUALIFICATION (Employee Number, Qualification Description, Qualification Year)

Figure 2.5 Employee model using relational notation.

2.4 **A More Complex Example**

Armed with the more concise relational notation, let's now look at a more complex example and introduce the rules of normalization as we proceed. The rules themselves are not too daunting, but we will spend some time looking at exactly what problems they solve.

The form in Figure 2.7 is based on one used in an actual survey of antibiotic drug prescribing practices in Australian public hospitals. The survey team wanted to determine which drugs and dosages were being used for various operations, to ensure that correct clinical decisions were being made and that patients and taxpayers were not paying for unnecessary (or unnecessarily expensive) drugs.

One form was completed for each operation. A little explanation is necessary to understand exactly how the form was used.

Each hospital in the survey was given a unique hospital number to distinguish it from other hospitals (in some cases two hospitals had the same name). All hospital numbers were prefixed "H" (for "hospital").

Operation numbers were assigned sequentially by each hospital.

EMPLOYEE
Employee Number: 5 Numeric—The number allocated to this employee by the Human Resources Department
Employee Name: 60 Characters—The name of this employee: the surname, a comma and space, the first given name plus a space and the middle initial if any
Department Number: The number used by the organization to identify the Department that pays this employee's salary

DEPARTMENT
Department Number: 2 Numeric—The number used by the organization to identify this Department
Department Name: 30 Characters—The name of this Department as it appears in company documentation
Department Location: 30 Characters—The name of the city where this Department is located

QUALIFICATION
Employee Number: 5 Numeric—The number allocated to the employee holding this qualification by the Human Resources Department
Qualification Description: 30 Characters—The name of this qualification
Qualification Year: Date Optional—The year in which this employee obtained this qualification

Figure 2.6 Employee model using list notation.

Hospital Number: H17	Hospital Name: St Vincent's		Operation Number: 48		
Hospital Category: P		Contact at Hospital: Fred Fleming			
Operation Name: Heart Transplant		Operation Code: 7A		Procedure Group: Transplant	
Surgeon Number: S15	Surgeon Specialty: Cardiology		Total Drug Cost: $75.50		
Drug Code	Full Name of Drug	Manufacturer	Method of Admin.	Cost of Dose ($)	Number of Doses
MAX 150mg	Maxicillin	ABC Pharmaceuticals	ORAL	$3.50	15
MIN 500mg	Minicillin	Silver Bullet Drug Co.	IV	$1.00	20
MIN 250mg	Minicillin	Silver Bullet Drug Co.	ORAL	$0.30	10

Figure 2.7 Drug expenditure survey.

Hospitals fell into three categories: "T" for "teaching," "P" for "public," and "V" for "private". All teaching hospitals were public ("T" implied "P").

The operation code was a standard international code for the named operation. Procedure group was a broader classification.

The surgeon number was allocated by individual hospitals to allow surgeons to retain a degree of anonymity. The prefix "S" stood for "surgeon." Only a single surgeon number was recorded for each operation.

Total drug cost was the total cost of all drug doses for the operation. The bottom of the form recorded the individual antibiotic drugs used in the operation. A drug code was made up of a short name for the drug plus the size of the dose.

As the study was extended to more hospitals, it was decided to replace the heaps of forms with a computerized database. Figure 2.8 shows the initial database design, using the relational notation. It consists of a single table, named **Operation** because each row represents a single operation. Do not be put off by all the columns; after the first ten, there is a lot of repetition to allow details of up to four drugs to be recorded against the operation. But it is certainly not elegant.

The data modeler (who was also the physical database designer and the programmer) took the simplest approach, exactly mirroring the form. Indeed, it is interesting to consider who really did the data modeling. Most of the critical decisions were made by the original designer of the form.

When we present this example in training workshops, we give participants a few minutes to see if they can improve on the design. We strongly suggest you do the same before proceeding. It is easy to argue *after* seeing a worked solution that the same result could be achieved intuitively.

OPERATION (Hospital Number, Operation Number, Hospital Name, Hospital Category, Contact Person, Operation Name, Operation Code, Procedure Group, Surgeon Number, Surgeon Specialty, Total Drug Cost,
Drug Code 1, Drug Name 1, Manufacturer 1, Method of Administration 1, Dose Cost 1, Number of Doses 1,
Drug Code 2, Drug Name 2, Manufacturer 2, Method of Administration 1, Dose Cost 1, Number of Doses 2,
Drug Code 3, Drug Name 3, Manufacturer 3, Method of Administration 3, Dose Cost 3, Number of Doses 3,
Drug Code 4, Drug Name 4, Manufacturer 4, Method of Administration 4, Dose Cost 4, Number of Doses 4)

Figure 2.8 Initial drug expenditure model.

2.5 **Determining Columns**

Before we get started on normalization proper, we need to do a little preparation and tidying up. Normalization relies on certain assumptions about the way data is represented, and we need to make sure that these are valid. There are also some problems that normalization does not solve, and it is better to address these at the outset, rather than carrying excess baggage through the whole normalization process. The following steps are necessary to ensure that our initial model provides a sound starting point.

2.5.1 **One Fact per Column**

First we make sure that each column in the table represents one fact only. The **Drug Code** column holds both a short name for the drug and a dosage size, two distinct facts. The dosage size in turn consists of a numeric size and a unit of measure. The three facts should be recorded in separate columns. We will see that this decision makes an important difference to the structure of our final model.

A more subtle example of a multifact column is the **Hospital Category**. We are identifying whether the hospital is public or private (first fact) as well as whether the hospital provides teaching (second fact). We should establish two columns, **Hospital Type** and **Teaching Status**, to capture these distinct ideas. (It is interesting to note that, in the years since the original form was designed, some Australian private hospitals have been accredited as teaching hospitals. The original design would not have been able to accommodate this change as readily as the "one-fact-per-column" design.)

The identification and handling of multifact columns is covered in more detail in Chapter 5.

2.5.2 **Hidden Data**

The second piece of tidying up involves making sure that we have not lost any data in the translation to tabular form. The most common problem here is that we cannot rely on the rows of the table being stored in any particular order. Suppose the original survey forms had been filed in order of return. If we wanted to preserve this data, we would need to add a **Return Date** or **Return Sequence** column. If the hospitals used red forms for emergency operations and blue forms for elective surgery, we would need to add a column to record the category if it was of interest to the database users.

2.5.3 **Derivable Data**

Remember our basic objective of nonredundancy. We should remove any data that can be derived from other data in the table and amend the columns accordingly. The **Total Drug Cost** is derivable by adding together the **Dose Costs** multiplied by the **Numbers of Doses**. We therefore remove it, noting in our supporting documentation how it can be derived (since it is presumably of interest to the database users, and we need to know how to reconstruct it when required).

We might well ask why the total was held in the first place. Occasionally, there may be a regulatory requirement to hold derivable data rather than calculating it whenever needed. In some cases, derived data is included unknowingly. Most often, however, it is added with the intention of improving performance. Even from that perspective, we should realize that there will be a trade-off between data retrieval (faster if we do not have to assemble the base data and calculate the total each time) and data update (the total will need to be recalculated if we change the base data). Far more importantly, though, performance is not our concern at the logical modeling stage. If the physical database designers cannot achieve the required performance, then specifying redundant data in the *physical* model is *one* option we might consider and properly evaluate.

We can also drop the practice of prefixing hospital numbers with "H" and surgeon numbers with "S." The prefixes add no information, at least when we are dealing with them as data in the database, in the context of their column names. If they were to be used without that context, we would simply add the appropriate prefix when we printed or otherwise exported the data.

2.5.4 **Determining the Primary Key**

Finally, we determine a **primary key**[4] for the table. The choice of primary keys is a critical (and sometimes complex) task, which is the subject of Chapter 6. For the moment, we will simply note that the primary key is a minimal set of columns that contains a different combination of values for each row of the table. Another way of looking at primary keys is that each value of the primary key uniquely identifies one row of the table. In this case, a combination of **Hospital Number** and **Operation Number** will do the job. If we nominate a particular hospital number and operation number, there will be at most one row with that particular combination of values. The purpose of the primary key is exactly this: to enable us to refer unambiguously to a specific row of a table ("show me the row for hospital number 33, operation 109"). We can check this with the business experts by asking: "Could there ever be more than one form with the same combination of hospital number and operation number?" Incidentally, any combination of columns that includes these two (e.g., **Hospital Number, Operation Number**, and **Surgeon Number**) will also identify only one row, but such combinations will not satisfy our definition (above), which requires that the key be minimal (i.e., no bigger than is needed to do the job).

Figure 2.9 shows the result of tidying up the initial model of Figure 2.8. We have replaced each **Drug Code** with its components (**Drug Short Name, Size of Dose**, and **Unit of Measure**) in line with our "one-fact-per-column" rule (Section 2.5.1). Note that **Hospital Number** and **Operation Number** are underlined. This is a standard convention for identifying the columns that form the primary key.

OPERATION (Hospital Number, Operation Number, Hospital Name, Hospital Type, Teaching Status, Contact Person, Operation Name, Operation Code, Procedure Group, Surgeon Number, Surgeon Specialty,
Drug Short Name 1, Drug Name 1, Manufacturer 1, Size of Dose 1, Unit of Measure 1, Method of Administration 1, Dose Cost 1, Number of Doses 1,
Drug Short Name 2, Drug Name 2, Manufacturer 2, Size of Dose 2, Unit of Measure 2, Method of Administration 2, Dose Cost 2, Number of Doses 2,
Drug Short Name 3, Drug Name 3, Manufacturer 3, Size of Dose 3, Unit of Measure 3, Method of Administration 3, Dose Cost 3, Number of Doses 3,
Drug Short Name 4, Drug Name 4, Manufacturer 4, Size of Dose 4, Unit of Measure 4, Method of Administration 4, Dose Cost 4, Number of Doses 4)

Figure 2.9   Drug expenditure model after tidying up.

---

[4]"Key" can have a variety of meanings in data modeling and database design. Although it is common for data modelers to use the term to refer only to primary keys, we strongly recommend that you acquire the habit of using the full term to avoid misunderstandings.

2.6 **Repeating Groups and First Normal Form**

Let's start cleaning up this mess. Earlier we saw that our first task in normalization was to put the data in tabular form. It might seem that we have done this already, but, in fact, we have only managed to hide a problem with the data about the drugs administered.

2.6.1 **Limit on Maximum Number of Occurrences**

The drug administration data is the major cause of the table's complexity and inelegance, with its **Drug Short Name 2**, **Drug Name 4**, **Number of Doses 3**, and so forth. The columns needed to accommodate up to four drugs account for most of the complexity. And why only four? Why not five or six or more? Four drugs represented a maximum arrived at by asking one of the survey teams, "What would be the maximum number of different drugs ever used in an operation?" In fact, this number was frequently exceeded, with some operations using up to ten different drugs. Part of the problem was that the question was not framed precisely enough; a line on the form was required for each *drug-dosage* combination, rather than just for each different drug. Even if this had been allowed for, drugs and procedures could later have changed in such a way as to increase the maximum likely number of drugs. The model rates poorly against the completeness and stability criteria.

With the original clerical system, this limit on the number of different drug dosage combinations was not a major problem. Many of the forms were returned with a piece of paper taped to the bottom, or with additional forms attached with only the bottom section completed to record the additional drug administrations. In a computerized system, the change to the database structure to add the extra columns could be easily made, but the associated changes to programs would be much more painful. Indeed, the system developer decided that the easiest solution was to leave the database structure unchanged and to hold multiple rows for those operations that used more than four combinations, suffixing the operation number with "A," "B," or "C" to indicate a continuation. This solution necessitated changes to program logic and made the system more complex.

So, one problem with our "repeating group" of drug administration data is that we have to set an arbitrary maximum number of repetitions, large enough to accommodate the greatest number that might ever occur in practice.

2.6.2 **Data Reusability and Program Complexity**

The need to predict and allow for the maximum number of repetitions is not the only problem caused by the repeating group. The data cannot necessarily be reused without resorting to complex program logic. It is relatively easy to write a program to answer questions like, "How many operations were performed by neurosurgeons?" or "Which hospital is spending the most money on drugs?" A simple scan through the relevant columns will do the job. But it gets more complicated when we ask a question like, "How much money was spent on the drug Ampicillin?" Similarly, "Sort into **Operation Code** sequence" is simple to handle, but "Sort into **Drug Name** sequence" cannot be done at all without first copying the data to another table in which each drug appears only once in each row.

You might argue that some inquiries are always going to be intrinsically more complicated than others. But consider what would have happened if we had designed the table on the basis of "one row per drug." This might have been prompted by a different data collection method—perhaps the hospital drug dispensary filling out one survey form per drug. We would have needed to allow a repeating group (probably with many repetitions) to accommodate all the operations that used each drug, but we would find that the queries that were previously difficult to program had become straightforward, and vice versa. Here is a case of data being organized to suit a specific set of processes, rather than as a resource available to all potential users.

Consider also the problem of updating data within the repeating group. Suppose we wanted to delete the second drug administration for a particular operation (perhaps it was a nonantibiotic drug, entered in error). Would we shuffle the third and fourth drugs back into slots two and three, or would our programming now have to deal with intermediate gaps? Either way, the programming is messy because our data model is inelegant.

2.6.3 Recognizing Repeating Groups

To summarize: We have a set of columns repeated a number of times—a "repeating group"—resulting in inflexibility, complexity, and poor data reusability. The table design hides the problem by using numerical suffixes to give each column a different name.

It is better to face the problem squarely and document our initial structure as in Figure 2.10. The braces (curly brackets) indicate a repeating group with an indefinite number of occurrences. This notation is a useful convention, but it describes something we cannot implement directly with a simple table. In technical terms, our data is *unnormalized*.

At this point we should also check whether there are any repeating groups that have not been marked as such. To do this, we need to ask whether there are any data items that could have multiple values for a given value of the key. For example, we should ask whether more than one

OPERATION (Hospital Number, Operation Number, Hospital Name, Hospital Category, Teaching Status, Contact Person, Operation Name, Operation Code, Procedure Group, Surgeon Number, Surgeon Specialty, {Drug Short Name, Drug Name, Manufacturer, Size of Dose, Unit of Measure, Method of Administration, Dose Cost, Number of Doses})

Figure 2.10   Drug expenditure model showing repeating group.

surgeon can be involved in an operation and, if so, whether we need to be able to record more than one. If so, the columns describing surgeons (**Surgeon Number** and **Surgeon Specialty**) would become another repeating group.

2.6.4   **Removing Repeating Groups**

A general and flexible solution should not set any limits on the maximum number of occurrences of repeating groups. It should also neatly handle the situation of few or no occurrences (some 75% of the operations, in fact, did not use any antibiotic drugs).

This brings us to the first step in normalization:

STEP 1: Put the data in table form by identifying and eliminating repeating groups.

The procedure is to split the original table into multiple tables (one for the basic data and one for each repeating group) as follows:

1. Remove each separate set of repeating group columns to a new table (one new table for each set) so that each occurrence of the group becomes a row in its new table.
2. Include the key of the original table in each new table, to serve as a cross-reference (we call this a **foreign key**).
3. If the sequence of occurrences within a repeating group has business significance, introduce a "Sequence" column to the corresponding new table.
4. Name each new table.
5. Identify and underline the primary key of each new table, as discussed in the next subsection.

Figure 2.11 shows the two tables that result from applying these rules to the **Operation** table.

We have named the new table **Drug Administration**, since each row in the table records the administration of a drug dose, just as each row in the original table records an operation.

OPERATION (<u>Hospital Number</u>, <u>Operation Number</u>, Hospital Name, Hospital Type, Teaching Status, Contact Person, Operation Name, Operation Code, Procedure Group, Surgeon Number, Surgeon Specialty)
DRUG ADMINISTRATION (<u>Hospital Number</u>, <u>Operation Number</u>, <u>Drug Short Name</u>, <u>Size of Dose</u>, <u>Unit of Measure</u>, <u>Method of Administration</u>, Dose Cost, Number of Doses, Drug Name, Manufacturer)

Figure 2.11   Repeating group removed to separate table.

2.6.5 **Determining the Primary Key of the New Table**

Finding the key of the new table was not easy (in fact this is usually the trickiest step in the whole normalization process). We had to ask, "What is the minimum combination of columns needed to uniquely identify one row (i.e., one specific administration of a drug)?" Certainly we needed **Hospital Number** and **Operation Number** to pin it down to one operation, but to identify the individual administration we had to specify not only the **Drug Short Name**, but also the **Size of Dose**, **Unit of Measure**, and **Method of Administration**—a six-column primary key.

In verifying the need for this long key, we would need to ask: "Can the same drug be administered in different dosages for the one operation?" (yes) and "Can the same drug and dose be administered using different methods for the one operation?" (yes, again).

The reason for including the primary key of the **Operation** table in the **Drug Administration** table should be fairly obvious; we need to know which operation each drug administration applies to. It does, however, highlight the importance of primary keys in providing the links between tables. Consider what would happen if we could have two or more operations with the same combination of hospital number and operation number. There would be no way of knowing which of these operations a given drug administration applied to.

To recap: primary keys are an essential part of normalization.

In determining the primary key for the new table, you will *usually* need to include the primary key of the original table, as in this case (**Hospital Number** and **Operation Number** form part of the primary key). This is not always so, despite what some widely read texts (including Codd's[5] original paper on normalization) suggest (see the example of insurance agents and policies in Section 13.6.3).

The sequence issue is often overlooked. In this case, the sequence in which the drugs were recorded on the form was not, in fact, significant,

---

[5]Codd, E., "A Relational Model of Data for Large Shared Data Banks," *Communications of the ACM* (June, 1970). This was the first paper to advocate normalization as a data modeling technique.

but the original data structure did allow us to distinguish between first, second, third, and fourth administrations. A sequence column in the **Drug Administration** table would have enabled us to retain that data if needed. Incidentally, the key of the **Drug Administration** table could then have been a combination of Hospital Number, Operation Number, and the sequence column.[6]

2.6.6 **First Normal Form**

Our tables are now technically in **First Normal Form** (often abbreviated to 1NF). What have we achieved?

- All data of the same kind is now held in the same place. For example, all drug names are now in a common column. This translates into elegance and simplicity in both data structure and programming (we could now sort the data by drug name, for example).
- The number of different drug dosages that can be recorded for an operation is limited only by the maximum possible number of rows in the **Drug Administration** table (effectively unlimited). Conversely, an operation that does not use any drugs will not require any rows in the **Drug Administration** table.

2.7 **Second and Third Normal Forms**

2.7.1 **Problems with Tables in First Normal Form**

Look at the **Operation** table in Figure 2.11.

Every row that represents an operation at, say, hospital number 17 will contain the facts that the hospital's name is St. Vincent's, that Fred Fleming is the contact person, that its teaching status is T, and that its type is P. At the very least, our criterion of nonredundancy is not being met. There are other associated problems. Changing any fact about a hospital (e.g., the contact person) will involve updating every operation for that hospital. And if we were to delete the last operation for a hospital, we would also be deleting the basic details of that hospital. Think about this for a moment. If we have a transaction "Delete Operation," its usual effect will be to delete the record of an operation only. But if the operation is the last for a

---

[6]We say "could" because we would now have a choice of primary keys. The original key would still work. This issue of multiple candidate keys is discussed in Section 2.8.3.

particular hospital, the transaction has the additional effect of deleting data about the hospital as well. If we want to prevent this, we will need to explicitly handle "last operations" differently, a fairly clear violation of our elegance criterion.

2.7.2 Eliminating Redundancy

We can solve all of these problems by removing the hospital information to a separate table in which each hospital number appears once only (and therefore is the obvious choice for the table's key). Figure 2.12 shows the result. We keep Hospital Number in the original **Operation** table to tell us which row to refer to in the **Hospital** table if we want relevant hospital details. Once again, it is vital that Hospital Number identifies one row only, to prevent any ambiguity.

We have gained quite a lot here. Not only do we now hold hospital information once only; we are also able to record details of a hospital even if we do not yet have an operation recorded for that hospital.

2.7.3 Determinants

It is important to understand that this whole procedure of separating hospital data relied on the fact that for a given hospital number there could be only one hospital name, contact person, hospital type, and teaching status. In fact we could look at the dependency of hospital data on hospital number as the cause of the problem. Every time a particular hospital number appeared in the **Operation** table, the hospital name, contact person, hospital type, and teaching status were the same. Why hold them more than once?

OPERATION (Hospital Number, Operation Number, Operation Name, Operation Code, Procedure Group, Surgeon Number, Surgeon Specialty)

HOSPITAL (Hospital Number, Hospital Name, Hospital Type, Teaching Status, Contact Person)

DRUG ADMINISTRATION (Hospital Number, Operation Number, Drug Short Name, Size of Dose, Unit of Measure, Method of Administration, Dose Cost, Number of Doses, Drug Name, Manufacturer)

Figure 2.12 Hospital data removed to separate table.

Formally, we say that Hospital Number is a **determinant** of the other four columns. We can show this as:

Hospital Number → Hospital Name, Contact Person, Hospital Type, Teaching Status

where we read "→" as "determines" or "is a determinant of."

Determinants need not consist of only one column; they can be a combination of two or more columns, in which case we can use a + sign to indicate such a combination. For example: Hospital Number + Operation Number → Surgeon Number.

This leads us to a more formal description of the procedure:

1. Identify any determinants, other than the (entire) primary key, and the columns they determine (we qualify this rule slightly in Section 2.8.3).
2. Establish a separate table for each determinant and the columns it determines. The determinant becomes the key of the new table.
3. Name the new tables.
4. Remove the determined columns from the original table. Leave the determinants to provide links between tables.

Of course, it is easy to *say* "Identify any determinants." A useful starting point is to:

1. Look for columns that appear by their names to be identifiers ("code," "number", "ID", and sometimes "Name" being obvious candidates). These may be determinants or components of determinants.
2. Look for columns that appear to describe something other than what the table is about (in our example, hospitals rather than operations). Then look for other columns that identify this "something" (Hospital Number in this case).

Our "other than the key" exception in step 1 of the procedure is interesting. The problems with determinants arise when the same value appears in more than one row of the table. Because hospital number 17 could appear in more than one row of the **Operation** table, the corresponding values of Contact Person and other columns that it determined were also held in more than one row—hence, the redundancy. But each value of the key itself can appear only once, by definition.

We have already dealt with "Hospital Number → Hospital Name, Contact Person, Hospital Type, Teaching Status."

Let's check the tables for other determinants.

Operation table:

Hospital Number + Surgeon Number → Surgeon Specialty

Operation Code → Operation Name, Procedure Group

Drug Administration table:

Drug Short Name → Drug Name, Manufacturer

Drug Short Name + Method of Administration + Size of Dose + Unit of Measure
→ Dose Cost

How did we know, for example, that each combination of **Drug Short Name, Method of Administration,** and **Size of Dose** would always have the same cost? Without knowledge of every row that might ever be stored in the table, we had to look for a general rule. In practice, this means asking the business specialist. Our conversation might have gone along the following lines:

- **Modeler:** What determines the Dose Cost?
- **Business Specialist:** It depends on the drug itself and the size of the dose.
- **Modeler:** So any two doses of the same drug and same size would always cost the same?
- **Business Specialist:** Assuming, of course, they were administered by the same method; injections cost more than pills.
- **Modeler:** But wouldn't cost vary from hospital to hospital (and operation to operation)?
- **Business Specialist:** Strictly speaking, that's true, but it's not what we're interested in. We want to be able to compare prescribing practices, not how good each hospital is at negotiating discounts. So we use a standardized cost.
- **Modeler:** So maybe we could call this column "Standard Dose Cost" rather than "Dose Cost." By the way, where does the standard cost come from?

Note that if the business rules were different, some determinants might well be different. For example, consider the rule "We use a standardized cost." If this did not apply, the determinant of **Dose Cost** would include **Hospital Number** as well as the other data items identified.

Finding determinants may look like a technical task, but in practice most of the work is in understanding the meaning of the data and the business rules.

For example, we might want to question the rule that **Hospital Number + Operation Number** determines **Surgeon Number**. Surely more than one surgeon could be associated with an operation. Or are we referring to the surgeon in charge, or the surgeon who is to be contacted for follow-up?

The determinant of **Surgeon Specialty** is interesting. **Surgeon Number** alone will not do the job because the same surgeon number could be allocated by more than one hospital. We need to add **Hospital Number** to form a true determinant. Think about the implications of this method of identifying surgeons. The same surgeon could work at more than one hospital, and would be allocated different surgeon numbers. Because we have no way of keeping track of a surgeon across hospitals, our system will not fully support queries of the type "List all the operations performed by a particular surgeon." As data modelers, we need to ensure the user understands this limitation of the data and that it is a consequence of the strategy used to ensure surgeon anonymity.

By the way, are we sure that a surgeon can have only one specialty? If not, we would need to show **Surgeon Specialty** as a repeating group. For the moment, we will assume that the model correctly represents reality, but the close examination of the data that we do at this stage of normalization often brings to light issues that may take us back to the earlier stages of preparation for normalization and removal of repeating groups.

2.7.4   **Third Normal Form**

Figure 2.13 shows the final model. Every time we removed data to a separate table, we eliminated some redundancy and allowed the data in the table to be stored independently of other data (for example, we can now hold data about a drug, even if we have not used it yet).

Intuitive designers call this "creating reference tables" or, more colloquially, "creating look-up tables." In the terminology of normalization, we say that the model is now in **third normal form** (3NF). We will anticipate a few questions right away.

2.7.4.1   What Happened to Second Normal Form?

Our approach took us directly from first normal form (data in tabular form) to third normal form. Most texts treat this as a two-stage process, and

OPERATION (<u>Hospital Number</u>, <u>Operation Number</u>, Operation Code, Surgeon Number)

SURGEON (<u>Hospital Number</u>, <u>Surgeon Number</u>, Surgeon Specialty)

OPERATION TYPE (<u>Operation Code</u>, Operation Name, Procedure Group)

STANDARD DRUG DOSAGE (<u>Drug Short Name</u>, <u>Size of Dose</u>, <u>Unit of Measure</u>, <u>Method of Administration</u>, Standard Dose Cost)

DRUG (<u>Drug Short Name</u>, Drug Name, Manufacturer)

HOSPITAL (<u>Hospital Number</u>, Hospital Name, Hospital Type, Teaching Status, Contact Person)

DRUG ADMINISTRATION (<u>Hospital Number</u>, <u>Operation Number</u>, <u>Drug Short Name</u>, <u>Size of Dose</u>, <u>Unit of Measure</u>, <u>Method of Administration</u>, Number of Doses)

Figure 2.13   Fully normalized drug expenditure model.

deal first with determinants that are part of the table's key and later with non-key determinants. For example, **Hospital Code** is part of the key of **Operation**, so we would establish the **Hospital** table in the first stage. Similarly, we would establish the **Drug** and **Standard Drug Dosage** tables as their keys form part of the key of the **Drug Administration** table. At this point we would be in Second Normal Form (2NF), with the **Operation Type** and **Surgeon** information still to be separated out. The next stage would handle these, taking us to 3NF.

But be warned: most explanations that take this line suggest that you handle determinants that are part of the key first, then determinants that are made up entirely from nonkey columns. What about the determinant of **Surgeon Specialty**? This is made up of one key column (**Hospital Number**) plus one nonkey column (**Surgeon Number**) and is in danger of being overlooked. Use the two-stage process to break up the task if you like, but run a final check on determinants at the end.

Most importantly, we only see 2NF as a stage in the process of getting our data fully normalized, never as an end in itself.

2.7.4.2 Is "Third Normal Form" the Same as "Fully Normalized"?

Unfortunately, no. There are three further well-established normal forms: Boyce-Codd Normal Form (BCNF), Fourth Normal Form (4NF), and Fifth Normal Form (5NF). We discuss these in Chapter 13. The good news is that in most cases, including this one, data in 3NF is already in 5NF. In particular, 4NF and 5NF problems usually arise only when dealing with tables in which every column is part of the key. By the way, "all key" tables are legitimate and occur quite frequently in fully normalized structures.

A Sixth Normal Form (6NF) has been proposed, primarily to deal with issues arising in representing time-dependent data. We look briefly at 6NF in Section 15.3.3.

2.7.4.3 What about Performance? Surely all Those Tables Will Slow Things Down?

There are certainly a lot of tables for what might seem to be relatively little data. This is partly because we deliberately left out quite a few columns, such as **Hospital Address**, which did not do much to illustrate the normalization process. This is done in virtually all illustrative examples, so they have a "stripped-down" appearance compared with those you will encounter in practice.

Thanks to advances in the capabilities of DBMSs, and the increased power of computer hardware, the number of tables is less likely to be an important determinant of performance than it might have been in the past.

But the important point, made in Chapter 1, is that *performance is not an issue at this stage.* We do not know anything about performance requirements, data and transaction volumes, or the hardware and software to be used. Yet time after time, trainee modelers given this problem will do (or not do) things "for the sake of efficiency." For the record, the actual system on which our example is based was implemented completely without compromise and performed as required.

Finally, recall that in preparing for normalization, we split the original Drug Code into Drug Short Name, Size of Dose, and Unit of Measure. At the time, we mentioned that this would affect the final result. We can see now that had we kept them together, the key of the **Drug** table would have been the original compound Drug Code. A look at some sample data from such a table will illustrate the problem this would have caused (Figure 2.14).

We are carrying the fact that "Max" is the short name for Maxicillin redundantly, and would be unable to neatly record a short name and its meaning unless we had established the available doses—a typical symptom of unnormalized data.

2.8 **Definitions and a Few Refinements**

We have taken a rather long walk through what was, on the surface, a fairly simple example. In the process, though, we have encountered most of the problems that arise in getting data models into 3NF. Because we will be discussing normalization issues throughout the book, and because you will encounter them in the literature, it is worth reviewing the terminology and picking up a few additional important concepts.

2.8.1 **Determinants and Functional Dependency**

We have already covered determinants in some detail. Remember that a determinant can consist of one or more columns and must comply with the following formula:

> For each value of the determinant, there can only be one value of some other nominated column(s) in the table at any point in time.

Drug Code	Drug Name
Max 50mg	Maxicillin
Max 100mg	Maxicillin
Max 200mg	Maxicillin

Figure 2.14 Drug table resulting from complex drug code.

Equivalently we can say that the other nominated columns are **functionally dependent** on the determinant. The determinant concept is what 3NF is all about; we are simply grouping data items around their determinants.

2.8.2 Primary Keys

We have introduced the underline convention to denote the primary key of each table, and we have emphasized the importance of primary keys in normalization. A **primary key** is a nominated column or combination of columns that has a different value for every row in the table. Each table has one (and only one) primary key. When checking this with a business person, we would say, "If I nominated, say, a particular account number, would you be able to *guarantee* that there was *never* more than one account with that number?" We look at primary keys in more detail in Chapter 6.

2.8.3 Candidate Keys

Sometimes more than one column or combination of columns could serve as a primary key. For example, we could have chosen Drug Name rather than Drug Short Name as the primary key of the **Drug** table (assuming, of course, that no two drugs could have the same name). We refer to such possible primary keys, whether chosen or not, as **candidate keys**. From the point of view of normalization, the important thing is that candidate keys that have not been chosen as the primary key, such as Drug Name, will be determinants of every column in the table, just as the primary key is. Under our normalization rules, as they stand, we would need to create a separate table for the candidate key and every other column (Figure 2.15).

All we have done here is to create a second table that will hold exactly the same data as the first—albeit with a different primary key.

To cover this situation formally, we need to be more specific in our rule for which determinants to use as the basis for new tables. We previously excluded the primary key; we need to extend this to all candidate keys. Our first step then should strictly begin:

"Identify any determinants, *other than candidate keys* . . ."

DRUG 1 (<u>Drug Short Name</u>, Drug Name, Manufacturer)

DRUG 2 (<u>Drug Name</u>, Drug Short Name, Manufacturer)

Figure 2.15 Separate tables for each candidate key.

2.8.4   **A More Formal Definition of Third Normal Form**

The concepts of determinants and candidate keys give us the basis for a more formal definition of Third Normal Form (3NF). If we define the term "nonkey column" to mean "a column that is not part of the primary key," then we can say:

A table is in 3NF if the only determinants of nonkey columns are candidate keys.[7]

This makes sense. Our procedure took all determinants *other* than candidate keys and removed the columns they determined. The only determinants left should therefore be candidate keys. Once you have come to grips with the concepts of determinants and candidate keys, this definition of 3NF is a succinct and practical test to apply to data structures. The oft-quoted maxim, "Each nonkey column must be determined by the key, the whole key, and nothing but the key," is a good way of remembering first, second, and third normal forms, but not quite as tidy and rigorous.

Incidentally, the definition of Boyce-Codd Normal Form (BCNF) is even simpler: a table is in BCNF if the only determinants of *any* columns (i.e., including key columns) are candidate keys. The reason that we defer discussion of BCNF to Chapter 13 is that identifying a BCNF problem is one thing; fixing it may be another.

2.8.5   **Foreign Keys**

Recall that when we removed repeating groups to a new table, we carried the primary key of the original table with us, to cross-reference or "point back" to the source. In moving from first to third normal form, we left determinants behind as cross-references to the relevant rows in the new tables.

These cross-referencing columns are called foreign keys, and they are our principal means of linking data from different tables. For example, Hospital Number (the primary key of **Hospital**) appears as a foreign key in the **Surgeon** and **Operation** tables, in each case pointing back to the relevant hospital information. Another way of looking at it is that we are using the foreign keys as substitutes[8] or abbreviations for hospital data; we can always get the full data about a hospital by looking up the relevant row in the **Hospital** table.

Note that "elsewhere in the data model" may include "elsewhere in the same table." For example, an **Employee** table might have a primary key of

---

[7]If we want to be even more formal, we should explicitly exclude trivial determinants: each column is, of course, a determinant of itself.

[8]The word we wanted to use here was "surrogates" but it carries a particular meaning in the context of primary keys—see Chapter 6.

Employee Number. We might also hold the employee number of each employee's manager (Figure 2.16). The **Manager's Employee Number** would be a foreign key. This structure appears quite often in models as a means of representing hierarchies. A common convention for highlighting the foreign keys in a model is an asterisk, as shown.

For the sake of brevity, we use the asterisk convention in this book. But when dealing with more complex models, and recording the columns in a list as in Figure 2.6, we suggest you mark each foreign key column by including in its description the fact that it forms all or part of a foreign key and the name of the table to which it points (Figure 2.17).

Some columns will be part of more than one primary key and, hence, potentially of more than one foreign key: for example, **Hospital Number** is the primary key of **Hospital**, but also part of the primary keys of **Operation**, **Surgeon**, and **Drug Administration**.

It is a good check on normalization to mark all of the foreign keys and then to check whether any column names appear more than once in the overall model. If they are marked as foreign keys, they are (probably) serving the required purpose of cross-referencing the various tables. If not, there are three likely possibilities:

1. We have made an error in normalization; perhaps we have moved a column to a new table, but forgotten to remove it from the original table.
2. We have used the same name to describe two different things; perhaps we have used the word "Unit" to mean both "unit of measure" and "(organizational) unit in which the surgeon works" (as in fact actually happened in the early stages of designing the more comprehensive version of this model).
3. We have failed to correctly mark the foreign keys.

In Chapter 3, foreign keys will play an important role in translating our models into diagrammatic form.

2.8.6 **Referential Integrity**

Imagine we are looking at the values in a foreign key column—perhaps the hospital numbers in the **Operation** table that point to the relevant **Hospital** records. We would expect every hospital number in the **Operation** table to

EMPLOYEE (<u>Employee Number</u>, Name, Manager's Employee Number*, . . .)

Figure 2.16 A foreign key convention.

DRUG ADMINISTRATION
Hospital Number: FK of Hospital, Part FK of Operation
Operation Number: Part FK of Operation
Drug Short Name: FK of Drug, Part FK of Standard Drug Dosage
Size of Dose: Part FK of Standard Drug Dosage
Unit of Measure: Part FK of Standard Drug Dosage
Method of Administration: Part FK of Standard Drug Dosage
Number of Doses

Figure 2.17   A more comprehensive foreign key convention.

have a matching hospital number in the **Hospital** table. If not, our database would be internally inconsistent as critical information about the hospital at which an operation was performed would be missing.

Modern DBMSs provide **referential integrity** features that ensure automatically that each foreign key value has a matching primary key value. Referential integrity is discussed in more detail in Section 14.5.4.

2.8.7 **Update Anomalies**

Discussions of normalization often refer to **update anomalies.** The term nicely captures most of the problems which normalization addresses, particularly if the word "update" is used in its broadest sense to include the insertion and deletion of data, and if we are talking about structures, which are at least in tabular form.

As we have seen, performing simple update operations on structures which are not fully normalized may lead to inconsistent or incomplete data. In the unnormalized and partially normalized versions of the drug expenditure model, we saw:

1. Insertion anomalies. For example, recording a hospital for which there were no operations would have required the insertion of a dummy operation record or other artifice.
2. Change anomalies. For example, the name of a drug could appear in many places; updating it in one place would have left other records unchanged and hence inconsistent.
3. Deletion anomalies. For example, deleting the record of the only operation performed at a particular hospital would also delete details of the hospital.

Textbook cases typically focus on such update anomalies and use examples analogous to the above when they want to show that a structure is not fully normalized.

2.8.8 **Denormalization and Unnormalization**

As we know, from time to time it is necessary to compromise one data modeling objective to achieve another. Occasionally, we will be obliged to implement database designs that are not fully normalized in order to achieve some other objective (most often performance). When doing this, it is important to look beyond "normalization," as a goal in itself, to the underlying benefits it provides: completeness, nonredundancy, flexibility of extending repeating groups, ease of data reuse, and programming simplicity. These are what we are sacrificing when we implement unnormalized,[9] or only partly normalized, structures.

In many cases, these sacrifices will be prohibitively costly, but in others, they may be acceptable. Figure 2.18 shows two options for representing data about a fleet of aircraft. The first model consists of a single table which is in 1NF, but not in 3NF; the second is a normalized version of the first, comprising four tables.

If we were to find (through calculations or measurement, not just intuition) that the performance cost of accessing the four tables to build up a picture of a given aircraft was unacceptable, we might consider a less-than-fully-normalized structure, although not necessarily the single table model of Figure 2.18(a). In this case, it may be that the **Variant**, **Model**, and **Manufacturer** tables are very stable, and that we are not interested in holding the data unless we have an aircraft of that type. Nevertheless, we would expect that there would be some update of this data, and we would still have to provide the less-elegant update programs no matter how rarely they were used.

(a) Unnormalized Model
AIRCRAFT (<u>Aircraft Tail Number</u>, Purchase Date, Model Name, Variant Code, Variant Name, Manufacturer Name, Manufacturer Supplier Code)
(b) Normalized Model
AIRCRAFT (<u>Aircraft Tail Number</u>, Purchase Date, Variant Code*)
VARIANT (<u>Variant Code</u>, Variant Name, Model Name*)
MODEL (<u>Model Name</u>, Manufacturer Code*)
MANUFACTURER (<u>Manufacturer Supplier Code</u>, Manufacturer Name)

Figure 2.18 Normalization of aircraft data.

---

[9]Strictly, unnormalized means "not in 1NF" and denormalized means "in 1NF but not fully normalized." However, these terms are often used loosely and interchangeably to refer to any structures that are not fully normalized. Unnormalized may be used to mean "prior to normalization" and denormalized to mean "after deliberate compromises to structures which were previously fully normalized."

Considered decisions of this kind are a far cry from the database design folklore that regards denormalization as the first tactic in achieving acceptable performance, and sometimes even as a standard implementation practice regardless of performance considerations. Indeed, the word "denormalization" is frequently used to justify all sorts of design modifications that have nothing to do with normalization at all. We once saw a data model *grow* from 25 to 80 tables under the guise of "denormalization for performance." (We would expect denormalization to *reduce* the number of tables.)

To summarize:

- Normalization is aimed at achieving many of the basic objectives of data modeling, and any compromise should be evaluated in the light of the impact on those objectives.

- There are other techniques for achieving better database performance, many of them affecting only the physical design. These should always be thoroughly explored before compromising the logical database design.

- The physical structure options and optimizers provided by DBMSs are reducing the importance of denormalization as a technique for improving performance.

- No change should ever be made to a logical database design without consultation with the data modeler.

2.8.9 Column and Table Names

In carrying out the normalization process, we took our column names from the original paper form, and we made up table names as we needed them. In a simple example such as this, we may not encounter too many problems with such a casual approach, yet we noted (in Section 2.8.5) that the word "unit" might refer to both the unit in which a surgeon worked and a unit of measure. A close look at the column names suggests that they do not fulfill their potential: for example the column name **Operation Code** suggests that the values in the column will be drawn from a set of codes—potentially useful information. But surely the same would apply to **Method of Administration**, which should then logically be named **Method of Administration Code**.

What we need is a consistent approach to column naming in particular, to convey the meaning of each column as clearly as possible[10] and to allow duplicates to be more readily identified. We look at some suitable rules and conventions in Chapter 5.

---

[10]As we shall see in Chapter 3, names alone are not sufficient to unambiguously define the meaning of columns; they need to be supported by definitions.

2.9 **Choice, Creativity, and Normalization**

Choice and creativity have not featured much in our discussion of normalization so far. Indeed, normalization by itself is a deterministic process, which makes it particularly attractive to teachers; it is always nice to be able to set a problem with a single right answer. The rigor of normalization, and the emphasis placed on it in teaching and research, has sometimes encouraged a view that data modeling as a whole is deterministic.

On the contrary, normalization is only one part of the modeling process. Let's look at our example again with this in mind.

We started the problem with a set of columns. Where did they come from? Some represented well-established classifications; Operation Code was defined according to an international standard. Some classified other data sought by the study—Hospital Name, Contact Person, Surgeon Specialty. And some were invented by the form designer (the *de facto* modeler): the study group had not asked for Hospital Number, Drug Short Name, or Surgeon Number.

We will look at column definition in some detail in Chapter 5; for the moment, let us note that there are real choices here. For example, we could have allocated nonoverlapping ranges of surgeon numbers to each hospital so that Surgeon Number alone was the determinant of Surgeon Specialty. And what if we had not invented a Hospital Number at all? Hospital Name and Contact Person would have remained in the **Operation** table, with all the apparent redundancy that situation would imply. We could not remove them because we would not have a reliable foreign key to leave behind.

All of these decisions, quite outside the normalization process, and almost certainly "sellable" to the business users (after all, they accepted the *unnormalized* design embodied in the original form), would have affected our final solution. The last point is particularly pertinent. We invented a Hospital Number and, at the end of the normalization process, we had a **Hospital** table. Had we not recognized the concept of "hospital" (and hence the need for a hospital number to identify it) before we started normalization, we would not have produced a model with a **Hospital** table. There is a danger of circular reasoning here; we implicitly recognize the need for a **Hospital** table, so we specify a Hospital Number to serve as a key, which in turn leads us to specify a **Hospital** table.

A particularly good example of concepts being embodied in primary keys is the old account-based style of banking system. Figure 2.19 shows

SAVINGS ACCOUNT (Savings Account Number, Name, Address, Account Class, Interest Rate, . . .)

Figure 2.19   Traditional savings account model.

part of a typical savings account file (a savings account *table*, in modern terms). Similar files would have recorded personal loan accounts, checking accounts, and so on. This file may or may not be normalized (for example, **Account Class** might determine **Interest Rate**), but no amount of normalizing will provide two of the key features of many modern banking data models: recognition of the concept of "customer," and integration of different types of accounts. Yet we can achieve this very simply by adding a **Customer Number** (uniquely identifying each customer) and replacing the various specific account numbers with a generic **Account Number**.

Let us be very clear about what is happening here. At some stage in the past, an organization may have designed computer files or manual records and invented various "numbers" and "identifiers" to identify individual records, forms, or whatever. If these identifiers are still around when we get to normalization, our new data model will contain tables that mirror these old classifications of data, which may or may not suit today's requirements. *In short, uncritical normalization perpetuates the data organization of the past.*

In our prenormalization tidying-up phase, we divided complex facts into more primitive facts. There is a degree of subjectivity in this process. By eliminating a multifact column, we add apparent complexity to the model (the extra columns); on the other hand, if we use a single column, we may hide important relationships amongst data, and will need to define a code for each allowable combination.

We will need to consider:

- The value of the primitive data to the business: A paint retailer might keep stock in a number of colors but would be unlikely to need to break the color codes into separate primary color columns (**Percentage Red**, **Percentage Yellow**, **Percentage Blue**); but a paint manufacturer who was interested in the composition of colors might find this a workable approach.
- Customary and external usage: If a way of representing data is well established, particularly outside the business, we may choose to live with it rather than become involved in "reinventing the wheel" and translating between internal and external coding schemes. Codes that have been standardized for electronic data interchange (e-business) are frequently overloaded, or suffer from other deficiencies, which we will discuss in Chapter 5. Nevertheless, the best trade-off often means accepting these codes with their limitations.

Finally, identification of repeating groups requires a decision about *generalization*. In the example we decide that (for example) **Drug Name 1**, **Drug Name 2**, **Drug Name 3**, and **Drug Name 4** are in some sense the "same sort of thing," and we represent them with a generic **Drug Name**. It is hard to dispute this case, but what about the example in Figure 2.20?

CURRENCY (<u>Currency ID</u>, <u>Date</u>, Spot Rate, Exchange Rate 3 Days, Exchange Rate 4 Days, Exchange Rate 5 Days, . . .)

Figure 2.20 Currency exchange rates.

Here we have different currency exchange rates, depending on the number of days until the transaction will be settled. There seems to be a good argument for generalizing most of the rates to a generic **Rate**, giving us a repeating group, but should we include **Spot Rate**, which covers settlement in two days? On the one hand, renaming it "Exchange Rate 2 Days" would probably push us towards including it; on the other, the business has traditionally adopted a different naming convention, perhaps because they see it as somehow different from the others. In fact, spot deals are often handled differently, and we have seen experienced data modelers in similar banks choose different options, without violating any rules of normalization.

Common examples of potential repeating groups include sequences of actions and roles played by people (Figure 2.21).

In this section, we have focused on the choices that are not usually explicitly recognized in the teaching and application of normalization theory, in particular the degree to which primary key selection preempts the outcome. It is tempting to argue that we might as well just define a table for each concept and allocate columns to tables according to common sense. This approach would also help to overcome another problem with the normalization process: the need to start with all data organized into a single table. In a complex real-world model, such a table would be unmanageably large.

In fact, this is the flavor of Chapter 3. However, normalization provides a complementary technique to check that columns are where they belong and that we have not missed any of the less obvious tables. The approach to data modeling projects described in Part 2 begins with top-down modeling, which gives us a first-cut set of tables, and then uses normalization as a test to ensure that these tables are free of the avoidable problems we have discussed in this chapter.

2.10 **Terminology**

In this chapter we have used terminology based around *tables*: more specifically *tables*, *columns*, and *rows*. These correspond fairly closely with the familiar (to older computer professionals) concepts of *files*, *data items* (or *fields*), and *records*, respectively.

APPLICATION (<u>Application ID</u>, Submission Date, Submitted By, Registration Date, Registered By, Examination Date, Examined By, Approval Date, Approved By, . . .)

SCHOOL (<u>School ID</u>, Principal Name, Principal's Contact Number, Deputy Principal Name, Deputy Principal's Contact Number, Secretary Name, Secretary's Contact Number, . . .)

Figure 2.21   Generalization produces repeating groups.

Most theoretical work on relational structures uses a different set of terms: *relations*, *attributes*, and *tuples*, respectively. This is because much of the theory of tabular data organization, including normalization, comes from the mathematical areas of relational calculus and relational algebra.

All that this means to most practitioners is a proliferation of different words for essentially the same concepts. We will stick with tables, columns, and rows, and we will refer to models in this form as relational models. If you are working with a relational DBMS, you will almost certainly find the same convention used, but be prepared to encounter the more formal relational terminology in books and papers, and to hear practitioners talking about files, records, and items. Old habits die hard!

2.11 **Summary**

Normalization is a set of techniques for organizing data into tables in such a way as to eliminate certain types of redundancy and incompleteness, and associated complexity and/or anomalies when updating it. The modeler starts with a single file and divides it into tables based on dependencies among the data items. While the process itself is mechanistic, the initial data will always contain assumptions about the business that will affect the outcome. The data modeler will need to verify and perhaps challenge these assumptions and the business rules that the data dependencies represent.

Normalization relies on correct identification of determinants and keys. In this chapter, we covered normalization to third normal form (3NF). A table is in 3NF if every determinant of a nonkey item is a candidate key. A table can be in 3NF but still not fully normalized. Higher normal forms are covered in Chapter 13.

In practice, normalization is used primarily as a check on the correctness of a model developed using a top-down approach.

Chapter 3
The Entity-Relationship Approach

"It is above all else the separation of designing from making and the increased importance of the drawing which characterises the modern design process."
– Bryan Lawson, How Designers Think

3.1 Introduction

This chapter presents a top-down approach to data modeling, supported by a widely used diagramming convention. In Chapter 2, the emphasis was on confirming that the data organization was technically sound. The focus of this chapter is on ensuring that the data meets business requirements.

We start by describing a procedure for representing existing relational models, such as those that we worked with in Chapter 2, in diagrammatic form. We then look at developing the diagrams directly from business requirements, and introduce a more business-oriented terminology, based around entity classes (things of interest to the business) and the relationships among them. Much of the chapter is devoted to the correct use of terminology and diagramming conventions, which provide a bridge between technical and business views of data requirements.[1]

3.2 A Diagrammatic Representation

Figure 3.1 is the model we produced in Chapter 2 for the drug expenditure example.

Imagine for a moment that you are encountering this model for the first time. Whatever its merits as a rigorous specification for a database designer, its format does not encourage a quick appreciation of the main concepts and

---

[1] It would be nice to be able to say (as many texts would) "a common language" rather than merely a "bridge between views," but in reality most nonspecialists do not have the ability, experience, or inclination to develop or interpret data model diagrams directly. We look at the practicalities of developing and verifying models in Chapter 10. There is further material on the respective roles of data modeling specialists and other stakeholders in Chapters 8 and 9.

OPERATION (<u>Hospital Number*</u>, <u>Operation Number</u>, Operation Code*, Surgeon Number*)

SURGEON (<u>Hospital Number*</u>, <u>Surgeon Number</u>, Surgeon Specialty)

OPERATION TYPE (<u>Operation Code</u>, Operation Name, Procedure Group)

STANDARD DRUG DOSAGE (<u>Drug Short Name*</u>, <u>Size of Dose</u>, <u>Unit of Measure</u>, <u>Method of Administration</u>, Standard Dose Cost)

DRUG (<u>Drug Short Name</u>, Drug Name, Manufacturer)

HOSPITAL (<u>Hospital Number</u>, Hospital Name, Hospital Category, Contact Person)

DRUG ADMINISTRATION (<u>Hospital Number*</u>, <u>Operation Number*</u>, <u>Drug Short Name*</u>, <u>Size of Dose*</u>, <u>Unit of Measure*</u>, <u>Method of Administration*</u>, Number of Doses)

Figure 3.1   Drug expenditure model in relational notation.

---

rules. For example, the fact that each operation can be performed by only one surgeon (because each row of the **Operation** table allows only one surgeon number) is an important constraint imposed by the data model, but is not immediately apparent. This is as simple a model as we are likely to encounter in practice. As we progress to models with more tables and more columns per table, the problem of comprehension becomes increasingly serious.

Process modelers solve this sort of problem by using diagrams, such as data flow diagrams and activity diagrams, showing the most important features of their models. We can approach data models the same way, and this chapter introduces a widely used convention for representing them diagrammatically.

3.2.1   **The Basic Symbols: Boxes and Arrows**

We start by presenting our model as a **data structure diagram** using just two symbols:

1. A "box" (strictly speaking, a rectangle)[2] represents a table.
2. An arrow[3] drawn between two boxes represents a foreign key pointing back to the table where it appears as a primary key.

The boxes are easy. Just draw a box for each table in the model (Figure 3.2), with the name of the table inside it.

---

[2]At this stage, we are producing a data structure diagram in which the boxes represent tables. Later in this chapter we introduce boxes with rounded corners to represent business entity classes.
[3]For the moment, we will refer to these lines as arrows, as it is useful at this stage to see them as "pointing" to the primary key.

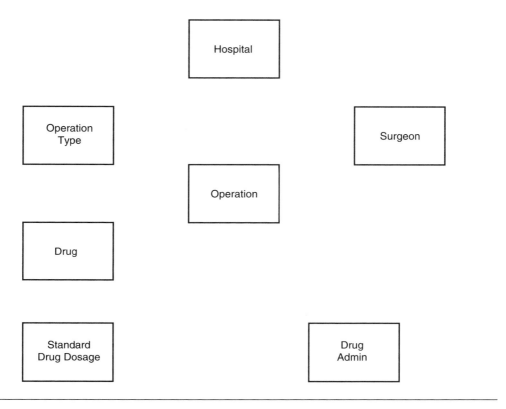

Figure 3.2 Boxes representing tables.

3.2.2 **Diagrammatic Representation of Foreign Keys**

To understand how to draw the arrows, look at the **Operation** and **Surgeon** tables. The primary key of **Surgeon** (Hospital Number + Surgeon Number) appears in the **Operation** table as a foreign key. Draw a line between the two boxes, and indicate the direction of the link by putting a "crow's foot"[4] at the foreign key end (Figure 3.3). You can think of the crow's foot as the tail of an arrow that is pointing back to the relevant surgeon for each operation.

---

[4]Some refer to these as "chicken feet." The shape would seem to be common to a wide range of birds, but we have only encountered these two variants. Excessive attention to matters of this kind is the sort of thing that gives data modelers a reputation for pedantry.

Figure 3.3 Foreign key represented by arrow and crow's foot.

3.2.3 **Interpreting the Diagram**

If presented only with this diagram, we could deduce at least four important things:

1. The model specifies a **Surgeon** table (hence we want to keep data about surgeons).
2. The model specifies an **Operation** table (hence we want to keep data about operations).
3. Each operation can be associated with only one surgeon (because the key of **Surgeon** can appear only once in each row of the **Operation** table, and this is reflected in the diagram by the crow's foot "pointing back" to a single **Surgeon** row).
4. Each surgeon could be associated with many operations (because there is nothing to stop many rows of the **Operation** table containing the same value for the foreign key of **Surgeon**; again, the positioning of the crow's foot at the **Operation** end of the arrow captures this).

The first two rules would have been obvious from the relational representation, the other two much less so. With the diagram, we have succeeded in summarizing the **relationships** between tables implied by our primary and foreign keys, without having to actually list any column names at all.

We could now ask a business specialist, referring to the diagram: "Is it true that each operation is performed by one surgeon only?" It is possible that this is not so, or cannot be relied upon to be so in future. Fortunately, we will have identified the problem while the cost of change is still only a little time reworking the model (we would need to represent the surgeon information as a repeating group in the **Operation** table, then remove it using the normalization rules).

Let us assume that the client in fact confirms that only one surgeon should be recorded against each operation but offers some explanation: while more than one surgeon could in reality participate in an operation, the client is only interested in recording details of the surgeon who *managed* the operation. Having made this decision, it is worth recording it on the diagram

Figure 3.4 Annotated relationship.

(Figure 3.4), first to avoid the question being revisited, and second to specify more precisely what data will be held. It is now clear that the database will not be able to answer the question: "In how many operations did surgeon number 12 at hospital number 18 *participate?*" It *will* support: "How many operations did surgeon number 12 at hospital number 18 *manage?*"

As well as annotating the diagram, we should change the name of the Surgeon Number column in the **Operation** table to "Managing Surgeon Number."

3.2.4 **Optionality**

The diagram may also raise the possibility of operations that do not involve any surgeons at all: "We don't usually involve a surgeon when we are treating a patient with a small cut, but we still need to record whether any drugs were used." In this case, some rows in the **Operation** table may not contain a value for Surgeon Number. We can show whether the involvement of a surgeon in an operation is **optional** or **mandatory** by using the conventions of Figure 3.5. Note that the commentary about the optionality would not normally be

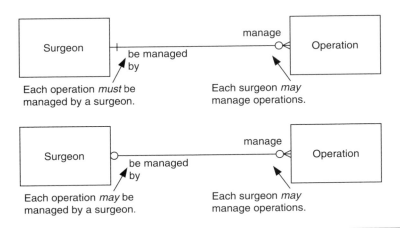

Figure 3.5 Optional and mandatory relationships.

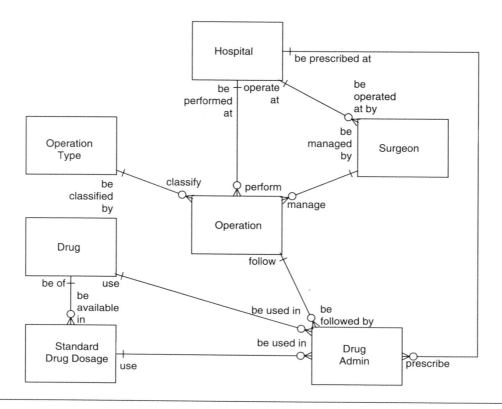

Figure 3.6 Diagram of drug expenditure model.

shown on such a diagram. You can think of the circle as a zero and the perpendicular bar as a one, indicating the minimum number of surgeons per operation or (at the other end of the arrow) operations per surgeon.

Our diagram now contains just about as much information about the **Surgeon** and **Operation** tables and their interrelationships as can be recorded without actually listing columns.[5] The result of applying the rules to the entire drug expenditure model is shown in Figure 3.6.

3.2.5 **Verifying the Model**

The diagram provides an excellent starting point for verifying the model with users and business specialists. Intelligent, thorough checking of each

---

[5]This is not quite all we can usefully record, but few documentation tools support much more than this. Chapter 7 discusses a number of alternatives and extensions to the conventions presented here.

arrow on the diagram will often reveal unsound assumptions and misunderstandings or, equally useful, increase stakeholders' confidence in the workability of the model.

We have already looked at the relationship between **Operation** and **Surgeon**. Now, let's consider the relationship between **Operation** and **Operation Type**. It prompts the question: "Are we sure that each operation can be of only one type?" This is the rule held in the model, but how would we represent a combined gall bladder removal and appendectomy? There are at least two possibilities:

1. Allow only "simple" operation types such as "Gall Bladder Removal" and "Appendectomy." If this course was selected, the model would need to be redesigned, based on the operation type information being a repeating group within the operation; or
2. Allow complex operation types such as "Combined Gall Bladder Removal and Appendectomy."

Both options are technically workable and the decision may be made for us by the existence of an external standard. If the database and associated system have already been implemented, we will probably be forced to implement option 2, unless we are prepared to make substantial changes. But option 1 is more elegant, in that, for example, a single code will be used for all appendectomies. Queries like, "List all operations that involved appendectomies," will therefore be simpler to specify and program.

Examining the relationship between the two tables led to thinking about the meaning of the tables themselves. Whatever decision we made about the relationship, we would need to document a clear definition of what was and what was not a legitimate entry in the **Operation Type** table.

3.2.6 **Redundant Arrows**

Look at the arrows linking the **Hospital**, **Operation**, and **Surgeon** tables. There are arrows from **Hospital** to **Surgeon** and from **Surgeon** to **Operation**. Also there is an arrow from **Operation** direct to **Hospital**. Does this third arrow add anything to our knowledge of the business rules supported by the model? It tells us that each operation must be performed at one hospital. But we can deduce this from the other two arrows, which specify that each operation must be managed by a surgeon and that each surgeon operates at a hospital. The arrow also shows that a program could "navigate" directly from a row in the **Operation** table to the corresponding row in the **Hospital** table. But our concern is with business rules rather than navigation. Accordingly, we can remove the "short-cut" arrow from the diagram without losing any information about the business rules that the model enforces.

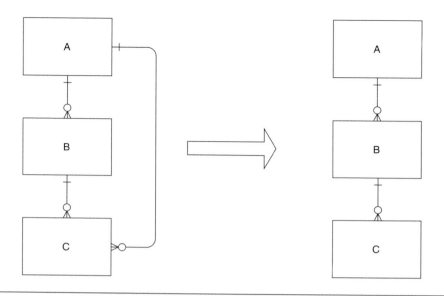

Figure 3.7 Removing redundant arrows.

Figure 3.7 summarizes the rule for removing redundant arrows, but the rule has some important caveats:

If it were possible for an operation to be recorded without a surgeon (i.e., if the link to the **Surgeon** table were *optional*), we could not remove the short-cut arrow (from **Operation** direct to **Hospital**). If we did, we could no longer count on being able to deduce from the other arrows the hospital at which an operation was performed.

If the arrow from **Surgeon** to **Hospital** was named (for example) "be trained at," then the direct link from **Operation** to **Hospital** would represent different information than the combined link. The former would identify the hospital at which the operation was performed, the latter which hospital trained the surgeon who performed the operation.

The value of recording names and optionality on the arrows should now be a little clearer. For one thing, they allow the correct decision to be made about which arrows on the diagram are redundant and can be removed. Figure 3.8 shows the result of applying the redundant arrow rule to the whole model.

3.3 **The Top-Down Approach: Entity-Relationship Modeling**

In the preceding section, a reasonably straightforward technique was used to represent a relational data model in diagrammatic form. Although the

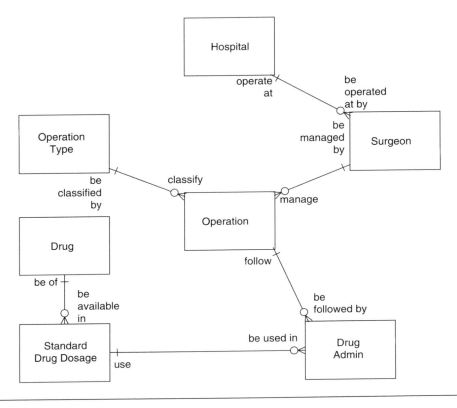

Figure 3.8 Drug expenditure model with redundant lines removed.

diagram contains little new information[6], it communicates some of the model's most important rules so much more clearly that you should never review or present a model without drawing one. In the past, databases were often designed without the use of diagrams, or the working diagrams were not kept. It is interesting to prepare a diagram for such a database and show it to programmers and analysts who have been working with the database for some time.[7] Frequently they have never explicitly considered many of the rules and limitations that the diagram highlights.

There is a good analogy with architecture here: we may have lost the plans for an existing building, but we can reconstruct them by examining

---

[6]The new information it contains is the names of the relationships (which can be captured by well-chosen names for foreign key columns) and whether relationships are optional or mandatory in the "many" direction (a relatively unimportant piece of information, captured largely to achieve symmetry with the "one" end of the relationship, where optionality reflects the fact that the foreign key columns need not contain a value).

[7]Techniques for developing diagrams for existing databases (as distinct from well-documented relational models) are covered in Section 9.5.

the existing structure and following some accepted diagramming conventions. The plans then form a convenient (and portable) summary of the building's design.

3.3.1 Developing the Diagram Top Down

The most interesting thing about the diagram is that it prompts a suspicion that normalization and subsequent translation into boxes and arrows was not necessary at all. If instead we had asked the client, "What things do you need to keep data about?" would we not have received answers such as, "hospitals, operations, and surgeons?" If we had asked how they were related, might we not have been able to establish that each operation was managed by one surgeon only, and so forth? With these questions answered, could we not draw the diagram immediately, without bothering about normalization?

In fact, this is the approach most often taken in practice, and the one that we describe in Part 2 of this book. The modeler develops a diagram that effectively specifies which tables will be required, how they will need to be related, and what columns they will contain. Normalization becomes a final check to ensure that the "grammar" of the model is correct. For experienced modelers, the check becomes a formality, as they will have already anticipated the results of normalization and incorporated them into the diagram.

The reason we looked at normalization first is that in order to produce a normalized model, you need to know what one looks like, just as an architect needs to have examined some completed buildings before attempting to design one. Ultimately, we want a design, made up of sound, fully normalized tables, that meets our criteria of completeness, nonredundancy, stability, flexibility, communication, rule enforcement, reusability, integration, and elegance—not a mish-mash of business concepts. The frequently given advice, "Ask what things the business needs to keep information about, and draw a box for each of these," is overly simplistic, although it indicates the general direction of the approach.

The need to produce a normalized model should be in the back of our minds, and we will therefore split up repeating groups and "reference tables" as we discover them. For example, we might identify a table called **Vehicle**. We recognize that some data will be the same for all vehicles of a particular type and that normalization would produce a **Vehicle Type** reference table for this data. Accordingly, a box named "Vehicle Type" is drawn. We are actually doing a little more than normalization here, as we do not actually know if there is an existing determinant of **Vehicle Type** in the data (e.g., Vehicle Model Number). No matter: we reserve the right to define one if we need it.

In dealing with a **Customer** table, we may recognize that a customer may have more than one occupation, and that data about occupations therefore forms a repeating group that normalization would remove. We can anticipate this and define a separate **Occupation** table, again without knowledge of actual columns and determinants.

The top-down approach also overcomes most of the limitations of normalization used by itself. We do not need to start with a formidably complex single table, nor do we need to accept the tables implicitly defined by our historical choice of determinants.

3.3.2 **Terminology**

As we shift our focus from the technicalities of table definition toward business requirements—and indeed toward the conceptual modeling stage—it helps to introduce a more business-oriented terminology. The relational models we looked at in Chapter 2 were built on three basic concepts: tables, columns, and keys.

Our terminology for the conceptual model is more business-oriented. Again, there are three basic concepts:

1. **Entity classes**: categories of things of interest to the business; represented by boxes on the diagram, and generally implemented as tables
2. **Attributes**: what we want to know about entity classes; not usually shown on the diagram and generally implemented as columns in tables
3. **Relationships**: represented by lines with crows' feet (we will drop the term "arrow" now that we are talking about conceptual models), and generally implemented through foreign keys.

Note the use of the word "generally" in the above descriptions of how the components of the conceptual model will be implemented. As we shall see later in this chapter, and in Chapters 11 and 12, there are some exceptions, which represent important transformations and design decisions as we move from the conceptual model to logical and physical models.

Do not be daunted by the new terms. Broadly speaking, we have just introduced a less technical language, to enable us to talk about (for example) "the relationship between a hospital and a surgeon," rather than "the existence of the primary key of **Hospital** as a foreign key in the **Surgeon** table."

The process of designing appropriate classes of entity classes, relationships, and attributes to meet a business problem is called **entity-relationship modeling** (E-R modeling for short) or, more generally, conceptual modeling.

(The latter term does not restrict us to using a particular set of conventions; as we shall see in Chapter 7, there are alternatives and extensions to the basic entity-relationship approach.) A data model in this format is often called an E-R[8] model or conceptual model, and the diagram an E-R diagram (ERD). The omission of the word "attribute" from these widely-used terms reflects the fact that attributes do not generally appear on the diagrams, which are usually the most visible deliverable of modeling. Of course, the conceptual model is not just the diagram; E-R modeling needs to produce (at a minimum) entity class definitions and attribute lists and definitions to supplement the diagram.

In the following sections, these new terms and their representation are examined in more detail.

3.4 **Entity Classes**

An **entity class** is a real-world class of things such as **Hospital**. We make the distinction between entities, such as "St. Vincent's Hospital" and entity classes (sometimes called entity types) such as "Hospital." In practice, many E-R modelers use the word entity loosely to mean entity class and use entity instance for those fairly rare occasions when they want to refer to a single instance. However, modelers with a background in object-oriented techniques are likely to use the term entity class more strictly, and they may refer to entity instances as entities. In the interests of clarity and of improving communication among modelers from different schools, we use the term entity class throughout this book.[9]

All entity classes will meet the criterion of being "a class of things we need to keep information about," as long as we are happy for "thing" to include more abstract concepts such as events (e.g., **Operation**) and classifications (e.g., **Operation Type**). However, the converse is not true; many classes that a user might nominate in response to the question, "What do you need to keep information about?" would not end up as entity classes.

Some concepts suggested by the user will be complex and will need to be represented by more than one entity class. For example, invoices would

---

[8]The term Entity Relationship Modeling originated with a paper by Peter Chen: P. Chen, "The Entity-Relationship Model—Toward a Unified View of Data," ACM Transactions on Database Systems, Vol. 1, No. 1. March 1976. The diagramming conventions proposed in that paper are in fact different from those used here. The Chen convention (recognizable by the use of diamonds for relationships) is widely used in academic work, but much less so in practice. The conventions that we use here reflect the Information Engineering (IE) approach associated with Finkelstein and Martin. The IE conventions in turn have much in common with the Data Structure Diagrams ("Bachman Diagrams") used to document conceptual schemas from the late 1960s.

[9]Strictly, we should also refer to "relationship classes" and "attribute classes" to be consistent with our use of the term "entity class." However, these terms are seldom used by practitioners.

not usually be represented by a single **Invoice** entity class, but by two entity classes: **Invoice** (holding invoice header information) and **Invoice Item** (the result of removing the repeating group of invoice items to form a separate entity class). Other user requirements will be derivable from more primitive data—for example **Quarterly Profit** might be derivable from sales and expense figures represented by other entity classes and their attributes.

Still other "real-world" classes will overlap and will therefore violate our nonredundancy requirement. If our model already had **Personal Customer** and **Corporate Customer** entity classes, we would not add a **Preferred Customer** entity class if such customers were already catered for by the original entity classes.[10]

Finally, some concepts will be represented by attributes or relationships. There is a degree of subjectivity in deciding whether some concepts are best represented as entity classes or relationships; is a marriage better described as a relationship between two people, or as "something we need to keep information about?"

There is almost always an element of choice in how data is classified into entity classes. Should a single entity class represent all employees or should we define separate entity classes for part-time and full-time employees? Should we use separate entity classes for insurance policies and cover notes, or is it better to combine them into a single **Policy** entity class? We will discuss ways of generating and choosing alternatives in Chapters 4 and 10; for the moment, just note that such choices do exist, even though they may not be obvious in these early examples.

Now a few rules for representing entity classes. Recommending a particular set of conventions is one of the best ways of starting an argument among data modelers, and there was a time when there seemed to be as many diagramming conventions as modelers. These days, the situation is somewhat better, thanks mainly to the influence of CASE tools, which enforce reasonably similar conventions. The rules for drawing entity classes and relationships presented in this chapter are typical of current practice.

3.4.1 **Entity Diagramming Convention**

In this book, entity classes are represented by boxes with rounded corners. We use the rounded corners to distinguish entity classes in conceptual models from tables (represented by square-cornered boxes) in logical and physical data models. The latter may include compromises required to

---

[10]This is not strictly true if we allow subtyping and, in particular, subtyping with multiple partitions. We look at these topics in Chapter 4.

achieve adequate performance or to suit the constraints of the implementation software.

There are no restrictions, other than those imposed by your documentation tools, on the size or color of the boxes. If drawing an entity class box larger or in another color aids communication, by all means do it. For example, you might have a **Customer** entity class and several associated entity classes resulting from removing repeating groups: **Address**, **Occupation**, **Dependant**, and so on. Just drawing a larger box for the **Customer** entity class might help readers approach the diagram in a logical fashion.

3.4.2 Entity Class Naming

The name of an entity class must be in the singular and refer to a single instance (in relational terms, a row)—not to the whole table. Thus, collective terms like File, Table, Catalog, History, and Schedule are inappropriate.

For example, we use:

Account rather than **Accounts**
Customer rather than **Customer File** or **Customer Table**, or even **Customer Record**
Product rather than **Product Catalog**
Historical Transaction rather than **Transaction History**
Scheduled Visit rather than **Visiting Schedule**

We do this for three reasons:

1. *Consistency*: It is the beginning of a naming standard for entity classes.
2. *Communication*: An entity class is "something we want to keep information about," such as a customer rather than a customer file.
3. *Generating business assertions*: As we will see in the following section and in Section 10.18, if we follow some simple rules in naming the components of an E-R model, we can automatically generate grammatically sound **assertions** which can be checked by stakeholders.

You should be aware of, and avoid, some common bad practices in entity class naming:

One is to name the entity class after the most "important" attribute—for example, **Dose Cost** rather than **Standard Drug Dosage**, or **Specialty** rather than **Surgeon**. This is particularly tempting when we have only one nonkey attribute. It looks much less reasonable later when we add further attributes, or if the original attribute is normalized out to another entity class. You should also avoid giving an entity class a name that reflects only a subset of the roles it plays in the business. For example, consider using **Material Item** rather than **Component**, **Person** rather than **Witness**, and **Stock Item** rather than **Returned Item**.

Another mistake is to name one entity class by adding a prefix to the name of another, for example, **External Employee** when there is already an **Employee** entity class. The natural assumption is that an external employee is a particular type of employee. Such naming should therefore be limited to cases where one entity class is a subtype of the other entity class (we look at subtypes in Chapter 4). It would be wrong to have entity classes named **Employee** and **External Employee** where the **Employee** entity class represented only *internal* employees, since it would be reasonable to infer that the **Employee** entity class included external employees as well. If an entity class representing only internal employees were required in this model it should be named **Internal Employee**.

A third is to abbreviate names unnecessarily. This is often done merely to save a few keystrokes. Modelers almost inevitably abbreviate inconsistently and without providing a list of abbreviation meanings. While the use of several abbreviations for the same word is perhaps more irritating than ambiguous, the opposite condition, of the same abbreviation being used for different words, is clearly ambiguous, but we have seen it more than once.

A list of abbreviation meanings might seem to be overkill, yet it is remarkable how much imagination is shown by analysts when choosing abbreviations, resulting in abominations that mean nothing to those attempting to understand the data structure. Some DBMSs impose stringent limits on the length of table and column names, requiring even more abbreviation. Given that developers and the writers of *ad hoc* queries may only have table and column names to work with, it is important that such names be unambiguous.

A good example of these perils occurred in a school administration system in which the names of the columns holding information about students' parents were prefixed by "M" and "F": M-Parent and F-Parent. Was that "mother" and "father" or "male" and "female"? It depended on who was entering the data.

Often in data modeling we have to discard familiar terms in favor of less widely used terms that do not carry the same diversity of meaning. This is particularly so for the most commonly used terms, which may have acquired all sorts of context-dependent meanings over a period of time. To a railroad company, the word "train" may mean a particular service (the 8.15 P.M. from Sydney to Melbourne), a physical object (Old Number 10), or perhaps a marketed product (the Orient Express).

Sometimes we have a choice of either restricting the meaning of an existing term or introducing a new term. The first approach produces a diagram that is more accessible to people familiar with the business, and apparently more meaningful; on the other hand, readers are less likely to look up the definition and may be misled. Keep this in mind: "communication" must include an understanding of the meaning of entity classes as well as a superficial comfort with the diagram.

3.4.3 **Entity Class Definitions**

Entity class names must be supported by definitions.

We cannot overemphasize the importance of good entity class definitions. From time to time, data modelers get stuck in long arguments without much apparent progress. Almost invariably, they have not put adequate effort into pinning down some working definitions, and they are continually making subtle mental adjustments, which are never recorded. Modelers frequently (and probably unwittingly) shift definitions in order to support their own position in discussion: "Yes, we could accommodate a patient who transfers hospitals while undergoing treatment by defining **Hospital** to mean the hospital where the treatment commenced," and later, "Of course we can work out how much each hospital spent on drugs; all the relevant hospitals are represented by the **Hospital** entity class."

As well as helping to clarify the modelers' thinking, definitions provide guidance on the correct use of the resulting database. Many a user interrogating a database through a query language has been misled because of incorrect assumptions about what its tables contained. And many a programmer or user has effectively changed the data model by using tables to hold data other than that intended by the modeler. The latter constitutes a particularly insidious compromise to a model. If someone (perhaps the physical database designer) proposes that the physical data model differ from the logical data model in some way, we can at least argue the case and ensure that the changes, if accepted, are documented and understood. However, bypassing a definition is far subtler, as the violation is buried in program specifications and logic. Because system enhancement cycles can be slow, users themselves may resort to reuse of data items for other purposes. In a typical case, a comment field was redefined by the users to hold a series of classification codes in the first line and the comment proper in the remaining lines.

The result can be inconsistent use of data by programmers and consequent system problems ("I assumed that surgeons included anyone who performed an operation," or "I used the **Surgeon** table for pharmacists; they're all prefixed with a 'P'"). The database may even be rendered unworkable because a business rule specified by the model does not apply under the (implicit) new definition. For example, the rule that each drug has only one manufacturer will be broken if the programmer uses the table to record generic drugs in violation of a definition that allows only for branded drugs. Changes of this kind are often made after a database has been implemented, and subsequently fails to support new requirements. A failure on the stability criterion leads to compromises in elegance and communication.

All of these scenarios are also examples of degradation in data quality. If a database is to hold good quality data, it is vital that definitions are not only well written but *used*.[11] This, of course, implies that all participants in the system-development process and all users of the resulting system have access to the same set of definitions, whether in a data dictionary or in another form of controlled but accessible project documentation.

A good entity class definition will clearly answer two questions:

1. What distinguishes instances of this entity class from instances of other entity classes?
2. What distinguishes one instance from another?

Good examples, focusing on the marginal cases, can often help clarify the answers to these questions. The primary key (if one is known at this stage) and a few other sample attributes can also do much to clarify the definition prior to the full set of attributes being defined.

Again a number of bad practices occur regularly, particularly if entity class definition is seen as a relatively meaningless chore rather than a key part of the modeling process:

- A glance at a thesaurus will reveal that many common words have multiple meanings, yet these same words are often used without qualification in definitions. In one model, an entity class named **Role** had the definition *"Part, task, or function,"* which, far from providing the reader with additional information as to what the entity class represented, widened the range of possibilities.

- Entity class definitions often do not make clear whether instances of the entity class are classes or individual occurrences. For example, does a **Patient Condition** entity class with a definition, *"A condition that a patient suffers,"* have instances like "Influenza" and "Hangnail" or instances like "Patient 123345's influenza that was diagnosed on 1/4/2004"? This sort of ambiguity is often defended by assertions that the identifier or other attributes of the entity class should make this clear. If the identifier is simply Patient Condition Identifier, we are none the wiser, and if the attributes are not well defined, as is often the case, we may still be in the dark.

- Another undesirable practice is using information technology terminology, and technical data modeling terms in entity class definitions. Terms such as "intersection entity," "cardinality," "optionality," "many-to-many relationship," or "foreign key" mean nothing to the average business person and should not appear in data definitions. If business users do not understand the definitions, their review of them will lack rigor.

---

[11] See, for example, Witt, G.C., "The Role of Metadata in Data Quality," *Journal of Data Warehousing* Vol. 3, No. 4 (Winter 1998).

Let's have a look at an example of a definition. We might define **Drug** as follows:

> "An antibiotic drug as marketed by a particular manufacturer. Variants that are registered as separate entries in *Smith's Index of Therapeutic Drugs* are treated as separate instances. Excluded are generic drugs such as penicillin. Examples are: Maxicillin, Minicillin, Extracycline."

Note that there is no rule against using the entity class name in the definition; we are not trying to write an English dictionary. However beware of using *other* entity class names in a definition. When a modeler chooses a name for an entity class, that entity class is usually not intended to represent every instance of anything that conforms to the dictionary definitions of that name. For example, the name "Customer" may be used for an entity class that only represents *some* of the customers of a business (e.g., loyalty program customers but not casual walk-in customers). If that entity class name is then used in a definition of another entity class, there is potential for confusion as to whether the common English meaning or the strict entity class definition is intended.

3.5 Relationships

In our drug expenditure model, the lines between boxes can be interpreted in real-world terms as relationships between entity classes. There are relationships, for example, between hospitals and surgeons and between operations and drug administrations.

3.5.1 Relationship Diagramming Conventions

We have already used a convention for annotating the lines to describe their meaning (relationship names), **cardinality** (the crow's foot can be interpreted as meaning "many," its absence as meaning "one"), and **optionality** (the circles and bars representing "optional" and "mandatory" respectively).

The convention is shown in Figure 3.9 and is typical of several in common use and supported by documentation tools. Note that the arrows and associated annotation would not normally be shown on such a diagram. Figure 3.10 shows some variants, including Unified Modeling Language (UML), which is now established as the most widely used alternative to the E-R conventions.[12] Use of this notation is discussed in Chapter 7.

---

[12]The diagrams shown are not exactly equivalent; each diagramming formalism has its own peculiarities in terms of what characteristics of a relationship can be captured and the exact interpretation of each symbol.

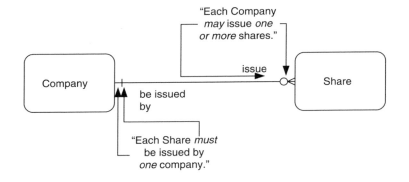

Figure 3.9 Relationship notation.

Note that we have named the relationship in both directions: "issue" and "be issued by." This enables us to interpret the relationship in a very structured, formal way:

"Each company may issue one or more shares."

and

"Each share must be issued by one company."

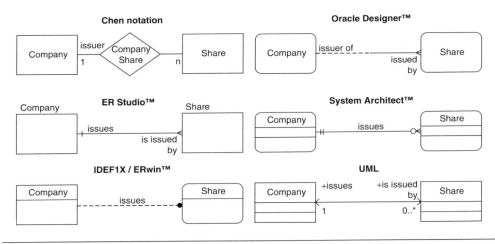

Figure 3.10 Some alternative relationship notations.[13]

---

[13]Note that these conventions and tools include many symbols other than those shown in this diagram, which is intended only to show the variation in representing the most common type of relationship. Note also that some tools allow alternative notations, (e.g., ERwin can alternatively use the System Architect relationship notation). For a more detailed comparison of some of the diagramming conventions used by practitioners in particular, we recommend Hay, D.C: *Requirements Analysis—From Business Views to Architecture*, Prentice-Hall, New Jersey, 2003, Appendix B.

The value of this **assertion** form is in improving communication. While diagrams are great for conveying the big picture, they do not encourage systematic and detailed examination, particularly by business specialists. If we record plural forms of entity class names in our documentation tool, generating these sentences can be an entirely automatic process. Of course, when reading from a diagram we just pluralize the entity class names ourselves. Some CASE tools do support such generation of assertions, using more or less similar formulae.

We like to use the expression "one or more" rather than "many," which may have a connotation of "a large number" ("Oh no, nobody would have *many* occupations, two or three would be the most"). We also like the "may" and "must" approach to describing optionality, rather than the "zero or more" and "one or more" wording used by some. "Zero or more" is an expression only a programmer could love, and our aim is to communicate with business specialists in a natural way without sacrificing precision.

An alternative to using "must" and "may" is to use "always" and "sometimes": "Each company sometimes issues one or more shares," and "Each share is always issued by one company." "Might" is also a workable alternative to "may."

In order to be able to automatically translate relationships into assertions about the business data, a few rules need to be established:

■ We have to select relationship names that fit the sentence structure. It is worth trying to use the same verb in both directions ("hold" and "be held by," or "be responsible for" and "be the responsibility of") to ensure that the relationship is not interpreted as carrying two separate meanings.

■ We have to name the relationships in both directions, even though this adds little to the meaning. We make a practice not only of placing each relationship name close to the entity class that is the object of the sentence, but also of arranging the names above and below the line so they are read in a clockwise direction when generating the sentence (as, for example, in Figure 3.9).

■ We need to be strict about using singular names for entity classes. As mentioned earlier, this discipline is worth following regardless of relationship naming conventions.

Finally, we need to show the optional/mandatory symbol at the crow's foot end of the relationship, even though this will not usually be enforceable by the DBMS (at the end without the crow's foot, "optional" is normally implemented by specifying the foreign key column as optional or **nullable**, that is, it does not have to have a value in every row). Despite this there are a number of situations, which we discuss in Section 14.5.3, in which the mandatory nature of a relationship at the crow's foot end is very important.

Figures 3.11 and 3.12 show some relationships typical of those we encounter in practice.

Note that:

- A crow's foot may appear at neither, one, or both ends of a relationship. The three alternatives are referred to as one-to-one, one-to-many, and many-to-many relationships, respectively.
- There may be more than one relationship between the same two entity classes.
- It is possible for the same entity class to appear at both ends of a relationship. This is called a "self-referencing" or "recursive" relationship.

When drawing one-to-many relationships, we suggest you locate the boxes so that the crow's foot points downwards (i.e., so that the box representing the entity class at the "many" end of the relationship is nearer the bottom of the page). This means that hierarchies appear in the expected

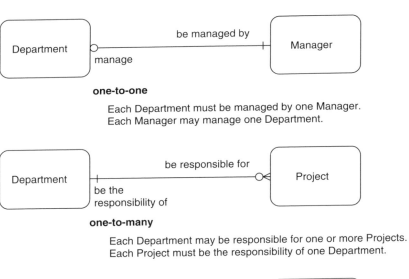

one-to-one

Each Department must be managed by one Manager.
Each Manager may manage one Department.

one-to-many

Each Department may be responsible for one or more Projects.
Each Project must be the responsibility of one Department.

many-to-many

Each Employee may be awarded one or more Qualifications.
Each Qualification may be awarded to one or more Employees.

Figure 3.11 Examples of relationships.

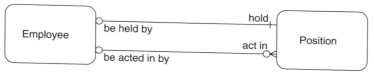

two relationships

Each Employee must hold one Position.
Each Position may be held by one Employee.

and

Each Employee may act in one or more Positions.
Each Position may be acted in by one Employee.

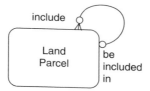

self-referencing one-to-many

Each Land Parcel may include one or more Land Parcels.
Each Land Parcel may be included in one Land Parcel.

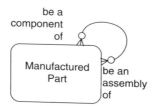

self-referencing many-to-many

Each Manufactured Part may be an assembly of one or more
Manufactured Parts.

Each Manufactured Part may be a component of one or more
Manufactured Parts.

Figure 3.12   More examples of relationships.

way, and diagrams are easier to compare. For horizontal relationship lines,
the convention (by no means followed by all modelers) is to orient the
crow's foot to the right. You will not always be able to follow these
conventions, especially when you use subtypes, which we introduce in
Chapter 4. Once again, do not sacrifice effectiveness of communication for
blind adherence to a layout convention.

Similarly, in laying out diagrams, it usually helps to eliminate crossing
lines wherever possible. But carrying this rule too far can result in large

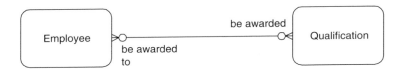

Figure 3.13 Many-to-many relationship.

numbers of close parallel lines not dissimilar in appearance (and compre-hensibility) to the tracks on a printed circuit board.

Another useful technique is to duplicate entity classes on the diagram to avoid long and difficult-to-follow relationship lines. You need to have a symbol (provided by some CASE tools) to identify a duplicated entity class; a dotted box is a good option.

3.5.2 **Many-to-Many Relationships**

Many-to-many relationships crop up regularly in E-R diagrams in practice. But if you look again at the drug expenditure diagram in Figure 3.8 you will notice that it contains only one-to-many relationships. This is no accident, but a consequence of the procedure we used to draw the diagram from normalized tables. Remember that each value of a foreign key pointed to *one* row (representing one entity instance), and that each value could appear *many* times; hence, we can only ever end up with one-to-many relationships when documenting a set of relational tables.

Look at the many-to-many relationship between **Employee** and **Qualification** in Figure 3.13.

How would we implement the relationship using foreign keys? The answer is that we cannot in a standard relational DBMS.[14] We cannot hold the key to **Qualification** in the **Employee** table because an employee could have several qualifications. The same applies to the **Qualification** table, which would need to record multiple employees. A normalized model cannot represent many-to-many relationships with foreign keys, yet such relationships certainly exist in the real world. A quick preview of the answer: although we cannot implement the many-to-many relationship with a foreign key, we *can* implement it with a table. But let us tackle the problem systematically.

---

[14]A DBMS that supports the SQL99 **set type constructor** feature enables implementa-tion of a many-to-many relationship without creating an additional table through storage of open-ended arrays in row/column intersections. This provides an alternative mechanism for storage of a many-to-many relationship (admittedly no longer in 1NF).

> **EMPLOYEE** (<u>Employee Number</u>, Employee Name, {Qualification ID,
> Qualification Name, Qualification Date})

Figure 3.14 Employee and Qualification unnormalized.

3.5.2.1 Applying Normalization to Many-to-Many Relationships

Although we cannot represent the many-to-many relationship between **Employee** and **Qualification** in a fully normalized logical model using only **Employee** and **Qualification** tables, we can handle it with an **unnormalized** representation, using a repeating group (Figure 3.14).

We have made up a few plausible columns to give us something to normalize!

Proceeding with normalization (Figure 3.15), we remove the repeating group and identify the key of the new table as Employee Number + Qualification ID (if an employee could receive the same qualification more than once, perhaps from different universities, we would need to include Qualification Date in the key to distinguish them).

Looking at our 1NF tables, we note the following dependency:

Qualification ID → Qualification Name

Hence, we provide a reference table for qualification details. The tables are now in 3NF. You may like to confirm that we would have reached the same result if we had represented the relationship initially with a repeating group of employee details in the **Qualification** table.

Unnormalised:
EMPLOYEE (<u>Employee Number</u>, Employee Name, {Qualification ID, Qualification Name, Qualification Date})

First Normal Form:
EMPLOYEE (<u>Employee Number</u>, Employee Name)
EMPLOYEE QUALIFICATION (<u>Employee Number*</u>, <u>Qualification ID</u>, Qualification Name, Qualification Date)

Second and Third Normal Forms:
EMPLOYEE (<u>Employee Number</u>, Employee Name)
EMPLOYEE QUALIFICATION RELATIONSHIP (<u>Employee Number*</u>, <u>Qualification ID*</u>, Qualification Date)
QUALIFICATION (<u>Qualification ID</u>, Qualification Name)

Figure 3.15 Normalization of Employee and Qualification.

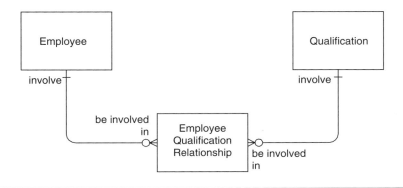

Figure 3.16   Many-to-many relationship resolved.

Naming the tables presents a bit of a challenge. **Employee** and **Qualification** are fairly obvious, but what about the other table? **Employee-Qualification Relationship**[15] is one option and makes some sense because this less obvious table represents the many-to-many relationship between the other two. The result is shown diagrammatically in Figure 3.16.

This example illustrates an important general rule. Whenever we encounter a many-to-many relationship between two entity classes, we can implement it by introducing a third table in addition to the tables derived from the two original entity classes. This third table is referred to variously as an **intersection table**, **relationship table**, **associative table**, or **resolution table**.[16] We call this process "resolving a many-to-many relationship." There is no need to go through the normalization process each time; we simply recognize the pattern and handle it in a standard way.

Note the optional/mandatory nature of the new relationships and how they derive from the optional/mandatory nature of the original many-to-many relationship:

- The "one" ends of the new relationships will always be mandatory (since an instance of the relationship without both of the original participating entity classes—in this case, an employee qualification relationship without both an employee and a qualification—does not make sense).

- The "many" ends of the new relationships will be optional or mandatory depending on the corresponding ends of the original relationship.

---

[15]Some modelers avoid the use of the word Relationship in a table name. We believe it is entirely appropriate if the table implements a relationship from the conceptual model. Using the term in the name of an *entity* is a different matter, though common practice, and there is an argument for using an alternative such as "cross-reference."

[16]In fact you will hear the terms used far more often in the context of entities, as discussed in the following section.

The nature of that correspondence is best illustrated by reference to Figures 3.13 and 3.16. The nature of the relationship to **Employee** will correspond to the nature of the original relationship at the **Qualification** end and the nature of the relationship to **Qualification** will correspond to the nature of the original relationship at the **Employee** end. Thus, if an employee had to have at least one qualification (i.e., the original relationship was mandatory at the **Qualification** end), the relationship between **Employee** and **Employee Qualification Relationship** would also be mandatory at the "many" end.

3.5.2.2 Choice of Representation

There is nothing (at least technically) to stop us from now bringing the conceptual model into line with the logical model by introducing an **Employee Qualification Relationship** *entity class* and associated relationships. Such entity classes are variously referred to as **intersection entities**, **associative entities**, **resolution entities**, or (occasionally and awkwardly) **relationship entities**.

So, we are faced with an interesting choice: we can represent the same "real-world" situation either with a many-to-many relationship or with an entity class and two new many-to-one relationships, as illustrated in Figure 3.17.

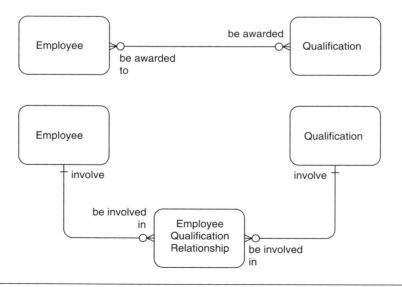

Figure 3.17 Many-to-many relationship or intersection entity class plus two one-to-many relationships.

Relationship	Intersection Entity Class
Students *enroll* in Subjects	Enrollment
Companies *employ* Persons	Employment
Employees *are responsible for* Assets	Responsibility

Figure 3.18   Intersection entity class names.

The many-to-many notation preserves consistency; we use a line to represent each real-world relationship, whether it is one-to-many or many-to-many (or one-to-one, for that matter). But we now have to perform some conversion to get to the relational representation required for the logical model. Worse, the conversion is not totally mechanical, in that we have to determine the key of the intersection table. In our example, this key might simply be **Employee Number** plus **Qualification ID**; however, if an employee can receive the same qualification more than once, the key of the intersection table must include **Qualification Date**. And how do we represent any nonkey attributes that might apply to the intersection entity class, such as **Qualification Date**? Do we need to allow entity classes *and* relationships to have attributes?[17]

On the other hand, if we restrict ourselves to one-to-many relationships, we seem to be stuck with the clumsy idea of an entity class whose name implies that it is a relationship. And if this box actually represents a real-world relationship rather than an entity class, what about the two one-to-many "relationships" with the original entity classes? Can we really interpret them as "real-world" relationships, or are they just "links" between relationships and entity classes?

One solution lies in the fact that there is usually some choice as to whether to classify a particular concept as an entity class or a relationship. For example, we could model the data relating prospective employees and job positions with either a relationship ("apply for/be applied for by") or an entity class (**Application**). Figure 3.18 shows some more examples.

The name of the many-to-many relationship is usually a good source of an appropriate entity class name. Perhaps we could use **Award** as an alternative to **Employee Qualification Relationship**.

Experienced data modelers take advantage of this choice, and become adept at selecting names that allow boxes to represent entity classes and lines to represent relationships. As a last resort, they would name the box representing a many-to-many relationship as "entity class-1 entity class-2 Relationship" (e.g., **Employee Asset Relationship**), and thereafter treat it as an *entity class*. This practice is so widespread that most data modelers refer to all boxes as entity classes and all lines as relationships. Many would

---

[17]Note that UML does allow relationships to have attributes (see Section 7.4.2).

be unaware that this is possible only because of choices they have made during the modeling process.

This may all sound a little like cheating! Having decided that a particular concept is going to be implemented by a foreign key (because of the way our DBMS works), we then decide that the concept is a relationship. Likewise, if a particular concept is to be implemented as a table, we decide to call the concept a real world entity class. And we may change our view along the way, if we discover, for example, that a relationship we originally thought to be one-to-many is in fact many-to-many.

We come back to the questions of design, choice, and creativity. If we think of the real world as being naturally preclassified into entity classes and relationships, and our job as one of analysis and documentation, then we are in trouble. On the other hand, if we see ourselves as designers who can choose the most useful representation, then this classification into entity classes and relationships is a legitimate part of our task.

Our own preference, reflected in Part 2 of the book, is to allow many-to-many relationships in the conceptual model, provided they do not have nonkey attributes. However, you may well be restricted by a tool that does not separate conceptual and logical models (and hence requires that the model be normalized), or one that simply does not allow many-to-many relationships in the conceptual model. In these cases, you will need to "resolve" all many-to-many relationships in the conceptual model.

3.5.3 **One-to-One Relationships**

Figure 3.19 shows some examples of one-to-one relationships.

One-to-one relationships occur far less frequently than one-to-many and many-to-many relationships, and your first reaction to a one-to-one relationship should be to verify that you have it right.

The third example in Figure 3.19 appears simply to be factoring out some attributes that apply only to government contracts. We see this sort of structure quite often in practice, and it always warrants investigation. Perhaps the modeler is anticipating that the attributes that have been factored out will be implemented as columns in a separate table and is making that decision prematurely. Or perhaps they want to capture the business rule that the attributes need to be treated as a group: either "all inapplicable" or "all applicable." In Chapter 4, we will look at a better way of capturing rules of this kind.

One-to-one relationships can be a useful tool for exploring alternative ways of modeling a situation, allowing us to "break up" traditional entity classes and reassemble them in new ways. They also present some special problems in implementation. In particular, note that you should not *automatically* combine the entity classes linked by a one-to-one relationship into

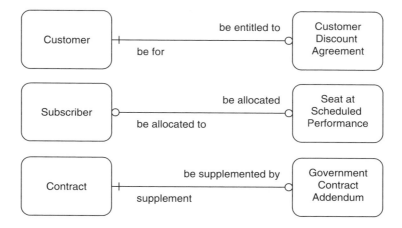

Figure 3.19   One-to-one relationships.

a single entity class or implement them as a single table, as is sometimes suggested.

We discuss the handling of one-to-one relationships in some detail in Sections 10.8 and 10.9.

3.5.4 **Self-Referencing Relationships**

We use the term **self-referencing** or **recursive** to describe a relationship that has the same entity class at both ends. Look at Figure 3.20 on the next page. This type of relationship is sometimes called a "head scratcher,"[18] not only because of its appearance, but because of the difficulty many people have in coming to grips with the recursive structure it represents.

We interpret this in the same way as any other relationship, except that both participants in the relationship are the same entity class:

"Each Employee may manage one or more Employees."
and
"Each Employee may be managed by one Employee."

The model represents a simple hierarchy of employees as might be shown on an organization chart. To implement the relationship using a foreign key, we would need to carry the key of **Employee** (say, Employee ID) as a foreign key *in the Employee table*. We would probably call it "Manager ID" or similar. We encountered the same situation in Section 2.8.5 when we discussed foreign keys that pointed to the primary key of the same table.

---

[18]We have also heard the terms "fish hook" and "pig's ear."

Figure 3.20 Self-referencing one-to-many relationship.

Note that the relationship is optional in both directions. This reflects the fact that the organizational hierarchy has a top and bottom (some employees have no subordinates, one employee has no manager). A mandatory symbol on a self-referencing relationship should always raise your suspicions, but it is not necessarily wrong if the relationship represents something other than a hierarchy.

Self-referencing relationships can also be many-to-many. Figure 3.21 shows such a relationship on a **Manufactured Part** entity class. In business terms, we are saying that a part can be made up of parts, which themselves can be made up of parts and so on. Furthermore, we allow a given part to be used in the construction of more than one part—hence, the many-to-many relationship.

This relationship, being many-to-many, cannot be implemented[19] by a single table with suitable foreign key(s). We can, however, resolve it in much the same way as a many-to-many relationship between two different entity classes.

Figure 3.22 shows an intuitive way of tackling the problem directly from the diagram. We temporarily split the **Manufactured Part** entity class in two, giving us a familiar two-entity class many-to-many relationship, which we resolve as described earlier. We then recombine the two parts of the split table, taking care not to lose any relationships.

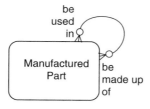

Figure 3.21 Self-referencing many-to-many relationship.

---

[19]Except in a DBMS that supports the SQL99 **set type constructor** feature.

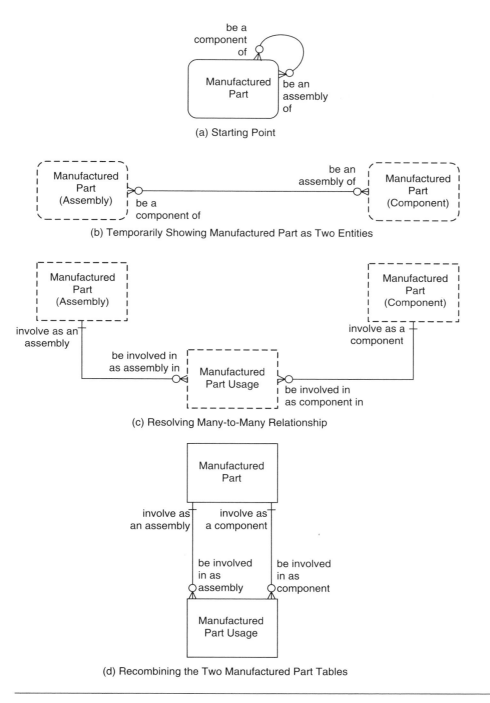

Figure 3.22 Resolving a self-referencing many-to-many relationship.

MANUFACTURED PART (<u>Manufactured Part Number</u>, Description,
{Component Manufactured Part Number, Quantity Used})
Removing repeating group . . .
MANUFACTURED PART (<u>Manufactured Part Number</u>, Description)
MANUFACTURED PART USAGE (<u>Assembly Manufactured Part Number*</u>, <u>Component</u>
<u>Manufactured Part Number*</u>, Quantity Used)

Figure 3.23   Using normalization to resolve a self-referencing many-to-many relationship.

Figure 3.23 shows the same result achieved by representing the structure with a repeating group and normalizing.

The structure shown in Figure 3.22(d) can be used to represent any self-referencing many-to-many relationship. It is often referred to as the **Bill of Materials** structure, because in manufacturing, a bill of materials lists all the lowest level components required to build a particular product by progressively breaking down assemblies, subassemblies, and so forth. Note that the **Manufactured Part Usage** table holds two foreign keys pointing to **Manufactured Part** (Assembly Manufactured Part Number and Component Manufactured Part Number) to support the two relationships.

Self-referencing relationships are an important part of the data modeler's tool kit and appear in most data models. They are used to represent three types of structure: hierarchies, networks, and (less commonly) chains. We discuss their use in greater detail in Chapter 10.

3.5.5 Relationships Involving Three or More Entity Classes

All our relationships so far have involved one or (more commonly) two entity classes. How would we handle a real world relationship involving three or more entity classes?

A welfare authority might need to record which services were provided by which organizations in which areas. Let us look at the problem from the perspective of the tables we would need in the logical model. Our three basic tables might be **Service**, **Organization**, and **Area**. The objective is to record each allowable combination of the three. For example, the Service "Child Care" might be provided by "Family Support Inc." in "Greentown." We can easily do this by defining a table in which each row holds an allowable combination of the three primary keys. The result is shown diagrammatically in Figure 3.24, and it can be viewed as an extension of the technique used to resolve two-entity class many-to-many relationships. The same principle applies to relationships involving four or more entity classes.

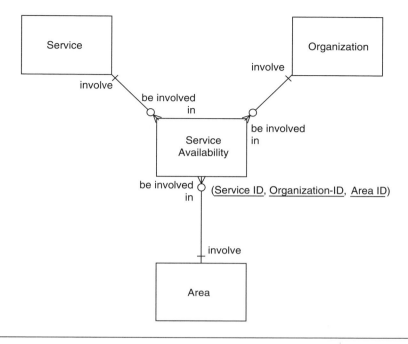

Figure 3.24 Intersection table representing a ternary (3-entity class) relationship.

Once more, in modeling the real world using an E-R model, we find ourselves representing a relationship with a box rather than a line. However, once again we can change our perspective and view the relationship as an entity class; in this case we might name it **Service Availability**, **Allowed Combination,** or similar.

We begin to encounter problems if we start talking about the cardinality and optionality of these higher degree relationships prior to their resolution. The concepts are certainly applicable,[20] but they are difficult to come to grips with for most data modelers,[21] let alone business specialists asked to verify the model. Nor do all diagramming conventions support the direct representation of higher degree relationships.[22] Our advice (reflecting common practice) is that, unless you are using such a convention, you should use an

---

[20]See, for example, Ferg, S., "Cardinality Concepts in Entity-Relationship Modeling," *Proceedings of the 10th International Conference on the Entity Relationship Approach*, San Mateo (1991); or Teorey: *Database Modeling and Design*, 3rd Edition, Morgan Kaufmann (1999).

[21]Hitchman, S. (1995): Practitioner perceptions on the use of some semantic concepts in the entity-relationship model, *European Journal of Information Systems, 4*, 31–40.

[22]UML and the Chen version of the E-R approach do.

intersection entity class to represent the relationships in the conceptual model, then work with the familiar two-entity-class relationships that result.

Whenever you encounter what appears to be a higher degree relationship, you should check that it is not in fact made up of individual many-to-many relationships among the participating entity classes. The two situations are not equivalent, and choosing the wrong representation may lead to normalization problems. This is discussed in some detail in Chapter 13.

Figure 3-25 shows a number of legitimate structures, with different cardinality and optionality.

3.5.6   **Transferability**

An important property of relationships that receives less attention than it should from writers and tool developers is **transferability**. We suspect there are two reasons for its neglect.

First, its impact on the design of a relational database is indirect. Changing a relationship from transferable to nontransferable will not affect the automatic part of the conversion of a conceptual model to relational tables.

Second, most diagramming tools do not support a symbol to indicate transferability. However, some do provide for it to be recorded in supporting documentation, and the Chen E-R conventions support the closely related concept of weak entity classes (Chapter 7).

3.5.6.1   The Concept of Transferability

Figure 3.26 illustrates the distinction between transferable and non-transferable relationships (see page 100).

The two models in this example appear identical in structure. However, let us impose the reasonable rule that public broadcasting licenses may be transferred from one person to another, while amateur radio licenses are nontransferable. Every time someone qualifies for an amateur license, a new one is issued.

3.5.6.2   The Importance of Transferability

The difference in transferability has some important consequences. For example, we could choose to identify amateur licenses with a two-column key of **Person ID** + **License No**, where **License No** was not unique in itself. We would expect the value of the key for a particular license to be stable[23]

---

[23]The importance of stability for primary keys is discussed in Section 6.2.4.

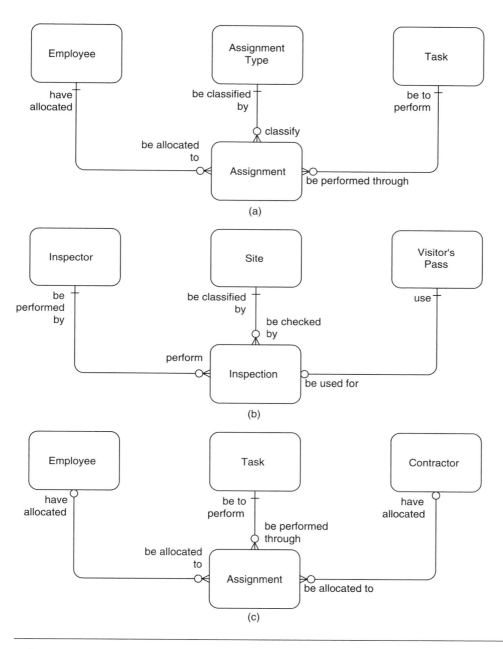

Figure 3.25 Structures interpretable as three-way relationships.

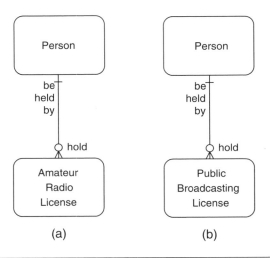

(a)   (b)

Figure 3.26   Nontransferable and transferable licenses.

because the **Person ID** associated with a license could not change. But if we used this key for public broadcasting licenses, it would not be stable, because the **Person ID** *would* change if the license were transferred. The crucial role of transferability in defining primary keys is discussed in some detail in Section 6.4.1.

Another difference is in handling historical data. If we wanted to keep an "audit trail" of changes to the data, we would need to provide for an ownership history of public broadcasting licenses, but not of amateur licenses. In Chapter 15, we look in detail at the modeling of historical data, and we frequently need to refer to the transferability of a relationship in choosing the appropriate structures.

Some DBMSs provide facilities, such as management of "delete" operations, that need to know whether relationships are transferable.

In Sections 10.8 and 10.9, we look in some detail at one-to-one relationships; transferability is an important criterion for deciding whether the participating entity classes should be combined.

3.5.6.3 Documenting Transferability

So, transferability is an important concept in modeling, and we will refer to it elsewhere in this book, particularly in our discussions of the time dimension in Chapter 15. We have found it very useful to be able to show on E-R diagrams whether or not a relationship is transferable. Unfortunately, as previously mentioned, most documentation tools do not support a transferability symbol.

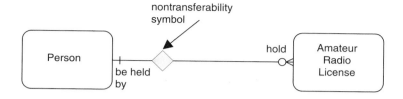

Figure 3.27   Nontransferability symbol.

Barker[24] suggests a symbol for nontransferability (the less common situation) as shown in Figure 3.27. He does not suggest a separate symbol to indicate that a relationship is transferable; transferability is the default.

Note that transferability, unlike optionality and cardinality, is *non-directional* in one-to-many relationships (we shall see in a moment that it can be directional in many-to-many relationships). Transferring a public broadcasting license from one person to another can equally be viewed as transferring the persons from one license to another. It is usually more natural and useful to view a transfer in terms of the entity class at the "many" end of the relationship being transferable. In relational model terms, this translates into a change in the value of the foreign key.

Nontransferable one-to-many relationships are usually, but not always, mandatory in the "one" direction. An example of an *optional* nontransferable relationship is shown in Figure 3.28. An insurance policy need not be sold by an agent (optionality), but if it is sold by an agent, it cannot be transferred to another (nontransferability).

One-to-one relationships may be transferable or nontransferable: The entity classes in a transferable relationship generally represent different real world concepts, whereas the entity classes in a nontransferable relationship often represent different parts of the same real-world concept.

Figure 3.28   Optional nontransferable relationship.

---

[24]Barker, R., *CASE Method Entity Relationship Modelling,* Addison Wesley (1990).

A point of definition: We regard establishment or deletion of a one-to-many relationship instance without adding or deleting entity instances as a transfer. (The terms "connect" and "disconnect" are sometimes used to describe these situations.) For example, if we could connect an agent to an existing policy that did not have an associated agent, or disconnect an agent from the policy, the relationship would be considered transferable. Obviously these types of transfers are only relevant to *optional* relationships.

Many-to-many relationships may be transferable or nontransferable. Often the only transactions allowed for a many-to-many relationship (particularly one that lists allowable combinations or some supports some other business rule—see Chapter 14) are creation and deletion. A many-to-many relationship may be transferable in only one direction. For example, a student may transfer his or her enrollment from one course to another course, but a student's enrollment in a course cannot be transferred to another student.

Transferability can easily be incorporated in the business sentences we generate from relationships:

Each public broadcasting license must be owned by one person *who may change over time.*

Each amateur radio license must be owned by one person *who must not change over time.*

In this book, we have shown the transferability of relationships diagrammatically only where it is relevant to a design decision.

3.5.7 Dependent and Independent Entity Classes

A concept closely related to transferability (but not the same!) is that of dependent and independent entity classes. It is useful primarily in allocating primary keys during the transition from a conceptual to a logical model (as we will see in Chapter 11).

An **independent entity class** is one whose instances can have an independent existence. By contrast a **dependent entity class** is one whose instances can only exist in conjunction with instances of another entity class, *and cannot be transferred between instances of that other entity.* In other words, an entity class is dependent if (and only if) it has a mandatory, nontransferable many-to-one (or one-to-one) relationship with another entity class.

For example, we would expect **Order Item** to be a dependent entity: order items cannot exist outside orders and cannot be transferred between orders.

Dependent entity classes can form hierarchies several levels deep, as well as being dependent on more than one owner entity.

3.5.8 **Relationship Names**

Finally, a few words on one of the areas most often neglected in modeling—the naming of relationships. It is usual in the early stages of modeling to leave relationships unnamed. This is fine while the basic entity classes are still being debated, but the final E-R model should always be properly annotated with meaningful relationship names (not "associated with" or "related to"). The exception to this rule is the two relationships that arise from resolving a many-to-many relationship, because the name of the relationship has usually been used to name the new entity class. We suggest "involve" and "be involved in" as workable names, as in Figure 3.16, but *only* for relationships that arise from resolving a many-to-many relationship.

A good example of the need for meaningful names is the relationship between **Country** and **Currency**, as might be required in a database to support foreign currency dealing. Figure 3.29 shows the two entity classes.

What is the relationship between these two entity classes? One-to-many? Many-to-many? We cannot answer these questions until the meaning of the relationship has been clarified. Are we talking about the fact that currency is *issued* by a country, is *legal tender* in the country, or is *able to be traded* in that country? The result of our investigation may well be that we identify more than one relationship between the same pair of entity classes.

There is an even more fundamental problem here that may affect cardinalities. What do we mean by "country"? Again, a word can have many meanings. Does the Holy See (Vatican City) qualify as a country? If the relationship is "issued by" do we define the Euro as being issued by multiple countries, or do we revise the definition (and name) of the Country entity class to accommodate "European Union," thus keeping the relationship as one-to-many?

The point is that definition of the relationship is closely linked to definitions of the participating entity classes. We focus on the entity class definitions first, but our analysis of the relationships may lead us to revise these definitions.

Let's look at some further examples of the way in which entity class and relationship definitions interact. Consider Figure 3.30: if the **Customer** entity class represents *all* customers, the relationships are correct since every purchase must be made by a customer but not every customer belongs to a loyalty program.

Figure 3.29 Unnamed relationship.

Figure 3.30   One use of a customer entity class.

However, if the business is an airline or a retail store, it may not keep records of customers other than those in loyalty programs. In this case, not all purchases are made by customers (*as defined in the model*), but all customers (*as defined in the model*) belong to loyalty programs. The relationships should now look like those in Figure 3.31.

An example of another type of entity class that can cause problems of definition is a **Position** entity class in a Human Resources model. Is a position a generic term like "Database Administrator," of which there may be more than one in the organization, or a specific budgeted position with a single occupant? We need to know before we can correctly draw the **Position** entity class's relationships.

3.6 **Attributes**

3.6.1 **Attribute Identification and Definition**

We have left the easiest concept until last (although we will have much more to say in Chapter 5). Attributes in an E-R model generally correspond to columns in a relational model.

We sometimes show a few attributes on the diagram for clarification of entity class meaning (or to illustrate a particular point), and some modeling tools support the inclusion of a nominated subset of attributes. But we do not generally show *all* of the attributes on the diagram, primarily because we would end up swamping our "big picture" with detail. They are normally recorded in simple lists for each entity class, either on paper or in an automated documentation tool such as a data dictionary, CASE tool, or other modeling tool.

Figure 3.31   Another use of a customer entity class.

Attributes represent an answer to the question, "What data do we want to keep about this entity class?" In the process of defining the attributes we may find common information requiring a reference table. If so, we normalize, then modify the model accordingly.

3.6.2 **Primary Keys and the Conceptual Model**

Recall that, in a relational model, every table must have a primary key. In E-R modeling, we can identify entity classes prior to defining their keys. In some cases, none of the attributes of an entity class (alone or in combination) is suitable as a primary key. For example, we may already have a company-defined **Employee ID** but it might not cover casual employees, who should also be included in our entity class definition. In such cases, we can invent our own key, *but we can defer this step until the logical modeling stage.* That way, we do not burden the business stakeholders with an attribute that is really a mechanism for implementation.

Since we will not have necessarily nominated primary keys for all entity classes at this stage, we cannot identify foreign keys. To do so, in fact, would be redundant, as the relationships in our conceptual model give us all the information we need to add these at the logical modeling stage. So, we do not include foreign keys in the attribute lists for each entity class.

Once again, your methodology or tools may require that you identify keys at the conceptual modeling stage. It is not a serious problem.

We discuss attributes in more detail in Chapter 5 and the selection of keys in Chapter 6.

3.7 **Myths and Folklore**

As with any relatively new discipline, data modeling has acquired its own folklore of "guidelines" and "rules." Some of these can be traced to genuine attempts at encouraging good and consistent practice. Barker[25] labels a number of situations "impossible" when a more accurate description would be "possible but not very common." The sensible data modeler will be alerted by such situations, but will not reject a model *solely* on the basis that it violates some such edict.

Here are a few pieces of advice, including some of the "impossible" relationships, which should be treated as warnings rather than prohibitions.

---

[25]Barker, R., *CASE Method Entity Relationship Modelling*, Addison Wesley (1990).

3.7.1 **Entity Classes without Relationships**

It is perfectly possible, though not common, to have an entity class that is not related to any other entity class. A trivial case that arises occasionally is a model containing only one entity class. Other counter-examples appear in models to support management information systems, which may require data from disparate sources, for example, **Economic Forecast** and **Competitor Profile**. Entity classes representing rules among types may be stand-alone if the types themselves are not represented by entity classes (see Section 14.5.2.3).

3.7.2 **Allowed Combinations of Cardinality and Optionality**

Figure 3.32 shows examples of relationships with combinations of cardinality and optionality we have seen described as impossible.

The problem with relationships that are mandatory in both directions may be the "chicken and egg" question: which comes first? We cannot record a customer without an account, and we cannot record an account without a customer. In fact, the problem is illusory, as we create both the customer and the account within one transaction. The database meets the stated constraints both at the beginning and the end of the transaction.

Remember also that self-referencing relationships need not only represent simple hierarchies but may model chains as in Figure 3.32(c).

3.8 **Creativity and E-R Modeling**

The element of choice is far more apparent in E-R modeling than in normalization, as we would expect. In E-R modeling we are defining our categories of data; in normalization these have been determined (often by someone else) before we start. The process of categorization is so subjective that even our broadest division of data, into entity classes and relationships, offers some choice, as we have seen.

It is helpful to think of E-R modeling as "putting a grid on the world." We are trying to come up with a set of nonoverlapping categories so that each fact in our world fits into one category only. Different modelers will choose differently shaped grids to achieve the same purpose. Current business terminology is invariably a powerful influence, but we still have room to select, clarify, and depart from this.

Consider just one area of our drug expenditure model—the classification of operations into operation types. As discussed earlier, we could

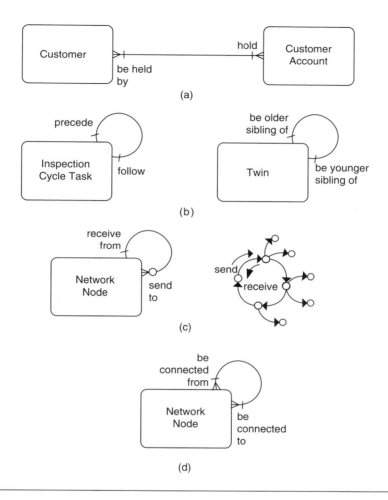

Figure 3.32   Examples of unusual but legitimate relationships.

define **Operation Type** to either include or exclude hybrid operations. If we chose the latter course, we would need to modify the model as in Figure 3.33(a) to allow an operation to be of more than one operation type.

Alternatively, we could define two levels of operation type: **Hybrid Operation Type** and **Basic Operation Type**, giving us the model in Figure 3.33(b). Or we could allow operation types to be either basic or hybrid, as in the original model, but record the component operations of hybrid operations, resulting in Figure 3.33(c).

Another option is to represent a hybrid operation as two separate operations, possibly an inelegant solution, but one we might end up adopting if we had not considered hybrid operations in our initial modeling

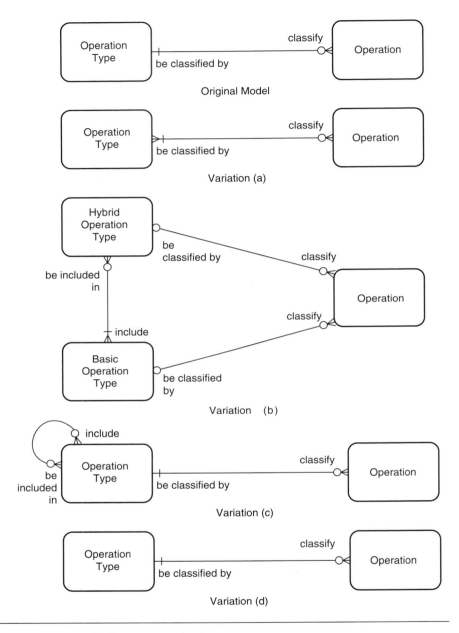

Figure 3.33 Alternative models for operations and operation types.

(Figure 3.33(d)). This diagram looks the same as the original, but the definitions of **Operation** and **Operation Type** will be different. This gives us five solutions altogether (including the original one), each with different implications. For example, Figure 3.33(b), Figure 3.33(c), and the original model allow us to record standard hybrids while the other options only allow their definition on an operation-by-operation basis. How many of these possibilities did you consider as you worked with the model?

Creativity in modeling is a progressively acquired skill. Once you make a habit of looking for alternative models, finding them becomes easier. You also begin to recognize common structures. The Operation Type example provides patterns that are equally relevant to dealing with customers and customer types or payments and payment types.

But we can also support the search for alternative models with some formal techniques. In the next chapter we will look at one of the most important of these.

3.9 **Summary**

Data models can be presented diagrammatically by using a box to represent each table and a line for each foreign key relationship. Further diagramming conventions allow the name, cardinality, and optionality of the relationships to be shown.

We can view the boxes as representing entity classes—things about which the business needs to keep information—and the lines as representing business relationships between entity classes. This provides a language and diagramming formalism for developing a conceptual data model "top down" prior to identifying attributes. The resulting model is often called an Entity-Relationship (E-R) model.

Entity class identification is essentially a process of classifying data, and there is considerable room for choice and creativity in selecting the most useful classification. Entity class naming and definition is critical.

Many-to-many "real-world" relationships may be represented directly or as a pair of one-to-many relationships and an intersection entity class.

Some modeling notations, including the E-R notation generally used in this book, do not directly support business relationships involving three or more entity classes. To model such a relationship in one of those notations, you must use an intersection entity class.

Much folklore surrounds relationships. Most combinations of optionality, cardinality, transferability, and recursion are possible in some context. The modeler should be alert for unusual combinations but examine each case from first principles.

Chapter 4
Subtypes and Supertypes

"A very useful technique … is to break the parts down into still smaller parts and then recombine these smaller units to form larger novel units."
– Edward de Bono, The Use of Lateral Thinking

"There is no abstract art. You must always start with something. Afterward you can remove all traces of reality."
– Pablo Picasso

4.1 Introduction

In this chapter, we look at a particular and very important type of choice in data modeling. In fact, it is so important that we introduce a special convention—subtyping—to allow our E-R diagrams to show several different options at the same time. We will also find subtyping useful for concisely representing rules and constraints, and for managing complexity.

Our emphasis in this chapter is on the conceptual modeling phase, and we touch only lightly on logical modeling issues. We look more closely at these in Chapter 11.

4.2 Different Levels of Generalization

Suppose we are designing a database to record family trees. We need to hold data about fathers, mothers, their marriages, and children. We have presented this apparently simple problem dozens of times to students and practitioners, and we have been surprised by the sheer variety of workable, if sometimes inelegant, ways of modeling it. Figure 4.1 shows two of the many possible designs.

Incidentally, the **Marriage** entity class is the resolution of a many-to-many relationship "be married to" between **Person** and **Person** in (a) and **Man** and **Woman** in (b). The many-to-many relationship arises from persons possibly marrying more than one other person, usually over time rather than concurrently.

Note the optionality of the relationships "mother of" and "father of," particularly in the first model, where they are self-referencing. (Recall our

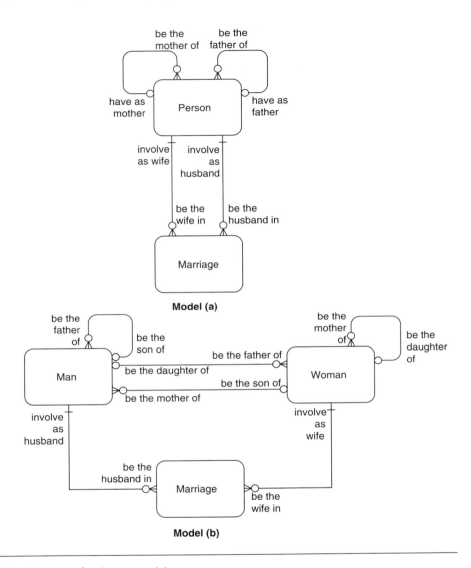

Figure 4.1 Alternative family tree models.

advice in Section 3.5.4 to beware of mandatory self-referencing relationships.) While the rule "every person must have a mother" may seem reasonable enough at first glance, it is not supported by the data available to us. We simply run out of data long before we need to face the real-world problem of, "Who was the first woman?" Eventually, we reach an ancestor whose mother we do not know.

The important issue, however, is our choice of entity classes. We cannot use the nouns ("mother," "father," "child") given in the problem description, because these will overlap; a given person can be both a mother and a child, for example. Implementing **Mother** and **Child** entity classes would therefore compromise our objective of nonredundancy, by holding details of some persons in two places. We need to come up with another set of concepts, and in Figure 4.1 we see two different approaches to the problem. The first uses the person concept; the second uses the two nonoverlapping concepts of man and woman.

Aside from this difference, the models are essentially the same (although they need not be). They appear to address our criterion of completeness equally well. Any person who can be represented by the first model can also be handled by the second, and vice versa. Neither model involves any redundant data. Although no attributes are shown, simple attributes such as Name, Birth Date, and Marriage Locality could be allocated to either model without causing any normalization problems.

The difference between the models arises from the level of generalization we have selected for the entity classes. **Person** is a **generalization** of **Man** and **Woman**, and, conversely, **Man** and **Woman** are **specializations** of **Person**. Recognizing this helps us to understand how the two models relate and raises the possibility that we might be able to propose other levels of generalization, and hence other models—perhaps specializing **Man** into **Married Man** and **Unmarried Man**, or generalizing **Marriage** to **Personal Relationship**.

It is important to recognize that our choice of level of generalization will have a profound effect not only on the database but on the design of the total system. The most obvious effect of generalization is to reduce the number of entity classes and, on the face of it, simplify the model. Sometimes this will translate into a significant reduction in system complexity, through consolidating common program logic. In other cases, the increase in program complexity from combining the logic needed to handle quite different subtypes outweighs the gains. You should be particularly conscious of this second possibility if you are using an algorithm to estimate system size and cost (e.g., in terms of function points). A lower cost estimate, achieved by deliberately reducing the number of entity classes through generalization, may not adequately take into account the associated programming complexity.

4.3 **Rules versus Stability**

To select the most appropriate level of generalization, we start by looking at an important difference between the models: the number and type of business rules (constraints) that each supports. The man-woman model has three entity classes and six relationships, whereas the person model has only two entity classes and four relationships. The man-woman model seems to be representing more rules about the data.

For example, the man-woman model insists that a marriage consists of one man and one woman, while the person model allows a marriage between two men or two women (one of whom would participate in the "wife" relationship and the other in the "husband" relationship, irrespective of gender). The person model would allow a person to have two parents of the same gender; the man-woman model insists that the mother must be a woman, and the father a man.

Under most present marriage laws at least, the man-woman model is looking pretty good! But remember that we can enforce rules elsewhere in the system as well. If we adopt the person-based model, we only need to write a few lines of program code to check the gender of marriage partners and parents when data is entered and return an error message if any rules are violated. We could even set up a table of allowed combinations, which was checked whenever data was entered. Or we could implement the rule outside the computerized component of the system, through (for example) manual review of input documents. The choice, therefore, is not whether to build the rules into the system, but whether the database structure, as specified by the data model, is the best place for them.

Recall that one of the reasons we give so much attention to designing a sound data model is the impact of changing the database structure after it is implemented. On the other hand, changing a few lines of program code, or data in a table, is likely to be much less painful. Accordingly, we included stability as one of the criteria for data model quality. But there is a natural trade-off between stability and enforcement of constraints.

Put simply, the more likely it is that a rule will change during the life of the system, the less appropriate it is to enforce that rule by data structures rather than some other mechanism. In our example, we need to trade off the power of representing the rules about marriage in data structures against the risk that the rules may change during the life of the system. In some jurisdictions, the man-woman model would already be unworkable. Once again there is a need for some forward thinking and judgment on the part of those involved in the modeling process.

Let us just look at how strongly the man-woman model enforces the constraint on marriages. The **Marriage** table will contain, as foreign keys, a Man ID and a Woman ID. Programs will be written to interpret these as pointers to the **Man** and **Woman** tables, respectively. If we want to record a marriage between two men without redesigning the database and programs, the most obvious "work around" is to record one as a man and one as a woman. What if both have previously been married to women? How will we need to modify reports such as "list all men?" Some complicated logic is going to be required, and our criterion of elegance is going to be severely tested.

We can express the flexibility requirement as a guideline:

Do not build a rule into the data structure of a system unless you are reasonably confident that the rule will remain in force for the life of the system.

As a corollary, we can add:

Use generalization to remove unwanted rules from the data model.

It is sometimes difficult enough to determine the *current* rules that apply to business data, let alone those that may change during the life of a system. Sometimes our systems are expected to outlast the strategic planning time frame of the business: "We're planning five years ahead, but we're expecting the system to last for ten."

The models developed by inexperienced modelers often incorporate too many rules in the data structures, primarily because familiar concepts and common business terms may themselves not be sufficiently general. Conversely, once the power of generalization is discovered, there is a tendency to overdo it. Very general models can seem virtually immune to criticism, on the basis that they can accommodate almost anything. This is not brilliant modeling, but an abdication of design in favor of the process modeler, or the user, who will now have to pick up all the business rules missed by the data modeler.

4.4 **Using Subtypes and Supertypes**

It is not surprising that many of the arguments that arise in data modeling are about the appropriate level of generalization, although they are not always recognized as such. We cannot easily resolve such disputes by turning to the rulebook, nor do we want to throw away interesting options too early in the modeling process. While our final decision might be to implement the "person" model, it would be nice not to lose the (perhaps unstable) rules we have gathered which are specific to men or women. Even if we do not implement the subtypes as tables in our final database design, we can document the rules to be enforced, by the DBMS (as integrity constraints) or by the process modeler.

So, we defer the decision on generalization, and treat the problem of finding the correct level as an opportunity to explore different options. To do this, we allow two or more models to exist on top of one another on the same E-R diagram. Figure 4.2 shows how this is achieved.

The ability to represent different levels of generalization requires a new diagramming convention, the box-in-box. You should be very wary about overcomplicating diagrams with too many different symbols, but this one literally adds another dimension (generalization/specialization) to our models.

We call the use of generalization and specialization in a model **subtyping**.

Man and **Woman** are **subtypes** of **Person**.

Person is a **supertype** of **Man** and of **Woman**.

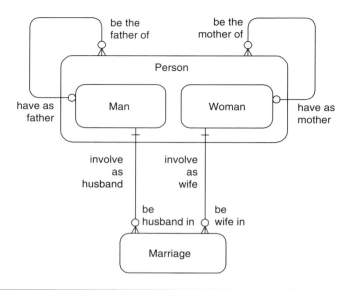

Figure 4.2 Different levels of generalization on a single diagram.

We note in passing at this stage that the diagram highlights *three* implementation options:

1. A single **Person** table
2. Separate **Man** and **Woman** tables
3. A **Person** table holding data common to both men and women, supplemented by **Man** and **Woman** tables to hold data (including foreign keys) relevant only to men or women, respectively.

We discuss the implications of the different options in some detail in Chapter 11.

We will now look at the main rules for using subtypes and supertypes.

4.5 **Subtypes and Supertypes as Entity Classes**

Much of the confusion that surrounds the proper use of subtypes and supertypes can be cleared with a simple rule: subtypes and supertypes are *entity classes*.

Accordingly:

1. We use the same diagramming convention (the box with rounded corners) to represent all entity classes, whether or not they are subtypes or supertypes of some other entity class(es).

2. Subtypes and supertypes must be supported by definitions.

3. Subtypes and supertypes can have attributes. Attributes particular to individual subtypes are allocated to those subtypes; common attributes are allocated to the supertype.

4. Subtypes and supertypes can participate in relationships. Notice in our family tree model how neatly we have been able to capture our "mother of" and "father of" relationships by tying them to entity classes at the most appropriate level. In fact, this diagram shows most of the sorts of relationships that seem to worry modelers, in particular the relationship between an entity class and its own supertype.

5. Subtypes can themselves have subtypes. We need not restrict ourselves to two levels of subtyping. In practice, we tend to represent most concepts at one, two, or three levels of generality, although four or five levels are useful from time to time.

Keep this basic rule in mind as we discuss these matters further in the following sections.

4.5.1 **Naming Subtypes**

It is important to remember that subtypes are entity classes when naming them. Too often we see subtypes named using adjectives instead of nouns [e.g., **Permanent** and **Temporary** as types of **Employee** (rather than **Permanent Employee** and **Temporary Employee**) or **Domestic** and **Overseas** as subtypes of **Customer** (rather than **Domestic Customer** and **Overseas Customer**)]. There are two good reasons for not doing this. The first is that an attribute list or other documentation about entity classes may show subtypes out of context (not associated with the supertype) and it can be difficult in this situation to establish what the subtype is supposed to be. The second reason is that most CASE tools and database development methodologies generate table names automatically from entity class names. Again, a table representing a subtype will not be obviously associated with the relevant supertype table (indeed there may be no such table) so its meaning may not be obvious to a programmer or query writer.

4.6 **Diagramming Conventions**

4.6.1 **Boxes in Boxes**

In this book, we use the "box-in-box" convention for representing subtypes. It is not the only option, but it is compact, widely used, and supported by

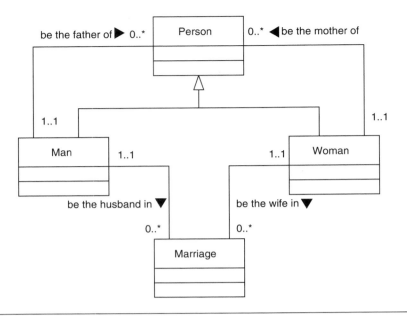

Figure 4.3 Family tree model in UML.

several popular documentation tools. Virtually all of the alternative conventions, including UML (see Figure 4.3), are based around lines between supertypes and subtypes. These are easily confused with relationships,[1] and can give the impression that the model allows redundant data. (In our example, **Person**, **Man**, and **Woman** would appear to overlap, until we recognized that the lines joining them represented subtype-supertype associations, rather than relationships.)

4.6.2 **UML Conventions**

Figure 4.3 illustrates how the model in Figure 4.2 could be represented in UML notation. The subtypes are represented by boxes outside rather than

---

[1]To add to the confusion, some practitioners and researchers use the term "relationship" broadly to include associations between subtypes and their supertypes. We believe the two concepts are sufficiently different to warrant different terms, but occasionally find ourselves talking loosely about a "subtype-supertype relationship" and unfortunately reinforcing the idea that these are relationships in the strict sense of the word. If you need a generic term, we suggest "association" as used in UML.

inside the supertype box. The unfilled arrowhead at the upper end of the line from **Person** to **Man** and **Woman** indicates that the latter are subtypes of **Person**.

4.6.3 **Using Tools That Do Not Support Subtyping**

Some documentation tools do not provide a separate convention for subtypes at all, and the usual suggestion is that they be shown as one-to-one relationships. This is a pretty poor option, but better than ignoring subtypes altogether. If forced to use it, we suggest you adopt a relationship name, such as "be" or "is," which is reserved exclusively for subtypes. (Which one you use depends on your formula for constructing business assertions to describe relationships, as discussed in Section 3.5.1.) Above all, do not confuse relationships with subtype-supertype associations just because a similar diagramming convention is used. This is a common mistake and the source of a great deal of confusion in modeling.

4.7 **Definitions**

Every entity class in a data model must be supported by a definition, as discussed in Section 3.4.3. To avoid unnecessary repetition, a simple rule applies to the definition of a subtype:

An entity class inherits the definition of its supertype.

In writing the definition for the subtype, then, our task is to specify what differentiates it from its sibling subtypes (i.e., subtypes at the same level and, if relevant, within the same partition—see Section 4.10.5). For example, if the entity class **Job Position** is subtyped into **Permanent Job Position** and **Temporary Job Position**, the definition of **Permanent Job Position** will be "a Job Position that . . . ." In effect we build a vocabulary from the supertypes, allowing us to define subtypes more concisely.

4.8 **Attributes of Supertypes and Subtypes**

Where do we record the attributes of an entity class that has been divided into supertypes and subtypes? In our example, it makes sense to document attributes that can apply to all persons against **Person** and those that can apply only to men or only to women against the respective entity classes. So we would hold Birth Date as an attribute of **Person**, and Maiden Name (family name prior to marriage)[2] as an attribute of **Woman**. By adopting this discipline, we are actually modeling constraints: "Only a woman can have a maiden name."

Sometimes we can add meaning to the model by representing attributes at two or more levels of generalization. For example, we might have an entity class **Contract**, subtyped into **Renewable Contract** and **Fixed-Term Contract**. These subtypes could include attributes Renewal Date and Expiry Date, respectively. We could then generalize these attributes to End Date, which we would hold as an attribute of **Contract**. You can think of this as subtyping at the attribute level. If an attribute's meaning is different in the context of different subtypes, it is vital that the differences be documented.

4.9 Nonoverlapping and Exhaustive

The subtypes in our family tree model obeyed two important rules:

1. They were **nonoverlapping**: a given person cannot be both a man and a woman.
2. They were **exhaustive**: a given person must be either a man or a woman, nothing else.

In fact, these two rules are necessary in order for each level of generalization to be a valid implementation option in itself.

Consider a model in which **Trading Partner** is subtyped into **Buyer** and **Seller**.

If a buyer can also be a seller, then the subtypes overlap. If we were to discard the supertype and implement the two subtypes, our database would hold redundant data: those trading partners who were both buyers and sellers would appear in both tables.

If we can have a trading partner who is neither a buyer nor a seller (perhaps an agent or intermediary), then if we were to discard the supertype and implement the two subtypes, our database would be incomplete. Agents or intermediaries who were not buyers or sellers would not appear in either the buyer or seller table.

---

[2]As an aside, Maiden Name is a culture-specific concept and term; it is likely that it will be irrelevant for a significant subclass of women (an opportunity for another level of subtyping?). And could we derive a maiden name from the father's family name (if that is indeed how we define Maiden Name)? But would we record a father if the only data we had for him was his family name, as a result of knowing his daughter's maiden name? "Simple" examples are not so simple!

With these restrictions in mind, let's take a harder look at the family tree model. Are we sure that we can classify every person as either a man or a woman? A look at medical data standards[3] will show that gender is a complex and controversial issue, not easily reduced to a simple division between "male" and "female." Different definitions may be useful for different purposes (for example a government agency may accept an individual's statement of their own gender; a sporting organization may base its determination on a medical assessment; a medical researcher may be interested only in chromosomes). In dealing with large numbers of people, we are going to encounter the less common (and even very rare) cases. If our modeling does not recognize them, our systems are not likely to be able to accommodate them easily.

Finally, what if we do not know the person's gender? Sometimes our data about the real world is incomplete, and we may not have enough information to classify all of the instances that we want to record. Implementing **Man** and **Woman** tables only would result in a database that was unable to hold what might be an important category of persons—those whose gender was unknown or uncertain.

Did we pick this example deliberately to be awkward (and perhaps provocative)? On the contrary, many situations that seem simple on the surface turn out to be far more complex when they are explored in detail, and many "obvious" definitions turn out to be difficult to pin down. We used this example for many years[4] without the assertion that there were only two genders ever being challenged. Then, in the space of a few months, we encountered several situations in which a naive approach to gender definition had caused real problems in established systems.

To summarize: in order to allow the subtypes at each level to represent a sound option for implementation, they must be nonoverlapping and exhaustive. This makes leveling of the model (as we move from the conceptual E-R model to the logical model, which may need to specify simple tables) considerably easier, but restricts our choice in selecting subtypes and, consequently, our ability to represent rules applying to specific subtypes. Whether the sacrifice is worth it is a contentious issue.

The most common argument against restrictions on subtyping is that we should not allow the facilities available for implementation (i.e., simple tables) to limit the power of our data modeling language. This is a nice idea in theory, but there are many facts about data that cannot be represented

---

[3] See for example the Australian Institute of Health and Welfare Data Dictionary www.aihw.gov.au and compare with ISO Standard 5218 http://www.fact-index. com/i/is/iso_5218.html.
[4] In earlier editions of this book, the complexities of gender were not discussed.

even by overlapping nonexhaustive subtypes. Genuine observance of this principle would seriously complicate our data modeling language and conventions with constructs that could not be translated into practical database designs using available technology. This has not stopped researchers from developing richer languages (see Chapters 7 and 14), but practitioners have been reluctant to extend their modeling much beyond that needed to specify a database design. Indeed, some practitioners do not even use subtypes.

Another more convincing argument is that the value of our models is reduced (particularly in the areas of communication and representation of constraints) if we cannot represent common but overlapping business concepts. This happens most often when modeling data about people and organizations. Typical businesses deal with people and organizations in many roles: supplier, customer, investor, account holder, guarantor, and so forth. Almost invariably the same person or organization can fill more than one of these roles; hence, we cannot subtype the entity classes **Person** and **Organization** into these roles without breaking the "no overlaps" rule. But leaving them out of the model may make them difficult to understand ("Where is 'Customer'?") and will limit our ability to capture important constraints ("Only a customer can have a credit rating."). This is certainly awkward, but in practice is seldom a problem outside the domain of persons and organizations. Some tactics for dealing with situations that seem to demand overlapping subtypes are discussed in the next section.

It is worth comparing the situation with process modeling. The rules for function decomposition and data flow diagrams do not normally allow functions at any level to overlap. Most of us do not even stop to consider this, but happily model nonoverlapping functions without thinking about it. Much the same applies in data modeling: we are used to modeling nonoverlapping entity classes in a level (subtype-free) model, and we tend to carry this over into the modeling of subtypes.

Some of the major documentation tool manufacturers have chosen the restrictive route, in part no doubt, because translation to relational tables is simpler. If you are using these tools, the choice will be made for you. UML allows overlapping and nonexhaustive subtypings, and provides for annotations that can be placed on the line linking the supertype to the set of subtypes to indicate whether the latter is overlapping or not and whether it is exhaustive or not. However, there is no requirement for those annotations to be added. As a result many UML modelers do not do so and their models are ambiguous.

The academic community has tended to allow the full range of options, in some cases recommending diagramming conventions to distinguish the different possible combinations of overlap and completeness.

On balance, our recommendation is that you discipline yourself to use only nonoverlapping, exhaustive subtypes, as we do in practice and in the remainder of this book.

4.10   **Overlapping Subtypes and Roles**

Having established a rule that subtypes must not overlap, we are left with the problem of handling certain real-world concepts and constraints that seem to require overlapping subtypes to model. As mentioned earlier, the most common examples are the various roles played by persons and organizations. Many of the most important terms used in business (Client, Employee, Stockholder, Manager, etc.) describe such roles, and we are likely to encounter at least some of them in almost every data modeling project. The way that we model (and hence implement) these roles can have important implications for an organization's ability to service its customers, manage risk, and comply with antitrust and privacy legislation.

There are several tactics we can use without breaking the "no overlaps" rule.

4.10.1   **Ignoring Real-World Overlaps**

Sometimes it is possible to model as if certain overlaps did not exist. We have previously distinguished real-world rules ("Every person must have a mother.") from rules about the data that we need to hold or are able to hold about the real world ("We only know some peoples' mothers."). Similarly, while a customer and a supplier may in fact be the same person, the business may be happy to treat them as if they were separate individuals. Indeed, this may be legally required. In such cases, we can legitimately model the roles as nonoverlapping subtypes. In the absence of such a legal requirement, we will need to look at the business value of knowing that a supplier and customer may be the same person or organization. We know of an organization that sued a customer for an outstanding debt unaware that the customer was also a supplier, and was deliberately withholding the money to offset money owed to them by the organization. Anecdotes of this kind abound and provide great material for people keen to point out bureaucratic or computer incompetence, but their frequency and impact on the business is often not sufficient to justify consolidating the data.

You obviously need to be careful in choosing not to reflect real-world overlap in the data model. Failure to recognize overlaps among parties is one of the most common faults in older database designs, and it is most unlikely that we can ignore all such overlaps. But neither should we automatically model all real-world overlaps. Sometimes it is possible to exclude a few important entity classes from the problem. If these are entity classes that are handled quite differently by the business, useful gains in simplicity and elegance may be achieved. A modern banking model is unlikely to treat borrowers, guarantors, and depositors as separate entity classes, but may well separate stockholders and suppliers.

Data modelers are inclined to reject such separation purely on the grounds of infidelity to the real world, rather than any negative impact on the resulting database or system. This is a simplistic argument, and not likely to convince other stakeholders.

4.10.2 Modeling Only the Supertype

One of the most common approaches to modeling the roles of persons and organizations is to use only a single supertype entity class to represent all possible roles. If subtyping is done at all, it is on the basis of some other criterion, such as "legal entity class type"—partnership, company, individual, etc. The supertype is typically named **Party**, **Involved Party**, or **Legal Entity**.

The problem of communicating this high-level concept to business people has been turned into an opportunity to influence thinking and terminology in some organizations. In particular, it can encourage a move from managing "customer" relationships to managing the total relationship with persons and organizations. A database that includes a table of parties rather than merely those who fulfill a narrower definition of "customer" provides the data needed to support this approach.

The major limitation of the approach is that we cannot readily capture in the model the fact that some relationships apply only to certain roles. These can still be documented, of course, along with other rules constraining the data, as formal constraints or supporting commentary (e.g., "**Market Segment** must be recorded if this **Party** interacts with the organization in the role of **Customer**"), but such relationships will not appear in the E-R Diagram.

4.10.3 Modeling the Roles as Participation in Relationships

In the supertype-only model described above, roles can often be described in terms of participation in relationships. For example, we can describe a customer as a party who maintains an account and a supplier as a party who participates in a contract for supply. The Chen notation, (introduced in Section 3.5.1 and discussed further in Chapter 7) includes a convention to support this (Figure 4.4).

If you are not using the Chen notation, then, rather than further complicate relationship notation for the sake of one section of a model, we

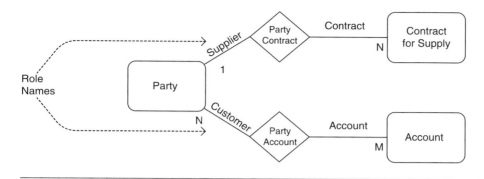

Figure 4.4 Chen convention for roles.

suggest you document such rules within the definition of the main entity class. For example, "A **Guarantor** is a **Party** who participates in the *guarantee* relationship with a **Loan**."

4.10.4 Using Role Entity Classes and One-to-One Relationships

An approach that allows us to record the business terminology as well as the specific attributes and relationships applicable to each role is shown in Figure 4.5. The role entity classes can be supertyped into **Party Role** to

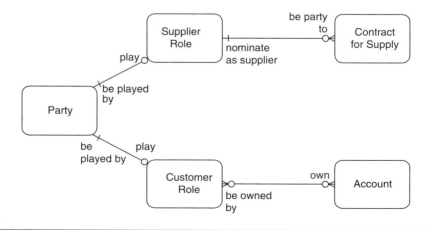

Figure 4.5 Role entity classes and one-to-one relationships.

facilitate communication, although we would be most unlikely to implement at this level, for we would then lose the distinction among roles that the role entity classes were designed to provide. However, intermediate supertyping is often useful. For example, we might decide that a single customer role would cover all roles involving participation in insurance policies, regardless of the type of policy or participation.

Note the entity class names. The word "role" is included to indicate that these entity classes do not hold the primary data about customers, suppliers, and so forth. There is a danger here of blurring the distinction between subtypes and one-to-one relationships.

Despite this inelegance in distinguishing relationships from subtypes, the role entity class approach is usually the neatest solution to the problem when there are significant differences in the attributes and relationships applicable to different roles.

4.10.5 **Multiple Partitions**

Several CASE tools[5] support a partial solution to overlapping subtypes by allowing multiple breakdowns (**partitions**) into complete, nonoverlapping subtypes (Figure 4.6). In the example, the two different subtypings of **Company** enable us to model the constraints that, for example:

- Only a public company can be listed on a stock exchange.
- Only an overseas company can be represented by a local company.

If a given company could be both public and local, for example, it would be difficult to model both of these constraints if we were restricted to a single partition.

The multiple partition facility is useful when we have two or three alternative ways of subtyping according to our rules. Translation to a relational model, however, is more difficult. We can do any one of the following:

1. Implement only the highest level supertype as a table (straightforward, but not always the best choice)
2. Select one partition and implement the subtypes as tables, (e.g., **Private Company** and **Public Company**)
3. Implement multiple levels selecting only some of the partitions, (e.g., implement only **Company**, **Private Company** and **Public Company** as tables)

---

[5]Including ERwin and ER/Studio.

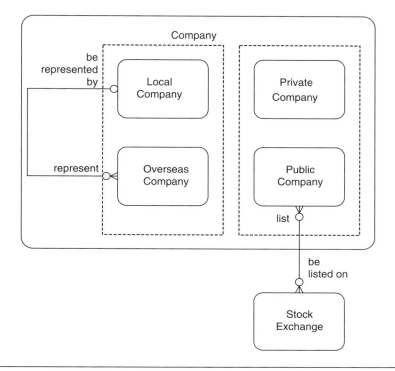

Figure 4.6 Multiple partitions.

4. Implement multiple levels and multiple partitions, (e.g., implement **Company**, **Local Company**, **Overseas Company**, **Private Company** and **Public Company** all as tables)

If we choose option 2 or 3, we need to ensure that relationships and attributes from the other partitions are reallocated to the chosen subtypes.

The multiple partition facility is less helpful in handling the roles problem, as we can end up with a less-than-elegant partitioning like the one in Figure 4.7.

4.11 **Hierarchy of Subtypes**

We have already used the term "subtype hierarchy." Each subtype can have only one immediate supertype (in a hierarchy, everybody has one immediate boss only, except the person at the top who has none). This follows from the "no overlap" requirement, as two supertypes that contained a

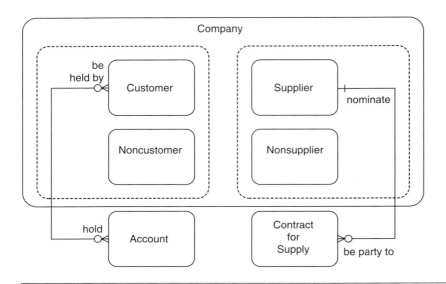

Figure 4.7 Representing roles using multiple partitions.

common subtype would overlap. Again, adherence to this rule produces a model that is more readily translated into an implementable form with each fact represented in one place only.

Few conventions or tools support multiple supertypes for an entity class, possibly because they introduce the sophistication of "multiple inheritance," whereby a subtype inherits attributes and relationships directly from two or more supertypes. Multiple inheritance is a major issue in object-oriented design. The object-oriented designers' problem is almost the opposite of ours; their programming languages provide the facilities, but the questions of how and where they should be used, if at all, are still contentious.

4.12 **Benefits of Using Subtypes and Supertypes**

We have introduced subtypes and supertypes as a means of comparing many possible options on the one diagram. Each level in each subtype hierarchy represents a particular option for implementing the business concepts embraced by the highest-level supertype. But subtypes and supertypes offer benefits not only in presenting options, but in supporting creativity and handling complexity as well.

4.12.1 **Creativity**

Our use of subtypes in the creative process has been a bit passive so far. We have assumed that two or more alternative models have already been designed, and we have used subtypes to compare them on the same diagram. This is a very useful technique when different modelers have been working on the same problem and (as almost always happens) produced different models. Generally, though, we use these conventions to enhance creativity in a far more active way. Rather than design several models and attempt to bring them together, we work with one multilevel model. As we propose entity classes we ask:

"Can this entity class be subtyped into more specific entity classes that represent distinct business concepts?" and,

"Are any of the entity classes candidates for generalization into a common supertype?"

The first question is usually reasonably straightforward to answer, although it may require some research and perhaps some thinking as to the best breakdown. However, the second frequently prompts us to propose new supertype entity classes that represent novel but useful classifications of data. Let us assume we already have a model that is complete and nonredundant. Experimenting with different supertypes will preserve these properties, and we can focus on other objectives, such as simplicity and elegance. "Taking the model down another level" by further subtyping existing entity classes will give us more raw material to work with. We will look at this technique more closely in Chapter 10. For the moment, take note that the use of subtyping and supertyping is one of the most important aids to creativity in modeling.

4.12.2 **Presentation: Level of Detail**

Subtypes and supertypes provide a mechanism for presenting data models at different levels of detail. This ability can make a huge difference to our ability to communicate and verify a complex model. If you are familiar with process modeling techniques, you will know the value of leveled data flow diagrams in communicating first the "big picture," then the detail as required. The concept is applied in many, many disciplines, from the hierarchy of maps in an atlas, to the presentation of a company's accounts. Subtypes and supertypes can form the basis of a similar *structured* approach to presenting data models.[6]

---

[6]First described in Simsion, G.C., "A Structured Approach to Data Modelling," *Australian Computer Journal* (August 1989).

We can summarize a data model simply by removing subtypes, choosing the level of summarization by how many levels of subtyping we leave. We can even vary this across the model: show the full detail in an area of interest, while showing only supertypes outside that area. For example, our model might contain (among other things) details of contracts and the employees who authorized them. The human resources manager might be shown a model in which all the subtypes of **Employee** were included, with a relationship to the simple supertype entity class **Contract**. Conversely, the contract manager might be shown a full subtyping of contracts, with a relationship to the supertype entity class **Employee** (Figure 4.8).

Each sees only what is of interest to them, without losing the context of external data.

In practice, when presenting a very high-level model, we often selectively delete those entity classes that do not fit into any of the major generalizations and that are not critical to conveying the overall "shape" of the model. In doing this, we lose the completeness of coverage that a strict supertype model provides. While the model no longer specifies a viable design, it serves as a starting point for understanding. Anyone who has tried to explain a data model for even a medium-sized application to a nontechnical person will appreciate the value of such a high-level starting point.

Documentation tools that can display and/or print multiple views of the same model by selective removal of entity classes and/or relationships are useful in this sort of activity.

4.12.3 **Communication**

Communication is not only a matter of dealing with complexity. Terminology is also frequently a problem. A vehicles manager may be interested in trucks, but the accountant's interest is in assets. Our subtyping convention allows **Truck** to be represented as a subtype of **Asset**, so both terms appear on the model, and their relationship is clear.

The ability to relate familiar and unfamiliar entity classes is particularly useful to the creative modeler, who may want to introduce an entity class that will not be immediately recognizable. By showing a new entity class in terms of old, familiar entity classes, the model can be verified without business people becoming stuck on the unfamiliar term. Perhaps our organization trades in bonds and bills, and we are considering representing both by a single entity class type **Financial Instrument**. To the organization, they are separate and have always been treated as such. By showing **Financial Instrument** subtyped into **Bond** and **Bill**, we provide a starting point for understanding. If they prefer, the business specialists need never use the new word, but can continue to talk about "bonds and bills."

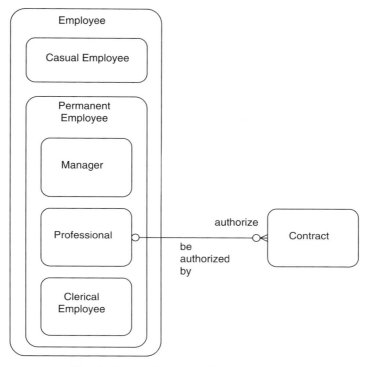

View (a) Human Resources Focus

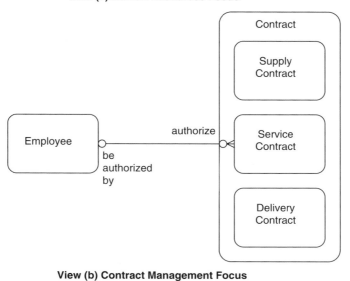

View (b) Contract Management Focus

Figure 4.8 Different views of a model.

In one organization, senior management wanted to develop a consolidated asset management system, but divisional management wanted local systems, arguing that their own requirements were unique. Rather than try to develop a consolidated model straightaway (with little cooperation), we developed two separate models, using local terminology, but with one eye on consistency. We then combined the models, preserving all the local entity classes but introducing supertypes to show the commonality. With the understanding that their specific needs had been accommodated (and the differences—and there were some—recognized), the managers agreed to proceed with the consolidated system.

When using subtypes and supertypes to help communicate a model, we need have no intention of implementing them as tables; communication is a sound enough reason in itself for including them.

4.12.4 **Input to the Design of Views**

Recall that relational DBMSs allow data to be accessed through *views*. Views can be specified to select only a subset of the rows in a table, or to combine rows from multiple tables, (i.e., to present subtypes or supertypes, respectively). In our original example, a **Person** table could be presented as separate **Man** and **Woman** views; alternatively **Man** and **Woman** tables could be combined to present a **Person** view.

There are some limitations on what we can do with views (in particular there are some important restrictions on the ability to update data through views) so using them does not absolve us from the need to select our base tables carefully. However, views do provide at least a partial means of implementing the subtypes and supertypes that we identify in conceptual modeling.

Looking at it from the other direction, using subtypes and supertypes to capture different perspectives on data gives us valuable input to the specification of useful views and encourages rigor in their definition.

4.12.5 **Classifying Common Patterns**

We can also use supertypes to help us classify and recognize common patterns. In the later chapters of this book, we look at a number of structures that appear again and again in models. In most cases, we first look at an example of the structure (such as the different ways of modeling **Operation Type** and **Operation** in Section 3.8), then we apply what we have learned to the general case (**Thing** and **Thing Type**, if you like). *Without generalization, we cannot apply what we learn in designing one* *model to the design of another.* Supertypes and subtypes provide a formal means of doing this.

We once had to review several models covering different stages in the brewing of beer. The models had been produced independently, but some common patterns began to emerge so that we developed a mental generic model roughly applicable to any stage. We could then concentrate on how the models differed. Reviewing one model, we asked why no samples were taken at this stage (since the high-level model included a **Sample** entity class). Later investigation showed that this was an oversight by the modeler, and we were congratulated on our knowledge of brewing. The other modelers had not noticed the omission because, without a high-level model, they were "too close to the problem"—unable to see the pattern for the detail.

4.12.6 Divide and Conquer

The structured approach to modeling gives us the ability to attack a model from the top down, the middle out, or the bottom up.

The top-down option is particularly important as it allows us to break a large modeling problem into manageable parts then to address the question: "What types of . . . do we need to keep information about?" Early analysis of a finance company might suggest the entity classes **Customer** and **Loan** (nothing terribly creative here). We could then tackle the questions: "What types of loan are we interested in (and how do they differ)?" and, "What type of customers are we interested in (and how do they differ)?" Alternatively, we might model the same business problem in terms of agreements and parties to agreements. Again, we can then proceed with more detailed analysis *within the high-level framework we have established.*

In developing large models, we may allocate different areas to different modelers, with some confidence that the results will all fit together in the end. This is much harder to achieve if we divide the task based on function or company structure rather than data ("Let us model the data for commercial lending first, then retail lending."). Because data is frequently used by more than one function or area, it will be represented in more than one model, usually in different ways. Often the reconciliation takes much longer than the initial modeling.

From a creative modeling perspective, a top-down approach based on specialization allows us to put in place a set of key concepts at the supertype level and to fit the rest of our results into this framework. There is a good analogy with architecture here: the basic shape of the building determines how other needs will be accommodated.

4.13 **When Do We Stop Supertyping and Subtyping?**

We once encountered a data model that contained more than 900 entity classes and took up most of a sizeable wall. The modelers had adopted the rule of "keep subtyping until there are no optional attributes,"[7] and had in fact run out of wall space before they ran out of optional attributes.

There is no absolute limit to the number of levels of subtypes that we can use to represent a particular concept. We therefore need some guidelines as to when to stop subtyping. The problem of when to stop supertyping is easier. We cannot go any higher than a single entity class covering all the business data—the "Thing" entity class. In practice, we will often go as high as a model containing only five to ten entity classes, if only for the purpose of communicating broad concepts.

Very high levels of supertyping are actually implemented sometimes. As we should expect, they are used when flexibility is paramount. Data dictionaries that allow users to define their own contents (or **metamodels** as they are often called) are one example.

No single rule tells us when to stop subtyping because we use subtypes for several different purposes. We may, for example, show subtypes that we have no intention of implementing as tables, in order to better explain the model. Instead, there are several guidelines. In practice, you will find that they seldom conflict. When in doubt, include the extra level(s).

4.13.1 **Differences in Identifiers**

If an entity class can be subtyped into entity classes whose instances are identified by different attributes, show the subtypes.

For example, we might subtype **Equipment Item** into **Vehicle** and **Machine** because vehicles were identified by registration number and machines by serial number. Conversely, if we have two entity classes that are identified by the same attribute(s), we should consider a common supertype.

Beware of circular thinking here! We are not talking about identifiers that have been created purely to support past or proposed database structures

---

[7]There is some research to suggest that subtypes should be preferred to optional attributes and relationships where users require a deep-level understanding of the model: Bodart, F., Patel, A., Sim, M., and R. Weber (2001): Should Optional Properties Be Used in Conceptual Modelling? A Theory and Three Empirical Tests. *Information Systems Research*, *12* (4): 384–405. We would caution against uncritically adopting this practice: researchers generally work with relatively simple models, and the results may not scale to more complex models.

or processing, but identifiers that have some standing within or outside the organization.

4.13.2   Different Attribute Groups

If an entity class can be subtyped into entity classes that have different attributes, consider showing the subtypes.

For example, **Insurance Policy** may be subtyped into **House Policy** (with attributes Construction Type, Floor Area, and so on) and **Motor Vehicle Policy** (with attributes Make, Model, Color, Engine Capacity, Modifications, Garaging Arrangements, and so on).

In practice, optional attributes are so common that strict enforcement of this rule will result in a proliferation of subtypes as discussed earlier; we should not need to draw two boxes just to show that a particular attribute can take a null value. However, if *groups of attributes* are always null or nonnull together, show the corresponding subtypes.

4.13.3   Different Relationships

If an entity class can be divided into subtypes such that one subtype may participate in a relationship while the other never participates, show the subtype.

Do not confuse this with a simple optional relationship. You need to look for groups that can never participate in the relationship. For example, a machine can never have a driver but a vehicle may have a driver (Figure 4.9).

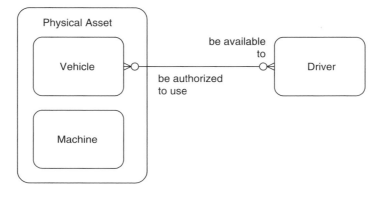

Figure 4.9   Subtyping based on relationship participation.

4.13.4 **Different Processes**

If some instances of an entity class participate in important processes, while others do not, consider subtyping. Conversely, entity classes that participate in the same process are candidates for supertyping.

Be very wary of supertyping entity classes that are not treated in a similar way by the business, regardless of superficial similarity of attributes, relationships, or names. For example, a wholesaler might propose entity classes **Supplier Order** (placed by the wholesaler) and **Customer Order** (placed by the customer). The attributes of both types of order may be similar, but the business is likely to handle them in quite different ways. If so, it is unlikely that there will be much value in introducing an **Order** supertype. Inappropriate supertyping of this kind is a common error in conceptual modeling.

4.13.5 **Migration from One Subtype to Another**

We should not subtype to a level where an entity occurrence may migrate from one subtype to another (at least not with a view to implementing the subtypes as separate tables). For example, we would not subtype **Account** into **Account in Credit** and **Overdrawn Account** because an account could move back and forth from subtype to subtype. Most modelers seem to observe this rule intuitively, but we note in passing that a family tree model based around **Man** and **Woman** entity classes may actually violate this rule (depending on our definitions, of course).

If we were to implement a database based on such unstable subtypes, we would need to transfer data from table to table each time the status changed. This would complicate processing and make it difficult to keep track of entity instances over time. More fundamentally, we would fail to distinguish the creation of a new entity instance from a change in status of an entity instance. We look further at this question when we discuss identity in Section 6.2.4.2.

4.13.6 **Communication**

As mentioned earlier, we may add both subtypes and supertypes to help explain the model. Sometimes it is useful to show only two or three illustrative subtypes. To avoid breaking the completeness rule, we then need to add a "miscellaneous" entity class. For example, we might show **Merchant Event** (in a credit card model) subtyped into **Purchase Authorization**, **Voucher Deposit**, **Stationery Delivery**, and **Miscellaneous Merchant Event**.

4.13.7   **Capturing Meaning and Rules**

In our discussions with business people, we are often given information that can conveniently be represented in the conceptual data model, even though we would not plan to include it in the final (single level) logical model. For example, the business specialist might tell us, "Only management staff may take out staff loans." We can represent this rule by subtyping **Staff Member** into **Manager** and **Nonmanager** and by tying the relationship to **Staff Loan** to **Manager** only (Figure 4.10). We would anticipate that these subtypes would not be implemented as tables in the logical model (the subtyping is likely to violate the "migration" rule), but we have captured an important rule to be included elsewhere in the system.

4.13.8   **A Pragmatic Approach**

Subtypes and supertypes are tools we use in the data modeling *process*, rather than structures that appear in the logical and physical models, at least as long as our DBMSs are unable to implement them directly. Therefore, we use them whenever they can help us produce a better final product, rather than according to a rigid set of rules. No subtyping or supertyping is invalid if it achieves this aim, and if it obeys the very simple rules of completeness and nonoverlap. In particular, there is nothing intrinsically wrong with subtypes or supertypes that do not have any attributes other than

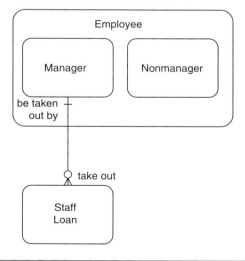

Figure 4.10   Using subtypes to represent rules.

those inherited or rolled-up, if they contribute to some other objective, such as communicating the model.

4.14 Generalization of Relationships

So far in this chapter we have focused on the level of generalization of entity classes and, to a lesser extent, attributes (which we cover in some detail in Section 5.6). Choosing the right level of generalization for relationships is also important and involves the same sorts of trade-off between enforcement of constraints and stability in the face of change.

However, our options for generalizing or specializing relationships are far more limited because we are only interested in relationships between the same pair of entity classes. Much of the time we have only one relationship to play with. For that reason, we do not have a separate convention for "subtyping" relationships.

But as we generalize entity classes, we find that the number of relationships between them increases, as a result of "rolling up" from the subtypes (Figure 4.11). Much of the time, we generalize relationships of the same name almost automatically, and this very seldom causes any problems. Most of us would not bother about the intermediate stage shown in Figure 4.11, but would move directly to the final stage.

As with entity classes, our decision needs to be based on commonality of use, stability, and enforcement of constraints. Are the individual relationships used in a similar way? Can we anticipate further relationships? Are the rules that are enforced by the relationships stable?

Let's look briefly at the main types of relationship generalization.

4.14.1 Generalizing Several One-to-Many Relationships to a Single Many-to-Many Relationship

Figure 4.12 shows several one-to-many relationships between **Customer** and **Insurance Policy** (see page 140). These can easily be generalized to a single many-to-many relationship.

Bear in mind the option of generalizing only some of the one-to-many relationships and leaving the remainder in place. This may be appropriate if one or two relationships are fundamental to the business, while the others are "extras." For example, we might choose to generalize the "beneficiary," "contact," and "security" relationships, but leave the "insure" relationship as it stands. This apparently untidy solution may in fact be more elegant from a programming point of view if many programs must navigate only the most fundamental relationship.

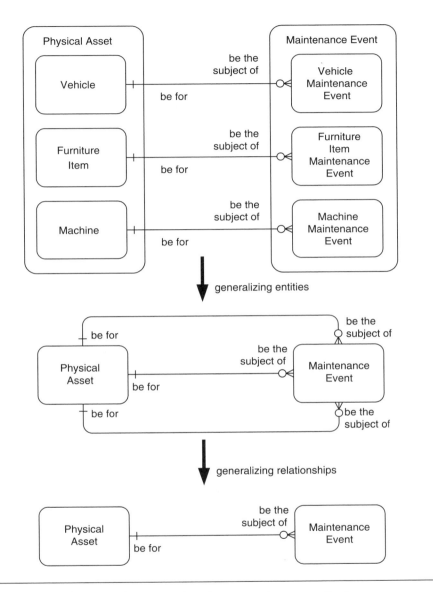

Figure 4.11   Relationship generalization resulting from entity class generalization.

4.14.2 **Generalizing Several One-to-Many Relationships to a Single One-to-Many Relationship**

Generalization of several one-to-many relationships to form a single one-to-many relationship is appropriate if the individual one-to-many relationships

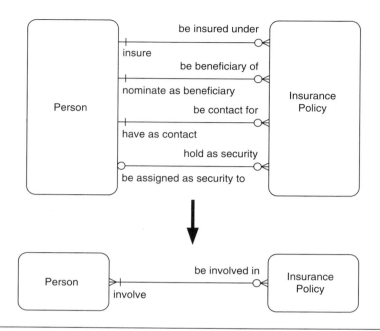

Figure 4.12   Generalization of one-to-many relationships.

are **mutually exclusive**, a more common situation than you might suspect. We can indicate this with an **exclusivity arc** (Figure 4.13).

We have previously warned against introducing too many additional conventions and symbols. However, the exclusivity arc is useful enough to justify the extra complexity, and it is even supported by some CASE tools.[8] As well as highlighting opportunities to generalize relationships, the exclusivity arc can suggest potential entity class supertypes. In Figure 4.13, we are prompted to supertype **Company**, **Individual**, **Partnership**, and **Government Body**, perhaps to **Taxpayer** (Figure 4.14).

We find that we use exclusivity arcs quite frequently during the modeling process. In some cases, they do not make it from the whiteboard to the final conceptual model, being replaced with a single relationship to the supertype. Of course, if your CASE tool does not support the convention and you wish to retain the arc, rather than supertype, you will need to record the rule in supporting documentation.

---

[8]Notably Oracle Designer from Oracle Corporation. UML tools we have reviewed support arcs but apparently only between pairs of relationships.

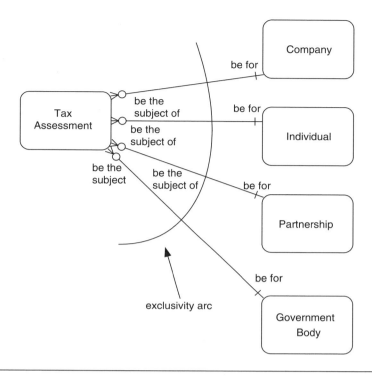

Figure 4.13 Diagramming convention for mutually exclusive relationships.

4.14.3 **Generalizing One-to-Many and Many-to-Many Relationships**

Our final example involves many-to-many relationships, along with two one-to-many relationships (see Figure 4.15 on next page). The generalization should be fairly obvious, but you need to recognize that if you include the one-to-many relationships in the generalization, you will lose the rules that only one employee can fill a position or act in a position. (Conversely, you will gain the ability to be able to break those rules.)

Figure 4.14 Entity class generalization prompted by mutually exclusive relationships.

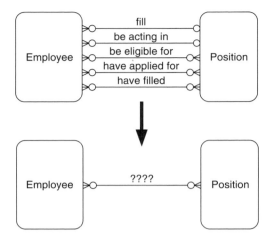

Figure 4.15   Generalizing one-to-many and many-to-many relationships.

4.15 **Theoretical Background**

In 1977 Smith and Smith published an important paper entitled "Database Abstractions: Aggregation and Generalization,"[9] which recognized that the two key techniques in data modeling were aggregation/disaggregation and generalization/specialization.

Aggregation means "assembling component parts," and **disaggregation** means, "breaking down into component parts." In data modeling terms, examples of disaggregation include breaking up **Order** into **Order Header** and **Ordered Item**, or **Customer** into Name, Address, and Birth Date. This is quite different from specialization and generalization, which are about classifying rather than breaking down. It may be helpful to think of disaggregation as "widening" a model and specialization as "deepening" it.

Many texts and papers on data modeling focus on disaggregation, particularly through normalization. Decisions about the level of generalization are often hidden or dismissed as "common sense." We should be very suspicious of this; before the rules of normalization were formalized, that process too was regarded as just a matter of common sense.[10]

---

[9]*ACM Transactions on Database Systems*, Vol. 2, No. 2 (1977).

[10]Research in progress by Simsion has shown that experienced modelers not only vary in the level of generalization that they choose for a particular problem, but also may show a bias toward higher or lower levels of generalization across different problems (see www.simsion.com.au).

In this book, and in day-to-day modeling, we try to give similar weight to the generalization/specialization and aggregation/disaggregation dimensions.

4.16 Summary

Subtypes and supertypes are used to represent different levels of entity class generalization. They facilitate a top-down approach to the development and presentation of data models and a concise documentation of business rules about data. They support creativity by allowing alternative data models to be explored and compared.

Subtypes and supertypes are not directly implemented by standard relational DBMSs. The logical and physical data models therefore need to be subtype-free.

By adopting the convention that subtypes are nonoverlapping and exhaustive, we can ensure that each level of generalization is a valid implementation option. The convention results in the loss of some representational power, but it is widely used in practice.

Chapter 5
Attributes and Columns

"There's a sign on the wall but she wants to be sure
'Cause you know sometimes words have two meanings"
– Page/Plant: Stairway to Heaven, © Superhype Publishing Inc.

"Sometimes the detail wags the dog"
– Robert Venturi

5.1 **Introduction**

In the last two chapters, we focused on entity classes and relationships, which define the high-level structure of a data model. We now return to the "nuts and bolts" of data: attributes (in the conceptual model) and columns (in the logical and physical models). The translation of attributes into columns is generally straightforward,[1] so in our discussion we will usually refer only to attributes unless it is necessary to make a distinction.

At the outset, we need to say that attribute definition does not always receive the attention it deserves from data modelers.

One reason is the emphasis on diagrams as the primary means of presenting a model. While they are invaluable in communicating the overall shape, they hide the detail of attributes. Often many of the participants in the development and review of a model see only the diagrams and remain unaware of the underlying attributes.

A second reason is that data models are developed progressively; in some cases the full requirements for attributes become clear only toward the end of the modeling task. By this time the specialist data modeler may have departed, leaving the supposedly straightforward and noncreative job of attribute definition to database administrators, process modelers, and programmers. Many data modelers seem to believe that their job is finished when a reasonably stable framework of entity classes, relationships, and primary keys is in place.

On the contrary, the data modeler who remains involved in the development of a data model right through to implementation will be in a good

---

[1]We discuss the specifics of the translation of attributes (and relationships) into columns, together with the addition of supplementary columns, in Chapter 11.

145

position to ensure not only that attributes are soundly modeled as the need for them arises, but to intercept "improvements" to the model before they become entrenched.

In Chapter 2 we touched on some of the issues that arise in modeling attributes (albeit in the context of looking at columns in a logical model). In this chapter we look at these matters more closely.

We look first at what makes a sound attribute and definition, and then introduce a classification scheme for attributes, which enables us to discuss the different types of attributes in some detail. The classification scheme also provides a starting point for constructing attribute names. Naming of attributes is far more of an issue than naming of entity classes and relationships, if only because the number of attributes in a model is so much greater.

The chapter concludes with a discussion of the role of generalization in the context of attributes. As with entity-relationship modeling, we have some quite firm rules for aggregation, whereas generalization decisions often involve trade-offs among conflicting objectives. And, as always, there is room for choice and sometimes creativity.

5.2 **Attribute Definition**

Proper definitions are an essential starting point for detailed modeling of attributes. In the early stages of modeling, we propose and record attributes before even the entity classes are fully defined, but our final model must include an unambiguous definition of each attribute. If we fail to do this, we are likely to overlook the more subtle issues discussed in this chapter and run the risk that the resulting columns in the database will be used inappropriately by programmers or users. Poor attribute definitions have the same potential to compromise data quality as poor entity class definitions (see Section 3.4.3). Definitions need not be long: a single line is often enough if the parent entity class is well defined.

In essence, we need to know what the attribute is intended to record, and how to interpret the values that it may take. More formally, a good attribute definition will:

1. Complete the sentence: "Assignment of a value to the <attribute name> for an instance of <entity class name> is a record of . . ."; for example: Assignment of a value to the **Fee Exemption Minimum Balance** for an instance of **Account** is a record of *the minimum amount which must be held in this Account at all times to qualify for exemption from annual account keeping fees.*" As in this example, the definition should refer to a single instance, (e.g., "The date of birth of this Customer," "The minimum amount of a transaction that can be made by a Customer against a Product of this type.")

2. Answer the questions "What does it mean to assign a value to this attribute?" and "What does each value that can be assigned to this attribute mean?"

It can be helpful to imagine that you are about to enter data into a data entry form or screen that will be loaded into an instance of the attribute. What information will you need in order to answer the following questions:

- What fact about the entity instance are you providing information about?
- What value should you enter to state that fact?

For a column to be completely defined in a logical data model, the following information is also required (although ideally your documentation tool will provide facilities for recording at least some of it in a more structured manner than writing it into the definition):

- What type of column it is (e.g., character, numeric)
- Whether it forms part of the primary key or identifier of the entity class
- What constraints (business rules) it is subject to, in particular whether it is mandatory (must have a value for each entity instance), and the range or set of allowed values
- Whether these constraints are to be managed by the system or externally
- The likelihood that these constraints will change during the life of the system
- (For some types of attribute) the internal and external representations (formats) that are to be used.

In a conceptual data model, by contrast, we do not need to be so prescriptive, and we are also providing the business stakeholders a view of how their information requirements will be met rather than a detailed first cut database design, so we need to provide the following information for each attribute:

- What type of attribute it is in business terms (see Section 5.4)
- Any important business rules to which it is subject.

5.3 Attribute Disaggregation: One Fact per Attribute

In Chapter 2 we introduced the basic rule for attribute disaggregation—one fact per attribute. It is almost never technically difficult to achieve this, and it generally leads to simpler programming, greater reusability of data, and easier implementation of change. Normalization relies on this rule being observed; otherwise we may find "dependencies" that are really dependencies on only part of an attribute. For example, **Bank Name** may be determined by a three-part **Bank-State-Branch Number**, but closer examination might show that the dependency is only on the "Bank" part of the Number.

Why, then, is the rule so often broken in practice? Violations (sometimes referred to as **overloaded attributes**) may occur for a variety of reasons, including:

1. Failing to identify that an attribute can be decomposed into more fundamental attributes that are of value to the business
2. Attempting to achieve greater efficiency through data compression
3. Reflecting the fact that the compound attribute is more often used by the business than are its components
4. Relying on DBMS or programming facilities to perform "trivial" decomposition when required
5. Confusing the way data is presented with the way it is stored
6. Handling variable length and "semistructured" attributes (e.g., addresses)
7. Changing the definition of attributes after the database is implemented as an alternative to changing the database design
8. Complying with external standards or practices
9. Perpetuating past practices, which may have resulted originally from 1 through 8 above.

In our experience, most problems occur as a result of attribute definition being left to programmers or analysts with little knowledge of data modeling. In virtually all cases, a solution can be found that meets requirements without compromising the "one fact per attribute" rule. Compliance with external standards or user wishes is likely to require little more than a translation table or some simple data formatting and unpacking between screen and database. However, as in most areas of data modeling, rigid adherence to the rule will occasionally compromise other objectives. For example, dividing a date attribute into components of Year, Month, and Day may make it difficult to use standard date manipulation routines. When conflicts arise, we need to go back to first principles and look at the total impact of each option.

The most common types of violation are discussed in the following sections.

5.3.1 Simple Aggregation

An example of simple aggregation is an attribute **Quantity Ordered** that includes both the numeric quantity and the unit of measure (e.g., "12 cases"). Quite obviously, this aggregation of two different facts restricts our ability to compare quantities and perform arithmetic without having to "unpack" the data. Of course, if the business was only interested in **Quantity Ordered** as, for example, text to print on a label, we would have an argument for treating it as a single attribute (but in this case we should surely review the attribute name, which implies that numeric quantity information is recorded). A good test as to whether an attribute is fully decomposed is to ask:

- Does the attribute correspond to a single business fact? (The answer should be "Yes.")
- Can the attribute be further decomposed into attributes that themselves correspond to meaningful business facts? (The answer should be "No.")
- Are there business processes that update only part of the attribute? (The answer should be "No.") We should also look at processes that read the attribute (e.g., for display or printing). However, if the reason for using only part of the attribute is merely to provide an abbreviation of the same fact as represented by the whole, there is little point in decomposing the attribute to reflect this.
- Are there dependencies (potentially affecting normalization) that apply to only part of the attribute? (The answer should be "No.")

Let's look at a more complex example in this light. A **Person Name** attribute might be a concatenation of salutation (Prof.), family name (Deng), given names (Chan, Wei), and suffixes, qualifications, titles, and honorifics (e.g., Jr., MBA, DFC). Will the business want to treat given names individually (in which case we will regard them as forming a repeating group and normalize them out to a separate entity class)? Or will it be sufficient to separate **First Given Name** (and possibly **Preferred Given Name**, which cannot be automatically extracted) from **Other Given Names**? Should we separate the different qualifications? It depends on whether the business is genuinely interested in individual qualifications, or simply wants to address letters correctly. To answer these questions, we need to consider the needs of all potential users of the database, and employ some judgment as to likely future requirements.

Experienced data modelers are inclined to err on the side of disaggregation, even if familiar attributes are broken up in the process. The situation has parallels with normalization, in which familiar concepts (e.g., Invoice) are broken into less obvious components (in this case Invoice Header, Invoice Item) to achieve a technically better structure. But most of us would not split **First Given Name** into **Initial** and **Remainder of Name**, even if there was a need to deal with the initials separately. We can verify this decision by using the questions suggested earlier:

- "Does **First Given Name** correspond to a single business fact?" Most people would agree that it does. This provides a strong argument that we are already at a "one fact per attribute" level.

■ "Can **First Given Name** be meaningfully decomposed?" **Initial** has some real-world significance, but only as an abbreviation for another fact. **Rest of Name** is unlikely to have any value to the business in itself.

■ "Are there business processes that change the initial or the rest of the name independently?" We would not expect this to be so; a change of name is a common business transaction, but we are unlikely to provide for "change of initial" or "change of rest of name" as distinct processes.

■ "Are there likely to be any other attributes determined by (i.e., dependent on) **Initial** or **Rest of Name?**" Almost certainly no.

On this basis, we would accept **First Given Name** as a "single fact" attribute. Note that it is quite legitimate in a *conceptual* data model to refer to aggregated attributes, such as a quantity with associated unit, or a person name, provided the internal structure of such attributes is documented by the time the logical data model is prepared. Such **complex attributes** are discussed in detail in Section 7.2.2.4.

Note also that there are numerous (in fact too many!) standards for representation of such common aggregates as person names and addresses, and these may be valuable in guiding your decisions as to how to break up such aggregates. ISO and national standards bodies publish standards that have been subject to due consideration of requirements and formal review. While there are also various XML schemas that purport to be standards, some do not appear to have been as rigorously developed, at least at the time of writing.

5.3.2 **Conflated Codes**

We encountered a conflated code in Chapter 2 with the **Hospital Type** attribute, which carried two pieces of information (whether the hospital was public or private and whether it offered teaching services or not). Codes of this kind are not as easy to spot as simple aggregations, but they lead to more awkward programming and stability problems.

The problems arise when we want to deal with one of the underlying facts in isolation. Values may end up being included in program logic ("If **Hospital Code** equals 'T' or 'P' then . . .") making change more difficult.

One apparent justification for conflated codes is their value in enforcing data integrity. Only certain combinations of the component facts may be allowable, and we can easily enforce this by only defining codes for those combinations. For example, private hospitals may not be allowed to have teaching facilities, so we simply do not define a code for "Private & Teaching."

This is a legitimate approach, but the data model should then specify a separate table to translate the codes into their components, in order to avoid the sort of programming mentioned earlier.

The constraint on allowed combinations can also be enforced by holding the attributes individually, and maintaining a reference table[2] of allowed combinations. Enforcement now requires that programmers follow the discipline of checking the reference table.

5.3.3 **Meaningful Ranges**

A special case of the conflated codes situation results from assigning meaning not only to the value of the attribute, but to the (usually numeric) range in which it falls.

For example, we may specify an attribute **Status Code** for an immigration application, then decide that values 10 through 50 are reserved for applications requiring special exemptions. What we actually have here is a hierarchy, with status codes subordinate to special exemption categories. In this example the hierarchy is two levels deep, but if we were to allocate meaning to subranges, sub-subranges, and so on, the hierarchy would grow accordingly. The obvious, and correct, approach is to model the hierarchy explicitly.

Variants of the "meaningful range" problem occur from time to time, and should be treated in the same way. An example is a "meaningful length"; in one database we worked with, a four-character job number identified a permanent job while a five-character job number indicated a job of fixed duration.

5.3.4 **Inappropriate Generalization**

Every COBOL programmer can cite cases where data items have been inappropriately redefined, often to save a few bytes of space, or to avoid reorganizing a file to make room for a new item. The same occurs under other file management and DBMSs, often even less elegantly. (COBOL at least provides an explicit facility for redefinition; relational DBMSs allow only one name for each column of a table,[3] although different names can be used for columns in views based on that table.)

---

[2]Normalization will not automatically produce such a table (refer to Section 13.6.2).
[3]Note that although object-relational DBMSs allow containers to be defined over columns, exploitation of this feature to use a column for multiple purposes goes against the spirit of the relational model.

The result is usually a data item that has no meaning in isolation but can only be interpreted by reference to other data items—for example, an attribute of **Client** which means "Gender" for personal clients and "Industry Category" for company clients. Such a generalized item is unlikely to be used anywhere in the system without some program logic to determine which of its two meanings is appropriate.

Again, we make programming more complex in exchange for a notional space saving and for enforcement of the constraint that the attributes are mutually exclusive. These benefits are seldom adequate compensation. In fact, data compression at the physical level may allow most of the "wasted" space to be retrieved in any case. On the other hand, few would argue with the value of generalizing, say, Assembly Price and Component Price if we had already decided to generalize the entity classes **Assembly** and **Component** to **Product**.

But not all attribute generalization decisions are so straightforward. In the next section, we look at the factors that contribute to making the most appropriate choice.

5.4 **Types of Attributes**

5.4.1 **DBMS Datatypes**

Each DBMS supports a range of **datatypes**, which affect the presentation of the column, the way the data is stored internally, what values may be stored, and what operations may be performed on the column. Presentation, constraints on values, and operations are of interest to us as modelers; the internal representation is primarily of interest to the physical database designer. Most DBMSs will provide at least the following datatypes:

- **Integer** signed whole number
- **Date** calendar date and time
- **Float** floating-point number
- **Char (n)** fixed-length character string
- **Varchar (n)** variable-length character string.

Datatypes that are supported by only some DBMSs include:

- **Smallint** 2-byte whole number
- **Decimal (p,s)** or **numeric (p,s)** exact numeric with s decimal places
- **Money** or **currency** money amount with 2 decimal places
- **Timestamp** date and time, including time zone
- **Boolean** logical Boolean (true/false)

- **Lseg** line segment in 2D plane
- **Point** geometric point in 2D plane
- **Polygon** closed geometric path in 2D plane.

Along with the name and definition, many modelers define the DBMS datatype for each attribute at the conceptual modeling stage. While this is important information once the DBMS and the datatypes it supports are known, such datatypes do not really represent business requirements as such but particular ways of supporting those requirements. For this reason we recommend that:

- Each attribute in the conceptual data model be categorized in terms of how the business intends to use it rather than how it might be implemented in a particular DBMS.
- Allocation of DBMS datatypes (or, if the DBMS supports them, user-defined datatypes) to attributes be deferred until the logical database design phase as described in Chapter 11.

For example, consider the attributes Order No and Order Quantity in Figure 5.1. A modeler fixated on the database rather than the fundamental nature of these attributes may well decide to define them both as integers. But we also need to recognize some fundamental differences in the way these attributes will be used:

- Order Quantity can participate in arithmetic operations, such as Order Quantity × Unit Price or sum (Order Quantity), whereas it does not make sense to include Order No in any arithmetic expressions.
- Inferences can legitimately be drawn from the fact that one Order Quantity is greater than another, thus the expressions Order Quantity > 2, Order Quantity < 10 and max (Order Quantity) make sense, as do attributes such as Minimum Order Quantity or Maximum Order Quantity. On the other hand, Order No > 2, Order No < 10, max (Order No), Minimum Order No and Maximum Order No are unlikely to have any business meaning. (If they do, we may well have a problem with meaningful ranges as discussed earlier.)
- Although the current set of Order Numbers may be solely numeric, there may be a future requirement for nonnumeric characters in Order Numbers. The use of integer for Order No effectively prevents the business taking up that option, but without an explicit statement to that effect.

ORDER (Order No, Customer No, Order Date, . . .)
ORDER LINE (Order No, Line No, Product Code, Order Quantity, . . .)

Figure 5.1 Integer attributes.

Attributes can usefully be divided into the following high-level classes:

- An **Identifier** exists purely to identify entity instances and does not imply any properties of those instances (e.g., Order No, Product Code, Line No).
- A **Category** can only hold one of a defined set of values (e.g., Product Type, Customer Credit Rating, Payment Method, Delivery Status).
- A **Quantifier** is an attribute on which some arithmetic can be performed (e.g., addition, subtraction), and on which comparisons other than "=" and "≠" can be performed (e.g., Order Quantity, Order Date, Unit Price, Discount Rate).
- A **Text Item** can hold any string of characters that the user may choose to enter (e.g., Customer Name, Product Name, Delivery Instructions).

This broad classification of attributes corresponds approximately to that advocated by Tasker.[4] As with taxonomies in general, it is by no means the only one possible, but is one that covers most practical situations and encourages constructive thinking.

In the following sections, we examine each of these broad categories in more detail and highlight some important subcategories. In some cases, recognizing an attribute as belonging to a particular subcategory will lead you directly to a particular design decision, in particular the choice of datatype; in other cases it will simply give you a better overall understanding of the data with which you are working.

Classifying attributes in this way offers a number of benefits:

- A better understanding by business stakeholders of what it is that we as modelers are proposing.
- A better understanding by process modelers of how each attribute can be used (the operations in which it can be involved).
- The ability to collect common information that might otherwise be repeated in attribute descriptions in one place in the model.
- Standardization of DBMS datatype usage.

5.4.2 **The Attribute Taxonomy in Detail**

5.4.2.1 Identifiers

Identifiers may be system-generated, administrator-defined, or externally defined. Examples of **system-generated identifiers** are Customer Numbers,

---

[4]Tasker, D., *Fourth Generation Data—A Guide to Data Analysis for New and Old Systems,* Prentice-Hall, Australia (1989) This book is currently out of print.

Order Numbers, and the like that are generated automatically without user intervention whenever a new instance of the relevant entity class is created. These are often generated in sequence although there is no particular requirement to do so. Again, they are often but not exclusively numeric: an example of a nonnumeric system-generated identifier is the booking reference "number" assigned to an airline reservation. In the early days of relational databases, the generation of such an identifier required a separate table in which to hold the latest value used; nowadays, DBMSs can generate such identifiers directly and efficiently without the need for such a table. System-generated identifiers may or may not be visible to users.

Administrator-defined identifiers are really only suitable for relatively low-volume entity classes but are ideal for these. Examples are Department Codes; Product Codes; and Room, Staff, and Class Codes in a school administration system. These can be numeric or alphanumeric. The system should provide a means for an administrative user of the system to create new identifiers when the system is commissioned and later as new ones are required.

Externally-defined identifiers are those that have been defined by an external party, often a national or international standards authority. Examples include Country Codes, Currency Codes, State Codes, Zip Codes, and so on. Of course, an externally-defined identifier in one system is a user-defined (or possibly system-generated) identifier in another; for example, Zip Code is externally-defined in most systems but may be administrator-defined in a Postal Authority system! Again, these can be numeric or alphanumeric. Ideally these are loaded into a system in bulk from a dataset provided by the defining authority.

A particular kind of identifier attribute is the **tie-breaker** which is often used in an entity class that has been created to hold a repeating group removed from another entity class (see Chapter 2). These are used when none of the "natural" attributes in the repeating group appears suitable for the purpose, or in place of a longer attribute. Line No in **Order Line** in Figure 5.1 is a tie-breaker. These are almost always system-generated and almost always numeric to allow for a simple means of generating new unique values.

It should be clear that identifiers are used in primary keys (and therefore in foreign keys), although keys may include other types of attribute. For example, a date attribute may be included in the primary key of an entity class designed to hold a version or snapshot of something about which history needs to be maintained (e.g., a **Product Version** entity class could have a primary key consisting of Product Code and Effective Date attributes).

Names are a form of identifier but may not be unique; a name is usually treated as a text attribute, in that there are no controls over what is entered (e.g., in an Employee Name or Customer Name attribute). However, you could identify the departments of an organization by their names alone rather than using a **Department Code** or **Department No**, although there are good reasons for choosing one of the latter, particularly as you move to defining a primary key.

We look at identifiers and the associated issue of primary keys in more detail in Chapter 6.

5.4.2.2 Categories

Categories are typically administrator-defined, but some may be externally defined. Externally (on screens and reports), they are represented using character strings (e.g., "Cash," "Check," "Credit Card," "Charge Card," "Debit Card") but may be represented internally using shorter codes or integer values. The internal representations may even be used externally if users are familiar with them and their meanings.

A particular kind of category attribute is the **flag**: this holds a Yes or No answer to a suitably worded question about the entity instance, in which case the question should appear as a legend on screens and reports alongside the answer (usually represented both internally and externally as either "Y" or "N"). Many categories, including flags, also need to be able to hold "Not applicable," "Not supplied," and/or "Unknown." You may be tempted to use nulls to represent any of these situations, but nulls can cause a variety of problems in queries, as Chris Date has pointed out eloquently;[5] if the business wishes to distinguish between any two or more of these, something other than null is required. In this case special symbols such as a dash or a question mark may be appropriate.

5.4.2.3 Quantifiers

Quantifiers come in a variety of forms:

- A **Count** enumerates a set of discrete instances (e.g., **Vehicle Count**, **Employee Count**); it answers a question of the form *"How many . . .?"* It represents a dimensionless (unitless) magnitude.

- A **Dimension** answers a question of the form *"How long . . .?"; "How high . . .?"; "How wide . . .?"; "How heavy . . .?";* and so forth. (e.g., **Room Width**, **Unit Weight**). It can only be interpreted in conjunction with a unit (e.g., feet, miles, millimeters).

- A **Currency Amount** answers a question of the form *"How much . . .?"* and specifies an amount of money (e.g., **Unit Price**, **Payment Amount**, **Outstanding Balance**). It requires a currency unit.

---

[5]Date, C.J. *Relational Database Writings 1989-1991*, Pearson Education POD, 1992, Ch. 12.

- A **Factor** is (conceptually) the result of dividing one magnitude by another (e.g., Interest Rate, Discount Rate, Hourly Rate, Blood Alcohol Concentration). It requires a unit (e.g., $/hour, meters/second) unless both magnitudes are of the same dimension, in which case it is a unit-less ratio (or percentage).

- A **Specific Time Point** answers a question of the form *"When . . .?"* in relation to a single event (e.g., Transaction Timestamp, Order Date, Arrival Year).

- A **Recurrent Time Point** answers a question of the form *"When . . .?"* in relation to a recurrent event (e.g., Departure TimeOfDay, Scheduled DayOfWeek, Mortgage Repayment DayOfMonth, Annual Renewal DayOfYear).

- An **Interval** (or **Duration**) answers a question of the form *"For how long . . .?"* (e.g., Lesson Duration, Mortgage Repayment Period). It requires a unit (e.g., seconds, minutes, hours, days, weeks, months, years).

- A **Location** answers a question of the form *"Where . . .?"* and may be a point, a line segment or a two-, three- (or higher) dimensional figure.

Where a quantifier requires units, there are two options:

1. Ensure that all instances of the attribute are expressed in the same units, which should, of course, be specified in the attribute definition.
2. Create an additional attribute in which to hold the units in which the quantifier is expressed, and provide conversion routines.

Obviously the first option is simpler but the second option offers greater flexibility. A common application of the second option is in handling currency amounts.

For many quantifiers it is important to establish and document what accuracy is required by the business. For example, most currency amounts are required to be correct to the nearest cent (or local currency equivalent) but some (e.g., stock prices) may require fractions of cents, whereas others may always be rounded to the nearest dollar. It should also be established whether the rounding is merely for purposes of display or whether arithmetic is to be performed on the rounded amount (e.g., in an Australian Income Tax return, Earnings and Deductions are rounded down to a whole dollar amount *before* computations using those amounts).

Time Points can have different accuracies and scope depending on requirements:

- A **Timestamp** (or **DateTime**) specifies the date and time when something happened.
- A **Date** specifies the date on which something happened but not the time.
- A **Month** specifies the month and year in which something happened.
- A **Year** specifies the year in which something happened (e.g., the year of arrival of an immigrant).

- A **Time of Day** specifies the time but not the date (e.g., in a timetable).
- A **Day of Week** specifies only the day within a week (e.g., in a timetable).
- A **Day of Month** specifies only the day within a month (e.g., a mortgage repayment date).
- A **Day of Year** specifies only the day within a year (e.g., an annual renewal date).
- A **Month of Year** specifies only the month within a year.

For quantifiers other than Currency Amounts and Points in Time we also need to define whether exact arithmetic is required or whether floating-point arithmetic can be used.

5.4.3 Attribute Domains

The term **domain** is unfortunately over-used and has a number of quite distinct meanings. We base our definition of "attribute domain" on the mathematical meaning of the term "domain" namely "the possible values of the independent variable or variables of a function"[6]—the variable in this case being an *attribute*. However many practitioners and writers appear to view this as meaning the set of values that may be stored in a particular *column* in the database. The same set of values can have different *meanings*, however, and it is the set of *meanings* in which we should be interested.

Consider the set of values {1, 2, . . . 8}. In a school administration application, for example, this might be the set of values allowed in any of the following columns:

- One recording payment types, in which 1 represents cash, 2 check, 3 credit card, and so on
- One recording periods, sessions, or timeslots in the timetabling module
- One recording the number of elective subjects taken by a student (maximum eight)
- One recording the grade achieved by a student in a particular subject

It should be clear that each of these sets of values has quite different meanings to the business. In a conceptual data model, therefore, we should not be interested in the set of values stored in a column in the database, but in the set (or range) of values or alternative meanings that are of interest to, or allowed by, the organization. While the four examples above all have the same set of stored values, they do not have the same set of

---

[6]*Concise Oxford English Dictionary,* 10th Ed. Revised, Oxford University Press 2002.

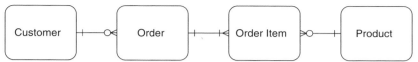

CUSTOMER (Customer No, Customer Name, Customer Type, Registered Business Address, Normal Delivery Address, First Contact Date, Preferred Payment Method)
PRODUCT (Product No, Product Type, Product Description, Current Price, Product Release Date)
ORDER (Order No, Order Date, Alternative Delivery Address, Payment Method)
ORDER ITEM (Item No, Ordered Quantity, Quoted Price, Promised Delivery Date, Actual Delivery Date)

Figure 5.2 A conceptual data model of a simple ordering application.

real-world values, so they do not really have the same domain. Put another way, it makes no sense to say that the "cash" payment type is the same as "Period 1" in the timetable.

This property of comparability is the heart of the **attribute domain** concept. Look at the conceptual data model in Figure 5.2.

In a database built from this model, we might wish to obtain a list of all customers who placed an order on the day we first made contact. The enquiry to achieve this would contain the (SQL) predicate Order Date = First Contact Date. Similarly a comparison between Order Date and Product Release Date is necessary for a query listing products ordered on the day they were released, a comparison between Order Date and Promised Delivery Date is necessary for a query listing "same day" orders, and a comparison between Promised Delivery Date and Actual Delivery Date is necessary for a query listing orders that were not delivered on time.

But now consider a query in which Order Date and Current Price are compared. What does such a comparison mean? Such a comparison ought to generate an SQL compile-time or run-time error. In at least one DBMS, comparison between columns with Date and Currency datatypes is quite legal, although the results of queries containing such comparisons are meaningless. Even if our DBMS rejects such mixed-type comparisons, it won't reject comparisons between Customer No and Product No if these have both been defined as numbers, or between Customer Name and Address.

In fact only the following comparisons are meaningful between the attributes in Figure 5.2:

■ Preferred Payment Method and Payment Method
■ Those between any pair of First Contact Date, Product Release Date, Order Date, Promised Delivery Date and Actual Delivery Date

- Current Price and Quoted Price
- Those between any pair of Registered Business Address, Normal Delivery Address, and Alternative Delivery Address.

Whether or not these comparisons are meaningful is completely independent of any implementation decisions we might make. It would not matter whether we implemented Price attributes in the database using specialized currency or money datatypes, integer datatypes (holding cents), or decimal datatypes (holding dollars and two decimal places); the meaningfulness of comparisons between Price attributes and other attributes is quite independent of the DBMS datatypes we choose. Meaningfulness of comparison is therefore a property of the attributes that form part of the conceptual data model rather than the database design.

You may be tempted to use an operation other than comparison to decide whether two attributes have the same domain, but beware. Comparison is the only operation that makes sense for *all* attributes and other operations may allow mixed domains; for example it is legal to multiply Ordered Quantity and Quoted Price although these belong to different domains.

How do attribute domains compare to the attribute types we described earlier in this chapter? An attribute domain is a lower level classification of attributes than an attribute type. One attribute type may include multiple attribute domains, but one attribute domain can only describe attributes of one attribute type.

What benefits do we get from defining the attribute domain of each attribute? The same benefits as those that accrue from attribute types (as described in Section 5.4.1) accrue in greater measure from the more refined classification that attribute domains allow. In addition they support quality reviews of process definitions:

- Only attributes in the same attribute domain can be compared.
- The value in an attribute can only be assigned to another attribute in the same attribute domain.
- Each attribute domain only accommodates some operations. For example, only some allow for ordering operations (>, <, between, order by, first value, last value).

The following "rules of thumb" are appropriate when choosing domains for attributes:

1. Each attribute used solely to identify an entity class should be assigned its own attribute domain (thus Customer No, Order No, and Product No should each be assigned a different attribute domain).
2. Each category attribute should be assigned its own attribute domain unless it shares the same possible values *and meanings* with another category attribute, in which case they share an attribute domain. (Thus Preferred

Payment Method and Payment Method share an attribute domain, but Customer Type and Product Type have their own attribute domains.)

3. All quantifier attributes of the same attribute type can be assigned the same attribute domain. For example:

   a. All counts can be assigned the same attribute domain.

   b. All currency amounts can be assigned the same attribute domain.

   c. All dates can be assigned the same attribute domain.

4. Text item attributes with different meanings should be assigned different attribute domains. (Thus Registered Business Address, Normal Delivery Address, and Alternative Delivery Address share an attribute domain, but Customer Name and Product Description have their own attribute domains.)

In the example shown in Figure 5.2, therefore, the attribute types and domains would be as listed in Figure 5.3.

High-Level Attribute Types	Detailed Attribute Types	Domains	Attributes
Identifiers	System-Generated Identifiers	Customer No	Customer No
		Order No	Order No
	Administrator-Defined Identifiers	Product No	Product No
	Tie-Breakers	Item No	Item No
Categories		Customer Type	Customer Type
		Payment Method	Payment Method
			Preferred Payment Method
		Product Type	Product Type
Quantifiers	Count	Count	Ordered Quantity
	Currency Amount	Currency Amount	Current Price
			Quoted Price
	Specific Time Point	Date	First Contact Date
			Product Release Date
			Order Date
			Promised Delivery Date
			Actual Delivery Date
Text Items		Customer Name	Customer Name
		Address	Registered Business Address
			Normal Delivery Address
			Alternative Delivery Address
		Product Description	Product Description

Figure 5.3 Attribute types and domains.

5.4.4 **Column Datatype and Length Requirements**

We now look at the translation of attribute types into column datatypes.

If your DBMS does not support UDTs (user-defined datatypes), you should assign to each column the appropriate DBMS datatype (as indicated in Sections 5.4.4.1 to 5.4.4.4).

If, however, you are using an SQL99-compliant DBMS that supports UDTs, you should do the following:

1. For each attribute type or attribute domain in the taxonomy, create a UDT based on the appropriate DBMS datatype.
2. Assign to each column the UDT corresponding to the attribute type of the attribute that it represents.

For example, if your model includes Identifier attributes, create one or more UDTs based on the char or varchar DBMS datatypes (either an Identifier UDT or Customer No, Product No, Order No UDTs, and so forth). Then, assign those UDTs to your Identifier attributes.

5.4.4.1 Identifiers

An **Identifier** should use the char or varchar datatype[7] (depending on the particular properties of these datatypes in the DBMS being used), unless it is known that nonnumeric values will never be required, in which case the integer datatype can be used. Even if only numeric values are used at present, this may not always be the case. For example, U.S. Zip codes are numeric; while nonnumeric codes may never be introduced in the United States, a U.S.-based company may want to allow for expansion into countries like Canada where nonnumeric codes are used. This is flexibility in exchange for rule enforcement—in this case probably a good exchange.

The length should be chosen to accommodate the maximum number of instances of the entity class required over the life of the system. As reuse of identifiers is not advisable, we are not talking about the maximum number of instances at any one time! The numbers of instances that can be accommodated by various lengths of (var)char and integer columns are shown in Figure 5.4, in which it is assumed that only letters and digits are used in a (var)char column. Of course, with an administrator-defined or externally defined identifier, there may already be a standard for the length of the identifier.

---

[7]Note that we are talking here about Identifier *attributes* in the conceptual data model, not about surrogate keys in the logical data model (see Chapter 7) for which there are other options.

5.4.4.2 Categories

If a **Category** attribute is represented internally using the same character strings as are used externally, the char or varchar datatype should be used with a length sufficient to accommodate the longest character string.

If (as is more usually the case) it is represented internally using a shorter code, the char or varchar datatype should again be used; now, however, the length depends on the number of values that may be required over the life of the system, according to Figure 5.4.

If integer values are to be used internally, the integer datatype should be used. Once again Figure 5.4 indicates how many values can be accommodated by each length of integer column.

Flags should be held in char(1) columns unless Boolean arithmetic is to be performed on them, in which case use integer1 and represent Yes by 1 and No by 0 (zero). However, these should still be represented in forms and reports using Y and N. Section 5.4.5 discusses conversion between external and internal representations.

5.4.4.3 Quantifiers

1. **Counts** should use the integer datatype. The length should be sufficient to accommodate the maximum value (e.g., if more than 32,767 use a 4-byte integer, otherwise if more than 127 use a 2-byte integer).
2. **Dimensions, Factors,** and **Intervals** should generally use a decimal datatype if available in the DBMS, unless exact arithmetic is not required, in which case the float datatype can be used. The decimal

Datatype	Length	Number accommodated
(var)char	1	36
	2	1,296
	3	46,656
	4	1,679,616
	5	60,466,176
	6	2,176,782,336
	7	78,364,164,096
	8	2.82×10^{12}
integer	1	127
	2	32,767
	4	2,147,483,647

Figure 5.4 Identifier capacities.

datatype requires the number of digits after the decimal point to be specified. If the decimal datatype is not available, the integer datatype must be used. A decision must then be made as to where the decimal point is understood to occur. (This will, of course, be the same for all instances of the attribute.) Then, data entry and display functionality must be programmed accordingly. For example, if there are two digits after the decimal point, any value entered by the user into the attribute must be multiplied by 100 and all values of the attribute must be displayed with a decimal point before the second-to-last digit. This is discussed further in Section 5.4.5. Note that use of a simple numeric datatype is only appropriate if all quantities to be recorded in the column use the same units. If a variety of units is required, you have a complex attribute with quantity and unit components (see Section 7.2.2.4).

3. **Currency Amounts** should use the currency datatype (if available in the DBMS) provided it will handle the business requirements. For example we may need to record amounts in different currencies and the DBMS's currency datatype may not handle this correctly. If a currency datatype is not available or does not support the requirements, the decimal datatype should be used with the appropriate number of digits after the decimal point (normally two) specified. If there is a requirement to record fractions of a cent and the DBMS currency datatype does not accommodate more than two digits after the decimal point, again the decimal datatype should be used. If the decimal datatype is not available, the integer datatype should be used in the same way as described for dimensions and factors.

4. **Timestamps** should use whichever datatype is defined in the DBMS to record date and time together (this datatype is often called simply "date"). If the business needs to record timestamps in multiple time zones, you need to ensure that the DBMS datatype supports this. As for the "year 2000" issue, as far as we are aware all commercial DBMSs record years using 4 digits, so that is one issue you should not need to worry about!

5. If there is a specific datatype in the DBMS to hold just a date without a time, this should be used for **Dates**. If not, the datatype defined in the DBMS to record date and time together can be used. The time should be standardized to 00:00 for each date recorded. This however can cause problems with comparisons. If an expiry date is recorded and an event occurs with a timestamp during the last day of the validity period, the comparison Event Timestamp <= Expiry Date will return False even though the event is valid. To overcome this, Expiry Dates using date/time datatypes need to be recorded as being at 00:00 on the day after the actual date (but displayed correctly!).

6. **Months** should probably use the datatype suitable for dates and standardize the day to the 1st of the month.

7. **Years** should use the integer2 datatype.

8. **Times of Day** can use the datatype defined in the DBMS to record date and time together if there is no specific datatype for time of day. The date should be standardized to some particular day throughout the system, such as 1/1/2000.

9. **Days of Week** should use the integer1 datatype and a standard sequential encoding starting at 0 or 1 representing Sunday or Monday. A suitable external representation is the first two letters of the day name. Conversion between external and internal representations is discussed in Section 10.5.3.

10. **Days of Month** should also use the integer1 datatype, but the internal and external representations can be the same.

11. **Days of Year** should probably use the datatype suitable for dates; the year should be standardized to some particular year throughout the system, such as 2000.

12. **Months of Year** should use the integer1 datatype and a standard sequential encoding starting at 1 representing January. The external representation should be either the integer value or the first three letters of the month name. Conversion between external and internal representations is discussed in Section 5.4.5.

13. If there is a specific datatype in the DBMS to hold position data, it should be used for **Locations**. If not, the most common solution is to use a coordinate system (e.g., represent a point by two decimal columns holding the x and y coordinates, a line segment by the x and y coordinates of each end, a polygon by the x and y coordinates of each vertex, and so on).

5.4.4.4 Text Attributes

Text attributes must use the char or varchar datatype (which of these is better depends on particular properties of these datatypes in the DBMS being used). The length should be sufficient to accommodate the longest character string that the business may need to record. The DBMS may impose an upper limit on the length of a (var)char column, but it may also provide a means of storing character strings of unlimited length; again, consult the documentation for that DBMS. If you need to store special characters, you will need to confirm whether the selected datatype will handle these; there may be an alternative datatype that does.

A particular type of text attribute is the **Commentary** (or comment) for when the business requires the ability to enter as much or as little text as each instance demands. If the DBMS does not provide a means of storing character strings of unlimited length, use the maximum length available in a standard varchar column. Do not make the common mistake of defining

Create PRODUCT_VIEW (Product_Code, Unit_Price, Obsolete_Flag) as

Select Product_Code, Unit_Price/100.00,

Case Obsolete_Flag when 1 then "Y" else "N" end. . .

Figure 5.5 Use of a view to convert from internal to external representation.

the commentary as a repeating char(80) (or thereabouts) column, which after normalization would be spread over multiple rows. This makes editing of a commentary nearly impossible since there is no word-wrap between rows as in a word processor.

5.4.5 Conversion Between External and Internal Representations

We have seen that a number of attribute types may have different external and internal representations. In a relational DBMS, SQL views can be used to manage the conversion from internal to external representation as in Figure 5.5.

This particular example uses an arithmetic expression to convert an amount stored as an integer to dollars and cents and a case statement to convert a flag stored as 0 or 1 to N or Y, respectively. Functions may also be used in views, particularly for date manipulation. None of these conversions will work in reverse however, so such a view is not updateable (e.g., one cannot enter Y into **Obsolete Flag** and have it recorded as 1). Such logic must therefore be written into the data entry screen(s) for the entity class in question. Ideally, there would only be one for each entity class.

5.5 Attribute Names

5.5.1 Objectives of Standardizing Attribute Names

Many organizations have put in place detailed standards for attribute naming, typically comprising lists of component words with definitions, standard abbreviations, and rules for stringing them together. Needless to say, there has been much "reinvention of the wheel." Names and abbreviations tend to be organization-specific, so most of the common effort has been in deciding sequence, connectors, and the minutiae of punctuation. IBM's "OF" language and the "reverse OF" language variant, originally proposed in the early 1970s, have been particularly influential, if only because the names that they generate often correspond to those that are already in use or that we would come up with intuitively. Attribute names constructed using the OF language consist of a single "class word" drawn from a short standard list (Date, Name, Flag, and so on) and one or more organization- defined "modifiers," separated by connectors (primarily "of" and "that is"—hence, the name). Examples of names constructed using the OF language are "Date of Birth," "Name of Person," and "Amount that is Discount of Product that is Retail." Some of these names are more natural and familiar than others!

Other standards include:

- The NIST Special Publication 500-149 "Guide on Data Entity Naming Conventions" from the U.S. National Institute of Standards and Technology
- ISO/IEC International Standard 11179-5, Information technology— Specification and standardization of data elements, Part 5: Naming and identification principles for data elements, International Organization for Standardization

The objectives of an attribute-naming standard are usually to:

- Reduce ambiguity in interpreting the meaning of attributes (the name serving as a short form of documentation)
- Reduce the possibility of "synonyms"—two or more attributes with the same meaning but different names
- Reduce the possibility of "homonyms"—two or more attributes with the same name but different meanings.

Consider the data shown in Figure 5.6. On the face of it, we can interpret this data without difficulty. However, we cannot really answer with confidence such questions as:

- How much of product FX-321-0138 has customer 36894 ordered?
- How much will that product cost that customer?
- When was that product delivered?

Customer	Product	Qty	Price	Discount	Date
36894	FX-321-0138	12	17.99	6.25	4/07/2002
47808	VL-108-7639	3	223.55	8.75	6/07/2002

Figure 5.6   Some data in a database.

The reason is that we do not know from the column names:

- What units apply to quantities in the **Qty** column?
- Is **Discount** a percentage or a $ amount?
- Is **Date** the date ordered, date required by, or date actually delivered?

This is as much a data quality problem as a failure to get correct and complete data into the database. (Data quality is not only about getting the right data into the system; it is also about correctly interpreting the data in the system.) Indeed data quality can be compromised by any of the following:

- Data-capture errors (not only invalid data getting into the database but also the failure of all required data to get into the database)
- Data-interpretation errors (when users misinterpret data)
- Data-processing errors (when developers misinterpret data processing requirements).

Thus, correct interpretation of data structures is essential by data entry personnel, data users, and developers. There are various views on how one might interpret the meaning of a data item in a database. Practitioners and writers often make statements to the effect that a "6" in the Quantity column means that Supplier x supplied Customer y with 6 of Product z (rather an overconfident view in the light of the prevalence of data quality problems!). A more realistic view is that a "6" in the Quantity column means either that the data entry person thought that was the right number to enter or that a programmer has written a program that puts "6" in that column for some reason.

So the issue becomes one of where people (data entry personnel or programmers) get their perceptions about what a data item means. Data entry persons and data users get their perceptions from onscreen captions, help screens, and (possibly) a user manual. Programmers get their perceptions from specifications written by process designers, and process designers in turn get their perceptions from table/column names and descriptions. This is all metadata. What it should tell a data entry person or user is how to put information in, how to express it, and what it means once it is in there. Likewise, what it should tell a developer is where to put information, how to represent it, and how to use it (again, what it means once it is in there).

5.5.2 **Some Guidelines for Attribute Naming**

The naming standard you adopt may be influenced by the facilities provided by your documentation tool or data dictionary and by established practices within your organization or industry, which are, ideally, the result of a well-thought-out and consistent approach. If you are starting with a blank slate, here are some basic guidelines and options:

1. Build a list of standard class words to be used for each attribute type, along the following lines:

   Identifiers: Number (or No), Code, Identifier (or Id), Tie-Breaker

   Categories: Type, Method, Status, Reason, and so forth.

   Counts: Count (*never* Number as in "Number of . . .")[8]

   Dimensions: Length, Width, Height, Weight, and so forth.

   Amounts: Amount, Price, Balance, and so forth.

   Factors: Rate, Concentration, Ratio, Percentage, and so forth.

   Specific Time Points: Timestamp, DateTime, Date, Month, Year

   Recurrent Time Points: TimeOfDay, DayOfWeek, DayOfMonth, DayOfYear, MonthOfYear

   Intervals: Duration, Period

   Positions: Point, LineSegment, Polygon, and so forth

   Texts: Name, Description, Comment, Instructions

   While it is desirable not to use different words for the same thing, it is more important to use terminology with which the business is comfortable. Thus, for example, Price is included as well as Amount since Unit Price Amount does not read as comfortably as Unit Price.

2. Select suitable qualifiers or modifiers to precede class words in attribute names (e.g., Registration in Registration Number and Purchase in Purchase Date). There may be value in building a standard list of modifiers, but the list should include all terms in common use in the business unless these are particularly ambiguous.

3. Sequence the qualifiers in each attribute name using the "reverse" variation of the IBM OF language. The traditional way of achieving this is to string together the words using "that is" and "of" as connectors, to produce an OF language name, then to reverse the order and eliminate the connectors. For example, an attribute to represent the average annual dividend amount for a stock could be (using the OF language):

   Amount of Dividend that is Average that is Annual of Stock

   Reversing gives:

   Stock Average Annual Dividend Amount

   This is pretty painful, but with a little practice you can move directly to the reverse OF language name, which usually sounds reasonable, at least to an information systems professional!

4. Determine a policy for inclusion of the name of the entity class in attribute names. This continues to be a matter of debate, probably because

---

[8]To avoid confusion with identifier attributes with names ending in "number."

there is no overwhelming reason for choosing one option over another. Workable variants include:

- Using the "home" entity class name as the first word or words of each attribute name. The "home" entity class of a foreign key is the entity class in which it appears as a primary key; the "home" entity class of an attribute inherited or rolled up from a supertype or a subtype is that supertype or subtype, respectively. So, attributes of Vehicle might include *Vehicle* Registration Number, *Asset* Purchase Date (inherited), *Truck* Capacity (rolled up), and Responsible *Organization Unit* Code (foreign key).
- Using home entity class names only in primary and foreign keys.
- Using home entity class names only in foreign keys.

5. In addition to using the home entity class name, prefix foreign keys according to the name of the relationship they implement, (e.g., *Issuing* Branch No, *Responsible* Branch No). This is not always easy, and it is reasonable to bend the rule if the relationship is obvious and the name clumsy, or if an alternative role name is available. For example, *Advanced* Customer No, meaning the key of the customer to whom a loan was advanced, could be better named Borrower (Customer) No.
6. Avoid abbreviations in attribute names, unless they are widely understood in your organization (by business people!) or you are truly constrained by your documentation tool or data dictionary. It is very likely that the DBMS will impose length and punctuation constraints. These apply to *columns*, not to attributes!
7. Look hard at any proposal to use "aliases" (i.e., synonyms to assist access). This is really a data dictionary (metadata repository) management issue rather than a modeling one, but take note that alias facilities are often established but relatively seldom used.
8. Establish a simple translation from attribute names to column names. Here is where abbreviations come in.

In the pursuit of consistency and purity, do not lose sight of one of the fundamental objectives of modeling: communication. Sometimes we must sacrifice rigid adherence to standards for familiarity and better-quality feedback from nontechnical participants in the modeling process. Conversely, it is sometimes valuable to introduce a new term to replace a familiar, but ambiguous term.

A final word on attribute names: If you are building your own data dictionary, do not use Attribute Name as the primary key for the table containing details of Attributes. Names and even naming standards will change from time to time, and we need to be able to distinguish a change in attribute name from the creation of a new attribute.[9] A simple meaningless

---

[9] We look at the problem of unstable primary keys (of which this is one example) in Chapter 6.

identifier will do the job; it need not be visible to anyone. Most documentation tools and data dictionaries support this; a few do not.

5.6   **Attribute Generalization**

5.6.1   **Options and Trade-Offs**

In Chapter 4 we looked at entity class generalization (and specialization, its converse), and we also looked at the use of supertypes and subtypes to represent the results. Recall that higher levels of generalization meant fewer entity classes, fewer rules within the data structure, and greater resilience to change. On the other hand, specialization provided a more detailed picture of data and enforcement of more business rules, but less stability in the face of changes to these rules.

The best design was necessarily a trade-off among these different features. Making the best choice started with being aware of the different possibilities (by showing them as subtypes and supertypes on the model), rather than merely recording the first or most obvious option.

Much the same trade-offs apply to attribute definition. In some cases, the decision is largely predetermined by decisions taken at the entity class level. We generalize two or more entity classes, then review their attributes to look for opportunities for generalization. In other cases, the discovery that attributes belonging to different entity classes are used in the same way may prompt us to consider generalizing their parent entity classes.

Conversely, close examination of the attributes of a single entity class may suggest that the entity class could usefully be subtyped. One or more attributes may have a distinct meaning for a specific subset of entity instances (e.g., **Ranking**, **Last Review Date**, and **Special Agreement Number** apply only to those Suppliers who have Preferred Supplier status). Often a set of attributes will be inapplicable under certain conditions. We need to look at the conditions and decide whether they provide a basis for entity class subtyping.

Generalizing attributes *within* an entity class can also affect the overall shape of the model. For example, we might generalize **Standard Price**, **Trade Price**, and **Preferred Customer Price** to **Price**. The generalized attributes will then become a repeating group, requiring us to separate them out in order to preserve first normal form (as discussed in Chapter 2).

Finally, at the attribute level, *consistency* (of format, coding, naming, and so on) is an important consideration, particularly when we are dealing with a large number of attributes. The starting point for consistency is generalization. Without recognizing that several attributes are in some sense similar, we cannot recognize the need to handle them consistently.

In turn, consistent naming practices may highlight opportunities for generalization.

Some examples will illustrate these ideas.

5.6.2 Attribute Generalization Resulting from Entity Generalization

Figure 5.7 shows a simple example of entity class generalization/specialization. The generalization of **Company** and **Person** to **Party** may have been suggested by their common attributes; equally, it may have resulted from our knowledge that the two are handled similarly. Alternatively, we may have worked top-down, starting with the **Party** entity class and looking for subtypes. The subtyping may have been prompted by noting that some of the attributes of **Party** were applicable only to people, and others only to companies.

Our initial task is to allocate attributes among the three entity classes. We have three options for each attribute:

1. Allocate the attribute to one of the subtypes only. We do this if the attribute can apply only to that subtype. For example, we may allocate Birth Date to **Person** only.
2. Allocate the attribute to the supertype only. We do this if the attribute can apply to all of the subtypes and has essentially the same meaning wherever it is used. For example, Address might be allocated to **Party**.
3. Allocate the attribute to more than one of the subtypes, indicating in the documentation that the attributes are related. We do this if the attribute has a different meaning in each case, but not so different that we cannot see any value in generalization. For example, we might allocate Name to both subtypes, on the basis that some processes will handle the names of both persons and companies in the same way (e.g., "Display party details.")

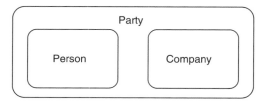

Figure 5.7 Allocating attributes among subtypes.

while others will be specific to company or person names (e.g., "Print envelope for person, including title.").

If we are thorough about this, handling of attributes when we level the model (by selecting the final level of generalization for each entity class) will be reasonably straightforward. If we follow the largely intuitive "inheritance" and "roll up" rules described in Chapter 11, the only issue in leveling the model will be what to do in situation 3 if we implement at the super-type level. We will then have to decide whether to specify a single generalized attribute or to retain the distinct attributes as rolled up from the subtypes.

A good guide is to look closely at the reasons for selecting the higher level of generalization for the entity class. Are we anticipating further, as yet unidentified, subtypes? If so, will they require a corresponding attribute? Have we decided that the subtypes are subject to common processes? How do these processes use the attribute in question? In practice, we tend to carry through the entity class generalization to the attribute more often than not.

We also find frequently that we have not been as thorough as we should have been in spotting possible attribute generalizations. Once the entity class level has been decided upon, it is worth reviewing all of the attributes "rolled up" from subtype entity classes to ensure that opportunities for generalization have not been overlooked.

5.6.3 **Attribute Generalization within Entity Classes**

Opportunities for attribute generalization can arise quite independently of entity class generalization. The following rather long (but instructive) example illustrates the key possibilities and issues. To best highlight some of the normalization issues, we present it in terms of manipulations to a logical model. In practice we would expect these decisions to be made at the conceptual modeling stage.

The **Financial Performance** table in Figure 5.8 represents data about budgeted and annual expenditure on a quarterly basis.

There are such obvious opportunities for column generalization here (most data modelers cannot wait to get started on a structure like this) that it is worth pointing out that the structure as it stands is a legitimate option, useable without further generalization. In particular, it is in at least first normal form. Technically, there are no repeating groups in the structure, despite the temptation to view, for example, the four material budget items as a repeating group. Doing this requires that we bring to bear our knowledge of the problem domain and recognize these columns as representing *at some level of generalization*, the "same thing."

Having conceded that the structure is at least workable, we can be a bit more critical and note some problems with resilience to change. Suppose we

FINANCIAL PERFORMANCE
(Department No, Year, Approved By,
First Quarter Material Budget Amount, Second Quarter Material Budget Amount,
Third Quarter Material Budget Amount, Last Quarter Material Budget Amount,
First Quarter Material Actual Amount, Second Quarter Material Actual Amount,
Third Quarter Material Actual Amount, Total Material Actual Amount,
First Quarter Labor Budget Amount, Second Quarter Labor Budget Amount,
Third Quarter Labor Budget Amount, Last Quarter Labor Budget Amount,
First Quarter Labor Actual Amount, Second Quarter Labor Actual Amount,
Third Quarter Labor Actual Amount, Total Labor Actual Amount,
Other Budget Amount, Other Actual Amount, Discretionary Spending Limit)

Figure 5.8   Financial performance table prior to generalization.

were to make a business decision to move to monthly rather than quarterly reporting, or to include some other budget category besides "labor," "material," and "other"—perhaps "external subcontracts." Changing the table structures and corresponding programs would be a major task, particularly if the possible generalizations had not been recognized even at the program level; in other words, if we had written separate program logic to handle each quarter or to handle labor figures in contrast to material figures. Perhaps this seems an unlikely scenario; on the contrary, we have seen very similar structures on many occasions in practice.

Let us start our generalization with the four material budget columns. We make two decisions here.

First, we confirm that there is value in treating all four in a similar way; that there are business processes that handle first, second, third, and last quarter budgets in much the same way. If this is so, we make the generalization to **Quarterly Material Budget Amount**, noting that the new column occurs four times. We flag this as a repeating group to be normalized out. Because sequence within the group is important, we need to add a new column **Quarter Number**. Another way of looking at this is that we have removed some information from the data structure (the words first, second, third, and last) and need to provide a new place to store that information—hence, the additional column.

Second, we relax the upper limit of four. We know that normalization is going to remove the constraint in any case, so we might as well recognize the situation explicitly and consider its consequences. In this example, the effect is that we are no longer constrained to quarterly budgets, so we need to change the names of the columns accordingly—"Material Budget Amount" and "Period Number."

We can now remove the repeating group, creating a new table **Material Budget Item** (Figure 5.9).

MATERIAL BUDGET ITEM (<u>Department No</u>, <u>Year</u>, <u>Period Number</u>, Material Budget Amount)

Figure 5.9 Material Budget Item Table.

The example, thus far, has illustrated the main impact of attribute generalization within an entity class:

- The increased flexibility obtainable through sensible generalization
- The need to add data items to hold information taken out of the data structure by generalization
- The creation of new entity classes to normalize out the repeating groups resulting from generalization.

Continuing with the financial results example, we could apply the same process to labor and other budget items, and to material, labor, and other actual items, producing a total of seven tables as in Figure 5.10.

In doing this, we would notice that there was no column named **Fourth Quarter Material Actual Amount**. Instead, we have **Total Material Actual Amount**.

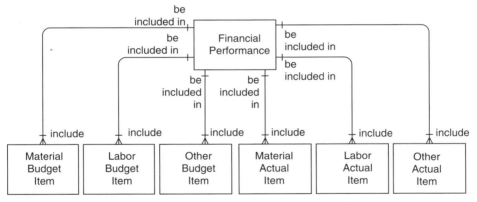

FINANCIAL PERFORMANCE (<u>Department No</u>, <u>Year</u>, Approved By, Discretionary Spending Limit)
MATERIAL BUDGET ITEM (<u>Department No</u>, <u>Year</u>, <u>Period Number</u>, Material Budget Amount)
LABOR BUDGET ITEM (<u>Department No</u>, <u>Year</u>, <u>Period Number</u>, Labor Budget Amount)
OTHER BUDGET ITEM (<u>Department No</u>, <u>Year</u>, <u>Period Number</u>, Other Budget Amount)
MATERIAL ACTUAL ITEM (<u>Department No</u>, <u>Year</u>, <u>Period Number</u>, Material Actual Amount)
LABOR ACTUAL ITEM (<u>Department No</u>, <u>Year</u>, <u>Period Number</u>, Labor Actual Amount)
OTHER ACTUAL ITEM (<u>Department No</u>, <u>Year</u>, <u>Period Number</u>, Other Actual Amount)

Figure 5.10 Budget and actual data separated.

This does not break any data modeling rules, since one value could be derived from the others. But if we choose to generalize, we will have to replace the "total" column with a "fourth quarter" column to make generalization possible. Even if we decide not to model the more generalized structure, we are likely to change the column anyway, for the sake of consistency. It is important to recognize that this "commonsense" move to consistency *relies on our having seen the possibility of generalization in the first place.* To achieve consistency, we need to recognize first that the columns (or the attributes which they implement) have something in common.

There is a flavor of creative data modeling here too. We deliberately choose a particular attribute representation in order to provide an opportunity for generalization.

Inconsistencies that become visible as a result of trying to generalize may suggest useful questions to be asked of the user. Why, for instance, are "other" budgets and expenditures recorded on an annual basis rather than quarterly? Do we want to bring them into line with labor and materials? Alternatively, do we need to provide for labor and materials also being reported at different intervals?

We can take generalization further, bringing together labor, material, and other budgets, and doing likewise for actuals. We gain the flexibility to introduce new types of financial reporting, but we will need to add a **Budget Type** column to replace the information lost from the data structure (Figure 5.11). Note that we can do this either by generalizing the tables in Figure 5.10, or generalizing the columns in the original model of Figure 5.8.

Finally, we could consider generalizing budget and actual data. After all, they are represented by identical structures. When we present this

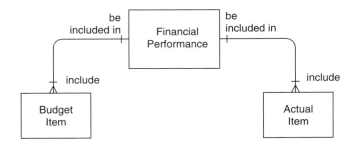

FINANCIAL PERFORMANCE (<u>Department No</u>, <u>Year</u>, Approved By, Discretionary Spending Limit)
BUDGET ITEM (<u>Department No</u>, <u>Year</u>, <u>Period Number</u>, <u>Budget Type</u>, Budget Amount)
ACTUAL ITEM (<u>Department No</u>, <u>Year</u>, <u>Period Number</u>, <u>Budget Type</u>, Actual Amount)

Figure 5.11   Generalization of labor, material, and other data.

BUDGET/ACTUAL ITEM (Department No, Year, Period Number, Budget Type, Budget/Actual Flag, Budget/Actual Amount)

Figure 5.12 Generalization of budget and actual amounts.

example in training courses, there is often strong support for doing this, as in Figure 5.12, perhaps because we have been doing so well with generalization to that point!

But we need to ask: Does the business have processes that treat budget and actual items in much the same way? Is there the possibility of a new category (in addition to "budget" and "actual") arising that can take advantage of existing processes? Chances are that the answer to both is no, and we may achieve only unnecessary obscurity by generalizing any further. The data model may look elegant, but the program logic needed to unravel the different data will be less so.

But before we abandon the idea completely, we could consider the option shown in Figure 5.13, which is different from the previous generalizations in that it *joins* Budget Item and Actual Item. This seems to make more sense.

To summarize: we need to look always at how the business treats the data, using commonality of shape only as a prompt, not as a final arbiter.

5.6.4 "First Among Equals"

Sometimes it is tempting to generalize a single-valued attribute and a similar multivalued attribute. For example, in Australia an organization can have only one Registered Business Name but may have more than one Trading Name. These could be modeled using a number of alternative patterns:

1. Separate attributes in **Organization** for Registered Business Name (single-valued) and Trading Names (multivalued—see Section 7.2.2.5). This is appropriate in the conceptual model and probably the best structure, as the representation is closest to what we observe in the real world.
2. A "child" entity class **Organization Name** at the "many" end of a one-to-many relationship with **Organization**, having a Name attribute and a Registered Business Name Flag attribute to indicate whether the name is the

BUDGET ITEM (Department No, Year, Period Number, Budget Item Type, Budget Amount, Actual Amount)

Figure 5.13 Joining budget item and actual item.

Registered Business Name. This is a less than ideal, but still acceptable, conceptual model and can be directly converted to an acceptable logical model.

3. A "child" table **Organization Name** with a primary key consisting of a foreign key to **Organization** and a Name No column, and a nonkey Name column. The **Organization** table has a Registered Business Name No column that identifies which row in the **Organization Name** table has the Registered Business Name; this is also an acceptable logical model, and if used unchanged as the physical data model is likely to achieve better overall performance for queries returning the Registered Business Name than the physical data model derived unchanged from pattern 2.

4. A Registered Business Name column in the **Organization** table and a Name column in a **Trading Name** table. This is the standard relational logical data model that corresponds to the conceptual data model in pattern 1 and as a physical data model is likely to achieve still better performance for queries that require only the Registered Business Name; however, an "all names" query is more complex (a UNION query is required).

5. Pattern 2 but with an additional Registered Business Name column in the **Organization** table to hold a copy of the Registered Business Name. Although this structure is technically fully normalized, it still has some redundancy so should not be acceptable as a logical model, although it is a workable physical model (provided the redundancy is documented so that inconsistency can be avoided).

5.6.5 **Limits to Attribute Generalization**

In the budgeting example of Section 5.6.3, we reached the point of limited further gains from generalization while we still had a number of distinct attributes. But there are situations in which a higher level of attribute generalization is justified. Figure 5.14 shows an example of a very high level of attribute generalization, in which all attributes are generalized to a

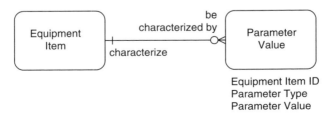

Figure 5.14 Highly generalized attributes.

single Parameter Value attribute and subsequently removed as a repeating group. We have called the new entity class **Parameter Value** rather than **Attribute**; an entity class named **Attribute** is not going to do much for communication with the uninitiated!

This is the attribute level equivalent of the **Thing** entity class (Chapter 4). It may be useful when structures are genuinely unstable and unpredictable. In this example, every time we purchase a new type of equipment, we might want to record new attributes: perhaps bandwidth, range, tensile strength, or mean time between failures. Rather than add new attributes to **Equipment Item**, we simply record new values for Parameter Type.

Commercial software packages may employ high levels of generalization to support "user-defined attributes." We have seen the technique used very successfully in product databases, allowing new products with unanticipated attributes to be defined very quickly without altering the database structure. But we have also seen it used far too often as a substitute for rigorous analysis. You need to keep in mind the following:

- Some of the entity class's attributes may be stable and handled in a distinct way. Model them separately, and do not include them in the generic repeating group.
- Consider subtyping **Parameter Value** based on attribute type, (e.g., **Quantity Parameter Value**, **Text Parameter Value**).
- You will need to add attributes to replace the information removed from the data structure. This includes anything you would normally specify for an attribute, including name, format, editing rules, and optionality. These become attributes initially of the **Parameter Value** entity class, then, through normalization, of a **Parameter Type** entity class (see Figure 5.15). **Parameter Type**s can be related to **Equipment Type**s to

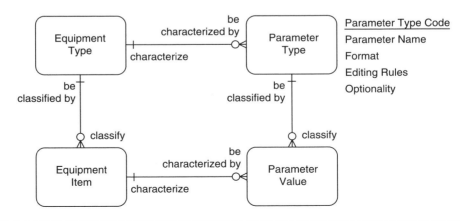

Figure 5.15   Highly generalized attributes with reference table.

specify which parameter types are applicable to each type of equipment (see Section 14.5.6 for further discussion of this technique).

■ The technique is only useful if the different parameter types can utilize common program code. If not, you may as well make the change to the system in the conventional fashion by modifying the database and writing the necessary code. Good candidates for the parameter approach are attributes that are simply entered and displayed, rather than those that drive or are involved in more complex logic.

■ Programs will need to be suitably parameter-driven, to the extent that you may need to support run-time decisions on screen and report formatting. You will need to look hard at how well your tool set supports the approach. Many program generators cannot effectively handle challenges of this kind. Even human programmers will need guidance from someone very familiar with the data model if they are to exploit it properly.

5.7 **Summary**

Proper definitions are an essential starting point for detailed modeling of attributes and can make a significant contribution to the quality of the data in the eventual system.

Each attribute should represent one fact type only. The most common types of violations are simple aggregations, complex codes, meaningful ranges, and inappropriate generalization.

We should create a complete business attribute taxonomy to cover all required attributes, with:

■ Usage requirements
■ Requirements for units, maximum value, accuracy, negative values, number of instances to be identified (as appropriate).

Then we should analyze how each attribute will be used, classifying it according to the taxonomy rather than using DBMS datatypes and specifying column lengths according to the business' capacity requirements. Each attribute then inherits the requirements of its classification. Any exception to those requirements should be handled using:

■ An additional classification, or
■ An override in the attribute description.

Name attributes according to whatever standard is in place or develop a standard according to the guidelines provided in Section 5.5.2.

There is value in exploring different levels of generalization for attributes. Attributes can be allocated to different levels of the entity class subtype hierarchy and will influence the choice of level for implementation. Attributes belonging to the same entity class may also be generalized, possibly resulting in repeating groups, which will be separated by normalization.

Chapter 6
Primary Keys and Identity

"The only thing we knew for sure about Henry Porter was that his name wasn't Henry Porter."
- Bob Dylan and Sam Shepard, Brownsville Girl, 1986, Special Rider Music

"No entity without identity."
- Slogan cited by P.F. Strawson in Contemporary British Philosophy[1]

6.1 Basic Requirements and Trade-Offs

There is no area of data modeling in which mistakes are more frequently made, and with more impact, than the specification of primary keys.

From a technical perspective, the job seems straightforward. For each table, we need to select (or create) a set of columns that have a different combination of values for each row of that table.

But from a business perspective, the purpose of the primary key is to identify the row corresponding to a particular entity instance in the real world—a client, a product, an item on an order. Unfortunately, this mapping from real-world identity to values in a database is not always straightforward. In the real world, we routinely cope with ambiguity and complexity in dealing with identity; we happily use the same name for more than one thing, or multiple names for the same thing, relying on context and questioning to clarify if necessary. In a database we need a simple, unambiguous identifier.

Most problems with primary keys arise from conflicts between technical soundness and ease of mapping to real-world identifiers.

Let us look first at the technical requirements.

To access data in a relational database, we need to be able to locate specific rows of a table by specifying values for their primary key column or columns. In particular:

- We must be able to unambiguously specify the row that corresponds to a particular real-world entity instance. When a payment for an account arrives, we need to be able to retrieve the single relevant row in the

---

[1] "Entity and Identity" in H.D. Lewis (Ed.) 4th Series, Allen and Unwin, London, 1976.

183

Account table by specifying the **Account Number** that was supplied with the payment.

■ Relationships are implemented using foreign keys (see Section 2.8.5), which must each point to one row only. Imagine the problems if we had an insurance policy that referred to customer number "12345" but found two or more rows with that value in the **Customer** table.

So we require that a primary key be *unique*. Even more fundamentally, we require that it be *applicable* to all instances of an entity (and hence to all rows in the table). It is not much good using **Registration Number** to identify vehicles if we need to keep track of unregistered vehicles. Applicability and uniqueness are essential criteria.

There are further properties that are highly desirable. We require that a primary key be *minimal*; we should not include more columns than are necessary for uniqueness. A key should also be *stable*; it should not change value over time. The stability requirement is frequently overlooked in data modeling texts and training courses (and indeed by all too many practitioners), but by observing it we can avoid the often complex program logic needed to accommodate changes in key values.

A very simple way of meeting all of the requirements is to invent a new column for each table, specifically to serve as its primary key, and to assign a different system-generated value to each row, and, by extension, to the corresponding entity instance. We refer to such a column as a **surrogate key**, which is typically named by appending "ID" (or, less often, "Number" or "No") to the table name. Familiar examples are customer IDs, employee IDs, and account numbers allocated by the system.

And here we strike the clash with business requirements. To begin with, primary keys are often confused with "available access mechanisms." The fact that the term "key" is often used loosely for both does not help. So, business stakeholders (and all too often technical people as well) may believe that using a surrogate key will preclude them from accessing the database using more familiar and convenient data. While this concern is based on a misunderstanding, it is a reflection of a real issue: each value of a surrogate key still needs to be matched to the real-world instance that it represents. Sometimes this is straightforward, as with internal account numbers that we generate ourselves; sometimes it is not, as with customers who cannot remember the numbers we have allocated them or the code that we have assigned to their country of origin. Often the necessary matching will incur costs in programming and database performance, as we have to match surrogate keys against real-world identifiers (so-called **natural keys**) in reference tables. So the physical database designer and programmers may also line up against the data modeler to support the use of natural keys.

Most arguments about primary keys come back to this choice between surrogate and natural keys. At the one extreme we have the argument that only surrogate keys should be used; at the other, a view that the natural key should always be the starting point, even if it needs to be modified or augmented to provide uniqueness. *Most serious mistakes in primary key selection are the result of ill-considered decisions to use natural keys without reference to whether or not they meet the basic requirements.* As a data modeler, you may well feel that the surrogate option offers a simple solution that eliminates the risk and complexities of using natural identifiers, and the need to read the rest of this chapter. However, if you take that option, you may find yourself revisiting the question at the physical design stage. In any event, you should read the section on surrogate keys and structured keys; there are still some decisions to be made!

In this chapter, we next look in detail at the technical criteria governing primary key selection. Going back to these basics can help resolve the majority of questions that arise in practice. We then explore the trade-offs involved with surrogate keys. We devote a full section to structured (multi-column) keys, in particular the choice between using a "stand-alone" key or one that incorporates the primary key of another table. Finally, we look at some issues that arise when there are multiple candidate keys available and at the impact of nullable (optional) columns in primary keys.

6.2 **Basic Technical Criteria**

6.2.1 **Applicability**

We must be able to determine a value for the primary key for every row of a table. Watch for the following traps when attempting to use columns derived from real-world attributes rather than surrogate keys.

6.2.1.1 Special Cases

Often our understanding of a business area is based on a few examples that may not be adequately representative. It is worth adopting the discipline of asking the business specialists, "Are there any cases in which we would not have a value for one of these attributes?" Do we ever encounter persons without a Social Security Number? Or flights without a flight number? Or sound recordings without a catalogue number? Surprisingly often, such special cases emerge. We are then faced with a choice of:

1. Setting up a mechanism to allocate values to these cases
2. Excluding them from the entity definition altogether
3. Rejecting the proposed primary key, usually in favor of a surrogate key.

Selecting option 2 will lead to a change to the conceptual model at the entity level as a new entity is added to cater to the special cases or the overall scope of the model is modified to exclude them.

6.2.1.2 Data Unavailable at Time of Entry

All components of a primary key need to be available at the time a row is first stored in the database. This can sometimes be a problem if we are building up data progressively. For example, we may propose Customer Number plus Departure Date as the primary key of **Travel Itinerary**. But will we always know the departure date at the time we first record information about an itinerary? Are we happy to hold off recording the travel plans until that date is available?

6.2.1.3 Broadening of Scope

One of the most common causes of problems with keys is a broadening of the original scope of a system, resulting in tables being used to hold data beyond that originally intended. Frequently, the primary key is not applicable to some of the instances embraced by the more general definition. For example, we may decide to market our products to individual persons, where in the past we only dealt with companies. In this case, a government-assigned Company Number will no longer be suitable as a primary key for **Customer**. Or our bookselling business may broaden its product range to include stationery, and International Standard Book Number will no longer be an appropriate key for **Product**.

One way of reducing the likelihood of being caught by scope changes is to be as precise as possible in entity class naming and definition: name the original entity class **Company** rather than **Customer**, or **Book Title** rather than **Product**. Then use supertyping to explore different levels of generalization, such as **Customer** and **Product**. The resulting model will prompt questions such as, "Are we potentially interested in customers who are not companies?" It now comes back to the familiar task of choosing a level of generalization, and a corresponding key, that will accommodate business change. We cannot expect to get it right every time, but most problems that arise in this area are a result of not having addressed the generalization issue at all, rather than coming up with the wrong answer.

6.2.2 **Uniqueness**

Uniqueness is the most commonly cited requirement of primary keys. To reiterate: *you cannot build a relational database without unique primary keys.*

Indeed, the term "unique primary key" is a tautology; if a combination of columns is not unique, it does not qualify to be called a primary key. There are three ways you can satisfy yourself that a key will be unique.

The first is that it is intrinsically unique, as a result of the nature of the real world. A fingerprint or signature might qualify under this criterion, as would coordinates of a location, if sufficiently precise. Such keys occur only rarely in practice.

The second is that you, as the designer, establish a mechanism for the allocation of key values and can therefore ensure that no value is allocated more than once. Surrogate keys, such as computer-generated sequential **Customer Numbers**, are the obvious examples. Another possibility is a **tie-breaker**—a (usually sequential) number added to an "almost unique" set of attributes. A common example is a numeric suffix added to a person's or organization's name, or part of the name ("Drummond0043"). Why use a tie-breaker when it would seem at least as easy to use a sequential number for the whole key? Performance, real or imagined, is usually the reason. The designer aims to be able to use a single index to provide access on both the primary key and a natural key (the first part of the primary key). In keeping with the "one fact per column" rule introduced in Section 2.5.1 (and discussed in detail in Section 5.3), a tie-breaker should be handled as a separate column, rather than simply appended to the natural key. And, as always with natural keys, you need to make sure that the stability requirement is met.

The third possibility is that someone else with the same intention as you has allocated the key values. Their surrogate key may have gained sufficient recognition for it to be treated as a natural key by others. A vehicle registration number is allocated by a state authority with the intention that it be unique in the issuing state. In these cases, the most common problem is a difference between our scope of interest and theirs. For example, we may be interested in vehicles in more than one state. We can address this problem by including in the key a column that identifies the issuer of the number, (e.g., **State of Registration**). If this column does not already exist, and we need to add it, we must update the conceptual model with a corresponding attribute and verify that we will in fact be able to capture its value in all circumstances. And again, we need to think about possible extensions to the scope of the system. Racehorse names may be unique within a country, but what happens if we want to extend our register to cover overseas events, or greyhounds?

The advantage of using someone else's scheme, particularly if it is widely accepted, is that the primary key will be useful in communicating with the world outside the system. Customers will be able to quote and verify registration numbers, and we avoid singularity problems (discussed in Section 6.3.2). But there is an element of faith in tying our primary key to another's decisions. We need to be reasonably confident that the key issuer's entity class definition will remain in line with our own, and that the key also meets basic standards of soundness. Many a system has been severely disrupted by an external decision to change a numbering scheme or to reuse old numbers.

If you are not using one of these three schemes, you need to ask yourself, "How can I *guarantee* that the key will be unique?" A common mistake is to use a "statistical reduction" approach, best illustrated by the problem of choosing a primary key for persons (customers, employees, and so forth). The modeler starts with a desire to use **Person Name** as the key, prompted by its obvious real-world significance as an identifier. We all know that names are not unique, but what about **Person Name** plus **Birth Date?** Or **Person Name** plus **Birth Date** plus **Zip Code** plus . . .? The problem is that while we can reduce the possibility of duplicates, we can never actually eliminate it, and it takes only one exception to destroy the integrity of the database. And do not forget that human beings are remarkably good at deliberately causing odd situations, including duplicates, if doing so is not actually impossible or illegal! The fact that a primary key of this type is almost unique might prompt you to use a tie-breaker as described above: note that while this will solve the uniqueness problem it will not solve the problem that **Person Name** and **Zip Code** are not *stable* (the values for a given person can change).

6.2.3 **Minimality**

A primary key should not include attributes beyond those required to ensure uniqueness. Having decided that Customer Number uniquely identifies a customer, we should not append Customer Name to the key. We refer to this property as **minimality** (more formally **irreducibility**). There are at least two reasons for requiring that primary keys be minimal.

First, whenever a primary key with an extra attribute appears as a foreign key, we will have normalization problems, as the extra attribute will be determined by the "real" key. For example, if we held both **Customer Number** and **Customer Name** in a **Purchase** table, we would be carrying **Customer Name** redundantly for each purchase made by the customer. A change of name would require a complex update procedure.

Second, it would be possible to insert multiple rows representing the same real-world object without violating the uniqueness constraint on the primary key (which can be routinely checked by DBMSs). If, for example, **Customer Name** were included in the primary key of the **Customer** table, it would then be possible to have two different rows with the same customer number but different names, which would be confusing, to say the least.

Minimality problems do not often occur, and they are usually a result of simple errors in modeling or documentation or of confusion about definitions, rather than an attempt to achieve any particular objective such as performance. They should be picked up by normalization, and there should be no argument about correcting them.

6.2.4   **Stability**

Stability is the subtlest of the design considerations for primary keys, and it is the one least discussed in the literature on data modeling and relational database theory—hence, the one most often violated. The idea is that a given real-world entity instance should keep the same value of the primary key for as long as it is recorded in the database. For example, a given customer should retain the same customer number for as long as he or she is a customer.

6.2.4.1   A Technical Perspective

The first reason for using stable primary keys is that they are used elsewhere as foreign keys. Changing the value of a primary key is therefore not a simple process because all of the foreign key references will also need to be updated. We will need program logic to deal with this,[2] and we will need to change that logic whenever another table carrying the relevant foreign key is added to the database design.

The foreign key maintenance problem is usually the most effective method of convincing programmers and physical database designers of the need for stable primary keys. But there is a more fundamental reason for not allowing changes to primary key values. Think about our customer example again. The customer may, over time, change his/her name, address, or even date of birth if it was stated or entered incorrectly. To match historical data—including data archived on paper, microfiche, tape, or other backup media—with the current picture, we require some attribute or combination of attributes that is not only unique, but does not change over time. The requirement for uniqueness points us to the primary key; to be able to relate current and historical data, we require that it be stable. Really, this is just the foreign key concept extended to include references from outside the database.

6.2.4.2   Reflecting Identity in the Real World

Another way of looking at stability is this: In a relational database, all of the nonkey columns hold data about real-world entity instances; but the key

---

[2]Such logic may be provided through "Update Cascade" facilities within the DBMS.

represents the *existence* of real-world entity instances. In other words, a new primary key value corresponds to a new entity instance being recorded in the database, while deletion of a primary key value corresponds to the record of an entity instance being deleted from the database. Without this discipline, it is difficult to distinguish a change of key value from the deletion of one entity instance and the addition of another.

Admittedly, it is possible to build workable databases without stable primary keys, and much complicated program logic has been written to support key changes. But the *simplest* approach is to adhere rigidly to the discipline of stable primary keys. Stability can always be achieved by using surrogate keys if necessary. There is invariably a payoff in terms of simpler, more elegant databases and systems. *In all of the examples in this book, we assume that the primary keys are stable.* If you require further convincing that unstable primary keys cause complexity, we suggest you try modifying some of the models of historical data in Chapter 15 to accommodate primary key changes.

Stability is very closely tied to the idea of identity. In the insurance business, for example, there are many options that we may want to add to or delete from a policy in order to provide the cover required by the client over the years. At some point, however, the business may decide that a particular change should not be accommodated under the original policy, and a replacement policy should be issued. It is important for the business to distinguish between changes and replacements to allow consistent compliance with legislation and management reporting. ("How many new policies did we issue this month? What is the average cost of issuing a new policy?") The supporting information systems need to reflect the distinction, and the primary key of **Policy** provides the mechanism. We can change virtually every nonkey attribute of a policy, but if the key value remains the same, we interpret the table row as representing the same policy. Conversely, we can leave all other attribute values unchanged, but if the key value changes, we interpret it as a new policy being recorded with identical characteristics to the old.

In some cases, such as persons, the definition of identity is so well entrenched that we would have to be creative modelers indeed to propose alternatives (although it is worth thinking about how a database would handle the situation of a police informer being given a "new identity," or even an employee who resigns and is later reemployed). In others, such as contracts, products, and organization units, a variety of definitions may be workable. Returning to the insurance policy example, what happens if the insurance company issues a temporary "cover note" to provide insurance cover while details of the actual policy are being finalized? Should the cover note and insurance policy be treated as different stages in the life-cycle of the same real-world entity instance, or as different instances? The decision is likely to have a profound impact on the way that we process—and even talk about—the data.

As data modelers we need to capture in entity definitions the essence of what distinguishes one instance from another, and define the primary key accordingly. Sometimes our work at this logical modeling stage will prompt some hard questions about the business and the associated conceptual model.

6.3 Surrogate Keys

As discussed earlier, the requirements of applicability, uniqueness, minimality, and stability seem to have a simple answer: just create a single primary key column for each table and use the system to generate a unique value for each occurrence. For example, we could specify Branch ID as the primary key of **Branch** and number the first Branch "1," the second "2," and so forth. We refer to all such columns as surrogate keys, although some modelers reserve the term for keys that are not only system-generated, but are kept invisible to system users.[3]

6.3.1 Performance and Programming Issues

The two arguments most commonly advanced against surrogate keys are programming complexity and performance. Frequently, we need to access a reference table to find the corresponding natural identifier. This situation occurs often enough that programmers are frequently opponents of surrogate keys. However, performance is not usually a problem if the reference tables are small and can reside in primary storage.

The more common performance-related issue with surrogate keys is the need for additional access mechanisms such as indexes to support access on both the surrogate and natural keys.

In databases handling high volumes of new data, problems may also arise with contention for "next available numbers." However, many DBMSs provide mechanisms specifically to generate unique key values efficiently.

6.3.2 Matching Real-World Identifiers

Simply specifying Supplier ID as the surrogate key of Supplier does not solve the problem of matching real-world suppliers with rows in a database table. However, in many cases we are able to "change the world" by making the surrogate key values generally available or even using them to supplant existing natural keys, and suggesting or insisting that they be used when data is to be retrieved. This is easier to insist upon if the keys are used only

---

[3]The choice of definition usually reflects a view as to how surrogate keys are to be used; those who choose to restrict the definition to "invisible" keys are usually advocating that system-generated keys should be invisible.

within our organization, rather than externally, or if there is some incentive for using them. In general it is relatively easy to get employees and suppliers to play by our rules; customers can be more difficult!

One of the most difficult problems with surrogate keys is the possibility of allocating more than one value to the same real-world object, a violation of **singularity**, which requires that each real-world object be represented by only one key value and, hence, only one row in the relevant database table. The problem can happen with natural keys as well as surrogate keys—for example, a person may have aliases (or misspellings)—but is less common. Merging two or more rows once the problem has been discovered can be a complicated business, especially if foreign keys also have to be consolidated. Mailing list managers (and recipients) will be familiar with this situation.

Problems with singularity arise when databases are merged. For example, it is common for organizations to consolidate customer files from different applications to support better customer management, but, in order for the exercise to be useful, they need to be able to identify situations in which records sourced from different databases refer to the same customer. It is a relatively simple matter to provide a new surrogate key for a merged customer record (row); the challenge, of course, is in matching the source records. This usually means using data such as names and addresses that fall short of providing a fully reliable identity, and possibly checking potential matches through direct customer contact.

At the organizational level, the consolidation of health care providers in the United States provides a good example of the challenges in customer identification that result from acquisitions and mergers. The *technical* solution is typically a Patient Master Index (PMI) that records the various databases in which data about each patient is held, together with the patient's "local" key in each database. But again, the real issue is in constructing the index, identifying where a patient record in one database refers to the same person as a patient record in another. And in a health care setting, getting it wrong can have serious ramifications.

In developing a new application, the best solution is good design of business processes, in particular data capture procedures, to ensure that duplicates are picked up at data entry time. For example, a company might ask a "new" customer, "Do you already have business with us?" and back this up with a check for matching names, addresses, and so forth. Making the employee who captures the details responsible for fixing any duplicates is one useful tactic in improving the quality of checking.

6.3.3 Should Surrogate Keys Be Visible?

It is often suggested that surrogate keys be hidden from system users and used only as a mechanism for navigation within the database.

The usual arguments are:

- If the surrogate keys are visible, users may begin to attribute meaning to them ("the contract number is between 5000 and 6000—hence, it is managed in London"). This meaning may not be reliable.
- We may wish to change the keys, perhaps as a result of not making adequate provision for growth or to consolidate existing databases.

We frequently see the first problem described above, and it usually arises when specific ranges of numbers are allocated to different locations, subtypes, or organization units. In these cases we *can* place a meaning on the code, but the meaning is "issued by," which is not necessarily equivalent to (for example) "permanently responsible for." The problem can be avoided by making it more difficult or impossible for the users to interpret the numbers by allocating multiple small ranges, or assigning available numbers randomly to sites. At the same time, we need to make sure the real information is available where it is required so the user does not need to resort to attempting to interpret the code.

The second problem described above should not often arise. Changing primary keys is a painful process even if the keys are hidden. We can insure against running out of numbers by allowing an extra digit or two. When designing the system, we should look at the likelihood of other databases being incorporated, and plan accordingly: simply adding a **Source** column to the primary key to identify the original database will usually solve the problem. If we have not made this provision, one of the simpler solutions is to assign new surrogate keys to one set of data and to provide a secondary access mechanism based on the old key, which is now held as a nonkey column.

The disadvantages of a visible key are usually outweighed by the advantage of being able to specify simply the row we want in a table—or, more generally, that the surrogate key can effectively supplant a less-suitable natural key. One example of surrogate keys that is in common use throughout the world is the booking number used in airline reservation systems (sometimes called a "record locator"). If a customer provides his or her record locator, access is available quickly and unambiguously to the relevant data. If the customer does not have the number available, the booking can be accessed by a combination of other attributes, but this is intrinsically a more involved process.

6.3.4 **Subtypes and Surrogate Keys**

If we decide to define a surrogate key at the supertype level, that key will be applicable to all of the subtypes. An interesting question then arises if we choose to implement a different table for each subtype: should we allow instances belonging to different subtypes to take the same key value? For example, if we implement **Criminal Case** and **Civil Case** tables, having previously defined a supertype **Legal Case**, should we allocate case numbers as in Figure 6.1(a) or as in 6.1(b)? If contention for "next available number," as described earlier in this section, is not a serious problem, we recommend you choose option (b). This provides some recognition of the supertype in our relational design. A supertype table can then be constructed using the "union" operator and easily joined to tables that hold case numbers as foreign keys (Figure 6.2).

6.3.4.1 Surrogate Key Datatypes

An appropriate datatype needs to be chosen for each surrogate key column. If the DBMS provides a specialized datatype for such columns (often in conjunction with an efficient mechanism for allocating new key values), you should use it, otherwise use an integer datatype that is sufficiently long (see Section 5.4.4).

6.4 Structured Keys

A **structured key** (sometimes called a "concatenated key" or "composite key") is technically just a key made up of more than one column. The term

CRIMINAL CASE

Case No	Date Scheduled
000001	01/02/93
000002	01/03/93
000003	01/04/93
000004	01/06/93

CIVIL CASE

Case No	Date Scheduled
000001	01/02/93
000002	01/03/93
000003	01/05/93
000004	01/07/93

(a) Primary keys allocated independently

CRIMINAL CASE

Case No	Date Scheduled
000001	01/02/93
000005	01/03/93
000006	01/04/93
000008	01/06/93

CIVIL CASE

Case No	Date Scheduled
000002	01/02/93
000003	01/03/93
000004	01/05/93
000007	01/07/93

(b) Primary keys allocated from a common source

Figure 6.1   Allocation of key values to subtypes.

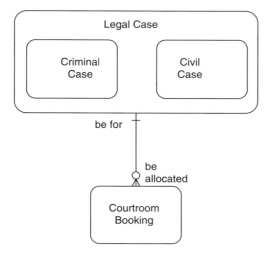

Original Tables:

CRIMINAL CASE (<u>Case No</u>, Scheduled Date, . . .)

CIVIL CASE (<u>Case No</u>, Scheduled Date, . . .)

COURTROOM BOOKING (<u>Courtroom No</u>, <u>Date</u>, <u>Period</u>, Case No*, . . .)

After Union of Criminal Case and Civil Case Tables:

LEGAL CASE (<u>Case No</u>, Scheduled Date, . . .)

COURTROOM BOOKING (<u>Courtroom No</u>, <u>Date</u>, <u>Period</u>, Case No*)

Figure 6.2 Combining subtypes.

also covers the situation in which several distinct attributes have been combined to form a single-column key, in contravention of the "one-fact-per-column" rule introduced in Section 2.5.1.

A structured key usually signifies that the entity instances that it represents can only exist in the context of some other entity instances. For example an order line (identified by a combination of **Order ID** and **Order Line Number**) can only exist in the context of an order.

What we are doing, technically, in these cases is including one or more mandatory foreign keys in the primary key for a table. Most experienced data modelers will automatically do this in at least some cases.

Structured keys often cause problems, but not because there is anything inherently wrong with multi-attribute keys. Rather, the problem keys usually fail to meet one or more of the basic requirements discussed earlier—in particular, stability.

In this section we look at the rationale for using structured keys, and the trade-offs involved.

6.4.1 **When to Use Structured Keys**

The rule for using structured keys is straightforward: you can include a foreign key in a primary key only if it represents a *mandatory non-transferable*[4] relationship.

The relationship needs to be mandatory because an optional relationship would mean that some rows would have a null value for the foreign key; hence, the primary key for those rows would be partially null. The problems of nulls in primary key columns are discussed in Section 6.7.

The reason for the nontransferability may not be so obvious. The problem with transferable relationships is that the value of the foreign key will need to change when the relationship is transferred to a new owner. For example, if an employee is transferred from one department to another, the value of Department ID for that employee will change. If the foreign key is part of the primary key, then we have a change in value of the primary key, and a violation of our stability criterion. In this example, Department ID should not form part of the primary key of **Employee**.

Another way of looking at this situation is that if we strictly follow the rule that primary key values cannot change (as we should), then structured keys can be used to *enforce* nontransferability (i.e., the structured key implements the rule that dependent entity instances cannot be transferred from one owner entity to another).

Figure 6.3 provides a more detailed example, using the notation for nontransferability introduced in Section 3.5.6. The **Stock Holding** entity class has mandatory, nontransferable relationships to both **Stock** and **Client.** In business terms:

1. An instance of **Stock Holding** cannot exist without corresponding instances of **Stock** and **Client.**
2. An instance of **Stock Holding** cannot be transferred to a different stock or client.

By contrast, the relationship from **Client** to **Investment Advisor** is optional and transferable, representing the business rules that:

1. We can hold information about a client who does not have an investment adviser.
2. A client can be transferred to a different investment adviser.

Accordingly, in constructing a primary key for a **Stock Holding** table, we could include the primary keys of the tables implementing the **Stock** and **Client** entity classes, but we would not include the primary key of the

---

[4]Transferability was introduced in Section 3.5.6.

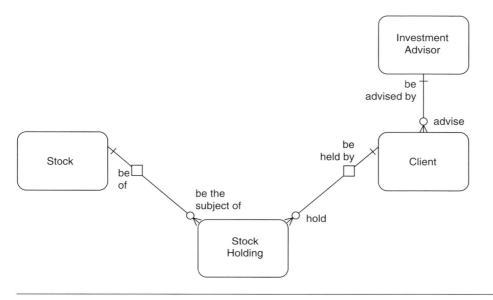

Figure 6.3   Transferable and nontransferable relationships.

table implementing the **Investment Advisor** entity class in the primary key of the **Client** table.

Incidentally, a very common case in which structured keys are suitable is that of an intersection table that supports a many-to-many relationship. This is because rows of the intersection table cannot exist without corresponding instances of the entity classes involved in the many-to-many relationship and cannot be reallocated to different instances of those entity classes.

In working through these examples, you should be aware of a real trap. Standard E-R diagrams do not include a symbol for nontransferability.[5] And many data modelers overlook the stability criterion for primary keys.

We therefore reemphasize: It is only safe to incorporate a foreign key into a primary key if that foreign key represents a *nontransferable* relationship.

6.4.2 **Programming and Structured Keys**

Structured keys may simplify programming and improve performance by providing more data items in a table row without violating normalization

---

[5]Some CASE tools and E-R modeling extensions do provide some support.

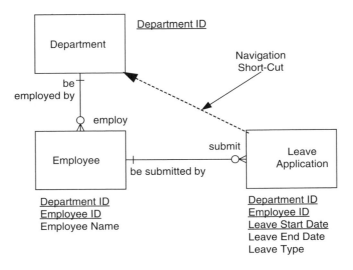

Figure 6.4 Navigation short cut supported by structured key.

rules. In Figure 6.4, we are able to determine the department from which a leave application comes without needing to access the **Employee** table. But can an employee transfer from one department to another? If so, the primary key of **Employee** will be unstable—almost certainly an unacceptable price to pay for a little programming convenience and performance. If performance was critically affected by the decision, it would probably be better to carry Department ID redundantly as a nonprimary-key item in the **Leave Application** table. In any event, these are decisions for the physical design stage!

6.4.3 **Performance Issues with Structured Keys**

Although performance is not our first concern as data modelers, it can provide a useful basis for deciding between alternatives that rate similarly against other criteria. (At the physical database design stage, we may need to reconsider the implications of structured keys as we explore compromises to improve performance.)

Structured keys may affect performance in three principal ways.

First, they may reduce the number of tables that need to be accessed by some transactions, as in Figure 6.4 (discussed above).

Second, they may reduce the number of access mechanisms that need to be supported. Take the Stock Holding example from Figure 6.3. If we proposed a stand-alone surrogate key for **Stock Holding**, it is likely that the physical database designer would need to construct three indexes: one for the surrogate key and one for each of the foreign keys to **Client** and **Stock**. But if we used Client ID + Stock ID + Date, the designer could probably get by with two indexes, resulting in a saving in space and update time.

Third, as the number of columns in a structured key increases, so does the size of table and index records. It is not unknown for a table at the bottom of a deep hierarchy to have six or more columns in its key. A key we encountered in an **Insurance Risk** table reflected the following hierarchy: State + Branch + District + Agent + Client + Policy Class + Original Issuer + Policy + Risk—a nine part key, used throughout the organization. In this case, the key had been constructed in the days of serial files and reflected neither a true hierarchy nor a nontransferable relationship. Very large keys are also common in data marts in which star schemas (see Chapter 16) are used.

When we encounter large keys, we have the option of introducing a stand-alone surrogate key at any point(s) in the hierarchy, reducing the size of the primary keys from that point downwards. Doing so will prevent us from fully enforcing nontransferability and will cost us an extra access mechanism. In the Compact Disk Library model of Figure 6.5 on the next page, we can add a surrogate key Track ID to **Track**, as the primary key, and use this to replace the large foreign key in **Performer Role**. The primary key of **Performer Role** would then become Track ID + Performer ID. However, the model would no longer enforce the fact that a track could not be transferred from one CD to another (and perhaps prompt us to rethink our definition of **Track**).

6.4.4 **Running Out of Numbers**

Structured keys are prone to a particular kind of stability problem—running out of numbers—which can ultimately require that we reallocate *all* key values. The more parts to a key, the more likely we are to exhaust all possible values for one of them. Of course, this may also imply running out of numbers for the relevant owner entity instances, but the impact on what is often only a reference table may be more local and manageable. Incidentally, the owner entity class may not actually be represented by a table in the database; its key may provide sufficient information in itself for our purposes.

If we do run out of numbers, it may be prohibitively expensive to redefine the key and amend the programs that use it. Experience suggests that we (or the system users) will be tempted to add new data and meaning to other parts of the key in order to keep the overall value unique. In turn, program logic now has to be amended to extract the meaning of the values held in these parts.

Most experienced data modelers have horror stories to tell in this area. One organization had a team of four staff members working full time on

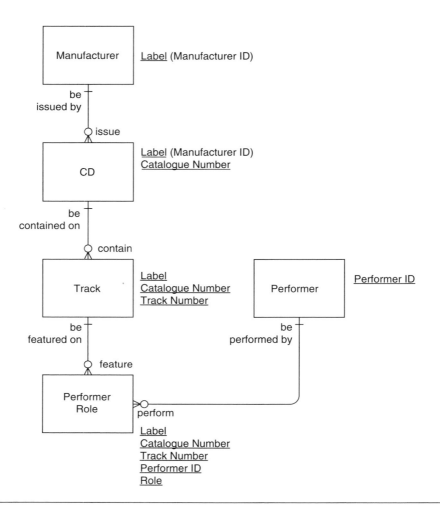

Figure 6.5 Large structured keys.

allocating location codes. Another had to completely redevelop a system because they ran out of insurance agent identifiers (the agent identifier consisted of a **State Code**, **Branch Code** within state, and **Agent Number** within state and branch; when all agent numbers for a particular branch had been allocated, new numbers were assigned by creating phantom branches and states). As a result of problems of this kind, it is often suggested that structured keys be avoided altogether. However, a structured key should involve no more risk than a single-column key, as long as we make adequate provision for growth of each component, and do not break the basic rules of column definition and key design.

6.5 **Multiple Candidate Keys**

Quite frequently we encounter tables in which there are two or more columns (or combinations of columns) that could serve as the primary key. There may be two or more natural keys or, more often, a natural and a surrogate key. We refer to each possible key as a **candidate key**. There are a few rules we need to observe and some traps to watch out for when there is more than one candidate key.

6.5.1 **Choosing a Primary Key**

We strongly recommend that you always nominate a single primary key for each table. One of the most important reasons for doing so is to specify how relationships will be supported; in nominating the primary key, you are specifying which columns are to be held elsewhere as foreign keys.[6]

The choice of primary key should be based on the requirements and issues discussed earlier in this section. In addition to comparing applicability, stability, structure, and meaningfulness, we should ask, "Does each candidate key represent the same thing for all time?" The presence of more than one candidate key may be a clue that an entity class should be split into two entity classes linked by a one-to-one transferable relationship.

If after this we still genuinely have two (or more) candidate keys for the same entity that are equally applicable and stable, the shortest of these may result in a significant saving in storage requirements, as primary keys are replicated in foreign keys and indexes.

6.5.2 **Normalization Issues**

Multiple candidate keys can be a sign of tables that are in third normal form but not Boyce-Codd normal form (this is discussed in Chapter 13). Tables with two or more candidate keys can also be a source of confusion in earlier stages of normalization. Some informal definitions of 3NF imply that a nonkey column (i.e., a column that is not part of the primary key) is not allowed to be a determinant of another nonkey column. ("Each nonkey item must depend on the key, the whole key, and *nothing but the key*.")

Look at the table in Figure 6.6:

---

[6]The SQL standard and some DBMSs allow relationships to be supported by foreign keys that point to candidate keys other than the primary key (Section 10.6.1.2). We recommend that use of this facility be restricted to the physical design stage.

CUSTOMER (<u>Customer No</u>, Tax File No, Name, Address, . . .)

Figure 6.6   Table with two candidate keys

Let us assume that every customer has a Tax File No, and that no two customers have the same Tax File No. A bit of thought will show that **Tax File No** (a nonkey item) is a determinant of **Name**, **Address**, and indeed every other column in the table. On the basis of our informal definition of 3NF, we would conclude that the table is not in third normal form, and remove **Name**, **Address**, and so on. to another table, with **Tax File No** copied across as the key.

We do *not* want to do this! It does not achieve anything useful. Remember our definition of 3NF in Chapter 2: Every determinant of a non-key item must be a candidate key. Our table satisfies this; it is only the "rough and ready" definition of 3NF that leads us astray.

6.6   Guidelines for Choosing Keys

Having read this far, you may feel that we have adequately made our point about primary key choice being complex and difficult! As in much of data modeling, there are certainly choices to be made, and when unusual circumstances arise, there is no substitute for a good understanding of the underlying principles.

However, we can usefully draw together the threads of the discussion so far and offer some general guidelines for choosing keys.

We divide the problem into two cases, based on the concepts of dependent and independent entity classes introduced in Section 3.5.7. Recall that a dependent entity class is one that has at least one many-to-one mandatory, nontransferable relationship with another entity class. An independent entity class has no such relationships.

A table representing a many-to-many relationship can be thought of as implementing an intersection entity class, which (as we saw in Section 3.5.2) will be dependent on the entity classes participating in the relationship. Accordingly, such a table will follow the rules for a dependent entity class.

6.6.1   Tables Implementing Independent Entity Classes

The primary key of a table representing an independent entity class must be one of the following:

1. A natural identifier: one or more columns in the table corresponding to attributes that are used to identify things in the real world: if you have

used the naming conventions outlined in Chapter 5, they will usually be columns with names ending in "Number," "Code," or "ID."

2. A surrogate key: a single column.

A sensible general approach to selecting the primary key of an independent entity class is to use natural identifiers when they are available and surrogate keys otherwise.

6.6.2 Tables Implementing Dependent Entity Classes and Many-to-Many Relationships

We have an additional option for the primary key of a table representing a dependent entity class or a many-to-many relationship in that we can include the foreign key(s) representing the relationships to the entity classes on which the entity class in question depends. Obviously, a single foreign key alone is not sufficient as a primary key, since that would only allow for one instance of the dependent entity for each instance of the associated entity.

The additional options for the primary key of the table representing a dependent entity class are as follows:

1. The foreign key(s) plus one or more existing columns. For example, a scheduled flight will be flown as multiple actual flights; there is therefore a one-to-many relationship between **Scheduled Flight** and **Actual Flight**. Actual flights can be identified by a combination of the Flight No (the primary key of **Scheduled Flight**) and the date on which the actual flight is flown.

2. Multiple foreign keys that together satisfy the criteria for a primary key. The classic example of this is the implementation of an intersection entity class (Section 3.5.2) (though this approach will not work for all intersection entity classes, some of which will require options 1 or 3, [i.e., the addition of an existing column (e.g., a date) or a surrogate key)].

3. The foreign key(s) plus a surrogate key. For example, a student could be identified by a combination of the Student ID issued by his or her college and the ID of the college that issued it (the foreign key representing the relationship between **Student** and **College**).

Our general rule is to include all foreign keys that represent dependency relationships, adding a surrogate or (if available) an existing column to ensure uniqueness if necessary. By doing this, we are enforcing nontransferability, as long as we stick to the general rule that primary key values cannot be changed.

We nearly always use primary keys containing foreign keys for tables representing dependent entity classes, but will sometimes find that such a table has an excellent stand-alone key available. We may then choose to trade enforcement of nontransferability for the convenience of using an available "natural" key. For example, it may not be possible for a passport to be transferred from one person to another; hence, we could include the key of **Person** in the key of **Passport**, but we may prefer to use a well-established stand-alone Passport Number (plus Issuer ID).

6.7 **Partially-Null Keys**

We complete this chapter by looking at an issue that arises from time to time: whether or not null values should be permitted in primary key columns.

There are plenty of good reasons why the entire primary key should never be allowed to be null (empty); we would then have a problem with interpreting foreign keys—does null mean "no corresponding row" or is it a pointer to the row with the null primary key?

But conventional data modeling wisdom also dictates that no *part* (i.e., no column) of a multicolumn primary key should ever be null. Some of the arguments are to do with sophisticated handling of different types of nulls, which is currently of more academic than practical relevance, since the null handling of most DBMSs is very basic. To our knowledge, no DBMS allows for any column of a primary key to be null. However, there are situations where not every attribute represented by a column of the primary key has a legitimate value for every instance. In these situations you may want to use some special value to indicate that there is no real-world value for those attributes in those instances. (We shall discuss possible special values shortly.)

The issue often arises when implementing a supertype whose subtypes have distinct primary keys. For example, an airline may want to implement a **Service** entity whose subtypes are **Flight Service** (identified by a Flight Number) and **Accommodation Service** (identified by an alphabetic Accommodation Service ID). The key for **Service** could be Flight Service No + Accommodation Service ID, where one value would always be logically null. This is a workable, if inelegant, alternative to generalizing the two to produce a single alphanumeric attribute.

A variant of this situation is shown in Figure 6.7. The keys for **Branch** and **Department** are legitimate as long as branches cannot be transferred from one division to another and departments cannot be transferred from one branch to another.

But if we decide to implement at the **Organization Unit** level, giving us a simple hierarchy, can we generalize the primary keys of the subtypes

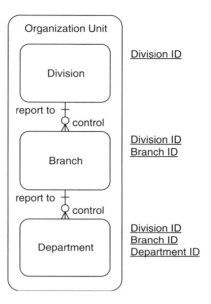

Figure 6.7   Use of a primary key with logically null attributes.

into a primary key for **Organization Unit**? The proposed key would be Division ID + Branch ID + Department ID. For divisions, Branch ID and Department ID would be logically null, and for branches Department ID would be logically null. Again, we have logically null values in the primary key; again, we have a solution that is workable and that has been employed successfully in practice.

The choice of key in this example has some interesting implications. The foreign key, which points to the next level up the hierarchy, is contained in the primary key (e.g., Branch ID "0219" contains the key of **Division** "02"). This limits us to three levels of hierarchy; our choice of primary key has imposed a constraint on the number of levels and their relationships. With a surrogate key, by contrast, any such limits would need to be enforced outside the data structure. This is another example of a structured key imposing constraints that we may or may not want to enforce for the life of the system.

What special values can we use to represent a logically-null primary key attribute given that our DBMS will almost certainly not allow us to use "null" itself? If the attribute is a text item or category (see Section 5.4.2), you might use a zero-length character string. If it is a quantifier, you can use zero if it does not represent a real-world value. If it does, you are reduced to either choosing some other special value, like –1 or 999999 or adding a flag column to indicate whether the original column holds a real-world value or not.

6.8 **Summary**

Primary keys must be applicable to all instances, unique, minimal, and stable. Stability is frequently overlooked, but stable keys provide a better representation of real-world identity and lead to simpler system designs.

Natural keys may offer simpler structures and performance advantages but are often unstable.

Surrogate keys are system-generated, meaningless keys and can be managed to ensure uniqueness and stability. They do not guarantee singularity (one key value per real-world entity instance). Surrogate keys may be made visible to users, but no meaning that is not constant over time for each instance should be attached to them.

Structured keys consist of two or more columns. Provided they satisfy the basic criteria of soundness, they can contribute to enforcing nontransferability and may offer better performance.

Primary keys must not be allowed to take a logically null value, but there are arguments for individual components being allowed to do so.

Chapter 7
Extensions and Alternatives

"The limits of my language mean the limits of my world."
– Ludwig Wittgenstein, Tractatus Logico-Philosophicus

7.1 Introduction

In Chapters 2 and 3, we introduced two closely-related languages or conventions for data modeling.

The Entity-Relationship (E-R) Model and its associated diagramming conventions are used to document an implementation-independent view of the data structures —a conceptual model—which is the key input to the logical design phase. Its principal concepts are entity classes, attributes, and relationships.

The Relational Model[1] is used to describe a relational database (existing or proposed). Its principal concepts are tables, columns, and keys (primary and foreign). It is the language we use for the logical data model.[2]

These conventions are by no means the only ones available for modeling data at the conceptual and logical levels. Since the advent of DBMSs, numerous alternatives have been proposed, and an enormous amount of effort on the part of both academics and practitioners has been devoted to debating their relative merits. In Chapter 4 we introduced a common extension to the basic E-R Model to represent subtypes and supertypes; as we discussed, not all practitioners use this extension, and different tools implement it in different ways.

Extensions to *conceptual* modeling languages are usually driven by two factors, sometimes synergistic, sometimes in conflict. The first is a desire to capture more meaning. The addition of subtypes is a nice example of this, as is the representation of constraints, such as relationships being mutually exclusive. The second is to improve stakeholders' ability to understand the model and, hence, their effectiveness in reviewing or contributing to it.

---

[1] Note the use of the capitalized "Model" to refer to a language and set of conventions, in contrast to the non-capitalized "model" which refers to a model of data to support a particular problem.
[2] The language we use for the *physical* data model is usually the Data Definition Language (DDL) supported by the DBMS, sometimes supplemented by data structure diagrams similar to those of the logical data model.

Extensions to *logical* modeling languages are often prompted by extensions (either real or desired) to DBMS capabilities. If a DBMS can implement a particular logical structure, we need to be able to specify it.

Remember that not all modelers make the distinction between conceptual and logical modeling and may therefore use the same language for both.

In practice, pragmatic considerations quickly narrow the choice. Most modelers will be specifying a logical model for implementation using a standard or extended relational DBMS, and the Relational Model will be the obvious choice. At the conceptual level, only a few sets of conventions are supported by CASE products. Many data modelers will have experience with only mainstream conventions. And, with some exceptions, there is relatively little value in capturing structures and constraints that will not affect the design of the database.

In this chapter we look at some of the more common alternatives and extensions, focusing on conceptual modeling.

We look first at some extensions to the E-R approach that we use generally in this book—in particular, facilities for the more sophisticated modeling of attributes. Each is supported by at least one popular CASE product. Even if you choose to skip over some of the material in this chapter because you are using a method or tool that does not support the extensions, we do suggest you read Section 7.2.2 on advanced attribute concepts, since we recommend that you use these concepts in the conceptual modeling stage, and we refer to them in Chapters 10 and 11.

We then look at the "true" E-R conventions, as proposed by Chen. To avoid ambiguity, we refer to these conventions as the Chen E-R Model.

UML (Unified Modeling Language) is the most-widely used alternative to the E-R and relational approaches, and it provides, as standard, a number of the constructs supported by Chen E-R and E-R extensions. It covers a number of activities and deliverables in systems analysis and design beyond data modeling. In this chapter we focus on some of the key issues for the data modeler.

Finally we look briefly at Object Role Modeling (ORM), which has been well researched, has CASE tool support, and is in use in some organizations.

We do not look at modeling languages for object-oriented (OO) databases; they represent a substantially different paradigm and the take-up of true OO DBMSs, at the time of writing, remains very low in comparison to relational products.

This chapter is not a tutorial or reference for any of these languages; at the end of the book we suggest some further reading if you wish to explore any of them in depth. Rather, we look at the key new facilities that they introduce to provide you with a starting point for approaching them—and perhaps a better appreciation of the comparative strengths and weaknesses of the approach that you use yourself. From time to time we find ourselves "borrowing" a concept from outside the language that we are using in order to describe a particular structure or rule that we encounter in practice. An understanding of other modeling languages will increase your ability to recognize and describe patterns and, hence, contribute to your skill as a modeler.

You should be aware that every approach comes with "baggage" in terms of associated methodologies and philosophies. For example, conventional E-R modeling is widely associated with Information Engineering methodologies and UML with object-oriented approaches. In many cases, these associations have more to do with the views of the language originators or proponents than with the languages themselves. In evaluating and learning from the languages and their proponents, it is important not to confuse the two.

7.2 Extensions to the Basic E-R Approach

7.2.1 Introduction

The basic E-R approach, which is widely used in practice, is not too different from the Bachman diagrams, which were used from the late 1960s to document prerelational (CODASYL)[3] database designs. In the transition to a conceptual modeling language, it has gained relatively little; doubtless, one of the reasons is that CASE tool vendors are not keen to support constructs that cannot be mechanically translated into relational structures. Perhaps the most consistent addition has been the inclusion of many-to-many relationships, which, as we saw in Chapter 3, cannot be implemented directly in a relational DBMS (or for that matter a network DBMS).

Perhaps for these reasons, too many modelers restrict themselves to only those concepts that were supported by the first generation of relational DBMSs. This is a mistake for two reasons:

1. The business is likely to see the data with which it deals in a much richer fashion than tables and columns. A conceptual model, which is designed to convey to the business the information concepts to be supported, should do likewise.

2. Many relational DBMSs now support these richer structures. If the business for which you are producing a logical data model intends to

---

[3]CODASYL from "Conference on Data Systems Languages" (specifically the Database Task Group which became the Data Description Language Committee) refers to a set of standards for "network" DBMSs in which the principal constructs were Record Types, Data Items, and Sets.

implement it on such a DBMS, it is similarly a mistake to constrain the logical data model to exclude structures that make business sense and that can be implemented directly. Even if the DBMS does not support a particular structure, there are simple techniques for converting these richer structures in the conceptual data model into simpler structures in the logical data model; these are described in Chapter 11.

7.2.2 **Advanced Attribute Concepts**

E-R modeling is subject in practice to a number of conventions that do not appear to have any basis other than conformity to the rather restrictive version of the relational model represented by the original SQL standard and implemented in the earliest versions of the various relational DBMS products. These restrictive conventions are inappropriate in a logical data model if the target DBMS implements any of the additional features of the SQL99 standard and, in any case, inappropriate in a conceptual data model, which should illustrate data structures as the business would naturally view them rather than as they will be implemented in a database.

Having said that, we are aware that some CASE tools continue to enforce these conventions; if you are using such a tool, you may not be able to take advantage of some of the suggestions in this section.

7.2.2.1 Category Attributes

A convention seems to have been established whereby a **category attribute** (see Section 5.4.2.2) such as Gender, Customer Type, or Payment Type is represented in a conceptual data model as a relationship to a classification entity class, which generally has Code and Meaning (or Description) attributes. It is not entirely clear why it is necessary to represent a single business concept by four modeling artifacts (the **classification** entity class, its Code and Meaning attributes, and the relationship between the entity class containing the category attribute and the classification entity class). If, as some modelers and CASE tools insist, the foreign key representing a relationship is shown as well as the relationship, the single business concept is represented by five modeling artifacts. This seems particularly inappropriate given that a classification table is not the only way to ensure that the column representing the category attribute is constrained to a discrete set of values.

Our recommendation is to represent each category attribute as just an attribute. If two different category attributes have the same set of meanings, this should be documented by assigning them the same attribute domain (see Section 5.4.3).

7.2.2.2 Derived Attributes

Given the focus on getting to a normalized logical data model, many modelers completely ignore derived attributes (those that can be calculated from others) yet such quantities often arise during the analysis process as explicit business requirements. Our view is that they should be included in a conceptual data model since a major but often overlooked contributor to poor data quality is inconsistent calculation of derived quantities. For example:

1. A derived quantity appears on a variety of different application screens and reports.
2. There are alternative methods of calculating that quantity, only one of which is correct.
3. As there is no definition of the derived quantity in any data model, each process analyst specifying a screen or report on which that quantity appears has defined the calculation method in the specification of that screen/ report and different stakeholders have reviewed those specifications.

Each derived quantity can be "normalized" to a single conceptual data model entity class, in the sense that:

1. Each instance of that entity class has only one value for that quantity.
2. There is no other attribute of that entity class, other than candidate keys, on which the derived quantity is functionally dependent.

Each derived quantity can be included in the conceptual data model as an attribute of that entity class with the following provisos:

1. It is marked to indicate that it is derived.
2. The single correct calculation method is recorded in the definition of the attribute.

To illustrate how this works, consider the logical data model in Figure 7.1: Four of these attributes appear to be derived. **Total Order Amount** is presumably the sum of the products of **Order Quantity** and **Quoted Price** in each associated order line, **Applicable Discount Rate** is presumably the minimum of the **Standard Discount Rate** for the customer and the **Maximum Discount Rate** for the product, and **Quoted Price** is presumably the **Standard Product Price** less the applicable discount. However, **YearToDate Total Sales Amount** could be based on:

- Orders raised, promised deliveries, or actual deliveries within the current year-to-date
- Either standard product prices or quoted prices
- Either current or historic standard product prices.

CUSTOMER (<u>Customer No</u>, Customer Name, Customer Address, Standard Discount Rate)
PRODUCT (<u>Product No</u>, Product Name, Standard Product Price, YearToDate Total Sales Amount, Maximum Discount Rate)
ORDER (<u>Order No</u>, Order Date, Customer No*, Delivery Charge, Total Order Amount)
ORDER LINE (<u>Order No</u>, <u>Product No</u>*, Order Quantity, Applicable Discount Rate, Quoted Price, Promised Delivery Date, Actual Delivery Date)

Figure 7.1 A logical data model of an ordering application.

The analyst should establish which of each of these sets of alternatives applies. Another issue that arises with YearToDate Total Sales Amount is that it may not actually be able to be calculated from other data. If order data is deleted before the year is out, the **Order** and **Order Line** tables may not contain all orders raised (or delivered against) within the year-to-date. Further, if YearToDate Total Sales Amount is based on historical standard product prices, these are not available to support such a calculation "on the fly." In each of these situations, YearToDate Total Sales Amount can be held in the **Product** table and added to as each order is raised (or delivered against, as the case may be).

In UML a derived attribute or relationship can be marked by preceding the name with a solidus or forward slash ("/"). There is no standard for marking derived attributes in E-R modeling and your E-R CASE tool may not support them. If so, they will need to be listed separately.

7.2.2.3 Attributes of Relationships

Consider the model in Figure 7.2. If we need to record the date that each student enrolled in each course, is that date an attribute of **Student** or of **Course**? It is in fact an attribute of the relationship between **Student** and **Course** as there is one Enrollment Date for each combination of **Student** and **Course**.

Figure 7.2 An E-R model of a simple education application.

Figure 7.3 A conceptual data model of a simple employee record application.

In E-R modeling, generally the only way to record the existence of such an attribute is to convert the many-to-many relationship into an entity class and two one-to-many relationships as described in Section 3.5.2, as the attribute can then be assigned to the intersection entity class. UML, by contrast, supports association classes, which are object classes tied to associations (which in UML includes relationships). The notation for an association class is illustrated later in this chapter in Figure 7.12.

Consider the model in Figure 7.3. If we need to record the date (if any) that an employee joined a union, is that an attribute of **Employee** or of **Union**? Because there can only be one Union Joining Date for each employee, most modelers would treat it as if it were an attribute of **Employee**. It is in fact better represented as an attribute of the relationship between **Employee** and **Union**: if a particular employee does not belong to a union, Union Joining Date must be null. By associating the attribute with the relationship, we enforce that rule.

In UML we can create an association class named **Employee Union Membership** and make Union Joining Date an attribute of that class. In E-R modeling we could do something similar by converting the relationship into an **Employee Union Membership** entity class with a one-to-many relationship (optional at the many end) between it and **Union** and a one-to-one relationship (optional at the **Employee Union Membership** end) between it and **Employee**. While this is valid in a conceptual data model, its principal disadvantage is the fact that any CASE tool is likely to create separate **Employee** and **Employee Union Membership** tables in the logical data model. (For that matter, this may well happen in a UML CASE tool if you model this relationship as we have suggested.)

If your CASE tool does not allow pairs of entity classes joined by one-to-one relationships to be implemented as single tables, you are probably better off documenting the business rule in text form.

7.2.2.4 Complex Attributes

Consider the following "attributes":

- Delivery Address
- Foreign Currency Amount

- Order Quantity
- Customer Name
- Customer Phone Number

In each case, how many attributes are there really? A Delivery Address (or any address for that matter) can be regarded as a single text attribute or as a set of attributes, such as:

- Apartment No
- Street No(s) with Street No Suffix
- Street Name and Street Type, with Street Name Suffix
- Locality Name and State Abbreviation
- Postal Code
- Country Name

This, of course, is just one example of what might be required.

Similarly **Foreign Currency Amount** will require not only a currency amount attribute but must indicate what currency is involved (e.g., USD, AUD, GBP). If we are in the business of selling bulk products, **Order Quantity** may involve different units (lb, tons, ft).

Customer Name may be a single attribute but is more likely to require **Surname, Given Name, Salutation, Honorifics** (e.g., Ph.D.), while **Phone Number** may require separate country and/or area codes.

The use of complex attributes can facilitate a top-down approach to modeling. In a five-day data modeling project that one of us reviewed, very little apparent progress had been made at the end of the first day, as the group had become bogged down in a debate about how addresses should be broken up. As a result there was nothing completed (neither a subject area model nor a high-level model) that could be reviewed by stakeholders outside the group. If that group had decided that an address was just a complex attribute with an internal structure that could be dealt with as a separate issue, they would have been able to produce a model including those entity classes for which addresses existed significantly sooner.

There are two significant other advantages in treating complex attributes as attributes rather than modeling their internal structure immediately. First, if requirement change or refinement during modeling leads to internal structure change (e.g., a decision is taken to allow for overseas addresses, which require a country name and nonnumeric postal codes), all that needs to be changed in the model is the internal structure of the appropriate attribute type (e.g., Address, Foreign Currency Amount), rather than changing each address (and possibly missing one or making slightly different changes to different addresses).

Second, if a complex attribute such as an address is optional, it is easier to document that fact directly rather than document that:

■ All individual attributes making up an address must be null if any of the essential parts of an address are null.

■ Any essential individual attribute of an address must be non-null if any other essential part of an address is non-null.

There are two distinct ways in which we can model complex attributes.

One is to include additional complex attribute types in the attribute taxonomy. We can then (for example) simply identify **Customer Address** and **Supplier Address** as being of the type "Address." Note that there may be more than one set of requirements for each major type of complex attribute, (e.g., some addresses may need to be formatted in a particular way for a particular purpose or have some properties that differ from others). In this situation, we need to create multiple attribute types, (e.g., U.S. Postal Address, Overseas Postal Address, Delivery Location Address.

Alternatively, we can model complex attributes as separate entity classes[4] and link those entity classes to the entity classes to which the complex attributes belong. Using addresses again as the example, we would create an **Address** entity class and relationships between it and **Customer**, **Employee**, **Supplier**, **Party Role**, and so on.

Your CASE tool will certainly allow you the second of these options and also the first if it supports attribute types, but a problem may arise when it comes to generate the logical data model from the conceptual data model. Whichever of these techniques you have used to model complex attributes, it may not support the transformations required to generate the appropriate structure in the logical data model if the DBMS for which the logical data model is being generated does not support complex attributes. The relevant transformations are described in Section 11.4.5.

7.2.2.5 Multivalued Attributes

Traditionally E-R modelers have included only single-valued attributes in conceptual data models. Whenever an attribute can have more than one value for an entity instance, a separate entity class is created to hold that attribute with a one-to-many relationship between the original "parent" entity class and the new "child" entity class, in a process equivalent to converting a relational data model to First Normal Form (in fact, we are anticipating the need to produce a normalized logical model). This practice, however, adds an extra box and an extra line to the model for the sake of one attribute.

---

[4]Somewhat analogous to the Row data type in SQL99.

While it is essential for a *logical data model* to be normalized if the DBMS on which it is to be implemented does not support multivalued attributes, there is no particular reason why a *conceptual data model* should be, so multivalued attributes are acceptable *if they are clearly marked as such*. However, in our experience object modelers sometimes include multivalued attributes without marking them to indicate that they are multivalued. Neither UML nor any of the E-R variants provides a notation for this purpose. One possible technique is to give such attributes plural names, [e.g., **Nicknames** as an attribute of **Employee**—using singular names for all other attributes of course].

Note that if an entity class has more than one multivalued attribute, you should ensure that such attributes are independent. If two multivalued attributes are dependent on each other, you should create a single multivalued complex attribute. For example, an **Employee** entity class should not be given separate multivalued attributes **Dependent Names** and **Dependent Birth Dates**; instead, you should create a **Dependents** multivalued complex attribute, each element of which is a dependent with name and birth date components.

Again, CASE tool support for multivalued attributes is not guaranteed, even if you are modeling in UML.

7.3 **The Chen E-R Approach**

In 1976, Peter Chen published an influential paper "The Entity-Relationship Approach: Towards a Unified View of Data."[5] He proposed a conceptual modeling language that could be used to specify either a relational or a network (CODASYL) database. The language itself continues to be widely used in academic work, but is much less common in industry. Arguably, the paper's greater contribution was the recognition of the value of separating conceptual design from logical and physical design.

However, in the space of a short academic paper, Chen introduced several interesting extensions, many of which have been adopted or adapted by later languages, notably UML.

7.3.1 **The Basic Conventions**

Chen E-R diagrams are immediately recognizable by the use of a diamond as the symbol for a relationship, and the Chen extensions relate largely

---

[5]*ACM Transactions on Database Systems*, Vol. 1, No. 1, March 1976.

to relationships. We included a simple example in Chapter 3, but only as an alternative way of representing something that we could already capture using our standard E-R conventions. The same basic symbol is used to represent all relationships, whether one-to-one, one-to-many or many-to-many—an important reflection of the desire to be true to real-world semantics rather than the constraints of a DBMS (which would have required that many-to-many relationships be represented as tables or record types).

7.3.2 **Relationships with Attributes**

In the Chen approach, relationships may have attributes. As discussed in 7.2.2.3, this facility is particularly useful for consistently representing many-to-many relationships, but it also has application in representing and enforcing constraints associated with one-to-many relationships.

Figure 7.4 shows an Employee-Asset example using the Chen convention. If we had started out thinking that the relationship was one-to-many but on checking with the user found that it was many-to-many, we would only need to make a minor change to the diagram (changing the "1" to "N"). This seems more appropriate than introducing a **Responsibility** entity class ("Fine," says the user, "but why didn't we need this entity class before?").

7.3.3 **Relationships Involving Three or More Entity Classes**

The Chen convention allows us to directly represent relationships involving more than two entity classes (as illustrated in Figure 7.5), rather than introducing an intersection entity class as is necessary in conventional E-R modeling (discussed in Section 3.5.2).

Figure 7.4 Chen convention for relationships (including relationships with attributes).

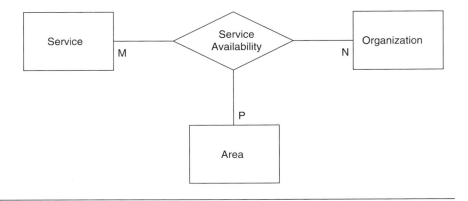

Figure 7.5 Ternary relationship documented using Chen E-R convention.

As in the case of many-to-many relationships, this convention enables us to be true to "real-world" classifications of concepts as entity classes or relationships, rather than being driven by implementation considerations, as discussed in Section 3.5.5.

7.3.4 **Roles**

The Chen conventions allow us to give a name to the role that an entity instance plays when it participates in a particular relationship. In Figure 7.6, we are able to note that a person who guarantees a loan contract is known as the guarantor. In our experience, this is an attractive feature when

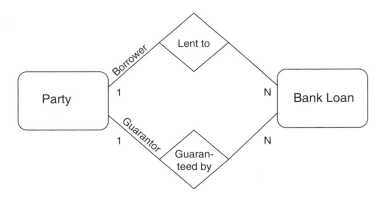

Figure 7.6 Bank loan and party entity classes.

dealing with relationships between generic parties, but of only occasional value elsewhere.

7.3.5 **The Weak Entity Concept**

Chen introduced the concept of a **weak entity** (class), an entity class that relies on another for its identification. For example, **Invoice Line** would be a weak entity class *if we decided to use the primary key of* **Invoice** *in constructing its primary key.* An entity class with a stand-alone key (i.e., a nonweak entity) is called a **regular entity**. The primary key of a weak entity class is sometimes called a **weak key**. These are useful terms to have in our vocabulary for describing models and common structures (for example, the split foreign key situation covered in Section 11.6.6).

Chen introduced special diagramming symbols to distinguish weak entities (Figure 7.7), but we find the nontransferability concept more useful at the conceptual modeling stage, since we prefer to defer definition of primary keys to the logical design stage. Of course, if you stick strictly to the practice of always enforcing nontransferability by using appropriately structured keys (see Section 6.4.1), then nontransferability and weakness will be one and the same.

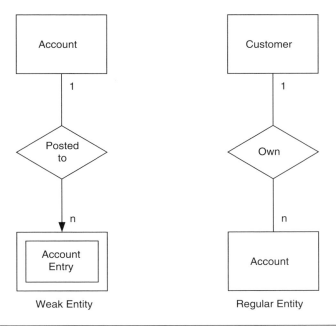

Figure 7.7 Chen's weak entity convention. Account has a stand-alone key; Account Entry does not.

7.3.6 **Chen Conventions in Practice**

The Chen approach offers some clear and useful advantages over the simple boxes and lines convention. Yet most practitioners do not use it, for three practical reasons. First, it simply puts too many objects on the page. With our boxes and lines convention, we tend to look at the boxes first, then the lines, allowing us to come to grips with the model in two logical stages. In our experience, diamonds make this much harder, and practical Chen models can be quite overwhelming. Some academics even extend the convention to include attributes, shown as circles connected to the entity classes and relationships—excellent for illustrating simple examples, but quite unwieldy for practical problems.

Second, many of the people who contribute to and verify the model will also need to see the final database design. End users may access it through query languages, and analysts will need to specify processes against it. If the final database design has the same general shape as the verified model, these people do not have the problem of coming to grips with two different views of their data.

Third, most documentation tools do not support the diamond convention. A few provide a special symbol for intersection entity classes, but still require one-to-many relationships to be documented using lines.

None of these problems need bother researchers, who typically work with fairly simple examples. And we would take issue with the second reason, the extreme version of which is to lose the distinction between conceptual modeling and logical database design. However, the reality is that the chief benefits of knowing the Chen conventions are likely to be the ability to read research papers and some useful tools for thinking.

7.4 **Using UML Object Class Diagrams**

UML has become increasingly popular in the last few years. UML is without doubt a very useful object-oriented application component design and development environment, and the growing object-oriented developer community has taken to it with justifiable enthusiasm.

You should have little trouble finding guides to UML and its use; however, the overwhelming majority of these are written by enthusiastic—even evangelical—advocates. Here we focus on some of the issues and limitations that the data modeler will also need to take into account in making the best use of UML, or in deciding whether to use it.

It is certainly possible to represent entity classes and relationships using UML class models, and indeed at least one UML CASE tool can use these to generate physical data models representing tables and columns in a manner indistinguishable from an E-R CASE tool. However, this overlooks a significant issue: UML class models are very much focused on the physical system to be built rather than on the business requirements that that system will support. For example, when drawing a class model, the dialogues with which you are presented to define association (relationship) characteristics include such system function concepts as navigability (or visibility) and privacy across the link in each direction.

As an example of this focus, we have observed that many UML class models produced by object modelers contain implementation classes as well as, or instead of, genuine business object classes. In much the same vein, UML **use cases** often focus on system dialogues apparently unsupported by any analysis of business functions and processes.

You may wish to use (or be required to use) a UML Object Class Diagram to represent data requirements. If you are using object classes, the UML symbols that we introduced in Chapter 3 (Figure 3.10) are appropriate as a representation of your entity classes and relationships (since each of your entity classes is treated as an object class).

7.4.1 A Conceptual Data Model in UML

Figure 7.8 shows a simple UML class model diagram. In this type of diagram each box represents an object class, and we can therefore represent each entity class using a box.

Each line between two boxes represents an association, of which there are many varieties, distinguishable by the symbols at the ends of the line; a line with only open arrowhead symbols on the line itself (as in Figure 7.8) or with no arrow heads represents a relationship. Cardinality (multiplicity in UML terminology) and optionality of a relationship is represented by one of the following legends placed somewhere near each end of the line:

- 0..1   optional "1" end
- 1...1 or 1   mandatory "1" end

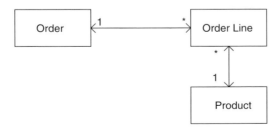

Figure 7.8 A simple UML class model.

- 0…* or *   optional "many" end
- 1…*   mandatory "many" end.

In fact, numerals other than 0 and 1 can be used (e.g., 2…4 indicates that each instance of the class at the other end of the relationship line must be associated with at least 2 but no more than 4 instances of the class at this end of the relationship line).

Attributes can be listed within a class box. Boxes can be divided into two or three "compartments" by means of horizontal lines; the lower compartment of a two-compartment box or the middle compartment of a three-compartment box is available for listing the object class's attributes (the lowest compartment of a three-compartment box is for the object class' methods or operations).

7.4.2   Advantages of UML

UML has many notational facilities not available in standard E-R modeling. In our experience the most useful of these for business information requirement modeling are derived attributes and relationships, association classes, *n*-ary relationships (those involving more than two entity classes), and on-diagram constraint documentation. Derived attributes are marked by preceding the attribute name with a solidus ("/"). Derived relationships can also be drawn. The name of such a relationship is similarly preceded by a solidus. Figure 7.9 features a derived attribute and a derived relationship. Association classes are a means of overcoming the dilemma as to whether to represent a many-to-many relationship as a relationship or as an entity class. In UML a class box can be drawn with a dashed line connecting it to

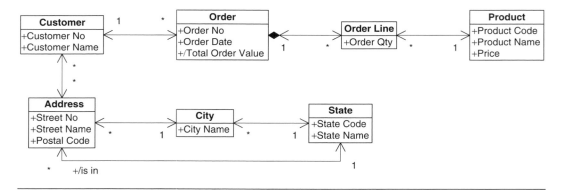

Figure 7.9   Derived attributes and relationships.

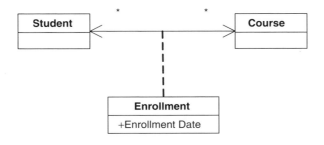

Figure 7.10 An association class.

an association line: any class represented in this way is known as an association class. Any attributes of the relationship can be listed within the association class box, yet the original many-to-many relationship continues to be depicted. This is obviously an improvement on the replacement of a many-to-many relationship by an entity class and two one-to-many relationships that is required in E-R diagramming if the many-to-many relationship has attributes. Association classes are not limited to many-to-many relationships. Figure 7.10 features an association class. Relationships can involve more than two entity classes in UML. An association class can also be used to document the attributes of such a relationship, as illustrated in Figure 7.11, which also shows that the Chen notation for a relationship has been adapted for this purpose. Constraints (business rules) can be documented on a UML class diagram using statements (in natural language or a formal constraint language) enclosed in braces ({ and }).

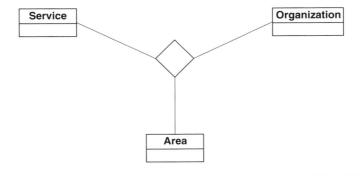

Figure 7.11 An n-ary relationship.

7.4.2.1 Use Cases and Class Models

If you are a data modeler working in a UML environment you may be expected to infer the necessary object classes by reading the Use Cases, as this is a claim often made for UML. Since a Use Case can and does contain anything its author wishes to include, the usefulness of a set of use cases for inferring object classes is not guaranteed; indeed, Alec Sharp has coined the term "useless cases"[6] to describe Use Cases from which nothing useful about object classes can be inferred.

Even if the Use Cases are useful for this purpose, the absence from UML of a "big picture" in the form of a function hierarchy correlated to entity classes via a "CRUD matrix" means that the question, "Have we yet identified all the Use Cases?" is not able to be answered easily and is sometimes not even asked.

Let us assume however that you have managed to convince the business stakeholders to submit to a second round of interviews and workshops to help you establish their information requirements and you are now developing UML class models. There are some features of the notation that have the potential to cause trouble.

7.4.2.2 Objects and Entity Classes

One of the most fundamental issues is how the concept of an object class relates to concepts in the E-R model. Many practitioners and CASE tool vendors state or imply that an object class is just an entity class. There are, however, other approaches that appear to define an object class as a cluster of related entity classes and processes that act on them, and still others that consider an object class to be a set of attributes that support a business process.

A significant contributor to this issue is the fact that the Object-Oriented Model is less prescriptive than the Relational Model and object modelers are relatively free to define the concept of an object class to suit their own needs or approaches. That flexibility can be used to advantage, however; an object class can include any set of things with similar behavior, be they entity classes, attributes, or relationships. Date and Darwen[7], for example, pursue this argument in interesting directions in their approach to reconciling the O-O and Relational Models. In Chapter 9 we introduce the concept of an Object Class Hierarchy, which can include entity classes, attributes, and

---

[6]Sharp, A: Developing Useful Use Cases—How to Avoid the "Useless Case" Phenomenon, *DAMA/MetaData Conference*, San Antonio, April 2002.

[7]Date, C., and Darwen, H: *Foundation for Future Database Systems: The Third Manifesto*, 2nd Edition, Addison-Wesley, 2000.

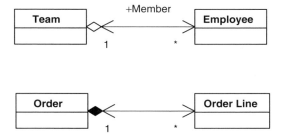

Figure 7.12   An aggregation and a composition.

relationships as a powerful means of capturing business data requirements in the earlier stages of modeling.

7.4.2.3 Aggregations and Compositions

The original UML specification[8] made a distinction between aggregation and composition but many UML modelers do not make such a distinction, perhaps because these terms have been used interchangeably so often. So what is the difference?

In an **Aggregation** each part instance may belong to more than one aggregate instance, and a part instance can have a separate existence. For example, an employee who is part of a team may be part of other teams and will continue to exist after any team to which he/she belongs is deleted.

In a **Composition**, by contrast, each part instance may belong to only one composite instance, and a part instance cannot have a separate existence, which means that a part instance can only be created as part of a composite instance and deletion of a composite instance deletes all of its associated part instances. For example, an order line that is part of an order may only be part of that order and is deleted when the order is deleted.

7.4.2.4 Qualified Associations

A **Qualified Association** is an association with identifying attributes. Unfortunately the designers of UML have chosen to use the same cardinality adornment symbols as for an unqualified association, but with a different meaning, as can be seen in Figure 7.13, in which a piece is rightly constrained

---

[8]Rumbaugh, Jacobson, and Booch (1998): *The Unified Modeling Language Reference Manual*, Addison Wesley.

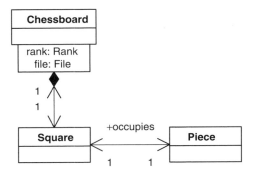

Figure 7.13 Qualified and unqualified associations.

to occupy only one square (at a time) and a square to hold only one piece (at a time) but a chessboard apparently has only one square. What these symbols are meant to convey is that a chessboard has only one square per combination of rank and file. This change of meaning of a symbol depending on context can only hinder understanding of the model by business stakeholders, so we recommend you do not use qualified associations.

7.4.2.5 Generalization and Inheritance

We saw in Section 4.9 that UML's representation of inheritance structures (superclasses and subclasses) can be ambiguous unless the modeler adopts a disciplined approach to representing them. To recap, the subtypes of a supertype do not have to be nonoverlapping or exhaustive in UML. There are symbols to distinguish these cases, but no compulsion to use them.

7.4.2.6 Diagram Understandability

UML exhibits two major weaknesses in terms of the understandability of diagrams, not only by business reviewers but by analysts and developers (although one of these is shared by some variants of E-R modeling).

One of these is the UML notation for relationship cardinality. The use of numerals and asterisks rather than graphic devices to indicate relationship cardinality is not only less intuitive (in that it engages the other side of the brain from the one that is dealing with the implications of a line between two boxes) but also has the potential to lead to confusing diagrams.[9]

---

[9]Currently at least one CASE tool may jumble up the cardinality notations of multiple relationship lines to or from the same box, may leave the cardinality notation behind if you move a relationship line, and may even allow one or more cardinality notations to disappear behind a box if you move a box or line.

UML's representation of inheritance structures (subtype boxes outside rather than inside supertype boxes) can (like some E-R variants) make it difficult to establish what relationships an entity class is involved in, particularly if the inheritance hierarchy is deep (subtypes themselves have subtypes and so on). In that situation the inheritance of a relationship by a subtype can only be inferred by tracing the generalization lines back through the hierarchy of supertypes.

7.5 **Object Role Modeling**

Object-Role Modeling (ORM) has a long history. Its ancestors include Binary Modeling and NIAM,[10] and (more so than most alternative languages) it has been used quite widely in practice and generated a substantial body of research literature.

Given the semantic richness of this notation, it perhaps deserves to be more popular than it is. Now that more tools (in particular Microsoft Visio for Enterprise Architects™) support ORM diagramming and the generation of business sentences and a relational logical data model from an ORM model, we may see more use made of ORM.

Figure 7.14 depicts an ORM model. In ORM ellipses represent object classes, which are either entity classes (sets of entity instances) or domains (sets of attribute values). Each multicompartment box represents a relationship between two or more object classes and enables the attributes of an entity class and the relationships in which it participates to be modeled in the same way. This confers a particular advantage in establishing which attributes and relationships of an entity class are mandatory and which are optional (by contrast, E-R modeling uses different mandatory/optional notations for attributes and relationships). ORM also provides a rich constraint language, an example of which is discussed in Section 14.6.2.

Perhaps the major disadvantage of ORM as a means of capturing business information requirements is that many more shapes are drawn on the page when compared to the E-R or UML representation of the same model. This may make it difficult for business stakeholders to come to grips with, at least initially. It also needs to be said that ORM's richness means that it takes longer to learn; we would be the last to suggest that data modelers should not invest time in learning their profession, but simpler languages have consistently proved more attractive.

---

[10]Variously standing for Natural Language Information Analysis Method, Nijssen's Information Analysis Method, and An Information Analysis Method.

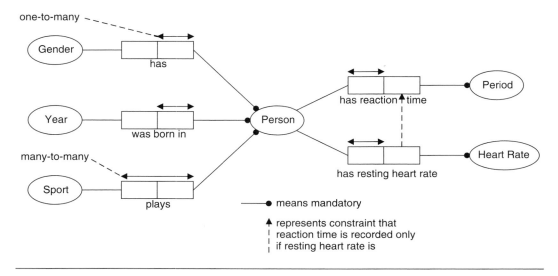

Figure 7.14 An ORM model.

7.6 **Summary**

There are a number of alternatives to the simple E-R modeling conventions for conceptual modeling. Relatively few, however, have a significant following in the practitioner community.

The Chen conventions provide for a more detailed and consistent representation of relationships but are not widely used in practice.

UML has a substantial following and offers a wide variety of constructs for representing concepts and constraints—which require skill to employ correctly and may be difficult for business stakeholders to grasp.

ORM is a powerful language that has been taken up only sporadically in industry. The lack of a distinction between entity classes and attributes is a key conceptual feature but can lead to diagrams becoming unacceptably complex.

The professional modeler, even if restricted to using a single language, will gain from an understanding of alternative conventions.

Part II
Putting It Together

Chapter 8
Organizing the Data Modeling Task

"The fact was I had the vision . . . I think everyone has . . . what we lack is the method."
– Jack Kerouac

"Art and science have their meeting point in method."
– Edward Bulwer-Lytton

8.1 Data Modeling in the Real World

In the preceding chapters, we have focused largely on learning the *language* of data modeling without giving much attention to the practicalities of modeling in a real business environment.

We are in a position not unlike that of the budding architect who has learned the drawing conventions and a few structural principles. The real challenges of understanding a set of requirements and designing a sound data model to meet them are still ahead of us.

As data modelers, we will usually be working in the larger context of an information systems development or enhancement project, or perhaps a program of change that may require the development of several databases. As such, we will need to work within an overall project plan, which will reflect a particular methodology, or at least someone's idea of how to organize a project.

Our first challenge, then, is to ensure that the project plan allows for the development and proper use of high quality data models.

The second challenge is to actually develop these models—or, more specifically, to develop a series of deliverables that will culminate in a complete physical data model and, along the way, provide sufficient information for other participants in the project to carry out their work.

This second part of the book is organized according to the framework for data model development that we introduced in Chapter 1. We commence by gaining an understanding of business requirements then by developing (in turn) conceptual, logical, and physical data models. Finally, we need to maintain the model or models as business requirements change, either before or after the formal completion of the project. Figure 8.1 provides a more detailed picture of these stages. You should note that data model development does not proceed in a strictly linear fashion; from time to time, discoveries we make about requirements or alternative designs will necessitate revisiting an earlier stage. If the project methodology is itself iterative, it will support this (and perhaps encourage too much data model volatility!); conversely if you are following a **waterfall** method (based on a single pass through each activity), you will need to ensure that mechanisms are in place to enable some iteration and associated revision of documentation.

Not all methodologies follow the framework exactly. The most common variations are the introduction of intermediate deliverables within the conceptual modeling stage (for example, a high-level model to support system scoping) and the use of an iterative approach in which the modeling stages are repeated, along with other project tasks, to achieve increasing

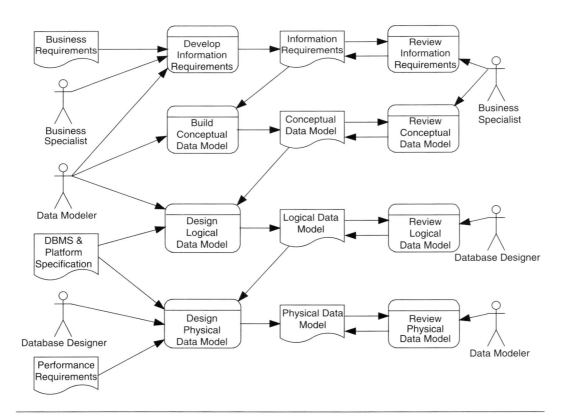

Figure 8.1   Data model development stages.

refinement or coverage. None of these variations changes the nature of the tasks, as we describe them, in any substantial way.

It is beyond the scope of this book to explore in detail the role of data modeling across the range of generic and proprietary methodologies and their local variants. In this chapter we look at the critical data modeling issues in project planning and management, with the aim of giving you the tools to examine critically any proposed approach from a data modeling perspective. We look in some detail at the often-neglected issue of managing change to the data model as it develops within and across the various stages.

8.2 **Key Issues in Project Organization**

As a data modeler, you may find yourself participating in the development of a project plan or (perhaps more likely) faced with an existing plan specifying how you will be involved and what you are expected to deliver. What should you look for and argue for? Here is a minimum list.

8.2.1 **Recognition of Data Modeling**

Let us repeat what we said in Chapter 1: No database was ever built without a data model. Unfortunately, many databases have been built from models that existed only in the minds of database technicians, and it is not uncommon for projects to be planned without allowing for a data model to be properly developed and documented by someone qualified to do so.

You are most likely to encounter such a situation in a "short and sharp" project that does not use a formal methodology, or loosely claims allegiance to a "prototyping," "agile," or "extreme" approach. Typically, the response to suggestions that a formal data modeling phase be included is that it will take too much time; instead, the database will be developed quickly and modified as necessary.

You should know the arguments by now: good data modeling is the foundation for good system design, and it is easier to get the foundations right at the outset than to try to move them later.

If these arguments are not effective, your options are to distance yourself from the project or to do what you can to make the best of the situation. If you opt for the latter, we recommend you rebadge yourself as a "logical database designer" and use the logical database design as the focus of discussion. The same quality issues and arguments will apply, but you will lack the discipline of staged development and deliverables.

8.2.2 **Clear Use of the Data Model**

It is not sufficient to develop a data model; it is equally important that its role and value be recognized and that it be used appropriately. We have seen projects in which substantial resources were devoted to the development of a data model, only for it to be virtually ignored in the implementation of the system. The scenario is typically one in which lip service is given to data modeling; perhaps it is part of a mandated methodology or policy, or the development team has been prevailed upon by a central data management or architectures function without truly understanding or being convinced of the place of data modeling in the project.

The crucial requirement is that the physical data model—as agreed to by the data modeler—is the ultimate specification for the database. Another take on this is that any differences between the logical and physical data models must have the data modeler's agreement.

Other important uses flow from this requirement. If process modelers and programmers know that the data model will truly form the specification for the database, they will refer to the model in their own work. If not, they will wait for the arrival of the "real" data structures.

It is not only project managers and database administrators who are guilty of breaking the link between data modeling and database implementation. On too many occasions we have seen data modelers deliver models that are incomplete or unworkable. Often this can be traced to a lack of understanding of database structures and a limited view of data modeling as "describing the real world," without adequate recognition that the description has to serve as a database specification. Such modelers may be only too pleased to have someone else take responsibility for the result.

Ernest Hemingway once suggested that screenwriters would do well to throw their manuscripts across the California state line and "get the hell out of there." This may or may not be good advice for screenwriters, but data modelers have a responsibility to see that their models are both implementable and implemented. As such, *the project plan must allow for data modeler involvement in performance design and tuning of the physical data model.*

8.2.3 **Access to Users and Other Business Stakeholders**

Good data modeling requires direct access to business stakeholders to ascertain requirements, verify models, and evaluate trade-offs. This is an ongoing process that does not stop until the physical data model is finalized.

It is not uncommon for data modelers to be expected to get their requirements from the process modelers or an individual charged with representing "the business." These situations are almost never satisfactory.

Getting information second hand usually means that the right questions about data are not asked and the right answers not obtained.

8.2.4 Conceptual, Logical, and Physical Models

While some tools and methodologies call for more or fewer stages of modeling, we recommend (along with most other writers and practitioners) that you employ a three-stage approach, delivering, in turn, a conceptual, logical, and physical model.

The separation of the modeling task into stages allows us to do a number of things:

- Divide the major design objectives into groups and work on each group in turn. We can thereby more easily trace the reasons for a design decision and are less likely to make decisions without clear justification.
- Defer some details of the design until they are needed, giving us the maximum time to gather information and explore possibilities.
- Use representation methods and techniques appropriate to the different participants in each stage.
- Establish some reference points to which we can return if the implementation environment changes. In particular, if performance requirements or facilities change, we can return to the logical model as the starting point for a new physical model, and if the DBMS changes, we can return to the conceptual model as the starting point for a new logical model.

In practice, we will often look beyond the stage that we are working on and come up with ideas of relevance to later stages. This is entirely normal in design activities: the discipline lies in noting the ideas for later reference, but not committing to them until the appropriate time. We call this "just in time design."

In the conceptual modeling activity, our focus is on designing a set of data structures that will meet business requirements (the determination of which forms the earlier "requirements" stage). The principal participants are business people, and we want them to be able to discuss and review proposed data concepts and structures without becoming embroiled in the technicalities of DBMS-specific constructs or performance issues. Plain language assertions, supported by diagrams, are our primary tools for presenting and discussing the conceptual model.

In the transition from conceptual to logical model, our principal concern is to properly map the conceptual model to the logical data structures supported by a particular DBMS. If the DBMS is relational, the logical model will be documented in terms of tables and columns; keys will need to be introduced; and many-to-many relationships will need to be resolved. If subtypes are not supported we will need to finalize the choice of implementation option.

In the transition from logical to physical model, our principal concern is performance. We may need to work creatively with the database designer to propose and evaluate changes to the logical model to be incorporated in the physical model, if these are needed to achieve adequate performance, and, similarly, we may need to work with the business stakeholders and process modelers or programmers to assess the impact of such changes on them. The physical model describes the actual implemented database including the tables (with names and definitions), their columns (with names, definitions and datatypes), primary and foreign keys, indexes, storage structures, and so on. This can be the DBMS catalogue provided that it has a human-readable view, although there are advantages in supporting it with a diagram showing the foreign key linkages between tables.

It is interesting to compare this widely-used partitioning of the data modeling task with the data component ("column 1") of the Zachman Enterprise Architecture Framework,[1] which specifies four levels of data model, namely the Planner's, Owner's, Designer's, and Builder's views (there is also a Subcontractor's view but it is not clear that that requires an additional model). While our conceptual model clearly corresponds to the Owner's view and our physical model corresponds to the Builder's view it is not clear in what way the Designer's view should differ from each of those. The Planner's view would appear to correspond to what we call an enterprise model (Chapter 17). Hay[2] has with some justification modified Zachman's Framework to include an Architect's view, eliminating the Subcontractor's view and shifting the Designer's and Builder's views each down a row.

8.2.5 Cross-Checking with the Process Model

The data and process models are interdependent. At regular intervals during the life cycle, we need to be able to verify the developing data model against the process model to ensure that:

1. We have included the data needed to support each process.
2. The process model is using the same data concepts and terminology as those that we have defined.

---

[1]This has been significantly extended since Zachman's initial paper on the Framework. The best current resource for information about the Framework is at www.zifa.com.

[2]Hay, D.C: *Requirements Analysis—From Business Views to Architecture*, Prentice-Hall, New Jersey, 2003.

Entity / Process	Customer	Order	Order Line	Invoice	Invoice Line	Product	Product Pack	Depot	Product Stock
Register new customer	C								
Take order	R	C	C			R	R		
Change order	R	U	U			R	R		
Make delivery	R	R	R	C	C	R	R	R	U
Make new stock						R	R	R	U
Record address change	U								
Update prices						R	U		

Figure 8.2 A portion of a CRUD matrix.

Several formal techniques are available for reconciling the two models. Probably the most widely used is the unfortunately-named "CRUD" matrix which maps processes against entity classes, showing whether they create, read, update, or delete (hence c, r, u, d) records of entity instances, as illustrated in Figure 8.2.

While there should be formal reviews and techniques to compare data and process models, there is also great value in having someone thoroughly familiar with the data model participating in day-to-day process and program design. A member of the data modeling team should be the first person contacted for clarification and explanation of data definitions and structures, and should participate in reviews and walkthroughs.

8.2.6 **Appropriate Tools**

If there is a single tool universally associated with data modeling, it is the whiteboard. It reflects a longstanding tradition of multiple stakeholders contributing to and reviewing models, a dynamic that can be difficult to reproduce with computer-based documentation tools. It also supports rapid turnover of candidate models, particularly in the early stages; an idea can be sketched, evaluated, modified, and perhaps discarded quickly and easily. Whiteboards place no constraints on modeling practices or notation, allowing flexibility to explore ideas without worrying about getting the grammar right. Of course, modelers also need to verify and cross-check models, produce complete and easily accessed documentation, and generate database schemas. These tasks can be better supported by automated tools. But in preparing for a data modeling project, or setting up an ongoing data modeling function, whiteboards, preferably with copying facilities, should be at the top of this list.

If a project is going to use CASE (computer-aided software engineering) tools, you will usually find yourself tightly tied to the tool-designer's view of how data modeling should be done. It is generally much more difficult to tailor an automated methodology to meet your personal preferences than it is to make changes to a written methodology.

Usually the tool has been chosen for a variety of reasons, which may or may not include how well it supports data modeling. The quality of data modeling support differs from tool to tool: the most common limitations are:

■ Use of a particular data modeling language. The most widely used tools support UML or an E-R variant, but some of the useful extensions (e.g., nontransferability or even subtyping) may not be available.

■ A mechanical translation from conceptual to logical model. In seeking to make the translation completely automatic, the tool designer is obliged to push certain design decisions back to the conceptual modeling stage. Some tools do not provide for a conceptual model at all; conceptual and logical modeling are combined into a single phase.

■ Poor support for:

   ◆ Recording and manipulating incomplete models ("sketch plans"). For this reason, many modelers defer recording the conceptual model in the CASE tool until it is substantially complete, relying on paper and whiteboards up to that point.

   ◆ Common conceptual model changes such as global renames and moving attributes between entity classes (from supertype to a subtype or *vice versa*, or from an entity class to its associated snapshot or *vice versa*).

   ◆ Synchronizing the logical schema and the database. A good tool will not only support rebuilding of the database but will enable data to be saved and reloaded when making design changes to a populated database.

8.3 **Roles and Responsibilities**

There is some debate about how many and what sort of people should participate in the development of a data model. The extremes are the specialist data modeler, working largely alone and gathering information from documentation and one-on-one interviews, and the joint applications development (JAD) style of session, which brings business people, data modelers, and other systems staff together in facilitated workshops.

We need to keep in mind two key objectives: (a) we want to produce the best possible models at each stage, and (b) we need to have them accepted by all stakeholders. Both objectives suggest the involvement of a fairly large group of people, first to maximize the "brainstorming" power and second to build commitment to the result. On the other hand, involvement need not mean *constant* involvement. Good ideas come not only from brainstorming sessions but also from reflection by individuals outside the sessions. Time outside group sessions is also required to ensure that models are properly checked for technical soundness (normalization, conformity to naming standards, and so forth). And some tasks are best delegated to one or two people, with the group being responsible for checking the result. These tasks include diagram production, detailed entity class and attribute definition, and follow-up of business issues that are beyond the expertise of the group.

Some decisions need to be made jointly with other specialists. For example, the choice of how to implement the various business rules (as program logic, data content, database design or outside the computerized system—covered in more detail in Chapter 14) needs to involve the process modeler as well as the data modeler. Performance tuning needs to involve the database administrator. Another key player may be the data administrator or architect, who will be interested in maintaining consistency in data definition across systems. However we organize the modeling task, we must ensure the involvement of these professionals.

Our own preference is to nominate a small core team, usually consisting of one or two specialist data modelers and a subject matter expert (generally from the business side). Another, larger team is made up of other stakeholders, including further owner/user representatives, process modelers, a representative of the physical database design team, and perhaps a more experienced data modeler. Other participants may include subject area specialists (who may not actually be users of the system), the project manager(s), and the data administrator. The larger team meets regularly to discuss the model. In the initial stages, their focus is on generating ideas and exploring major alternatives. Later, the emphasis shifts to review and verification. The smaller team is responsible for managing the process, developing ideas into workable candidate models, ensuring that the models are technically sound, preparing material for review, and incorporating suggestions for change.

Support for the final model by all stakeholders, particularly the process modelers and physical database designers, is critical. Many good data models have been the subject of long and acrimonious debate, and sometimes rejection, after being forced upon process modelers and physical database designers who have not been involved in their development. This is particularly true of innovative models. Other stakeholders may not have shared in the flashes of insight that have progressively moved the model away from familiar concepts, nor may they be aware of the problems or limitations of those concepts. Taking all stakeholders along with the process stage by stage is the best way of overcoming this. A good rule is to involve anyone likely to be in a position to criticize or reject the model and anyone likely to ask, "Why wasn't I asked?" If this seems to be excessive, be assured that the cost of doing so is likely to be far less than that of trying to force the model on these people later.

8.4 **Partitioning Large Projects**

Larger applications are often partitioned and designed in stages. There are essentially two approaches:

1. Design the processes that *create* entity instances before those that read, update, and delete them. Achieving this is not quite as simple as it might appear, as some entity instances cannot be created without referring to other entity classes. In the data model of Figure 8.3, we will not be able to create an instance of **Contribution** without checking **Employee** and **Fund** to ensure that the contribution refers to valid instances of these. We would therefore address these "reference" entity classes and associated processes first.

   Generally, this approach leads to us starting at the top of the hierarchy and working down. In Figure 8.3 we would commence detailed modeling around **Fund Type** and **Fund**, **Employer**, or **Account**, at the top of the hierarchy, moving to **Person** only when **Fund** and **Fund Type** were completed, and **Account Entry** only when all the other entity classes were fully specified.

   The attraction of the approach is that it progressively builds on what is already in place and (hopefully) proven. If we follow the same sequence for *building* the system (as we will have to do if we are prototyping), we should avoid the problems of developing transactions that cannot be tested because the data they read cannot be created.

2. Design core processes first and put in place the necessary data structures to support them. In Figure 8.3 we might commence with the "Record Contribution" process, which could require virtually all of the entity classes in the model. This puts pressure on the data modeler to deliver quite a complete design early (and we need to plan accordingly), but it also provides considerable input on the workability of the high level model. If we follow the same sequence for development, we may have to use special programs (e.g., database utilities) to populate the reference tables for testing. While this approach is less elegant, it has the advantage of addressing the more critical issues first, leaving the more straightforward handling of reference data until later. As a result, rework may be reduced.

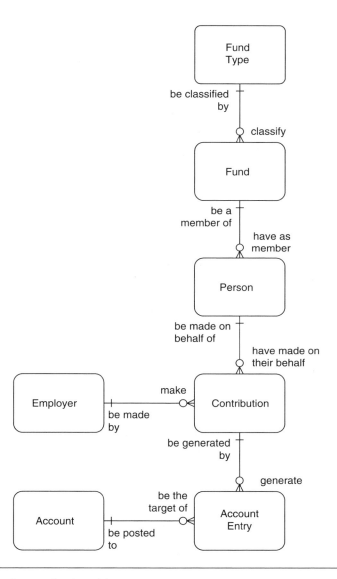

Figure 8.3 Pension fund model.

There are as many variations on these broad options as there are systems development methodologies. Some rigorously enforce a sequence derived from "Create, Read, Update, Delete" dependencies, while others allow more flexibility to sequence development to meet business priorities. As data modelers, our preference is for the second approach, which tends to raise critical data modeling issues early in the process before it is too late or expensive to address them properly. Whichever approach you use, the important thing is to be conscious of the quality and reliability of the data model at each stage, and to ensure that the process modeler understands the probability of change as later requirements are identified.

8.5 Maintaining the Model

However well your data model meets the business requirements, changes during its development are inevitable. Quite apart from actual changes in scope or requirements that may arise during the project, your understanding of requirements will grow as you continue to work with stakeholders. At the same time, the stakeholders' increasing understanding of the implications of the system proposed may prompt them to suggest changes to the data structures originally discussed. Most modelers (and indeed most designers in any field) have had the experience of finding a better way of handling a situation even after they have ostensibly completed their work in an area.

Another reason why significant changes to a model are likely to occur during its development is because it makes good sense to publish an early draft to ensure that scope and requirements are "in the ballpark" rather than leaving publication until you are confident that all details have been captured.

Here we show the rules for managing some common changes and then look at some more general principles. We cover them in this chapter because they are relevant across all phases of a modeling project.

8.5.1 Examples of Complex Changes

Some model changes, such as the addition of an attribute to an entity class to support a previously unsupported requirement, can be made without any need to consider the impact of the change on the rest of the model. Two common types of change that do require such consideration are those involving generalization and those involving entity class or attribute renaming. These are discussed in the following sections.

8.5.1.1 Changes Resulting from Generalization

One of the most common forms of generalization results from the recognition of similarities between two entity classes and the subsequent creation of a supertype of which those entity classes become subtypes. This requires a number of individual changes to the data model:

- Add the supertype.
- Mark each of the original entity classes as a subtype of that supertype.

- Move each of the common attributes (renaming, if necessary, to a more general name) from one of the original entity classes to the supertype.
- Move each of the common relationships (renaming, if necessary, to a more general name) from one of the original entity classes to the supertype.
- Remove the common attributes from the other original entity class(es).
- Remove the common relationships from the other original entity class(es).

Another form of generalization is the merging of two or more entity classes, when each has a set of attributes and relationships that corresponds to those of the other entity class(es). The changes required in this situation are:

- Add the generalized entity class.
- Move all the attributes (renaming each, if necessary, to a more general name) from one of the original entity classes to the generalized entity class.
- Move all the relationships (renaming each, if necessary, to a more general name) from one of the original entity classes to the generalized entity class.
- Remove the original entity classes.
- Remove the common relationships from the other original entity class(es).
- Add a category attribute distinguishing the original entity classes to support any business rules referring to those classes.

Figure 8.4 shows an example of a conceptual model to support various types of insurance claims (see next page). This model could benefit from some generalization in both of the ways described above.

For example, **Compensation Claim Item, Service Claim Item**, and **Equipment Claim Item** can be generalized by creating the supertype **Claim Item**. This requires the following individual changes:

- Add the **Claim Item** entity class.
- Mark **Compensation Claim Item, Service Claim Item**, and **Equipment Claim Item** as subtypes of **Claim Item**.
- Add the attributes Claim Date, Claimed Amount, Claim Item Status, and Details to **Claim Item**.
- Remove those attributes from **Compensation Claim Item, Service Claim Item**, and **Equipment Claim Item**.

By way of contrast, since **Registered Practitioner** and **Registered Equipment Supplier** have corresponding attributes they might be generalized into the single entity class **Registered Service Provider** without being

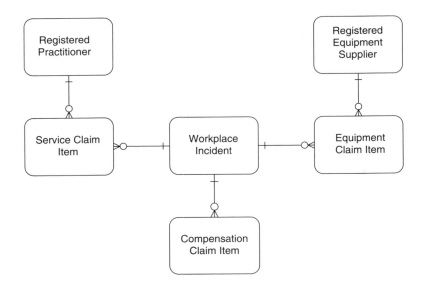

REGISTERED PRACTITIONER (Practitioner Registration No, Practitioner Name, Registered Address Street No, Registered Address Street Name, Registered Address Locality Name, Registered Address Postal Code, Contact Phone No)

REGISTERED EQUIPMENT SUPPLIER (Supplier Registration No, Supplier Name, Registered Address Street No, Registered Address Street Name, Registered Address Locality Name, Registered Address Postal Code, Contact Phone No)

WORKPLACE INCIDENT (Incident Date, Incident TimeOfDay, Incident Nature, Injury Nature, Injured Body Part, Injury Severity, Employee Time Off Start Date, Claim No, Claim Status, Employee Time Off End Date, Incapacity Duration, Details)

COMPENSATION CLAIM ITEM (Claim Date, Compensation Type, Period Start Date, Period End Date, Claimed Amount, Claim Item Status, Details)

SERVICE CLAIM ITEM (Claim Date, Service Type, Service Start Date, Service End Date, Claimed Amount, Claim Item Status, Details)

EQUIPMENT CLAIM ITEM (Claim Date, Equipment Type, Acquisition Type, Equipment Use Start Date, Equipment Use End Date, Claimed Amount, Claim Item Status, Details)

Figure 8.4 A model requiring generalization.

retained as subtypes thereof. This requires the following individual changes:

- Add the **Registered Service Provider** entity class.
- Add the attributes Service Provider Registration No, Service Provider Name, Registered Address Street No, Registered Address Street Name, Registered Address Locality Name, Registered Address Postal Code, and Contact Phone No to **Registered Service Provider**.

- Move the relationship between **Registered Practitioner** and **Service Claim Item** from **Registered Practitioner** to **Registered Service Provider**.
- Move the relationship between **Registered Equipment Supplier** and **Equipment Claim Item** from **Registered Equipment Supplier** to **Registered Service Provider**.
- Record in the "off-model" business rules list the rules that:
  - ◆ Only **Registered Service Providers** of type **Registered Practitioner** can be associated with a **Service Claim Item**.
  - ◆ Only **Registered Service Providers** of type **Registered Equipment Supplier** can be associated with a **Equipment Claim Item**.
- Add the attribute Service Provider Type to **Registered Service Provider** to support those business rules.
- Remove the entity classes **Registered Practitioner** and **Registered Equipment Supplier**.

The results of both these generalization activities are illustrated in Figure 8.5.

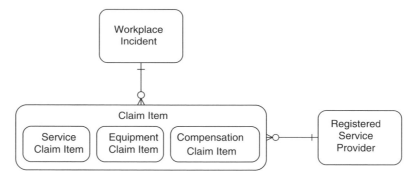

REGISTERED SERVICE PROVIDER (Service Provider Type, Service Provider Registration No, Service Provider Name, Registered Address Street No, Registered Address Street Name, Registered Address Locality Name, Registered Address Postal Code, Contact Phone No)

WORKPLACE INCIDENT (Incident Date, Incident TimeOfDay, Incident Nature, Injury Nature, Injured Body Part, Injury Severity, Employee Time Off Start Date, Claim No, Claim Status, Employee Time Off End Date, Incapacity Duration, Details)

CLAIM ITEM (Claim Date, Claimed Amount, Claim Item Status, Details)

COMPENSATION CLAIM ITEM (Compensation Type, Period Start Date, Period End Date)

SERVICE CLAIM ITEM (Service Type, Service Start Date, Service End Date)

EQUIPMENT CLAIM ITEM (Equipment Type, Acquisition Type, Equipment Use Start Date, Equipment Use End Date)

Figure 8.5 The same model after generalization.

8.5.1.2 Changes to Generalized Structures

Among the changes to an already-generalized structure that may trigger consequential changes are adding an attribute, relationship, or new subtype to a supertype.

If you add an attribute or relationship to a supertype, you must check the attributes and relationships of each subtype of that supertype to determine whether any are now superfluous. Note that the subtype attributes and relationships may not have the same name as those of the supertype. For example if Period Start Date and Period End Date are added to **Claim Item** in Figure 8.3, then:

- Period Start Date and Period End Date should be removed from **Compensation Claim Item**.
- Service Start Date and Service End Date should be removed from **Service Claim Item**.
- Equipment Use Start Date and Equipment Use End Date should be removed from **Equipment Claim Item**.

If you add a new subtype to a supertype, you must check each attribute and relationship of the supertype to determine whether any are not appropriate for the new subtype. If any are not appropriate, there are three options:

- Move the attribute or relationship to each existing subtype.
- Create an intermediate subtype as a supertype of the existing subtypes.
- Rename the attribute or relationship to something more general (if possible).

For example, if we need to add the subtype **Electric Locomotive Class** to the model in Figure 8.6, we discover that the attribute Engine Model does not apply to the new subtype. We can either move that attribute to **Diesel-Electric Locomotive Class** and **Diesel-Hydraulic Locomotive Class** or create an additional **Diesel Locomotive Class** subtype of **Locomotive Class** to hold that attribute and make **Diesel-Electric Locomotive Class** and **Diesel-Hydraulic Locomotive Class** subtypes of **Diesel Locomotive Class**.

LOCOMOTIVE CLASS (Wheel Arrangement, Wheel Diameter, Engine Model, Tractive Effort, Power, Length, Weight, Body Style, Manufacturer, Duty Type, Maximum Speed)
DIESEL-ELECTRIC LOCOMOTIVE CLASS (Generator Model, Traction Motor Model)
DIESEL-HYDRAULIC LOCOMOTIVE CLASS (Transmission Model)

Figure 8.6 Adding a new subtype to a supertype.

Since there is nothing resembling an engine in an electric locomotive, we cannot rename Engine Model to something more general.

8.5.1.3 Entity Class or Attribute Renaming

A major issue to be considered when model reviewers (or indeed the modeler) decide that an entity class or attribute should be renamed is the extent to which other uses of the same words should be changed to correspond. For example, when the model of which Figure 8.4 is a fragment was reviewed, one reviewer stated that the attributes Start Date and End Date used in a particular entity class representing a business rule (not shown in Figure 8.4) should instead be Effective Date and Expiry Date, while another stated that all occurrences of the attributes Start Date and End Date throughout the model should be renamed thus. The real requirement was somewhere between those conservative and radical viewpoints. This was that Start Date and End Date should be renamed to Effective Date and Expiry Date in all business rule entity classes and in the entity class recording insurance policies but *not* in **Workplace Incident** or in any of the **Claim Item** entity classes.

It is important when renaming any entity class or attribute to check not only all entity classes or attributes with names incorporating the same words but relationship names and descriptions of entity classes and attributes.

Some renaming will have semantic implications—or at least alert us to deeper issues. For example, in Figure 8.4 we were advised that Incapacity Duration was really Incapacity Lost Time Duration, which meant that it was derivable from Employee Time Off Start Date and Employee Time Off End Date (given that weekends and public holidays were also recorded).

8.5.2 **Managing Change in the Modeling Process**

It should be obvious from the foregoing examples and discussion that many changes to the data model are "long transactions." Can we keep track if there are likely to be interruptions? These can occur not only in the guise of visitors, phone calls, meetings, breaks, and so on, but also as a result of noticing, while making one change, that other changes are required.

For this reason alone, we recommend that you produce a list of intended changes before actually making them. Doing this yields a number of advantages. For a start noone who has reviewed an earlier version of the model will be prepared to review the revised model unless they are furnished with a list of the changes. Secondly, we can sort changes by entity class and check for any conflicting changes. For example, we may have been asked by one reviewer to remove an attribute but by another to rename it or change one of its properties. We can obtain a "second opinion" of our intended changes before we make them. And if we decide that a change is inappropriate or ill-formed, we can reverse it more easily if we have a statement of what changes we have made. Finally, we can check off the changes on the list as we make them and avoid forgetting to make intended changes due to interruptions.

Each change decision should be listed in business terms, followed by the individual types of model change that are required, for example:

Addition of entity classes or relationships
Changes to the attributes of an entity class
Moving attributes/relationships
Changing relationship cardinality
Changing identification data items
Renaming

8.6 Packaging It Up

In the remainder of this part of the book, we discuss the stages in the data modeling process and the deliverables that we believe need to be produced. At the end of a data modeling project, the final deliverables will be the sum of the outputs of the individual stages—a substantial body of documentation that will include not only what is required directly by the project, but also interim outputs produced along the way. The latter provide at least a partial audit trail of design decisions and a basis for making changes in a controlled manner in the future.

The list below summarizes the central deliverables; whatever formal or informal methodology you are using, it should deliver these as a minimum.

1. A broad summary of requirements covering scope, objectives, and future business directions. These should provide the justification for the overall approach taken—for example, highly generic or customer-centered.

2. Inputs to the model: interview summaries, reverse-engineered models, process models, and so forth. Normally these are appended to the main documentation and referred to as necessary in definitions.

3. A conceptual data model in the form of a fully annotated entity-relationship diagram, UML class diagram, or alternative.

4. Entity class definitions, attribute lists, and attribute definitions for every entity class in the model.

5. Documentation of constraints and business rules other than those implicit in items 3 and 4 (see Section 14.4).

6. A logical data model suitable for direct implementation as a logical database design. If our target DBMS is a conventional relational

product, the model will not include subtypes and should be fully normalized.

7. Design notes covering decisions made in translating the conceptual model to a logical model—in particular, implementation of subtypes and choice of primary keys.

8. Cross-reference to the process model, proving that all processes are supported.

9. As necessary, higher level and local versions of the model to facilitate presentation.

10. A physical data model with documentation explaining all changes from the logical data model.

This is quite a lot of documentation. Items 1 to 9 are certainly more than a database designer needs to produce a physical database design. *But database designers are not the only audience for data models.*

Some of the additional documentation is to allow the business stakeholders to verify that the database will meet their requirements. Some is aimed at process modelers and program designers, to ensure that they will understand the model and use it as intended. This role of data model documentation is often overlooked, but it is absolutely critical; many a good model has been undermined because it was incorrectly interpreted by programmers. The documentation of source material provides some traceability of design decisions and allows proposals to change or compromise the model to be assessed in terms of the business requirements that they affect.

8.7 **Summary**

Data modeling is generally performed in the context of an information systems project with an associated methodology and toolset. The data modeler will need to work within these constraints, but needs to ensure that the appropriate inputs and resources are available to support the development of a sound data model, and that the model is used correctly as a basis for database design. Regular cross-checking against the process model is essential.

The data modeling task is usually assigned to a small team, with regular input from and review by a larger group of stakeholders.

Remember that changes to a data model can be complex, so plan, document, and review changes before making them.

Chapter 9
The Business Requirements

"The greater part of all mischief in the world arises from the fact that men do not sufficiently understand their own aims."
- Johann Wolfgang von Goethe

"The real voyage of discovery consists not in seeking new landscapes but in having new eyes."
- Marcel Proust

9.1 Purpose of the Requirements Phase

There are two extreme views of the requirements phase and its deliverables.

The first is that we do not need a separate requirements phase and associated "statement of requirements" at all. Rather, requirements are captured in the conceptual data modeling phase and represented in the conceptual data model. This approach is prescribed by many data modeling texts and methodologies and, accordingly, widely used in practice. Sometimes, it reflects a view that the purpose of data modeling is to document data structures that are "out there," independent of other business requirements. You should know by now that we do not subscribe to this view of modeling.

A more persuasive argument for proceeding straight to modeling is that it is common for designers in other fields to start designing before they have a complete understanding of requirements. Architects may begin sketching plans well before they have a complete understanding of all of the client's needs. The evolving plan becomes the focus of the dialogue between client and architect. As the architect cannot refer back to a complete statement of requirements, the client must take a large share of the responsibility for confirming that the design meets his or her needs.

The strongest arguments for this approach are:

1. Many requirements are well-known to the designer and client ("The house must be structurally sound; the shower requires both hot and cold water.") and it would be impractical to try to document them in full.

2. Some requirements are only relevant to specific design alternatives ("The shelves in this cupboard should be widely spaced," only makes sense in the context of a design that includes the cupboard).

251

3. Some requirements may emerge only when the client has seen an actual design ("I like to sleep in complete darkness." or "I don't want to hear the kids practicing piano.").

The second extreme position is that we should develop a rigorous and complete statement of business requirements sufficient to enable us to develop and evaluate data models without needing to refer back to the client. For the reasons described above, such a comprehensive specification is unlikely to be practical, but there are good reasons for having at least some written statement of requirements. In particular:

1. There are requirements—typically high-level business directions and rules—that will influence the design of the conceptual data model, but that cannot be captured directly using data modeling constructs. We cannot directly capture in an E-R model requirements such as, "We need to be able to introduce new products without redesigning the system." or, "The database will be accessed directly by end-users who would have difficulty coming to grips with unfamiliar terminology or sophisticated data structures."

2. There are requirements we *can* represent directly in the model, but in doing so, we may compromise other goals of the model. For example, we can capture the requirement, "All transactions (e.g., loans, payments, purchases) must be able to be conducted in foreign currencies." We can do so by introducing a generic **Transaction** entity class with appropriate currency-related attributes as a high level supertype. However, if there is no other reason for including this entity class, we may end up unnecessarily complicating the model.

3. Expressing requirements in a form other than a data model provides a degree of traceability. We can go back to the requirements documentation to see why a particular modeling decision was taken or why a particular alternative was chosen.

4. If only a data model is produced, the opportunity to experiment confidently with alternative designs may be lost; the initial data model effectively *becomes* the business requirement.

Our own views have, over the years, moved toward a more formal and comprehensive specification of requirements. In earlier editions of this book we devoted only one section ("Inputs to the Modeling Task") to the analysis of requirements prior to modeling. We now view requirements gathering as an important task in its own right, primarily because good design begins with an understanding of the big picture rather than with narrowly focused questions.

In this chapter, we look at a variety of techniques for gaining a holistic understanding of the relevant business area and the role of the proposed information system. That understanding will take the form of (a) written structured deliverables and (b) knowledge that may never be formally recorded, but that will inform data modelers' decisions. Data modeling is a creative process, and the knowledge of the business that modelers hold in their heads is an essential input to it.

We do not expect to uncover every requirement. On the contrary, we soon reach a point where data modeling becomes the most efficient way of capturing detail. As a rough guide, once you are able to propose a "first cut" set of entity classes (but not necessarily relationships or attributes) and justify their selection, you are ready to start modeling.

This chapter could have been titled "What Do You Do Before You Start Modeling?" Certainly that would capture the spirit of what the chapter is about, but we recognize that it is difficult to keep data modelers from modeling. Most of us will use data models as one tool for capturing requirements—and experimenting with some early solutions—during this phase. There is nothing wrong with this as long as modeling does not become the dominant technique, and the models are treated as inputs to the formal conceptual modeling phase rather than preempting it.

Finally, this early phase in a project provides an excellent opportunity to build relationships not only with the business stakeholders but with the other systems developers. Process modelers in particular also need a holistic view of the business, and it makes sense to work closely with them at this time and to agree on a joint set of deliverables and activities. Virtually all of the requirements-gathering activities described in this chapter can profitably be undertaken jointly with the process modelers. If the process modelers envisage a radical redesign of business processes, it is important that the data modeling effort reflects the new way of working. The common understanding of business needs and the ability to work effectively together will pay off later in the project.

9.2 **The Business Case**

An information system is usually developed in response to a problem, an opportunity, or a directive/mandate, the statement of which should be supported by a formal **business case**. The business case typically estimates the costs, benefits, and risks of alternative approaches and recommends a particular direction. It provides the logical starting point for the modeler seeking to gain an overall understanding of the context and requirements.

In reviewing a business case, you should take particular note of the following matters:

1. The broad justification for the application, who will benefit from it, and (possibly) who will be disadvantaged. This background information is

fundamental to understanding where business stakeholders are coming from in terms of their commitment to the system and likely willingness to contribute to the models. People who are going to be replaced by the system are unlikely to be enthusiastic about ensuring its success.

2. The business concepts, rules, and terminology, particularly if this is your first encounter with the business area. These will be valuable in establishing rapport in the early meetings and workshops with stakeholders.

3. The critical success factors for the system and for the area of the business in general, and the data required to support them.

4. The intended scope of the system, to enable you to form at least a preliminary picture of what data will need to be covered by the model.

5. System size and time frames, as a guide to planning the data modeling effort and resources.

6. Performance-related information—in particular, throughputs and response times. At the broadest level, this will enable you to get a sense of the degree to which performance issues are likely to dominate the modeling effort.

7. Management information requirements that the system is expected to meet in addition to supporting operational processes.

8. The expected lifetime of the application and changes likely to occur over that period. This issue is often not well addressed, but there should at least be a statement of the payback period or the period over which costs and benefits have been calculated. Ultimately, this information will influence the level of change the model is expected to support.

9. Interfaces to other applications, both internal and external—in particular, any requirement to share or transfer data (including providing data for data warehouses and/or marts). Such requirements may constrain data formats to those that are compatible with the other applications.

9.3 Interviews and Workshops

Interviews and workshops are essential techniques for requirements gathering. In drawing up interview and workshop invitation lists, we recommend that you follow the advice in Section 8.3 and include (a) the people whom you believe collectively understand the requirements of the system and (b) anyone likely to say, after the task is complete, "why wasn't I asked?"

Including the latter group will add to the cost and time of the project, and you may feel that the additional information gained does not justify the expense. We suggest you consider it an early investment in "change management"—the cost of having the database and the overall system accepted by those whom it will affect. People who have been consulted and (better still) who have contributed to the design of a system are more likely to be committed to its successful implementation.

Be particularly wary of being directed to the "user representative"—the single person delegated to answer all of your questions about the business—while the real users get on with their work. One sometimes wonders why this all-knowing person is so freely available!

9.3.1 Should You Model in Interviews and Workshops?

Be very, very careful about using data models as your means of communication during these initial interviews or workshops. In fact, use anything *but* data models: UML Use Cases and Activity Diagrams, plain text, data flow diagrams, event diagrams, function hierarchies, and/or report layouts.

Data models are *not* a comfortable language for most business people, who tend to think more in terms of activities. Too often we have seen well-intentioned business people trying to fulfill a facilitator's or modeler's request to "identify the things you need to keep information about," and then having their suggestions, typically widely-used business terms, rejected because they were not proper entity classes. Such a situation creates at least four problems:

1. It is demotivating not only to the stakeholder who suggested the term but to others in the same workshop.
2. Whatever is offered in a workshop is presumably important to the stakeholder and probably to the business in general and will therefore need to be captured eventually, yet such an approach fails to capture any terms other than entity classes.
3. By drawing the model now, you are making it harder (both cognitively and politically) to experiment with other options later.
4. Future requirement gathering sessions focused on attributes, relationships, categories, and so on may also be jeopardized.

Instead, you need to be able to accept all terms offered by stakeholders, be they entity classes, attributes, relationships, classification schemes, categories or even instances of any of these. Later in this chapter (Section 9.7), we look at a formal technique for doing this without committing to a model.

Because "on the fly" modeling is so common (and we may have failed to convince you to avoid it), it is worth looking at the problems it can cause a bit more closely.

In a workshop, the focus is usually on moving quickly and on capturing the "boxes and lines." There is seldom the time or the patience to accurately define each entity class. In fact what generally happens is that each participant in the workshop assumes an implicit definition of each entity class. If a relationship is identified between two entity classes that have names but only ambiguous definitions (or none), any subsequent attempt to achieve an agreed detailed definition of either of those entity classes (which is in effect a redefinition of that entity class) may change the cardinality and optionality of that relationship. This is not simply a matter of rework: We have observed that the need to review the associated relationships is often overlooked when an entity is defined or redefined, risking inconsistency in the resulting model.

You may recall that, in Section 3.5.8 (Figures 3.30 and 3.31), we presented an example in which the cardinality and optionality of two relationships depended on whether the definition of one entity class (**Customer**) included all customers or only those belonging to a loyalty program.

Similarly while a particular attribute might be correctly assigned to an entity class while it has a particular implicit definition, a change to (or refinement of) that definition might mean that that attribute is no longer appropriate as an attribute of that entity class. As an example, consider an entity class named **Patient Condition** in a health service model. If the assumption is made that this entity class has instances such as "Patient 123345's influenza that was diagnosed on 1/4/2004," it is reasonable to propose attributes like First Symptom Date or Presenting Date, but such attributes are quite inappropriate if instances of this entity class are simply conditions that such patients can suffer, such as "Influenza" and "Hangnail." In this case, those attributes should instead be assigned to the relationship between **Patient** and **Patient Condition** (or the intersection entity class representing that relationship).

9.3.2 **Interviews with Senior Managers**

CEOs and other senior managers may not be familiar with the details of process and data but are usually the best placed to paint a picture of future directions. Many a system has been rendered prematurely obsolete because information known to senior management was not communicated to the modeler and taken into account in designing the data model.

Getting to these people can be an organizational and political problem but one that must be overcome. Keep time demands limited; if you are working for a consultancy, bring in a senior partner for the occasion; explain in concise terms the importance of the manager's contribution to the success of the system.

Approach the interview with top management forearmed. Ensure that you are familiar with their area of business and focus on future directions. What types of regulatory and competitive change does the business face?

How does the business plan to respond to these challenges? What changes may be made to product range and organizational structure? Are there plans to radically reengineer processes? What new systems are likely to be required in the future?

By all means ask if their information needs are being met, but do not make this the sole subject of the interview. Senior managers are far less driven by structured information than some data warehouse vendors would have us believe. We recall one consultant being summarily thrown out by the chief executive of a major organization when he commenced an interview with the question: "What information do you need to run your business?" (To be fair, this is an important question, but many senior managers have been asked it one too many times without seeing much value in return.)

Above all, be aware of what the project as a whole will deliver for the interviewee. Self-interest is a great motivator!

9.3.3 Interviews with Subject Matter Experts

Business experts, end users, and "subject matter experts" are the people we speak to in order to understand the data requirements in depth. Do not let them design the model—at least not yet! Instead, encourage them to talk about the processes and the data they use and to look critically at how well their needs are met.

A goal and process based approach is often the best way of structuring the interview. "What is the purpose of what you do?" is not a bad opening question, leading to an examination of how the goals are achieved and what data is (ideally) required to support them.

9.3.4 Facilitated Workshops

Facilitated workshops are a powerful way of bringing people together to identify and verify requirements. Properly run, they can be an excellent forum for brainstorming, for ensuring that a wide range of stakeholders have an opportunity to contribute, and for identifying and resolving conflicts.

Here are a few basic guidelines:

- Use an experienced facilitator if possible and spend time with them explaining what you want from the workshop. (The cost of bringing in a suitable person is usually small compared with the cost of the participants' time.)
- If your expertise is in data modeling, avoid facilitating the workshop yourself. Facilitating the workshop limits your ability to contribute and

ask questions, and you run the risk of losing credibility if you are not an expert facilitator.

■ Give the facilitator time to prepare an approach and discuss it with you. The single most important factor in the success of a workshop is preparation.

■ Appoint a note-taker who understands the purpose of the workshop and someone to assist with logistics (finding stationery, chasing "no-shows," and so forth).

■ Avoid "modeling as you go." Few things destroy the credibility of a "neutral" facilitator more effectively than their constructing a model on the whiteboard that noone in the room could have produced, in a language noone is comfortable using.

■ Do not try to solve everything in the workshop, particularly if deep-seated differences surface or there is a question of "saving face." Make sure the problem is recognized and noted; then, organize to tackle it outside the workshop.

9.4 Riding the Trucks

A mistake often made by systems analysts (including data modelers) is to rely on interviews with managers and user representatives rather than direct contact with the users of the existing and proposed system. One of our colleagues used to call such direct involvement "riding the trucks," referring to an assignment in which he had done just that in order to understand an organization's logistics problems.

We would strongly encourage you to spend time with the hands-on users of the existing system as they go about their day-to-day work. Frequently such people will be located outside of the organization's head office; even if the same functions are ostensibly performed at head office, you will invariably find it worthwhile to visit a few different locations. On such visits, there is usually value in conducting interviews and even workshops with the local management, but the key objective should be to improve your understanding of system requirements and issues by watching people at work and questioning them about their activities and practices.

Things to look for, all of which can affect the design of the conceptual data model, include:

■ Variations in practices and interpretation of business rules at different locations

■ Variations in understanding of the meaning of data—particularly in interpretation and use of codes

- Terminology used by the real users of the system
- Availability and correct use of data (on several occasions we have heard, "Noone ever looks at this field, so we just make it up.")
- Misuse or undocumented use of data fields ("Everyone knows that an 'F' at the beginning of the comment field signifies a difficult customer.")

While you will obviously keep your eyes open for, and take note of, issues such as the above, the greatest value from "riding the trucks" comes from gaining a real sense of the purpose and operation of the system.

It is not always easy to get access to these end-users. Travel, particularly to international locations, may be costly. Busy users—particularly those handling large volumes of transactions, such as customer service representatives or money market dealers—may not have time to answer questions. And managers may not want their own vision of the system to be compromised by input from its more junior users.

Such obstacles need to be weighed against the cost of fixing or working around a data model based on an incorrect understanding of requirements. Unfortunately, data modelers do not always win these arguments. If you cannot get the access you want through formal channels, you may be able to use your own network to talk informally to users, or settle for discussions with people who have had that access.

9.5 **Existing Systems and Reverse Engineering**

Among the richest sources of raw material for the data modeler are existing file and database designs. Unfortunately, they are often disregarded by modelers determined to make a fresh start. Certainly, we should not incorporate earlier designs uncritically; after all, the usual reason for developing a new database is that the existing one no longer meets our requirements. There are plenty of examples of data structures that were designed to cope with limitations of the technology being carried over into new databases because they were seen as reflecting some undocumented business requirement. But there are few things more frustrating to a user than a new application that lacks facilities provided by the old system.

Existing database designs provide a set of entity classes, relationships, and attributes that we can use to ask the question, "How does our new model support this?" This question is particularly useful when applied to attributes and an excellent way of developing a first-cut attribute list for each entity class. A sound knowledge of the existing system also provides common ground for discussions with users, who will frequently express their needs in terms of enhancements to the existing system.

The existing system may be manual or computerized. If you are very fortunate, the underlying data model will be properly documented. Otherwise, you should produce at least an E-R diagram, short definitions, and attribute lists by "reverse engineering," a process analogous to an architect drawing the plan of an existing building.

The job of reverse engineering combines the diagram-drawing techniques that we discussed in Chapter 3 with a degree of detective work to determine the meaning of entity classes, attributes, and relationships. Assistance from someone familiar with the database is invaluable. The person most able to help is more likely to be an analyst or programmer responsible for maintenance work on the application than a database administrator.

You will need to adapt your approach to the quality of available documentation, but broadly the steps are as follows:

1. Represent existing files, segments, record types, tables, or equivalents as entity classes. Use subtypes to handle any redefinition (multiple record formats with substantially different meanings) within files.

2. Normalize. Recognize that here you are "improving" the system, and the resulting documentation will not show up any limitations due to lack of normalization. It will, however, provide a better view of data requirements as input to the new design. If your aim is purely to document the capabilities of the existing system, skip this step.

3. Identify relationships supported by "hard links." Non-relational DBMSs usually provide specific facilities ("sets," "pointers," and so forth) to support relationships. Finding these is usually straightforward; determining the meaning of the relationship and, hence, assigning a name is sometimes less so.

4. Identify relationships supported by foreign keys. In a relational database, all relationships will be supported in this way, but even where other methods for supporting relationships are available, foreign keys are often used to supplement them. Finding these is often the greatest challenge for the reverse engineer, primarily because data item (column) naming and documentation may be inconsistent. For example, the primary key of **Employee** may be Employee Number, but the data item Authorized By in another file may in fact be an employee number and, thus, a foreign key to **Employee**. Common formats are sometimes a clue, but they cannot be totally relied upon.

5. List the attributes for each entity class and define each entity class and attribute.

6. The resulting model should be used in the light of outstanding requests of system enhancement and of known limitations. The proposal for the new system is usually a good source of such information.

9.6   **Process Models**

If you are using a process-driven approach to systems development, as outlined briefly in Section 1.9.1, you will have valuable input in the form of the data used by the processes, as well as a holistic view of requirements conveyed by the higher level documentation. The data required by individual processes may be documented explicitly (e.g., as data stores) or implicitly within the process description (e.g., "Amend product price on invoice."). Even if you have adopted a data-driven approach, in which data modeling precedes process modeling, you should plan to verify the data model against the process model when it is available and allow time for enhancement of the data model. In any case, you should not go too far down the track in data modeling without some sort of process model, even if its detailed development is not scheduled until later.

We find a one or two level data flow diagram or interaction diagram a valuable adjunct to communicating the impact of different data models on the system as a whole. In particular, the processes in a highly generic system will look quite different from those in a more traditional system and will require additional data inputs to support "table driven" logic. A process model shows the differences far better than a data model alone (Figures 9.1 and 9.2).

9.7   **Object Class Hierarchies**

In this section, we introduce a technique for eliciting and documenting information that can provide quite detailed input to the conceptual data model, without committing us to a particular design. Its focus is on capturing business terms and their definition.

The key feature of this technique is that no restrictions are placed on what types of terms are identified and defined. A term proposed by a stakeholder may ultimately be modeled as an entity class but may just as easily become an attribute, relationship, classification scheme, individual category within a scheme, or entity instance. This means that we need a "metaterm" to embrace all these types of terms, and since at least some in the object-oriented community have stated that "everything is an object (class)," we use the term **object class** for that purpose. It is essential to organize the terms collected. We do this by classifying them using an **Object Class Hierarchy** that tends to bring together related terms and synonyms. While each enterprise's set of terms will naturally differ, there are some high-level object classes that are applicable to virtually all enterprises and can therefore be reused by each project. Let us consider the various ways in which we might classify terms before we actually lay out a suggested set of high-level object classes.

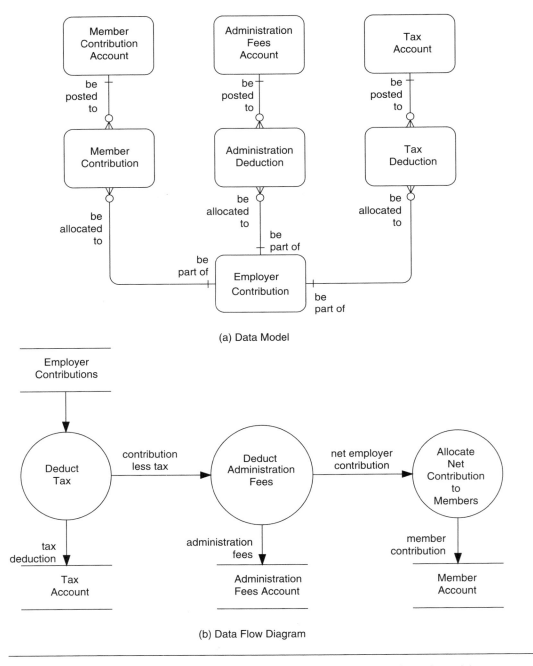

(a) Data Model

(b) Data Flow Diagram

Figure 9.1   Data flow diagrams used to supplement data models: "Traditional" model.

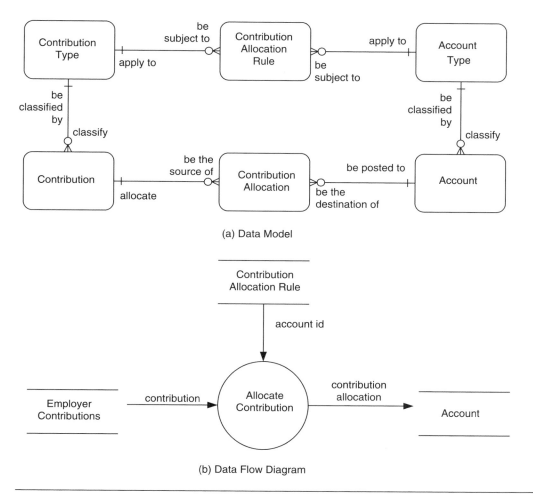

(a) Data Model

(b) Data Flow Diagram

Figure 9.2   Data flow diagrams used to supplement data models: "Generic" model.

9.7.1 **Classifying Object Classes**

The most obvious way of classifying terms is as entity classes (and instances thereof), attributes, relationships, classification schemes, and categories within schemes. There are then various ways in which we can further classify entity classes.

One way is based on the life cycle that an entity class exhibits. Some entity classes represent data that will need to be in place before the enterprise starts business (although this does not preclude addition to or modification of these once business gets under way). These include:

- Classification systems (e.g., **Customer Type**, **Transaction Type**)
- Other reference classes (e.g., **Organization Unit**, **Currency**, **Country**, **Language**)
- The service/product catalogue (e.g., **Installation Service**, **Maintenance Service**, **Publication**)
- Business rules (e.g., **Maximum Discount Rate**, **Maximum Credit Limit**)
- Some parties (e.g., **Employee**, **Regulatory Body**).

Other entity classes are populated as the enterprise does business, with instances that are generally long-lived. These include:

- Other parties (e.g., **Customer**, **Supplier**, **Other Business Partner**)
- Agreements (e.g., **Supply Contract**, **Employment Contract**, **Insurance Policy**)
- Assets (e.g., **Equipment Item**).

Still other entity classes are populated as the enterprise does business, but with instances that are generally transient (although information on them may be retained for some time). These include:

- Transactions (e.g., **Sale**, **Purchase**, **Payment**)
- Other events (e.g., **Equipment Allocation**).

Another way of classifying entity classes is by their degree of independence. Independent entity classes (with instances that do not depend for their existence on instances of some other entity class) include parties, classification systems, and other reference classes. By contrast, dependent entity classes include transactions, historic records (e.g., **Historic Insurance Policy Snapshot**), and aggregate components (e.g., **Order Line**). Attributes and relationships are of course also dependent as their instances cannot exist in the absence of "owning" instances of one or two entity classes respectively.

A third way of classifying entity classes is by the type of question to which they enable answers (or which column(s) they correspond to in Zachman's Architecture Framework):[1]

- Parties enable answers to "Who?" questions.

---

[1]Zachman's framework (at www.zifa.com) supports the classification of the components of an enterprise and its systems; its six columns broadly address the questions, "What?", "How?", "Where?", "Who?", "When?", and "Why?" Note that in general entity classes fall into column 1 ("What") of the framework, but that the things they describe may fall into any of the columns.

- Products and Services and Assets and Equipment enable answers to "What?" questions.
- Events enable answers to "When?" questions.
- Locations enable answers to "Where?" questions.
- Classifications and Business Rules enable answers to "How?" and "Why?" questions.

Another way of looking at question types is:

- Events and Transactions enable answers to "What happened?" questions.
- Business Rules enable answers to "What is (not) allowed?" questions.
- Other entity classes enable answers to "What is/are/was/were?" questions.

9.7.2   A Typical Set of Top-Level Object Classes

The different methods of classification described in the preceding section will actually generate quite similar sets of top-level object classes when applied to most enterprises. The following set is typical:

- **Product/Service**: includes all product types and service types that the enterprise is organized to provide
- **Party**: includes all individuals and organizations with which the enterprise does business (some organizations prefer the term **Entity**)
- **Party Role**: includes all roles in which parties interact with the enterprise [e.g., **Customer (Role)**, **Supplier (Role)**, **Employee (Role)**, **Service Provider (Role)**]
- **Location**: includes all physical addresses of interest to the enterprise and all geopolitical or organizational divisions of the earth's surface (e.g., **Country**, **Region**, **State**, **County**, **Postal Zone**, **Street**)
- **Physical Item**: includes all equipment items, furniture, buildings, and so on of interest to the enterprise
- **Organizational Influence**: includes anything that influences the actions of the enterprise, its employees and/or its customers, or how those actions are performed, such as:
  - Items of legislation or government policy that govern the enterprise's operation
  - Organizational policies, performance indicators, and so forth used by the enterprise to manage its operation
  - Financial accounts, cost centers, and so forth (although this collection might be placed in a separate top-level object class)

- ◆ Business Rules: standard amounts and rates used in calculating prices or fees payable, maxima and minima (e.g., **Minimum Credit Card Transaction Amount**, **Maximum Discount Rate**, **Maximum Session Duration**) and equivalences (e.g., between Qantas™ Frequent Flier Silver Status and OneWorld™ Frequent Flier Ruby Status)
- ◆ Any other external issues (political, industrial, social, economic, demographic, or environmental) that influence the operation or behavior of the enterprise

- ■ **Event**: includes all financial transactions, all other actions of interest by customers (e.g., **Complaint**), all service provisions by the enterprise or its agents, all tasks performed by employees, and any other events of interest to the enterprise
- ■ **Agreement**: includes all contracts and other agreements (e.g., insurance policies, leases) between the enterprise (or any legally-constituted parts thereof) and parties with which it does business and any contracts between other parties in which the enterprise has an interest
- ■ **Initiative**: includes all programs and projects run by the enterprise
- ■ **Information Resource**: includes all files, libraries, catalogues, copies of publications, and so on
- ■ **Classification**: includes all classification schemes (entity classes with names ending in "Type," "Class," "Category," "Reason," and so on)
- ■ **Relationship**: includes all relationships between parties other than agreements, all roles played by parties with respect to events (e.g., **Claimant**, **Complainant**), agreements (**Insurance Policy Beneficiary**) or locations (e.g., **Workplace Supervisor**), and any other relationships of interest to the enterprise (except equivalences, which are Business Rules)
- ■ **Detail**: includes all detail records (e.g., **Order Line**) and all attributes other than Business Rules identified by the enterprise as being important (e.g., **Account Balance**, **Annual Sales Total**)

A number of things should be noted in connection with this list:

1. A particular enterprise may not need all the top-level classes in this list and may need others not in this list, but you should avoid creating too many top-level classes (more than 20 is probably too many).
2. Terms listed as included within each top-level class are not meant to be exhaustive.
3. Object classes may include low-level subtypes that would never appear as tables in a logical data model or even entity classes in a conceptual data model.
4. Relationships do not have to be "many-to-many."
5. Attributes may include calculated or derived attributes, such as aggregates (e.g., **Total Order Amount**).

9.7.3 **Developing an Object Class Hierarchy**

Terms (or object classes) are best gathered in a series of workshops, each covering a specific business function or process, with the appropriate stakeholders in attendance. Remember that any term offered by a stakeholder, however it might eventually be classified, should be recorded. This should be done in a manner visible to all participants (a whiteboard or in a document or spreadsheet on a computer attached to a projector). Rather than attempt to achieve an agreed definition and position in the hierarchy of each term as it is added, it is better to just list them in the first instance, and then, after a reasonable number have been gathered, group terms by their most appropriate top-level class.

Definitions should then be sought for each term within a top-level class before moving on to the next top-level class. In this way it is easier to ensure that definitions of different classes within a given top-level class do not overlap.

Some terms may be already defined in existing documentation, such as policy manuals or legislation. For each of these, identify the corresponding documentation if possible, or delegate an appropriate workshop participant to examine the documentation and supply the required definition. Other terms may lend themselves to an early consensus within the workshop group as a whole. If, however, discussion takes more than five or ten minutes and no consensus is in sight, move on to the next item, and, before the end of the workshop, deal with outstanding terms in one of the following ways:

1. Assign terms to breakout groups within the workshop to agree on definitions and report back to the plenary group with their results
2. Assign terms to appropriate workshop participants (or groups thereof) to agree on definitions and report back to the modeler for inclusion in the next iteration of the Object Class Hierarchy
3. Agree that the modeler will take on the job of coming up with a suggested definition and include it in the next iteration.

The key word here is iteration. Workshop results should be fed back as soon as possible to participants. The consolidated Object Class Hierarchy (including results from all workshop groups) should be made available to each participant, instead of, or in addition to, the separate results from that participant's workshop, and each participant should review the hierarchy before attending one or more follow-up workshops in which necessary changes to the hierarchy as perceived by the modeler can be negotiated.

However there is work for the modeler to do before feeding results back:

1. We will usually need to introduce intermediate classes to further organize the object classes within a top-level classification. If, for example, a large

number of **Party Role**s have been identified, we might organize them into intermediate classifications such as **Client (Customer) Role**s, **Enterprise Employee Role**s, and **Third Party Service Provider Role**s. In turn we might further categorize **Enterprise Employee Role**s according to the type of work done, and **Third Party Service Provider Role**s according to the type of service provided.

2. All **Classification** classes should be categorized according to the object classes that they classify. For example, classifications of **Party Role**s (e.g., **Customer Type**) should be grouped under the intermediate class **Party Role Classification** and classifications of **Event**s (e.g., **Transaction Type**) should be grouped under the intermediate class **Event Classification**.

3. If there is more than one **Classification** class associated with a particular object class (e.g., **Claim Type**, **Claim Decision Type,** and **Claim Liability Status** might all classify **Claim**s) then they should be grouped into a common class (e.g., **Claim Classification**). This intermediate class would in turn belong to a higher level intermediate class. In this example, **Claim** might be a subclass of **Event**, in which case **Claim Classification** would be a subclass of **Event Classification**. So we would have a hierarchy from **Classification** to **Event Classification** to **Claim Classification** to **Claim Type**, **Claim Decision Type**, and **Claim Liability Status.**

4. All **Relationship** classes should similarly be categorized by the classes that they associate: relationships between parties grouped under **Inter-Party Relationship**, roles played by parties with respect to events grouped under **Party Event Role**, roles played by parties with respect to agreements grouped under **Party Agreement Role,** and so on.

5. All of these intermediate classes and any other additional classes created by the modeler rather than supplied by stakeholders should be clearly marked as such.

6. Any synonyms identified should be included as facts about classes.

7. All definitions not explicitly agreed on at the workshop should be added.

8. The source of each definition (the name or job title of the person who supplied it or the name of the document from which it was taken) should be included.

Figure 9.3 shows a part of an object class hierarchy using these conventions.

The follow-up workshop will inevitably result in not only changes to definitions (and possibly even names) of classes, but also in reclassification of classes as stakeholders develop more understanding of the exact meaning of each class. The extent to which this occurs will dictate how many

Class	Source	Synonym	Definition
Administrative Area			Any area that may be gazetted or otherwise defined for a particular administrative purpose.
Country	ISO 3166		A country as defined by International Standard ISO 3166:1993(E/F) and subsequent editions.
Jurisdiction			A formally recognized administrative or territorial unit used for the purpose of applying or performing a responsibility. Jurisdictions include States, Territories, and Dominions.
Australian State	GNR	State	A state of Australia.
County	RGD GNR		A basic division of an Australian State, further divided into Parishes, for administrative purposes.
Parish	RGD GNR		An area formed by the division of a county.
Portion	RGD		A land unit capable of separate disposition created by the Crown within the boundaries of a Parish.

Figure 9.3 Part of an object class hierarchy—indentation shows the hierarchical relationships.

additional review cycles are required. In each new published version of the Object Class Hierarchy, it is important to identify:

1. New classes (with those added by the modeler marked as such)
2. Renamed classes
3. New definitions (with the source—person or document—of each definition)
4. Classes moved within the hierarchy (i.e., reclassified)
5. Deleted classes (These are best collected under an additional top-level class named **Deleted Class**.)

Given the highly intensive and iterative nature of this process, we do not recommend a CASE tool for recording and presenting this information, unless it provides direct access to the repository for textual entry of names, definitions, and superclass/subclass associations. We have found that, compared with some commonly-used CASE tools, a spreadsheet not only provides significantly faster data entry and modification facilities but requires significantly less effort in tidying up outputs for presentation back to stakeholders.

9.7.4 Potential Issues

The major issue that we have found arising from this process has been debate about which top-level class a given class really belongs to, and it has been tempting to allow "multiple inheritance" whereby a class is assigned to multiple top-level classes. In most cases in our experience the "class" in question turns out to be, in fact, two different classes. Among the situations in which this issue arises, we have found the same name used by the business for:

- Both types and instances (e.g., **Stock Item**, used for both entries in the stock catalogue and issues of items of stock from the warehouse in response to requisitions)
- Both events and the documents raised to record those events (e.g., **Application for License**)
- Planned or required events or rules about events and the events themselves (e.g., **Crew Member Recertification**, used by an airline for the requirement for regular recertification and the occurrence of a recertification of a particular crew member).

9.7.5 Advantages of the Object Class Hierarchy Technique

We have found that the process we have described inspires a high level of business buy-in, as it is neither too technical nor too philosophical but visibly useful. The use of the general term "object class" provides a useful separation from the terminology of the conceptual data model and does not constrain our freedom to explore alternative data classifications later.

At the enterprise level (see Chapter 17), an object class model can offer significant advantages over traditional E-R-based enterprise data models, particularly as a means of classifying existing data.

9.8 Summary

In requirements gathering, the modeler uses a variety of sources to gain a holistic understanding of the business and its system needs, as well as detailed data requirements. Sources of requirements and ideas include system users, business specialists, system inputs and outputs, existing databases, and process models.

An object class hierarchy can provide a focus for the requirements gathering exercise by enabling stakeholders to focus on data and its definitions without preempting the conceptual model.

Chapter 10
Conceptual Data Modeling

"Our job is to give the client not what he wants, but what he never dreamed he wanted."
- Denys Lasdun, An Architect's Approach to Architecture[1]

"If you want to make an apple pie from scratch, you must first create the universe."
- Carl Sagan

10.1 Designing Real Models

Conceptual data modeling is the central activity in a data modeling project. In this phase we move from requirements to a solution, which will be further developed and tuned in later phases.

In common with other design processes, development of a conceptual data model involves three main stages:

1. Identification of requirements (covered in Chapter 9)
2. Design of solutions
3. Evaluation of the solutions.

This is an iterative process (Figure 10.1). In practice, the initial requirements are never comprehensive or rigorous enough to constrain us to only one possible design. Draft designs will prompt further questions, which will, in turn, lead to new requirements being identified. The architecture analogy is again appropriate. As users, we do not tell an architect the exact dimensions and orientation of each room. Rather we specify broader requirements such as, "We need space for entertaining," and, "We don't want to be disturbed by the children's play when listening to music." If the architect returns with a plan that includes a wine cellar, prompted perhaps by his or her assessment of our lifestyle, we may decide to revise our requirements to include one.

In this chapter, we look at the design and evaluation stages.

The design of conceptual models is the most difficult stage in data model development to learn (and to teach). There is no mechanical transformation from requirements to candidate solutions. Designing a conceptual data model

---

[1]*RIBA Journal, 72(4), 1965*

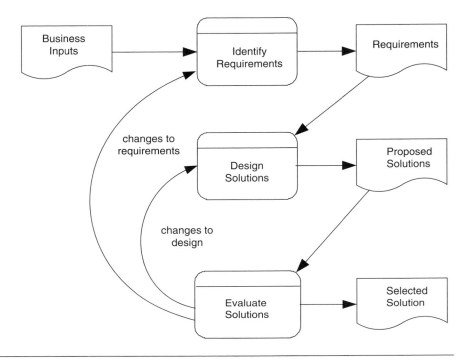

Figure 10.1   Data modeling as a design activity.

from first principles involves conceptualization, abstraction, and possibly creativity, skills that are hard to invoke on a day-to-day basis without considerable practice. Teachers of data modeling frequently find that students who have understood the theory (sometimes in great depth) become "stuck" when faced with the job of developing a real model.

If there is a single secret to getting over the problem of being stuck, it is that data modeling practitioners, like most designers, seldom work from first principles, but adapt solutions that have been used successfully in the past. The development and use of a repertoire of standard solutions ("patterns") is so much a part of practical data modeling that we have devoted a large part of this chapter to it.

We look in some detail at two patterns that occur in most models, but are often poorly handled: hierarchies and one-to-one relationships.

Evaluation of candidate models presents its own set of challenges. Reviews with users and business specialists are an essential part of verifying a data model, particularly as formal statements of user requirements do not normally provide a sufficiently detailed basis for review (as discussed in Section 9.1).

Several years ago, one of us spent some time walking through a relatively simple model with a quite sophisticated user—a recent MBA with exposure to formal systems design techniques—including data modeling. He was fully convinced that the user understood the model, and it was only some years later that the user confessed that her sign-off had been entirely due to her faith that he personally understood her requirements, rather than to her seeing them reflected in the data model.

We can do better than this, and in the second part of this chapter, we focus on a practical technique—business assertions—for describing a model with a set of plain language statements, which can be readily understood and verified by business people whether or not they are familiar with data modeling.

10.2 **Learning from Designers in Other Disciplines**

Once we recognize that we are performing a design task, we achieve at least two things:

1. We gain a better perspective on the nature of the task facing us. On the one hand, design can be intimidating; creating something new seems a more difficult task than describing something that already exists. On the other hand, most of us successfully create designs in other areas every day—be they report layouts or the menu for a dinner party.

2. As a relatively new profession, we can learn from designers in other disciplines. We have leaned heavily on the architecture analogy throughout this book, and for good reason. Time and again this analogy has helped us to solve problems with our own approaches and to communicate the approaches and their rationale to others.

There is a substantial body of literature on how designers work. It is useful not only as a source of ideas, but also for reassurance that what you are doing is reasonable and normal—especially when others are expecting you to proceed in a linear, mechanical manner. Designers' preferences and behavior include:

- Working with a limited "brief": in Chapter 9 we discussed the problem of how much to include in the statement of requirements; many designers prefer to work with a very short brief and to gain understanding from the client's reaction to candidate designs.
- A preference for early involvement with their clients, before the clients have had an opportunity to start solving the problem themselves.
- The use of patterns at all levels from overall design to individual details.
- The heavy use of diagrams to aid thinking (as well as communication).

- The deliberate production of alternatives, though this is by no means universal: many designers focus on one solution that seems "right" while recognizing that other solutions are possible.
- The use of a central idea ("primary generator") to help focus the thinking process: for example, an architect might focus on "seminar rooms off a central hub"; a data modeler might focus on "parties involved in each transaction."

10.3 **Starting the Modeling**

Despite the availability of documentation tools, the early work in data modeling is usually done with whiteboard and marker pen. Most experienced data modelers initially draw only entity classes and partly annotated relationships. Crow's feet are usually shown, but optionality and names are only added if they serve to clarify an obviously difficult or ambiguous concept. The idea is to keep the focus on the big picture, moving fairly quickly and exploring alternatives, rather than becoming bogged down in detail.

We cannot expect our users to have the data model already in their minds, ready to be extracted with a few well-directed questions ("What things do you want to keep data about? What data do you want to keep about them? How are those things related?"). Unfortunately, much that is written and taught about data modeling makes this very naive assumption. Experienced data modelers do not try to solicit a data model directly, but take a holistic approach. Having established a broad understanding of the client's requirements, they then propose designs for data structures to meet them.

This puts the responsibility for coming up with the entity classes squarely on the data modeler's shoulders. In the first four chapters, we looked at a number of techniques that generated new entity classes: normalization produces new tables by disaggregating existing tables, and supertyping and subtyping produce new entity classes through generalizing and specializing existing entity classes. But we have to start with something!

It is at this point that an Object Class Hierarchy, as described in Section 9.7, delivers one of its principal advantages. Rather than starting with a blank whiteboard, the Object Class Hierarchy can be used as a source of the key entity classes and relationships.

To design a data model from "first principles," we generalize (more precisely, *classify*) instances of things of interest to the business into entity classes. We have a lot of choice as to how we do this, even given the constraint that we do not want the same fact to be represented by more than one entity class. Some classification schemes will be much more useful than others, but, not surprisingly, there is no rule for finding the *best* scheme, or even recognizing it if we do find it. Instead, we have a set of guidelines that are essentially the same as those we use for selecting good supertypes (Chapter 4). The most important of these is that we group together things that the business handles in a similar manner (and about which it will, therefore, need to keep similar data).

This might seem a straightforward task. On the contrary, "similarity" can be a very subjective concept, often obscured by the organization's structure and procedures. For example, an insurance company may have assigned responsibility for handling accident and life insurance policies to separate divisions, which have then established quite different procedures and terminology for handling them. It may take a considerable amount of investigation to determine the underlying degree of similarity.

10.4 **Patterns and Generic Models**

10.4.1 **Using Patterns**

Experienced data modelers rarely develop their designs from first principles. Like other designers, they draw on a "library" of proven structures and structural components, some of them formally documented, others remembered from experience or observation. We already have a few of these from the examples in earlier chapters. For example, we know the general way of representing a many-to-many relationship or a simple hierarchy. In Part III, you will find data modeling structures for dealing with (for example) the time dimension, data warehousing, and the higher normal forms. These structures are patterns that you can come to use and recognize.

Until relatively recently (as recently as the first edition of this book in 1994) there was little acknowledgment of the importance of patterns. Most texts treated data modeling as something to be done from first principles, and there were virtually no published libraries of data modeling patterns to which practitioners could refer. What patterns there were tended to exist in the minds of experienced data modelers (sometimes without the data modelers being aware of it).

That picture has since changed substantially. A number of detailed data models—generally aimed at particular industries such as banking, health care, or oil—can now be purchased or, in some cases, have been made available free of charge through industry bodies. Many of these provide precise definitions and coding schemes for attributes to facilitate data comparison and exchange. Some useful books of more general data modeling patterns have been published.[2] And the object-oriented theorists and practitioners, with their focus on reuse, have contributed much to the theory and body of experience around patterns.[3] The practicing data modeler

---

[2]Refer to "Further Reading" at the end of this book.
[3]Fowler, M., *Analysis Patterns: Reusable Object Models*, Addison-Wesley (1997).

should be in a position to use general patterns from texts such as this book, application-specific patterns from books and industry, patterns from their own experience, and, possibly, organization-specific patterns recorded in an enterprise data model.

10.4.2 **Using a Generic Model**

In practice, we usually try to find a generic model that broadly meets the users' requirements, then tailor it to suit the particular application, drawing on standard structures and adapting structures from other models as opportunities arise. For example, we may need to develop a data model to support human resource management. Suppose we have seen successful human resources models in the past, and have (explicitly or just mentally) generalized these to produce a generic model, shown in part in Figure 10.2.

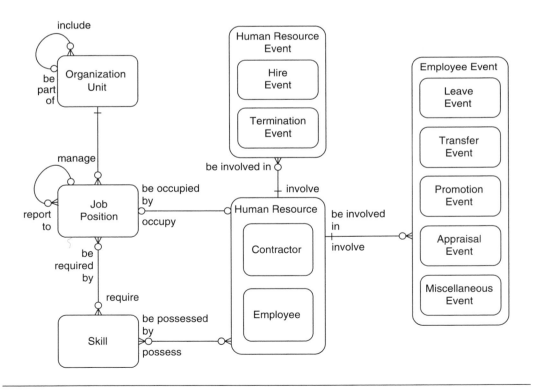

Figure 10.2 Generic human resources model.

The generic model suggests some questions, initially to establish scope (and our credibility as modelers knowledgeable about the data issues of human resource management). For example:

"Does your organization have a formally-defined hierarchy of job positions?" "Yes, but they're outside the scope of this project." We can remove this part of the model.

"Do you need to keep information about leave taken by employees?" "Yes, and one of our problems is to keep track of leave taken without approval, such as strikes." We will retain **Leave Event**, possibly subtyped, and add **Leave Approval**. Perhaps **Leave Application** with a status of approved or not approved would be better, or should this be an attribute of **Leave Event**? Some more focused questions will help with this.

"Could Leave be approved but not taken?" "Certainly." *"Can one application cover multiple periods of leave?"* "Not currently. Could our new system support this?"

And so on. Having a generic model in place as a starting point helps immensely, just as architects are helped by being familiar with some generic "family home" patterns. Incidentally, asking an experienced modeler for his or her set of generic models is likely to produce a blank response. Experienced modelers generally carry their generic models in their heads rather than on paper and are often unaware that they use such models at all.

10.4.3 **Adapting Generic Models from Other Applications**

Sometimes we do not have an explicit generic model available but can draw an analogy with a model from a different field. Suppose we are developing a model to support the management of public housing. The users have provided some general background on the problem in their own terms. They are in the business of providing low-cost accommodation, and their objectives include being able to move applicants through the waiting list quickly, providing accommodation appropriate to clients' needs, and ensuring that the rent is collected.

We have not worked in this field before, so we cannot draw on a model specific to public housing. In looking for a suitable generic model, we might pick up on the central importance of the rental agreement. We recall an insurance model in which the central entity class was **Policy**—an agreement of a different kind, but nevertheless one involving clients and the organization (Figure 10.3). This model suggests an analogous model for rental agreement management (Figure 10.4).

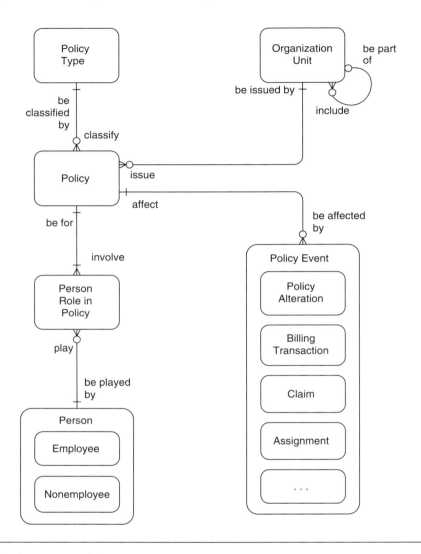

Figure 10.3   Insurance model.

We proceed to test and flesh out the model with the business specialist:

"Who are the parties to a rental agreement? Only persons? Or families or organizations?" "Only individuals (tenants) can be parties to a rental agreement, but other occupiers of the house are noted on the agreement. We don't need to keep track of family relationships."

"Are individual employees involved in rental agreements? In what role?" "Yes, each agreement has to be authorized by one of our staff."

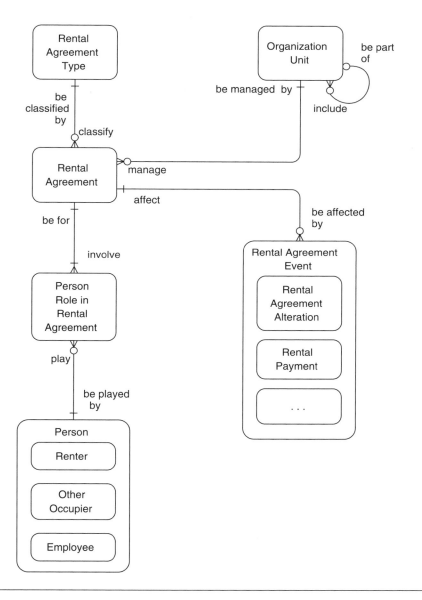

Figure 10.4   Rental agreement model based on insurance model.

"How do we handle changes to rental agreements? Do we need to keep a history of changes?" "Yes, it's particularly important that we keep a history of any changes to rent. Sometimes we establish a separate agreement for payment of arrears."

What do we do here? Can we treat a rental arrears agreement as a subtype of **Agreement**? We can certainly try the idea.

"How do rental arrears agreements differ from ordinary rental agreements?" "They always relate back to a basic rental agreement. Otherwise, administration is much the same—sending the bill and collecting the scheduled repayments."
Let's check the cardinality of the relationship:

"Can we have more than one rental arrears agreement for a given basic rental agreement?" "No, although we may modify the original rental arrears agreement later."

The answer provides some support for treating rental arrears agreements similarly to basic rental agreements. Now we can look for further similarities to test the value of our subtyping and refine the model.

"Do we have different types of rental arrears agreements? Are people directly involved in rental arrears agreements, or are they always the same as those involved in the basic rental agreement?"

And so on. Figure 10.5 shows an enhanced model including the **Rental Arrears Agreement** concept.

10.4.4 Developing a Generic Model

As we gained experience with using this model in a variety of business situations, we would develop a generic "agreement" model, rather than drawing analogies or going through the two-stage process of generalizing from **Policy** to **Agreement**, then specializing to **Rental Agreement**.

With this model in mind, we can approach data modeling problems with the question: "What sort of agreements are we dealing with?" In some cases, the resulting model will be reasonably conventional, as with our housing example, where perhaps the only unusual feature is the handling of arrears repayment agreements. In other cases, approaching a problem from the perspective of agreements might lead to a new way of looking at it. The new perspective may offer an elegant approach; on the other hand, the result of "shoe-horning" a problem to fit the generic model may be inelegant, inflexible, and difficult to understand. For example, the "agreement" perspective could be useful in modeling foreign currency dealing, where

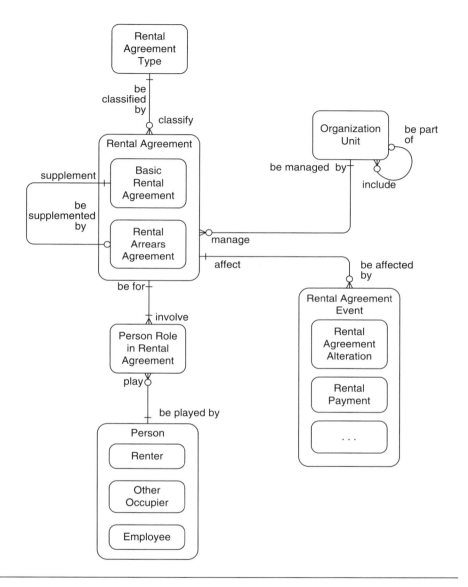

Figure 10.5   Inclusion of rental arrears agreement.

deals could be modeled as Agreements, but less useful in a retail sales model. Certainly a sale constitutes an agreement to purchase, but the concepts of alterations, parties to agreements, and so on may be less relevant in this context.

Generic models can also be suggested by answers to the "What is our business?" type of question. Business people addressing the question are consciously trying to cut through the detail to the "essence" of the business, and the answers can be helpful in establishing a stable generic model. For example, during the development of a model to support money market dealing, a business specialist offered the explanation that the fundamental objective was to "trade cash flows." This very simple unifying idea (a "primary generator" in design theory) suggested a generic model based on the entity classes **Deal** and **Cash Flow**, and ultimately provided the basis for a flexible and innovative system. Often these insights will come not from those who are close to the problem and burdened with details of current procedures, but from more senior managers, staff who have recently learned the business, consultants, and even textbooks.

Even among very experienced modelers, there is a tendency to adopt an "all purpose" generic model. We have seen some particularly inelegant data models resulting from trying to force such a model to fit the problem. In our housing model, for example, there is unlikely to be much value in including **Employment Agreement** and **Supplier Agreement** under the **Agreement** supertype, unless we can establish that the business treats these entity classes in a common way. The high-level classes, which we suggest for developing an object class hierarchy in Section 9.7, should only carry over to the conceptual model if they correspond to entity classes of genuine use to the business *at that level of generalization.*

Sometimes an organization will develop a generic enterprise model covering its primary business activities, with the intention of coordinating data modeling at the project level (data models of this kind are discussed in Chapter 17). Such a model may be an excellent representation of the core business but inappropriate for support functions such as human resource management or asset management.

The best approach is to consciously build up your personal library of generic models and to experiment with more than one alternative when tackling problems in practice. This is not only a good antidote to the "shoehorning" problem; it also encourages exploration of different approaches and often provides new insights into the problem. Frequently, the final model will be based primarily on one generic model but will include ideas that have come from exploring others.

10.4.5 **When There Is Not a Generic Model**

From time to time, we encounter situations for which we cannot find a suitable generic model as a starting point. Such problems should be viewed, of course, as opportunities to develop new generic models. There are essentially two approaches, the first "bottom up" and the second "top down." We look at these in the following sections.

10.5   **Bottom-Up Modeling**

With the bottom-up approach, you initially develop a very "literal" model, based on existing data structures and terminology, then use subtyping and supertyping to move toward other options.

We touched on this technique in Chapter 4, but it is so valuable that it is worth working through an example that is complex enough to illustrate it properly. Figure 10.6 shows a form containing information about products sold by an air conditioning systems retailer.

Figure 10.7 is a straightforward model produced by normalizing the repeating groups contained in the form (note that we have already departed from strictly literal modeling by generalizing the specific types of tax, delivery, and service charges).

There is a reasonably obvious opportunity to generalize the various charges and discounts into a supertype entity class **Additional Charge or Discount**. In turn, this decision would suggest separating Insurance Charge from **Product**, even though it is not a repeating group, in order to represent all price variations consistently (Figure 10.8).

We could also consider including Unit Price and renaming the supertype **Price Component,** depending on how similarly the handling of Unit Price was to that of the price variations.

Looking at the subtypes of **Additional Charge or Discount**, we might consider an intermediate level of subtyping, to distinguish charges and discounts directly related to sale of the original product from stand-alone services (Figure 10.9).

This, in turn, might prompt a more adventurous generalization; why not broaden our definition of **Product** to embrace services as well? We would then need to change the name of the original entity class **Product** to (say) **Physical Product**. Figure 10.10 shows the result.

Note that we started with a very straightforward model, based on the original form. This is the beauty of the technique; we do not need to be creative "on the fly" but can concentrate initially on getting a model that

Product No.:	450TE	Volume	2-4		5%
Type:	Air Conditioning Unit– Industrial	Discount	5-10		10%
Unit Price:	$420		Over 10		12%
Sales Tax:	3% (except VT/ND: 2%)	Service	09	Install	$35
Delivery Charge:	$10	Charges	01	Yearly Service	$40
Remote Delivery:	$15		05	Safety Check	$10
Insurance:	5%				

Figure 10.6   Air conditioning product form.

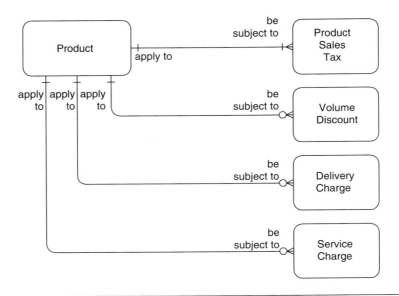

Figure 10.7   Literal model of air conditioning products.

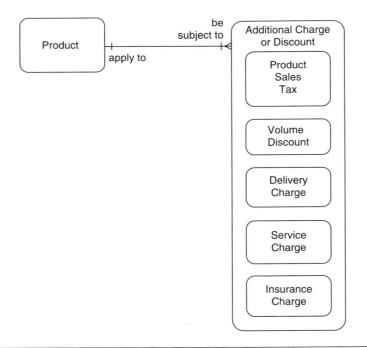

Figure 10.8   Generalizing additional charges.

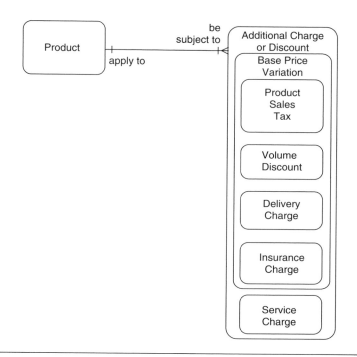

Figure 10.9 Separating service charges.

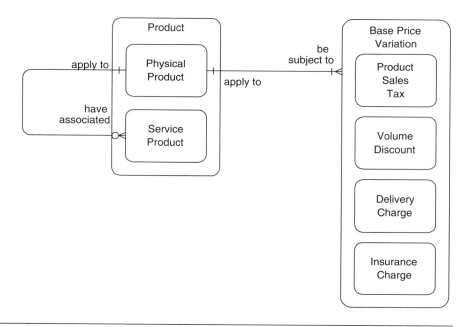

Figure 10.10 Redefining product to include services.

is complete and nonredundant, and on clarifying how data is currently represented. Later we can break down the initial entity classes and reassemble them to explore new ways of organizing the data. The approach is particularly useful if we are starting from existing data files.

Note also that we ended up with a new definition of **Product**. Ideally, we would never give more than one meaning to the same word, even over time. However the desire to keep the model reasonably approachable through use of familiar terminology often means that a term will need to change meaning as we develop it. We could have encountered the same situation with **Service Product**, had we decided to regard delivery as a type of service. Just remember to keep the definitions up to date!

10.6 **Top-Down Modeling**

The top-down approach to an unfamiliar problem is an extreme version of the generic model approach; we simply use a model that is generic enough to cover at least the main entity classes in any business or organization. The ultimate extreme is that suggested in many texts: by asking, "What 'things' are of interest to the business?" we are effectively starting from the single entity class **Thing**, and looking for subtypes. We can usually be a little more specific than this!

An object class hierarchy developed as part of the requirements phase (as described in Section 9.7) can provide an excellent basis, starting with the highest level classes defined by the business.

Just be aware that this technique used by itself may not challenge current views of data. If you want to explore alternatives, it can be useful to experiment with alternative supertypes and intermediate classifications, once you have finished the top-down identification of entity classes.

10.7 **When the Problem Is Too Complex**

Sometimes it is possible to be overwhelmed by the complexity of the business problem. Perhaps we are attempting to model the network managed by a large and diverse telecommunications provider. Unless we are very experienced in the area, we will be quickly bogged down in technical detail, terminology, and traditional divisions of responsibilities. A useful strategy in these circumstances is to develop a first-cut generic model as a basis for classifying the detail.

Paradoxically, a good way to achieve this is by initially *narrowing* our view. We select a specific (and, as best as we can judge) typical area and model it in isolation. We then generalize this to produce a generic model, which we then use as a basis for investigating other areas. In this way we are able to focus on similarities and differences and on modifying and fleshing out our base model.

Obviously, the choice of initial area is important. We are looking for business activities that are representative of those in other areas. In other words we anticipate that when generalized they will produce a useful generic model. There is a certain amount of circular thinking here but, in practice, selection is not too difficult. Many organizations are structured around products, customer types, or geographic locations. Often, each organization unit has developed its own procedures and terminology. Selecting an organizational unit, then generalizing out these factors, is usually a good start. Often the *second* area that we examine will provide some good pointers on what can usefully be generalized.

In our telecommunications example, we might start by modeling the part of the network that links customers to local exchanges or, perhaps, only that part administered by a particular local branch. Part of an initial model is shown in Figure 10.11.

Testing this model against the requirements of the Trunk Network Division, which has an interest in optical fiber and its termination points, suggests that **Cable Pair** can usefully be generalized to **Physical Bearer**, and **Cable Connection Point** to **Connection Point,** to take account of alternative technologies (Figure 10.12).

But we are now able to ask some pointed questions of the next division: What sort of bearers do you use? How do they terminate or join?

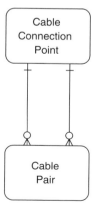

Figure 10.11 Local exchange network model.

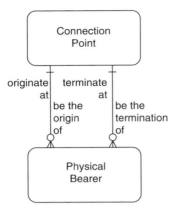

Figure 10.12 Generalized network model.

This is a very simple generic model, but not much simpler than many that we have found invaluable in coming to grips with complex problems. And its use is not confined to telecommunications networks. What about other networks, such as electricity supply, railways, or electrical circuits? Or, more creatively, could the model be applied to a retail distribution network?

10.8 Hierarchies, Networks, and Chains

In this section and the next, we take a detour from the generalities of conceptual modeling for a closer look at some common structures that we introduced in Section 3.5.4.

Hierarchies, networks, and chains are all modeled using self-referencing (single entity) relationships (Figure 10.13). Note that these inevitably have important business rules constraining how each member of the hierarchy may relate to others. These are discussed in Section 14.6.1.

The more we generalize our entity classes, the more we encounter these structures.

Figure 10.14 shows an organization structure at two levels of generalization (see page 292).

If we choose to implement the model using **Branch**, **Department**, and **Section** entity classes, we do not require any self-referencing relationships. But if we choose the higher level of generalization, the relationships between branches, departments, and sections become self-referencing relationships among organization units.

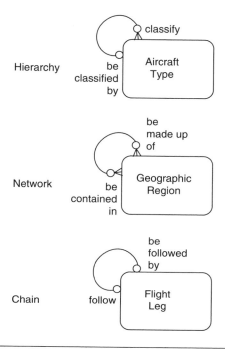

Figure 10.13 Self-referencing relationships.

10.8.1 **Hierarchies**

Hierarchies are characterized by each instance of the entity class having any number of subordinates but only one superior of the same entity class. Accordingly, we use one-to-many relationships to represent them.

Examples of the types of hierarchies we need to model in practice are

"Contains"—e.g., **System** may contain (component) **System**s; **Location** may contain (smaller) **Location**s.

"Classifies"—e.g., **Equipment Type** may classify (more specific) **Equipment Type**s; **Employee Type** may classify (more specific) **Employee Type**s.

"Controls"—e.g., **Organization Unit** may control (subordinate) **Organization Unit**s; **Network Node** may control (subordinate) **Network Node**s.

Implementation of one-to-many self-referencing relationships is straightforward and was covered in Sections 2.8.5 and 3.5.4. (Basically, we hold a foreign key such as "Superior Organization Unit.")

Programming against such structures is less straightforward if we want to retain the full flexibility of the structure (in particular, the unlimited number of levels). Some programming languages do not provide good

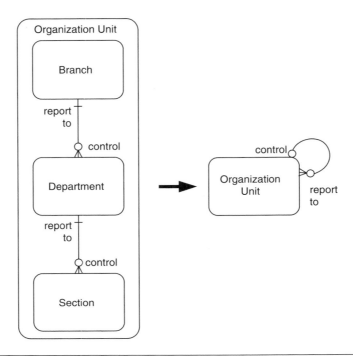

Figure 10.14 Self-referencing relationship resulting from generalization.

support for recursion. Screen and report design is also more difficult if we want to allow for a variable number of levels.

The important thing here, as always, is to make the options clear by showing the subtypes and their explicit relationships as well as the more general entity class. One way of limiting the number of levels is to use a structured primary key, as discussed in Section 6.7.

Note that hierarchies may not be of consistent depth. For example, if not all branches are divided into departments and not all departments are divided into sections, the organization unit hierarchy in Figure 10.14 will be one, two, or three deep in different places. If the DBMS does not provide a specialized extension for hierarchy navigation, such hierarchies can be difficult to query. In this case a query might have to be a union of three separate queries, one to handle each depth.

A neat solution to this problem is provided if each organization unit without a parent holds its own primary key, rather than null in the foreign key representing the self-referencing relationship. It is then possible to write a simple (nonunion) query that assumes the full depth (in this case three levels).

Should you be concerned about such implementation issues during the conceptual modeling phase? Strictly, the answer is *no*, but we have found many data modelers to be a little cavalier in their use of self-referencing relationships, sometimes to represent quite stable two- or three-level hierarchies. It is worth being aware that hierarchies may be difficult to query and that you may therefore be called upon to justify your decisions and perhaps provide some suggestions as to how the model can be queried.

10.8.2 Networks (Many-to-Many Relationships)

Networks differ from hierarchies in that each entity instance may have more than one superior. We therefore model them using many-to-many relationships, which can be resolved as discussed in Section 3.5.4.

Like hierarchical structures, they are easy to draw and not too difficult to implement, but they can provide plenty of headaches for programmers and users of query languages. Again, modelers frequently fail to recognize underlying structures that could lead to a simpler system. In particular, multiple hierarchies are often generalized to networks without adequate consideration. For example, it might be possible for an employee to have more than one superior, which suggests a network structure. But further investigation might show that individual employees could report to at most three superiors—their manager as defined in the organization hierarchy, a project manager, and a technical mentor. This structure could be more accurately represented by three hierarchies (Figure 10.15) leaving us the option of direct implementation using three foreign keys or generalization to a many-to-many relationship.

Be careful in defining self-referencing many-to-many relationships to ensure that they are asymmetric. The relationship must have a different name in each direction. Figure 10.16 shows the reason. If we name the relationship "in partnership with," we will end up recording each partnership twice. We discuss symmetric and asymmetric relationships in more detail in Section 14.6.1.

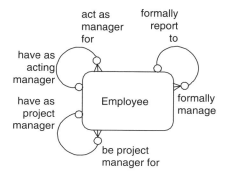

Figure 10.15 Multiple hierarchies.

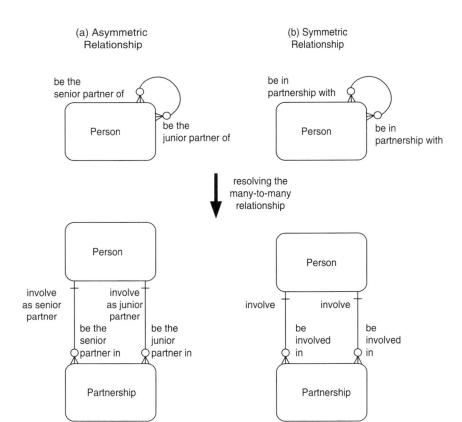

Figure 10.16 Symmetry leading to duplication.

Partnership		
Senior Partner	Junior Partner	Date Established
Anne	Mary	6/2/1953
Fred	Sue	3/8/1982
Anne	Jane	7/5/1965

Partnership		
Person 1	Person 2	Date Established
Anne	Mary	6/2/1953
Fred	Sue	3/8/1982
Anne	Jane	7/5/1965
Mary	Anne	6/2/1953
Sue	Fred	3/8/1982
Jane	Anne	7/5/1965

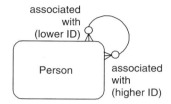

Figure 10.17 Deliberate creation of asymmetry.

Sometimes we need to impose this asymmetry on a symmetric world, as in Figure 10.17. Here, we deliberately make the "associated with" relationship asymmetric, using an identifier (**Person ID**) as a means of determining which role each entity instance plays. The identifier chosen needs to be stable or we will have some complicated processing to do when values change. (Stability of identifiers is discussed in Section 6.2.4.)

10.8.3 **Chains (One-to-One Relationships)**

Chains (sometimes called *linked lists*) occur far less frequently than hierarchies and networks. In a chain, each entity instance is associated with a maximum of one other instance of the same entity class in either direction. Chains are therefore modeled using one-to-one relationships. Implementation using a foreign key presents us with the same problem as for transferable one-to-one relationships; we end up implementing a one-to-*many* relationship whether we like it or not. Other mechanisms, such as unique indexes on the foreign key attribute, will be needed to enforce the one-to-one constraint.

A frequently used alternative is to group the participants in each chain and to introduce a sequence number to record the order (Figure 10.18).

This is another example of deviating from the conventional implementation of relationships, but, unlike some of the other variations we have looked at, it is usually well supported by DBMSs. Inserting a new instance in the chain will involve resequencing—an inelegant option unless we regard the use of floating point sequence numbers (i.e., using decimals) as elegant.

10.9 **One-to-One Relationships**

There is little to stop us from taking any entity class and splitting it into two or more entity classes linked by a one-to-one relationship, provided (for the

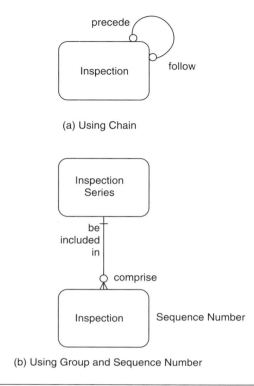

(a) Using Chain

(b) Using Group and Sequence Number

Figure 10.18 Chaining and grouping.

sake of nonredundancy) that each nonkey attribute appears in only one of the new entity classes.

The main consequence of splitting an entity class in this way is that inserting and deleting full rows in the resulting database becomes a little more complicated. We now have to update two or more tables instead of one. The sacrifice in simplicity and elegance means that we should have a good reason for introducing one-to-one relationships. Once again, there are few absolute rules, but several useful guidelines.

10.9.1 **Distinct Real-World Concepts**

Be very wary of combining entity classes that represent concepts commonly accepted as distinct just because the relationship between them appears to be one-to-one (e.g., **Person** and **Passport**, **Driver** and **Racing Car**), particularly in the earlier stages of modeling. Closer examination may suggest supertypes in which only one of the pair participates, or even that the relationship is actually one-to-many or many-to-many. Combining the entity classes will hide these possibilities.

The entity class **Telephone Exchange** provides a nice example; chances are it can profitably be broken into entity classes representing locations, nodes, switching equipment, buildings, and possibly more.

In many of these cases, transferability (as discussed below) will dictate that the entity classes remain separate. Relationships that are optional in both directions suggest entity classes that are independently important. And look also at the cardinality; could we envisage a change to the business that would make the relationship one-to-many or many-to-many?

10.9.2 Separating Attribute Groups

In Section 4.13.2 we discussed the situation in which a group of attributes would be either applicable or not applicable to a particular entity instance. For example, in a **Client** entity, the attributes Incorporation Date, Company Registration No, and Employee Count might only be applicable if the client was a company rather than a person. We saw that this situation suggested a sub-typing strategy—in this case, subtyping **Client** into **Company Client** and **Personal Client** to represent the "all applicable or none applicable" rule.

But sometimes we can better handle an attribute group by removing it to a separate entity class. For example, we might have a number of attributes associated with a client's credit rating—perhaps Rating, Source, Last Update Date, Reason for Check. If these were recorded for only some clients, we could model two subtypes: **Client with Credit Rating** and **Client without Credit Rating**. But this seems less satisfactory than the previous example. For a start, a given client could migrate from one entity class to another when a credit rating was acquired. An alternative is to model a separate **Credit Rating** entity class, linked to the **Client** entity class through a one-to-one relationship (Figure 10.19). Note the optional and mandatory symbols, showing that a client *may* have a credit rating.

Which is the better approach? The subtyping approach is based on specialization, the one-to-one relationship on disaggregation, so they are

Figure 10.19 Separate entity class for credit rating attributes.

fundamentally different. But both allow us to represent the constraint that the attribute group applies to only certain instances. A few guidelines will help.

Look at the name of the attribute group. Does it suggest an entity class in its own right (e.g., **Credit Rating**) or a set of data items that applies only to certain stable subtypes (e.g., additional company data)? In the first case, we would prefer a one-to-one relationship—in the second, subtypes.

In Section 4.13.5 we introduced the guideline that real-world instances should not migrate from one subtype to another—or at least that such subtypes would not remain as tables in the logical model. A company will not become a person, but a client may acquire a credit rating. So, the "never applicable to this instance" situation suggests subtyping; the "not currently applicable to this instance" situation suggests the one-to-one approach.

Remember also that our subtyping rules restrict us to nonoverlapping subtypes. If there is more than one relevant attribute group, we will have trouble with the subtyping approach. But there is no limit to the number of one-to-one relationships that an entity class can participate in. This is a good technique to bear in mind when faced with alternative useful breakdowns into subtypes based on attribute groups.

10.9.3 **Transferable One-to-One Relationships**

Transferable one-to-one relationships should always be modeled as such and never combined into a single entity class. Figure 10.20 shows a transferable one-to-one relationship between parts and bins. If we were to combine the two entity classes, then transferring parts from one bin to another would involve not only updating **Bin No**, but all other attributes "belonging to" the bin.

Another way of looking at transferability is that the relationship will be many-to-many over time.

Figure 10.20 is an excellent counterexample to the popular view that one-to-one relationships that are mandatory in both directions should always be reduced to a single entity class. In fact, we may want to model *three* entity classes. Suppose that **Bin Capacity** was defined as the number of

Figure 10.20 Transferable one-to-one relationship.

parts that could be stored in a bin (and could not be calculated from the attributes of **Bin** and **Part**). Should we now hold Bin Capacity as an attribute of **Part** or of **Bin**? Updating the attribute when a part moves from one bin to another is untidy. We might want to consider modeling a separate entity class with a key of Part No + Bin No as the most elegant solution to the problem.

We discuss this example from a normalization perspective in Section 13.5.

10.9.4   Self-Referencing One-to-One Relationships

Self-referencing one-to-one relationships cannot be collapsed into a single entity class. These were discussed in Section 10.8.3.

10.9.5   Support for Creativity

If splitting an entity class or combining entity classes linked by a one-to-one relationship helps to develop a new and potentially useful model of the business area, then there is no need for further justification. (Of course, the professional modeler will try to look behind his or her intuition to understand the original motivation for proposing the split—e.g., are there really two concepts that the business handles differently?)

The value of one-to-one relationships in fostering creativity is best illustrated by an example. Figure 10.21 shows a simple banking model, including provision for regular transfers of funds from one account to another.

There does not appear to be much scope for generalization or specialization here. But there is an opportunity to break **Account** into two parts— the "accounting part," which is basically the balance, and the "contractual part," which covers interest rates, fees, and so forth—giving us the model in Figure 10.22. We now have some more material for generalization. We might

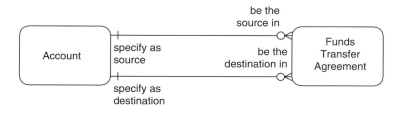

Figure 10.21 Funds transfer model.

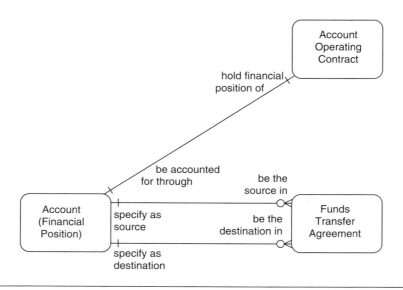

Figure 10.22 Separating components of account.

choose to regard both account operating contracts and funds transfer agreements as *agreements* between the bank and the customer (Figure 10.23); we are now on our way to exploring a new view of data. Many banks have, in fact, implemented systems based on this new view, usually after a far longer and more painful creative process than described here!

Of course, you do not need to use one-to-one relationships to arrive at a new view. But they often provide a starting point and can be particularly useful "after the event" in showing how a new model relates to the old. But on what basis do we decide to break an entity class into two entity classes linked by a one-to-one relationship? Or, conversely, on what basis do we combine the entity classes participating in a one-to-one relationship?

10.10 **Developing Entity Class Definitions**

Definitions, even if initially very rough, should be noted as entity classes are identified, and written up more fully at the end of each session or day. It is surprising how much disagreement can arise overnight!

One useful way of getting to a first-cut definition is to write down a few candidate subtypes or examples, some of which are expected to fit the ultimate definition, and some of which are expected to be outside the

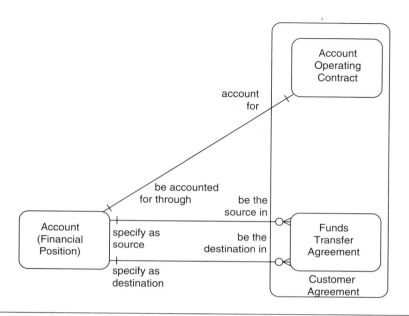

Figure 10.23 Generalizing customer agreements.

definition or "borderline." Then take a vote of participants in the modeling session: include or exclude? This is a very effective way of highlighting areas of agreement and disagreement, and it often produces some surprises. For the entity class **Asset,** we might suggest **Building**, **Vehicle**, **Consumable**, **Employee**, **Cash on Hand**, and **Bank Account Balance** as potential subtypes. A vote might unanimously support inclusion of **Building**, **Vehicle**, **Cash,** and **Bank Account Balance** and exclusion of **Employee**, but disagreement may arise concerning **Consumable**. Further discussion might indicate that some participants were assuming a strict accounting definition of asset, while others (perhaps unfamiliar with accounting) have taken a more flexible view. Once any disagreements are resolved, the examples can be included permanently in the definition.

We provide some rules for forming entity class definitions in Section 10.18.2.1.

10.11 **Handling Exceptions**

One of the frustrations of data modeling is to produce a model that seems to handle every case except one or two. In general we should welcome these exceptions. Better to discover them now than to have them appear as new requirements after the database is built. Usually we face a choice:

1. Make the model more flexible by generalizing the structures to accommodate the exceptions. This often makes the model more difficult to understand by introducing obscure terminology and may make the common cases more complicated to specify and process.
2. Add new structures specifically to cope with the exceptions. The result may be a more complex model and less elegant processing when common cases and exceptions need to be handled together (e.g., in calculating totals).
3. Optimize for the common situation, and accept that exceptions will not be as well handled. Perhaps most wine can be classified as being from one vintage only or from unspecified vintages ("nonvintage"), but a very few wines are blends from specific years. We could record these exceptions with a vintage year of (say) "2001/2003"—possibly a reasonable compromise between complexity of structure and processing. (You might find it a useful exercise to reflect on how you would explain the implications of this choice to a business stakeholder.)

But sometimes the exceptions are historical and unlikely to recur. In these situations, the best decision may require intervention at the business level. Perhaps those few unusual insurance policies can be paid out at less cost to the business than that of accommodating them in the information system. Perhaps they could be handled outside the computerized system. This solution may be attractive from an operational, day-to-day, processing perspective, but it can play havoc with reporting as the exceptions have to be "added in." It is the data modeler's duty to suggest these options, rather than assuming that every problem requires a data modeling solution.

The option of deferring the exceptions to a later stage of systems development is usually unrealistic, though often proposed as an easy way to avoid facing the problem. If the data model cannot handle the exceptions from the outset, we will not be able to accommodate them later without database changes and probable disruption to existing programs.

10.12 **The Right Attitude**

We began this first part of the chapter by looking at some lessons from design in general. We conclude with a look at "attitude," specifically in the context of data modeling.

We are indebted to Clare Atkins of Nelson Marlborough Institute of Technology in New Zealand—who has taught data modeling for many years—for suggesting some of the factors that make up a good attitude to the data modeling task.

10.12.1 **Being Aware**

A big part of improving your modeling skill and being able to explain your decisions is simply being conscious of what you are doing. As you model, it is worth asking:

- What process am I following?
- What heuristics am I using?
- What patterns am I using?
- What do I not know yet? Where am I guessing?
- What have I done that I could use again? (Write it down!)
- How did I do? What would I do differently next time?

If you want to be forced to do all of these things, take any opportunity to teach an "apprentice" modeler and explain to him or her what you are doing as you go. Meetings with a mentor or experienced modeler in a quality assurance role can also help.

10.12.2 **Being Creative**

If we have not stressed it enough already, modeling is a creative process. You need to ask:

- Am I deliberately creating alternative models, or am I getting "anchored" on one design?
- Have I stepped back from the problem, or am I still modeling the traditional view?
- Have I "fallen in love" with a particular design at the expense of others?
- Am I trying to force this model to fit a pattern?
- Why do I prefer this design to another?
- Have I asked for a second or third opinion and opened my mind to it?

10.12.3 **Analyzing or Designing**

Data modeling is, overall, a design activity, but it includes the task of understanding requirements. There is a time to ask and to listen, a time to propose, and even a time to persuade. What is important is recognizing which you are doing (analysis or design) to ensure that adequate attention is given to both. Literal modeling (the model *is* the user requirement) is one extreme;

uninformed design (the model *ignores* the user requirement) is the other. The key questions are:

- Am I balancing analysis and design?
- Am I analyzing or designing right now?

10.12.4. **Being Brave**

Designers, particularly if they are proposing an unfamiliar or radical solution, need to have a level of self-confidence. The requirement to get others' agreement to a model should not cause you to neglect your professional duty to produce the highest quality model (and we use the word "quality" in the sense of "fit for purpose"). Rather, it should alert you to the need to present the model and its rationale clearly and persuasively.
You need to ask:

- Do I believe in the model?
- Are there areas of which I am unsure, and am I prepared to admit this?
- Can I explain how the model works?
- Can I explain the design decisions?
- Can I explain how the model provides a better solution than alternatives?
- Am I prepared to modify the model in the face of sound criticism?

10.12.5 **Being Understanding and Understood**

Many a data modeler has been frustrated to see a quality solution or approach rejected in favor of one proposed by someone with more power or persuasive skills. (This does not just happen to data modelers!) Data modelers need to be aware of the context in which they are operating. If you are a student studying data modeling and this sounds irrelevant to you, take note that one of our very experienced colleagues helped a student with an assignment, and the student was failed. The model was too sophisticated for the context, and, by the time the professional modeler entered into an argument with the professor, there was too much "face" at stake!
You should be asking:

- How will this model be used? Who will use it?
- Have I involved all stakeholders? Will anyone say, "Why wasn't I asked?"
- Can I communicate the model to all stakeholders?

- Will anyone have reasons for not liking the model (too hard to program against, difficult to understand . . .)?
- Is there any history in the organization or project of data models being misunderstood, ignored, or rejected?
- Will the model surprise anyone? Will anyone have to change their plans?

10.13   **Evaluating the Model**

Having developed one or more candidate conceptual models, we still need to select the most appropriate alternative and verify that it meets the business' needs. If we do the job thoroughly at this point, we will then need only to review the design decisions that we make as we proceed from the conceptual to logical and physical models, rather than reviewing those later models in their entirety.

If we have developed more than one candidate model, our first task is to select the best option. In practice, this situation seldom occurs; alternative models are usually eliminated as modeling progresses, typically on the basis of elegance and simplicity in meeting the requirements. (In architecture, it would be unusual to arrive at more than one *detailed* design.) However, if there are still two or more candidates in contention, it will be necessary to discuss with the stakeholders the trade-offs they represent and reach a decision as to which one to use.

The trade-off between stability and enforcement of rules can be deferred to some extent, as the model at this stage will still contain subtypes; the decision as to which level(s) of generalization to implement takes place at the "conceptual to logical" stage, described in the next chapter.

In reviewing the model, we are asking stakeholders to verify that:

1. It is complete, meaning all business requirements are met.
2. Each component[4] of the model is correctly defined.
3. It does not contain any components that are not required.

In our experience, this level of verification is often not achieved. The quality assurance of the conceptual model is frequently carried out in a fairly haphazard manner even when requirements gathering and modeling have been performed rigorously. Typically, some diagrams and supporting text are supplied to stakeholders in the proposed system, who raise any issues that are obvious to them. Once those issues are addressed, the model becomes part of a signed-off specification.

---

[4]In this context we are using the term "component" to refer to all artifacts in a model, such as entity classes, attributes, associations/relationships, and constraints.

Several factors can contribute to this less-than-rigorous scenario:

1. The desire to achieve a formal sign-off and get on with the project; this in turn may be a result of not allowing sufficient time for review.
2. A reluctance on the part of the modelers to encourage criticism of their work.
3. Failure on the part of the reviewers to fully understand the model and its implications.

In the remainder of this chapter, we focus on the last of these factors and look at a number of techniques and approaches for communicating with people who are not fluent in the language of modeling. We present the last of these—the translation of the model into plain language assertions—in some detail, and we recommend it as the central, mandatory technique to be supported by the other techniques at the modeler's discretion.

10.14 **Direct Review of Data Model Diagrams**

The traditional method of data model review is to present the data model diagram with supporting attribute lists and definitions.

Those of us who work with data models on a daily basis can easily forget how difficult it is for others to understand them. Research has shown clearly that nonspecialists who have been shown data modeling conventions cannot be relied upon to interpret models correctly.[5] Our own experience supports this.

Consider the following:

1. It is not uncommon for reviewers to make such fundamental errors as interpreting lines as data flows (particularly if modeling variants using arrowheads are used).
2. Some discipline is required to ensure that all components of a two-dimensional diagram are covered.
3. There is always a trade-off between including detail on the diagram and recording it in a separate textual document. On the one hand, the cluttered appearance of even a moderately complex model when all attributes are shown (let alone all the business rules to which those attributes are subject) can act as a strong disincentive to review the

---

[5]See Shanks, G., Nuredini, J., Tobin, D., Moody, D., and Weber, R. Representing Things and Properties in Conceptual Modelling: An Empirical Evaluation, *Proc. European Conference on Information Systems*, Naples, June 2003.

diagram for a person who does not deal with such diagrams as part of their daily work.

4. Splitting a complex model (e.g., into subject areas) or removing detail from the diagram may make the model less intimidating, but there is a risk that reviewers will comment on "missing" detail, only to find that they did not look in the right place.

5. Some diagramming conventions (including UML and some variants of the E-R notation) include detail that is not relevant to business reviewers—in particular, information relevant only to physical schema or process design.

There is a simple lesson here: do not send out the data model to stakeholders asking for their feedback. Including an explanation of the diagramming conventions does not alleviate the problem; on the contrary it constitutes an admission that we are expecting people to understand a model immediately after learning the language. Remember too that if reviewers have to be told that their comments are based on misunderstandings, they will quickly lose interest in contributing.

"Walking through" a data model diagram with the stakeholder(s) is a big improvement and provides an opportunity to explain issues and design decisions that span more than one entity class or relationship, and to test your understanding of the requirements on which the model is explicitly or implicitly based. You should interpret the model in business terms to the user, rather than simply presenting the conventions and working through entity class by entity class. In particular, discuss design decisions and their rationale, instead of presenting your best solution without background.

For example: "This part of the model is based around the 'Right of Abode' concept rather than the various visas, passports, and special authorities. We've done this because we understand that new ways of authorizing immigrants to stay in the country may arise during the life of the system. Is this so? Here is how we've defined Right of Abode. Are there any ways of staying in the country that wouldn't fit this definition? We also thought of using a 'travel document' concept instead, but rejected it because an authority doesn't always tie to one document only, and perhaps there might not be a document at all in some cases. Did we understand that correctly?"

Having walked through the model, it now makes sense to let the stakeholder take it away if he or she wants to think about it further. In this situation (by contrast to simply sending the data model out) an explanation of the diagramming conventions such as that in Figure 10.24 does make a useful addition to the documentation.

A final warning: if the reviewers do not find something wrong with the model, or do not prompt you to improve it in some way, you should be very suspicious about their level of understanding.

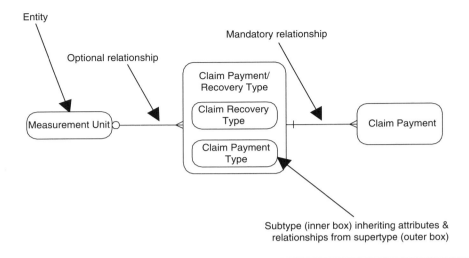

Figure 10.24 A typical guide to notations used in a data model.

10.15 **Comparison with the Process Model**

One of the best means of verifying a data model is to ensure that it includes all the necessary data to support the process model. This is particularly effective if the process model has been developed relatively independently, as it makes available a second set of analysis results as a cross-check. (This is not an argument in favor of data and process modelers working separately; if they work effectively together, the verification will take place progressively as the two models are developed.)

There will be little value in checking against the process model if an extreme form of data-driven approach has been taken and processes have been mechanically derived from the data model.

There are a number of formal techniques for mapping process models against data models to ensure consistency. They include matrices of processes mapped against entity classes, entity life cycles, and state transition diagrams.

Remember however, that the final database may be required to support processes as yet undefined and, hence, not included in the process model. Support for the process model is therefore a necessary but not sufficient criterion for accepting a data model.

10.16 **Testing the Model with Sample Data**

If sample data is available, there are few better ways of communicating and verifying a data model than to work through where each data item would be held. The approach is particularly appropriate when the data model represents a new and unfamiliar way of organizing data: fitting some existing data to the new model will provide a bridge for understanding, and may turn up some problems or oversights.

We recall a statistical analysis system that needed to be able to cope with a range of inputs in different formats. The model was necessarily highly generalized and largely the work of one specialist modeler. Other participants in its development were at least a little uncomfortable with it. Half an hour walking through the model with some typical inputs was far more effective in communicating and verifying the design than the many hours previously spent on argument at a more abstract level (and it revealed areas needing more work).

10.17 **Prototypes**

An excellent way of testing a sophisticated model, or part of a model, is to build a simple prototype. Useful results can often be achieved in a few days, and the exercise can be particularly valuable in winning support and input from process modelers, especially if they have the job of building the prototype.

One of the most sophisticated (and successful) models in which we have been involved was to support a product management database and associated transaction processing. The success of the project owed much to the early production of a simple PC prototype, prior to the major task of developing a system to support fifteen million accounts. A similar design, which was not prototyped, failed at a competitor organization, arguably because of a lack of belief in its workability.

10.18 **The Assertions Approach**

In this section, we look at a rigorous technique for reviewing the detail of data models by presenting them as a list of plain language assertions. In Section 3.5, we saw that if we named a relationship according to some simple rules, we could automatically generate a plain language statement that fully described the relationship, including its cardinality and optionality, and, indeed, some CASE products provide this facility.

The technique described here extends the idea to cover the entire data model diagram. It relies on sticking to some fairly simple naming conventions, consistent with those we have used throughout this book. Its great strength is that it presents the entire model diagram in a nondiagrammatic linear form, which does not require any special knowledge to navigate or interpret. We have settled, after some experimentation, on a single numbered list of assertions with a check box against each in which reviewers can indicate that they agree with, disagree with, or do not understand the assertion.

The assertions cover the following metadata:

1. Entity classes, each of which may be a subtype of another entity class
2. Relationships with cardinality and optionality at each end (the technique is an extension of that described in Section 3.5)
3. Attributes of entity classes (and possibly relationships), which may be marked as mandatory or optional (and possibly multivalued)
4. Intersection entity classes implementing binary "many-to-many" relationships or n-ary relationships
5. Uniqueness constraints on individual attributes or subsets of the attributes and relationships associated with an entity class
6. Other constraints.

10.18.1 **Naming Conventions**

In order to be able to generate grammatically sensible assertions, we have to take care in naming the various components of the model. If you are following the conventions that we recommend, the following rules should be familiar to you:

- Entity class names must be singular and noncollective, (e.g., **Employee** or **Employee Transaction** but not **Employees, Employee Table,** nor **Employee History**).
- Entity class definitions must be singular and noncollective, (e.g., for an entity class named **Injury Nature**, "*a type of injury that can be incurred by a worker,*" not "*a reference list of the injuries that can be incurred by a worker,*" nor "*injuries sustained by a worker*"). They should also be indefinite, (i.e., commencing with "*a*" or "*an*" rather than "*the*"—hence "a type of injury incurred by a worker" rather than "the type of injury incurred by a worker").
- Relationship names must be in infinitive form, (e.g., "*deliver*" rather than "*delivers*" or "*deliverer*" and "*be delivered by*" rather than "is delivered by" or "*delivery*"). There is an alternative set of assertion forms to support attributes of relationships; if this is used, alternative relationship names must also be provided in the 3rd person singular form ("*delivers,*" "*is delivered by*").
- Attribute definitions must refer to a single instance, (e.g., for an attribute named **Total Price**, "*the price paid inclusive of tax*" not "*the prices paid*

inclusive of tax"). They should also be definite, (i.e., commencing with "the" rather than "*a*" or "*an*" —hence "*the price paid inclusive of tax*" rather than "*a price paid inclusive of tax*").

■ Attribute and entity class constraints must start with "*must*" or "*must not*" and any other data item referred to should also be qualified so as to make clear precisely which instance of that data item we are referring to, (e.g., "*[End Date] must not be earlier than the corresponding Start Date*" rather than "*must not be earlier than Start Date*").

10.18.2 **Rules for Generating Assertions**

In the assertion templates that follow:

1. The symbols < and > are used to denote placeholders for which the nominated metadata items can be substituted.
2. The symbols { and } are used to denote sets of alternative wordings separated by the | symbol, (e.g., {A|An} indicates that either "*A*" or "*An*" may be used). Which alternative is used may depend on:
    a. The context, (e.g., "*A*" or "*An*" is chosen to correspond to the name that follows).
    b. A property of the component being described, (e.g., "*must*" or "*may*" is chosen depending on the optionality of the relationship being described).

The examples should make these conventions clear.

10.18.2.1 Entity Class Assertions

For each entity class, we can make an assertion of the form:

"{A|An} <Entity Class Name> is <Entity Class Definition>."
(*e.g.*, "*A Student is an individual person who has enrolled in a course at Smith College.*")

For each entity class that is marked as a subtype (subclass) of another entity class, we can make an assertion of the form:

"{A|An} <Entity Class Name> is a type of <Superclass Name>, namely <Entity Class Definition>."
(*e.g.*, "*A Distance Learning Student is a type of Student, namely a student who does not attend classes in person but who uses the distance learning facilities provided by Smith College.*")

10.18.2.2 Relationship Assertions

For each relationship, we can make an assertion of the form:
"Each <Entity Class 1 Name> {must | may} <Relationship Name> {just one <Entity Class 2 Name> | one or more <Entity Class 2 Plural Name>} that {may | must not}[6] change over time."
(e.g., *"Each Professor may teach one or more Classes that may change over time."*)

For recursive relationships, however, this assertion type reads better if worded as follows

"Each <Entity Class 1 Name> {must | may} <Relationship Name> {just one other <Entity Class 2 Name> | one or more other <Entity Class 2 Plural Name>} that {may | must not} change over time."
(e.g., *"Each Employee may report to just one other Employee that may change over time."*)

We found in practice that the form of this assertion for optional relationships (i.e., with "may" before the relationship name) was not strong enough to alert reviewers who required that the relationship be mandatory, so an additional assertion was added for each optional relationship:

"Not every <Entity Class 1 Name> has to <Relationship Name> {{a | an} <Entity Class 2 Name> | <Entity Class 2 Plural Name>}." (nonrecursive) or
"Not every <Entity Class 1 Name> has to <Relationship Name> {another <Entity Class 2 Name> | other <Entity Class 2 Plural Name>}." (recursive)
(e.g., *"Not every Organization Unit has to consist of other Organization Units."*)

We have also found that those relationships that are marked as optional solely to cope with population of one entity class occurring before the other (e.g., a new organization unit is created before employees are reassigned to that organization unit) require an additional assertion of the form:

"Each <Entity Class 1 Name> should ultimately <Relationship Name> {{a | an} <Entity Class 2 Name> | <Entity Class 2 Plural Name>}."
(e.g., *"Each Organization Unit should ultimately be assigned Employees."*)

---

[6]Depending on whether the relationship is transferable or non-transferable.

10.18.2.3. Attribute Assertions

For each single-valued attribute of an entity class, we can make assertions[7] of the form:

"Each <Entity Class Name> {must | may} have {a | an} <Attribute Name> which is <Attribute Definition>.

 No <Entity Class Name> may have more than one <Attribute Name>."
(e.g., *"Each Student must have a Home Address, which is the address at which the student normally resides during vacations.*

 No Student may have more than one Home Address.")

Note that the must/may choice is based on whether the attribute is marked as optional. Again, the "may" form of this assertion is not strong enough to alert reviewers who required that the attribute be mandatory, so we added for each optional attribute:

"Not every <Entity class Name> has to have {a | an} <Attribute Name>."
(e.g., *"Not every Service Provider has to have a Contact E-mail Address."*)

This particular type of assertion highlights the importance of precise assertion wording. Originally this assertion type read:

"{A | An} <Entity Class Name> does not have to have {a | an} <Attribute Name>."
(e.g., *"A Service Provider does not have to have a Contact E-mail Address."*)

However, that led to one reviewer commenting, "Yes they do have to have one in case they advise us of it." Clearly that form of wording allowed for confusion between provision of an attribute for an entity class and population of that attribute.

If the model includes multivalued attributes, then for each such attribute we can make assertions[8] of the form:

"Each <Entity Class Name> {must | may} have <Attribute Plural Name> which are <Attribute Definition>.

 {A | An} <Entity Class Name> may have more than one <Attribute Name>."
(e.g., *"Each Flight may have Operating Days, which are the days on which that flight operates.*

 Each Flight may have more than one Operating Day.")

---

[7]These are not alternatives; both assertions must be made.
[8]Again these are not alternatives; both assertions must be made.

If the model includes attributes of relationships, then for each single-valued attribute of a relationship, we can make assertions of the form:

"Each combination of <Entity Class 1 Name> and <Entity Class 2 Name> {must|may} have {a|an} <Attribute Name> which is <Attribute Definition>.

No combination of <Entity Class 1 Name> and <Entity Class 2 Name> may have more than one <Attribute Name>."
(e.g., *"Each combination of Student and Course must have an Enrollment Date, which is the date on which the student enrolls in the course.*

No combination of Student and Course may have more than one Enrollment Date.")

Similarly, if the model includes multivalued attributes as well as attributes of relationships, then for each such attribute, we can make assertions[9] of the form:

"Each combination of <Entity Class 1 Name> and <Entity Class 2 Name> {must|may} have <Attribute Plural Name> which are <Attribute Definition>.

A combination of <Entity Class 1 Name> and <Entity Class 2 Name> may have more than one <Attribute Name>."
(e.g., *"Each combination of Student and Course may have Assignment Scores which are the scores achieved by that student for the assignments performed on that course.*

A combination of Student and Course may have more than one Assignment Score.")

All assertions about relationships we have previously described relied on the relationship being named in each direction using the infinitive form (the form that is grammatically correct after "may" or "must"); if a 3rd person singular form ("is" rather than "be," "reports to" rather than "report to") of the name of each relationship with attributes is also recorded, alternative assertion forms are possible. If the attribute is single-valued:

"Each <Entity Class 1 Name> that <Relationship Alternative Name> {a|an} <Entity Class 2 Name> {must|may} have {a|an} <Attribute Name> which is <Attribute Definition>.

No <Entity Class 1 Name> that <Relationship Alternative Name> {a|an} <Entity Class 2 Name> may have more than one <Attribute Name> for that <Entity Class 2 Name>."

---

[9]Again these are not alternatives; both assertions must be made.

(e.g., *"Each Student that enrolls in a Course must have an Enrollment Date, which is the date on which the student enrolls in the course.*

No Student that enrolls in a Course may have more than one Enrollment Date for that Course.")

If the attribute is multivalued:

"Each <Entity Class 1 Name> that <Relationship Alternative Name> {a | an} <Entity Class 2 Name> {must | may} have <Attribute Plural Name> which are <Attribute Definition>.

A <Entity Class 1 Name> that <Relationship Alternative Name> {a | an} <Entity Class 2 Name> may have more than one <Attribute Name> for that <Entity Class 2 Name>."

(e.g., *"Each Student that enrolls in a Course may have Assignment Scores, which are the scores achieved by that student for the assignments performed on that course.*

Each Student that enrolls in a Course may have more than one Assignment Score for that Course.")

Note that each derived attribute should include in its <Attribute Definition> the calculation or derivation rules for that attribute.

If the model includes the attribute type of each attribute (see Section 5.4), then for each attribute of an entity class we can make an assertion of the form:

"The <Attribute Name> of {a | an} <Entity Class Name> is (and exhibits the properties of) {a | an} <Attribute Type Name>."

(e.g., *"The Departure Time of a Flight is (and exhibits the properties of) a TimeOfDay."*)

The document containing the assertions should then contain in its front-matter a list of all attribute types used and their properties. If these are negotiable with stakeholders they should be included as assertions, (i.e., each should be given a number and a check box).

10.18.2.4. Intersection Assertions

There are three types of intersection entity class to consider:

1. Those implementing a binary many-to-many relationship for which only one combination of each pair of instances is allowed (i.e., if implemented in a relational database, the primary key would consist only of the foreign keys of the tables representing the two associated entity classes). The classic example is **Enrollment** where each **Student** may only enroll once in each **Course.**

2. Those implementing a binary many-to-many relationship for which more than one combination of each pair of instances is allowed (i.e., if implemented in a relational database the primary key would consist not only of the foreign keys of the tables representing the two associated entity classes, but also an additional attribute, usually a date). The classic example is **Enrollment** where a **Student** may enroll more than once in each **Course**.

3. Those implementing an n-ary relationship.

For each attribute of an intersection entity class of the first type, we can make assertions[10] of the form:

"There can only be one <Data Item Name> for each combination of <Associated Entity Class 1 Name> and <Associated Entity Class 2 Name>.

For any particular <Associated Entity Class 1 Name> a different <Data Item Name> can occur for each <Associated Entity Class 2 Name>.

For any particular <Associated Entity Class 2 Name> a different <Data Item Name> can occur for each <Associated Entity Class 1 Name>." (e.g., *"There can only be one Conversion Factor for each combination of Input Measurement Unit and Output Measurement Unit.*

For any particular Input Measurement Unit a different Conversion Factor can occur for each Output Measurement Unit.

For any particular Output Measurement Unit a different Conversion Factor can occur for each Input Measurement Unit.")

Note that <Data Item Name> can be:

1. An attribute name
2. The name of an entity class associated with the intersection entity class via a nonidentifying relationship.[11]

For each attribute of an intersection entity class of the second or third type, we can make assertions[12] of the form:

"There can only be one <Data Item Name> for each combination of <Identifier Component 1 Name>, <Identifier Component 2 Name>, . . . and <Identifier Component n Name>.

---

[10]Again, these are not alternatives; all assertions must be made.
[11]For example the intersection entity class **Enrollment** may have identifying relationships to **Student** and **Course** but a nonidentifying relationship to **Payment Method** and attributes of Enrollment Date and Payment Date. <Data Item Name> can refer to any of those last three.
[12]Again these are not alternatives; all assertions must be made.

For any particular combination of <Identifier Component 1 Name> . . . and <Identifier Component n-1 Name> a different <Data Item Name> can occur for each <Identifier Component *m* Name>."

Note that:

1. There is an <Identifier Component Name> for each part of the identifier of the intersection entity class, and it is expressed as one of:

   a. The name of an entity class associated with the intersection entity class via an identifying relationship
   b. The name of the attribute included in the identifier of the intersection entity class.

2. An assertion of the second form above must be produced for each identifier component of each intersection entity class, in which the name of that identifier component is substituted for <Identifier Component m Name>, and all other identifier components appear in the list following "combination of."

Thus, in the case of Enrollment where a Student may enroll more than once in each Course:

"There can only be one Achievement Score for each combination of Student, Course, and Enrollment Date.

For any particular combination of Course and Enrollment Date, a different Achievement Score can occur for each Student.

For any particular combination of Student and Enrollment Date, a different Achievement Score can occur for each Course.

For any particular combination of Student and Course, a different Achievement Score can occur for each Enrollment Date."

10.18.2.5. Constraint Assertions

For each attribute of an entity class on which there is a uniqueness constraint, we can make an assertion of the form:

"No two <Entity Class Plural Name> can have the same <Attribute Name>."
(e.g., *"No two Students can have the same Student Number."*)

For each set of data items of an entity class on which there is a uniqueness constraint, we can make an assertion of the form:

"No two <Entity Class Plural Name> can have the same combination of <Data Item 1 Name>, <Data Item 2 Name>, . . . and <Data Item n Name>."

(e.g., *"No two Payment Rejections can have the same combination of Payment Transaction and Payment Rejection Reason."*)

Note that each <Data Item Name> can be:

1. An attribute name
2. The name of another entity class associated with this entity class via a relationship.

For each other constraint[13] on an attribute, we can make an assertion of the form:

"The <Attribute Name> of {a | an} <Entity Class Name> <Attribute Constraint>."

As these can vary considerably in their syntax, we provide a number of examples:

"The Unit Price of a Stock Item must not be negative."
"The End Date & Time of an Outage Period must be later than the Start Date & Time of the same Outage Period."
"The Alternative Date of an Examination must be entered if the Deferral Flag is set but must not be entered if the Deferral Flag is not set."
"The Test Day of a Test Requirement must be specified if the Test Frequency is Weekly, Fortnightly, or Monthly. If the Test Frequency is Monthly, this day can be either the nth day in the month or the nth occurrence of a specified day of the week."
"The Test Frequency of a Test Requirement may be daily, weekly, fortnightly, monthly, a specified number of times per week or year, or every n days."

The last example shows how a category attribute having a defined discrete set of values can be documented for confirmation by reviewers.

For each other constraint on an entity class, we can make an assertion of the form:

"{A | An} <Entity Class Name> <Entity Class Constraint>."
(e.g., *"A Student Absence may not overlap in time another Student Absence for the same Student."*)

It can also be useful to use this template to include additional statements to support design decisions, such as:

---

[13]Note that these may exist in many forms, as described in Chapter 14.

"A Sampling/Analysis Assignment covers sampling and/or analysis relating to all Sampling Points at one or more Plants, therefore there is no need to identify which Sampling Points at a Plant are covered by an Assignment."

10.19 **Summary**

Data modeling is a design discipline. Data modelers tend to adapt generic models and standard structures, rather than work from first principles. Innovative solutions may result from employing generic models from other business areas. New problems can be tackled top-down from very generic supertypes, or bottom-up by modeling representative areas of the problem domain and generalizing.

Verification of the conceptual model requires the informed participation of business stakeholders. Direct review of data model diagrams is not sufficient: it needs to be supplemented by other techniques, which can include explanation by the modeler, comparison with the process model, testing with sample data, and development of prototypes. Plain language assertions, generated directly from metadata, provide a powerful way of presenting a model in a form suitable for detailed verification.

Chapter 11
Logical Database Design

"Utopia to-day, flesh and blood tomorrow."
– Victor Hugo, Les Miserables

11.1 Introduction

If we have produced a conceptual data model and had it effectively reviewed and verified as described in Chapter 10, the next step is to translate it into a logical data model suitable for implementation using the target DBMS.

In this chapter we look at the most common situation (in which the DBMS is relational) and describe the transformations and design decisions that we need to apply to the conceptual model to produce a logical model suitable for direct implementation as a relational database. As we shall see in Chapter 12, it may later be necessary to make some changes to this initial relational model to achieve performance goals; for this purpose we will produce a physical data model.

The advantages of producing a logical data model as an intermediate deliverable rather than proceeding directly to the physical data model are:

1. Since it has been produced by a set of well-defined transformations from the conceptual data model, the logical data model reflects business information requirements without being obscured by any changes required for performance; in particular, it embodies rules about the properties of the data (such as functional dependencies, as described in Section 2.8.1). These rules cannot always be deduced from a physical data model, which may have been denormalized or otherwise compromised.

2. If the database is ported to another DBMS supporting similar structures (e.g., another relational DBMS or a new version of the same DBMS having different performance properties), the logical data model can be used as a baseline for the new physical data model.

The task of transforming the conceptual data model to a relational logical model is quite straightforward—certainly more so than the conceptual modeling stage—and is, even for large models, unlikely to take more than a few days. In fact, many CASE tools provide facilities for the logical data model to be generated automatically from the conceptual model. (They generally

321

achieve this by bringing forward some decisions to the conceptual modeling stage, and/or applying some default transformation rules, which may not always provide the optimum result.)

We need to make a number of transformations; some of these lend themselves to alternatives and therefore require decisions to be made, while others are essentially mechanical. We describe both types in detail in this chapter. Generally the decisions do not require business input, which is why we defer them until this time.

If you are using a DBMS that is not based on a simple relational model, you will need to adapt the principles and techniques described here to suit the particular product. However, the basic Relational Model currently represents the closest thing to a universal, simple view of structured data for computer implementation, and there is a good case for producing a relational data model as an interim deliverable, even if the target DBMS is not relational. From here on, unless otherwise qualified, the term "logical model" should be taken as referring to a relational model.

Similarly, if you are using a CASE tool that enforces particular transformation rules, or perhaps does not even allow for separate conceptual and logical models, you will need to adapt your approach accordingly.

In any event, even though this chapter describes what is probably the most mechanical stage in the data modeling life cycle, your attitude should not be mechanistic. Alert modelers will frequently uncover problems and challenges that have slipped through earlier stages, and will need to revisit requirements or the conceptual model.

The remainder of this chapter is in three parts.

The next section provides an overview of the transformations and design decisions in the sequence in which they would usually be performed.

The following sections cover each of the transformations and decisions in more detail. A substantial amount of space is devoted to subtype implementation, a central decision in the logical design phase. The other critical decision in this phase is the definition of primary keys. We discussed the issues in detail in Chapter 6, but we reiterate here: poor choice of primary keys is one of the most common and expensive errors in data modeling.

We conclude the chapter by looking at how to document the resulting logical model.

11.2 Overview of the Transformations Required

The transformations required to convert a conceptual data model to a logical model can be summarized as follows:

1. Table specification:
   a. Exclusion of entity classes not required in the database

b. Implementation of classification entity classes, for which there are two options

c. Removal of derivable many-to-many relationships (if our conceptual modeling conventions support these)[1]

d. Implementation of many-to-many relationships as intersection tables

e. Implementation of n-ary relationships (if our conceptual modeling conventions support these)[2] as intersection tables

f. Implementation of supertype/subtypes: mapping one or more levels of each subtype hierarchy to tables

g. Implementation of other entity classes: each becomes a table.

2. Basic column specification:

a. Removal of derivable attributes (if our conceptual modeling conventions support these)[3]

b. Implementation of category attributes, for which there are two options

c. Implementation of multivalued attributes (if our conceptual modeling conventions support these),[4] for which there are multiple options

d. Implementation of complex attributes (if our conceptual modeling conventions support these),[5] for which there are two options

e. Implementation of other attributes as columns

f. Possible introduction of additional columns

g. Determination of column datatypes and lengths

h. Determination of column nullability.

At this point, the process becomes iterative rather than linear, as we have to deal with some interdependency between two tasks. We cannot specify foreign keys until we know the primary keys of the tables to which they point; on the other hand, some primary keys may include foreign key columns (which, as we saw in Section 6.4.1, can make up part or all of a table's primary key).

What this means is that we cannot first specify all the primary keys across our model, then specify all the foreign keys in our model—or the reverse. Rather, we need to work back and forth.

---

[1] UML supports derived relationships; E-R conventions generally do not.

[2] UML and Chen conventions support n-ary relationships; E-R conventions generally do not.

[3] UML supports derived attributes; E-R conventions generally do not.

[4] UML supports multivalued attributes.

[5] Although not every CASE tool currently supports complex attributes, there is nothing in the UML or E-R conventions to preclude the inclusion of complex attributes in a conceptual model

First, we identify primary keys for tables derived from independent entity classes (recall from Section 3.5.7 that these are entity classes that are not at the "many" end of any nontransferable mandatory many-to-one relationships;[6] loosely speaking, they are the "stand-alone" entity classes). Now we can implement all of the foreign keys pointing back to those tables. Doing this will enable us to define the primary keys for the tables representing any entity classes dependent on those independent entity classes and then implement the foreign keys pointing back to them. This is described, with an example, in Section 11.5.

So, the next step is:

3. Primary key specification (for tables representing independent entity classes):

   a. Assessment of existing columns for suitability
   b. Introduction of new columns as surrogate keys.

Then, the next two steps are repeated until all relationships have been implemented.

4. Foreign key specification (to those tables with primary keys already identified):

   a. Removal of derivable one-to-many relationships (if our conceptual modeling conventions support these)[7]
   b. Implementation of one-to-many relationships as foreign key columns
   c. Implementation of one-to-one relationships as foreign keys or through common primary keys

5. Primary key specification (for those tables representing entity classes dependent on other entity classes for which primary keys have already been identified):

   a. Inclusion of foreign key columns representing mandatory relationships
   b. Assessment of other columns representing mandatory attributes for suitability
   c. Possible introduction of additional columns as "tie-breakers."

We counsel you to follow this sequence, tempting though it can be to jump ahead to "obvious" implementation decisions. There are a number of

---

[6]An entity class that *is* at the "many" end of a non-transferable mandatory many-to-one relationship may be assigned a primary key, which includes the foreign key implementing that relationship.
[7]UML supports derived relationships; E-R conventions generally do not.

dependencies between the steps and unnecessary mistakes are easily made if some discipline is not observed.

11.3 Table Specification

11.3.1 The Standard Transformation

In general, each entity class in the conceptual data model becomes a table in the logical data model and is given a name that corresponds to that of the source entity class (see Section 11.7).

There are, however, exceptions to this "one table per entity" picture:

1. Some entity classes may be excluded from the database
2. Classification entity classes (if included in the conceptual model) may not be implemented as tables
3. Tables are created to implement many-to-many relationships and n-ary relationships (those involving more than two entity classes)
4. A supertype and its subtypes may not all be implemented as tables.

We discuss these exceptions and additions below in the sequence in which we recommend you tackle them. In practice, the implementation of subtypes and supertypes is usually the most challenging of them.

Finally, note that we may also generate some classification tables during the next phase of logical design (see Section 11.4.2), when we select our method(s) of implementing category attributes.

11.3.2 Exclusion of Entity Classes from the Database

In some circumstances an entity class may have been included in the conceptual data model to provide context, and there is no actual requirement for that application to maintain data corresponding to that entity class. It is also possible that the data is to be held in some medium other than the relational database: nondatabase files, XML streams, and so on.

11.3.3 Classification Entity Classes

As discussed in Section 7.2.2.1, we do not recommend that you specify classification entity classes purely to support category attributes during the conceptual modeling phase. If, however, you are working with a conceptual model that contains such entity classes, you should not implement them as tables at this stage but defer action until the next phase of logical design (column specification, as described in Section 11.4.2) to enable all category attributes to be looked at together and consistent decisions made.

11.3.4 **Many-to-Many Relationship Implementation**

11.3.4.1 The Usual Case

We saw in Section 3.5.2 how a many-to-many relationship can be represented as an additional entity class linked to the two original entity classes by one-to-many relationships. In the same way, each many-to-many relationship in the conceptual data model can be converted to an intersection table with two foreign keys (the primary keys of the tables implementing the entity classes involved in that relationship)

The issues described in Section 3.5.2 with respect to the naming of intersection entity classes apply equally to the naming of intersection tables.

11.3.4.2 Derivable Many-to-Many Relationships

Occasionally, you may discover that a many-to-many relationship that you have documented can be derived from attributes of the participating entity classes. Perhaps we have proposed **Applicant** and **Welfare Benefit** entity classes and a many-to-many relationship between them (Figure 11.1).

On further analysis, we discover that eligibility for benefits can be determined by comparing attributes of the applicant with qualifying criteria for the benefit (e.g., **Birth Date** compared with **Eligible Age** attributes).

APPLICANT (Applicant ID, Name, Birth Date, . . .)
WELFARE BENEFIT (Benefit ID, Minimum Eligible Age, Maximum Eligible Age . . .)

Figure 11.1   Derivable many-to-many relationship.

In such cases, if our chosen CASE tool does not allow us to show many-to-many relationships in the conceptual data model without creating a corresponding intersection table in the logical data model, we should delete the relationship on the basis that it is derivable (and hence redundant); we do not want to generate an intersection table that contains nothing but derivable data.

If you are using UML you can specifically identify a relationship as being derivable, in which case the CASE tool should not generate an intersection table. If you look at any model closely, you will find opportunities to document numerous such many-to-many "relationships" derivable from inequalities ("greater than," "less than") or more complex formulae and rules. For example:

Each **Employee Absence** may occur during one or more **Strike**s and Each **Strike** may occur during one or more **Employee Absence**s (derivable from comparison of dates).

Each **Aircraft Type** may be able to land at one or more **Airfield**s and Each **Airfield** may be able to support landing of one or more **Aircraft Type**s (derivable from airport services and runway facilities and aircraft type specifications).

If our chosen CASE tool does not allow us to show many-to-many relationships in the conceptual data model without including a corresponding intersection table in the logical data model, what do we say to the business reviewers? Having presented them with a diagram, which they have approved, we now remove one or more relationships.

It is certainly not appropriate to surreptitiously amend the model on the basis that "we know better." Nor is it appropriate to create two conceptual data models, a "business stakeholder model" and an "implementation model." Our opposition to these approaches is that the first involves important decisions being taken without business stakeholder participation, and the second complicates the modeling process for little gain. We have found that the simplest and most effective approach in this situation is to remove the relationship(s) from the conceptual data model but inform business stakeholders that we have done so and explain why. We show how the relationship is derivable from other data, and demonstrate, using sample transactions, that including the derivable relationship will add redundancy and complexity to the system.

11.3.4.3   Alternative Implementations

In Chapter 12 we shall see that a DBMS that supports the SQL99 **set type constructor** feature enables implementation of a many-to-many relationship without creating an additional table. However, we do not recommend that you include such a structure in your logical data model. The decision as to whether to use such a structure should be taken at the physical database design stage.

11.3.5 Relationships Involving More Than Two Entity Classes

The E-R conventions that we use in this book do not support the direct representation of relationships involving three or more entity classes ("n-ary relationships"). If we have encountered such relationships at the conceptual modeling stage, we will have been forced to represent them using intersection entity classes, anticipating the implementation. There is nothing more to do at this stage, since the standard transformation from entity class to table will have included such entity classes. However, you should check for normalization; such structures provide the most common situations of data that is in third normal form but not in fourth or fifth normal form (Chapter 13).

If you are using UML (or other conventions that support n-ary relationships), you will need to resolve the relationships [i.e., represent each n-ary relationship as an intersection table (Section 3.5.5)].

11.3.6 Supertype/Subtype Implementation

The Relational Model and relational DBMSs do not provide direct support for subtypes or supertypes. Therefore any subtypes that were included in the conceptual data model are normally replaced by standard relational structures in the logical data model. Since we are retaining the documentation of the conceptual data model, we do not lose the business rules and other requirements represented by the subtypes we created in that model. This is important since there is more than one way to represent a supertype/subtype set in a logical data model and the decisions we make to represent each such set may need to be revisited in the light of new information (such as changes to transaction profiles, other changes to business processes, or new facilities provided by the DBMS) or if the system is ported to a different DBMS. Indeed if the new DBMS supports subtypes directly, supertypes and subtypes can be retained in the logical data model; the SQL99[8] standard provides for direct support of subtypes and at least one object-relational DBMS provides such support.

11.3.6.1 Implementation at a Single Level of Generalization

One way of leveling a hierarchy of subtypes is to select a single level of generalization. In the example in Figure 11.2, we can do this by discarding **Party**, in which case we implement only its subtypes, **Individual** and

---

[8]ANSI/ISO/IEC 9075.

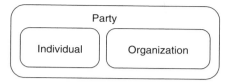

Figure 11.2   A simple supertype/subtype set.

Organization, or by discarding **Individual** and **Organization** and implementing only their supertype, **Party**.

Actually, "discard" is far too strong a word, since all the business rules and other requirements represented by the subtypes have been retained in the conceptual data model.

We certainly will not discard any attributes or relationships. Tables representing subtypes *inherit* the attributes and relationships of any "discarded" supertypes, and tables representing supertypes *roll up* the attributes and relationships of any "discarded" subtypes. So if we implement **Individual** and **Organization** as tables but not **Party**, each will inherit all the attributes and relationships of **Party**. Conversely, if we implement **Party** as a table but not **Individual** or **Organization**, we need to include in the **Party** table any attributes and relationships specific to **Individual** or **Organization**. These attributes and relationships would become *optional* attributes and relationships of **Party**. In some cases, we might choose to combine attributes or relationships from different subtypes to form a single attribute or relationship. For example, in rolling up **Purchase** and **Sale** into **Financial Transaction** we might combine Price and Sale Value into Amount. This is generalization at the attribute level and is discussed in more detail in Section 5.6, while relationship generalization is discussed in Section 4.14.

If we implement at the supertype level, we also need to add a Type column to allow us to preserve any distinctions that the discarded subtypes represented and that cannot be derived from existing attributes of the supertype. In this example we would introduce a Party Type column to allow us to distinguish those parties that are organizations from those who are individuals.

If we are rolling up two or more levels of subtypes, we have some choice as to how many Type columns to introduce. For a generally workable solution, we suggest you simply introduce a single Type column based on the lowest level of subtyping. Look at Figure 11.3 on the next page. If you decide to implement at the **Party** level, add a single Party Type column, which will hold values of "Adult," "Minor," "Private Sector Organization," and "Public Sector Organization." If you want to distinguish which of these are persons and which are organizations, you will need to introduce an additional reference table with four rows as in Figure 11.4.

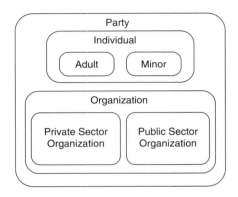

Figure 11.3 A more complex supertype/subtype structure.

11.3.6.2 Implementation at Multiple Levels of Generalization

Returning to the example in Figure 11.2, a third option is to implement all three-entity classes in the Party hierarchy as tables. We link the tables by carrying the foreign key of **Party** in the **Individual** and **Organization** tables. The appeal of this option is that we do not need to discard any of our concepts and rules. On the other hand, we can easily end up with a proliferation of tables, violating our aim of simplicity. And these tables will usually not correspond on a one-to-one basis with familiar concepts; the **Individual** table in this model does not hold all the attributes of individuals, only those that are not common to all parties. The concept of an individual is represented by the **Party** and **Individual** tables in combination.

Figure 11.6 illustrates all three options for implementing the supertype/subtype structure in Figure 11.5. (As described in Section 4.14.2, the exclusivity arc drawn across a set of relationships indicates that they are mutually exclusive.)

11.3.6.3 Other Options

There may be other options in some situations.

Party Type	Organization/Individual Indicator
Private Sector Organization	Organization
Public Sector Organization	Organization
Adult	Individual
Minor	Individual

Figure 11.4 Reference table of party types.

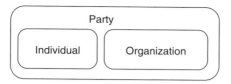

PARTY (Party ID, First Contact Date)
INDIVIDUAL (Family Name, Given Name, Gender, Birth Date)
ORGANIZATION (Registered Name, Incorporation Date, Employee Count)

Figure 11.5 A conceptual data model with a supertype/subtype set.

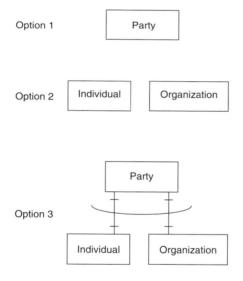

Option 1:
PARTY (Party ID, First Contact Date, Family Name, Given Name, Gender, Birth Date, Registered Name, Incorporation Date, Employee Count)
Option 2:
INDIVIDUAL (Party ID, First Contact Date, Family Name, Given Name, Gender, Birth Date)
ORGANIZATION (Party ID, First Contact Date, Registered Name, Incorporation Date, Employee Count)
Option 3:
PARTY (Party ID, First Contact Date)
INDIVIDUAL (Party ID, Family Name, Given Name, Gender, Birth Date)
ORGANIZATION (Party ID, Registered Name, Incorporation Date, Employee Count)

Figure 11.6 Implementing a supertype/subtype set in a logical data model.

First, we may create a table for the supertype and tables for only *some* of the subtypes. This is quite common when some subtypes do not have any attributes or relationships in addition to those of the supertype, in which case those subtypes do not need separate tables.

Second, if a supertype has three or more subtypes and some of those subtypes have similar attributes and relationships, we may create single tables for similar subtypes and separate tables for any other subtypes, with or without a table for the supertype. In this case we are effectively recognizing an intermediate level of subtyping and should consider whether it is worth including it in the conceptual model. For example in a financial services conceptual data model the **Party Role** entity class may have **Customer, Broker, Financial Advisor, Employee, Service Provider**, and **Supplier** subtypes. If we record similar facts about brokers and financial advisors, it may make sense to create a single table in which to record both these roles; similarly, if we record similar facts about service providers and suppliers, it may make sense to create a single table in which to record both these roles.

11.3.6.4   Which Option?

Which option should we choose for each supertype hierarchy?

An important consideration is the enforcement of referential integrity (see Section 14.5.4). Consider this situation:

1. The database administrator intends to implement referential integrity using the DBMS referential integrity facilities
2. The target DBMS only supports standard referential integrity between foreign keys and primary keys.[9]

In this case, each entity that is at the "one" end of a one-to-many relationship must be implemented as a table, whether it is a supertype or a subtype, so that the DBMS can support referential integrity of those relationships.

This is because standard DBMS referential integrity support allows a foreign key value to be any primary key value from the one associated table. If a subtype is represented by a subset of the rows in a table implementing the supertype rather than as its own separate table, any foreign keys implementing relationships to that subtype can have any primary key value including those of the other subtypes. Referential integrity on a relationship

---

[9]That is without any selection of rows from the referenced table (i.e., only the rows of a subtype) or multiple referenced tables (i.e., all the rows of a supertype). The authors are not aware of any DBMSs that provide such facilities.

to that subtype can therefore only be managed by either program logic or a combination of DBMS referential integrity support and program logic.

By contrast if the supertype is represented by multiple subtype tables rather than its own table, any foreign key implementing relationships to that supertype can have any value from any of the subtype tables. Referential integrity on a relationship to that supertype can therefore only be managed in program logic.

Another factor is the ability to present data in alternative ways. As mentioned in Chapter 1, we do not always access the tables of a relational database directly. Usually, we access them through **views**, which consist of data from one or more tables combined or selected in various ways. We can use the standard facilities available for constructing views to present data at the subtype or supertype level, regardless of whether we have chosen to implement subtypes, supertype, or both. However, there are some limitations. Not all views allow the data presented to be updated. This is sometimes due to restrictions imposed by the particular DBMS, but there are also some logical constraints on what types of views can be updated. In particular these arise where data has been combined from more than one table, and it is not possible to unambiguously interpret a command in terms of which underlying tables are to be updated. It is beyond the scope of this book to discuss view construction and its limitations in any detail. Broadly, the implications for the three implementation options described above are:

1. Implementation at the supertype level: if we implement a **Party** table, a simple selection operation will allow us to construct **Individual** and **Organization** views. These views will be logically updateable.

2. Implementation at the subtype level: if we implement separate **Individual** and **Organization** tables, a **Party** view can be constructed using the "union" operator. Views constructed using this operator are not updateable.

3. Implementation of both supertype and subtype tables: if we implement **Individual**, **Organization**, and **Party** tables, full views of **Individual** and **Organization** can be constructed using the "join" operator. Some views using this operator are not updateable, and DBMSs differ on precisely what restrictions they impose on "join" view updateability. They can be combined using the "union" operator to produce a Party view, which again will not be updateable.

Nonrelational DBMSs offer different facilities and may make one or other of the options more attractive. The ability to construct useful, updateable views becomes another factor in selecting the most appropriate implementation option.

What is important, however, is to recognize that views are not a substitute for careful modeling of subtypes and supertypes, and to consider the appropriate level for implementation. Identification of useful data classifications is part of the data modeling process, not something that should be left to some later task of view definition. If subtypes and supertypes are not recognized in the conceptual modeling stage, we cannot expect the process model to take advantage of them. There is little point in constructing views unless we have planned to use them in our programs.

11.3.6.5 Implications for Process Design

If a supertype is implemented as a table and at least one of its subtypes is implemented as a table as well, any process creating an instance of that subtype (or one of *its* subtypes) must create a row in the corresponding supertype table as well as the row in the appropriate subtype table(s). To ensure that this occurs, those responsible for writing detailed specifications of programs (which we assume are written in terms of table-level transactions) from business-level process specifications (which we assume are written in terms of entity-level transactions) must be informed of this rule.

11.4 Basic Column Definition

11.4.1 Attribute Implementation: The Standard Transformation

With some exceptions, each attribute in the conceptual data model becomes a column in the logical data model and should be given a name that corresponds to that of the corresponding attribute (see Section 11.7).

The principal exceptions to this are:

1. Category attributes
2. Derivable attributes
3. Attributes of relationships
4. Complex attributes
5. Multivalued attributes.

The following subsections describe each of these exceptions.

We may also add further columns for various reasons. The most common of these are surrogate primary keys and foreign keys (covered in Sections 11.5 and 11.6 respectively), but there are some additional situations, discussed in Section 11.4.7. The remainder of Section 11.4 looks at some issues applicable to columns in general.

Note that in this phase we may end up specifying additional tables to support category attributes.

11.4.2 **Category Attribute Implementation**

In general, DBMSs provide two distinct methods of implementing a category attribute (see Section 5.4.2.2):

1. As a foreign key to a classification table
2. As a column on which a constraint is defined limiting the values that the column may hold.

The principal advantage of the classification table method is that the ability to change codes or descriptions can be granted to users of the database rather than them having to rely on the database administrator to make such changes. However, if any procedural logic depends on the value assigned to the category attribute, such changes should only be made in controlled circumstances in which synchronized changes are made to procedural code.

If you have adopted our recommendation of showing category attributes in the conceptual data model as attributes rather than relationships to classification entity classes (see Section 7.2.2.1), and you select the "constraint on column" method of implementation, your category attributes become columns like any other, and there is no more work to be done. If, however, you select the "classification table" method of implementation, you must:

1. Create a table for each domain that you have defined for category attributes, with **Code** and **Meaning** columns.
2. Create a foreign key column that references the appropriate domain table to represent each category attribute.[10]

For example, if you have two category attributes in your conceptual data model, each named **Customer Type** (one in the **Customer** entity class and the other in an **Allowed Discount** business rule entity class recording the maximum discount allowed for each customer type), then each of these should belong to the same domain, also named "Customer Type." In this case, you must create a **Customer Type** table with **Customer Type Code** and **Customer Type Meaning** columns and include foreign keys to that table in your **Customer** and **Allowed Discount** tables to represent the **Customer Type** attributes.

By contrast, if you have modeled category attributes in the conceptual data model as relationships to classification entity classes, and you select the classification table option, your classification entity classes become

---

[10]Strictly speaking, we should not be specifying primary or foreign keys at this stage, but the situation here is so straightforward that most of us skip the step of initially documenting only a relationship.

tables like any other and the relationships to them become foreign key columns like any other. If, however, you select the "constraint on column" option, you must not create tables for those classification entity classes but you must represent each relationship to a classification entity class as a simple column, not as a foreign key column.

11.4.3 Derivable Attributes

Since the logical data model should not specify redundant data, derivable attributes in the conceptual data model should not become columns in the logical data model. However, the designer of the physical data model needs to be advised of derivable attributes so as to decide whether they should be stored as columns in the database or calculated "on the fly." We therefore recommend that, for each entity class with derivable attributes, you create a view based on the corresponding table, which includes (as well as the columns of that table) a column for each derived attribute, specifying how that attribute is calculated. Figure 11.7 illustrates this principle.

11.4.4 Attributes of Relationships

If the relationship is many-to-many or "n-ary," its attributes should be implemented as columns in the table implementing the relationship. If the relationship is one-to-many, its attributes should be implemented as columns in the table implementing the entity class at the "many" end. If the relationship is one-to-one, its attributes can be implemented as columns in either of the tables used to implement one of the entity classes involved in that relationship.

Table: **ORDER LINE** (Order No, Product No, Order Quantity, Applicable Discount Rate, Quoted Price, Promised Delivery Date, Actual Delivery Date)

View: **ORDER LINE VIEW** (Order No, Product No, Order Quantity, Applicable Discount Rate, Quoted Price, Promised Delivery Date, Actual Delivery Date, Total Item Cost = Order Quantity * Quoted Price * (1- Applicable Discount Rate/100.0))

Figure 11.7 A table and a view defining a derivable attribute.

11.4.5 **Complex Attributes**

In general, unless the target DBMS provides some form of **row datatype** facility (such as Oracle™'s "nested tables"), built-in complex datatypes (such as foreign currencies or timestamps with associated time zones), or **constructors** with which to create such datatypes, each component of a complex attribute (see Section 7.2.2.4) will require a separate column. For example, a currency amount in an application dealing with multiple currencies will require a column for the amount and another column in which the currency unit for each amount can be recorded. Similarly, a time attribute in an application dealing with multiple time zones may require a column in which the time zone is recorded as well as the column for the time itself. Addresses are another example of complex attributes. Each address component will require a separate column.

An alternative approach where a complex attribute type has many components (e.g., addresses) is to:

1. Create a separate table in which to hold the complex attribute
2. Hold only a foreign key to that table in the original table.

11.4.6 **Multivalued Attribute Implementation**

Consider the conceptual data model of a multi-airline timetable database in Figure 11.8. A flight (e.g., AA123, UA345) may operate over multiple flight legs, each of which is from one port to another. Actually a flight has no real independent existence but is merely an identifier for a series of flight legs. Although some flights operate year-round, others are seasonal and may therefore have one or more operational periods (in fact two legs of a flight may have different operational periods: the Chicago-Denver flight may only continue to Los Angeles in summer). And of course not all flights are daily, so we need to record the days of the week on which a flight (or rather its legs) operates. In the conceptual data model we can do this using the multivalued attribute {Week Days}. At the same time we should record for the convenience of passengers on long-distance flights what meals are served (on a trans-Pacific flight there could be as many as three). The {Meal Types} multivalued attribute supports this requirement.

In general, unless the target DBMS supports the SQL99 **set type constructor** feature, which enables direct implementation of multivalued attributes, normal practice is to represent each such attribute in the logical data model using a separate table. Thus, the {Meal Types} attribute of the **Flight Leg** entity class could be implemented using a table (with the name

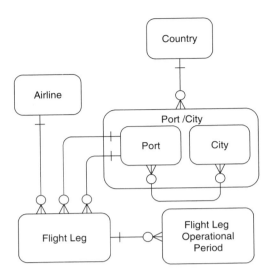

PORT/CITY (Code, Name, Time Zone)
COUNTRY (Code, Name)
AIRLINE (Code, Name)
FLIGHT LEG (Flight Number, Leg Number, Departure Local TimeOfDay, Arrival Local
Time TimeOfDay, Arrival Additional Day Count, Aircraft Type, {Meal Types})
FLIGHT LEG OPERATIONAL PERIOD (Start Date, End Date, {Week Days})

Figure 11.8   Implementing a multivalued attribute.

Flight Leg Meal Type, i.e., the singular form of the attribute name prefixed
by the name of its owning entity class) with the following columns:

1. A foreign key to the **Flight Leg** table (representing the entity class
   owning the multivalued attribute)
2. A column in which a single Meal Type can be held (with the name Meal
   Type, i.e., the singular form of the attribute name).

The primary key of this table can simply be all these columns.
Similarly normal practice would be to represent the {Week Days} attrib-
ute in the logical data model using a **Flight Leg Operational Period Week
Day** table with a foreign key to **Flight Leg Operational Period** and a Week
Day column.
However, the case may be that:

1. The maximum number of values that may be held is finite and small.
2. There is no requirement to sort using the values of that attribute.

Then, the designer of the physical data model may well create, rather than an additional table, a set of columns (one for each value) in the original table (the one implementing the entity class with the multivalued attribute). For example, {Week Days} can be implemented using seven columns in the **Flight Leg Operational Period** table, one for each day of the week, each holding a flag to indicate whether that flight leg operates on that day during that operational period.

If the multivalued attribute is textual, the modeler may even implement it in a single column in which all the values are concatenated, or separated if necessary by a separator character. This is generally only appropriate if queries searching for a single value in that column are not rendered unduly complex or slow. If this is likely to occur, it may be better from a pragmatic point of view to model such attributes this way in the logical data model as well, to avoid the models diverging so much. For example, {Meal Types} can be implemented using a single Meal Types column in the **Flight Leg** table, since there is a maximum of three meals that can be served on one flight leg.

By way of another example, an **Employee** entity class may have the attribute Dependent Names, which could be represented by a single column in the **Employee** table, which would hold values such as "Peter" or "Paul, Mary."

11.4.7 **Additional Columns**

In some circumstances additional columns may be required. We have already seen in Section 11.3.6.1 the addition of a column or columns to identify subtypes in a supertype table. Other columns are typically required to hold data needed to support system administration, operation, and maintenance. The following examples will give you a flavor.

A very common situation is when a record is required of who inserted each row and when, and of who last updated each row and when. In this case, you can create a pair of DateTime columns, usually named along the lines of Insert DateTime and Last Update DateTime, and a pair of text columns, usually named along the lines of Insert User ID and Last Update User ID. Of course, if a full audit trail of all changes to a particular table is required, you will need to create an additional table with the following columns:

1. Those making up a foreign key to the table to be audited
2. An Update DateTime column, which together with the foreign key columns makes up the primary key of this table
3. An Update User ID column
4. The old and/or new values of the remaining columns of the table to be audited.

The **Meaning** attribute in a classification entity class in the conceptual data model is usually a relatively short text that appears as the interpretation of the code in screens and reports. If the differences between some meanings require explanation that would not fit in the **Meaning** column, then an additional, longer **Explanation** column (to expand upon **Meaning**) may need to be added.

By contrast, additional columns holding abbreviated versions of textual data may be needed for any screens, other displays (such as networked equipment displays), reports, and other printouts (such as printed tickets) in which there may be space limitations. A typical example is location names: given the fact that these may have the same initial characters (e.g., Carlton and Carlton North) simple truncation of such names may produce indistinguishable abbreviations.

Another situation in which additional columns may be required is when a numeric or date/time attribute may hold approximate or partly-defined values such as "At least $10,000," "Approximately $20,000," "some time in 1968," "25th July, but I can't remember which year." To support values like the first two examples, you might create an additional text column in which a qualifier of the amount in the numeric column can be recorded. To support values like the other two examples, you might store the year and month/day components of the date in separate columns.

11.4.8 **Column Datatypes**

If the target DBMS and the datatypes available in that DBMS are known, the appropriate DBMS datatype for each domain (see Section 5.4.3) can be identified and documented. Each column representing an attribute should be assigned the appropriate datatype based on the domain of the corresponding attribute. Each column in a foreign key should be given the same datatype as the corresponding column in the corresponding primary key.

11.4.9 **Column Nullability**

If an attribute has been recorded as mandatory in the business rule documentation accompanying the conceptual data model, the corresponding column should be marked as mandatory in the logical data model; the standard method for doing this is to follow the column name and its datatype with the annotation "NOT NULL." By contrast, if an attribute has been recorded as optional, the corresponding column should be marked as optional using the annotation "NULL."

Any row in which no value has been assigned to that attribute for the entity instance represented by that row will have a null marker rather than a value assigned to that column. Nulls can cause a variety of problems in queries, as Chris Date has pointed out.[11]

Ranges (see Section 12.6.6) provide a good example of a situation in which it is better to use an actual value rather than a null marker in a column representing an optional attribute. The range end attribute is often optional because there is no maximum value in the last range in a set. For example, the **End Date** of the current record in a table that records current and past situations is generally considered to be optional as we have no idea when the current situation will change. Unfortunately, to use a null marker in **End Date** complicates any queries that determine the date range to which a transaction belongs, like the first query in Figure 11.9. Loading a "high value" date (a date that is later than the latest date that the application could still be active) into the **End Date** column of the current record enables us to use the second, simpler, query in Figure 11.9.

11.5 **Primary Key Specification**

We set out the rules for primary key specification in Chapter 6. Recall that in that chapter we discussed the possibility that the primary key of a table may include foreign keys to other tables. However, at this point in the translation to a logical model, we haven't defined the foreign keys—and cannot do so until we have defined the primary keys of the tables being referenced. We resolve this "chicken and egg" situation with an iterative approach.

At the start of this step of the process, you can only determine primary keys for those tables that correspond to independent entity classes (see Chapter 6), since, as we have seen, the primary keys of such tables will not include foreign keys. You therefore first select an appropriate primary key for each of these tables, if necessary adding a surrogate key column as a key in its own right or to supplement existing attributes.

Having specified primary keys for at least some tables, you are now in a position to duplicate these as foreign keys in the tables corresponding to related entity classes. Doing that is the subject of the next section.

You are now able to determine the primary keys of those tables representing entity classes dependent on the entity classes for which you have already identified primary keys (since you now have a full list of columns for these tables, including foreign keys). You can then duplicate these in turn as foreign keys in the tables corresponding to related entity classes. You then repeat this step, "looping" until the model is complete.

---

[11]Date, C.J. *Relational Database Writings 1989–1991*, Pearson Education POD, 1992.

select TRANSACTION.*, HISTORIC_PRICE.PRICE
from TRANSACTION, HISTORIC_PRICE
where TRANSACTION.TRANSACTION_DATE between
HISTORIC_PRICE.START_DATE and HISTORIC_PRICE.END_DATE
or TRANSACTION.TRANSACTION_DATE >
HISTORIC_PRICE.START_DATE and HISTORIC_PRICE.END_DATE is null;

select TRANSACTION.*, HISTORIC_PRICE.PRICE
from TRANSACTION, HISTORIC_PRICE
where TRANSACTION.TRANSACTION_DATE between
HISTORIC_PRICE.START_DATE and HISTORIC_PRICE.END_DATE;

Figure 11.9 Queries involving date ranges.

This may sound complicated but, in practice, this iterative process moves quickly and naturally, and the discipline will help to ensure that you select sound primary keys and implement relationships faithfully. The process is illustrated in Figure 11.10:

1. **Policy Type** and **Person** are obviously independent, and **Organization Unit** is at the "many" end of a transferable relationship, so we can identify primary keys for them immediately.
2. **Policy** is at the "many" end of a nontransferable relationship so depends on **Policy Type** having a defined primary key.
3. **Policy Event** and **Person Role in Policy** are at the "many" ends of nontransferable relationships so depend on **Policy** and **Person** having defined primary keys.

11.6 **Foreign Key Specification**

Foreign keys are our means of implementing one-to-many (and occasionally one-to-one) relationships. This phase of logical design requires that we know the primary key of the entity class at the "one" end of the relationship, and, as discussed in Section 11.2, definition of primary keys is, in turn, dependent on definition of foreign keys. So, we implement the relationships that meet this criterion, then we return to define more primary keys.

This section commences with the basic rule for implementing one-to-many relationships. This rule will cover the overwhelming majority of situations. The remainder of the section looks at a variety of unusual

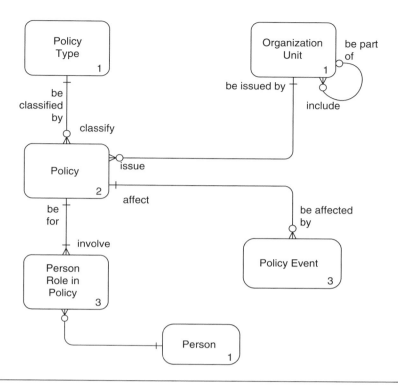

Figure 11.10   Primary and foreign key specification.

situations. It is worth being familiar with them because they do show up from time to time, and, as a professional modeler, you need to be able to recognize and deal with them.

11.6.1 **One-to-Many Relationship Implementation**

11.6.1.1 The Basic Rule

In Section 3.2 we saw how to translate the links implied by primary and foreign keys in a relational model into lines representing one-to-many relationships on an E-R diagram. This is a useful technique when we have an existing database that has not been properly documented in diagrammatic form. The process of recovering the design in this all-too-frequent situation is an example of the broader discipline of "reverse engineering" and is one of the less glamorous tasks of the data modeler (Section 9.5).

When moving from a conceptual to a logical data model, however, we work from a diagram to tables and apply the following rule (illustrated in Figure 11.11):

A one-to-many relationship is supported in a relational database by holding the primary key of the table representing the entity class at the "one" end of the relationship as a foreign key in the table representing the entity class at the "many" end of the relationship.

In the logical data model, therefore, we create, in the table representing the entity class at the "many" end of the relationship, a copy of the primary key of the entity class at the "one" end of the relationship. (Remember that the primary key may consist of more than one column, and we will, of course. need to copy all of its columns to form the foreign key.) Each foreign key column should be given the same name as the primary key column from which it was derived, possibly with the addition of a prefix. Prefixes are necessary in two situations:

1. If there is more than one relationship between the same two entity classes, in which case prefixes are necessary to distinguish the two different foreign keys, for example **Preparation Employee ID** and **Approval Employee ID**.
2. A self-referencing relationship (see Section 3.5.4) will be represented by a foreign key which contains the same column(s) as the primary key of the same table, so a prefix will be required for the column names of the foreign key; typical prefixes are "Parent," "Owner," "Manager" (in a organizational reporting hierarchy).

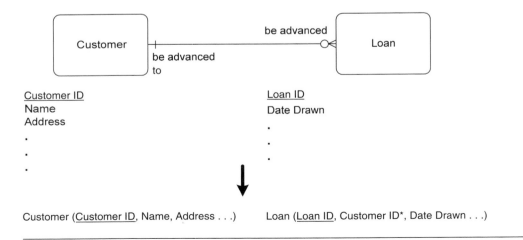

Figure 11.11 Deriving foreign keys from relationships.

Note the use of the asterisk; as mentioned in Chapter 3, this is a convention sometimes used to indicate that a column of a table is all or part of a foreign key. Different CASE tools use different conventions.

A column forming part of a foreign key should be marked as NOT NULL if the relationship it represents is mandatory at the "one" end; conversely, if the relationship is optional at the "one" end, it should be marked as NULL.

11.6.1.2 Alternative Implementations

In Chapter 12 we shall see that a DBMS that supports the SQL99 **set type constructor** feature enables implementation of a one-to-many relationship within one table. However, we do not recommend that you include such a structure in your logical data model; the decision as to whether to use such a structure should be made at the physical database design stage.

Some DBMSs (including DB2) allow a one-to-many relationship to be implemented by holding a copy of *any* candidate key of the referenced table, not just the primary key. (The candidate key must have been defined to the DBMS as unique.) This prompts two questions:

1. How useful is this?
2. Does the implementation of a relationship in this way cause problems in system development?

The majority of database designs cannot benefit from this option. However, consider the following tables from a public transport management system (Figure 11.12):

There are two alternative candidate keys for **Actual Vehicle Trip** (in addition to the one chosen):

Route No + Trip No + Trip Date, and
Route No + Direction Code + Trip Date + Actual Departure TimeOfDay

However, in the system as built these were longer than the key actually chosen (by one and three bytes respectively). Since a very large number of records would be stored, the shortest key was chosen to minimize the data storage costs of tables, indexes, and so on. There was a requirement to identify which **Actual Vehicle Trip** each **Passenger Trip** took place on.

SCHEDULED VEHICLE TRIP (<u>Route No</u>, <u>Trip No</u>, Direction Code, Scheduled Departure TimeOfDay)

ACTUAL VEHICLE TRIP (<u>Vehicle No</u>, <u>Trip Date</u>, <u>Actual Departure TimeOfDay</u>, Route No, Direction Code, Trip No)

PASSENGER TRIP (<u>Ticket No</u>, <u>Trip Date</u>, <u>Trip Start Time</u>, Route No, Direction Code)

Figure 11.12   Tables with candidate keys.

In a DBMS that constrains a foreign key to be a copy of the primary key of the other table, Vehicle No and Actual Departure TimeOfDay would have had to be added to the **Passenger Trip** table at a cost of an extra four bytes in each of a very large number of rows. The ability to maintain a foreign key that refers to any candidate key of the other table meant that only Trip No needed to be added at a cost of only one extra byte.

Of course, exploitation of this option might be difficult if the CASE tool being used to build the application did not support it. Beyond the issue of tool support, there do not appear to be any technical problems associated with this option. However, it is always sensible to be as simple and consistent as possible; the less fancy stuff that programmers, users, and DBAs have to come to grips with, the more time they can devote to using the data model properly!

11.6.2 **One-to-One Relationship Implementation**

A one-to-one relationship can be supported in a relational database by implementing both entity classes as tables, then using the same primary key for both. This strategy ensures that the relationship is indeed one-to-one and is the preferred option.

In fact, this is the way we retain the (one-to-one) association between a supertype and its subtypes when both are to be implemented as tables (see Section 11.3.6.2).

However we cannot use the same primary key when dealing with a *transferable* one-to-one relationship. If we used Part No to identify both **Part** and **Bin** in our earlier example (reproduced in Figure 11.13), it would not be stable as a key of **Bin** (whenever a new part was moved to a bin, the key of that bin would change).

In this situation we would identify **Bin** by Bin No and **Part Type** by Part No, and we would support the relationship with a foreign key: either Bin No in the **Part Type** table or Part No in the **Bin** table. Of course, what we are really supporting here is not a one-to-one relationship any more, but a one-to-many relationship. We have flexibility whether we like it or not! We will need to include the one-to-one rule in the business rule documentation. A relational DBMS will support such a rule by way of a unique index on the foreign key, providing a simple practical solution. Since we have a choice as to the direction of the one-to-many relationship, we will need to

Figure 11.13 A one-to-one relationship.

consider other factors, such as performance and flexibility. Will we be more likely to relax the "one part per bin" or the "one bin per part" rule?

Incidentally, we once struck exactly this situation in practice. The database designer had implemented a single table, with a key of **Bin No**. Parts were thus effectively identified by their bin number, causing real problems when parts were allocated to a new bin. In the end, they "solved" the problem by relabeling the bins each time parts were moved!

11.6.3 **Derivable Relationships**

Occasionally a one-to-many relationship can be derived from other data in one or more of the tables involved. (We discussed derivable many-to-many relationships in Section 11.3.4.2.) The following example is typical. In Figure 11.14, we are modeling information about diseases and their groups (or categories), as might be required in a database for medical research.

During our analysis of attributes we discover that disease groups are identified by a range of numbers (**Low No** through **High No**) and that each disease in that group is assigned a number in the range. For example, 301 through 305 might represent "Depressive Illnesses," and "Post-Natal Depression" might be allocated the number 304. Decimals can be used to avoid running out of numbers. We see exactly this sort of structure in many classification schemes, including the Dewey decimal classification used in libraries. We can use either **High No** or **Low No** as the primary key; we have arbitrarily selected **Low No**.

If we were to implement this relationship using a foreign key, we would arrive at the tables in Figure 11.15.

However, the foreign key **Disease Group Low No** in the **Disease** table is derivable; we can determine which disease group a given disease belongs to by finding the disease group with the range containing its disease no. It therefore violates our requirement for nonredundancy.

In UML we can mark the relationship as derivable, in which case no foreign key is created, but many CASE tools will generate a foreign key to represent each relationship in an Entity-Relationship diagram (whether you want it or not). In this case, the best option is probably to retain the relationship in the diagram and the associated foreign key in the logical

Figure 11.14 Initial E-R model of diseases and groups.

DISEASE (<u>Disease No</u>, Disease Group Low No*, Disease Name, . . .)
DISEASE GROUP (<u>Disease Group Low No</u>, Disease Group High No, . . .)

Figure 11.15 Relational model of diseases and groups.

data model and to accept some redundancy in the latter as the price of automatic logical data model generation.

Including a derivable foreign key may be worthwhile if we are generating program logic based on navigation using foreign keys. But carrying redundant data complicates update and introduces the risk of data inconsistency. In this example, we would need to ensure that if a disease moved from one group to another, the foreign key would be updated. In fact this can happen only if the disease number changes (in which case we should regard it as a new disease—see Section 6.2.4.2: if we were unhappy with this rule, we would need to allocate a surrogate key) or if we change the boundaries of existing groups. We may well determine that the business does not require the ability to make such changes; in this case the derivable foreign key option becomes more appealing.

Whether or not the business requires the ability to make such changes, the fact that **Disease No** must be no less than **Disease Group Low No** and no greater than the corresponding **Disease Group High No** should be included in the business rule documentation (see Chapter 14).

The above situation occurs commonly with dates and date ranges. For example, a bank statement might include all transactions for a given account between two dates. If the two dates were attributes of the **Statement** entity class, the relationship between **Transaction** and **Statement** would be derivable by comparing these dates with the transaction dates. In this case, the boundaries of a future statement might well change, perhaps at the request of the customer, or because we wished to notify them that the account was overdrawn. If we choose the redundant foreign key approach, we will need to ensure that the foreign key is updated in such cases.

11.6.4 **Optional Relationships**

In a relational database, a one-to-many relationship that is optional at the "many" end (as most are) requires no special handling. However, if a one-to-many relationship is optional at the "one" end, the foreign key representing that relationship must be able to indicate in some way that there is no associated row in the referenced table. The most common way of achieving this is to make the foreign key column(s) "nullable" (able to be null or empty in some rows). However, this adds complexity to queries. A simple join of the two tables (an "inner join") will only return rows with

Figure 11.16 Optional relationship.

nonnull foreign keys. For example, if nullable foreign keys are used, a simple join of the **Agent** and **Policy** tables illustrated in Figure 11.16 will only return those policies actually sold by an agent. One of the major selling points of relational databases is the ease with which end-users can query the database. The novice user querying this data to obtain a figure for the total value of policies is likely to get a value significantly less than the true total. To obtain the true total it is necessary to construct an outer join or use a union query, which the novice user may not know about.

A way around this problem is to add a "Not Applicable" row to the referenced table and include a reference to that row in each foreign key that would otherwise be null. The true total can then be obtained with only a simple query. The drawback is that other processing becomes more complex as we need to allow for the "dummy" agent.

11.6.4.1 Alternatives to Nulls

In Section 11.4.9 we discussed some problems with nulls in nonkey columns. We now discuss two foreign key situations in which alternatives to nulls can make life simpler.

Optional Foreign Keys in Hierarchies

In a hierarchy represented by a recursive relationship, that relationship must be optional at both ends as described in Section 3.5.4. However, we have found that making top-level foreign keys self-referencing rather than null (see the first two rows in Figure 11.17) can simplify the programming of queries that traverse a varying number of levels. For example, a query to return the H/R Department and all its subordinate departments does not need to be a UNION query as it can be written as a single query that traverses the maximum depth of the hierarchy.

Other Optional Foreign Keys

If a one-to-many relationship is optional at the "one" end, a query that joins the tables representing the entity classes involved in that relationship may need to take account of that fact, if it is not to return unexpected results. For example, consider the tables in Figure 11.18 on page 351. If we wish to list all employees and the unions to which they belong, the first query in Figure 11.18 will only return four employees (those that belong to unions)

ORG UNIT (<u>Org Unit ID</u>, Org Unit Name, Parent Org Unit ID*)

Org Unit ID	Org Unit Name	Parent Org Unit ID
1	Production	1
2	H/R	2
21	Recruitment	2
22	Training	2
221	IT Training	22
222	Other Training	22

Figure 11.17 An alternative simple hierarchy table.

rather than all of them. By contrast an outer join, indicated by the keyword "left"[12] as in the second query in Figure 11.18, will return all employees.

If users are able to access the database directly through a query interface, it is unreasonable to expect all users to understand this subtlety. In this case, it may be better to create a dummy row in the table representing the entity class at the "one" end of the relationship and replace the null foreign key in all rows in the other table by the key of that dummy row, as illustrated in Figure 11.19. The first, simpler, query in Figure 11.18 will now return all employees.

11.6.5 Overlapping Foreign Keys

Figure 11.20 is a model for an insurance company that operates in several countries. Each agent works in a particular country, *and sells only to customers in that country*. Note that the E-R diagram *allows* for this situation but does not enforce the rule (see page 352).

If we apply the rule for representing relationships by foreign keys, we find that the Country ID column appears twice in the **Policy** table—once to support the link to **Agent** and once to support the link to **Customer**. We can distinguish the columns by naming one Customer Country ID and the other Agent Country ID. But because of our rule that agents sell only to customers in their own country, both columns will always hold the same value. This seems a clear case of data redundancy, easily solved by combining the two columns into one. Yet, there are arguments for keeping two separate columns.

The two-column approach is more flexible; if we change the rule about selling only to customers in the same country, the two-column model will

---

[12]The keyword "right" may also be used if all rows from the second table are required rather than all rows from the first table.

Surname	Initial	Union Code
Chekov	P	APF
Kirk	J	null
McCoy	L	null
Scott	M	ETU
Spock	M	null
Sulu	H	APF
Uhura	N	TCU

Union Code	Union Name
APF	Airline Pilots' Federation
ETU	Electrical Trades Union
TCU	Telecommunications Union

select   SURNAME, INITIAL, UNION_NAME

from   EMPLOYEE join UNION on

EMPLOYEE.UNION_CODE = UNION.UNION_CODE;

select   SURNAME, INITIAL, UNION_NAME

from   EMPLOYEE left join UNION on

EMPLOYEE.UNION_CODE = UNION.UNION_CODE;

Figure 11.18   Tables at each end of an optional one-to-many relationship.

easily support the new situation. But here we have the familiar trade-off between flexibility and constraints; we can equally argue that the one-column model does a better job of enforcing an important business rule, if we are convinced that the rule will apply for the life of the database.

There is a more subtle flexibility issue: What if one or both of the relationships from **Policy** became optional? Perhaps it is possible for a policy to be issued without involving an agent. In such cases, we would need to hold a null value for the foreign key to **Agent**, but this involves "nulling out" the value for Country ID, part of the foreign key to **Customer**. We would end up losing our link to **Customer**. We have been involved in some long arguments about this one, the most common suggestion being that we only need to set the value of Agent ID to null and leave Country ID untouched.

Surname	Initial	Union Code
Chekov	P	APF
Kirk	J	N/A
McCoy	L	N/A
Scott	M	ETU
Spock	M	N/A
Sulu	H	APF
Uhura	N	TCU

Union Code	Union Name
APF	Airline Pilots' Federation
ETU	Electrical Trades Union
TCU	Telecommunications Union
N/A	Not applicable

Figure 11.19   A dummy row at the "one" end of an optional one-to-many relationship.

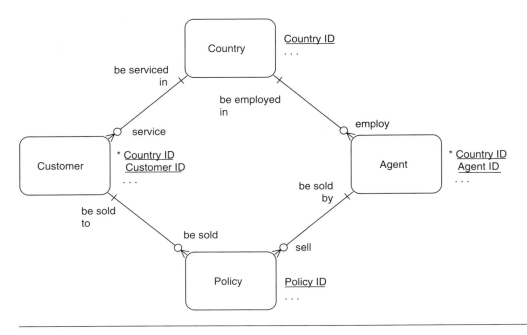

Figure 11.20 E-R model leading to overlapping foreign keys.

But this involves an inconsistency in the way we handle foreign keys. It might not be so bad if we only had to tell *programmers* to handle the situation as a special case ("Don't set the whole of the foreign key to null in this instance"), but these days program logic may be generated automatically by a CASE tool that is not so flexible about handling nonstandard situations. The DBMS itself may recognize foreign keys and rely on them not overlapping in order to support referential integrity (Section 14.5.4).

Our advice is to include both columns and to include the rule that agents and customers must be from the same country in the business rule documentation (see Chapter 14).

Of course, we can alternatively use stand-alone keys for **Customer** and **Agent**. In this case the issue of overlapping foreign keys will not arise, but again the rule that agents and customers must be from the same country should be included in the business rule documentation.

11.6.6 **Split Foreign Keys**

The next structure has a similar flavor but is a little more complex. You are likely to encounter it more often than the overlapping foreign key problem, once you know how to recognize it!

Figure 11.21 shows a model for an organization that takes orders from customers and dispatches them to the customers' branches. Note that the primary key of **Branch** is a combination of Customer No and Branch No, a choice that would be appropriate if we wanted to use the customers' own branch numbers rather than define new ones ourselves. In translating this model into relational tables, we need to carry two foreign keys in the **Ordered Item** table. The foreign key to **Order** is Order No, and the foreign key to **Branch** is Customer No + Branch No.

Our **Ordered Item** table, including foreign keys (marked with asterisks), is shown in Figure 11.22.

But let us assume the reasonable business rule that the customer who places the order is also the customer who receives the order. Then, since each order is placed and received by one customer, Order No is a determinant of Customer No. The **Ordered Item** table is therefore not fully normalized, as Order No is a determinant but is not a candidate key of the table.

We already have a table with Order No as the key and Customer No as a non-key item. Holding Customer No in the **Ordered Item** table tells us nothing new and involves us in the usual problems of un-normalized structures. For example, if the Customer No for an order was entered incorrectly, it would need to be corrected for every item in that order. The obvious solution seems to be to remove Customer No from the **Ordered Item** table. But this causes its own problems.

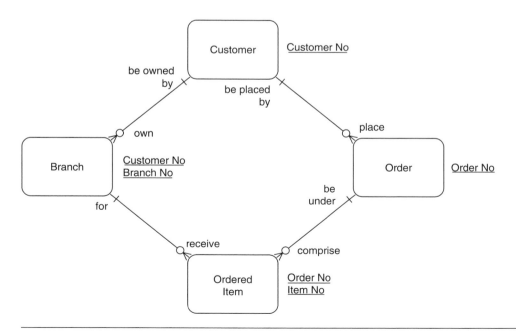

Figure 11.21 E-R model leading to split foreign key.

ORDERED ITEM (<u>Order No*</u>, <u>Item No</u>, Product, Customer No*, Branch No*)

Figure 11.22 Ordered item table.

First, we have broken our rule for generating a foreign key for each one-to-many relationship. Looked at another way, if we were to draw a diagram from the tables, would we include a relationship line from **Ordered Item** to **Branch**? Not according to our rules, but we started off by saying there *was* a relationship between the two; Branch No is in the **Ordered Item** table to support a relationship to **Branch**.

But there is more to the problem than a diagramming nicety. Any CASE tool that generates foreign keys automatically from relationships is going to include Customer No in the **Ordered Item** table. A program generator that makes the usual assumption that it can find the full primary key of **Branch** in the **Ordered Item** table will be in trouble if Customer No is excluded. Again, standard facilities for enforcing referential integrity are most unlikely to support the special situation that arises if Customer No is excluded.

Whether we include or exclude Customer No, we strike serious problems. When you encounter this situation, which you should pick up through a normalization check after generating the foreign keys, we strongly suggest you go back and select different primary keys. In this case, a stand-alone Branch No as the primary key of **Branch** will do the job. (The original Branch No and Customer No will become nonkey items, forming a second candidate key.) You will lose the constraint that the customer who places the order receives the order. This will need to be included in the business rule documentation (see Chapter 14).

11.7 **Table and Column Names**

There are two factors affecting table and column names:

1. The target DBMS (if known) may impose a limit on the length of names, may require that there are no spaces or special characters other than underlines in a name, and may require names to be in all uppercase or all lowercase.

2. There may be a standard in force within the organization as to how tables and columns are named.

If there is no name length limit and no table/column naming standard, the best approach to table and column naming is to use the corresponding entity class or attribute name, with spaces and special characters replaced by underlines if necessary (e.g., the entity class **Organization Unit** would be represented by the table **organization_unit)**. An alternative, provided the target DBMS supports mixed-case names, is to delete all spaces and special characters and capitalize the first letter of each word in the name[13] (e.g., **OrganizationUnit**).

In our experience, installation table/column naming standards often require that table names all start with a particular prefix, typically "t_" or "Tbl." Our example table name would then be **t_organization_unit** or **TblOrganizationUnit,** respectively.

If the target DBMS imposes a name length limit, it is usually necessary to abbreviate the words that make up table and column names. If so, two principles should be observed:

1. Use abbreviations consistently.
2. Do not also abbreviate entity class and attribute names as these are for use by the business, not the database.

11.8 **Logical Data Model Notations**

How should a logical data model be presented to users and reviewers? There is a choice of diagrammatic and textual notations.

An Entity-Relationship diagram can be used to present a logical data model using the following conventions:

1. Each table is represented by a box as if it were an entity class.
2. Each foreign key in a table is represented by a line from that table to the referenced table, marked as "optional many" at the foreign key end and either "mandatory one" or "optional one" at the primary key end, depending on whether the column is mandatory (NOT NULL) or optional (NULL), which will have been derived from the optionality of the relationship that the particular foreign key represents.
3. All columns (including foreign keys) should be listed either on the diagram (inside the box representing the table) or in a separate list depending on the facilities provided by the chosen CASE tool and the need to produce an uncluttered diagram that fits the page.

If this notation is chosen, it is important to be able to distinguish the logical data model diagram from the conceptual data model diagram. Your chosen CASE tool may provide different diagram templates for the two types of model with different notations, but in any case, be sure to label clearly each diagram as to whether it is conceptual or logical.

---

[13]The so-called "CamelCase."

> **EMPLOYEE** (<u>Employee Number</u>, Employee Name, Department Number)
> **DEPARTMENT** (<u>Department Number</u>, Department Name, Department Location)
> **QUALIFICATION** (<u>Employee Number</u>, <u>Qualification Description</u>, Qualification Year)

Figure 11.23 Employee model using relational notation.

Some UML CASE tools (e.g., Rational Rose™) provide a quite different diagram type for the logical data model; although it consists of boxes and lines, the boxes look quite different from those used in a class model.

The textual notations available also depend on the CASE tool chosen but generally conform to one of three formats:

1. "Relational" notation in Figure 11.23 in which each table name is listed and followed on the same line by the names of each of its columns, the entire set of column names enclosed in parentheses or braces.
2. "List" notation as in Figure 11.24 in which each table name and column name appears in a line on its own, and the datatype and length (and possibly the definition) of each column is shown.
3. DDL (data description language) as in Figure 11.25 in which the instructions to the DBMS to create each table and its columns are couched.

EMPLOYEE
<u>Employee Number</u>: 5 Numeric—The number allocated to this employee by the Human Resources Department
Employee Name: 60 Characters—The name of this employee: the surname, a comma and space, the first given name plus a space and the middle initial if any
Department Number: The number used by the organization to identify the Department that pays this employee's salary

DEPARTMENT
<u>Department Number</u>: 2 Numeric—The number used by the organization to identify this Department
Department Name: 30 Characters—The name of this Department as it appears in company documentation
Department Location: 30 Characters—The name of the city where this Department is located

QUALIFICATION
<u>Employee Number</u>: 5 Numeric—The number allocated to the employee holding this qualification by the Human Resources Department
<u>Qualification Description</u>: 30 Characters—The name of this qualification
Qualification Year: Date Optional—The year in which this employee obtained this qualification

Figure 11.24 Employee model using list notation.

```
create table EMPLOYEE (
EMPLOYEE_NUMBER integer not null,
EMPLOYEE_NAME char(60) not null,
DEPARTMENT_NUMBER integer not null);
alter table EMPLOYEE add constraint PK1 primary key (EMPLOYEE_NUMBER);

create table DEPARTMENT (
DEPARTMENT_NUMBER: integer not null,
DEPARTMENT_NAME char(30) not null,
DEPARTMENT_LOCATION: char(30) not null);
alter table DEPARTMENT add constraint PK2 primary key (DEPARTMENT_NUMBER);

create table QUALIFICATION (
EMPLOYEE_NUMBER integer not null,
QUALIFICATION_DESCRIPTION char(30) not null,
QUALIFICATION_YEAR date null);
alter table QUALIFICATION add constraint PK3 primary key (EMPLOYEE_NUMBER,
QUALIFICATION_DESCRIPTION);
alter table EMPLOYEE add constraint FK1 foreign key (DEPARTMENT_NUMBER)
references DEPARTMENT;
alter table QUALIFICATION add constraint FK2 foreign key (EMPLOYEE_NUMBER)
references EMPLOYEE;
```

Figure 11.25   Employee model using DDL notation.

11.9 **Summary**

The transformation from conceptual model to logical model is largely mechanical, but there are a few important decisions to be made by the modeler.

Subtypes and supertypes need to be "leveled." Tables can represent a selected single level of generalization or multiple levels of generalization.

The allowed values of category attributes need to be specified either by a constraint on the relevant column or by the addition of a new table to hold them.

Care needs to be taken in the interdependent tasks of primary key specification and implementation of relationships using foreign keys.

At all stages of this phase, there are exceptions and unusual situations that the professional modeler needs to be able to recognize and deal with.

Chapter 12
Physical Database Design

"'Necessity is the mother of invention' is a silly proverb. 'Necessity is the mother of futile dodges' is much nearer to the truth."
– Alfred North Whitehead

"Judgment, not passion, should prevail."
– Epicharmus

12.1 Introduction

The transition from logical to physical database design marks a change in focus and in the skills required. To this point, our goal has been to develop a set of data structures independent of any particular DBMS, without explicit regard for performance. Now our attention shifts to making those structures perform on a particular hardware platform using the facilities of our selected DBMS. Instead of business and generic data structuring skills, we require a detailed knowledge of general performance tuning techniques and of the facilities provided by the DBMS. Frequently this means that a different, more technical, person will take on the role of database design. In this case, the data modeler's role will be essentially to advise on the impact of changes to tables and columns, which may be required as a last resort to achieve performance goals.

An enduring myth about database design is that the response time for data retrieval from a normalized set of tables and columns will be longer than acceptable. As with all myths there is a grain of truth in the assertion. Certainly, if a large amount of data is to be retrieved, or if the database itself is very large and either the query is unduly complex or the data has not been appropriately indexed, a slow response time may result. However, there is a lot that can be done in tuning the database and in careful crafting of queries, before denormalization or other modification of the tables and columns defined in a logical data model becomes necessary. This has become increasingly true as overall computer performance has improved and DBMS designers have continued to develop the capabilities of their optimizers (the built-in software within a DBMS that selects the most efficient means of executing each query).

Before we go any further, we need to clarify some terminology that we touched on in Chapter 1.

The data modeler's focus will be on the tables and columns (and the views based on them). He or she will typically refer to the tables and columns delivered by the physical database design process as the **Physical Data Model** to distinguish it from the Logical Data Model. As we saw in the previous chapter, the **Logical Data Model** is an ideal structure, which reflects business information requirements and makes assertions about data properties such as functional dependency, without being obscured by any changes required for performance.

The database designer will be interested not only in the tables and columns but also in the infrastructure components—indexes and physical storage mechanisms—that support data management and performance requirements. Since program logic depends only on tables and columns (and views based on them), that set of components is often referred to as the **Logical Schema**[1] while the remainder may be referred to as the **Physical Schema**.[2]

These alternative uses of the terms "logical" and "physical" can easily lead to confusion!

In this chapter we review the inputs that the physical database designer requires in addition to the Logical Data Model, then we look at a number of options available for achieving performance goals. We divide these options into three broad categories:

1. Design decisions that do not affect program logic (i.e., that preserve the structure of the Logical Data Model)
2. Approaches to redesigning queries themselves to run faster (rather than changing the database structure)
3. Design decisions that entail changes to the structures specified in the Logical Data Model.

Finally, we look at the definition of views.

If you are a specialist data modeler, you may be tempted to skip this chapter, since much of it relates to the tools and work of the physical database designer. We encourage you not to do so. One of the key factors in getting good outcomes in physical database design is the level of communication and respect between the database designer and the data modeler. That means understanding what the other party does and how they do it. Good architects maintain an up-to-date knowledge of building materials.

On the other hand, if you are responsible for physical database design, you need to recognize that this chapter merely scratches the surface of the many features and facilities available to you in a modern DBMS. Many of these are DBMS-specific, and accordingly better covered in vendor manuals or guides for the specific product. Specialist physical database designers generally focus on one (or a limited number) of DBMSs, in contrast to modelers whose specialization is more likely to be in a specific business domain.

---

[1]Equivalent to the ANSI/SPARC Conceptual Schema and External Schemas.
[2]Equivalent to the ANSI/SPARC Internal Schema.

12.2 **Inputs to Database Design**

As well as the logical data model, the database designer will require other information to be able to make sound design decisions:

1. The Process Model, detailing input processes (creation and updating of rows in tables) and output requirements (retrieval of data from the database), enabling the database designer to establish:
   a. The circumstances in which rows are added to each table: how frequently on average and at peak times (e.g., 1 per day or 100 per second), and how many at a time, plus such details as whether the primary key of an added row depends on the time that it is added, so that rows added at about the same time have similar primary keys (which can impact performance both through contention and the need to rebalance the primary key index)
   b. The circumstances in which rows are updated in each table: how frequently on average and at peak times plus the likelihood that rows with similar primary keys are updated at about the same time, which may affect locking (see Section 12.5.1)
   c. The circumstances in which rows are deleted from each table: how frequently and how many at a time (deletes, like inserts, affect all indexes on the table)
   d. The circumstances in which rows are retrieved from each table: what columns in the table are used for selecting rows, how many rows are retrieved, what other tables are referenced, what columns in the referring and referenced tables are correlated or "joined"
2. The Process/Entity Matrix[3] or mapping that shows which processes access each entity class and how (create, update, retrieve), providing the database designer with a list of the processes that create, update, and retrieve each entity class
3. Nonstructural data requirements:
   a. Retention: how long data in each table is to be retained before deletion or archiving, whether there is a requirement for data to be removed from a table within a certain time frame
   b. Volumes: how many rows are likely to be included in each table at system roll-out, how many additional rows are likely to be created within a given time period (retention and volumes enable the database designer to establish how big each table will be at various times during the life of the application)

---

[3]Often referred to as a "CRUD" matrix (Create, Read, Update, Delete). See Section 8.2.5.

    c. Availability: whether data is required on a "24 × 7" basis, and if not, for how long and how frequently the database can be inaccessible by users, enabling the database designer to plan for:

       i. Any batch processes specified in the process model

      ii. Downtime during which the database can be reorganized; (i.e., data and indexes redistributed more evenly across the storage medium)

     iii. Whether data needs to be replicated at multiple sites to provide fallback in the event of network failure

    d. Freshness: how up-to-date the data available to those retrieving it has to be, enabling the database designer to decide whether it is feasible to have separate update and retrieval copies of data (see Section 12.6.4)

    e. Security requirements, driving access permissions and possibly prompting table partitioning and creation of views reflecting different subsets of data available to different classes of users

4. Performance requirements: usually expressed in terms of the Response Time, the time taken by each defined exchange in each application/user dialog, (i.e., the time between the user pressing the Enter key and the application displaying the confirmation of the creation or updating of the data in the database or the results of the query). These enable the database designer to focus on those creates, updates, and retrieval queries that have the most critical performance requirements (beware of statements such as "all queries must exhibit subsecond response time"; this is rarely true and indicates that the writer has not bothered to identify the critical user operations; we once encountered this statement in a contract that also contained the statement "The application must support retrieval queries of arbitrary complexity.")

5. The target DBMS: not only the "brand" (e.g., DB2™, Informix™, Oracle™, SQL Server™, Access ™, and so on), but the version, enabling the database designer to establish what facilities, features, and options are provided by that DBMS

6. Any current or likely limitations on disk space: these will be a factor in choosing one or the other option where options differ in their use of disk space (see, for example, Section 12.6.8)

7. Any likely difficulties in obtaining skilled programming resources: these may prompt the avoidance of more complex data structures where these impact programming complexity (see, for example, Sections 12.6.4 and 12.6.5).

12.3 **Options Available to the Database Designer**

The main challenge facing the database designer is to speed up those transactions with critical performance requirements. The slowest activities in a database are almost always the reading of data from the storage medium into main memory and the writing of data from main memory back to the storage medium, and it is on this data access (also known as "I/O"—input/output) that we now focus.

Commercial relational DBMSs differ in the facilities and features they offer, the ways in which those facilities and features are implemented, and the options available within each facility and feature. It is beyond the scope and intention of this book to detail each of these; in any case, given the frequency with which new versions of the major commercial DBMSs are released, our information would soon be out-of-date. Instead, we offer a list of the most important facilities and features offered by relational DBMSs and some principles for their use. This can be used:

1. By the database designer, as a checklist of what facilities and features to read up on in the DBMS documentation
2. By the data modeler who is handing over to a database designer, as a checklist of issues to examine during any negotiations over changes to tables and columns.

We first look at those design decisions that do not affect program logic. We then look at ways in which queries can be crafted to run faster. We finally look at various types of changes that can be made to the logical schema to support faster queries when all other techniques have been tried and some queries still do not run fast enough. This is also the sequence in which these techniques should be tried by the database designer.

Note that those design decisions that do not affect program logic can be revisited and altered after a database has been rolled out with minimal, if any, impact on the availability of the database and, of course, none on program logic. Changes to the logical schema, however, require changes to program logic. They must therefore be made in a test environment (along with those program changes), tested, packaged, and released in a controlled manner like any other application upgrade.

12.4   Design Decisions Which Do Not Affect Program Logic

The discussion in this section makes frequent reference to the term **block**. This is the term used in the Oracle™ DBMS product to refer to the smallest amount of data that can be transferred between the storage medium and main memory. The corresponding term in IBM's DB2™ DBMS is **page**.

12.4.1   Indexes

Indexes provide one of the most commonly used methods for rapidly retrieving specified rows from a table without having to search the entire table.

Each table can have one or more indexes specified. Each index applies to a particular column or set of columns. For each value of the column(s), the index lists the location(s) of the row(s) in which that value can be found. For example, an index on **Customer Location** would enable us to readily locate all of the rows that had a value for **Customer Location** of (say) New York.

The specification of each index includes:

- The column(s)
- Whether or not it is unique, (i.e., whether there can be no more than one row for any given value) (see Section 12.4.1.3)
- Whether or not it is the sorting index (see Section 12.4.1.3)
- The structure of the index (for some DBMSs: see Sections 12.4.1.4 and 12.4.1.5).

The advantages of an index are that:

- It can improve data access performance for a retrieval or update
- Retrievals which only refer to indexed columns do not need to read any data blocks (access to indexes is often faster than direct access to data blocks bypassing any index).

The disadvantages are that each index:

- Adds to the data access cost of a create transaction or an update transaction in which an indexed column is updated
- Takes up disk space
- May increase lock contention (see Section 12.5.1)
- Adds to the processing and data access cost of reorganize and table load utilities.

Whether or not an index will actually improve the performance of an individual query depends on two factors:

- Whether the index is actually used by the query
- Whether the index confers any performance advantage on the query.

12.4.1.1 Index Usage by Queries

DML (Data Manipulation Language)[4] only specifies what you want, not how to get it. The optimizer built into the DBMS selects the best available

---

[4]This is the SQL query language, often itself called "SQL" and most commonly used to retrieve data from a relational database.

access method based on its knowledge of indexes, column contents, and so on. Thus index usage cannot be explicitly specified but is determined by the optimizer during DML compilation. How it implements the DML will depend on:

- The DML clauses used, in particular the predicate(s) in the WHERE clause (See Figure 12.1 for examples)
- The tables accessed, their size and content
- What indexes there are on those tables.

Some predicates will preclude the use of indexes; these include:

- Negative conditions, (e.g., "not equals" and those involving NOT)
- LIKE predicates in which the comparison string starts with a wildcard
- Comparisons including scalar operators (e.g., +) or functions (e.g., datatype conversion functions)
- ANY/ALL subqueries, as in Figure 12.2
- Correlated subqueries, as in Figure 12.3.

Certain update operations may also be unable to use indexes. For example, while the retrieval query in Figure 12.1 can use an index on the **Salary** column if there is one, the update query in the same figure cannot.

Note that the DBMS may require that, after an index is added, a utility is run to examine table contents and indexes and recompile each SQL query. Failure to do this would prevent any query from using the new index.

12.4.1.2   Performance Advantages of Indexes

Even if an index is available and the query is formulated in such a way that it can use that index, the index may not improve performance if more than a certain proportion of rows are retrieved. That proportion depends on the DBMS.

```
select    EMP_NO, EMP_NAME, SALARY
from      EMPLOYEE
where     SALARY > 80000;

update    EMPLOYEE
set       SALARY = SALARY* 1.1
```

Figure 12.1   Retrieval and update queries.

```
select    EMP_NO, EMP_NAME, SALARY
from      EMPLOYEE
where     SALARY > all
 (select  SALARY
from      EMPLOYEE
where     DEPT_NO = '123');
```

Figure 12.2 An ALL subquery.

12.4.1.3 Index Properties

If an index is defined as **unique**, each row in the associated table must have a different value in the column or columns covered by the index. Thus, this is a means of implementing a uniqueness constraint, and a unique index should therefore be created on each table's primary key as well as on any other sets of columns having a uniqueness constraint. However, since the database administrator can always drop any index (except perhaps that on a primary key) at any time, a unique index cannot be relied on to be present whenever rows are inserted. As a result most programming standards require that a uniqueness constraint is explicitly tested for whenever inserting a row into the relevant table or updating any column participating in that constraint.

The **sorting index** (called the **clustering index** in DB2) of each table is the one that controls the sequence in which rows are stored during a bulk load or reorganization that occurs during the existence of that index. Clearly there can be only one such index for each table. Which column(s) should the sorting index cover? In some DBMSs there is no choice; the index on the primary key will also control row sequence. Where there is a choice, any of the following may be worthy candidates, depending on the DBMS:

- Those columns most frequently involved in inequalities, (e.g., where > or >= appears in the predicate)
- Those columns most frequently specified as the sorting sequence

```
select      EMP_NO, EMP_NAME
from        EMPLOYEE as E1
where       exists
 (select*
from        EMPLOYEE as E2
where       E2.EMP_NAME = E1.EMP_NAME
and         E2.EMP_NO <> E1.EMP_NO);
```

Figure 12.3 A correlated subquery.

- The columns of the most frequently specified foreign key in joins
- The columns of the primary key.

The performance advantages of a sorting index are:

- Multiple rows relevant to a query can be retrieved in a single I/O operation
- Sorting is much faster if the rows are already more or less[5] in sequence.

By contrast, creating a sorting index on one or more columns may confer no advantage over a nonsorting index if those columns are mostly involved in index-only processing, (i.e., if those columns are mostly accessed only in combination with each other or are mostly involved in = predicates).

Consider creating other (nonunique, nonsorting) indexes on:

- Columns searched or joined with a low hit rate
- Foreign keys
- Columns frequently involved in aggregate functions, existence checks or DISTINCT selection
- Sets of columns frequently linked by AND in predicates
- **Code & Meaning** columns for a classification table if there are other less-frequently accessed columns
- Columns frequently retrieved.

Indexes on any of the following may not yield any performance benefit:

- Columns with low cardinality (the number of different values is significantly less than the number of rows) unless a bit-mapped index is used (see Section 12.4.1.5)
- Columns with skewed distribution (many occurrences of one or two particular values and few occurrences of each of a number of other values)
- Columns with low population (NULL in many rows)
- Columns which are frequently updated
- Columns which take up a significant proportion of the row length
- Tables occupying a small number of blocks, unless the index is to be used for joins, a uniqueness constraint, or referential integrity, or if index-only processing is to be used
- Columns with the "varchar" datatype.

---

[5]Note that rows can get out of sequence between reorganizations.

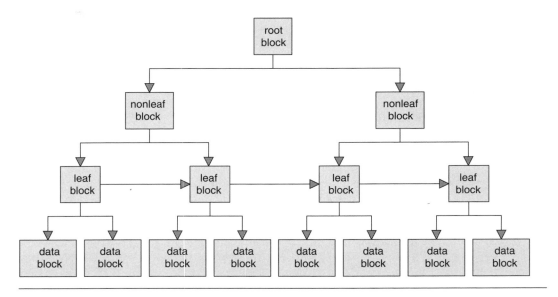

Figure 12.4 Balanced tree index structure.

12.4.1.4 Balanced Tree Indexes

Figure 12.4 illustrates the structure of a **Balanced Tree index**[6] used in most relational DBMSs. Note that the depth of the tree may be only one (in which case the index entries in the root block point directly to data blocks), two (in which case the index entries in the root block point to leaf blocks in which index entries point to data blocks), three (as shown) or more than three (in which the index entries in nonleaf blocks point to other nonleaf blocks). The term "balanced" refers to the fact that the tree structure is symmetrical. If insertion of a new record causes a particular leaf block to fill up, the index entries must be redistributed evenly across the index with additional index blocks created as necessary, leading eventually to a deeper index.

Particular problems may arise with a balanced tree index on a column or columns on which INSERTs are sequenced, (i.e., each additional row has a higher value in those column[s] than the previous row added). In this case, the insertion of new index entries is focused on the rightmost (highest value) leaf block, rather than evenly across the index, resulting in more frequent redistribution of index entries that may be quite slow if the entire index is not in main memory. This makes a strong case for random, rather than sequential, primary keys.

---

[6]Often referred to as a "B-tree Index."

12.4.1.5   Bit-Mapped Indexes

Another index structure provided by some DBMSs is the **bit-mapped index**. This has an index entry for each value that appears in the indexed column. Each index entry includes a column value followed by a series of bits, one for each row in the table. Each bit is set to one if the corresponding row has that value in the indexed column and zero if it has some other value. This type of index confers the most advantage where the indexed column is of low cardinality (the number of different values is significantly less than the number of rows). By contrast such an index may impact negatively on the performance of an insert operation into a large table as every bit in every index entry that represents a row after the inserted row must be moved one place to the right. This is less of a problem if the index can be held permanently in main memory (see Section 12.4.3).

12.4.1.6   Indexed Sequential Tables

A few DBMSs support an alternative form of index referred to as **ISAM** (**Indexed Sequential Access Method**). This may provide better performance for some types of data population and access patterns.

12.4.1.7   Hash Tables

Some DBMSs provide an alternative to an index to support random access in the form of a hashing algorithm to calculate block numbers from key values. Tables managed in this fashion are referred to as **hashed random** (or "hash" for short). Again, this may provide better performance for some types of data population and access patterns. Note that this technique is of no value if partial keys are used in searches (e.g., "Show me the customers whose names start with 'Smi'") or a range of key values is required (e.g., "Show me all customers with a birth date between 1/1/1948 and 12/31/1948"), whereas indexes do support these types of query.

12.4.1.8   Heap Tables

Some DBMSs provide for tables to be created without indexes. Such tables are sometimes referred to as **heaps**.

If the table is small (only a few blocks) an index may provide no advantage. Indeed if all the data in the table will fit into a single block, accessing a row via an index requires two blocks to be read (the index block and the data block) compared with reading in and scanning (in main memory) the one block: in this case an index degrades performance. Even if the data in the table requires two blocks, the average number of blocks read to access a single row is still less than the two necessary for access via an index. Many reference (or classification) tables fall into this category.

Note however that the DBMS may require that an index be created for the primary key of each table that has one, and a classification table will certainly require a primary key. If so, performance may be improved by one of the following:

1. Creating an additional index that includes both code (the primary key) and meaning columns; any access to the classification table which requires both columns will use that index rather than the data table itself (which is now in effect redundant but only takes up space rather than slowing down access)
2. Assigning the table to main memory in such a way that ensures the classification table remains in main memory for the duration of each load of the application (see Section 12.4.3).

12.4.2 **Data Storage**

A relational DBMS provides the database designer with a variety of options (depending on the DBMS) for the storage of data.

12.4.2.1 Table Space Usage

Many DBMSs enable the database designer to create multiple **table spaces** to which tables can be assigned. Since these table spaces can each be given different block sizes and other parameters, tables with similar access patterns can be stored in the same table space and each table space then tuned to optimize the performance for the tables therein. The DBMS may even allow you to interleave rows from different tables, in which case you may be able to arrange, for example, for the **Order Item** rows for a given order to follow the **Order** row for that order, if they are frequently retrieved together. This reduces the average number of blocks that need to be read to retrieve an entire order. The facility is sometimes referred to as **clustering,** which may lead to confusion with the term "clustering index" (see Section 12.4.1.3).

12.4.2.2 Free Space

When a table is loaded or reorganized, each block may be loaded with as many rows as can fit (unless rows are particularly short and there is a limit imposed by the DBMS on how many rows a block can hold). If a new row is inserted and the sorting sequence implied by the primary index dictates that the row should be placed in an already full block, that row must be placed in another block. If no provision has been made for additional rows, that will be the last block (or if that block is full, a new block following the last block). Clearly this "overflow" situation will cause a degradation over time of the sorting sequence implied by the primary index and will reduce any advantages conferred by the sorting sequence of that index.

This is where **free space** enters the picture. A specified proportion of the space in each block can be reserved at load or reorganization time for rows subsequently inserted. A fallback can also be provided by leaving every nth block empty at load or reorganization time. If a block fills up, additional rows that belong in that block will be placed in the next available empty block. Note that once this happens, any attempt to retrieve data in sequence will incur extra block reads.

This caters, of course, not only for insertions but for increases in the length of existing rows, such as those that have columns with the "varchar" (variable length) datatype.

The more free space you specify, the more rows can be fitted in or increased in length before performance degrades and reorganization is necessary. At the same time, more free space means that any retrieval of multiple consecutive rows will need to read more blocks. Obviously for those tables that are read-only, you should specify zero free space. In tables that have a low frequency of create transactions (and update transactions that increase row length) zero free space is also reasonable since additional data can be added after the last row.

Free space can and should be allocated for indexes as well as data.

12.4.2.3   Table Partitioning

Some DBMSs allow you to divide a table into separate **partitions** based on one of the indexes. For example, if the first column of an index is the state code, a separate partition can be created for each state. Each partition can be independently loaded or reorganized and can have different free space and other settings.

12.4.2.4   Drive Usage

Choosing where a table or index is on disk enables you to use faster drives for more frequently accessed data, or to avoid channel contention by distributing across multiple disk channels tables that are accessed in the same query.

12.4.2.5 Compression

One option that many DBMSs provide is the compression of data in the stored table, (e.g., shortening of null columns or text columns with trailing space). While this may save disk space and increase the number of rows per block, it can add to the processing cost.

12.4.2.6 Distribution and Replication

Modern DBMSs provide many facilities for distributing data across multiple networked servers. Among other things distributing data in this manner can confer performance and availability advantages. However, this is a specialist topic and is outside the scope of this brief overview of physical database design.

12.4.3 **Memory Usage**

Some DBMSs support multiple **input/output buffers** in main memory and enable you to specify the size of each buffer and allocate tables and indexes to particular buffers. This can reduce or even eliminate the need to swap frequently-accessed tables or indexes out of main memory to make room for other data. For example, a buffer could be set up that is large enough to accommodate all the classification tables in their entirety. Once they are all in main memory, any query requiring data from a classification table does not have to read any blocks for that purpose.

12.5 **Crafting Queries to Run Faster**

We have seen in Section 12.4.1.1 that some queries cannot make use of indexes. If a query of this kind can be rewritten to make use of an index, it is likely to run faster. As a simple example, consider a retrieval of employee records in which there is a Gender column that holds either "M" or "F." A query to retrieve only male employees could be written with the predicate GENDER <> 'F' (in which case it cannot use an index on the Gender column) or with the predicate GENDER = 'M' (in which case it can use that index). The optimizer (capable of recasting queries into logically equivalent forms that will perform better) is of no help here even if it "knows" that there are currently only "M" and "F" values in the Gender column, since it has no way of knowing that some other value might eventually be loaded into that column. Thus GENDER = 'M' is not logically equivalent to GENDER <> 'F'.

There are also various ways in which subqueries can be expressed differently. Most noncorrelated subqueries can be alternatively expressed as a join. An IN subquery can always be alternatively expressed as an EXISTS subquery, although the converse is not true. A query including "> ALL (SELECT . . .)" can be alternatively expressed by substituting "> (SELECT MAX(. . .))" in place of "> ALL (SELECT . . .)."

Sorting can be very time-consuming. Note that any query including GROUP BY or ORDER BY will sort the retrieved data. These clauses may, of course, be unavoidable in meeting the information requirement. (ORDER BY is essential for the query result to be sorted in a required order since there is otherwise no guarantee of the sequencing of result data, which will reflect the sorting index only so long as no inserts or updates have occurred since the last table reorganization.) However, there are two other situations in which unnecessary sorts can be avoided.

One is DISTINCT, which is used to ensure that there are no duplicate rows in the retrieved data, which it does by sorting the result set. For example, if the query is retrieving only addresses of employees, and more than one employee lives at the same address, that address will appear more than once unless the DISTINCT clause is used. We have observed that the DISTINCT clause is sometimes used when duplicate rows are impossible; in this situation it can be removed without affecting the query result but with significant impact on query performance.

Similarly, a UNION query without the ALL qualifier after UNION ensures that there are no duplicate rows in the result set, again by sorting it (unless there is a usable index). If you know that there is no possibility of the same row resulting from more than one of the individual queries making up a UNION query, add the ALL qualifier.

12.5.1 **Locking**

DBMSs employ various **locks** to ensure, for example, that only one user can update a particular row at a time, or that, if a row is being updated, users who wish to use that row are either prevented from doing so, or see the pre-update row consistently until the update is completed. Many business requirements imply the use of locks. For example, in an airline reservation system if a customer has reserved a seat on one leg of a multileg journey, that seat must not be available to any other user, but if the original customer decides not to proceed when they discover that there is no seat available on a connecting flight, the reserved seat must be released.

The lowest level of lock is **row-level** where an individual row is locked but other rows in the same block are still accessible. The next level is the **block-level lock**, which requires less data storage for management but locks all rows in the same block as the one being updated. **Table locks** and **table space locks** are also possible. Locks may be **escalated**, whereby a lock at one level is converted to a lock at the next level to improve performance. The designer may also specify **lock acquisition** and **lock release** strategies for transactions accessing multiple tables. A transaction can either acquire all locks before starting or acquire each lock as required, and it can either release all locks after committing (completing the update transaction) or release each lock once no longer required.

12.6 Logical Schema Decisions

We now look at various types of changes that can be made to the logical schema to support faster queries when the techniques we have discussed have been tried and some queries still do not run fast enough.

12.6.1 Alternative Implementation of Relationships

If the target DBMS supports the SQL99 **set type constructor** feature:

1. A one-to-many relationship can be implemented within one table.
2. A many-to-many relationship can be implemented without creating an additional table.

Figure 12.5 illustrates such implementations.

12.6.2 Table Splitting

Two implications of increasing the size of a table are:

1. Any Balanced Tree index on that table will be deeper, (i.e., there will be more nonleaf blocks between the root block and each leaf block and, hence, more blocks to be read to access a row using that index).
2. Any query unable to use any indexes will read more blocks in scanning the entire table.

Thus, all queries—those that use indexes and those that do not—will take more time. Conversely, if a table can be made smaller, most, if not all, queries on that table will take less time.

Department No	Department Code	Department Name	Employee Group	
			Employee No	**Employee Name**
123	ACCT	Accounts	37289	J Smith
			41260	A Chang
			50227	B Malik
135	PRCH	Purchasing	16354	D Sanchez
			26732	T Nguyen

Employee No	Employee Name	Assignment Group	
		Project No	**Assignment Date**
50227	B Malik	1234	27/2/95
		2345	2/3/95
37289	J Smith	1234	28/2/95

Figure 12.5   Alternative implementations of relationships in an SQL99 DBMS.

12.6.2.1   Horizontal Splitting

One technique for reducing the size of a table accessed by a query is to split it into two or more tables with the same columns and to allocate the rows to different tables according to some criteria. In effect we are defining and implementing subtypes. For example, although it might make sense to include historical data in the same table as the corresponding current data, it is likely that different queries access current and historical data. Placing current and historical data in different tables with the same structure will certainly improve the performance of queries on current data. You may prefer to include a copy of the current data in the historical data table to enable queries on all data to be written without the UNION operator. This is duplication rather than splitting; we deal with that separately in Section 12.6.4 due to the different implications duplication has for processing.

12.6.2.2   Vertical Splitting

The more data there is in each row of a table, the fewer rows there are per block. Queries that need to read multiple consecutive rows will therefore need to read more blocks to do so. Such queries might take less time if the rows could be made shorter. At the same time shortening the rows reduces the size of the table and (if it is not particularly large) increases the likelihood that it can be retained in main memory. If some columns of a table constitute a significant proportion of the row length, and are accessed significantly less frequently than the remainder of the columns of that table, there may be a case for holding those columns in a separate table using the same primary key.

For example, if a classification table has Code, Meaning, and Explanation columns, but the Explanation column is infrequently accessed, holding that column in a separate table on the same primary key will mean that the classification table itself occupies fewer blocks, increasing the likelihood of it remaining in main memory. This may improve the performance of queries that access only the Code and Meaning columns. Of course, a query that accesses all columns must join the two tables; this may take more time than the corresponding query on the original table. Note also that if the DBMS provides a long text datatype with the property that columns using that datatype are not stored in the same block as the other columns of the same table, and the Explanation column is given that datatype, no advantage accrues from splitting that column into a separate table.

Another situation in which vertical splitting may yield performance benefits is where different processes use different columns, such as when an **Employee** table holds both personnel information and payroll information.

12.6.3 **Table Merging**

We have encountered proposals by database designers to merge tables that are regularly joined in queries.

An example of such a proposal is the merging of the **Order** and **Order Line** tables shown in Figure 12.6. Since the merged table can only have one set of columns making up the primary key, this would need to be Order No and Line No, which means that order rows in the merged table would need a dummy Line No value (since all primary key columns must be nonnull); if that value were 0 (zero), this would have the effect of all **Order Line** rows following their associated **Order** row if the index on the primary key were also the primary index. Since all rows in a table have the same columns, **Order** rows would have dummy (possibly null) Product Code, Unit Count, and

Separate: **ORDER** (<u>Order No</u>, Customer No, Order Date)
  ORDER LINE (<u>Order No, Line N</u>o, Product Code, Unit Count, Required By Date)
Merged: **ORDER/ORDER LINE** (<u>Order No, Line No</u>, Customer No, Order Date, Product Code, Unit Count, Required By Date)

Figure 12.6 Separate and merged order and order line tables.

Required By Date columns while **Order Line** rows would have dummy (again possibly null) Customer No and Order Date columns. Alternatively, a single column might be created to hold the Required By Date value in an **Order** row and the Order Date value in an **Order Line** row.

The rationale for this approach is to reduce the average number of blocks that need to be read to retrieve an entire order. However, the result is achieved at the expense of a significant change from the logical data model. If a similar effect can be achieved by interleaving rows from different tables in the same table space as described in Section 12.4.2.1, this should be done instead.

12.6.4 **Duplication**

We saw in Section 12.6.2.1 how we might separate current data from historical data to improve the performance of queries accessing only current data by reducing the size of the table read by those queries. As we indicated then, an alternative is to duplicate the current data in another table, retaining all current data as well as the historical data in the original table. However, whenever we duplicate data there is the potential for errors to arise unless there is strict control over the use of the two copies of the data. The following are among the things that can go wrong:

1. Only one copy is being updated, but some users read the other copy thinking it is up-to-date.
2. A transaction causes the addition of a quantity to a numeric column in one copy, but the next transaction adds to the same column in the other copy. Ultimately, the effect of one or other of those transactions will be lost.
3. One copy is updated, but the data from the other copy is used to overwrite the updated copy, in effect wiping out all updates since the second copy was taken.

To avoid these problems, a policy must be enforced whereby only one copy can be updated by transactions initiated by users or batch processes (the current data table in the example above). The corresponding data in the other copy (the complete table in the example above) is either automatically updated simultaneously (via a DBMS trigger, for example) or, if it is acceptable for users accessing that copy to see data that is out-of-date, replaced at regular intervals (e.g., daily).

Another example of an "active subset" of data that might be copied into another table is data on insurance policies, contracts, or any other agreements or arrangements that are reviewed, renewed, and possibly changed on a cyclical basis, such as yearly. Toward the end of a calendar month the data for those policies that are due for renewal during the next calendar month could become a "hot spot" in the table holding information about all policies. It may therefore improve performance to copy the policy data for the next renewal month into a separate table. The change over from one month to the other must, of course, be carefully managed, and it may make sense to have "last month," "this month," and "next month" tables as well as the complete table.

Another way in which duplication can confer advantages is in optimization for different processes. We shall see in Section 12.6.7 how hierarchies in particular can benefit from duplication.

12.6.5 **Denormalization**

Technically, **denormalization** is any change to the logical schema that results in it not being fully normalized according to the rules and definitions discussed in Chapters 2 and 13. In the context of physical database design, the term is often used more broadly to include the addition of derivable data of any kind, including that derived from multiple rows.

Four examples of strict violations of normalization are shown in the model of Figure 12.7:

1. It can be assumed that Customer Name and Customer Address have been copied from a **Customer** table with primary key Customer No.
2. Customer No has been copied from the **Order** table to the **Order Line** table.
3. It can be assumed that Unit Price has been copied from a **Product** table with primary key Product Code.
4. Total Price can be calculated by multiplying Unit Price by Unit Count.

Changes such as this are intended to offer performance benefits for some transactions. For example, a query on the **Order Line** table which also requires the Customer No does not have to also access the **Order** table. However, there is a down side: each such additional column must be carefully controlled.

1. It should not be able to be updated directly by users.

ORDER (<u>Order No</u>, Customer No, Customer Name, Customer Address, Order Date)
ORDER LINE (<u>Order No</u>, <u>Line No</u>, Customer No, Customer Name, Customer Address, Product Code, Unit Count, Unit Price, Total Price, Required By Date)

Figure 12.7   Denormalized Order and Order Line Tables.

2. It must be updated automatically by the application (via a DBMS trigger, for example) whenever there is a change to the original data on which the copied or derived data is based.

The second requirement may slow down transactions other than those that benefit from the additional data. For example, an update of Unit Price in the **Product** table will trigger an update of Unit Price and Total Price in every row of the **Order Line** table with the same value of Product Code. This is a familiar performance trade-off; enquiries are made faster at the expense of more complex (and slower) updating.

There are some cases where the addition of redundant data is generally accepted without qualms and it may indeed be included in the logical data model or even the conceptual data model. If a supertype and its subtypes are all implemented as tables (see Section 11.3.6.2), we are generally happy to include a column in the supertype table that indicates the subtype to which each row belongs.

Another type of redundant data frequently included in a database is the aggregate, particularly where data in many rows would have to be summed to calculate the aggregate "on the fly." Indeed, one would never think of not including an Account Balance column in an **Account** table (to the extent that there will most likely have been an attribute of that name in the **Account** entity class in the conceptual data model), yet an account balance is the sum of all transactions on the account since it was opened. Even if transactions of more than a certain age are deleted, the account balance will be the sum of the opening balance on a statement plus all transactions on that statement.

Two other structures in which redundant data often features are Ranges and Hierarchies. We discuss these in the next two sections.

12.6.6 **Ranges**

There are many examples of ranges in business data. Among the most common are date ranges. An organization's financial year is usually divided into a series of financial or accounting periods. These are contiguous, in that the first day of one accounting period is one day later than the last day of the previous one. Yet we usually include both first and last day columns in an accounting period table (not only in the physical data model, but probably in the logical and conceptual data models as well), even though one of these is redundant in that it can be derived from other data. Other examples of date ranges can be found in historical data:

1. We might record the range of dates for which a particular price of some item or service applied.

2. We might record the range of dates for which an employee reported to a particular manager or belonged to a particular organization unit.

Time ranges (often called "time slots") can also occur, such as in scheduling or timetabling applications. Classifications based on quantities are often created by dividing the values that the quantity can take into "bands" (e.g., age bands, price ranges). Such ranges often appear in business rule data, such as the duration bands that determine the premiums of short-term insurance policies.

Our arguments against redundant data might have convinced you that we should not include range ends as well as starts (e.g., **Last Date** as well as **First Date**, **Maximum Age** as well as **Minimum Age**, **Maximum Price** as well as **Minimum Price**). However, a query that accesses a range table that does not include both end and start columns will look like this:

```
select      PREMIUM_AMOUNT
from        PREMIUM_RULE as PR1
where       POLICY_DURATION >= MINIMUM_DURATION
and         POLICY_DURATION < MIN
   (select  PR2.MINIMUM_DURATION
   from     PREMIUM_RULE as PR2
   where    PR2.MINIMUM_DURATION > PR1.MINIMUM_DURATION);
```

However, if we include the range end **Maximum Duration** as well as the range start **Minimum Duration** the query can be written like this:

```
select      PREMIUM_AMOUNT
from        PREMIUM_RULE
where       POLICY_DURATION between MINIMUM_DURATION
and         MAXIMUM_DURATION;
```

The second query is not only easier to write but will take less time to run (provided there is an index on **POLICY DURATION**) unless the **Premium Rule** table is already in main memory.

12.6.7 **Hierarchies**

Hierarchies may be specific, as in the left-hand diagram in Figure 12.8, or generic, as in the right-hand diagram. Figure 12.9 shows a relational implementation of the generic version.

Generic hierarchies can support queries involving traversal of a fixed number of levels relatively simply, (e.g., to retrieve each top-level organization unit together with the second-level organization units that belong to it).

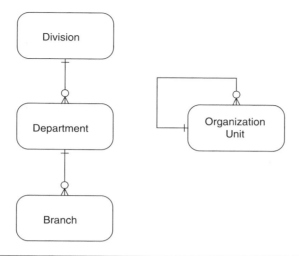

Figure 12.8 Specific and generic hierarchies.

Often, however, it is necessary to traverse a varying number of levels, (e.g., retrieve each top-level organization unit together with the bottom-level organization units that belong to it). Queries of this kind are often written as a collection of UNION queries in which each individual query traverses a different number of levels.

There are various alternatives to this inelegant approach, including some nonstandard extensions provided by some DBMSs. In the absence of these, the simplest thing to try is the suggestion made in Section 11.6.4.1 as to population of the recursive foreign key (**Parent Org Unit ID** in the table shown in Figure 12.9). The revised table is shown in Figure 12.10.

If that does not meet all needs, one of the following alternative ways of representing a hierarchy in a relational table, each of which is illustrated in Figure 12.11, may be of value:

ORG UNIT (<u>Org Unit ID</u>, Org Unit Name, Parent Org Unit ID)

Org Unit ID	Org Unit Name	Parent Org Unit ID
1	Production	null
2	H/R	null
21	Recruitment	2
22	Training	2
221	IT Training	22
222	Other Training	22

Figure 12.9 A simple hierarchy table.

ORG UNIT (Org Unit ID, Org Unit Name, Parent Org Unit ID)

Org Unit ID	Org Unit Name	Parent Org Unit ID
1	Production	1
2	H/R	2
21	Recruitment	2
22	Training	2
221	IT Training	22
222	Other Training	22

Figure 12.10   An alternative way of implementing a hierarchy.

1. Include not only a foreign key to the parent organization unit but foreign keys to the "grandparent," "great-grandparent" . . . organization units (the number of foreign keys should be one less than the maximum number of levels in the hierarchy).

2. As a variation of the previous suggestion, include a foreign key to each "ancestor" at each level.

3. Store all "ancestor"/"descendant" pairs (not just "parents" and "children") together with the difference in levels. In this case the primary key must include the level difference as well as the ID of the "descendant" organization unit.

As each of these alternatives involves redundancy, they should not be directly updated by users; instead, the original simple hierarchy table shown in Figure 12.9 should be retained for update purposes and the additional table updated automatically by the application (via a DBMS trigger, for example).

Still other alternatives can be found in Joe Celko's excellent book on this subject.[7]

12.6.8   **Integer Storage of Dates and Times**

Most DBMSs offer the "date" datatype, offering the advantages of automatic display of dates in a user-friendly format and a wide range of date and time arithmetic. The main disadvantage of storing dates and times using the "date" datatype rather than "integer" is the greater storage requirement, which in one project in which we were involved increased the total data storage requirement by some 15%. In this case, we decided to store dates in the critical large tables in "integer" columns in which were loaded the

---

[7]Celko, J. *Joe Celko's Trees and Hierarchies in SQL for Smarties*, Morgan Kaufmann, 2004.

ORG UNIT (<u>Org Unit ID</u>, Org Unit Name, Parent Org Unit ID, Grandparent Org Unit ID)

Org Unit ID	Org Unit Name	Parent Org Unit ID	Grandparent Org Unit ID
1	Production	null	null
2	H/R	null	null
21	Recruitment	2	null
22	Training	2	null
221	IT Training	22	2
222	Other Training	22	2

ORG UNIT (<u>Org Unit ID</u>, Org Unit Name, Level 1 Org Unit ID, Level 2 Org Unit ID)

Org Unit ID	Org Unit Name	Level 1 Org Unit ID	Level 2 Org Unit ID
1	Production	1	null
2	H/R	2	null
21	Recruitment	2	21
22	Training	2	22
221	IT Training	2	22
222	Other Training	2	22

ORG UNIT (<u>Org Unit ID</u>, <u>Level Difference</u>, Org Unit Name, Ancestor Org Unit ID)

Org Unit ID	Level Difference	Org Unit Name	Ancestor Org Unit ID
1	1	Production	null
2	1	H/R	null
21	1	Recruitment	2
22	1	Training	2
221	1	IT Training	22
221	2	IT Training	2
222	1	Other Training	22
222	2	Other Training	2

Figure 12.11   Further alternative ways of implementing a hierarchy.

number of days since some base date. Similarly, times of day could be stored as the number of minutes (or seconds) since midnight. We then created views of those tables (see Section 12.7) in which datatype conversion functions were used to derive dates in "dd/mm/yyyy" format.

12.6.9 **Additional Tables**

The processing requirements of an application may well lead to the creation of additional tables that were not foreseen during business information analysis and, hence, do not appear in the conceptual or logical data models. These can include:

- Summaries for reporting purposes
- Archive retrieval
- User access and security control data
- Data capture control, logging, and audit data
- Data distribution control, logging, and audit data
- Translation tables
- Other migration/interface support data
- Metadata

12.7 Views

The definition of **Views** (introduced in Chapter 1) is one of the final stages in database design, since it relies on the logical schema being finalized.

Views are "virtual tables" that are a selection of rows and columns from one or more real tables and can include calculated values in additional virtual columns. They confer various advantages, among them support for users accessing the database directly through a query interface. This support can include:

- The provision of simpler structures
- Inclusion of calculated values such as totals
- Inclusion of alternative representations of data items (e.g., formatting dates as integers as described in Section 12.6.8)
- Exclusion of data for which such users do not have access permission.

Another function that views can serve is to isolate not only users but programmers from changes to table structures. For example, if the decision is taken to split a table as described in Section 12.6.2 but access to that table was previously through a view that selected all columns of all rows (a so-called "base view"), the view can be recoded as a union or join of the two new tables. For this reason, installation standards often require a base view for every table. Life, however, is not as simple as that, since there are two problems with this approach:

- Union views and most join views are not updateable, so program code for update facilities must usually refer to base tables rather than views.
- As we show in Section 12.7.3, normalized views of denormalized tables lose any performance advantages conferred by that denormalization.

Some standards that we do recommend, however, are presented and discussed in the next four sections.

12.7.1 Views of Supertypes and Subtypes

However a supertype and its subtypes have been implemented, each of them should be represented by a view. This enables at least "read" access by users to all entity classes that have been defined in the conceptual data model rather than just those that have ended up as tables.

If we implement only the supertype as a table, views of each subtype can be constructed by selecting in the WHERE clause only those rows that belong to that subtype and including only those columns that correspond to the attributes and relationships of that subtype.

If we implement only the subtypes as tables, a view of the supertype can be constructed by a UNION of each subtype's base view.

If we implement both the supertype and the subtypes as tables, a view of each subtype can be constructed by joining the supertype table and the appropriate subtype table, and a view of the supertype can be constructed by a UNION of each of those subtype views.

12.7.2 Inclusion of Derived Attributes in Views

If a derived attribute has been defined as a business information requirement in the conceptual data model it should be included as a calculated value in a view representing the owning entity class. This again enables user access to all attributes that have been defined in the conceptual data model.

12.7.3 Denormalization and Views

If we have denormalized a table by including redundant data in it, it may be tempting to retain a view that reflects the normalized form of that table, as in Figure 12.12.

However a query of such a view that includes a join to another view so as to retrieve an additional column will perform that join even though the additional column is already in the underlying table. For example, a query to return the name and address of each customer who has ordered product "A123" will look like that in Figure 12.13 and will end up reading the **Customer** and **Order** tables as well as the **Order Line** table to obtain Customer Name and Customer Address, even though those columns have been

<u>Tables:</u>
CUSTOMER (<u>Customer No</u>, Customer Name, Customer Address)
ORDER (<u>Order No</u>, Customer No, Customer Name, Customer Address, Order Date)
ORDER LINE (<u>Order No</u>, <u>Line No</u>, Customer No, Customer Name, Customer Address, Product Code, Unit Count, Required By Date)
<u>Views:</u>
CUSTOMER (<u>Customer No</u>, Customer Name, Customer Address)
ORDER (<u>Order No</u>, Customer No, Order Date)
ORDER LINE (<u>Order No</u>, <u>Line No</u>, Product Code, Unit Count, Required By Date)

Figure 12.12 Normalized views of denormalized tables.

```
select CUSTOMER_NAME, CUSTOMER_ADDRESS
from ORDER LINE join ORDER on
ORDER LINE. ORDER_NO = ORDER.ORDER_NO join CUSTOMER on
ORDER.CUSTOMER_NO = CUSTOMER.CUSTOMER_NO
where PRODUCT_CODE = 'A123';
```

Figure 12.13 Querying normalized views.

copied into the **Order Line** table. Any performance advantage that may have accrued from the denormalization is therefore lost.

12.7.4 **Views of Split and Merged Tables**

If tables have been split or merged, as described in Sections 12.6.2 and 12.6.3, views of the original tables should be provided to enable at least "read" access by users to all entity classes that have been defined in the conceptual data model.

12.8 **Summary**

Physical database design should focus on achieving performance goals while implementing a logical schema that is as faithful as possible to the ideal design specified by the logical data model.

The physical designer will need to take into account (among other things) stated performance requirements, transaction and data volumes, available hardware and the facilities provided by the DBMS.

Most DBMSs support a wide range of tools for achieving performance without compromising the logical schema, including indexing, clustering, partitioning, control of data placement, data compression, and memory management.

In the event that adequate performance across all transactions cannot be achieved with these tools, individual queries can be reviewed and sometimes rewritten to improve performance.

The final resort is to use tactics that require modification of the logical schema. Table splitting, denormalization, and various forms of data duplication can provide improved performance, but usually at a cost in other areas. In some cases, such as hierarchies of indefinite depth and specification of ranges, data duplication may provide a substantial payoff in easier programming as well as performance.

Views can be utilized to effectively reconstruct the conceptual model but are limited in their ability to accommodate update transactions.

Part III
Advanced Topics

Chapter 13
Advanced Normalization

"Everything should be made as simple as possible, but not simpler."
- Albert Einstein (attrib.)

"The soul never thinks without a picture."
- Aristotle

13.1 **Introduction**

In Chapter 2 we looked at normalization, a formal technique for eliminating certain problems from data models. Our focus was on situations in which the same facts were carried in more than one row of a table—resulting in wasted space, more complex update logic, and the risk of inconsistency. In data structures that are not fully normalized, it can also be difficult to store certain types of data independently of other types of data. For example, we might be unable to store details of customers unless they currently held accounts with us, and similarly, we could lose customer details when we deleted their accounts. All of these problems, with the exception of the wasted space, can be characterized as "update anomalies."

The normalization techniques presented in Chapter 2 enable us to put data into third normal form (3NF). However, it is possible for a set of tables to be in 3NF and still not be *fully* normalized; they can still contain the problems of the kind that we expect normalization to remove.

In this chapter, we look at three further stages of normalization: Boyce-Codd normal form (BCNF), fourth normal form (4NF), and fifth normal form (5NF).

We then discuss in more detail a number of issues that were mentioned only briefly in Chapter 2. In particular, we look further at the limitations of normalization in eliminating redundancy and allowing us to store data independently and at some of the pitfalls of failing to follow the rules of normalization strictly.

Before proceeding, we should anticipate the question: Are there normal forms beyond 5NF? Until relatively recently, we would have answered, "No," although from time to time we would see proposals for further normal forms intended to eliminate certain problems which could still exist in a 5NF structure. In most cases these problems were of a different kind to those that we aim to eliminate by normalization, and the proposals did not win much support in the academic or practitioner communities. More recently, however, Date et al.[1] proposed a sixth normal form (6NF), which has gained some acceptance. The issues that it addresses relate to time-dependent data, and we therefore discuss it in Chapter 15.

13.2 Introduction to the Higher Normal Forms

We have left the discussion of the normal forms beyond 3NF until this chapter, not because the problems they address are unimportant, but because they occur much less frequently. Most tables in 3NF are already in BCNF, 4NF, and 5NF. The other reason for handling the higher normal forms separately is that they are a little more difficult to understand, particularly if we use only the relational notation, as in Chapter 2. Diagrams, which were not introduced until Chapter 3, make understanding much easier.

If you are a practicing data modeler, you are bound to encounter normalization problems beyond 3NF from time to time. Recognizing the patterns will save a lot of effort. And, because each higher normal form includes all the lower normal forms, you only need to be able to prove that a structure is in 5NF to be certain that it is also in 1NF through 4NF.

13.2.1 Common Misconceptions

Before we start on the specifics of each of the higher normal forms, it is worth clearing up a few common misconceptions.

The first is that 4NF and 5NF are impossibly difficult for practitioners to understand. When running seminars for experienced data modelers we sometimes ask whether they have a practical understanding of the higher normal forms. It is not unusual to find that *no one* in the audience is prepared to claim that knowledge.

The reality is that 4NF and 5NF are often not well-taught—sometimes because the teachers themselves do not understand them. But while the formal definitions can be hard work, the structural problems that they address are relatively simple to grasp, particularly if they are translated into entity-relationship terms. If you observe the rule, "Do not resolve several

---

[1]Date C.J., Darwen H., Lorentzos N, *Temporal Data and the Relational Model*. Morgan Kaufmann, 2002.

distinct many-to-many relationships with a single entity," you are well on the way to ensuring you have 5NF structures. But we would like you to understand it a little more deeply than that!

The general lack of understanding of the higher normal forms has led to all sorts of data modeling guidelines and decisions, most of them bad, being paraded under the banner of 4NF and 5NF. Unsound data structures have been defended on the basis that they were required to achieve someone's spurious definition of 4NF or 5NF. And we have even seen perfectly sound design practices rejected on the basis that they lead to (incorrectly defined) 4NF or 5NF structures, which in turn are seen to be academic or detrimental to performance. If nothing else, an understanding of the higher normal forms will ensure that you are not swayed by arguments of this kind.

Practitioners are frequently advised to normalize "only as far as third normal form" on the basis that further normalization offers little benefit or that it incurs serious performance costs. The argument that normalization beyond 3NF is not useful is only true in the sense that normalization to 3NF will remove most, and *usually* all, of the problems associated with unnormalized data. In other words, once we have put our data in 3NF, it is very often already in 5NF. But those data structures that are in 3NF but *not* in 5NF still exhibit serious problems of very much the same type that we address in the earlier stages of normalization: redundancy; insertion, update, and deletion complexity and anomalies; and difficulty in storing facts independently of other facts.

The performance argument is no more valid for the higher normal forms than it is for 3NF. As with the other normal forms and good design practices in general, we may ultimately need to make compromises to achieve adequate performance, but our starting point should always be fully normalized structures. Denormalization should be a last resort because the resulting redundancy, complexity, and incompleteness are likely to be expensive to manage.

The most common reason for not looking beyond 3NF is plain ignorance: not knowing how to proceed any further!

Finally, you can expect to hear modelers argue that a formal knowledge of normalization is unnecessary, as they can arrive at normalized structures through proper application of top-down techniques. This looks like a convenient excuse for avoiding a potentially difficult subject, but there is some truth in the argument.[2] Most of the time, *good* data modelers are able to achieve normalized structures without going through a formal normalization process. However, if you understand normalization, you are in a position to

---

[2]If you are using the Object Role Modeling (ORM) technique, mentioned in Chapter 7, rather than E-R, this argument carries more weight, as the various business rules relevant to normalization are rigorously checked during the conceptual modeling stages to allow a mechanical translation to normalized structures.

tackle certain types of modeling problems from an alternative (and very rigorous) perspective, to check your intuition and patterns, and to verify and justify your decisions. You will also have a deeper understanding of what makes a sound (or unsound) data structure. For a professional data modeler, this should be core knowledge.

13.3 Boyce-Codd Normal Form

13.3.1 Example of Structure in 3NF but Not in BCNF

Look at the model in Figure 13.1, which represents data about an organization's branches and how each branch services its customers.

Figure 13.2 shows the **Branch-Customer Relationship** table.

Note three things about this table:

1. The table enforces the rule that each branch will serve a customer through only one salesperson, as there is only one **Salesperson No** for each combination of **Customer No** and **Branch No**. This rule cannot be deduced from the diagram alone. We need the additional information

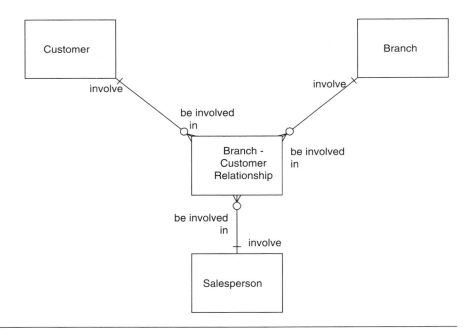

Figure 13.1 Customers, salespersons, and branches.

BRANCH-CUSTOMER RELATIONSHIP (<u>Customer No</u>, <u>Branch No</u>, Visiting Frequency, Relationship Establishment Date, Salesperson No)

Figure 13.2 Branch-Customer relationship table.

---

that **Customer No** and **Branch No** form the primary key of the table, so each combination can occur only once. (If the primary key also included **Salesperson No**, then the table would support multiple salespersons for each combination of branch and customer.)

2. The table is in 3NF; there are no repeating groups, and every determinant of a nonkey item is a candidate key.

3. If we are given the additional information that each salesperson works for one branch only, then the table will still have some normalization problems. The fact that a particular salesperson belongs to a particular branch will be recorded in every row in which that salesperson's identifier appears.

The underlying reason for the normalization problems is that we have a dependency between **Salesperson No** and **Branch No**; **Salesperson No** is a **determinant** of Branch No. (A reminder on the terminology: this means that for every **Salesperson No**, there is only one corresponding **Branch No**.) The unusual feature here is that **Branch No** is part of the key. In all our examples so far, we have dealt with determinants of *nonkey* items. We now have a real problem. What we would like to do is set up a reference table with **Salesperson No** as the key (Figure 13.3).

But this does not really help. Although we can now record which branch a salesperson belongs to, regardless of whether he or she is serving any customers, we cannot take anything out of the original table. We would like to remove **Branch No**, but that would mean destroying the key.

The trick is to recognize that the original table has another candidate key. We could just as well have used a combination of **Salesperson No** and **Customer No** as the primary key (Figure 13.4, next page).

The new key suggests a new name for the table: **Customer-Salesperson Relationship**. But now we are no longer in 3NF (in fact not even in 2NF). **Salesperson No** is a determinant of **Branch No**, so we need to split these columns off to another table (Figure 13.5, next page).

We now have our **Salesperson** reference table, including the foreign key to **Branch**, and we have eliminated the problem of repeated data.

SALESPERSON (<u>Salesperson No</u>, Branch No)

Figure 13.3 Salesperson table.

CUSTOMER-SALESPERSON RELATIONSHIP (<u>Customer No</u>, <u>Salesperson No</u>, Visiting Frequency, Relationship Established Date, Branch No)

Figure 13.4 Changing the primary key.

Technically, we have resolved a situation in which the tables were in 3NF but not BCNF.

13.3.2 Definition of BCNF

For a table to be in BCNF, we require that the following rule be satisfied:
Every determinant must be a candidate key.

In our example, Salesperson No was a determinant of Branch No, but was not a candidate key of **Branch-Customer Relationship**. Compare this with the definition of 3NF: "Every determinant of a *nonkey* column must be a candidate key." If you compare the two definitions it should be clear that BCNF is stronger than 3NF in the sense that any table in BCNF will also be in 3NF.

Situations in which tables may be in 3NF but not BCNF can only occur when we have more than one candidate key—to be more precise, *overlapping* candidate keys. We can often spot them more quickly in diagrammatic form. In Figure 13.1, the **Branch-Customer-Relationship** box indicates a three-way relationship between **Branch**, **Customer**, and **Salesperson**. Approaching the problem from an Entity-Relationship perspective, we would normally draw the model as in Figure 13.6, recognizing the direct relationship between **Salesperson** and **Branch**. Any proposed relationship between **Customer-Salesperson Relationship** and **Branch** would then be seen as derivable from the separate relationships between **Customer-Salesperson Relationship** and **Salesperson**, and between **Salesperson** and **Branch**. Taking this top-down approach, we would not have considered holding Branch No as an attribute of **Customer-Salesperson Relationship**, and the BCNF problem would not have arisen.

You may find it interesting to experiment with different choices of keys for the various tables in the flawed model of Figure 13.1. In each case, you

CUSTOMER-SALESPERSON RELATIONSHIP (<u>Customer No</u>, <u>Salesperson No</u>, Visiting Frequency, Relationship Established Date)
SALESPERSON (<u>Salesperson No</u>, Branch No)

Figure 13.5 Normalized tables.

will find that a normalization rule is violated or a basic business requirement not supported.

13.3.3 Enforcement of Rules versus BCNF

There are some important issues about rules here, which can easily be lost in our rather technical focus on dependencies and normalization. In the original table, we enforced the rule that a given customer was only served by one salesperson from each branch. Our new model no longer enforces that rule. It is now possible for a customer to be supported by several salespersons from the same branch. We have traded the enforcement of a rule for the advantages of normalization. It is almost certainly a good trade, because it is likely to be easier to enforce the rule within program logic than to live with the problems of redundant data, update complexity, and unwanted data dependencies.

But do not lose sight of the fact that changing a data structure, for whatever reason, changes the rules that it enforces. For example, in Figure 13.6, we enforce the rule that each salesperson is employed by a single branch;

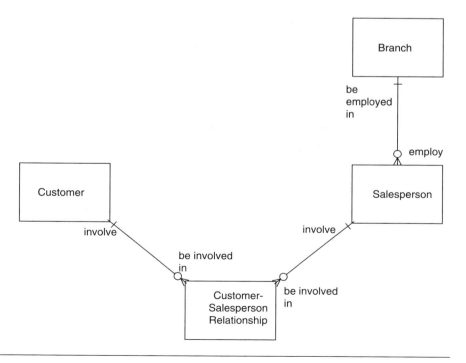

Figure 13.6 Revised model for customer-salesperson-branch.

in the original example, the rule was perhaps implied by the description, but certainly not enforced by the model.

13.3.4 **A Note on Domain Key Normal Form**

We complete our discussion of this example with a slightly academic aside. You may occasionally see references to Domain Key Normal Form (DKNF), which requires that "All constraints are a consequence of domains or keys."[3] The idea of a constraint being a consequence of a domain[4] in the sense of a set of allowed values is a familiar one; if we say that the value of **Contract Status** must be drawn from a domain containing only the values "Pending," "Active," and "Closed," then **Contract Status** is *constrained* to those three values. The idea of a constraint being a consequence of the choice of keys is less obvious, but our example nicely illustrates it: if we choose a combination of **Branch No** and **Customer No** as the key of **Branch-Customer Relationship** in Figure 13.1, we are able to enforce the constraint that each customer is served by only one salesperson from each branch, but if we choose a combination of **Customer No** and **Salesperson No** as the key, we do not enforce the constraint.

Academic interest in DKNF seems to have faded, and it has never been used much by practitioners. We mention it here primarily to highlight the important impact that key choice and normalization have on the enforcement of constraints.

13.4 **Fourth Normal Form (4NF) and Fifth Normal Form (5NF)**

Let us start our discussion of fourth and fifth normal forms with some good news. Once data structures are in BCNF, remaining normalization problems come up almost exclusively when we are dealing with "key only" tables—that is, tables in which every column is part of the key. Even then, for practical purposes (see Section 13.4.3), they only apply to tables with three or more columns (and, hence, a three-or-more-part key). We will discuss 4NF and 5NF together because the reason these two forms are defined

---

[3]Fagin, R., "A Normal Form for Relational Databases That Is Based on Domains and Keys," *ACM Transactions on Database Systems* (September 1981).

[4]Not to be confused with the term "domain" in the sense of "problem domain" (the subset of interest of an organization or its data) in which sense it is also used by data modeling practitioners.

separately has more to do with the timing of their discovery than anything else. We will not bother too much about a formal definition of 4NF because the 5NF definition is simpler and covers 4NF as well. (As mentioned earlier, any structure in 5NF is automatically in 4NF and all the lower normal forms. In Chapter 2, we similarly skipped over 2NF and proceeded directly to 3NF.)

13.4.1 **Data in BCNF but Not in 4NF**

Suppose we want to record data about financial market dealers, the instruments they are authorized to trade, and the locations at which they are allowed to operate. For example, Smith might be authorized to deal in stocks in New York and in Government Bonds in London.

Let us suppose for the moment that:

Each instrument can be traded only at a specified set of locations, and

Each dealer is allowed to trade in a specified set of instruments.

So, if we wanted to know whether Smith could deal in Government Bonds in Sydney, we would ask:

Can Government Bonds be traded in Sydney?

Can Smith deal in Government Bonds?

If the answer to both questions was, "Yes," then we would deduce that Smith could indeed deal in Government Bonds in Sydney. Figures 13.7(a) and (b) show data models for this situation. In (b), the many-to-many relationships shown in (a) are resolved using all-key tables.

If we wanted to know all of the authorized combinations of dealer, location, and instrument, we could *derive* a list by combining (joining) the two tables to produce the single table in Figure 13.8 (see page 401).

But what if this derived table was offered up as a solution in itself? It should be reasonably clear that it suffers from normalization-type problems of redundancy and nonindependence of facts. Any authorized combination of instrument and location (e.g., the fact that Government Bonds can be traded in New York) will have to be repeated for each dealer permitted to trade in that instrument. This is the familiar normalization problem of the same fact being held in more than one row. Adding or deleting a combination will then involve updating multiple rows. A similar problem applies to combinations of dealer and instrument. Note that the derived table carries more column values than the two original tables. This is hardly surprising considering that it contains duplicated data, but we have often seen derivable tables offered up on the basis that they will save space.

Using the three-column table, we cannot record the fact that an instrument is allowed to be traded at a particular location unless there is at least one dealer who can trade in that instrument. Options can be traded in Tokyo, but this fact is not reflected in the derived table. Nor can we record the fact that the dealer can trade in a particular instrument unless that instrument

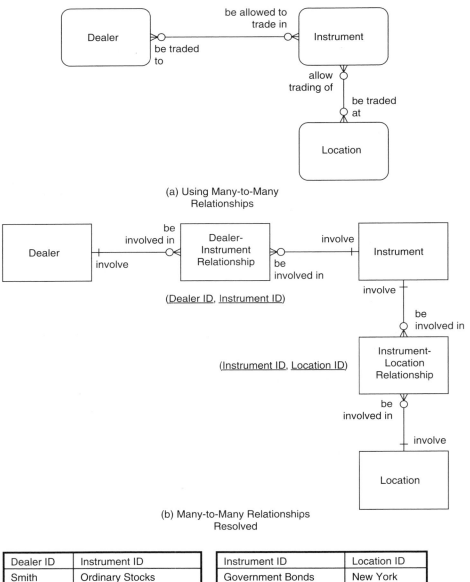

(a) Using Many-to-Many
Relationships

(b) Many-to-Many Relationships
Resolved

Dealer ID	Instrument ID
Smith	Ordinary Stocks
Smith	Government Bonds
Bruce	Futures
Bruce	Government Bonds

Instrument ID	Location ID
Government Bonds	New York
Government Bonds	London
Government Bonds	Sydney
Futures	Singapore
Futures	Tokyo
Options	Tokyo

Figure 13.7   Dealing model with sample data.

Dealer	Instrument ID	Location ID
Dealer	Instrument ID	Location ID
Smith	Government Bonds	New York
Smith	Government Bonds	London
Smith	Government Bonds	Sydney
Bruce	Futures	Singapore
Bruce	Futures	Tokyo
Bruce	Government Bonds	New York
Bruce	Government Bonds	London
Bruce	Government Bonds	Sydney

Figure 13.8 Allowed combinations of Dealer, Instrument, and Location.

can be traded at a minimum of one location. The derived table does not show that Smith is authorized to trade in ordinary stocks.

So our derived table appears to be unnormalized, but on checking, we find that it is in BCNF. Technically, our normalization problem is the result of a **multivalued dependency** (MVD)[5] and our table is not in 4NF (which specifies, roughly speaking, that we should not have any nontrivial multivalued dependencies).

Rather than get sidetracked by more formal definitions of 4NF and multivalued dependencies, let us refer back to the diagrams. In our one-table solution, we have tried to resolve two many-to-many relationships with a single table, rather than with two separate tables. The simple message is *not* to do this! Another way of looking at it is that we should record *underlying* rules rather than *derived* rules. This is a basic principle of data modeling we have encountered before when eliminating derivable attributes and relationships. It also provides a good starting point for understanding 5NF.

13.4.2 **Fifth Normal Form (5NF)**

Throughout the various stages of normalization, at least one thing has remained constant: each new stage involves splitting a table into two or more new tables. Remember: "Normalization is like marriage; you always end up with more relations."

We have taken care not to lose anything in splitting a table; we could always reconstruct the original table by *joining* (matching values in) the

---

[5]Instrument ID is said to **multidetermine** Location ID and Dealer ID, and conversely, Location ID and Dealer ID each **multidetermine** Instrument ID.

new tables. In essence, normalization splits each table into underlying tables from which the original table can be derived, if necessary.

The definition of 5NF picks up on this idea and essentially tells us to keep up this splitting process until we can go no further. We only stop splitting when one of the following is true:

■ Any further splitting would lead to tables that could not be joined to produce the original table.

■ The only splits left to us are trivial.

"Trivial" splits are defined as being splits based on candidate keys, such as those shown in Figure 13.9. A nontrivial split results in two or more tables with different keys, none of which is a candidate key of any other table.

The definition of 5NF differs in style from our definitions for earlier stages in normalization. Rather than picking a certain type of anomaly to be removed, 5NF defines an end-point after which any further "normalization" would cause us to lose information. Applying the definition to the dealing authority problem, we have shown that the three-key table can be split into two without losing information; hence, we perform the split.

The 5NF definition enables us to tackle a more complex version of the dealing authority problem. Suppose we introduce an additional rule: each dealer can only operate at a specified set of locations. The new model is shown in Figures 13.10(a) and (b).

Now that we have *three* separate relationships, could we resolve them all with one entity? We hope your intuitive answer based on the preceding discussion is, "No." The resulting three-column table would have to be

EMPLOYEE (Employee Number, Name, Birth Date)

can be trivially split into:

EMPLOYEE-NAME (Employee Number, Name)

EMPLOYEE-BIRTH (Employee Number, Birth Date)

(a) Split Based on Primary Key

DEPARTMENT (Department Number, Department Name, Location Code, Manager Employee Number)

assuming Department Name is a candidate key, can be trivially split into:

DEPARTMENT-LOCATION (Department Number, Department Name, Location Code)

DEPARTMENT-MANAGER (Department Name, Manager Employee Number)

(b) Split Based on Non Primary Candidate Key

Figure 13.9 Trivial table splits.

equivalent to the three separate tables and, hence, could be broken down into them. Figure 13.11 on the next page shows the combined table, which still exhibits normalization problems. Changing one of the underlying rules may require multiple rows to be added or deleted, and we cannot record rules that do not currently lead to any valid combinations.

For example, deleting the rule that Smith can trade in Tokyo requires only one row to be removed from the underlying tables, but two from the derived

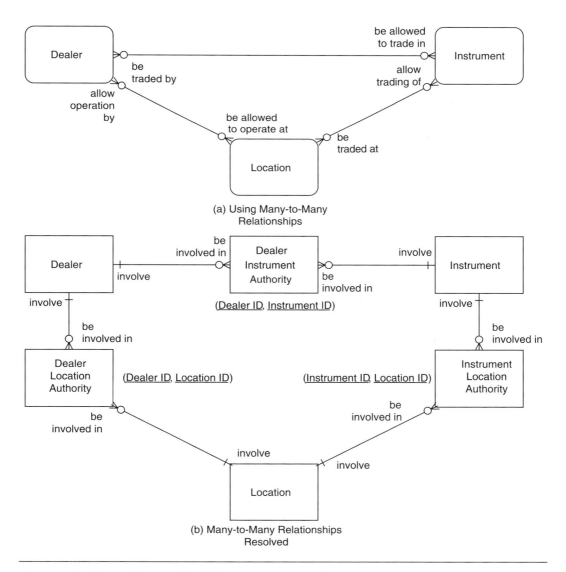

Figure 13.10   Dealing model with three many-to-many relationships.

table. As populations are increased from a few sample rows to hundreds or thousands of rows, the differences become correspondingly greater.

Technically, the three-column derived table is in 4NF, as there are no multivalued dependencies (you may have to take our word on this!). But because we can split the table into three new tables and reconstruct it, it is not yet in 5NF. Splitting the table into three solves the problem.

In simple terms, then, the definition of 4NF effectively says that two many-to-many relationships cannot be resolved with one table. Satisfying 5NF requires that *two or more* many-to-many relationships are not resolved by a single table.

13.4.3 **Recognizing 4NF and 5NF Situations**

The first step in handling 4NF and 5NF problems is recognizing them. In relational notation, we can spot all-key tables with three or more columns; in a diagram, we look for three- or more-way intersection entity classes. We are indebted to Chris Date (see Further Reading) for bringing to our attention the possibility of 4NF and 5NF being violated in situations other than those involving only "all key" tables. We will not pursue these cases here; suffice to say that:

■ The examples we have seen and those that we have been able to construct involve business rules which we would not seriously contemplate enforcing in the data structure.

■ We have yet to encounter an example in practice.

Dealer ID	Location ID	Instrument ID
Smith	Sydney	90-Day Bills
Smith	Sydney	180-Day Bills
Smith	Tokyo	90-Day Bills
Smith	Tokyo	10-Year Bonds
Philip	Sydney	180-Day Bills
Philip	Perth	180-Day Bills

This table is derivable from the following tables.

Dealer ID	Location ID
Smith	Sydney
Smith	Tokyo
Philip	Sydney
Philip	Perth

Dealer ID	Instrument ID
Smith	90-Day Bills
Smith	180-Day Bills
Smith	10-Year Bonds
Philip	180-Day Bills

Location ID	Instrument ID
Sydney	90-Day Bills
Sydney	180-Day Bills
Tokyo	90-Day Bills
Tokyo	10-Year Bonds
Perth	180-Day Bills

Figure 13.11   Allowed combinations derivable from underlying rules.

Figure 13.12 shows some variations to the basic three-way intersection entity pattern, which may be less easy to recognize (see following page).

Each of the structures in Figure 13.12 contains an all-key table representing a three-way intersection entity and may therefore exhibit 4NF or 5NF problems. Of course, some three-way relationships are perfectly legitimate. The problems arise only when they are derivable from simpler, more fundamental relationships.

If, in our dealer authority example, authorities were decided on a case-by-case basis independently of underlying rules, then the three-way relationship entity would be valid. Figure 13.13 on page 407 shows a table of values assigned in this way. You may find it an interesting exercise to try to break the table down into "underlying" tables; it cannot be done because there are no underlying rules beyond "any combination may be independently deemed to be allowed." Any set of two-column tables will either fail to cover some permitted combinations or generate combinations that are not permitted. For example, our "underlying" tables would need to record that:

1. Smith can deal in Sydney (first row of table).
2. Smith can deal in 180-day Bills (third row of table).
3. 180-day bills can be traded in Sydney (fourth row of table).

With these three facts we would derive a three-column table that recorded that Smith can deal in 180-day bills in Sydney, which, as we can see from the original table, is not true.

We have gone as far as we can in table splitting, and our tables are therefore in 5NF.

13.4.4 Checking for 4NF and 5NF with the Business Specialist

In determining whether all-key tables are in 4NF and 5NF, we suggest that you do not bother with the multivalued dependency concept. It is not an easy idea to grasp and certainly not a good starting point for dialogue with a nontechnical business specialist. And, after all that, you have only established 4NF, with 5NF still in front of you! Move straight to the 5NF definition, and look to see if there are simpler business rules underlying those represented by the multiway relationship. Ask the following questions: On what (business) basis do we add a row to this table? On what basis do we delete rows? Do we apply any rules? Understanding the business reasons behind changes to the table is the best way of discovering whether it can be split further.

Do not expect the answers to these business questions to come easily. Often the business rules themselves are not well understood or even well defined. We have found it helpful to present business specialists with pairs

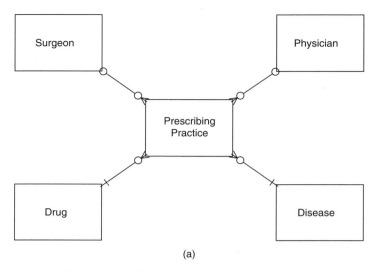

(a)

Note: Relationships to Physician and Surgeon are mutually exclusive.
Structure emerges clearly if we use the "exclusivity arc" as described
in Section 4.14.2, or generalize Surgeon and Physician to Medical Practitioner.

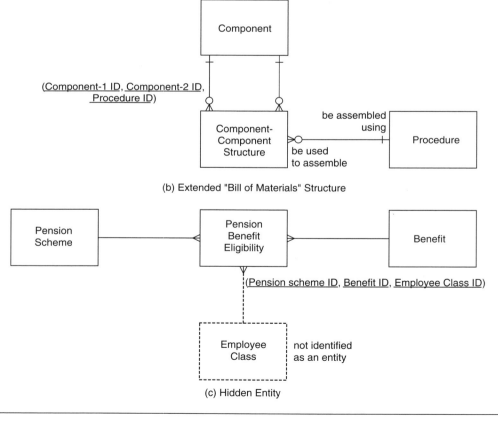

Figure 13.12 Structures possibly not in 4NF or 5NF.

Dealer ID	Location ID	Instrument ID
Smith	Sydney	90-Day Bills
Smith	Tokyo	90-Day Bills
Smith	Tokyo	180-Day Bills
Philip	Sydney	180-Day Bills

Figure 13.13   Nonderivable combinations.

of attribute values, or, equivalently, with a null value in one of the columns of a three-column table, and ask "Does this mean anything by itself?" Another useful technique is to look for possible nonkey columns. Remember that 4NF and 5NF problems are generally associated with all-key tables.

13.5   Beyond 5NF: Splitting Tables Based on Candidate Keys

In defining 5NF, we indicated that the task of normalization was complete when the only ways of further splitting tables either resulted in our losing information or were based on candidate keys. Because it represents the point at which our simple splitting process can take us no further, 5NF is usually considered synonymous with "fully normalized."

However, as we saw in Chapter 10 in our discussion of one-to-one relationships, sometimes we *do* want to split tables based on candidate keys. In Section 10.9.3, we looked at an example of a manufacturing business that stored parts in bins according to the following rules:

1. Each type of part is stored in one bin only.
2. Each bin contains one type of part only.

It is interesting to reexamine this example from a normalization perspective. We might be offered the following table to represent data about parts and bins (Figure 13.14):

In checking normalization, our first reaction is likely to be that **Bin No** determines **Bin Height**, **Bin Width**, and **Bin Depth**. But **Bin No** is a candidate key, so technically we do not have a problem. Nevertheless, most experienced data modelers would still feel uncomfortable about this structure, and with

PART (<u>Part No</u>, Bin No, Bin Height, Bin Width, Bin Depth, Part Name, Quantity)

Figure 13.14   Parts and bins.

good reason. Think about the problem of moving parts from one bin to another. Suppose, for example, we want to swap the parts stored in two bins. We would expect this to involve changing only the bin numbers for the relevant parts. But with this structure, we will also need to update (swap) the values for **Bin Height**, **Bin Width**, and **Bin Depth**, and of any other columns that "belong to" bins rather than parts. If we split bin and part data into separate tables, we can avoid this problem, and this is indeed the best approach.

But what distinguishes this example from the trivial employee example in the previous section where we did not split the original table? The difference is basically that **Bin No** and **Part No** represent different things in the real world, *and the relationship between them is transferable* (i.e., a part may move from one bin to another and vice versa). Although the 5NF rule does not *require* us to split the data into separate tables, it does not prohibit us from doing so. The two resulting tables are still in 5NF.

This issue is seldom discussed in texts on normalization, and you need to be aware of it, if only to back up your intuition when another modeler or a database designer argues that the two tables should be combined. In practice, if you start with an E-R diagram, you will almost certainly identify separate entity classes, with a one-to-one relationship between them, rather than a single entity.

13.6 **Other Normalization Issues**

In this section, we look more closely at some normalization issues that we have mentioned only in passing so far. We start by examining some common misconceptions about what is achieved by normalization. We then look at some of the less usual situations that may arise when applying the standard rules of normalization.

13.6.1 **Normalization and Redundancy**

Normalization plays such an important role in reducing data redundancy that it is easy to forget that a model can be fully normalized and still allow redundant data. The most common situations are as follows.

13.6.1.1 Overlapping Tables

Normalization does not address data redundancy resulting from overlapping classifications of data. If we recognize **Teacher Number** and **Student Number** as keys when normalizing data, we will build a **Teacher** table and a **Student** table. But if a teacher can also be a student, we will end up holding the values of any common attributes (such as **Address**) in both tables.

13.6.1.2 Derivable Data

If the value of one column can be calculated from others, normalization by itself will not eliminate the redundancy. If the underlying column values and the result are all within one row, normalization will remove the calculated value to a separate table (Figure 13.15), but we will still need to observe that the table itself is redundant and remove it.

Better to remove the derivable item at the outset rather than going through this procedure! Normalization will not help at all with values calculated from multiple rows (possibly from more than one table), such as "Total Quantity of this Item Outstanding" or "Total Charge on an Invoice Header."

Another example of data derivable across multiple rows is a table used to translate contiguous numeric ranges—for example, Australian postal code ranges to States—and including columns **First Number** and **Last Number**. The value of **Last Number** is incremented by one to derive the next **First Number**; hence, if the **Last Number** column was removed, we could recreate it by subtracting one from the next highest **First Number** (Figure 13.16). (We do *not* need to have the rows sequenced to achieve this.) This is, however, hardly elegant programming. And can we rely on the organization that defines the ranges to maintain the convention that they are contiguous? In this case, holding redundant data is likely to represent the best tradeoff.

Repeated data of this kind does not show up as the simple dependencies that we tackle with normalization. As discussed in Chapter 2, the best approach is to remove columns representing *derivable* data (as distinct from dependent data), prior to starting normalization. But sometimes the

---

ORDER ITEM (<u>Order No</u>, <u>Item No</u>, Ordered Quantity, Delivered Quantity, Outstanding Quantity)

Outstanding Quantity = Ordered Quantity less Delivered Quantity

Hence (Ordered Quantity, Delivered Quantity) determines Outstanding Quantity

Normalizing:

ORDER ITEM (<u>Order No</u>, <u>Item No</u>, Ordered Quantity, Delivered Quantity)

OUTSTANDING ORDER (<u>Ordered Quantity</u>, <u>Delivered Quantity</u>, Outstanding Quantity)

Outstanding Order table contains no useful information and can be removed on this basis

---

Figure 13.15 Removing derivable data.

Australian Postal Code Table

First Number	Last Number	State
2000	2999	New South Wales
3000	3999	Victoria
4000	4999	Queensland
5000	5999	South Australia
etc.		

Figure 13.16 Data derivable across rows.

distinction may be hard to make. And, as in the example of Figure 13.16, the sacrifice in programming simplicity and stability may not justify the reduction in redundancy. If in doubt, leave the questionable columns in, then review again after normalization is complete.

13.6.2 Reference Tables Produced by Normalization

Each stage in normalization beyond 1NF involves the creation of "reference" tables (often referred to as "look-up" tables as some data is removed from the original table to another table where it can be "looked up" by citing the relevant value of the primary key). As well as reducing data redundancy, these tables allow us to record instances of the reference data that do not currently appear in the unnormalized table. For example, we could record a hospital for which there were no operations or a customer who did not hold any accounts with us. We become so used to these reference tables appearing during the normalization process that it is easy to miss the fact that normalization alone will not always generate all the reference tables we require.

Imagine we have the table of employee information shown in Figure 13.17:

Normalization gives us a table of all the employees and their names and another table of all the skill names and their descriptions. We have not only eliminated duplicate rows but are now able to record a skill even though no employee has that skill. However, if we remove **Skill Description** from the

SKILL HELD (<u>Employee No</u>, <u>Skill Name</u>, Skill Description, Employee Name)
Normalizing:
SKILL HELD (<u>Employee No</u>, <u>Skill Name</u>)
EMPLOYEE (<u>Employee No</u>, Employee Name)
SKILL (<u>Skill Name</u>, Skill Description)

Figure 13.17 Normalization producing reference table.

problem, normalization will no longer give us a **Skill** table (which would contain the single column Skill Name). If we want such a list, we can certainly specify an all-key table consisting of Skill Name only. But normalization will not do it for us.

In discussing 4NF and 5NF situations, we raised the possibility of finding a nonkey column. If such a column, dependent on the full key, was added, our 4NF and 5NF problems would disappear. So why not just introduce a dummy column? The problem is much the same as the one we encountered with employees and skills: normalization will provide an internally consistent model, but will not generate the reference tables we require.

Suppose, for example, we found in our dealing model (Figure 13.10) that there was a rule that limited the amount of any deal for each combination of dealer, location, and instrument. We now need the three-key table to hold the Limit column, even if our underlying rules are as in Figure 13.10, giving us the model in Figure 13.18 on the following page. This one can be a bit tricky to draw. Modelers often show relationships from the basic tables (**Dealer**, **Instrument**, **Location**) rather than the intersection tables. We have shown it first with *all* foreign-key relationships, including redundant relationships, then with redundant relationships removed. We have left off relationship names in the interest of minimizing clutter.

Can we now eliminate the three outside intersection tables, giving us the model in Figure 13.19? (see page 413)

At first glance, the answer may appear to be, "Yes." It would seem that we could find all allowable combinations of (say) dealer and location just by searching the relevant columns of the three-column rule table. The problem is that some of the underlying (two-column) rules may not have given rise to any rows in the rule table. For example, a dealer may be authorized to deal in New York but may not yet be authorized to deal in any of the instruments available in that city.

In this example, if we started with just the rule table (including the Limit column), no rule of normalization would lead us to the two-column intersection tables—the "reference" tables. This is because they contain separate and additional facts to the information in the original table. But it is also the sort of thing that is easily missed.

The message here is that normalization is an adjunct to E-R modeling, not a substitute. In the two examples discussed here, we need to identify the reference tables as entity classes during the conceptual modeling phase.

13.6.3 Selecting the Primary Key after Removing Repeating Groups

In Chapter 2, we highlighted the importance of correctly identifying primary keys at each stage of the normalization process. Once the tables are in 1NF,

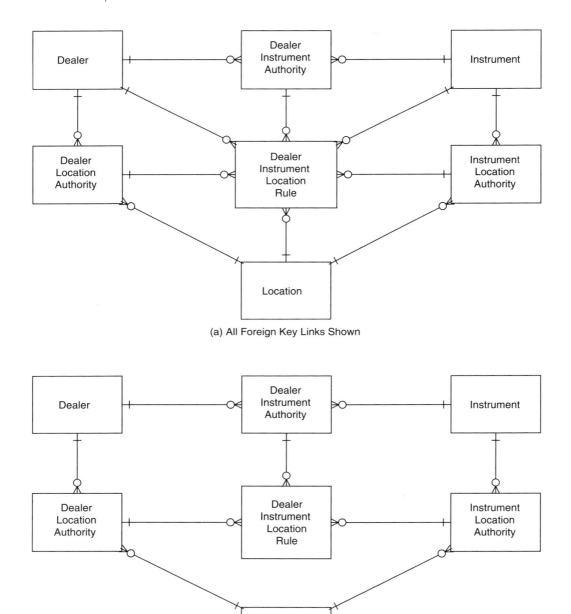

(a) All Foreign Key Links Shown

(b) Derivable Links Removed

Figure 13.18 Dealing model including dealer instrument location rule table.

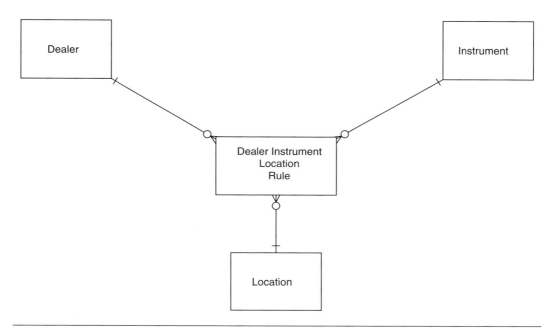

Figure 13.19 Dealing model with two-way intersection tables removed.

this is usually straightforward; in progressing to BCNF, we identify determinants that become primary keys, and the new tables we create in moving beyond BCNF are generally "all key."

The point, therefore, at which mistakes in primary key identification are most often made is in moving from unnormalized structures to 1NF. We should already have a key for the original file or list (we do not use the word table here, as tables do not have repeating groups); the problem is to identify a key for the new table that represents the repeating group. The simplest approach is to look at the repeating group before removing it and ask: what identifies one occurrence in the group within the context of a given record in the file? Then, ask whether the context is necessary at all; in other words: do we need to add the primary key of the original file or not?

On most occasions, we *do* need to include the primary key of the original file. But this is not always so, and you will eventually get into trouble if you do so unthinkingly. Figure 13.20 on the next page shows normalization of a simple file of insurance agents and the policies they have sold. The key of **Policy** is Policy No alone. Although Agent No must be included in the **Policy** table as a foreign key, it is not part of the primary key. Note that the result depends on the two business rules stated underneath the original model in Figure 13.20.

Surprisingly, a number of texts and papers do not recognize this possibility or, through choice of examples, encourage a view that it does not occur.

AGENT (<u>Agent No</u>, Name, {Policy No, Customer ID, Insured Amount })
Policy No uniquely identifies Policy
Each policy is sold by only one agent

Normalizing:
AGENT (<u>Agent No</u>, Agent Name)
POLICY (<u>Policy No</u>, Customer ID, Insured Amount, Agent No*)

Figure 13.20   Repeating group table with stand-alone key.

13.6.4   Sequence of Normalization and Cross-Table Anomalies

We conclude this chapter with an example that illustrates the importance of rigorously following the rules of normalization, and of developing a sound E-R model at the outset.

Let us go back to the customer-salesperson example we used to illustrate BCNF earlier in this chapter (shown again in Figure 13.21):

Recall that we ended up with two tables and observed that the structure did not appear to enforce our original business rule that each branch serviced a customer through one salesperson only.

But think about the consequences of relaxing the rule. Let us assume that Relationship Established Date is the date that the *branch* established a relationship with the customer. Then, for a given customer, we will end up carrying that same date for each salesperson within the branch (exactly the sort of redundancy that we would expect normalization to eliminate). But both tables are fully normalized.

We can see the problem more clearly if we go back to our original single table (Figure 13.22).

If we now normalize, taking into account the revised rule, we see that Customer No + Branch No is a determinant of Relationship Established Date and is no longer a candidate key. We therefore need to set up a separate table for these items, removing Relationship Established Date from the original table. Salesperson No is still a determinant of Branch No, so we set up another table

CUSTOMER-SALESPERSON RELATIONSHIP (<u>Customer No</u>, <u>Salesperson No</u>, Visiting Frequency, Relationship Established Date)
SALESPERSON (<u>Salesperson No</u>, Branch No)

Figure 13.21   Customer-salesperson model.

CUSTOMER-SALESPERSON RELATIONSHIP (Customer No, Salesperson No, Visiting Frequency, Relationship Established Date, Branch No)

Figure 13.22   Original customer-branch-salesperson model (not fully normalized).

for these items, removing **Branch No** from the original table. The result is shown in Figure 13.23.

There are at least three lessons here:

1. If you find during normalization that business rules on which you have relied are incorrect, go back to the E-R model and revise it accordingly; then renormalize. Be very careful about "patching" the logical model.
2. Normalization alone is not completely reliable if you start with data already divided into more than one table. But in practice, this is what we do virtually all of the time. So we need to analyze our E-R diagrams for problems as well as going through the steps of normalization.
3. Try to identify all the determinants at the start, and do not remove any part of them until all the columns they determine have first been removed. In this example, if we had removed **Branch No** first, we would have missed the "**Branch No** + **Customer No** determines **Relationship Established Date**" dependency.

13.7 **Advanced Normalization in Perspective**

Earlier in this chapter (Section 13.2.1), we noted that many modelers claim that they produce normalized structures intuitively, without recourse to normalization theory. And in teaching the higher normal forms and some of the more subtle aspects of normalization, we are frequently challenged by experienced data modelers as to their value in practice.

As we have seen, most of the problems that normalization addresses are more easily seen and resolved in the context of an E-R diagram. But much

CUSTOMER-SALESPERSON RELATIONSHIP (Customer No, Salesperson No, Visiting Frequency)
CUSTOMER-BRANCH RELATIONSHIP (Customer No, Branch No, Relationship Established Date)
SALESPERSON (Salesperson No, Branch No)

Figure 13.23   Fully normalized customer-branch-salesperson model.

of data modeling is about understanding, recognizing, and reusing patterns. The real value of the normalization to practitioners is in increasing their store of patterns, and backing it up with a deep understanding of the advantages and disadvantages of those patterns. When we see a three-way intersection entity, we automatically know to ask whether it can be derived from underlying relationships. If it is derivable, we can quote exactly the types of problems that will occur if it is not broken down into individual tables. (If we have forgotten, we need only look up a text on 4NF or 5NF, having classified the problem.) These patterns are useful enough that every professional data modeler needs to have them in his or her armory.

13.8 Summary

Tables in third normal form may not be in Boyce Codd, fourth, and fifth normal forms. Such tables will have problems with redundancy and incompleteness. The higher normal forms are frequently misunderstood by practitioners and, hence, ignored, or they are cited to support unsound modeling practices.

Boyce Codd Normal Form requires that every determinant be a candidate key. A table in 3NF will be in BCNF unless a key item is determined by a nonkey item. This will only occur if the table has multiple overlapping candidate keys. The problem is fixed by replacing the primary key with another candidate key and renormalizing.

A table in BCNF will usually only exhibit 4NF and 5NF problems if it has three or more columns, all of which are part of the key and can be derived from "underlying" tables. In entity-relationship terms, 4NF and 5NF problems arise when two or more many-to-many relationships are (incorrectly) resolved using a single entity.

To use normalization as the prime modeling technique, we need to start with all data in a single table. In practice, we commence with an E-R model, which will embody numerous assumptions. Normalization will not challenge these.

Normalization by itself does not remove all redundancy from a model nor guarantee completeness.

Chapter 14
Modeling Business Rules

"He may justly be numbered among the benefactors of mankind, who contracts the great rules of life into short sentences."
– Samuel Johnson

14.1 Introduction

Information systems contain and enforce *rules* about the businesses they support. (Some writers prefer the word *constraints*; we use the two interchangeably). For example, a human resource management system might incorporate the following rules (among others):

> *"Each employee can belong to at most one union at one time."*
> *"A minimum of 4% of each employee's salary up to $80,000 must be credited to the company pension fund."*
> *"If salary deductions result in an employee's net pay being negative, include details in an exception report."*
> *"At most two employees can share a job position at any time."*
> *"Only employees of Grade 4 and above can receive entertainment allowances."*
> *"For each grade of employee, a standard set of base benefits applies."*
> *"Each employee must have a unique employee number."*
> *"An employee's employment status must be either Permanent or Casual."*
> *"Employee number 4787 has an annual salary of $82,000."*

What is a rule? Systems contain information in various forms (data structure, data content, program logic, procedure manuals), which may be:

1. Assertions that something has happened (e.g., a particular customer has placed an order for a particular product)
2. Information about how the system[1] is to behave in particular situations (e.g., if the user attempts to raise an order without any products specified, reject it).

---

[1]We are using the term "system" in its broadest sense to mean not only the database and programs that operate upon it but the people who interact with it.

We refer to information of the second type as **rules**. Thus, it is fair to say that all of the statements listed in italics above are rules since each describes in some way how the system is to behave. Even the last, which is quite specific, affects the outcome of a process in the payroll system.

In this chapter we begin with a broad look at business rules then focus on the types of rules that are of particular concern to the data modeler. We look at what rules can be captured in E-R and relational models, and we discuss the problem of documenting those that cannot.

We then look at where and how rules should be implemented within an application, focusing on options available within popular DBMSs.

But before we get into the detail of rules, an important caveat. As discussed in Section 1.4, a new database is usually developed for the purpose of supporting a new way of doing business. Some of the recent writing on business rules has overlooked the fact that our job is to model what will be, not what was. And as people in a position to see what may be possible, we should be proactive in suggesting new possibilities and new rules to the business.

14.2 **Types of Business Rules**

Given our definition of a business rule as information about how the system is to behave in a particular situation, we can see that there are a number of different types of business rules.

14.2.1 **Data Rules**

First, there are rules that constrain the data the system can handle and how items of data relate to each other. These fall into two categories:

1. **Data validation rules** (strictly speaking data update rules), which determine what data may be recorded in the database and what changes may be made to that data
2. **Data derivation rules**, which specify the methods by which derived data items (on screens, in reports, and possibly in the database itself) are calculated.

Two specific types of data validation rules are of particular interest:

1. **Structural** or **cardinality rules**, which determine how many of a particular data item can be recorded in the database in association with some other data item

2. **Referential integrity rules**, which require that both entity instances involved in each relationship instance must exist.

Examples of cardinality rules include *"Each employee can belong to at most one union at any time"* and *"At most two employees can share a job position at any time."* Some "laws of physics" fall under this heading, such as *"Each employee can only be in one place at the one time"*: while hardly a business rule, it is presumably a requirement of the system that we cannot enter data that indicates that an employee was in two different places at the same time.

Strictly speaking, we should distinguish between rules about real-world objects and rules about the data that represents those objects. In most cases, the distinction is academic, but, as we see in Section 14.5.8, there are sometimes requirements to record information about real-world objects that have broken the rules.

Examples of data validation rules include *"Each employee must have a unique employee number,"* *"An employee's employment status must be either Permanent or Casual,"* and *"Only employees of Grade 4 and above can receive entertainment allowances."* It is likely to be a requirement of the system that any attempt to record two employees with the same employee number, an employee with an employment status other than Permanent or Casual, or an entertainment allowance for an employee of Grade 3 will be rejected.

An example of a data derivation rule is *"An employee's gross monthly salary is the sum of 1/12 of their annual salary plus 52/12 of the total of each of the nontaxable weekly allowances for each week for which that allowance applies less the total of each of the before-tax deductions for each week for which that deduction applies."*

In a relational database there is an implicit referential integrity rule for each foreign key, which states that each instance of that foreign key must match one of the primary keys in the referenced table (e.g., we cannot have an order without an associated customer). There is no need to explicitly document these rules if the relevant relationships or foreign keys are fully documented, although there may occasionally be a requirement to relax such rules. Referential integrity is discussed further in Section 14.5.4.

The rule *"Only employees of Grade 4 and above can receive entertainment allowances"* includes two items ("Grade 4" and allowance type "entertainment") that could be recorded in any of a number of places, including the database. So we also need to consider **data that supports data rules**, which are most often data validation rules like this one, but possibly cardinality rules (e.g., "What is the maximum number of unions an employee can belong to at one time?") or data derivation rules (e.g., "Is allowance *x* nontaxable and, hence, included in the calculation of an employee's gross monthly salary?") We discuss the options for recording data of this kind in Section 14.5.7.

14.2.2 **Process Rules**

A system will also be constrained by **process rules**, such as "*A minimum of 4% of each employee's salary up to $80,000 must be credited to the company pension fund*" and "*If salary deductions result in an employee's net pay being negative, include details in an exception report.*" Rules of this kind determine what processing the system is to do in particular circumstances.

The first of the preceding examples includes two numbers (4% and $80,000), which may or may not be recorded as data in the database itself. We discuss **data that supports process rules** in Section 14.5.7.

Another example of a process rule that requires some data somewhere is "*For each grade of employee, a standard set of base benefits applies.*" To support this rule, we need to record the base benefits for each grade of employee.

"*Employee number 4787 has annual salary $82,000*" is, as already indicated, a process rule. It is reasonable to expect that the data to support this process rule is going to be held in the database.

14.2.3 **What Rules Are Relevant to the Data Modeler?**

The data modeler should be concerned with both data and process rules and the data that supports them with one exception: other than in making a decision where and how the data supporting a process rule is to be recorded, it is not in the data modeler's brief to either model or decide on the implementation of any process rules. References to "business rules" in the rest of this chapter therefore include only the various *data rule* types listed above, whereas references to "data that supports rules" covers both data that supports process rules and data that supports data rules.

14.3 **Discovery and Verification of Business Rules**

While the business people consulted will volunteer many of the business rules that a system must support, it is important to ensure that all bases have been covered. Once we have a draft data model, the following activities should be undertaken to check in a systematic way that the rules it embodies correctly reflect the business requirements.

14.3.1 **Cardinality Rules**

We can assemble a candidate set of cardinality rules by constructing assertions about each relationship as described in Sections 3.5.1 and 10.18.2.2.

We should also check the cardinality of each *attribute* (how many values it can have for one entity instance). This should be part of the process of normalization, as described in Chapter 2. However, if you have worked top-down to develop an Entity-Relationship model, you need to check whether each attribute can have more than one value for each instance of the entity class in which it has been placed. For example, if there is a **Nickname** attribute in the **Employee** entity class and the business needs to record all nicknames for those employees that have more than one, the data model needs to be modified, either by replacing **Nickname** by the multivalued attribute **Nicknames** (in a conceptual data model or in a logical data model in which these are allowable—see Section 11.4.6) or by creating a separate entity for nicknames (related to the **Employee** entity class). To establish attribute cardinalities, we can ask questions in the following form for each attribute:

"Can an employee have more than one nickname?"
"If so, is it necessary to record more than one in the database?"

14.3.2 **Other Data Validation Rules**

Other data validation rules can be discovered by asking, for each entity class:

"What restrictions are there on adding an instance of this entity class?"
"What restrictions are there on the values that may be assigned to each attribute of a new instance of this entity class?"
"What restrictions are there on the values that may be assigned to each attribute when changing an existing instance of this entity class?" (The answer to this question is often the same as the answer to the previous question but on occasion they may differ; in particular, some attributes once assigned a value must retain that value without change.)
"What restrictions are there on removing an instance of this entity class?"

14.3.3 **Data Derivation Rules**

Data derivation rules are best discovered by analyzing each screen and each report that has been specified and by listing each value therein that does not correspond directly to an attribute in the data model. For each value, it is necessary to establish with the business exactly how that value is to be derived from the data that is in the database. In the case of a data warehouse (Chapter 16), or any other database in which we decide to hold summary data, we will need to ask similar questions and document the answers.

14.4 **Documentation of Business Rules**

14.4.1 **Documentation in an E-R Diagram**

Only a few types of business rules can be documented in an E-R diagram:

1. The referential integrity rules implicit in each relationship (see Section 14.5.4)
2. The cardinalities of each relationship (as discussed in Section 3.2.3): these are (of course) cardinality rules
3. Whether each relationship is mandatory or optional (as also discussed in Section 3.2.4): these are data validation rules, since they determine restrictions on the addition, changing, and/or removal of entity instances
4. Various limitations on which entity instances can be associated with each other (by specifying that a relationship is with a subtype of an entity class rather than the entity class itself; this is discussed further in Section 14.4.3): these are also data validation rules
5. The fact that an attribute is restricted to a discrete set of values (a data validation rule) *can* be documented by adding an entity class to represent the relevant set of categories and a relationship from that entity class to one containing a category attribute—the familiar "reference table" structure (see Section 14.5.5)—although, as discussed in Section 7.2.2.1, we do not recommend this in a conceptual data model.

Further business rules can conveniently be documented in the attribute lists supporting an E-R diagram. Most documentation tools will allow you to record:

6. Whether each attribute is optional (nullable) (a data validation rule)
7. The DBMS datatype of each attribute (e.g., if the attribute is given a numeric datatype, this specifies a data validation rule that nonnumerics cannot be entered; if a date datatype, that the value entered must be a valid date).

If the transferability notation (see Section 3.5.6) is available, an additional type of business rule can be documented:

8. Whether each relationship is transferable (a data validation rule).

14.4.2 **Documenting Other Rules**

Unfortunately, there are many other types of rules, including all data derivation rules and the following types of data validation rules, which are not so readily represented in an E-R diagram or associated attribute list, or at least not in a manner amenable to direct translation into relational database constraints (we can always record them as text in definitions):

1. Nondiscrete constraints on attribute values (e.g., *"The Unit Price of a Product must be positive"*)

2. Attribute constraints dependent on values of other attributes in the same entity instance (e.g., *"The End Date must be later than the Start Date"*)

3. Most attribute constraints that are dependent on values of attributes in different entity instances, including instances of different entity classes (e.g., *"The amount of this allowance for this employee cannot exceed the maximum for this employee grade"*)—exceptions that *can* be modeled in an E-R diagram are referential integrity (see Section 14.5.4) and those involving allowable combinations of values of different attributes (see Section 14.5.6)

4. Cardinality/optionality constraints such as *"There can be no more than four subjects recorded for a teacher"* or *"There must be at least two subjects recorded for each teacher"* (actually the first of these could be documented using a repeating group with four items but, as discussed in Section 2.6, repeating groups generally have serious drawbacks)

5. Restrictions on updatability (other than transferability) such as *"No existing transaction can be updated,"* *"This date can only be altered to a date later than previously recorded,"* and *"This attribute can only be updated by the Finance Manager."*

E-R diagrams do not provide any means of documenting these other rule types, yet such rules tell us important information about the data, its meaning, and how it is to be correctly used. They logically belong with the data model, so some supplementary documentation technique is required. Some other modeling approaches recognize this need. ORM (Object Role Modeling, discussed briefly in Section 7.5) provides a well-developed and much richer language than the E-R Model for documenting constraints, and the resulting models can be converted to relational database designs fairly mechanically. UML also provides some constraint notations, although in general the ability of UML CASE tools to automatically implement constraints in the resulting database is less developed than for ORM. We can also choose to take advantage of one or more of the techniques available to specify *process* logic: decision tables, decision trees, data flow diagrams, function decompositions, pseudo-code, and so on. These are particularly relevant for rules we would like to hold as data in order to facilitate change, but which would more naturally be represented within program logic. The important thing is that whichever techniques are adopted, they be readily understood by all participants in the system development process.

It is also important that rules not be ignored as "too hard." The rules are an integral part of the system being developed, and it is essential to be able to refer back to an agreed specification.

Plain language is still one of the most convenient and best understood ways to specify rules. One problem with plain language is that it provides plenty of scope for ambiguity. To address this deficiency, Ross[2] has developed a very sophisticated diagrammatic notation for documenting rules of all types. While he has developed a very thorough taxonomy of rules and a wide range of symbols to represent them, the complexity of the diagrams produced using this technique may make them unsuitable as a medium for discussion with business people.

Ross' technique may be most useful in documenting rules for the benefit of those building a system and in gaining an appreciation of the types of rules we need to look for. The great advantage of using plain language for documentation is that the rules remain understandable to all participants in the system development process. The downside is the possibility of making ambiguous statements, but careful choice of wording can add rigor without loss of understanding.

Data validation rules that cannot be represented directly in the data model proper should be documented in text form against the relevant entity classes, attributes, and relationships (illustrated in Figure 14.1). Data derivation rules should be documented separately only if the derived data items have not been included in the data model as we recommended in Section 7.2.2.2.

Where there is any doubt about the accuracy of a rule recorded against the model, you should obtain and list examples. These serve not only to clarify and test the accuracy of the specified requirements and verify that the rules are real and important, but provide ammunition to fire at proposed solutions. On occasions, we have seen requirements dropped or significantly modified after the search for examples failed to turn up any, or confirmed that the few cases from which the rules had been inferred were in fact the only cases!

14.4.3 **Use of Subtypes to Document Rules**

Subtypes can be used in a conceptual data model to document limitations on which entity instances can be associated with each other (outlined in Chapter 4). Figure 14.2 on page 426 illustrates the simplest use of subtypes to document a rule. The initial model relates workers and annual leave applications, but we are advised that only certain types of workers— employees—can submit annual leave applications. A straightforward subtyping captures the rule.

Nonemployee Worker is not an elegant classification or name, and we should be prompted to ask what other sorts of workers the user is

---

[2]Ross, R.G., *The Business Rule Book: Classifying, Defining & Modeling Rules,* Business Rule Solutions (1997).

Entity Class/Data Item	Constraints
Student Absence	No date/time overlaps between records for the same Student
be for Student	Mandatory; Student must already exist
Start Date	Mandatory; must be valid date; must be within reasonable range
End Date	If entered: must be valid date; must be not be before Start Date; must be within reasonable range
First Timetable Period No	Mandatory; integer; must be between 1 and maximum timetable period no inclusive
Last Timetable Period No	If entered: integer; must be between 1 and maximum timetable period no inclusive; must not be less than First Timetable Period No
be classified by Student Absence Reason	Mandatory; Student Absence Reason must already exist
Notification Date	If entered: must be valid date; must be within reasonable range
Absence Approved Flag	If entered: must be Yes or No
Student Absence Reason	
Absence Reason Code	Mandatory; must be unique
Description	Mandatory; must be unique

Figure 14.1 Some data validation rules.

interested in. Perhaps we might be able to change the entity class name to **Contractor**.

Note that, as described in Chapter 11, we have a variety of options for implementing a supertype/subtype structure; inclusion of subtypes in the model does not necessarily imply that each will be implemented in a separate table. We may well decide not to, perhaps because we can envision other worker types in the future, or due to a relaxation of the rule as to who can submit leave applications. We would then implement the rule either within program logic, or through a table listing the types of workers able to submit annual leave applications.

This simple example provides a template for solving more complex problems. For example, we might want to add the rule that *"Only noncitizens require work permits."* This could be achieved by using the partitioning convention introduced in Chapter 4 to show alternative subtypings (see Figure 14.3, page 427).

Note that the relationship from **Noncitizen** to **Work Permit** is *optional*, even though the original rule could have been interpreted as requiring it to be mandatory. We would have checked this by asking the user: "Could we ever want to record details of a noncitizen who did not have a work permit (perhaps prior to their obtaining one)?"

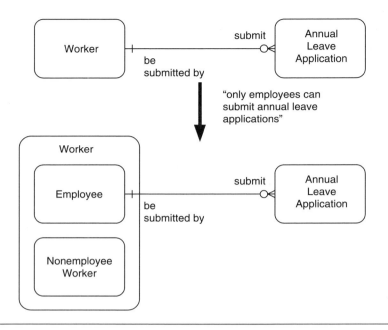

Figure 14.2   Using subtypes to model rules.

Suppose we wanted to model the organizational structure of a company so as to enforce the rule that an employee could be assigned only to a lowest level organizational unit. This kind of structure also occurs in hierarchical charts of accounts, in which transactions can be posted only to the lowest level.

Figure 14.4 on page 428 shows the use of subtypes to capture the rule. Note that the structure itself defines a **Lowest Level Organization Unit** as an **Organizational Unit** that cannot control other **Organizational Unit**s (since it lacks the "control" relationship). Once again, we might not implement the subtypes, perhaps because a given lowest level organizational unit could later control other organization units, thus changing its subtype. (Section 4.13.5 discusses why we want to avoid instances changing from one subtype to another.)

Wherever subtyping allows you to capture a business rule easily in a conceptual data model, we recommend that you do so, *even if you have little intention of actually implementing the subtypes as separate tables in the final database design*. Even if you plan to have a single table in the database holding many different types of real-world objects, documenting those real-world objects as a single entity class is likely to make the model incomprehensible to users. Do not omit important rules that can be readily documented using subtypes simply because those subtypes are potentially

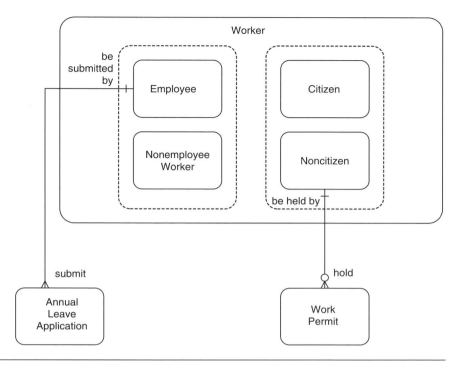

Figure 14.3   Using alternative subtypings to model rules.

volatile. This is an abdication of the data modeler's responsibility for doing detailed and rigorous analysis and the process modelers will not thank you for having to ask the same questions again!

14.5 **Implementing Business Rules**

Deciding how and where each rule is to be implemented is one of the most important aspects of information system design. Depending on the type of rule, it can be implemented in one or more of the following:

- The structure of the database (its tables and columns)
- Various properties of columns (datatype, nullability, uniqueness, referential integrity)
- Declared constraints, enforced by the DBMS
- Data values held in the database
- Program logic (stored procedures, screen event handling, application code)

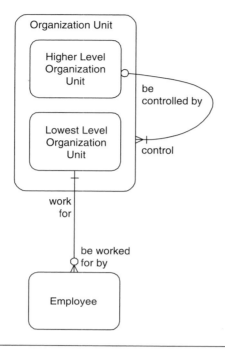

Figure 14.4 Using unstable subtypes to capture rules.

- Inside specialized "rules engine" software
- Outside the computerized component of the system (manual rules, procedures).

14.5.1 **Where to Implement Particular Rules**

Some rules by their nature suggest one of the above techniques in particular. For example, the rule *"Each employee can belong to at most one union at one time"* is most obviously supported by data structure (a foreign key in the **Employee** table representing a one-to-many relationship between the **Union** and **Employee** entity classes). Similarly, the rule *"If salary deductions result in an employee's net pay being negative, include details in an exception report"* is clearly a candidate for implementation in program logic. Other rules suggest alternative treatments; for example, the values 4% and $80,000 supporting the rule *"A minimum of 4% of each employee's salary up to $80,000 must be credited to the company pension fund"* could be held as data in the database or constants in program logic.

14.5.1.1 Choosing from Alternatives

Where there are alternatives, the selection of an implementation technique should start with the following questions:

1. How readily does this implementation method support the rule?
2. How volatile is the rule (how likely is it to change during the lifetime of the system)?
3. How flexible is this implementation method (how easily does it lend itself to changing a rule)?

For example, changing the database structure after a system has been built is a very complex task whereas changing a data value is usually very easy. Changes to program logic involve more work than changing a data value but less than changing the database structure (which will involve program logic changes in at least one program—and possibly many). Changes to column properties can generally be made quite quickly but not as quickly as changing a data value.

Note that rules implemented primarily using one technique may also affect the design of other components of the system. For example, if we implement a rule in data structure, that rule will also be reflected in program structure; if we implement a rule using data values, we will need to design the data structure to support the necessary data, and design the programs to allow their processing logic to be driven by the data values.

This is an area in which it is crucial that data modelers and process modelers work together. Many a data model has been rejected or inappropriately compromised because it placed demands upon process modelers that they did not understand or were unprepared to meet.

If a rule is volatile then we may need to consider a more flexible implementation method than the most obvious one. For example, if the rule "*Each employee can belong to at most one union at one time*" might change during the life of the system, then rather than using an inflexible data structure to implement it, the alternative of a separate **Employee Union Membership** table (which would allow an unlimited number of memberships per employee) could be adopted. The current rule can then be enforced by adding a unique index to the Employee No column in that table. Removal of that index is quick and easy, but we would then have no limit on the number of unions to which a particular employee could belong. If a limit other than one were required, it would be necessary to enforce that limit using program logic, (e.g., a stored procedure triggered by insertion to, or update of, the **Employee Union Membership** table).

Here, once again, there are alternatives. The maximum number of union memberships per employee could be included as a constant in the program logic or held as a value in the database somewhere, to be referred to by the program logic. However, given the very localized effect of stored procedures, the resultant ease of testing changes to them, and the expectation that changes to the rule would be relatively infrequent (and not require direct user control), there would be no great advantage in holding the limit in a table.

One other advantage of stored procedures is that, if properly associated with triggers, they always execute whenever a particular data operation takes place and are therefore the preferred location for rule enforcement logic (remember that we are talking about *data* rules). Since the logic is now only in one place rather than scattered among all the various programs that might access the data, the maintenance effort in making changes to that logic is much less than with traditional programming.

Let us look at the implementation options for some of the other rules listed at the start of this chapter:

"At most two employees can share a job position at any time" can be implemented in the data structure by including two foreign keys in the **Job Position** table to the **Employee** table. This could be modeled as such with two relationships between the **Job Position** and **Employee** entity classes. If this rule was volatile and there was the possibility of more than two employees in a job position, a separate **Employee Job Position** table would be required. Program logic would then be necessary to impose any limit on the number of employees that could share a job position.

"Only employees of Grade 4 and above can receive entertainment allowances" can be implemented using a stored procedure triggered by insertion to or update of the **Employee Allowance** table (in which each individual employee's allowances are recorded). This and the inevitable other rules restricting allowances to particular grades could be enforced by explicit logic in that procedure or held in an **Employee Grade Allowance** table in which legitimate combinations of employee grades and allowance types could be held (or possibly a single record for each allowance type with the range of legitimate employee grades). Note that the recording of this data in a table in the database does not remove the need for a stored procedure; it merely changes the logic in that procedure.

"For each grade of employee, a standard set of base benefits applies" can be implemented using a stored procedure triggered by insertion to the **Employee** table or update of the Grade column in that table. Again the base benefits for each grade could be explicitly itemized in that procedure or held in an **Employee Grade** table in which the benefits for each employee grade are listed. Again, the recording of this data in a table in the database does not remove the need for a stored procedure; it merely changes the logic in that procedure.

"Each employee must have a unique employee number" can be implemented by addition of a unique index on Employee No in the **Employee** table. This would, of course, be achieved automatically if Employee No was declared to be the primary key of the **Employee** table, but additional unique indexes can be added to a table for any other columns or combinations of columns that are unique.

"An employee's employment status must be either Permanent or Casual" is an example of restricting an attribute to a discrete set of values. Implementation options for this type of rule are discussed in Section 14.5.5.

A detailed example of alternative implementations of a particular set of rules is provided in Section 14.5.2.

14.5.1.2 Assessment of Rule Volatility

Clearly we need to assess the volatility (or, conversely, stability) of each rule before deciding how to implement it. Given a choice of "flexible" or "inflexible," we can expect system users to opt for the former and, consequently, to err on the side of volatility when asked to assess the stability of a rule. But the net result can be a system that is far more sophisticated and complicated than it needs to be.

It is important, therefore, to gather reliable evidence as to how often and in what way we can expect rules to change. Figure 14.5 provides an illustration of the way in which the volatility of rules can vary.

History is always a good starting point. We can prompt the user: "This rule hasn't changed in ten years; is there anything that would make it more likely to change in the future?" Volume is also an indication. If we have a large set of rules, of the same type or in the same domain, we can anticipate that the set will change.

Type of Rule	Example	Volatility
Laws of nature: violation would give rise to a logical contradiction	A person can be working in no more than one location at a given time	Zero
Legislation or international or national standards for the industry or business area	Each customer has only one Social Security Number	Low
Generally accepted practice in the industry or business area	An invoice is raised against the customer who ordered the goods delivered	Low[3]
Established practice (formal procedure) within the organization	Reorder points for a product are centrally determined rather than being set by warehouses	Medium
Discretionary practices: "the way it's done at the moment"	Stock levels are checked weekly	High

Figure 14.5 Volatility of rules.

---

[3]This is the sort of rule that is likely to be cited as non-volatile—and even as evidence that data structures are intrinsically stable. But breaking it is now a widely known business process reengineering practice.

When you find that a rule is volatile, at least to the extent that it is likely to change over the life of the system, it is important to identify the components that are the cause of its volatility. One useful technique is to look for a more general "higher-level" rule that *will* be stable.

For example, the rule "*5% of each contribution must be posted to the Statutory Reserve Account*" may be volatile. But what about "*A percentage of each contribution must be posted to the Statutory Reserve Account?*" But perhaps even this is a volatile instance of a more general rule: "*Each contribution is divided among a set of accounts, in accordance with a standard set of percentages.*" And will the division always be based on percentages? Perhaps we can envision in the future deducting a fixed dollar amount from each contribution to cover administration costs.

This sort of exploration and clarification is essential if we are to avoid going to great trouble to accommodate a change of one kind to a rule, only to be caught by a change of a different kind.

It is important that volatile rules can be readily changed. On the other hand, stable rules form the framework on which we design the system by defining the boundaries of what it must be able to handle. Without some stable rules, system design would be unmanageably complex; every system would need to be able to accommodate any conceivable possibility or change. We want to implement these stable rules in such a way that they cannot be easily bypassed or inadvertently changed.

In some cases, these two objectives conflict. The most common situation involves rules that would most easily be enforced by program logic, but which need to be readily updateable by users. Increased pressure on businesses to respond quickly to market or regulatory changes has meant that rules that were once considered stable are no longer so. One solution is to hold the rules as data. If such rules are central to the system, we often refer to the resulting system as being "table-driven." Note, however, that no rule can be implemented by data values in the database alone. Where the data supporting a rule is held in the database, program logic must be written to use that data. While the cost of changing the rule during the life of the system is reduced by opting for the table-driven approach, the sophistication and initial cost of a table-driven system is often significantly greater, due to the complexity of that program logic.

A different sort of problem arises when we want to represent a rule within the data structure but cannot find a simple way of doing so. Rules that "almost" follow the pattern of those we normally specify in data models can be particularly frustrating. We can readily enforce the rule that only one person can hold a particular job position, but what if the limit is two? Or five? A minimum of two? How do we handle more subtle (but equally reasonable) constraints, such as "*The customer who receives the invoice must be the same as the customer who placed the order?*"

There is room for choice and creativity in deciding how each rule will be implemented. We now look at an example in detail, then at some commonly encountered issues.

14.5.2 **Implementation Options: A Detailed Example**

Figure 14.6 shows part of a model to support transaction processing for a medical benefits (insurance) fund. Very similar structures occur in many systems that support a range of products against which specific sets of transactions are allowed. Note the use of the exclusivity arc introduced in Section 4.14.2 to represent, for example, that each dental services claim must be lodged by either a Class A member or a Class B member.

Let us consider just one rule that the model represents: "*Only a Class A member can lodge a claim for paramedical services.*"

14.5.2.1 Rules in Data Structure

If we implement the model at the lowest level of subtyping, the rule restricting paramedical services claims to Class A members will be implemented in the data structure. The **Paramedical Services Claim** table will hold a foreign key supporting the relationship to the **Class A Member** table. Program logic will take account of this structure in, for example, the steps taken to process a paramedical claim, the layout of statements to be

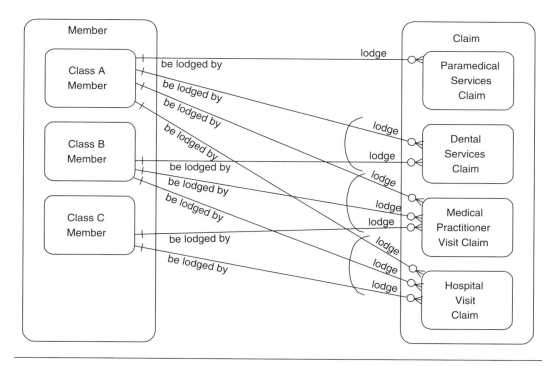

Figure 14.6 Members and medical insurance claims.

sent to Class B members (no provision for paramedical claims), and in ensuring that only Class A members are associated with paramedical claims, through input vetting and error messages. If we are confident that the rule will not change, then this is a sound design and the program logic can hardly be criticized for inflexibility.

Suppose now that our assumption about the rule being stable is incorrect and we need to change the rule to allow Class B members to claim for paramedical services. We now need to change the database design to include a foreign key for Class B members in **Paramedical Claim**. We will also need to change the corresponding program logic.

In general, changes to rules contained within the data structure require the participation of data modelers and database administrators, analysts, programmers, and, of course, the users. Facing this, we may well be tempted by "quick and dirty" approaches: "Perhaps we could transfer all Class B members to Class A, distinguishing them by a flag in a spare column." Many a system bears the scars of continued "programming around" the data structure rather than incurring the cost of changes.

14.5.2.2 Rules in Programs

From Chapter 4, we know broadly what to do with unstable rules in data structure: we generalize them out. If we implement the model at the level of Member, the rules about what sort of claims can be made by each type of member will no longer be held in data structure.

Instead, the model holds rules including:

"Each Paramedical Claim must be lodged by one Member."
"Each Dental Claim must be lodged by one Member."

But we do need to hold the original rules somewhere. Probably the simplest option is to move them to program logic. The logic will look a little different from that associated with the more specific model, and we will essentially be checking the claims against the new attribute **Member Type**.

Enforcement of the rules now requires some discipline at the programming level. It is technically possible for a program that associates any sort of claim with any sort of member to be written. Good practice suggests a common module for checking, but good practice is not always enforced!

Now, if we want to change a rule, only the programs that check the constraints will need to be modified. We will not need to involve the data modeler and database administrator at all. The amount of programming work will depend on how well the original programmers succeeded in localizing the checking logic. It may include developing a program to run periodic checks on the data to ensure that the rule has not been violated by a rogue program.

14.5.2.3 Rules in Data

Holding the rules in program logic may still not provide sufficient responsiveness to business change. In many organizations, the amount of time required to develop a new program version, fully test it, and migrate it into production may be several weeks or months.

The solution is to hold the rules in the data. In our example, this would mean holding a list of the valid member types for each type of claim. An **Allowed Member Claim Combination** table as in Figure 14.7 will provide the essential data.

But our programs will now need to be much more sophisticated. If we implement the database at the generalized Member and Claim level (see Figure 14.8, next page), the program will need to refer to the **Allowed Member Claim Combination** table to decide which subsets of the main tables to work with in each situation.

If we implement at the subtype level, the program will need to decide at run time which *tables* to access by referring to the **Allowed Member Claim Combination** table. For example, we may want to print details of all claims made by a member. The program will need to determine what types of claims can be made by a member of that type, and then it must access the appropriate claim tables. This will involve translating Claim Type Codes and Member Type Codes into table names, which we can handle either with reference tables or by translation in the program. In-program translation means that we will have to change the program if we add further tables; the use of reference tables raises the possibility of a system in which we could add new tables without changing any program logic. Again, we would need to be satisfied that this sophisticated approach was better overall than simply implementing the model at the supertype level. Many programming languages (in particular, SQL) do not comfortably support run-time decisions about which table to access.

The payoff for the "rules in data" or "table-driven" approach comes when we want to change the rules. We can leave both database administrators and programmers out of the process, by handling the change with conventional transactions. Because such changes may have a significant business impact, they are typically restricted to a small subset of users or to a system administrator. Without proper control, there is a temptation for individual users to find "novel" ways of using the system, which may invalidate assumptions made by the system builders. The consequences may

ALLOWED MEMBER CLAIM COMBINATION (<u>Claim Type Code</u>, <u>Member Type Code</u>)

Figure 14.7 Table of allowed claim types for each member type.

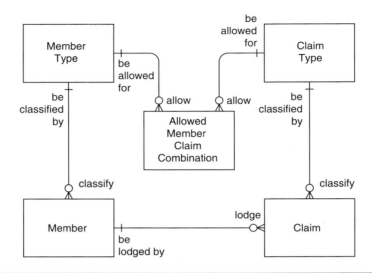

Figure 14.8   Model at claim type and member type level.

include unreliable, or uninterpretable, outputs and unexpected system behavior.

For some systems and types of change, the administrator needs to be an information systems professional who is able to assess any systems changes that may be required beyond the changes to data values (not to mention taking due credit for the quick turnaround on the "systems maintenance" requests). In our example, the tables would allow a new type of claim to be added by changing data values, but this might need to be supplemented by changes to program logic to handle new processing specific to claims of that type.

14.5.3   Implementing Mandatory Relationships

As already discussed, a one-to-many relationship is implemented in a relational database by declaring a column (or set of columns) in the table at the "many" end to be a foreign key and specifying which table is referenced. If the relationship is mandatory at the "one" end, this is implemented by declaring the foreign key column(s) to be nonnullable; conversely, if the relationship is optional at the "one" end, this is implemented by declaring the foreign key column(s) to be nullable. However if the relationship is mandatory at the "many" end, additional logic must be employed.

Relationships that are mandatory at the "many" end are more common than some modelers realize. For example, in Figure 14.9, the relationship between **Order** and **Order Line** is mandatory at the "many" end since an order without anything ordered does not make sense. The relationship between **Product** and **Product Size** is mandatory at the "many" end for a rather less obvious reason. In fact, intuition may tell us that in the real world not every product is available in multiple sizes. If we model this relationship as optional at the "many" end then we would have to create two relationships from **Order Line**—one to **Product Size**, (to manage products that are available in multiple sizes) and one to **Product** (to manage products that are not). This will make the system more complex than necessary. Instead, we establish that a **Product Size** record is created for each product, even one that is only available in one size.

To enforce these constraints it is necessary to employ program logic that allows neither an **Order** row to be created without at least one **Order Line** row nor a **Product** row to be created without at least one **Product Size** row. In addition (and this is sometimes forgotten), it is necessary to prohibit the deletion of either the last remaining **Order Line** row for an **Order** or the last remaining **Product Size** row for a **Product**.

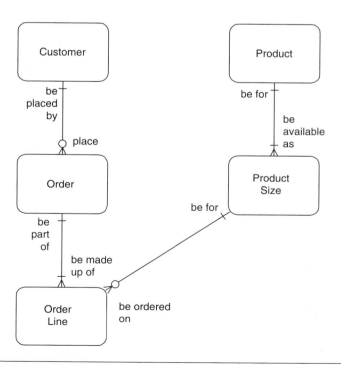

Figure 14.9 An order entry model.

14.5.4 **Referential Integrity**

14.5.4.1 What It Means

The business requirements for referential integrity are straightforward. If a column supports a relationship (i.e., is a foreign key column), the row referred to:

- Must exist at all times that the reference does
- Must be the one that was intended at the time the reference was created or last updated.

14.5.4.2 How Referential Integrity Is Achieved in a Database

These requirements are met in a database as follows.

Reference Creation: If a column is designed to hold foreign keys the only values that may be written into that column are primary key values of existing records in the referenced table. For example, if there is a foreign key column in the **Student** table designed to hold references to families, only the primary key of an *existing* row in the **Family** table can be written into that column.

Key Update: If the primary key of a row is changed, all references to that row must also be changed in the same update process (this is known as **Update Cascade**). For example, if the primary key of a row in the **Family** table is changed, any row in the **Student** table with a foreign key reference to that row must have that reference updated at the same time. Alternatively the primary key of any table may be made nonchangeable (**No Update**) in which case no provision needs to be made for Update Cascade on that table. You should recall from Chapter 6 that we strongly recommend that all primary keys be nonchangeable (stable).

Key Delete: If an attempt is made to delete a record and there are references to that record, one of three policies must be followed, depending on the type of data:

1. The deletion is prohibited (**Delete Restrict**).
2. All references to the deleted record are replaced by nulls (**Delete Set Null**).
3. All records with references to the deleted record are themselves deleted (**Delete Cascade**).

Alternatively, we can prohibit deletion of data from any table irrespective of whether there are references (**No Delete**), in which case no provision needs to be made for any of the listed policies on that table.

14.5.4.3 Modeling Referential Integrity

Most data modelers will simply create a relationship in an E-R model or (in a relational model) indicate which columns in each table are foreign keys. It is then up to the process modeler or designer, or sometimes even the programmer or DBA, to decide which update and delete options are appropriate for each relationship/foreign key. However, since the choice should be up to the business and it is modelers rather than programmers or DBAs who are consulting with the business, it should be either the data modeler or the process modeler who determines the required option in each case. Our view is that even though updating and deleting of records are processes, the implications of these processes for the integrity of data are such that the data modeler has an obligation to consider them.

14.5.5 **Restricting an Attribute to a Discrete Set of Values**

14.5.5.1 Use of Codes

Having decided that we require a category attribute such as **Account Status**, we need to determine the set of possible values and how we will represent them. For example, allowed statuses might be "Active," "Closed," and "Suspended." Should we use these words as they stand, or introduce a coding scheme (such as "A," "C," and "S" *or* "1," "2," and "3" to represent "Active," "Closed," and "Suspended")?

Most practitioners would introduce a coding scheme automatically, in line with conventional practice since the early days of data processing. They would also need to provide somewhere in the system (using the word "system" in its broadest sense to include manual files, processes, and human knowledge) a translation mechanism to code and decode the fully descriptive terms.

Given the long tradition of coding schemes, it is worth looking at what they actually achieve.

First, and most obviously, we save space. "A" is more concise than "Active." The analyst responsible for dialogue design may well make the coding scheme visible to the user, as one means of saving key strokes and reducing errors.

We also improve flexibility, in terms of our ability to add new codes in a consistent fashion. We do not have the problem of finding that a new value of **Account Status** is a longer word than we have allowed for.

Probably the most important benefit of using codes is the ability to change the text description of a code while retaining its meaning. Perhaps we wish to rename the "Suspended" status "Under Review." This sort of thing happens as organizational terminology changes, sometimes to conform to industry standards and practices. The coding approach provides us with a level of insulation, so that we distinguish a change in the meaning of a code (update the **Account Status** table) from a change in actual status of an account (update the **Account** table).

To achieve this distinction, we need to be sure that the code can remain stable if the full description changes. Use of initial letters, or indeed anything derived from the description itself, will interfere with this objective. How many times have you seen coding schemes that only partially follow some rule because changes or later additions have been impossible to accommodate?

The issues of code definition are much the same as those of primary key definition discussed in Chapter 6. This is hardly surprising, as a code is the primary key of a computerized or external reference table.

14.5.5.2 Simple Reference Tables

As soon as we introduce a coding scheme for data, we need to provide for a method of coding and decoding. In some cases, we may make this a human responsibility, relying on users of the computerized system to memorize or look up the codes themselves. Another option is to build the translation rules into programs. The third option is to include a table for this purpose as part of the database design. Such tables are commonly referred to as **reference tables**. Some DBMSs provide alternative translation mechanisms, in which case you have a fourth option to choose from. The advantage of all but the first option is that the system can ensure that only valid codes are entered.

In fact, even if we opt for full text descriptions in the category attribute rather than codes, a table of allowed values can be used to ensure that only valid descriptions are entered. In either case referential integrity (discussed in Section 14.5.4) should be established between the category attribute and the table of allowed values.

As discussed in Section 7.2.2.1, even though we may use entity classes to represent category attributes in the logical data model, we recommend that you omit these "category entity classes" from the conceptual data model in order to reduce the complexity of the diagram, and to avoid pre-empting the method of implementation.

There are certain circumstances in which the reference table approach should be strongly favored:

1. If the number of different allowed values is large enough to make human memory, manual look-up, and programming approaches cumbersome. At 20 values, you are well into this territory.
2. If the set of allowed values is subject to change. This tends to go hand in hand with large numbers of values. Changing a data value is simpler

than updating program logic, or keeping people and manual documents up-to-date.

3. If we want to hold additional information (about allowed values) that is to be used by the system at run-time (as distinct from documentation for the benefit of programmers and others). For example, we may need to hold a more complete description of the meaning of each code value for inclusion in reports or maintain "Applicable From" and "Applicable To" dates.

4. If the category entity class has relationships with other entity classes in the model, besides the obvious relationship to the entity class holding the category attribute that it controls (see Section 14.5.6).

Conversely, the reference table approach is less attractive if we need to "hard code" actual values into program logic. Adding new values will then necessitate changes to the logic, so the advantage of being able to add values without affecting programs is lost.

14.5.5.3 Generalization of Reference Tables

The entity classes that specify reference tables tend to follow a standard format: **Code**, **Full Name** (or **Meaning**), and possibly **Description**. This suggests the possibility of generalization, and we have frequently seen models that specify a single supertype reference table (which, incidentally, should not be named "Reference Table," but something like "**Category**," in keeping with our rule of naming entity classes according to the meaning of a single instance).

Again, we need to go back to basics and ask whether the various code types are subject to common processes. The answer is usually "Yes," as far as their update is concerned, but the inquiry pattern is likely to be less consistent. A consolidated reference table offers the possibility of a generic code update module and easy addition of new code types, not inconsiderable benefits when you have seen the alternative of individual program modules for each code type. Views can provide the subtype level pictures required for enquiry.

Be ready for an argument with the physical database designer if you recommend implementation at the supertype level. The generalized table will definitely make referential integrity management more complex and may well cause an access bottleneck. As always, you will want to see evidence of the real impact on system design and performance, and you will need to negotiate trade-offs accordingly. Programmers may also object to the less obvious programming required if full advantage is to be taken of the generalized design. On the other hand, we have seen generalization of all reference tables proposed by database administrators as a standard design rule.

As usual, recognizing the possibility of generalization is valuable even if the supertype is not implemented directly. You may still be able to write or clone generic programs to handle update more consistently and at reduced development cost.

14.5.6 Rules Involving Multiple Attributes

Occasionally, we encounter a rule that involves two or even more attributes, usually but not always from the same entity class. If the rule simply states that only certain combinations of attribute values are permissible, we can set up a table of the allowed combinations. If the attributes are from the same entity class, we can use the referential integrity features of the database management system (see Section 14.5.4) to ensure that only valid combinations of values are recorded. However, if they are from different entity classes enforcement of the rule requires the use of program logic, (e.g., a stored procedure).

We can and should include an entity class in the data model representing the table of allowed combinations, and, if the controlled attributes are from the same entity class, we should include a relationship between that entity class and the **Allowed Combination** entity.

Some DBMSs provide direct support for describing constraints across multiple columns as part of the database definition. Since such constraints are frequently volatile, be sure to establish how easily such constraints can be altered.

Multiattribute constraints are not confined to category attributes. They may involve range checks ("*If Product Type is 'Vehicle,' Price must be greater than $10,000*") or even cross-entity constraints ("*Only a Customer with a credit rating of 'A' can have an Account with an overdraft limit of over $1000*"). These too can be readily implemented using tables specifying the allowed combinations of category values and maxima or minima, but they require program logic to ensure that only allowed combinations are recorded. Once again the DBMS may allow such constraints to be specified in the database definition.

As always, the best approach is to document the constraints as you model and defer the decision as to exactly how they are to be enforced until you finalize the logical database design.

14.5.7 Recording Data That Supports Rules

Data that supports rules often provides challenges to the modeler. For example, rules specifying allowed combinations of three or more categories (e.g., **Product Type**, **Customer Type**, **Contract Type**) may require analysis as to whether they are in 4th or 5th normal form (see Chapter 13).

Another challenge is presented by the fact that many rules have exceptions. Subtypes can be valuable in handling rules with exceptions. Figure 14.10 is a table recording the dates on which post office branches are closed. (A bit

POST OFFICE CLOSURE (<u>Branch No</u>, <u>Date</u>, Reason)

Post Office Closure		
Branch	Date	Reason
18	12/19/2004	Maintenance
63	12/24/2004	Local Holiday
1	12/25/2004	Christmas
2	12/25/2004	Christmas
3	12/25/2004	Christmas
4	12/25/2004	Christmas
5	12/25/2004	Christmas
6	12/25/2004	Christmas

Figure 14.10 Post office closures model.

of creativity may already have been applied here; the user is just as likely to have specified a requirement to record when the post offices were *open*).

Look at the table closely. There is a definite impression of repetition for national holidays, such as Christmas Day, but the table is in fact fully normalized. We might see what appears to be a dependency of **Reason** on **Date**, but this only applies to some rows of the table.

The restriction "only some rows" provides the clue to tackling the problem. We use subtypes to separate the two types of rows, as in Figure 14.11 on the following page.

The **National Branch Closure** table is not fully normalized, as **Reason** depends only on **Date**; normalizing gives us the three tables of Figure 14.12 (page 445).

We now need to ask whether the **National Branch Closure** table holds any information of value to us. It is fully derivable from a table of branches (which we probably have elsewhere) and from the **National Closure** data. Accordingly, we can delete it. We now have the two-table solution of Figure 14.13 (page 446).

In solving the problem of capturing an underlying rule, we have produced a far more elegant data structure. Recording a new national holiday, for example, now requires only the addition of one row. In effect we found an unnormalized structure hidden within a more general structure, with all the redundancy and update anomalies that we expect from unnormalized data.

14.5.8 **Rules That May Be Broken**

It is a fact of life that in the real world the existence of rules does not preclude them being broken. There is a (sometimes subtle) distinction between the rules that describe a desired situation (e.g., a customer's accounts should not exceed their overdraft limits) and the rules that describe reality (some accounts will in fact exceed their overdraft limits).

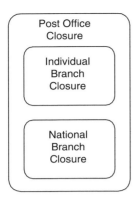

INDIVIDUAL BRANCH CLOSURE (Branch No, Date, Reason)

NATIONAL BRANCH CLOSURE (Branch No, Date, Reason)

Individual Branch Closure		
Branch No	Date	Reason
18	12/21/93	Maintenance
63	12/23/93	Local Holiday

National Branch Closure		
Branch No	Date	Reason
1	12/25/93	Christmas
2	12/25/93	Christmas
3	12/25/93	Christmas
4	12/25/93	Christmas
5	12/25/93	Christmas
6	12/25/93	Christmas

Figure 14.11 Subtyping post office closure.

We may *record* the first kind of rule in the database (or indeed elsewhere), but it is only the second type of rule that we can sensibly *enforce* there.

A local government system for managing planning applications did not allow for recording of land usage that broke the planning regulations. As a result data entry personnel would record land details using alternative usage codes that they knew would be accepted. In turn the report that was designed to show how many properties did not conform to planning regulations regularly showed 100% conformity!

To clarify such situations, each rule discovered should be subject to the following questions:

"Is it possible for instances that break this rule to occur?"

"If so, is it necessary to record such instances in the database?"

If the answer to both questions is "Yes," the database needs to allow nonconforming instances to be recorded. If the rule is or includes a referential integrity rule, DBMS referential integrity enforcement cannot be used.

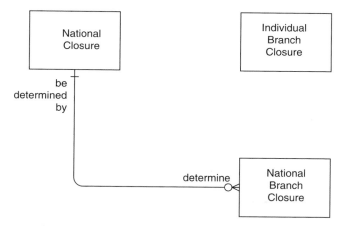

INDIVIDUAL BRANCH CLOSURE (<u>Branch No</u>, <u>Date</u>, Reason)
NATIONAL BRANCH CLOSURE (<u>Branch No</u>, <u>Date</u>)
NATIONAL CLOSURE (<u>Date</u>, Reason)

Individual Branch Closure		
Branch No	Date	Reason
18	12/21/93	Maintenance
63	12/23/93	Local Holiday

National Closure	
Date	Reason
12/25/93	Christmas

National Branch Closure	
Branch No	Date
1	12/25/93
2	12/25/93
3	12/25/93
4	12/25/93
5	12/25/93
6	12/25/93

Figure 14.12   Post office closures—normalized after subtyping.

14.5.9 Enforcement of Rules Through Primary Key Selection

The structures available to us in data modeling were not designed as a comprehensive "tool kit" for representing rules. To some extent, the types of rules we are able to model are a by-product of database management system design, in which other objectives were at the fore. Most of these are well-understood (cardinality, optionality, and so forth), but others arise from quite subtle issues of key selection.

In Section 11.6.6, we looked at an apparently simple customer orders model reproduced with different primary keys in Figure 14.14 (page 447).

By using a combination of **Customer No** and **Order No** as the key for **Order** and using **Customer** and **Branch No** as the key for **Branch**, as shown, we are able to enforce the important constraint that the customer who placed the

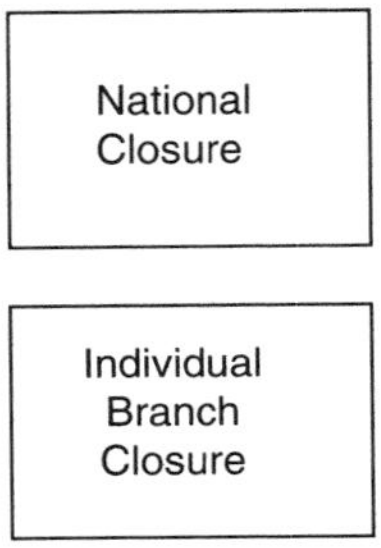

```
┌─────────────────┐
│                 │
│  National       │
│  Closure        │
│                 │
└─────────────────┘

┌─────────────────┐
│                 │
│  Individual     │
│  Branch         │
│  Closure        │
│                 │
└─────────────────┘
```

INDIVIDUAL BRANCH CLOSURE (<u>Branch No</u>, <u>Date</u>, Reason)

NATIONAL CLOSURE (<u>Date</u>, Reason)

Individual Branch Closure		
Branch	Date	Reason
18	12/21/93	Maintenance
63	12/23/93	Local Holiday

National Closure	
Date	Reason
12/25/93	Christmas

Figure 14.13   Final post office closure model.

order also received the order (because the Customer No in the **Ordered Item** table is part of the foreign key to both **Order** and **Branch**). But this is hardly obvious from the diagram or even from fairly close perusal of the attribute lists, unless you are a fairly experienced and observant modeler. Do not expect the database administrator, user, or even your successor to see it.

We strongly counsel you not to rely on these subtleties of key construction to enforce constraints. Clever they may be, but they can easily be overridden by other issues of key selection or forgotten as time passes. It is better to handle such constraints with a check within a common program module and to strongly enforce use of that module.

14.6 Rules on Recursive Relationships

Two situations in which some interesting rules are required are:

■ Recursive relationships (see Section 3.5.4), which imply certain constraints on the members thereof

■ Introduction of the time dimension, which adds complexity to basic rules.

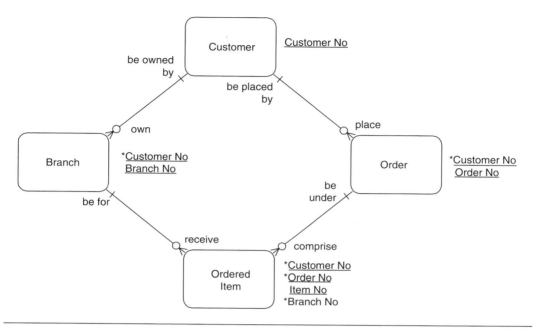

Figure 14.14 Constraint enforced by choice of keys.

We discuss the time dimension in Chapter 15, so we will defer discussion of time-related business rules until that chapter (Section 15.9 if you want to look ahead!).

Recursive relationships are often used to model hierarchies, which have an implicit rule that instance *a* cannot be both above and below instance *b* in the hierarchy (at least at any one time). This may seem like stating the obvious, but without implementation of this rule, it is possible to load contradictory data. For example, if the hierarchy is a reporting hierarchy among employees, we could specify in John Smith's record that he reports to Susan Brown and in Susan Brown's record that she reports to John Smith. We need to specify and implement a business rule to ensure that this situation does not arise.

14.6.1 **Types of Rules on Recursive Relationships**

The relationship just described is **asymmetric**: if *a* reports to *b*, *b* cannot report to *a*. It is actually more complicated than that. It is equally contradictory to specify that John Smith reports to Susan Brown, Susan Brown reports to Miguel Sanchez, and Miguel Sanchez reports to John Smith. You should be able to see that we need to restrict anyone from being recorded as reporting to anyone below them in the hierarchy to whatever depth the hierarchy might extend.

The technical term for relationships of this kind is **acyclic**.

This relationship is also **irreflexive** (cannot be self-referencing): an employee cannot report to himself or herself.

It is also **intransitive**: if a is recorded as reporting to b, and b is recorded as reporting to c, we cannot then record a as reporting to c. However, not all acyclic relationships are intransitive: if the relationship "is an ancestor of"[4] rather than "reports to," we can record that a is an ancestor of b, b is an ancestor of c, and a is an ancestor of c. In fact the first two statements taken together imply the third statement, which makes "is an ancestor of" a **transitive** relationship. This means that the third statement (a is an ancestor of c) is redundant if the other statements are also recorded. You should prevent the recording of redundant instances of a transitive relationship. Technically speaking you could achieve this by marking the relationship as intransitive although to the business this would be a false statement.

Note that a recursive relationship may be neither transitive nor intransitive—for example, the relationship "shares a border with" on the entity class **Country**. France shares a border with Germany, and Germany shares a border with Switzerland. This does not prevent France sharing a border with Switzerland but does not imply it either; that is a separate fact, which should be recorded.

This relationship is also **symmetric**: if country a shares a border with country b, country b must share a border with country a. With symmetric relationships we again have the issue of redundancy. Recording that the United States shares a border with Canada and that Canada shares a border with the United States is redundant. Symmetric relationships therefore need to be managed carefully; you should not only prevent the reverse form of a relationship instance also being recorded but you should go further and ensure that each relationship instance be recorded in only one way. For example, you can require that the name of the first country in the statement alphabetically precedes that of the second country. So, if "France shares a border with Germany" were entered, this would be stored as such in the appropriate table (if not already present), but if "Germany shares a border with France" were entered, it would be stored as "France shares a border with Germany" (again, if not already present). This automatically prevents redundancy. We saw an example of symmetric relationships in Section 10.8.2.

Again, there are relationships which are neither symmetric nor asymmetric; we have seen the relationship "likes" on the entity class **Person** cited in course material as an example of a symmetric relationship but

---

[4]Although we recommend in Section 3.5.1 that relationships be named "be an ancestor of," "be a parent of," and so on, we use an alternative form in this section to make the discussion more readable.

the fact that Joe likes Maria does not imply that Maria likes Joe.[5] Perhaps a more useful relationship for some business purposes might be the relationship "requires a visa from citizens of" on the entity class **Country**. If Country *a* requires visas from citizens of country *b*, this does not prevent country *b* requiring visas from citizens of country *a* but does not imply it either; that is a separate fact, which should be recorded.

A **reflexive** relationship is one in which a self-referencing instance is implied for each instance of the entity class participating in the relationship. An example of a reflexive relationship is "allows work by citizens of" on the entity class **Country**. While it would be necessary to record for each country those other countries whose citizens may work in that country, it should not be necessary to record that each country allows its own citizens to work in that country.

Again, there are relationships that are neither reflexive nor irreflexive; again, we have seen the relationship "likes" on the entity class **Person** incorrectly cited in course material as an example of a reflexive relationship, but not everyone likes himself or herself.

Asymmetric relationships must be irreflexive. There are also **antisymmetric** relationships, which may include self-referencing instances but not instances that are reflections of other instances. Examples are hard to come by; one possibility is the relationship "teaches." One can teach oneself a skill but if I teach you a skill, you cannot then teach it to me.

14.6.2 **Documenting Rules on Recursive Relationships**

ORM (Object Role Modeling) refers to constraints on recursive relationships as **ring constraints** and allows you to specify each ring constraint as acyclic, irreflexive, intransitive, symmetric, asymmetric, or antisymmetric (or one of the allowable combinations: acyclic intransitive, asymmetric intransitive, symmetric intransitive, and symmetric irreflexive). If you are not using ORM, your best option is to include in the description of the relationship whether it is subject to a ring constraint and, if so, which type(s). This assumes, of course, that the parties responsible for implementing constraints are familiar with those terms!

14.6.3 **Implementing Constraints on Recursive Relationships**

Implementing constraints on recursive relationships is a complex subject outside the scope of this book; while it is relatively simple to constrain an

---

[5]The poetic term is "unrequited love."

irreflexive relationship (the foreign key to the parent row cannot have the same value as the primary key in the same row), constraining an acyclic relationship is very complex.

14.6.4 **Analogous Rules in Many-to-Many Relationships**

Analogous rules may apply to recursive many-to-many relationships that have been modeled using an intersection entity class or table. For example, the Bill of Materials model [Section 3.5.4 Figure 3.22(d)] is subject to a cyclic ring constraint: an assembly cannot consist of any subassembly that includes the original assembly as a component.

In fact any table with two foreign keys to the same other table (or entity class with two one-to-many relationships to the same other entity class) may also be subject to ring constraints. For example, a **Flight Leg** entity class will have two relationships to a **Port** entity class (identifying origin and destination). These two relationships are jointly subject to an irreflexive ring constraint; no scheduled commercial flight leg can have the same port as both origin and destination.

14.7 **Summary**

Both E-R and relational data models can capture a variety of business rules in their structures, definitions, and supporting documentation. The data in the resulting database will also serve to enforce business rules.

There are various techniques for discovery, verification, and documentation of business rules.

A conventional information system may implement rules in the data structure, declared constraints, data in the database, program logic or specialized "rules engine" software. Rules held in data structure are difficult to circumvent or change. Rules held in data values are more readily changed but may demand more sophisticated programming.

Chapter 15
Time-Dependent Data

". . . the flowing river of time more closely resembles a giant block of ice with every moment frozen into place."
- Brian Greene, The Future of the Cosmos, 2004

"History smiles at all attempts to force its flow into theoretical patterns or logical grooves; it plays havoc with our generalizations, breaks all our rules; history is baroque."
- Will Durrant, The Lessons of History, 1968

15.1 The Problem

Few areas of data modeling are the subject of as much confusion as the handling of time-related and time-dependent data.

Perhaps we are modeling data for an insurance company. It is certainly important for us to know the current status of a client's insurance policy—how much is insured and what items are covered. But in order to handle claims for events that happened some time ago, we need to be able to determine the status at any given date in the past.

Or, we may want to support planning of a railway network and to be able to represent how the network will look at various times in the future.

Or, we might want to track deliveries of goods around the world and need to take into account different time zones when recording dates of dispatch and receipt.

Underlying each of these problems is the concept of effective dates and times (past or future) and how we handle them in a data model.

A closely related issue is the maintenance of an **audit trail**: a history of database changes and of the transactions that caused them. What cash flows contributed to the current balance? Why was a customer's credit rating downgraded?

The difficulties that even experienced data modelers encounter in these areas are often the result of trying to find a simple recipe for "adding the time dimension" to a model. There are two fundamental problems with this approach: first, the conceptual model usually includes time-dependent data even before we have explicitly considered the time dimension, and second, we seldom need to maintain a full history and set of past positions for *everything* in the database.

In this chapter we look at some basic principles and structures for handling time-related data. You should be able to solve most problems you encounter in practice by selectively employing combinations of these. We look at some techniques specific to data warehouses in Chapter 16. Once again, the choice of the best approach in a given situation is not always straightforward, and, as in all our modeling, we need to actively explore and compare alternatives.

15.2 **When Do We Add the Time Dimension?**

At what stage in modeling should we consider time-related issues? As we pointed out in the introduction to this chapter, the inclusion of the time dimension in a model is not a stand-alone task, but rather something that we achieve using a variety of techniques as modeling proceeds. Many of our decisions will be responses to specific business needs and should therefore be made during the conceptual modeling phase.

We may also need to implement certain time-related data to assist with the administration and audit of the database. For example, we may include in every table a column to record the date and time when that table was last updated. Often, such decisions are not in the hands of the individual modeler, but they are the result of data administration policies applicable to all databases developed in the organization. Business interest in such data is usually peripheral; stakeholders will have an interest in the overall improvement in (for example) auditability, but not in the mechanism used to achieve it. If the changes to data structures are largely mechanical, and the data is not of direct interest to the business, it makes sense to perform these additions during the transformation from conceptual to logical model.

In this chapter we focus on the issues of most interest to the modeler, which should generally be tackled at the conceptual modeling stage. However, in many examples we have shown the resulting *logical* models, in order to show primary and foreign keys, and have included some nonkey columns in the diagrams. In doing this, our aim is to give you a better appreciation of how the structures work.

15.3 **Audit Trails and Snapshots**

Let us start with a very simple example—a single table. Our client is an investor in shares (stocks), and the table **Share Holding** represents the client's holdings of each share type (Figure 15.1). As it stands, the

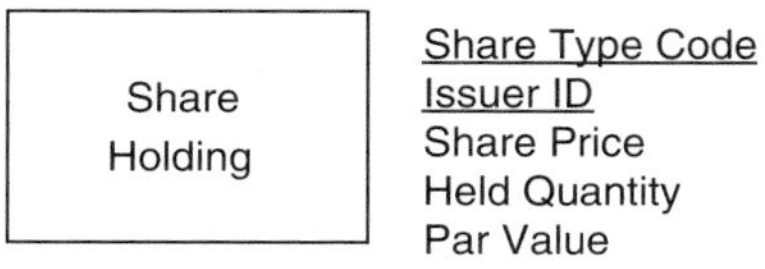

Share Holding	Share Type Code Issuer ID Share Price Held Quantity Par Value

Figure 15.1 Model of current share holdings.

model enables us to record the *current* quantity and price of each type of share.

We assume that the primary key has been properly chosen and, therefore, that the type and issuer of a share cannot change. We will add the business rule that the par value (nominal issue value) of a share also cannot change. But quantities and prices certainly may change over time, and we may need to hold data about past holdings and prices to support queries such as, "How many shares in company *xyz* did we hold on July 1, 2002?" or, "By how much has the total value of our investments changed in the past month?"

There are essentially two ways of achieving this:

1. Record details of each *change* to a share holding—the "audit trail" approach.
2. Include an **Effective Date** attribute in the **Share Holding** table, and record new instances either periodically or each time there is a change—the "snapshot" approach.

If you are familiar with accounting, you can think of these as "income statement" and "balance sheet" approaches, respectively. Balance sheets are snapshots of a business' position at particular times, while income (profit and loss) statements summarize changes to that position.

15.3.1 **The Basic Audit Trail Approach**

We will start with the audit trail approach. Let's make the reasonable assumption that we want to keep track not only of changes, but of the events that cause them. This suggests the three-table model of Figure 15.2. Note that **Share Holding** represents *current* share holdings.

This is the basic audit trail solution, often quite workable as it stands. But there are a number of variations we can make to it.

The **Event** table implements a very generic entity class that could well be subtyped to reflect different sets of attributes and associated processes. In this example we might implement tables that represented subtypes **Purchase**, **Sale**, **Rights Issue**, **Bonus Issue**, and so on.

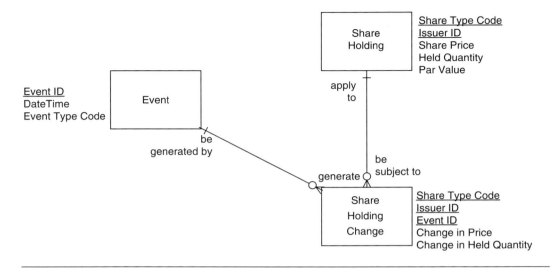

Figure 15.2 Basic audit trail approach.

There is often value in grouping events into higher-level events or, conversely, breaking them down into component events. For example, we might group a number of different share purchases into the aggregate event "company takeover" or break them down into individual parcels. We can model this with a variable or fixed-depth hierarchy (e.g., a recursive relationship on **Event**, or separate tables for **Aggregate Event**, **Basic Event**, and **Component Event**).

In some circumstances we may not require the **Event** table at all. Attributes of the **Share Holding Change** entity class (typically DateTime or External Reference Number) can sometimes provide all the data we need about the source of the change. For example, values may change or be recorded at predetermined intervals. We might record share prices on a daily basis, rather than each time there was a movement.

Another possibility is that each event affects only one share holding—(i.e., generates exactly one share holding change). We can very often propose workable definitions of **Event** to make this so. For example, we could choose to regard a bundled purchase of shares of different types as several distinct "purchase events." This makes the relationship between **Event** and **Share Holding Change** mandatory, nontransferable, and one-to-one and suggests combining the two tables (see Section 10.9). Figure 15.3 shows the result.

Even if some types of events do cause more than one change (for example, exercising options would mean a reduction in the holding of options and an increase in the number of ordinary shares), we can extend the model to accommodate them as in Figure 15.4.

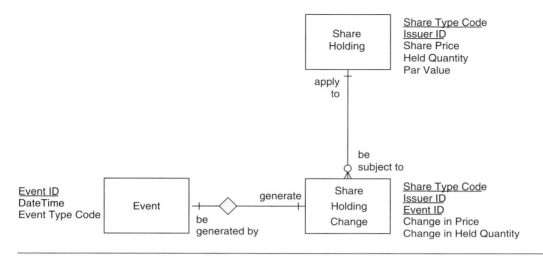

Figure 15.3 Event defined as generating only one change.

Returning to the model in Figure 15.2, **Share Holding Change** can also be divided into two tables (reflecting subtypes in the conceptual model) to distinguish price changes from quantity changes (Figure 15.5).

With only two attributes, our choices are straightforward, but as the number of attributes increases so does the variety of subtyping options.

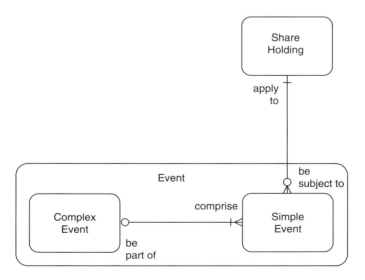

Figure 15.4 Separating complex and simple events.

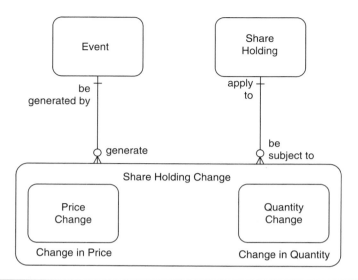

Figure 15.5 Subtyping to reflect different types of changes.

During conceptual modeling, it can be helpful to look at the different types of events (whether formal subtypes or not) and the combination of attributes that each affects. This will often suggest subtypes based on groups of attributes that are affected by particular types of events. For example, **Share Acquisition** might be suggested by the **Event** subtypes **Share Purchase**, **Bonus Issue**, **Rights Issue**, and **Transfer In**. But you do need to look closely at the stability of these groups of attributes. If they reflect well-established business events, there may be no problem, but if they are based around, for example, the sequence of events in an extended interaction (e.g., a customer applying for and being granted or refused a loan), we may find ourselves having to change the database structure simply because we want to update a column at a different point in the interaction.

The **Share Holding** table not only contains the current values of all attributes, but is the only place in which any static attributes (other than the primary key) need to be held. For example, the Par or Issue Value of the share never changes and therefore should not appear in **Share Holding Change**.

Instead of defining **Share Holding** as representing current share holdings, we could have used it to represent *initial* share holdings (Figure 15.6).

In one way this is more elegant, as updates will need only to create rows in the **Event** and **Share Holding Change** tables; they will not need to update the **Initial Share Holding** table. On the other hand, inquiries on the current position require that it be built up by applying all changes to the initial holding.

The definition of **Initial Share Holding** may need to take into account share holdings that were in place before the database and associated

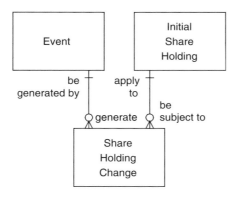

Figure 15.6 Model based on changes to initial share holding.

system were implemented. Do we want to record the actual initial purchases (perhaps made many years ago) and all subsequent events and changes? Or is it more appropriate to "draw a line" at some point in time and record the quantities held at that time as initial share holdings? Similar questions will arise if we choose to remove (and presumably archive) events that are no longer of interest to us.

One very important assumption in the model of Figure 15.6 is that instances of **Event** and **Share Holding Change** cannot themselves be updated (or, at least, that we are not interested in keeping any history of such changes). Imagine for a moment that we *could* update the column values in **Share Holding Change**. Then we would need to extend the model to include **Share Holding Change Change** to keep track of these changes, and so on, until we reached a nonupdatable table—one in which each row, once recorded, never changed. So, an interesting feature of the audit trail approach to modeling time-dependent data is that it relies on defining some data that is invariant.

In our example, it is difficult to envision any business event that would cause the values of **Share Holding Change** columns to change. But there is always the possibility that we record some data in error (perhaps we have miskeyed a price change). We then have essentially three options:

1. Correct the data without keeping a history of the change. This is a simple solution, but it will cause reconciliation problems if reports have been issued or decisions made based on the incorrect data.
2. Maintain a separate history of "changes to changes." This complicates the model but does separate error corrections from business changes.
3. Allow for a "reversal" or "correction" event, which will create another **Share Holding Change** row. This is the approach used in accounting.

It is often the cleanest way of avoiding both the problems inherent in option 1 and situations where the correction event can cause more complex changes to the database (e.g., reversal of commission and government tax).

Any of these approaches may be used, depending on the circumstances. The important thing is to plan explicitly for changes resulting from error corrections as well as those caused by the more usual business events.

15.3.2 **Handling Nonnumeric Data**

You may have noticed that we conveniently chose numeric attributes (Share Quantity and Share Price) as the time-dependent data in the example. It makes sense to talk about the change (increase or decrease) to a numeric attribute. But how do we handle changes to the value of nonnumeric attributes (for example, Custodian Name)? One approach is to hold the value prior to the change, rather than the amount of change. The value *after* the change will then be held either in the next instance of **Share Holding Change** or in (Current) **Share Holding**. For example, if the value of Custodian Name was changed from "National Bank" to "Rural Bank," the sequence of updates would be as follows (in terms of the model in Figure 15.7):

1. Update Custodian Name in the relevant row of the **Share Holding** table to "Rural Bank."
2. Create a new row in the **Share Holding Change** table, with relevant values of Share Type Code, Issuer ID and Event ID, and "National Bank" as the value for Previous Custodian Name.

Holding the prior value is also an option when dealing with numeric data. We could just as well have held Previous Price instead of Change in Price. One will be derivable from the other, and selecting the best option usually comes down to which is more commonly required by the business processes, and perhaps maintaining a consistency of approach—elegance again!

Note that if we were using the approach based on an **Initial Share Holding** table (Figure 15.6), we would need to record the values *after* the change in the **Share Holding Change** table.

15.3.3 **The Basic Snapshot Approach**

The idea of holding prior values rather than changes provides a nice lead-in to the "snapshot" approach.

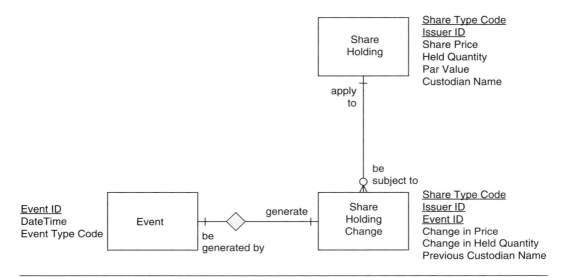

Figure 15.7 Change to numeric and nonnumeric data.

One of the options available to us is to consistently hold prior values rather than changes, to the extent that "no change" is represented by the prior value being the same as the new value. If we take this approach, then **Share Holding Change** starts to look very like **Current Share Holding**. The only difference in the attributes is the inclusion of the event identifier or effective date, and the exclusion of data that is not time-dependent, such as Par Value.

Share Holding Change is now badly named, as we are representing past positions, rather than changes. **Historical Share Holding** is more appropriate (Figure 15.8). This change of name reflects a change in the flavor of the model. Queries of the form, "What was the position at a particular date?" are now supported in a very simple way (just find the relevant **Historical Share Holding**), while queries about changes are still supported, but require some calculation to assemble the data.

If typical updates to share holdings involve changes to only a small number of attributes, this snapshot approach will be less tidy than an audit trail with subtypes. We will end up carrying a lot of data just to indicate "no change." If we wanted to eliminate this redundancy, we could split **Historical Share Holding** into several tables, each with only one nonkey column. In our simplified example with two nonkey columns, this would mean replacing **Historical Share Holding** with a **Historical Share Price** table and a **Historical Held Quantity** table. In doing this we would be going beyond Fifth Normal Form (Chapter 13) insofar as we were performing further table splits based on keys. This type of further normalization—and the formal concept of Sixth Normal Form—has been explored by

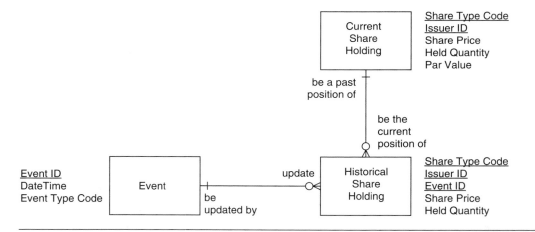

Figure 15.8 Basic snapshot approach.

Date et al. (see reference in "Further Reading"). In considering such a tactic, remember that historical share holdings should be created but not updated; hence, we are not avoiding any update anomalies. Look also at the complexity of programming needed to assemble a complete snapshot. Much that has been written on organizing time-dependent data is based on the premise that direct DBMS support for such data manipulation is available.

Note that the event associated with a particular historical share holding is the event that ended that set of attribute values, not the event that set them up. The relationship name "update" (in contrast to "create") reflects this. Another option is to link events to the historical share holding they *create*. In this case, we will also need to link **Current Share Holding** to **Event** (Figure 15.9).

This gives us yet another option, with some advantages in elegance if the business is more interested (as it often is) in the event that *led* to a particular position.

Note that the two relationships to **Event** are now optional. This is because the initial share holding (which may be an instance of either **Current Share Holding** or **Historical Share Holding**) may represent an opening position, not created by any event we have recorded. Of course, we have the option of defining an "initialize" or "transfer in" event to set up the original holdings, in which case the two relationships would become mandatory.

The model as it now stands has at least two weaknesses. The first is the inelegance of having two separate relationships to **Current Share Holding** and **Historical Share Holding**. The second is more serious. Each time we create a new current share holding, we will need to create a historical share holding that is a copy of the previous current share holding. This is very

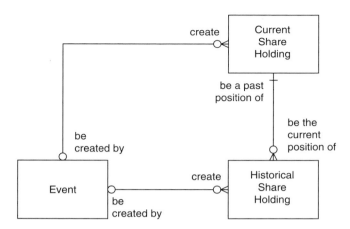

Figure 15.9   Linking events to the positions they create.

close to breaking our rule of not transferring instances from one entity class to another (Section 4.13.5).

We can overcome both problems by generalizing the two relationships, along with the two entity classes. We do this by first splitting out the time-dependent portion of **Current Share Holding**, using a one-to-one relationship, according to the technique described in Section 10.9. The result is shown in Figure 15.10.[1]

Historical Share Holding will have basically the same attributes as this extracted part of **Current Share Holding**, and there may well be important processes (e.g., portfolio valuation plotted over time) that treat the two in much the same way.

The **Share Holding (Fixed)** entity class represents attributes that are not time-dependent, or for which we require only one value (perhaps the current value, perhaps the original value). If there are no such attributes apart from the key, we will not require this entity class at all. Nor will we require it if we take the "sledge hammer" approach of assuming at the outset that *all* data is time-dependent and that we need to record all historical values.

We have now come quite some distance from our original audit trail approach. The path we took is a nice example of the use of creative modeling techniques. Along the way we have seen a number of ways of handling historical data, even for the simplest one-entity model. The one-entity

---

[1]In adding a supertype at this stage we are effectively working backwards from the logical model to the conceptual model. The model we show represents an interim stage and shows both foreign keys and subtyping, which you would not normally expect to see together in a final model (unless of course your DBMS directly supports subtypes).

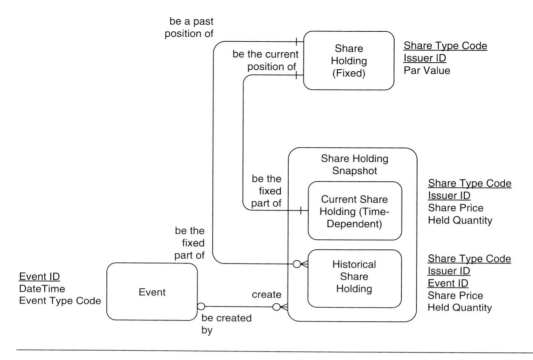

Figure 15.10 Separating time-dependent and static data.

example is quite general and can easily be adapted to handle future positions (for example, the results of a planned share purchase) as well as (or instead of) past positions.

We often arrive at models like those discussed here without ever explicitly considering the time dimension. For example, a simple model of bank accounts and transactions is an example of the audit trail approach, and a **Staff Appraisal** entity class, which represents multiple appraisals of the same person over time, is an example of the snapshot approach.

15.4 **Sequences and Versions**

In our examples so far, we have used the term "time-dependent" in a very literal way to mean that events, snapshots, and changes have an attribute of **Date** or **DateTime**. We can equally apply these rules to sequences that are not explicitly or visibly tied to dates and times. For example, we may wish to keep track of software according to **Version Number** or to record the effect of events that can be placed in sequence without specifying absolute times—perhaps the stages in a human-computer dialogue.

15.5 **Handling Deletions**

Sometimes entity instances become obsolete in the real world. Consider the case of the Soviet Union. If we have a table of countries and there are references to that table in—for example, our **Employee** table (country of birth), **Customer** table (country in which the business is registered) or **Product** table (country of manufacture)—we cannot simply delete the record for the Soviet Union from our country table unless there are no records in any other table that refer to the Soviet Union. In fact we cannot rely on there being no such records so we must design for the situation in which a country is no longer current but there are records that continue to refer to it (after all there may be employees who were born in what was then the Soviet Union).

Often these noncurrent entity instances will still have relevance in the context of relationships with other entity classes. For example, although the country "Soviet Union" may no longer exist and, hence, be flagged as noncurrent, it will still have meaning as a place of birth for a visa applicant.

A simple solution in this case is to include a Current Flag attribute in the **Country** table, which can be set to mark a country as no longer current (or obsolete). This enables us to include logic that, for example, prevents the Soviet Union from being recorded as either the country of registration of a new customer or the country of manufacture of a product (unless we were dealing in antiques!). We would still wish to be able to record the Soviet Union as the country of birth of a new employee.

It is possible for an entity instance to be deleted and then reinstated. In these cases we can simply keep a history of the Current Flag attribute in the same way that we would for any other attribute.

15.6 **Archiving**

In modeling time-dependent data, you need to take into account any archiving requirements and the associated deletion of data from the database.

Snapshot approaches are generally amenable to having old data removed; it is even possible to retain selected "snapshots" from among the archived data. For example, we might remove daily snapshots from before a particular date but retain the snapshots from the first day of each month to provide a coarse history.

Audit trail approaches can be less easy to work with. If data is to be removed, it will need to be summarized into an aggregate "change" or "event" or into a "starting point snapshot." Similarly, if a coarse history is required, it will be necessary to summarize intermediate events.

15.7 **Modeling Time-Dependent Relationships**

15.7.1 **One-to-Many Relationships**

We have now had a fairly good look at the simplest of models, the one-entity model. If we can extend this to a model of two entity classes linked by a relationship, we have covered the basic building blocks of a data model and should be able to cope with any situation that arises. In fact, handling relationships requires no new techniques at all if we think in terms of a relational model where they are represented by foreign keys; a change to a relationship is just a change to a (foreign key) data item.

So let's develop the share holding example further to include an entity class representing the company that issued the shares (Figure 15.11).

We can use any of the preceding approaches to represent a history of changes to **Company** and **Share Holding**. Figure 15.12 shows the result of applying a version of the snapshot approach. The **Event**, **Share Holding Snapshot**, and **Company Snapshot** entity classes are a result of using the techniques for one-entity models. The new problem is what to do with the relationship between **Company** and **Share Holding**. In this case, we note that the "issued by" relationship is *nontransferable* and, hence, is part of the *fixed* data about share holdings. (The foreign key Company ID will not change value for a given **Share Holding**.)

We already hold Company ID in **Share Holding (Fixed)**, and the relationship is therefore between **Share Holding (Fixed)** and **Company (Fixed)**, as shown.

But what if the relationship were transferable? In Figure 15.13 we include the entity class **Location**, and the rule that shareholdings can be

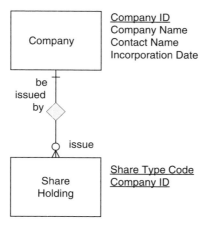

Figure 15.11 Companies and shares—current position.

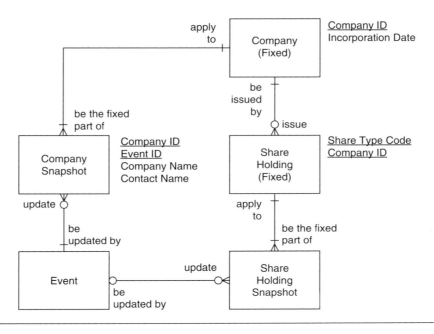

Figure 15.12 Basic snapshot approach applied to nontransferable relationship.

transferred from one location to another. Each shareholding *snapshot* is now related to a single instance of **Location**. A new shareholding snapshot is created whenever a share holding is moved from one location to another. From a relational model perspective, the foreign key to **Location** is now

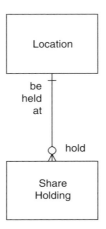

Figure 15.13 Location and shareholding—current data.

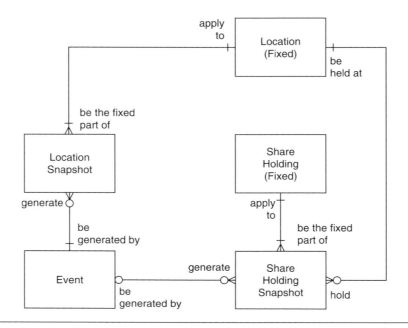

Figure 15.14 Basic snapshot approach applied to transferable relationship.

time-dependent and therefore needs to be an attribute of **Share Holding Snapshot** (Figure 15.14).

The effects on the original relationship under the two options (transferable and nontransferable) are summarized in Figure 15.15. Note the use of the nontransferability symbol introduced in Section 3.5.6.

You might find it interesting to compare this result with the often-quoted guideline, "When you include the time dimension, one-to-many relationships become many-to-many." If you think of **Shareholding Snapshot** as an intersection entity class, you will see that this guideline only applies to *transferable* relationships.

This makes sense. If a relationship is nontransferable, it will not change over time; hence, there is no need to record its history.

15.7.2 **Many-to-Many Relationships**

Many-to-many relationships present no special problems, as we can start by resolving them into two one-to-many nontransferable relationships, plus an intersection entity class.

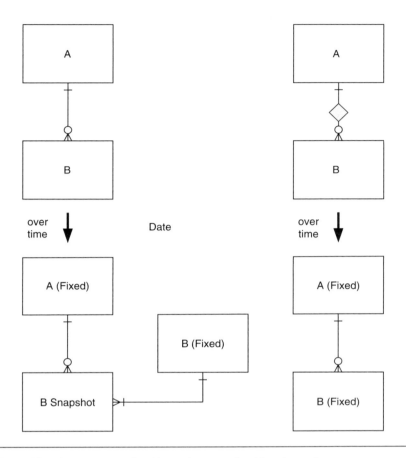

Figure 15.15 Adding history to transferable and nontransferable relationships.

Figure 15.16 on the next page shows a worked example using the snapshot approach (we have left out the individual histories of the **Employee** and **Equipment Item** entity classes).

In the simplest case, when the intersection entity class does not contain any attributes other than the key, we need only keep track of the periods for which the entity instance (i.e., the relationship) exists. We can use either of the structures in Figure 15.17. Option 1 is based on an audit trail of changes, option 2 on periods of currency. Note that while option 1 allows us to easily determine which are the current responsibilities of an employee, establishing what were an employee's responsibilities at an earlier date involves complex query programming, since one has to select from the set of **Responsibility** rows with Effective Date earlier than the date in question, the one with the latest Effective Date. By contrast option 2 supports both types

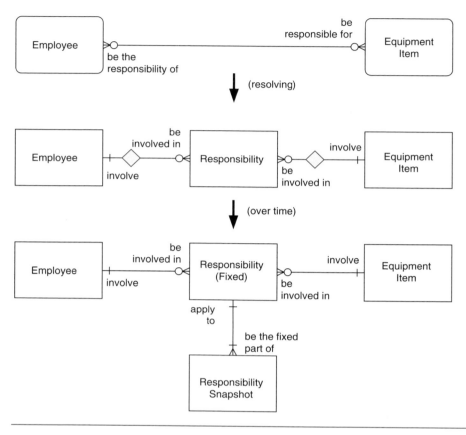

Figure 15.16   History of many-to-many relationships.

of query with relatively easy programming, in each case selecting the one **Responsibility** row for which the date in question (which may be today) is between **Effective Date** and **Expiry Date**. For this reason many database designs to support history include **Expiry Date** as well as **Effective Date** even though it is technically redundant (this has already been discussed in Section 12.6.6). Our recommendation is to include **Expiry Date** in the logical data model if you intend it to appear in the database although some would argue that it should be deferred until the physical data model.

15.7.3   **Self-Referencing Relationships**

Handling self-referencing relationships is no different in principle from handling relationships between two entity classes, but it is easy to get confused. Figure 15.18 on page 470 shows solutions to the most common situations.

Option 1:
RESPONSIBILITY (<u>Employee ID</u>, <u>Equipment ID</u>, <u>Effective Date</u>, Currency Indicator)
Option 2:
RESPONSIBILITY (<u>Employee ID</u>, <u>Equipment ID</u>, <u>Effective Date</u>, Expiry Date)

Figure 15.17 Alternatives for handling history of simple intersection entity class.

15.8 **Date Tables**

Occasionally, we need to set up a table called **Date** or something similar, to record such data as whether a given date is a public holiday. (Incidentally, we have often seen this table named "Calendar"—a violation of our rule that names should reflect a single instance, covered in Section 3.4.2.)

There is no problem with the table as such, but a difficulty does arise when we note that the primary key is **Date** and that this column appears in tables throughout the data model where, technically, it is a foreign key to the **Date** table. According to our diagramming rules, we should draw relationships between the **Date** table and all the tables in which the foreign key appears, a tedious and messy exercise.

Our advice is to break the rules and not to worry about drawing the relationships. The rules that the relationships enforce (i.e., ensuring that only valid dates appear) are normally handled by standard date-checking routines; our explicit relationships add virtually nothing except unnecessary complexity. The situation is different if the dates are a special subset—for example, public holidays. In this case, you should name the table appropriately (**Public Holiday**) and show any relationships that are constrained to that subset (e.g., **Public Holiday Bonus** *paid for work on* **Public Holiday**).

15.9 **Temporal Business Rules**

Consider the model fragment (see Figure 15.19, page 471) of a database to manage employees. This has been developed using the "snapshot" approach to handle a full history of changes affecting those employees.

A number of business rules apply to these tables:

1. Employee Snapshot:
  a. No two **Employee Snapshot** rows for the same employee can overlap in time. If this were to occur we could not establish the correct name, address, salary amount, commission amount or union membership for the period covered by the overlapping rows. Note that this rule is not enforced by the fact that Snapshot Effective Date is part of the primary key of **Employee Snapshot**, a common misconception.

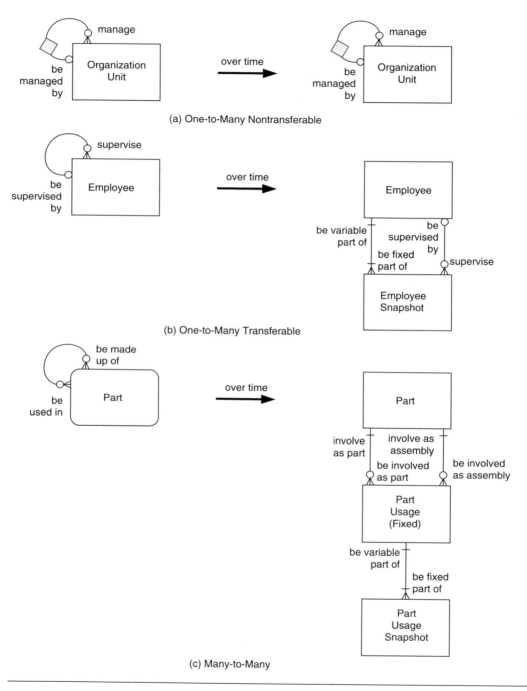

(a) One-to-Many Nontransferable

(b) One-to-Many Transferable

(c) Many-to-Many

Figure 15.18   History of self-referencing relationships.

EMPLOYEE (Employee ID, Commencement Date, Termination Date)
EMPLOYEE SNAPSHOT (Employee ID, Snapshot Effective Date, Snapshot Expiry Date, Employee Name, Employee Address, Weekly Salary Amount, Weekly Commission Amount, Union Code)
EMPLOYEE PROJECT ASSIGNMENT (Employee ID, Project ID, Start Date, End Date)
EMPLOYEE ALLOWANCE (Employee ID, Allowance Code, Start Date, End Date, Weekly Allowance Amount)

Figure 15.19   A model holding a full history of changes affecting employees.

b. No **Employee Snapshot** row can have a Snapshot Effective Date earlier than the Commencement Date of the corresponding employee.

c. No **Employee Snapshot** row can have a Snapshot Expiry Date later than the Termination Date of the corresponding employee.

d. If at least one of the **Employee** attributes now in **Employee Snapshot** is mandatory (e.g., Employee Name), the Snapshot Effective Date of each **Employee Snapshot** row must be no later than one day after the Snapshot Expiry Date of the previous **Employee Snapshot** row for the same employee. Combined with the first business rule, Snapshot Effective Date must be exactly one day after the relevant Snapshot Expiry Date.

One way of avoiding rules a, c, and d, of course, is to remove Snapshot Expiry Date from **Employee Snapshot**, but we will almost certainly pay a price in more complex programming.

2. Employee Project Assignment:

a. If there is a business rule to the effect that an employee may only be assigned to one project at a time, no two **Employee Project Assignment** rows for the same employee can overlap in time.

b. No two **Employee Project Assignment** rows for the same employee/project combination can overlap in time.

c. No two **Employee Project Assignment** rows for the same employee/project combination should between them cover a single unbroken time period. In other words, we should not use two rows to represent a fact that could be captured in a single row. Violation of this rule can lead to misleading query results. For example, consider a query on the table in Figure 15.20 intended to return all employee project assignments as at 06/30/2001 along with the dates on which each employee started that assignment. Such a query would correctly show RICHB76 as having started on project 234 on 01/12/2001 but incorrectly show WOODI02 as having started on project 123 on 06/13/2001 rather than 01/23/2001. Of course, if **Employee Project Assignment** was defined to mean "An assignment

EMPLOYEE PROJECT ASSIGNMENT

Employee ID	Project ID	Start Date	End Date
WOODI02	123	01/23/2001	06/12/2001
WOODI02	123	06/13/2001	07/31/2001
RICHB76	234	01/12/2001	06/30/2001
RICHB76	234	09/12/2001	09/30/2001

Figure 15.20   Expressing one fact with two rows.

to a project under a specific set of terms and conditions" and the new row reflected a change in terms and conditions, the above rule would now read "no two **Employee Project Assignment** rows for the same combination of employee, project, and set of terms and conditions should between them cover a single unbroken time period." Then, we would need to interpret the results of our query in this light.

   d. No **Employee Project Assignment** row can have a Start Date earlier than the Commencement Date of the corresponding employee.

   e. No **Employee Project Assignment** row can have an End Date later than the Termination Date of the corresponding employee.

   f. If there is a business rule to the effect that an employee must be assigned to at least one project at all times during his or her employment (unlikely in the past but more likely nowadays), there must be no date between the Commencement Date and Termination Date of an employee that is not also between the Start Date and End Date of at least one **Employee Project Assignment** row for the same employee. If Termination Date is null, there must be an **Employee Project Assignment** row for the same employee with a null End Date.

If an employee may only be assigned to one project at a time, removal of End Date from **Employee Project Assignment** is again an option which avoids rules a, b, d, and e.

3. Employee Allowance: the rules that apply to this table are analogous to those that apply to **Employee Project Assignment**. Note that the equivalent of rule c is that no two **Employee Allowance** rows for the same employee/allowance type/allowance amount combination should between them cover a single unbroken time period. (Two rows for the same employee/allowance type combination could between them cover a single unbroken time period if the allowance amount were different in two rows.)

Note that the business may be quite happy with the notion that all changes nominally occur at the end of each business day, that is that the time of day is of no interest or relevance. If the time as well as the date of a change is relevant, an issue arises of how one defines a gap in the last rule quoted for each table. The easiest way to deal with this issue in our experience is to require that Snapshot Effective DateTime is equal to Snapshot Expiry DateTime in the previous row. A slight problem then occurs. Any enquiry about the state of affairs at one of the time points recorded in Snapshot Effective DateTime will return two records per employee: one for the snapshot that expires at that time and one for the snapshot that becomes effective at that time. A convention needs to be established so that in such circumstances, only the first (or second) of the records is actually used in the query result.

The rules in this example are typical of those that you will encounter in models of time-dependent data and are special cases of the general data rules discussed in Chapter 14, and thus subject to the same guidelines for documentation and enforcement. If historical data is always created by update transactions, then a natural place to implement many of these rules is in common logic associated with database updates.

15.10 Changes to the Data Structure

Our discussion so far has related to keeping track of changes to data *content* over time. From time to time, we need to change a data model—and, hence, the logical database *structure*—to reflect a new requirement or changes to the business.

Handling this falls outside the realm of data modeling and is a serious challenge for the database administrator. The problem is not only to implement the changes to the database and the (often-considerable) consequent changes to programs. The database administrator also needs to ensure the ongoing usefulness of archived data, which remains in the old format. Usually, this means archiving copies of the original programs and of any data conversion programs.

15.11 Putting It into Practice

In this chapter, we have worked through a number of options for incorporating time and history in data models. In practice, we suggest that you do not worry too much about these issues in your initial modeling. On the other hand, you should not consciously try to exclude the time dimension. You will find that you automatically include much time-related data through the use of familiar structures such as account entries, transactions, and events.

You should then review the model to ensure that time-related needs are met. The best approach often does not become clear until attributes are well-defined and functional analysis has identified the different event types and their effects on the data.

Keep in mind that every transaction that changes or deletes data without leaving a record of the previous position is destroying data the organization has paid to capture. It is important to satisfy yourself and the user that such data is no longer of potential value to the organization before deciding that it will be deleted without trace.

15.12 **Summary**

There are numerous options for modeling historical and future (planned or anticipated) data. The most appropriate technique will vary from case to case, even within the same model.

The two basic approaches are the "audit trail," which records a history of changes, and the "snapshot," which records a series of past or future positions. Other variations arise from different levels of generalization and aggregation for events and changes and from the choice of whether to treat current positions separately or as special cases of historical or future positions.

Transferable relationships that are one-to-many with the time factor excluded become many-to-many over time. Nontransferable relationships remain one-to-many.

Other time-related issues of relevance to the data modeler include the documentation of associated business rules, management of data and time information, and dealing with archived data in the face of changes to the structure of the operational version of the databases.

Chapter 16
Modeling for Data Warehouses and Data Marts

"The structure of language determines not only thought, but reality itself."
- Noam Chomsky

"The more constraints one imposes, the more one frees oneself of the chains that shackle the spirit."
- Igor Stravinsky, Poetics of Music

16.1 Introduction

Data warehouses and data marts emerged in the 1990s as a practical solution to the problem of drawing together data to support management and (sometimes) external reporting requirements. One widely used architecture for a data warehouse and associated data marts is shown in Figure 16.1.

The terminology in the diagram is typical, but the term **data warehouse** is sometimes used loosely to include data marts as well. And while we are clarifying terms, in this chapter we use the term **operational** to distinguish databases and systems intended to support transaction processing rather than management queries.

The diagram shows that data is extracted periodically from operational databases (and sometimes external sources), consolidated in the data warehouse, and then extracted to data marts, which serve particular users or subject areas. In some cases the data marts may be fed directly, without an intermediate data warehouse, but the number of load programs (more precisely **extract/transformation/load** or ETL programs) needed can grow quickly as the number of source systems and marts increases. In some cases data marts may be developed without a data warehouse, but within a framework of data standards, to allow a data warehouse to be added later or to enable data from different marts to be consolidated. Another option is for the data marts to be logical views of the warehouse; in this scenario there is no physical data mart, but rather a window into the data warehouse with data being selected and combined for each query.

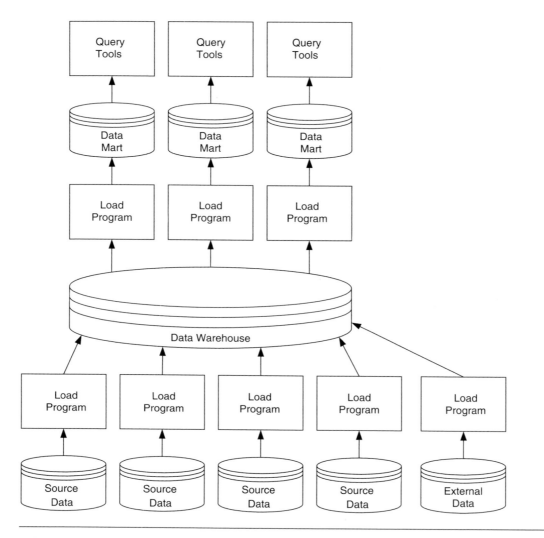

Figure 16.1   Typical data warehouse and data mart architecture.

It is beyond the scope of this chapter to contribute to the ongoing debate about the relative advantages of these and other data warehouse architectures. (Some suitable references are listed in Further Reading.) Unless otherwise noted, our discussion in this chapter assumes the simple architecture of Figure 16.1, but you should have little trouble adapting the principles to alternative structures.

Data warehouses are now widely used and generally need to be developed in-house, primarily because the mix of source systems (and associated operational databases) varies so much from organization to organization. Reporting requirements, of course, may also vary. This is good news for data modelers because data warehouses and data marts are databases, which, of course, must be specified by data models. There may also be some reverse engineering and general data management work to be done in order to understand the organization and meaning of the data in the source systems (as discussed in Chapter 17).

Data modeling for data warehouses and marts, however, presents a range of new challenges and has been the subject of much debate among data modelers and database designers. An early quote indicates how the battle lines were drawn:

> *"Forget everything you know about entity relationship data modeling . . . using that model with a real-world decision support system almost guarantees failure."*[1]

On the other side of the debate were those who argued that "a database is a database" and nothing needed to change.

Briefly, there are two reasons why data modeling for warehouses and marts is different. First, the requirements that data warehouses and marts need to satisfy are different (or at least differ in relative importance) from those for operational databases. Second, the platforms on which they are implemented may not be relational; in particular, data marts are frequently implemented on specialized **multidimensional DBMS**s.

Many of the principles and techniques of data modeling for operational databases are adaptable to the data warehouse environment but cannot be carried across uncritically. And there are new techniques and patterns to learn.

Data modeling for data warehouses and marts is a relatively new discipline, which is still developing. Much has been written, and will continue to be written, on the subject, some of it built on sound foundations, some not. In this chapter we focus on the key requirements and principles to provide you with a basis for evaluating advice, leveraging what you already know about data modeling, and making sound design decisions.

We first look at how the requirements for data marts and data warehouses differ from those for operational databases. We then reexamine the rules of data modeling and find that, although the basic objectives (expressed as evaluation criteria/quality measures) remain the same, their relative importance changes. As a result, we need to modify some of the rules and add some general guidelines for data warehouse and data mart modeling. Finally, we look specifically at the issues of organizing

---

[1]Kimball, R., and Strehlo, K., "Why Decision Support Fails and How to Fix It," *Datamation* (June 1, 1994.)

data to suit the multidimensional database products that underpin many data marts.

16.2 Characteristics of Data Warehouses and Data Marts

The literature on data warehouses identifies a number of characteristics that differentiate warehouses and marts from conventional operational databases. Virtually all of these have some impact on data modeling.

16.2.1 Data Integration: Working with Existing Databases

A data warehouse is not simply a collection of copies of records from source systems. It is a database that "makes sense" in its own right. We would expect to specify one **Product** table even if the warehouse drew on data from many overlapping **Product** tables or files with inconsistent definitions and coding schemes. The data modeler can do little about these historical design decisions but needs to define target tables into which all of the old data will fit, after some translation and/or reformatting. These tables will in turn need to be further combined, reformatted, and summarized as required to serve the data marts, which may also have been developed prior to the warehouse. (Many organizations originally developed individual data marts, fed directly from source systems—and often called "data warehouses"—until the proliferation of ETL programs forced the development of an intermediate warehouse.) Working within such constraints adds an extra challenge to the data modeling task and means that we will often end up with less than ideal structures.

16.2.2 Loads Rather Than Updates

Data marts are intended to support queries and are typically updated through periodic batch loading of data from the warehouse or directly from operational databases. Similarly, the data warehouse is likely to be loaded from the operational databases through batch programs, which are not expected to run concurrently with other access. This strategy may be adopted not only to improve efficiency and manage contention for data resources, but also to ensure that the data warehouse and data marts are not "moving targets" for queries, which generally need to produce consistent results.

Recall our discussion of normalization. One of the strongest reasons for normalizing beyond first normal form was to prevent "update anomalies" where one occurrence of an item is updated but others are left unchanged. In the data warehouse environment, we can achieve that sort of consistency in a different way through careful design of the load programs—knowing that no other update transactions will run against the database.

Of course, there is no point in abandoning or compromising normalization just because we can tackle the problem in another (less elegant) way. There needs to be some payoff, and this may come through improved performance or simplified queries. And if we chose to "trickle feed" the warehouse using conventional transactions, update anomalies could become an issue again.

16.2.3 Less Predictable Database "Hits"

In designing an operational database, we usually have a good idea of the type and volumes of transactions that will run against it. We can optimize the database design to process those transactions simply and efficiently, sometimes at the expense of support for lower-volume or unpredicted transactions.

Queries against a data mart are less predictable, and, indeed, the ability to support *ad hoc* queries is one of the major selling points of data marts. A design decision (such as use of a repeating group, as described in Chapter 2) that favors one type of query at the expense of others will need to be very carefully thought through.

16.2.4 Complex Queries—Simple Interface

One of the challenges of designing data marts and associated query tools is the need to support complex queries and analyses in a relatively simple way. It is not usually reasonable to expect users of the facility to navigate complex data structures in the manner of experienced programmers, yet typical queries against a fully normalized database may require data from a large number of tables. (We say "not *usually* reasonable" because some users of data marts, such as specialist operational managers, researchers, and data miners may be willing and able to learn to navigate sophisticated structures if the payoff is sufficient.)

Perhaps the central challenge for the data mart modeler comes from the approach that tool vendors have settled on to address the problem. Data mart query tools are generally intended for use with a multidimensional database based on a central "fact" table and associated look-up tables called **dimension tables** or just **dimensions.** (Figure 16.2 in Section 16.6.2 shows an example.) The data modeler is required to fit the data into this shape. We can see this as an interesting variation of the "elegance" objective discussed in Chapter 1. From a user perspective, the solution is elegant, in that it is easy to understand and use and is consistent from one mart to the next. From the data modeler's perspective, some very inelegant decisions may need to be taken to meet the constraint.

16.2.5 History

The holding of historical information is one of the most important characteristics of a data warehouse. Managers are frequently interested in trends, whereas operational users of data may only require the current position. Such information may be built up in the data warehouse over a period of time and retained long after it is no longer required in the source systems. The challenge of modeling time-dependent data may be greater for the data warehouse designer than for the operational database designer.

16.2.6 Summarization

The data warehouse seldom contains complete copies of all data held (currently or historically) in operational databases. Some is excluded, and some may be held only in summary form. Whenever we summarize, we lose information, and the data modeler needs to be fully aware of the impact of summarization on all potential users.

16.3 Quality Criteria for Warehouse and Mart Models

It is interesting to take another look at the evaluation or quality criteria for data models that we identified in Chapter 1, but this time in the context of the special requirements of data warehouses and marts. All remain relevant, but their relative importance changes. Thus, our trade-offs are likely to be different.

16.3.1 Completeness

In designing a data warehouse, we are limited by the data available in the operational databases or from external sources. We have to ask not only,

"What do we want?" but also, "What do we have?" and, "What can we get?" Practically, this means acquainting ourselves with the source system data either at the outset or as we proceed. For example:

User: "I want to know what percentage of customers spend more than a specified amount on CDs when they shop here."

Modeler: "We only record sales, not customers, so what we can tell you is what percentage of sales exceed a certain value."

User: "Same thing, isn't it?"

Modeler: "Not really. What if the customer buys a few CDs in the classical section then stops by the rock section and buys some more?"

User: "That'd actually be interesting to know. Can you tell us how often that happens? And what about if they see another CD as they're walking out and come back and buy it. They see the display by the door . . ."

Modeler: "We can get information on that for those customers who use their store discount card, because we can identify them . . ."

The users of data warehouses, interested in aggregated information, *may* not make the same demands for absolute accuracy as the user of an operational system. Accordingly, it may be possible to compromise completeness to achieve simplicity (as discussed below in Section 16.3.3). Of course, this needs to be verified at the outset. There are examples of warehouses that have lost credibility because the outputs did not balance to the last cent. What we cannot afford to compromise is good documentation, which should provide the user with information on the currency, completeness, and quality of the data, as well as the basic definitions.

Finally, we may lose data by summarizing it to save space and processing. The summarization may take place either when data is loaded from operational databases to the warehouse (a key design decision) or when it is loaded from the warehouse to the marts (a decision more easily reversed).

16.3.2 **Nonredundancy**

We can be a great deal less concerned about redundancy in data warehouses and data marts than we would be with operational databases. As discussed earlier, since data is loaded through special ETL programs or utilities, and not updated in the usual sense, we do not face the same risk that fields may be updated inconsistently. Redundancy does, of course, still cost us in storage space, and data warehouses can be very large indeed.

Particularly in data marts, denormalization is regularly practiced to simplify structures, and we may also carry derived data, such as commonly used totals.

16.3.3 **Enforcement of Business Rules**

We tend not to think of a data warehouse or mart as *enforcing* business rules in the usual sense because of the absence of traditional update transactions.

Nevertheless, the data structures will determine what sort of data can be loaded, and if the data warehouse or mart implements a rule that is not supported by a source system, we will have a challenge to address! Sometimes, the need to simplify data leads us to (for example) implement a one-to-many relationship even though a few real world cases are many-to-many. Perhaps an insurance policy can occasionally be sold by more than one salesperson, but we decide to build our data mart around a **Policy** table with a **Salesperson** dimension. We have specified a tighter rule, and we are going to end up trading some "completeness" for the gain in simplicity.

16.3.4 **Data Reusability**

Reusability, in the sense of reusing data captured for operational purposes to support management queries, is the *raison d'être* of most data warehouses and marts. More so than in operational databases, we have to expect the unexpected as far as queries are concerned. Data marts may be constructed to support a particular set of queries (we can build another mart if necessary to support a new requirement), but the data warehouse itself needs to be able to feed virtually any conceivable mart that uses the data that it holds. Here is an argument *in favor of* full normalization in the data warehouse, and against any measures that irrecoverably lose data—such as summarization with removal of the source data.

16.3.5 **Stability and Flexibility**

One of the challenges of data warehouse design is to accommodate changes in the source data. These may reflect real changes in the business or simply changes (including complete replacement) to the operational databases.

Much of the value of a data warehouse may come from the build-up of historical data over a long period. We need to build structures that not only accommodate the new data, but also allow us to retain the old.

It is a maxim of data warehouse designers that "data warehouse design is never finished." If users gain value from the initial implementation, it is almost inevitable that they will require that the warehouse and marts be extended—often very substantially. Many a warehouse project has delivered a warehouse that cannot be easily extended, requiring new warehouses to be constructed as the requirements grow. The picture in Figure 16.1 becomes much less elegant when we add multiple warehouses in the middle, possibly sharing common source databases and target data marts.

16.3.6 Simplicity and Elegance

As discussed earlier, data marts often need to be restricted to simple structures that suit a range of query tools and are relatively easy for end-users to understand.

16.3.7 Communication Effectiveness

It is challenging enough to communicate "difficult" data structures to professional programmers, let alone end-users, who may have only an occasional need to use the data marts. Data marts that use highly generalized structures and unfamiliar terminology, or that are based on a sophisticated original view of the business, are going to cause problems.

16.3.8 Performance

Query volumes against data marts are usually very small compared with transaction volumes for operational databases. Response times can usually be much greater than would be acceptable in an operational system, but the time required to process large tables in their entirety—as is required for many analyses if data has not been summarized in advance—may still be unacceptable.

The data warehouse needs to be able to accept the uploading of large volumes of data, usually within a limited "batch window" when operational databases are not required for real-time processing. It also needs to support reasonably rapid extraction of data for the data marts. Data loading may use purpose-designed ETL utilities, which will dictate how data should be organized to achieve best performance.

16.4 The Basic Design Principle

The architecture shown in Figure 16.1 has evolved from earlier approaches in which the data warehouse and data marts were combined into a single database.

The separation is intended to allow the data warehouse to act as a bridge or clearinghouse between different representations of the data, while the data marts are designed to present simpler views to the end-users.

The basic rule for the data modeler is to respect this separation.

Accordingly, we design the data warehouse much as we would an operational database, but with a recognition that the relative importance of the various design objectives/quality criteria (as reviewed in the previous section) may be different. So, for example, we may be more prepared to accept a denormalized structure, or some data redundancy—provided, of course, there is a corresponding payoff. Flexibility is paramount. We can expect to have to accommodate growth in scope, new and changed operational databases, and new data marts.

Data marts are a different matter. Here we need to fit data into a quite restrictive structure, and the modeling challenge is to achieve this without losing the ability to support a reasonably wide range of queries. We will usually end up making some serious compromises, which may be acceptable for the data mart but would not be so for an operational database or data warehouse.

16.5 Modeling for the Data Warehouse

Many successful data warehouses have been designed by data modelers who tackled the modeling assignment as if they were designing an operational database. We have even seen examples of data warehouses that had to be completely redesigned according to this traditional approach after ill-advised attempts to apply modeling approaches borrowed from the data mart theory. Conversely, there is a strong school of thought that argues that the data warehouse model can usefully anticipate some common data manipulation and summarization.

Both arguments have merit, and the path you take should be guided by the business and technical requirements in each case. That is why we devoted so much space at the beginning of this chapter to differences and goals; it is a proper appreciation of these rather than the brute application of some special technique that leads to good warehouse design.

We can, however, identify a few general techniques that are specific to data warehouse design.

16.5.1 An Initial Model

Data warehouse designers usually find it useful to start with an E-R model of the total business or, at least, of the part of the business that the data warehouse may ultimately cover. The starting point may be an existing enterprise data model (see Chapter 17) or a generalization of the data structures in the most important source databases. If an enterprise data model is used, the data modeler will need to check that it aligns reasonably closely with existing structures rather than representing a radical "future vision." Data warehouse designers are not granted the latitude of data modelers starting with a blank slate!

16.5.2 Understanding Existing Data

In theory, we could construct a data warehouse without ever talking to the business users, simply by consolidating data from the operational databases. Such a warehouse would (again in theory) allow any query possible within the limitations of the source data.

In practice, we need user input to help select what data will be relevant to the data mart users (the extreme alternative would be to load every data item from every source system), to contribute to the inevitable decisions on compromises, and, of course, to "buy in" and support the project.

Nevertheless, a good part of data warehouse design involves gaining an understanding of data from the source systems and defining structures to hold and consolidate it. Usually the most effective approach is to use the initial model as a starting point and to map the existing structures against it. Initially, we do this at an entity level, but as modeling proceeds in collaboration with the users, we add attributes and possibly subtypes.

16.5.3 Determining Requirements

Requirements are likely to be expressed in a different way to those for an operational database. The emphasis is on identifying business measures (such as monthly turnover) and the base data needed to derive them. Much of this discussion will naturally be at the attribute level. Prototype data marts can be invaluable in helping potential users to articulate their requirements. The data modeler also needs to have one eye on the source data structures and the business rules they implement, in order to provide the user with feedback as to what is likely to be possible and what alternatives may be available.

16.5.4 Determining Sources and Dealing with Differences

One of the great challenges of data warehouse design is in making the most of source data in legacy systems. If we are lucky, some of the source data structures may be well designed, but we are likely to have to contend with overloaded attributes (see Section 5.3), poor documentation of definitions and coding schemes, and (almost certainly) inconsistency across databases.

Our choice of source for a data item—and, hence, its definition in the data warehouse—will depend on a number of factors:

1. The objective of minimizing the number of source systems feeding the data warehouse, in the interests of simplicity; reduced need for data integration; and reduced development, maintenance, and running costs.

2. The "quality" of the data item—a complex issue involving primarily the accuracy of the item instances (i.e., whether they accurately reflect the real world), but also timeliness (when were they last updated?)—and compatibility with other items (update cycles again). Timing differences can be a major headache. The update cycles of data vary in many organizations from real-time to annually. Because of this, the "same" data item may hold different values in different source databases.

3. Whether multiple sources can be reconciled to produce a better overall quality. We may even choose to hold two or more versions of the "same" attribute in the warehouse, to enable a choice of the most appropriate version as required.

4. The compatibility of the coding scheme with other data. Incompatible coding schemes and data formats are relatively straightforward to handle—*as long as the mapping between them is simple.* If the underlying definitions are different, it may be impossible to translate to a common scheme without losing too much meaning. It is easy to translate country codes as long as you can agree what a country is! One police force recognizes three eye colors, another four.[2]

5. Whether overloaded attributes can be or need to be unpacked. For example, one database may hold name and address as a single field,[3] while another may break each down into smaller fields—initial, family name, street number, and so on. Programmers often take serious liberties with data definitions and many a field has been redefined well beyond its original intent. Usually, the job of unpacking it into primitive attributes is reasonably straightforward once the rules are identified.

In doing the above, the data warehouse designer may need to perform work that is, more properly, the responsibility of a data management or data

---

[2]For a fascinating discussion of how different societies classify colors and a detailed example of the challenges that we face in coming up with classification schemes acceptable to all, see Chapter 2 of *Language Universals and Linguistic Typology* by Bernard Comrie, Blackwell, Oxford 1981, ISBN 0-631-12971-5.

[3]We use the general term "field" here rather than "column" as many legacy databases are not relational.

administration team. Indeed, the problems of building data warehouses in the absence of good data management groundwork have often led to such teams being established or revived.

16.5.5 **Shaping Data for Data Marts**

How much should the data warehouse design anticipate the way that data will be held in the data marts? On the one hand, the data warehouse should be as flexible as possible, which means not organizing data in a way that will favor one user over another. Remember that the data warehouse may be required not only to feed data marts, but may also be the common source of data for other analysis and decision support systems. And some data marts offer broader options for organizing data.

On the other hand, if we can be reasonably sure that all users of the data will first perform some common transformations such as summarization or denormalization, there is an argument for doing them once—as data is loaded into the warehouse, rather than each time it is extracted. And denormalized data can usually be renormalized without too much trouble. (Summarization is a different matter: base data cannot be recovered from summarized data.) The data warehouse can act as a stepping-stone to greater levels of denormalization and summarization in the marts. When data volumes are very high, there is frequently a compelling argument for summarization to save space and processing.

Another advantage of shaping data at the warehouse stage is that it promotes a level of commonality across data marts. For example, a phone company might decide not to hold details of all telephone calls but rather only those occurring during a set of representative periods each week. If the decision was made at the warehouse stage, we could decide once and for all what the most appropriate periods were. All marts would then work with the same sampling periods, and results from different marts could be more readily compared.

Sometimes the choice of approach will be straightforward. In particular, if the data marts are implemented as views of the warehouse, we will need to implement structures that can be directly translated into the required shape for the marts.

The next section discusses data mart structures, and these can, with appropriate discretion, be incorporated into the data warehouse design.

Where you are in doubt, however, our advice is to lean toward designing the data warehouse for flexibility, independent of the data marts. One of the great lessons of data modeling is that new and unexpected uses will be found for data, once it is available, and this is particularly true in the context of data warehouses. Maximum flexibility and minimum anticipation are good starting points!

16.6 **Modeling for the Data Mart**

16.6.1 **The Basic Challenge**

In organizing data in a data mart, the basic challenge is to present it in a form that can be understood by general business people. A typical operational database design is simply too complex to meet this requirement. Even our best efforts with views cannot always transform the data into something that makes immediate sense to nonspecialists. Further, the query tools themselves need to make some assumptions about how data is stored if they are going to be easy to implement and use, and if they are going to produce reports in predictable formats. Data mart users also need to be able to move from one mart to another without too much effort.

16.6.2 **Multidimensional Databases, Stars and Snowflakes**

Developers of data marts and vendors of data mart software have settled on a common response to the problem of providing a simple data structure: a **star schema** specifying a multidimensional database. Multidimensional databases can be built using conventional relational DBMSs or specialized multidimensional DBMSs optimized for such structures.

Figure 16.2 shows a star schema. The structure is very simple: a **fact table** surrounded by a number of **dimension tables**.

The format is not difficult to understand. The fact tables hold (typically) transaction data, either in its raw, atomic form or summarized. The dimensions effectively classify the data in the fact table into categories, and make it easy to formulate queries based on categories that aggregate data from the fact table: "What percentage of sales were in region 13?" or "What was the total value of sales in region 13 to customers in category B?"

With our user hats on, this looks fine. Putting our data modeling hats on, we can see some major limitations—at least compared with the data structures for operational databases that we have been working with to date.

Before we start looking at these "limitations," it is interesting to observe that multidimensional DBMSs have been around long enough now that there are professional designers who have modeled only in that environment. They seem to accept the star schema structure as a "given" and do not think of it as a limiting environment to work in. It is worth taking a leaf from their book if you are a "conventional" modeler moving to data mart design. Remember that relational databases themselves are far from comprehensive in the structures that they support—many DBMSs do not directly support subtypes for example—yet we manage to get the job done!

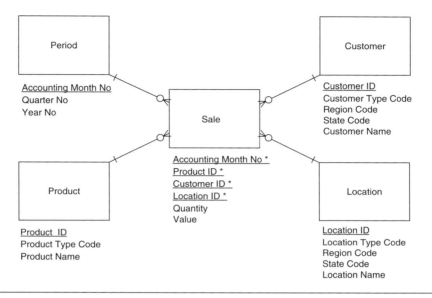

Figure 16.2   A star schema: the fact table is Sale.

16.6.2.1   One Fact Table per Star

While there is usually no problem implementing multiple stars, each with its own fact table (within the same[4] or separate data marts), we can have only one fact table in each star. Figure 16.3 illustrates the key problem that this causes.

It is likely that we will hold numeric data and want to formulate queries at both the loan and transaction level. Some of the options we might consider are the following:

1. Move the data in the **Loan** table into the **Transaction** table, which would then become the fact table. This would mean including all of the data about the relevant loan in each row of the **Transaction** table. If there is a lot of data for each loan, and many transactions per loan, the space requirement for the duplicated data could be unacceptable. Such denormalization would also have the effect of making it difficult to hold loans that did not have any transactions against them. Our solution might require that we add "dummy" rows in the **Transaction** table, containing only loan data. Queries about loans and transactions would

---

[4]Multiple stars in the same data mart can usually share dimension tables.

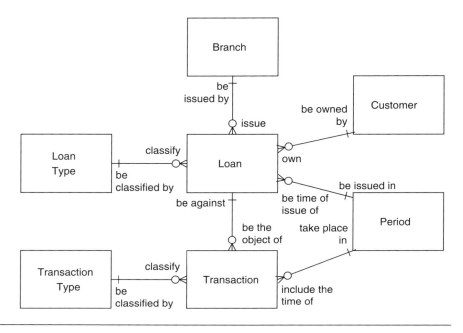

Figure 16.3 Which is the fact table—Loan or Transaction?

be more complicated than would be the case with a simple loan or transaction fact table.

2. Nominate the **Loan** table as the fact table, and hold transaction information in a summarized form in the **Loan** table. This would mean holding totals rather than individual items. If the maximum number of transactions per loan was relatively small (perhaps more realistically, we might be dealing with the number of assets securing the loan), we could hold a repeating group of transaction data in the **Loan** table—as always with some loss of simplicity in query formulation.

3. Implement separate star schemas, one with **Loan** as a fact table and the other with **Transaction** as a fact table. We would probably turn **Loan** into a dimension for the Transaction schema, and we might hold summarized transaction data in the **Loan** table.

16.6.2.2 One Level of Dimension

A true star schema supports only one level of dimension. Some data marts do support multiple levels (usually simple hierarchies). These variants are generally known as **snowflake** schemas (Figure 16.4).

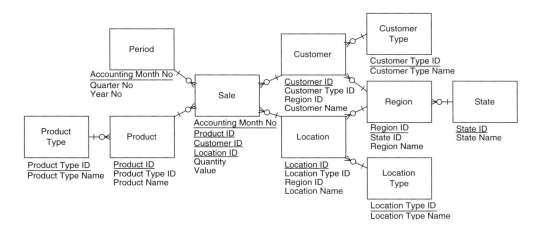

Figure 16.4 A snowflake schema—Sale is the fact table.

To compress what may be a multilevel hierarchy down to one level, we have to denormalize (specifically from fully normalized back to first normal form). Figure 16.5 provides an example.

While we may not need to be concerned about update anomalies from denormalizing, we do need to recognize that space requirements can sometimes become surprisingly large if the tables near the top of the hierarchy contain a lot of data. We may need to be quite brutal in stripping these down to codes and (perhaps) names, so that they function only as categories. (In practice, space requirements of dimensions are seldom as much of a problem as those of fact tables.)

Another option is to summarize data from lower-level tables into higher-level tables, or completely ignore one or more levels in the hierarchy (Figure 16.6). This option will only be workable if the users are not interested in some of the (usually low-level) classifications.

16.6.2.3 One-to-Many Relationships

The fact table in a star schema is in a many-to-one relationship with the dimensions. In the discussion above on collapsing hierarchies, we also assumed that there were no many-to-many relationships amongst the dimensions, in which case simple denormalization would not work.

What do we do if the real-world relationship is many-to-many, as in Figure 16.7? Here, we have a situation in which, most of the time, sales are made by only one salesperson, but, on occasion, more than one salesperson shares the sale.

One option is to ignore the less common case and tie the relationship only to the "most important" or "first" salesperson. Perhaps we can

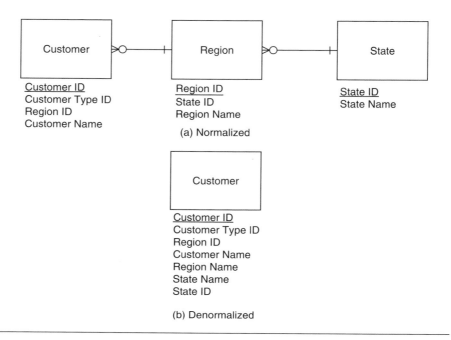

Figure 16.5   Denormalizing to collapse a hierarchy of dimension tables.

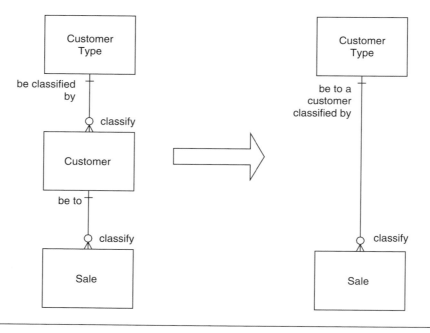

Figure 16.6   (a) Ignoring one or more levels in the hierarchy.

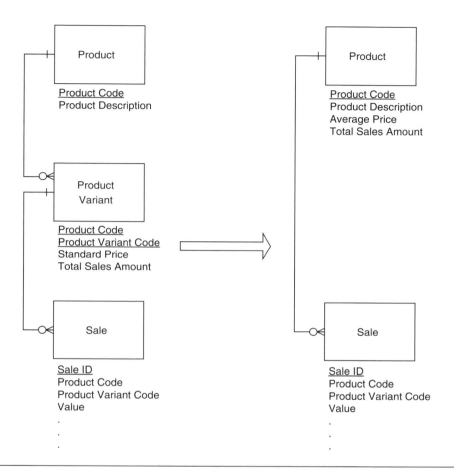

Figure 16.6 (b) Summarizing data from lower-level tables into higher-level tables.

compensate to some degree by carrying the number of salespersons involved in the **Sale** table, and even by carrying (say) the percentage involvement of the key person. For some queries, this compromise may be quite acceptable, but it would be less than satisfactory if a key area of interest is sales involving multiple salespersons.

We could modify the **Salesperson** table to allow it to accommodate more than one salesperson, through use of a repeating group. It is an inelegant solution and breaks down once we want to include (as in the previous section) details from higher-level look up tables. Which region's data do we include—that of the first, the second, or the third salesperson?

Another option is to in effect resolve the many-to-many relationship and treat the **Sale-by-Salesperson** table as the fact table (Figure 16.8). We will probably need to include the rest of the sale data in the table.

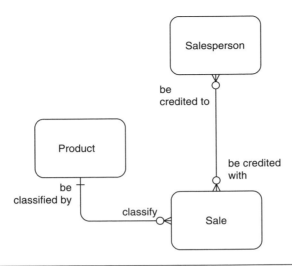

Figure 16.7   Many-to-many relationship between dimension and fact tables.

Once again, we have a situation in which there is no single, mechanical solution. We need to talk to the users about how they want to "slice and dice" the data and work through with them the pros and cons of the different options.

16.6.3 **Modeling Time-Dependent Data**

The basic issues related to the modeling of time, in particular the choice of "snapshots" or history are covered in Chapter 15 and apply equally to data warehouses, data marts, and operational databases. This section covers a few key aspects of particular relevance to data mart design.

16.6.3.1 Time Dimension Tables

Most data marts include one or more dimension tables holding time periods to enable that dimension to be used in analysis (e.g., "What percentage or sales were made by salespeople in Region X *in the last quarter?*"). The key design decisions are the level of granularity (hours, days, months, years) and how to deal with overlapping time periods (financial years may overlap with calendar years, months may overlap with billing periods, and so on). The finer the granularity (i.e., the shorter the periods), the fewer problems we have with overlap and the more precise our queries can be. However,

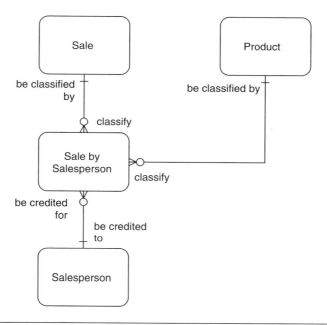

Figure 16.8   Treating the sale-by-salesperson table as the fact table.

query formulation may be more difficult or time-consuming in terms of specifying the particular periods to be covered.

Sometimes, we will need to specify a hierarchy of time periods (as a snowflake or collapsed into a single-level denormalized star). Alternatively, or in addition, we may specify multiple time dimension tables, possibly covering overlapping periods.

16.6.3.2   Slowly-Changing Dimensions

One of the key concerns of the data mart designer is how quickly the data in the dimension tables will change, and how quickly fact data may move from one dimension to another.

Figure 16.9 shows a simple example of the problem in snowflake form for clarity. This might be part of a data mart to support analysis of customer purchasing patterns over a long period.

It should be clear that, if customers can change from one customer group to another over time and our mart only records the current group, we will not be able to ask questions such as, "What sort of vehicles did people buy while they were in group 'A'?" (We *could* ask, "What sort of vehicles did people *currently* in group 'A' buy over time?"—but this may well be less useful.)

Figure 16.9 Slowly changing dimensions.

In the operational database, such data will generally be supported by many-to-many relationships, as described in Chapter 15, and/or matching of timestamps and time periods. There are many ways of reworking the structure to fit the star schema requirement. For example:

1. Probably the neatest solution to the problem as described is to carry *two* foreign keys to **Customer Group** in the **Purchase** table. One key points to the customer group to which the customer belonged at the time of the purchase; the other points to the customer group to which the customer currently belongs. In fact, the information supported by the latter foreign key may not be required by the users, in which case we can delete it, giving us a very simple solution.

   Of course, setting up the mart in this form will require some translation of data held in more conventional structures in the operational databases and (probably) the data warehouse.

2. If the dimension changes sufficiently slowly in the time frames in which we are interested, then the amount of error or uncertainty that it causes may be acceptable. We may be able to influence the speed of change by deliberately selecting or creating dimensions (perhaps at the data warehouse stage) which change relatively slowly. For example, we may be able to classify customers into broad occupational groups ("professional," "manual worker," "technician") rather than more specific occupations, or even develop lifestyle profiles that have been found to be relatively stable over long periods.

3. We can hold a history of (say) the last three values of Customer Group in the **Customer** table. This approach will also give us some information on how quickly the dimension changes.

16.7 **Summary**

Logical data warehouse and data mart design are important subdisciplines of data modeling, with their own issues and techniques.

Data warehouse design is particularly influenced by its role as a staging point between operational databases and data marts. Existing data structures in operational databases or (possibly) existing data marts will limit the freedom of the designer, who will also need to support high volumes of data and load transactions. Within these constraints, data warehouse design has much in common with the design of operational databases.

The rules of data mart design are largely a result of the star schema structure—a limited subset of the full E-R structures used for operational database design—and lead to a number of design challenges, approaches, and patterns peculiar to data marts. The data mart designer also has to contend with the limitations of the data available from the warehouse.

Chapter 17
Enterprise Data Models and Data Management

"Always design a thing by considering it in its next larger context—a chair in a room, a room in a house, a house in an environment, an environment in a city plan."

- Eliel Saarinen

17.1 Introduction

So far, we have discussed data modeling in the context of database design; we have assumed that our data models will ultimately be implemented more or less directly using some DBMS. Our interest has been in the data requirements of individual application systems.

However, data models can also play a role in data planning and management for an enterprise as a whole. An **enterprise data model** (sometimes called a **corporate data model**) is a model that covers the whole of, or a substantial part of, an organization. We can use such a model to:

- Classify or index existing data
- Provide a target for database and systems planners
- Provide a context for specifying new databases
- Support the evaluation and integration of application packages
- Guide data modelers in the development or implementation of individual databases
- Specify data formats and definitions to support the exchange of data between applications and with other organizations
- Provide input to business planning
- Specify an organization-wide database (in particular, a data warehouse)

These activities are part of the wider discipline of **data management**—the management of data as a shared enterprise resource—that warrants a book in itself.[1] In this chapter, we look briefly at data management in

---

[1]A useful starting point is *Guidelines to Implementing Data Resource Management*, 4th Edition, Data Management Association, 2002.

general, then discuss the uses of enterprise data models. Finally, we examine how development of an enterprise data model differs from development of a conventional project-level data model.

But first, a word of warning: far too many enterprise data models have ended up "on the shelf" after considerable expenditure on their development. The most common reason, in our experience, is a lack of a clear idea of how the model is to be used. It is vital that any enterprise data model be developed in the context of a data management or information systems strategy, within which its role is clearly understood, rather than as an end in itself.

17.2 Data Management

17.2.1 Problems of Data Mismanagement

The rationale for data management is that data is a valuable and expensive resource that therefore needs to be properly managed. Parallels are often drawn with physical assets, people, and money, all of which need to be managed explicitly if the enterprise is to derive the best value from them. As with the management of other assets, we can best understand the need for data management by looking at the results of not doing it.

Databases have traditionally been implemented on an application-by-application basis—one database per application system. Indeed, databases are often seen as being "owned" by their parent applications. The problem is that some data may be required by more than one application. For example, a bank may implement separate applications to handle personal loans and savings accounts, but both will need to hold data about customers. Without some form of planning and control, we will end up holding the same data in both databases. And here, the element of choice in data modeling works against us; we have no guarantee that the modelers working on different systems will have represented the common data in the same way, particularly if they are software package developers working for different vendors. Differences in data models can make data duplication difficult to identify, document, and control.

The effects of duplication and inconsistency across multiple systems are similar to those that arise from poor data modeling at the individual system level.

There are the costs of keeping multiple copies of data in step (and repercussions from data users—including customers, managers, and regulators—if we do not). Most of us have had the experience of notifying an organization of a change of address and later discovering that only some of their records have been updated.

Pulling data together to meet management information needs is far more difficult if definitions, coding, and formats vary. An airline wants to know the total cost of running each of its terminals, but the terminals are identified in different ways in different systems—sometimes only by a series of account numbers. An insurance company wants a breakdown of profitability by product, but different divisions have defined "product" in different ways. Problems of this kind constitute *the* major challenge in data warehouse development (Chapter 16).

Finally, poor overall data organization can make it difficult to use the data in new ways as business functions change in response to market and regulatory pressures and internal initiatives. Often, it seems easier to implement yet another single-purpose database than to attempt to use inconsistent existing databases. A lack of central documentation also makes reuse of data difficult; we may not even know that the data we require is held in an existing database. The net result, of course, is still more databases, and an exacerbation of the basic problem. Alternatively, we may decide that the new initiative is "too hard" or economically untenable.

We have seen banks with fifty or more "Branch" files, retailers with more than thirty "Stock Item" files, and organizations that are supposedly customer-focused with dozens of "Customer" files. Often, just determining the scope of the problem has been a major exercise. Not surprisingly, it is the data that is most central to an organization (and, therefore, used by the greatest number of applications) that is most frequently mismanaged.

17.2.2 **Managing Data as a Shared Resource**

Data management aims to address these issues by taking an organization-wide view of data. Instead of regarding databases as the sole property of their parent applications, we treat them as a shared resource. This may entail documenting existing databases; encouraging development of new, sharable databases in critical areas; building interfaces to keep data in step; establishing standards for data representation; and setting an overall target for data organization. The task of data management may be assigned to a dedicated data management (or "data administration" or "information architecture") team, or be included in the responsibilities of a broader "architectures" group.

17.2.3 **The Evolution of Data Management**

The history of data management as a distinct organizational function dates from the early 1970s. In an influential paper, Nolan[2] identified "Data

---

[2]Nolan: Managing the Crisis in Data Processing, *Harvard Business Review*, 5(2), March–April, 1979.

Resource Management" as the fifth stage in his Stages of Growth model (the last being "Maturity"). Many medium and large organizations established data management groups, and data management began to emerge as a discipline in its own right.[3]

In the early days of data management, some organizations pursued what seemed to be the ideal solution: development of a single shared database, or an integrated set of "subject databases" covering all of the enterprise's data requirements. Even in the days when there were far fewer information systems to deal with, the task proved overwhelmingly difficult and expensive, and there were few successes. Today, most organizations have a substantial base of "legacy" systems and cannot realistically contemplate replacing them all with new applications built around a common set of data structures.

Recognizing that they could not expect to design and build the enterprise's data structures themselves, data managers began to see themselves as akin to town planners (though the term "architect" has continued to be more widely used—unfortunately, in our view, as the analogy is misleading). Their role was to define a long-term target (town plan) and to ensure that individual projects contributed to the realization of that goal.

In practice, this meant requiring developers to observe common data standards and definitions (typically specified by an enterprise-wide data model), to reuse existing data where practicable, and to contribute to a common set of data documentation. Like town planners, data managers encountered considerable resistance along the way, as builders asserted their preference for operating without outside interference and appealed to higher authorities for special dispensation for their projects.

This approach, too, has not enjoyed a strong record of success, though many organizations have persisted with it. A number of factors have worked against it, in particular the widespread use of packaged software in preference to in-house development, and greater pressure to deliver results in the short-to-medium term.

In response to such challenges, some data managers have chosen to take a more proactive and focused role, initiating projects to improve data management in specific areas, rather than attempting to solve all of an organization's data management problems. For example, they might address a particularly costly data quality problem, or establish data standards in an area in which data matching is causing serious difficulties. Customer Relationship Management (CRM) initiatives fall into this category, though in many cases they have been initiated and managed outside the data management function.

---

[3]The Data Management Association (DAMA) at www.dama.org is a worldwide body that supports data management professionals.

More recently we have seen a widespread change in philosophy. Rather than seek to consolidate individual databases, organizations are looking to keep data in step through messages passed amongst applications. In effect, there is a recognition that applications (and their associated databases) will be purchased or developed one at a time, with relatively little opportunity for direct data sharing. The proposed solution is to accept the duplication of data, which inevitably results, but to put in place mechanisms to ensure that when data is updated in one place, messages (typically in XML format) are dispatched to update copies of the data held by other applications. For some data managers, this approach amounts to a rejection of the data management philosophy. For others, it is just another mechanism for achieving similar ends. What is clear is that while the technology and architecture may have changed, the basic issues of understanding data meaning and formats within and across applications remain. To some extent at least, the problem of data specification moves from the databases to the message formats.

An enterprise data model has been central to all of the traditional approaches to data management, and, insofar as the newer approaches also require enterprise-wide data definitions, is likely to continue to remain so.

In the following sections, we examine the most important roles that an enterprise data model can play.

17.3 **Classification of Existing Data**

Most organizations have a substantial investment in existing databases and files. Often, the documentation of these is of variable quality and held locally with the parent applications.

The lack of a central, properly-indexed register of data is one of the greatest impediments to data management. If we do not know what data we have (and where it is), how can we hope to identify opportunities for its reuse or put in place mechanisms to keep the various copies in step? The problem is particularly apparent to builders of data warehouses (Chapter 16) and reporting and analysis applications which need to draw data from existing operational files and databases. Just finding the required data is often a major challenge. Correctly interpreting it in the absence of adequate documentation can prove an even greater one, and serious business mistakes have been made as a result of incorrect assumptions.

Commercial data dictionaries and "repositories" have been around for many years to hold the necessary **metadata** (data about data). Some organizations have built their own with mixed success. But data inventories are of limited value without an index of some kind; we need to be able to ask, "What files or databases hold data about flight schedules?" or, "Where is **Country Code** held?" remembering that **Country Code** may be called "CTRY-ID" in one system and "E12345" in another. Or an attribute named "Country Code" may mean something entirely different to what we expect. We recall encountering a **Vehicle ID** attribute, which in fact identified salespersons; the salesperson was the "vehicle" by which the sale was made.

Probably the cleanest method of indexing a data inventory is to map each item to the relevant component of an enterprise data model.

In developing an enterprise data model specifically to index existing data, remember that the mapping between the model and existing data structures will be simpler if the two are based on similar concepts. Avoid radically new, innovative enterprise data models unless there is an adequate payoff! Of course, if the business has changed substantially since the databases were built, the enterprise data model may well, by necessity, differ significantly from what is currently in place. It then becomes an important tool for assessing the completeness and quality of information systems support for the business.

One of the most effective approaches to building an indexed inventory of data is to develop a fairly generalized enterprise data model and to devote the major effort to improving documentation of individual databases. The enterprise model is mapped against existing data at the entity class level and serves as a coarse index to identify databases in which any required data may be held; the final assessment is made by close examination of the local documentation.

The Object Class Hierarchy technique described in Section 9.7 is a good method of developing an enterprise data model that classifies data in the same way that the business does.

17.4 **A Target for Planning**

Just as a town plan describes where we aim to be at some future date, an enterprise data model can describe how we intend to organize our total set of computerized data at some point in the future.

It is here that enterprise data modelers have frequently encountered trouble. It is one thing to start with a blank sheet of paper and develop an ideal model that may be conceptually quite different from the models on which existing applications are based. It is quite another to migrate from existing databases and files to new ones based on the model, or to find package vendors who share the same view of data organization.

There is a natural (and often economically sound) reluctance to replace current databases that are doing an adequate job. We may need to accept, therefore, that large parts of an enterprise model will remain unimplemented.

This leads to a second problem: should implementers of new applications aim to share data from existing databases, or should they build new databases following the specification of the enterprise data model? The former approach perpetuates the older structures; the latter increases the problems of data duplication. We have even seen developers refusing to use databases that had been designed in accordance with an enterprise data model because the enterprise model had since changed.

Third, in many business areas, the most cost-effective approach is to purchase a packaged application. In these cases, we have little choice about the underlying data models (except insofar as we may be able to choose among packages that are better or worse matches with the enterprise data model). With one purchase decision, we may render a large part of the enterprise data model irrelevant.

Enterprise data modelers frequently find themselves fighting both systems developers and users who want economical solutions to their local problems and who feel constrained by the requirement to fit in with a larger plan. There are arguments for both sides. Without an overall target, it will certainly be difficult to achieve better sharing of data. But too often data modelers forget the basic tenet of creative data modeling: there may be more than one good answer. We have seen data modelers arguing against purchase of a package because it does not fit "their" enterprise model, when in fact the underlying database for the package is built on a sound model and could readily be incorporated into the existing set of databases.

The "town planning" paradigm mentioned earlier, if pragmatically applied, can help us develop a target that balances the ideal vision with the practicalities of what is in place or available. The target needs to be a combination of existing databases that are to be retained, databases to be implemented as components of packages, and databases to be developed in-house. It is, in fact, an enterprise data model produced within the constraints of other commitments, the most important being the existing systems and the applications development strategy. Some of it will be less than ideal; the structures that fit in best will often differ from those we would use if we had started with a "clean slate."

In developing this sort of model, you should set a specific date—typically, three to five years hence—and aim to model how the organization's data will look at that time. Some areas of the model can be very precise indeed, as they merely document current databases; others may be very broad because we intend to purchase a package whose data structure is as yet unknown.

Such a model represents a realistic target that can be discussed in concrete terms with systems planners, developers, and users, and can be used as a basis for assessing individual proposals.

17.5 A Context for Specifying New Databases

17.5.1 Determining Scope and Interfaces

In specifying a new database, three fundamental questions we need to ask are:

1. What is included?
2. What is excluded?
3. What do we have to fit in with?

These questions need to be answered early in a systems development or acquisition project as an important part of agreeing expectations and budgets and of managing overlaps and interfaces among databases. Once a project team has planned and budgeted to design their own database (and all the associated processing to maintain it) in isolation, it can be virtually impossible to persuade them to use existing files and databases. Similarly, once it has been decided (even if only implicitly) not to include certain data, it is very difficult to change the decision.

A "big picture" of an organization's overall data requirements—an enterprise data model—can be an invaluable aid to answering questions of scope and overlap, and highlighting data issues before it is too late to address them.

17.5.2 Incorporating the Enterprise Data Model in the Development Life Cycle

Here is how a large organization might ensure that databases are specified in the context of an overall data plan.

The organization requires that every information systems project beyond a certain size receive funding approval from a committee of senior managers,[4] which looks at proposals in terms of overall costs and benefits to the business. The committee's charter is far broader than data management; its prime concern is that the organization's total investment in information systems is well directed, and that local needs do not override the best interests of the organization as a whole. (For example, they may enforce a preferred supplier policy for hardware.)

---

[4]It has been an almost universal practice in organizations with a substantial investment in information technology to establish a permanent committee to review investment proposals and projects. Increasingly, we are seeing the senior executive team taking on this role as a part of their management and governance responsibilities.

The committee requires that each proposal include a brief "data management" statement, prepared in consultation with the data management group. This involves project and data management representatives looking at the enterprise data model and identifying the entity classes that will be required by the proposed system. The resulting "first-cut" data model for the system is a subset of the enterprise data model produced by "slicing" in two dimensions: horizontally, to select which entity classes are to be included, and vertically, to select which subtypes of those entity classes are applicable to the project. For example, the project might decide that it requires the entity class **Physical Asset** (horizontal selection), but only in order to keep data about vehicles (vertical selection). This exercise may lead to reconsideration of system scope, perhaps to include other subtypes that are handled similarly. For example, it might turn out that with some minor enhancements the vehicle management system could handle all movable assets.

The data management group then advises on whether and in what form the required data is currently held, by reference to the data inventory. This, in turn, provides a basis for deciding where data will be sourced, and what new data structures the project will build. Where data is to be duplicated, the need for common representation and/or interfaces can be established. The results of the discussions form the data management statement.

From time to time, disagreements as to data sourcing arise, typically because the project prefers to "roll its own," and the data management group favors data reuse. Ultimately, the committee decides, but following a formal procedure ensures that the implications of each option are laid out and discussed.

In practice, this can be a very simple process, with the data management statement typically taking less than a day to prepare. But it can make a real difference to the scope and cost of projects, and to the integration of systems. It does, however, depend upon having an enterprise data model, and someone in authority who is interested in *overall* costs and benefits to the organization rather than the cost-justification of each project in isolation.

The first-cut project data model can also be a valuable tool for estimating and budgeting. It is possible to make an estimate of system size in terms of function points[5] using only a data model and some rules of thumb, such as average number of functions per entity class. The accuracy of the estimate depends very much on how well data boundaries are defined; the enterprise model approach does much to assist this.

Another benefit of an early look at project data requirements in the context of an enterprise data model is that the terminology, definitions, and

---

[5]The function point approach to estimating system size is credited to Albrecht (Albrecht, A.J.: Measuring Application Development Productivity, in GUIDE/SHARE: Proceedings of the IBM Applications Development Symposium (Monterey, Calif.), 1979, pp. 83–92. For an evaluation of Function Point Analysis using both the traditional approach and one based on the E-R model and a starting point for further reading, see Kemerer, Chris F.: Reliability of function points measurement, Communications of the ACM, New York, Feb. 1993.

data structures of the enterprise data model are communicated to the project team before they embark on a different course. The value of this in improving the quality and compatibility of databases is discussed in the next section.

17.6 **Guidance for Database Design**

An enterprise data model can provide an excellent starting point for the development of project-level data models (and, hence, database designs).

An enterprise data model takes a broad view of the business (and is likely to incorporate contributions from senior management and strategic planners) that might not otherwise be available to data modelers working on a specific project. In particular, it may highlight areas in which change can be expected. This is vital input to decisions as to the most appropriate level of generalization.

Because an enterprise data model is usually developed by very experienced data modelers, it should specify sound data structures and may include good and perhaps innovative ideas.

The enterprise data model can also provide standard names and definitions for common entity classes and attributes. Pulling together data from multiple databases or transferring data from one to another is much easier if definitions, formats, and coding are the same. More and more, we need to be able to exchange data with external bodies, as well as among our own databases. The enterprise data model can be the central point for specifying the necessary standard definitions and formats.

Achieving genuine consistency demands a high level of rigor in data definition. We recall an organization that needed to store details of languages spoken. One database treated Afghani as a single language, while another treated it as two—Pushtu and Pashto. What might seem to be an academic difference caused real problems when transferring data from one system to another or attempting to answer simple questions requiring data from both databases. In cases of code sets like this, reference to an external standard can sometimes assist in resolving the problem. Often decisions at this level of detail are not taken in the initial enterprise modeling exercise but are "fed back" to the model by project teams tackling the issue, for the benefit of future project data modelers.

17.7 **Input to Business Planning**

An enterprise data model provides a view of an important business resource (data) from what is usually a novel perspective for business specialists.

As such, it may stimulate original thinking about the objectives and organization of the business.

In business, new ideas frequently arise through generalization: a classic example is redefining a business as "transportation" rather than "trucking." We as modelers make heavy use of generalization and are able to support it in a formal way through the use of supertypes.

So, we find that even if the more specialized entity classes in an enterprise data model represent familiar business concepts, their supertypes may not. Or, commonly, the supertypes represent critical high-level concepts that cut across organizational boundaries and are not managed well as a whole. In a bank, we may have **Loan** (whereas, individual organization units manage only certain types of loan), and in a telecommunications company we may have **Customer Equipment Item** (whereas, different organization units manage different products).

We have seen some real breakthroughs in thinking stimulated by well-explained enterprise data models. Some of these have been attributable to a multidisciplinary, highly skilled enterprise modeling team looking closely at a business's aims and objectives as input to the modeling exercise. Others have appeared as a result of the actual modeling.

Nevertheless, we would not encourage enterprise data modeling for this reason alone. Better results can usually be achieved by the use of specific business planning and modeling techniques. We need to remember that data modeling was developed as a stage in database design, and its conventions and principles reflect this. Normalization is unlikely to help you set your business direction!

Unfortunately, there is a tendency among data modelers to see a business only from the perspective of data and to promote the data model as representing a kind of "business truth." Given the element of choice in modeling, the argument is hard to sustain. In fact, enterprise data models usually encourage a view of the business based on common *processes*, as distinct from products, customers, or projects. For example, the high-level supertype **Policy** in an insurance model might suggest common handling of all policies, rather than distinct handling according to product or customer type. Sometimes the new view leads to useful improvements; sometimes it is counterproductive. The business strategy that allows for the most elegant handling of data certainly has its advantages, but these may be of relatively minor importance in comparison to other considerations, such as business unit autonomy.

17.8 **Specification of an Enterprise Database**

The last use of an enterprise data model was historically the first. The dream in the early days of DBMSs was to develop a database embracing all of an organization's computer data, fully normalized, nonredundant, and serving the needs of all areas of the organization.

As mentioned earlier, a number of organizations actually attempted this, almost invariably without success.

A variant is the "subject database" approach, in which the enterprise data model is carved up into smaller, more manageable components, which are to be built one at a time. The difficulty lies in deciding how to partition the data. If we partition the data on an application-by-application basis, we end up with duplication, resulting from data being required by more than one application (the same as if we had developed application databases without any plan).

An alternative approach is to divide the data by supertypes: thus, a bank might plan subject databases for Loans, Customers, Transactions, Branches, and so on. The problem here is that most practical systems require data from many of these subject databases. To implement a new loan product, the bank would probably require all of the databases mentioned above.

In practice, the subject database approach encountered much the same difficulties as the enterprise database approach: complexity, unacceptably long time frames to achieve results, and incompatibility with packaged software.

A less ambitious variant is to focus on a few important reference databases, holding widely used but centrally updated data, typically of low to medium volume. These databases are usually implementations of entity classes near the top of the one-to-many relationship hierarchy. Examples include data about products, organizational structure, regulations, and staff, as well as common codes and their meanings. Customer data does not quite fit the criteria but, since most organizations these days are customer-focused, support can frequently be gained for a customer database project.

Although reference databases may have a potentially large user base, it is almost always a mistake to develop them (or indeed databases of any kind) in isolation. "If we build it they will come," is not a sound motto for a data management group. Successful projects deliver a *system*, even if this only provides for update and basic inquiries on the data. For example, rather than deliver a product database, we should aim to deliver a product management system for the marketing division. By doing this, we bring the subject database initiative into the mainstream of systems development and can manage it using well-understood procedures and roles. Most importantly, organizations have proved more reluctant to abandon the development of a conventional system with specific user sponsorship than an infrastructure project whose benefits may be less obvious and less clearly "owned."

Since the mid-1990s, we have seen the concept of enterprise-wide databases become relevant once again, this time in the context of Enterprise Resource Planning (ERP) applications. These applications are intended to provide support for a substantial part of an organization's information processing and reporting. Accordingly, they are large, complex, highly customizable, and provided only by a relatively small number of vendors able to make the necessary investment in their development.

It is well beyond the scope of this book to cover the range of issues that arise in the selection and implementation of ERP packages. From the data manager's perspective, the vendor of the ERP package should have solved many of the problems of data integration. (However, not all ERP packages have been developed top-down using a single high-quality data model.) The customizability of ERP packages usually means that there are important data modeling choices still to be made, particularly in terms of attribute definition and coding. And it is unusual for ERP to provide a complete solution; most enterprises will continue to need supplementary applications to support at least some aspects of their business. An enterprise data model, reflecting the data structures of the ERP package, can be an important tool in integrating such applications.

17.9 **Characteristics of Enterprise Data Models**

Although enterprise data models use the same building blocks—entity classes, relationships, and attributes—as individual database models, they differ in several ways. Most of the differences arise from the need to cover a wide area, but without the detail needed to specify a database.

Ultimately, the level of detail in an enterprise data model depends upon its role in the data management strategy—in other words, what it is going to be used for. An extreme example is the organization that produced, after considerable effort and investment, an enterprise data model with only six entity classes. But suppose the organization was a bank, and the entity classes were **Customer**, **Product**, **Service**, **Contract**, **Account**, and **Branch**. If the model was successfully used to win agreement throughout the organization on the meaning of these six terms, drove the rationalization of the databases holding the associated data, and encouraged a review of the way each group of data was managed, then the six-entity-class model would have justified its cost many times over.

More typical enterprise data models contain between 50 and 200 entity classes. This relatively low number (in comparison with the model that would result from consolidating all possible project-level models) is achieved by employing a high level of generalization—often higher than we would select for implementation. Traditionally, enterprise models focused on entity classes rather than attributes, in line with their role of providing guidance on data structures or classifying existing data. Today, with the greater emphasis on message-based data integration, central definition of attributes is gaining greater importance, and the entity classes in the model may be regarded by its users as little more than "buckets" to hold the standards for message construction.

Even a highly generalized enterprise data model may still be too complicated to be readily understood. Many business specialists have been permanently discouraged from further participation in the modeling process by a forbiddingly complex "circuit diagram" of boxes and lines. In these cases, it is worth producing a very high-level diagram showing less than ten very generalized entity classes. Ruthless elimination of entity classes that are not critical to communicating the key concepts is essential. Such a diagram is intended solely as a starting point for understanding, and you should therefore make decisions as to what to generalize or eliminate on this basis alone.

17.10 Developing an Enterprise Data Model

In developing an enterprise data model, we use the same basic techniques and principles as for a project-level model. The advice in Chapter 10 about using patterns and exploring alternatives remains valid, but there are some important differences in emphasis and skills.

17.10.1 The Development Cycle

Project-level models are developed reasonably quickly to the level of detail necessary for implementation. Later changes tend to be relatively minor (because of the impact on system structure) and driven by changes to business requirements.

In contrast, enterprise models are often developed progressively over a long period. The initial modeling exercise may produce a highly generalized model with few attributes. But project teams and architects using the enterprise model as a starting point will need to "flesh it out" by adding subtypes, attributes, and new entity classes resulting from detailed analysis and normalization. To do so, they will spend more time analyzing the relevant business area, and will be able to cross-check their results against detailed function models. They may also receive better quality input from users, who have a more personal stake in specifying a system than in contributing to the planning exercise that produced the enterprise data model.

The results of project-level modeling can affect the enterprise model in two ways. First, more detailed analysis provides a check on the concepts and rules included in the enterprise model. Perhaps a one-to-many relationship is really many-to-many, or an important subtype of an entity class has been overlooked. The enterprise model will need to be corrected to reflect the new information.

Second, the additional subtypes, entity classes, and attributes that do not conflict with the enterprise model, but add further detail, may be incorporated into the enterprise model. Whether this is done or not depends on the data management strategy and often on the resources and tools available to maintain a more complex model. Many organizations choose to record only data of "corporate significance" in the enterprise data model, leaving "local" data in project models.

In planning an enterprise modeling exercise, then, you need to recognize that development will extend beyond the initial study, and you need to put in place procedures to ensure that later "field work" by project teams is appropriately incorporated.

17.10.2 **Partitioning the Task**

Project-level data models are usually small enough that one person or team can undertake all of the modeling. While a model may be notionally divided into sections that are examined one at a time, this is usually done by the team as a whole rather than by allocating each section to a different modeler.

With enterprise models, this is not always possible. For many reasons, including time constraints, skill sets, and organizational politics, we may need to divide up the task, and have separate teams develop parts of the model in parallel.

If doing this, consider partitioning the task by supertype, rather than by functional area, as data is often used by more than one functional area. You might, for example, assign a team to examine Physical Assets (supertype) rather than Purchasing (functional area). Although this approach may be less convenient from an organizational perspective, it means that different teams will not be modeling the same data. The element of choice in modeling inevitably leads to different models of the same data and long arguments in their reconciliation. We have seen teams spend far longer on reconciliation than on modeling, and enterprise modeling projects abandoned for this reason.

If you choose to partition by functional area, ensure that you have an agreed framework of supertypes in place before starting, and meet very regularly to fit results into the framework and identify any problems.

The initial high-level model is essential whichever approach is taken. Its development provides a great opportunity for creative exploration of options—so great that enterprise data modeling project teams frequently spend months arguing or become seriously stuck at this point looking for the "perfect" solution. Beware of this. Document the major options and move quickly to collect more detailed information to allow them to be better evaluated.

17.10.3 **Inputs to the Task**

Few things are more helpful to enterprise data modelers than a clearly documented business strategy that is well supported by management. In developing an enterprise model, overall business objectives need to take the place of system requirements in guiding and verifying the model. The best answer to, "Why did you choose this particular organization of data?" is, "Because it supports the following business objectives in the following way."

Business objectives prompt at least three important questions for the data modeler:

1. What data do we need to *support* the achievement of each objective? A welfare organization might need a consolidated register of welfare recipients to achieve the objective: "Reduce the incidence of persons illegally claiming more than one benefit."
2. What data do we need to *measure* the achievement of each objective? A police force may have the objective of responding to urgent calls as quickly as possible and could specify the key performance indicator (KPI): "Mean time to respond to calls classified as urgent." Base data needed to derive the KPI would include time taken to respond to each call and categories of calls.
3. How will pursuit of the objectives change our data requirements over time? An investment bank may have the objective of providing a full range of investment products for retail and commercial clients. Meeting the objective could involve introduction of new products and supporting data.

Ideally, the enterprise data model will be developed within the context of a full information systems planning project, following establishment of a comprehensive business plan. In many cases, however, data modeling studies are undertaken in relative isolation, and we need to make the best of what we have, or attempt to put together a working set of business objectives as part of the project. Interviews with senior staff can help, but it is unrealistic to expect an enterprise modeling project to produce a business strategy as an interim deliverable!

The best approach in these cases is to make maximum use of whatever is available: company mission statement, job descriptions, business unit objectives, annual plans. Interviews and workshops can then be used to verify and supplement these.

One of the most difficult decisions facing the enterprise modeling team is what use to make of existing project-level models, whether implemented or not, and any earlier attempts at enterprise or business unit models. We find the best approach is to commit only to taking them into account, without undertaking to include any structures uncritically. These existing models are then used as an important source of requirements, and for verification, but are not allowed to stand in the way of taking a fresh look at the business.

The situation is different if our aim is to produce a realistic target for planning that incorporates databases to which we are committed. In this case, we will obviously need to copy structures from those databases directly into the enterprise model.

17.10.4 Expertise Requirements

Data modelers working at the project level can reasonably be forgiven any initial lack of familiarity with the area being modeled. The amount of knowledge required is limited by the scope of the project, and expertise can be gained as the model is developed, typically over several weeks or months.

In the case of an enterprise data model, the situation is quite different. A wide range of business areas need to be modeled, with limited time available for each. And we are dealing with senior members of the organization whose time is too precious to waste on explaining basic business concepts.

Conducting an interview with the finance manager without any prior knowledge of finance will achieve two things: a slightly improved knowledge of finance on the part of the interviewer, and a realization on the part of the finance manager that he/she has contributed little of value to the model. On the other hand, going into the interview with a good working knowledge of finance in general, and of the company's approach in particular, will enable the interview to focus on rules specific to the business, and will help build credibility for the model and data management.

In enterprise data modeling, then, modeling skills need to be complemented by business knowledge. The modeling team will usually include at least one person with a good overall knowledge of the business. In complex businesses, it can be worthwhile seconding business specialists to the team on a temporary basis to assist in examining their area of expertise. We find that there is also great value in having someone whose knowledge of the business area was acquired outside the organization: experienced recruits, consultants, and MBAs are often better placed to take an alternative or more general view of the organization and its data.

17.10.5 External Standards

External data standards are an important, but often overlooked, input to an enterprise data model. There is little point in inventing a coding scheme if a perfectly good (and hopefully well-thought-out) one is accepted as an industry, national, or international standard, nor in rewriting definitions and inventing data names for entity classes and attributes.

A major payoff in using external standards is in facilitating electronic communication with business partners and external resources. The enterprise model can be the means by which the necessary standards are made available to development teams, with the data management team taking responsibility for ascertaining which standards are most appropriate for use by the business.

17.11 Choice, Creativity, and Enterprise Data Models

Enterprise data models can be a powerful means of promulgating innovative concepts and data structures. Equally, they can inhibit original thought by presenting each new project with a *fait accompli* as far as the overall structure of its model is concerned. In our experience, both situations are common and frequently occur together in the one organization.

With their access to the "big picture" and strong data modeling skills, an enterprise data modeling team is in a good position to propose and evaluate creative approaches. They are more likely than a conventional application project team to have the necessary access to senior management to win support for new ideas. Through the data management process, they have the means to at least encourage development teams to adopt them. Some of the most significant examples of business benefits arising from creative modeling have been achieved in this way.

On the other hand, an enterprise data model may enshrine poor or outdated design and inhibit innovation at the project level. There needs to be a means by which the enterprise model can be improved by ideas generated by systems developers, and at least some scope for breaking out of the enterprise data modeling framework at the project level. Too often, a lack of provision for changing the enterprise data model in response to ideas from project teams has led to the demise of data management as the model ages.

It is vital that both systems developers and enterprise modelers clearly understand the choice factor in modeling and recognize that:

- If the project model meets the user requirements but differs from the enterprise model, the enterprise model is not necessarily wrong.
- If the enterprise model meets business requirements but the project model differs, it too is not necessarily wrong.

Indeed, both models may be "right," but in the interests of data management we may need to agree on a common model, ideally one that incorporates the best of both.

A genuine understanding of these very basic ideas will overcome many of the problems that occur between enterprise modelers and project teams and provide a basis for workable data management standards and procedures.

17.12 **Summary**

Enterprise data models cover the data requirements of complete enterprises or major business units. They are generally used for data planning and coordination rather than as specifications for database design.

An enterprise data model should be developed within the context of a data management strategy. Data management is the management of data as an enterprise resource, typically involving central control over its organization and documentation and encouraging data sharing across applications.

An enterprise data model can be mapped against existing data and thereafter used as an index to access it. It may also serve as a starting point for detailed project-level data modeling, incorporating ideas from senior business people and experienced data modelers.

Development of an enterprise data model requires good business skills as well as modeling expertise. If the task is partitioned, it should be divided by data supertype rather than functional area.

While enterprise data models can be powerful vehicles for promulgating new ideas, they may also stifle original thinking by requiring conformity.

Further Reading

Chapter 1

Virtually every textbook on data modeling or database design offers an overview of the data modeling process. However, data modeling is seldom presented as a design activity, and issues of choice and quality criteria are, therefore, not covered.

If you are interested in reading further on the question of choice in data modeling, we would recommend a general book on category theory first:

Lakoff, G.: *Women, Fire and Dangerous Things: What Categories Reveal about the Mind*, University of Chicago Press (1987). The first part of the book is the more relevant.

William Kent's 1978 book *Data and Reality* is a classic in the field, lucidly written, covering some of the basic issues of data representation in a style accessible and relevant to practitioners. A new edition appeared in 2000: Kent, W.: *Data and Reality*, 1st Books Library (2000).

The literature on data modeling and choice is largely written from a philosophical perspective. The following paper is a good starting point:

Klein, H., and Hirschheim, R.A. (1987): A comparative framework, of data modelling paradigms and approaches, *The Computer Journal*, *30*(1): 8–15.

If your appetite for the philosophical foundations of data modeling has been whetted, we would suggest the following book and papers as a starting point, recognizing that you are now heading firmly into academic territory.

Hirschheim, Klein, and Lyytinen: *Information Systems Development and Data Modeling: Conceptual and Philosophical Foundations*, Cambridge University Press, Cambridge (1995).

Weber, R.: The Link between Data Modeling Approaches and Philosophical Assumptions: A Critique, *Proceedings of the Association of Information Systems Conference*, Indianapolis (1997) 306–308.

Milton, S., Kazmierczak, E., and Keen, C. (1998): Comparing Data Modelling Frameworks Using Chisholm's Ontology, *6th European Conference on Information Systems*, pp. 260–272, "Euro-Arab Management School, Granada, Spain, Aix-en-Provence, France.

A number of papers, particularly by our former colleagues Graeme Shanks and Daniel Moody, have looked at data model quality. As a starting point, we would suggest:

Moody, D., and Shanks, G. (1998): What makes a good data model? A framework for evaluating and improving the quality of entity relationship models, *The Australian Computer Journal, 30*(3): 97–110.

Chapter 2

Most textbooks on data modeling cover basic normalization, and you may find that a different presentation of the material will reinforce your understanding. Beyond that, the logical next step is to read Chapter 13 in this book and then refer to the suggestions for further reading in connection with that chapter.

More broadly, in Chapter 2 we have worked with the Relational Model for data representation. This originated with Edgar (Ted) Codd, and his writings, and those of his colleague Chris Date, are the seminal references on the Relational Model. Codd's original paper was "A relational model of data for large shared data banks," *Communications of the ACM* (June, 1970).

For a comprehensive treatment of the relational model, we strongly recommend:

Date, C.J.: *Fundamentals of Database Systems,* 8th Edition, Pearson Addison Wesley (2003).

This book also provides an excellent background for working with RDBMSs—and with physical database designers.

Chapter 3

Most data modeling textbooks cover E-R modeling conventions, usually in less detail than we do in Chapters 3 and 4. At this point, the next logical step is to learn about using them in practice to model real business situations, the subject of Chapter 10.

It would also make sense to familiarize yourself with the conventions supported by your CASE tool or in your place of work. This is particularly relevant if you are using UML or other alternative notation. We provide an overview of the most common alternatives in Chapter 7.

A good CASE-tool-oriented reference is Barker's *CASE Method: Entity Relationship Modelling,* Addison Wesley (1990). There is much excellent advice here even if you are not using the Oracle CASE method or tool.

Chapter 7

The starting point for the Chen approach is the original paper, "The entity-relationship approach: Towards a unified view of data," *ACM Transactions on Database Systems*, Vol. 1, No. 1, March 1976. For more detail, we suggest:

Batini, Ceri, and Navathe, *Conceptual Database Design—An Entity-Relationship Approach,* Addison Wesley (1992).

There is now an extensive body of literature on UML. The logical starting point is the original specification: Rumbaugh, Jacobson, and Booch: *The Unified Modeling Language Reference Manual*, Addison Wesley (1998).

The definitive reference for Object Role Modeling is Halpin, T: *Information Modeling and Relational Database: From Conceptual Analysis to Logical Design*, 3rd Edition, Morgan Kaufmann (2001). See also *www.orm.net*

Chapter 8

If your organization recommends or prescribes a particular methodology, then the documentation of that methodology is your logical next port of call.

If you are interested in how data modeling fits into a broader range of methodologies than we discuss here, the definitive reference is:

Avison, D. and Fitzgerald, G.: *Information Systems Development: Methodologies, Techniques and Tools,* 3rd edition, Maidenhead, McGraw-Hill (2003).

Chapter 9

For a comprehensive coverage of requirements analysis and much else, Hay, D.C.: *Requirements Analysis—From Business Views to Architecture*, Prentice-Hall, New Jersey (2003).

Chapter 10

If you are interested in design in general, a good starting point is:

Lawson, B.: *How Designers Think*, 3rd Edition, Architectural Press, Oxford, UK (1997).

Two books of data modeling patterns should be owned by every professional data modeler:

Hay, D.C.: *Data Model Patterns: Conventions of Thought*, Dorset House (1995).

Silverston, L.: *The Data Model Resource Book—A Library of Universal Models for all Enterprises,* Volumes 1 and 2, John Wiley & Sons (2001).

The assertions approach has much in common with the Business Rules Approach advocated by the Business Rules Group's first paper,[1] which

---

[1]*Defining Business Rules ~ What Are They Really?* available at *www.businessrulesgroup.org*.

categorizes Business Rules as Structural Assertions (Terms and Facts), Action Assertions (Constraints), and Derivations.

The assertion forms that we have suggested here are nearly all Facts, with those we have labeled as Constraints corresponding to the Business Rules Group definition of Constraint and those we have labeled as Attribute Assertions corresponding to the Business Rule Group definition of Derivation when used as suggested for derived attributes.

A set of Action Assertion templates, known as RuleSpeak™, is available from Ronald Ross of the Business Rules Group at *http://www.brsolutions.com/rulespeak_download.shtml*. The approach is described in more detail in:

Ross, R.: *Principles of the Business Rule Approach,* Addison Wesley (2003).

Chapter 12

As suggested throughout this chapter, the next logical step in improving your ability to contribute to physical data modeling is to become familiar with the DBMS(s) that your organization uses. Your source may be the official manual or one of the many third-party books covering specific products. Just be careful that your reading material reflects the version of the software that you are using.

We would also recommend:

Shasha, D., and Bonnet, P.: *Database Tuning—Principles, Experiments and Troubleshooting Techniques,* Morgan Kaufmann (2003).

A feature of this book is a number of "experiments" or benchmarks that show the real (as distinct from folkloric) improvements that are obtained from various design decisions.

Chapter 13

Normalization is one of the most widely covered areas of data modeling theory, and you will have little trouble finding texts and papers covering the higher normal forms with far more theoretical detail than presented here. However, unless you have a strong background in mathematics, you are likely to find many of them very hard going and, perhaps, not worth the considerable effort required. (Conversely, if you *can* manage the mathematics, we would encourage you to take advantage of the opportunity to leverage your mathematical knowledge to strengthen your modeling skills.)

Kent, W.: "A Simple Guide to the Five Normal Forms of Relational Database Theory," *Communications of the ACM* (February 1983) is a very readable paper at a similar level to this chapter.

Chris Date is one of the most lucid and insightful writers on the technicalities of relational data organization and the Relational Model in general.

In addition to his classic *Fundamentals of Database Systems* (8th Edition, Pearson Addison Wesley 2003), we would recommend the "Selected Writings" series—in particular, the earlier books—for articles covering a variety of important topics.

Most authors stick strictly with the relational notation and do not offer a lot of context. For example, 4NF and 5NF problems usually show only one table to start with; this is technically adequate, but it can be hard coming to grips with the problem unless you imagine the columns as foreign keys to "context" tables. If you have trouble following such examples, you are not alone! We suggest you draw a data structure diagram of the problem and add extra reference tables as we did in our 4NF and 5NF examples to show context.

Chapter 15

The time dimension has been the subject of a number of papers. Many of them propose extensions to DBMSs to better support time-related data. From a practitioner's perspective, they may make interesting reading but are of limited value unless the suggestions have been incorporated in the DBMSs available to them.

Chris Date, Hugh Darwen, and Nikos Lorentzos's book *Temporal Data and the Relational Model* (Morgan Kaufmann, 2003) is perhaps the most up-to-date and erudite publication on the topics in this chapter, particularly temporal business rules. Date has summarized these issues in the 8th edition of his *Introduction to Database Systems.*

Chapter 16

As mentioned earlier, there is a substantial body of literature on the design of data warehouses and marts. William Inmon and Ralph Kimball have been key contributors to the practitioner-oriented literature and offer markedly different views on architecture in particular. We suggest you look for the most recent and relevant publications from both authors.

For an introductory book on the related subject of data mining, we suggest:

Delmater and Hancock: *Data Mining Explained*, Digital Press (2001).

Chapter 17

A useful starting point is *Guidelines to Implementing Data Resource Management, 4th Edition*, Data Management Association, 2002.

Index

Two Scoops of Django

Best Practices For Django 1.6

Daniel Greenfeld
Audrey Roy

Two Scoops of Django: Best Practices for Django 1.6
Second Edition, 20140124

by Daniel Greenfeld and Audrey Roy

First Printing, January 2014

For more information, visit `https://twoscoopspress.com`.

For Malcolm Tredinnick
1971-2013
We miss you.

http://2scoops.co/malcolm-tredinnick-memorial

Contents

List of Figures

List of Tables

Authors' Notes

About the Dedication

Malcolm Tredinnick wasn't just a Django core developer and reviewer of "Two Scoops of Django: Best Practices for Django 1.5." To us, he was much, much more.

Daniel had worked with Malcolm Tredinnick in the summer of 2010, but we first met him in person at DjangoCon 2010. He was funny and charming, sharply opinionated but always a gentleman; we instantly became close friends.

In 2012, when we co-organized the first PyCon Philippines, as soon as we told him about it, Malcolm instantly declared he was coming. He gave two memorable talks and ran an impromptu all-day Django tutorial. He also pushed and encouraged the local community to work on Filipino language translations for Django, including Tagalog, Tausug, Cebuano, and more.

After the conference, we started working on a book about Django best practices. We gathered friends and colleagues to help us as technical reviewers. Malcolm Tredinnick became the most active of them. He was our mentor and forced us to dig deeper and work harder. He did this while working a day job as the leader of a combined Rails and Haskell team; Malcolm was a true programming language polyglot.

For our book, he provided so much assistance and guidance we tried to figure out a way to include him in the author credits. When we told him about our dilemma, he laughed it off saying, "For a book called 'Two Scoops', you can't have three authors." We suggested he share credit with us on a second book, and he refused, saying he preferred to just comment on our work. He said that he wanted people to have proper references, and for him, simply reviewing our work was contributing to the greater good. Eventually the two of us quietly planned to somehow coerce him into being a co-author on a future work.

After months of effort, we released the first iteration on January 17th, 2013. Malcolm stepped back from Two Scoops of Django, but we stayed in touch. Since Malcolm was unable to attend PyCon US 2013 we weren't sure when we would meet him again.

Two months later, on March 17th, 2013, Malcolm passed away.

We knew Malcolm for less than three years and yet he made an incredible difference in our lives. We've heard many similar stories in the community about Malcolm; He was a friend and mentor to countless others around the world. His last lesson to us went beyond code or writing, he taught us to never take for granted friends, family, mentors, and teachers.

A Few Words From Daniel Greenfeld

In the spring of 2006, I was working for NASA on a project that implemented a Java-based RESTful web service that was taking weeks to deliver. One evening, when management had left for the day, I reimplemented the service in Python in 90 minutes.

I knew then that I wanted to work with Python.

I wanted to use Django for the web front-end of the web service, but management insisted on using a closed-source stack because "Django is only at version 0.9x, hence not ready for real projects." I disagreed, but stayed happy with the realization that at least the core architecture was in Python. Django used to be edgy during those heady days, and it scared people the same way that Node.js scares people today.

Nearly eight years later, Django is considered a mature, powerful, secure, stable framework used by incredibly successful corporations (Instagram, Pinterest, Mozilla, etc.) and government agencies (NASA, et al) all over the world. Convincing management to use Django isn't hard anymore, and if it is hard to convince them, finding jobs which let you use Django has become much easier.

In my 7+ years of building Django projects, I've learned how to launch new web applications with incredible speed while keeping technical debt to an absolute minimum.

My goal in this book is to share with you what I've learned. My knowledge and experience have been gathered from advice given by core developers, mistakes I've made, successes shared with others, and an enormous amount of note taking. I'm going to admit that the book is opinionated, but many of the leaders in the Django community use the same or similar techniques.

This book is for you, the developers. I hope you enjoy it!

A Few Words From Audrey Roy

I first discovered Python in a graduate class at MIT in 2005. In less than 4 weeks of homework assignments, each student built a voice-controlled system for navigating between rooms in MIT's Stata Center, running on our HP iPaqs running Debian. I was in awe of Python and wondered why it wasn't used for everything. I tried building a web application with Zope but struggled with it.

A couple of years passed, and I got drawn into the Silicon Valley tech startup scene. I wrote graphics libraries in C and desktop applications in C++ for a startup. At some point, I left that job and picked up painting and sculpture. Soon I was drawing and painting frantically for art shows, co-directing a 140-person art show, and managing a series of real estate renovations. I realized that I was doing a lot at once and had to optimize. Naturally, I turned to Python and began writing scripts to generate some of my artwork. That was when I rediscovered the joy of working with Python.

Many friends from the Google App Engine, SuperHappyDevHouse, and hackathon scenes in Silicon Valley inspired me to get into Django. Through them and through various freelance projects and partnerships I discovered how powerful Django was.

Before I knew it, I was attending PyCon 2010, where I met my husband Daniel Greenfeld. We met at the end of James Bennett's "Django In Depth" tutorial, and now this chapter in our lives has come full circle with the publication of this book.

Django has brought more joy to my life than I thought was possible with a web framework. My goal with this book is to give you the thoughtful guidance on common Django development practices that are normally left unwritten (or implied), so that you can get past common hurdles and experience the joy of using the Django web framework for your projects.

Introduction

Our aim in writing this book is to write down all of the unwritten tips, tricks, and common practices that we've learned over the years while working with Django.

While writing, we've thought of ourselves as scribes, taking the various things that people assume are common knowledge and recording them with simple examples.

A Word About Our Recommendations

Like the official Django documentation, this book covers how to do things in Django, illustrating various scenarios with code examples.

Unlike the Django documentation, this book recommends particular coding styles, patterns, and library choices. While core Django developers may agree with some or many of these choices, keep in mind that many of our recommendations are just that: personal recommendations formed after years of working with Django.

Throughout this book, we advocate certain practices and techniques that we consider to be the best approaches. We also express our own personal preferences for particular tools and libraries.

Sometimes we reject common practices that we consider to be anti-patterns. For most things we reject, we try to be polite and respectful of the hard work of the authors. There are the rare, few things that we may not be so polite about. This is in the interest of helping you avoid dangerous pitfalls.

We have made every effort to give thoughtful recommendations and to make sure that our practices are sound. We've subjected ourselves to harsh, nerve-wracking critiques from Django and

Python core developers whom we greatly respect. We've had this book reviewed by more technical reviewers than the average technical book, and we've poured countless hours into revisions. That being said, there is always the possibility of errors or omissions. There is also the possibility that better practices may emerge than those described here.

We are fully committed to iterating on and improving this book, and we mean it. If you see any practices that you disagree with or anything that can be done better, we humbly ask that you send us your suggestions for improvements.

Please don't hesitate to tell us what can be improved. We will take your feedback constructively. Errata will be published at `http://www.2scoops.co/1.6-errata/`.

Why Two Scoops of Django?

Like most people, we, the authors of this book, love ice cream. Every Saturday night we throw caution to the wind and indulge in ice cream. Don't tell anyone, but sometimes we even have some when it's not Saturday night!

Figure 1: Throwing caution to the wind.

We like to try new flavors and discuss their merits against our old favorites. Tracking our progress through all these flavors, and possibly building a club around it, makes for a great sample Django project.

When we do find a flavor we really like, the new flavor brings a smile to our face, just like when we find great tidbits of code or advice in a technical book. One of our goals for this book is to write the kind of technical book that brings the ice cream smile to readers.

Best of all, using ice cream analogies has allowed us to come up with more vivid code examples. We've had a lot of fun writing this book. You may see us go overboard with ice cream silliness here and there; please forgive us.

Before You Begin

If you are new to Django, this book will be helpful large parts will be challenging for you. This book is not a tutorial. To use this book to its fullest extent, you should have an understanding of the Python programming language and have at least gone through the 6 page Django tutorial: `https://docs.djangoproject.com/en/1.6/intro/tutorial01/`. Experience with object-oriented programming is also very useful.

This Book Is Intended for Django 1.6 and Python 2.7.x/3.3.x

This book should work well with the Django 1.6 series, less so with Django 1.5, and so on. Even though we make no promises about functional compatibility, at least the general approaches from most of this book stand up over every post-1.0 version of Django.

As for the Python version, this book is tested on Python 2.7.x and Python 3.3.x.

None of the content in this book, including our practices, the code examples, and the libraries referenced applies to Google App Engine (GAE). If you try to use this book as a reference for GAE development, you may run into problems.

Each Chapter Stands on Its Own

Unlike tutorial and walkthrough books where each chapter builds upon the previous chapter's project, we've written this book in a way that each chapter intentionally stands by itself.

We've done this in order to make it easy for you to reference chapters about specific topics when needed while you're working on a project.

The examples in each chapter are completely independent. They aren't intended to be combined into one project, and are not a tutorial. Consider them useful, isolated snippets that illustrate and help with various coding scenarios.

Conventions Used in This Book

Code blocks like the following are used throughout the book:

```
EXAMPLE 0.1

class Scoop(object):
    def __init__(self):
        self._is_yummy = True
```

To keep these snippets compact, we sometimes violate the PEP 8 conventions on comments and line spacing. Code samples are available online at http://2scoops.co/1.6-code.

Special "Don't Do This!" code blocks like the following indicate examples of bad code that you should avoid:

```
BAD EXAMPLE 0.1

# DON'T DO THIS!
from rotten_ice_cream import something_bad
```

We use the following typographical conventions throughout the book:

- ➤ Constant width for code fragments or commands.
- ➤ *Italic* for filenames.
- ➤ **Bold** when introducing a new term or important word.

Boxes containing notes, warnings, tips, and little anecdotes are also used in this book:

> ## TIP: Something You Should Know
>
> Tip boxes give handy advice.

> ### WARNING: Some Dangerous Pitfall
> Warning boxes help you avoid common mistakes and pitfalls.

> ### PACKAGE TIP: Some Useful Django Package Recommendation
>
> Indicates notes about useful third-party packages related to the current chapter, and general notes about using various Django packages.
>
> We also provide a complete list of packages recommended throughout the book in Appendix A: *Packages Mentioned In This Book*.

We also use tables to summarize information in a handy, concise way:

	Daniel Greenfeld	Audrey Roy
Can be fed coconut ice cream	No	Yes
Favorite ice cream flavors of the moment	Cappuccino Fudge, and anything with white chocolate	Pink Peppermint, Chocolate Hazelnut

Authors' Ice Cream Preferences

Core Concepts

When we build Django projects, we keep the following concepts in mind.

Keep It Simple, Stupid

Kelly Johnson, one of the most renowned and prolific aircraft design engineers in the history of aviation, said it this way about 50 years ago. Centuries earlier, Leonardo da Vinci meant the same thing when he said "Simplicity is the ultimate sophistication."

When building software projects, each piece of unnecessary complexity makes it harder to add new features and maintain old ones. Attempt the simplest solution, but take care not to implement overly simplistic solutions that make bad assumptions. This concept is sometimes abbreviated as 'KISS'.

Fat Models, Helper Modules, Thin Views, Stupid Templates

When deciding where to put a piece of code, we like to follow the "Fat Models, Helper Modules, Thin Views, Stupid Templates" approach.

We recommend that you err on the side of putting more logic into anything but views and templates. The results are pleasing. The code becomes clearer, more self-documenting, less duplicated, and a lot more reusable.

As for template tags and filters, they should contain the least amount of logic possible to function. We cover this further in chapter 13, *Template Tags and Filters*.

Start With Django by Default

Before we consider switching out core Django components for things like alternative template engines, different ORMs, or non-relational databases, we first try an implementation using standard Django components. If we run into obstacles, we explore all possibilities before replacing core Django components.

See chapter 16, *Tradeoffs of Replacing Core Components* for more details.

Be Familiar with Django's Design Philosophies

It is good to periodically read the documentation on Django's design philosophy because it helps us understand why Django provides certain constraints and tools. Like any framework, Django is more than just a tool for providing views, it's a way of doing things designed to help us put together maintainable projects in a reasonable amount of time.

https://docs.djangoproject.com/en/1.6/misc/design-philosophies/

The Twelve Factor App

A comprehensive approach to web-based application design, the *Twelve Factor Approach* is growing in popularity amongst many senior and core Django developers. It is a methodology for building deployable, scalable applications worth reading and understanding. Parts of it closely match the practices espoused in Two Scoops of Django, and we like to think of it as suggested reading for any web-based application developer.

See http://12factor.net

Our Writing Concepts

When we wrote this book, we wanted to provide to the reader and ourselves the absolute best material possible. To do that, we following the following concepts:

Provide the Best Material

We've done our absolute best to provide the best material possible, going to the known resources on every topic covered to vet our material. We weren't afraid to ask questions! Then we distilled the articles, responses and advice of experts into the content that exists in the book today. When that didn't suffice, we come up with our own solutions and then vetted them with various subject matter experts. It has been a lot of work, and we hope you are pleased with the results.

If you are curious about the differences between this edition (Django 1.6) and the previous edition (Django 1.5) of the book, you can find the short-list of changes at:

> ➤ http://2scoops.co/1.6-change-list

Stand on the Shoulders of Giants

While we take credit and responsibility for our work, we certainly did not come up all with the practices described in this book on our own.

Without all of the talented, creative, and generous developers who make up the Django, Python, and general open-source software communities, this book would not exist. We strongly believe in recognizing the people who have served as our teachers and mentors as well as our sources for information, and we've tried our best to give credit whenever credit is due.

Listen to Our Readers and Reviewers

In the previous edition of this book, we received a huge amount of feedback from a veritable legion of readers and reviewers. This allowed us to greatly improve the quality of the book. It is now at a level that we hoped for but never expected to achieve.

In return, we've shared credit at the back of the book and are continually working on ways to pay it forward by improving the lives of developers around the world.

If you have any questions, comments, or other feedback about this edition, please share your input by submitting issues in our issue tracker, at:

➤ `https://github.com/twoscoops/two-scoops-of-django-1.6/issues`

Also, at the end of the book is a link to leave a review for Two Scoops of Django on Amazon. Doing this will help others make an informed decision about whether this book is right for them.

Publish Errata

Nothing is perfect, even after extensive review cycles. We will be publishing errata at:

➤ `http://2scoops.co/1.6-errata`

1 | Coding Style

A little attention to following standard coding style guidelines will go a long way. We highly recommend that you read this chapter, even though you may be tempted to skip it.

1.1   The Importance of Making Your Code Readable

Code is read more than it is written. An individual block of code takes moments to write, minutes or hours to debug, and can last forever without being touched again. It's when you or someone else visits code written yesterday or ten years ago that having code written in a clear, consistent style becomes extremely useful. Understandable code frees mental bandwidth from having to puzzle out inconsistencies, making it easier to maintain and enhance projects of all sizes.

What this means is that you should go the extra mile to make your code as readable as possible:

- Avoid abbreviating variable names.
- Write out your function argument names.
- Document your classes and methods.
- Refactor repeated lines of code into reusable functions or methods.
- Keep functions and methods short. A good rule of thumb is scrolling should not be necessary to read an entire function or method.

When you come back to your code after time away from it, you'll have an easier time picking up where you left off.

Take those pesky abbreviated variable names, for example. When you see a variable called `balance_sheet_decrease`, it's much easier to interpret in your mind than an abbreviated variable like `bsd` or `bal_s_d`. These types of shortcuts may save a few seconds of typing, but that savings comes at the expense of hours or days of technical debt. It's not worth it.

1.2   PEP 8

PEP 8 is the official style guide for Python. We advise reading it in detail and learn to follow the PEP 8 coding conventions: http://www.python.org/dev/peps/pep-0008/

PEP 8 describes coding conventions such as:

- ➤ "Use 4 spaces per indentation level."
- ➤ "Separate top-level function and class definitions with two blank lines."
- ➤ "Method definitions inside a class are separated by a single blank line."

All the Python files in your Django projects should follow PEP 8. If you have trouble remembering the PEP 8 guidelines, find a plugin for your code editor that checks your code as you type.

When an experienced Python developer sees gross violations of PEP 8 in a Django project, even if they don't say something mean, they are probably thinking bad things. Trust us on this one.

WARNING: Don't Change an Existing Project's Conventions

The style of PEP 8 applies to new Django projects only. If you are brought into an existing Django project that follows a different convention than PEP 8, then follow the existing conventions.

Please read the "A Foolish Consistency is the Hobgoblin of Little Minds" section of PEP 8 for details about this and other reasons to break the rules:

- ➤ http://2scoops.co/hobgoblin-of-little-minds

PACKAGE TIP: Use flake8 For Checking Code Quality

Created and maintained by noted Python developer Tarek Ziadé, this is a very useful command-line tool for checking code quality in projects.

1.2.1   The 79 Character Limit

According to PEP 8, the limit of text per line is 79 characters. This exists because it's a safe value that most text-wrapping editors and developer teams can accommodate without hurting the understandability of code.

However, PEP 8 also has a provision for relaxing this limit to 99 characters for exclusive team projects. We interpret this to mean projects that are not open source.

Our preference is as follows:

➤ On open-source projects, there should be a hard 79 character limit. Our experience has shown that contributors or visitors to these projects will grumble about line length issues.
➤ On private projects, we relax the limit to 99 characters, taking full advantage of modern monitors.

Please read `http://www.python.org/dev/peps/pep-0008/#maximum-line-length`.

TIP: Aymeric Augustin on Line Length Issues

Django core developer Aymeric Augustin says, "Fitting the code in 79 columns is never a good reason to pick worse names for variables, functions, and classes. It's much more important to have readable variable names than to fit in an arbitrary limit of hardware from three decades ago."

1.3   The Word on Imports

PEP 8 suggests that imports should be grouped in the following order:

❶ Standard library imports
❷ Related third-party imports
❸ Local application or library specific imports

When we're working on a Django project, our imports look something like the following:

EXAMPLE 1.1
```
# Stdlib imports
from __future__ import absolute_import
from math import sqrt
from os.path import abspath
```

```
# Core Django imports
from django.db import models
from django.utils.translation import ugettext_lazy as _

# Third-party app imports
from django_extensions.db.models import TimeStampedModel

# Imports from your apps
from splits.models import BananaSplit
```

(Note: you don't actually need to comment your imports like this. The comments are just here to explain the example.)

The import order here is:

❶ Standard library imports.
❷ Imports from core Django.
❸ Imports from third-party apps including those unrelated to Django.
❹ Imports from the apps that you created as part of your Django project. (You'll read more about apps in chapter 4, *Fundamentals of App Design*.)

1.4   Use Explicit Relative Imports

When writing code, it's important to do so in such a way that it's easier to move, rename, and version your work. In Python, explicit relative imports remove the need for hardcoding a module's package, separating individual modules from being tightly coupled to the architecture around them. Since Django apps are simply Python packages, the same rules apply.

To illustrate the benefits of explicit relative imports, let's explore an example.

Imagine that the following snippet is from a Django project that you created to track your ice cream consumption, including all of the waffle/sugar/cake cones that you have ever eaten.

Oh no, your cones app contains hardcoded imports, which are bad!

```
BAD EXAMPLE 1.1
# cones/views.py
from django.views.generic import CreateView

# DON'T DO THIS!
# Hardcoding of the 'cones' package
# with implicit relative imports
from cones.models import WaffleCone
from cones.forms import WaffleConeForm
from core.views import FoodMixin

class WaffleConeCreateView(FoodMixin, CreateView):
    model = WaffleCone
    form_class = WaffleConeForm
```

Sure, your cones app works fine within your ice cream tracker project, but it has those nasty hardcoded imports that make it less portable and reusable:

➤ What if you wanted to reuse your cones app in another project that tracks your general dessert consumption, but you had to change the name due to a naming conflict (e.g. a conflict with a Django app for snow cones)?

➤ What if you simply wanted to change the name of the app at some point?

With hardcoded imports, you can't just change the name of the app; you have to dig through all of the imports and change them as well. It's not hard to change them manually, but before you dismiss the need for explicit relative imports, keep in mind that the above example is extremely simple compared to a real app with various additional helper modules.

Let's now convert the bad code snippet containing hardcoded imports into a good one containing explicit relative imports. Here's the corrected example:

```
EXAMPLE 1.2
# cones/views.py
from __future__ import absolute_import
from django.views.generic import CreateView
```

```
# Relative imports of the 'cones' package
from .models import WaffleCone
from .forms import WaffleConeForm
from core.views import FoodMixin


class WaffleConeCreateView(FoodMixin, CreateView):
    model = WaffleCone
    form_class = WaffleConeForm
```

Another concrete advantage is that we can immediately tell our local/internal imports from global/external imports, highlighting the Python package as a unit of code.

TIP: Use "from __future__ import absolute_import"

Python 3 updates and improves how imports work, and in a good way. Fortunately, it's been back-ported to Python 2.7 via the use of the from __future__ import abso-lute_import statement. Even if you don't plan to use Python 3, this is a great feature and allows for the *explicit relative* imports demonstrated in the table below.

To summarize, here's a table of the different Python import types and when to use them in Django projects:

Code	Import Type	Usage
`from core.views import FoodMixin`	absolute import	Use when importing from outside the current app
`from .models import WaffleCone`	explicit relative	Use when importing from another module in the current app
`from models import WaffleCone`	implicit relative	Often used when importing from another module in the current app, but not a good idea

Table 1.1: Imports: Absolute vs. Explicit Relative vs. Implicit Relative

Get into the habit of using explicit relative imports. It's very easy to do, and using explicit relative imports is a good habit for any Python programmer to develop.

> ### TIP: Doesn't PEP 328 Clash with PEP 8?
>
> See what Guido Van Rossum, BDFL of Python says about it:
> - http://2scoops.co/guido-on-pep-8-vs-pep-328

Additional reading: http://www.python.org/dev/peps/pep-0328/

1.5 Avoid Using Import *

In 99% of all our work, we explicitly import each module:

EXAMPLE 1.3

```python
from django import forms
from django.db import models
```

Never do the following:

BAD EXAMPLE 1.2

```python
# ANTI-PATTERN: Don't do this!
from django.forms import *
from django.db.models import *
```

The reason for this is to avoid implicitly loading all of another Python module's locals into and over our current module's namespace, which can produce unpredictable and sometimes catastrophic results.

We do cover a specific exception to this rule in chapter 5, *Settings and Requirements Files*.

Let's look at the bad code example above. Both the Django forms and Django models libraries have a class called CharField. By implicitly loading both libraries, the models library overwrote the forms version of the class. This can also happen with Python built-in libraries and other third-party libraries overwriting critical functionality.

WARNING: Python Naming Collisions

You'll run into similar problems if you try to import two things with the same name, such as:

```
BAD EXAMPLE 1.3

# ANTI-PATTERN: Don't do this!
from django.forms import CharField
from django.db.models import CharField
```

Using import * is like being that greedy customer at an ice cream shop who asks for a free taster spoon of all thirty-one flavors, but who only purchases one or two scoops. Don't import everything if you're only going to use one or two things.

If the customer then walked out with a giant ice cream bowl containing a scoop of every or almost every flavor, though, it would be a different matter.

Figure 1.1: Using import * in an ice cream shop.

1.6 Django Coding Style Guidelines

It goes without saying that it's a good idea to be aware of common Django style conventions. In fact, internally Django has its own set of style guidelines that extend PEP 8:

> ➤ http://2scoops.co/1.6-coding-style

While the following are not specified in the official standards, you may want to follow them in your projects:

> ➤ Use underscores (the '_' character) in URL pattern names rather than dashes as this is friendlier to more IDEs and text editors. Note that we are referring to the name argument of `url()` here, not the actual URL typed into the browser. Dashes in actual URLs are fine.
> ➤ For the same reason, use underscores rather than dashes in template block names.

1.7 Never Code to the IDE (or Text Editor)

There are developers who make decisions about the layout and implementation of their project based on the features of IDEs (Integrated Development Environment). This can make discovery of project code extremely difficult for anyone whose choice of development tool doesn't match the original author.

Always assume that the developers around you like to use their own tools and that your code and project layout should be transparent enough that someone stuck using Notepad or Nano will be able to navigate your work.

For example, introspecting **template tags** or discovering their source can be difficult and time consuming for developers not using a very, very limited pool of IDEs. Therefore, we follow the commonly-used naming pattern of `<app_name>_tags.py`.

1.8 Summary

This chapter covered our preferred coding style and explained why we prefer each technique.

Even if you don't follow the coding style that we use, please follow a consistent coding style. Projects with varying styles are much harder to maintain, slowing development and increasing the chances of developer mistakes.

2 | The Optimal Django Environment Setup

This chapter describes what we consider the best local environment setup for intermediate and advanced developers working with Django.

2.1 Use the Same Database Engine Everywhere

A common developer pitfall is using **SQLite3** for local development and **PostgreSQL** (or another database besides SQLite3) in production. This section applies not only to the SQLite3/PostgreSQL scenario, but to any scenario where you're using two different databases and expecting them to behave identically.

Here are some of the issues we've encountered with using different database engines for development and production:

2.1.1 Fixtures Are Not a Magic Solution

You may be wondering why you can't simply use **fixtures** to abstract away the differences between your local and production databases.

Well, fixtures are great for creating simple hardcoded test data sets. Sometimes you need to prepopulate your databases with fake test data during development, particularly during the early stages of a project.

Fixtures are not a reliable tool for migrating large data sets from one database to another in a database-agnostic way. They are simply not meant to be used that way. Don't mistake the ability of fixtures to create basic data (dumpdata/loaddata) with the capability to migrate production data between database tools.

2.1.2   You Can't Examine an Exact Copy of Production Data Locally

When your production database is different from your local development database, you can't grab an exact copy of your production database to examine data locally.

Sure, you can generate a SQL dump from production and import it into your local database, but that doesn't mean that you have an exact copy after the export and import.

2.1.3   Different Databases Have Different Field Types/Constraints

Keep in mind that different databases handle typing of field data differently. Django's ORM attempts to accommodate those differences, but there's only so much that it can do.

For example, some people use SQLite3 for local development and PostgreSQL in production, thinking that the Django ORM gives them the excuse not to think about the differences. Eventually they run into problems, since SQLite3 has dynamic, weak typing instead of strong typing.

Yes, the Django ORM has features that allow your code to interact with SQLite3 in a more strongly typed manner, but form and model validation mistakes in development will go uncaught (even in tests) until the code goes to a production server. You may be saving long strings locally without a hitch, for example, since SQLite3 won't care. But then in production, your PostgreSQL or **MySQL** database will throw constraint errors that you've never seen locally, and you'll have a hard time replicating the issues until you set up an identical database locally.

Most problems usually can't be discovered until the project is run on a strongly typed database (e.g. PostgreSQL or MySQL). When these types of bugs hit, you end up kicking yourself and scrambling to set up your local development machine with the right database.

TIP: Django+PostgreSQL Rocks

Most Django developers that we know prefer to use PostgreSQL for all environments: development, staging, QA, and production systems.

Depending on your operating system, use these instructions:

> ➤ Mac: Download the one-click Mac installer at http://postgresapp.com
> ➤ Windows: Download the one-click Windows installer at
>   http://postgresql.org/download/windows/
> ➤ Linux: Install via your package manager, or follow the instructions at
>   http://postgresql.org/download/linux/

PostgreSQL may take some work to get running locally on some operating systems, but we find that it's well worth the effort.

2.2   Use Pip and Virtualenv

If you are not doing so already, we strongly urge you to familiarize yourself with both pip and virtualenv. They are the de facto standard for Django projects, and most companies that use Django rely on these tools.

Pip is a tool that fetches Python packages from the Python Package Index and its mirrors. It is used to manage and install Python packages. It's like easy_install but has more features, the key feature being support for virtualenv.

Virtualenv is a tool for creating isolated Python environments for maintaining package dependencies. It's great for situations where you're working on more than one project at a time, and where there are clashes between the version numbers of different libraries that your projects use.

For example, imagine that you're working on one project that requires Django 1.5 and another that requires Django 1.6.

> ➤ Without virtualenv (or an alternative tool to manage dependencies), you have to reinstall Django every time you switch projects.
> ➤ If that sounds tedious, keep in mind that most real Django projects have at least a dozen dependencies to maintain.

Pip is already included in Python 3.4 and higher. Further reading and installation instructions can be found at:

> ➤ pip: http://pip-installer.org
> ➤ virtualenv: http://virtualenv.org

TIP: virtualenvwrapper

For developers using Mac OS X or Linux, or those with advanced Windows skills and ample patience, we also highly recommend **virtualenvwrapper** by Doug Hellmann: http://virtualenvwrapper.readthedocs.org

Personally, we think virtualenv without virtualenvwrapper can be a pain to use, because every time you want to activate a virtual environment, you have to type something long like:

EXAMPLE 2.1

```
$ source ~/.virtualenvs/twoscoops/bin/activate
```

With virtualenvwrapper, you'd only have to type:

EXAMPLE 2.2

```
$ workon twoscoops
```

Virtualenvwrapper is a popular companion tool to pip and virtualenv and makes our lives easier, but it's not an absolute necessity.

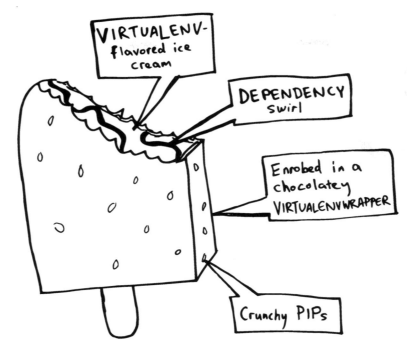

Figure 2.1: Pip, virtualenv, and virtualenvwrapper in ice cream bar form.

2.3 Install Django and Other Dependencies via Pip

The official Django documentation describes several ways of installing Django. Our recommended installation method is with pip and requirements files.

To summarize how this works: a requirements file is like a grocery list of Python packages that you want to install. It contains the name and desired version of each package. You use pip to install packages from this list into your virtual environment.

We cover the setup of and installation from requirements files in chapter 5, *Settings and Requirements Files.*

> **TIP: Setting PYTHONPATH**
>
> If you have a firm grasp of the command line and environment variables, you can set your virtualenv PYTHONPATH so that the *django-admin.py* command can be used to serve your site and perform other tasks. Some people have found that with the latest version of pip they can even do it with just running "`pip install -e .`".
>
> If you don't know how to set this or it seems complicated, don't worry about it and stick with *manage.py*.
>
> Additional reading:
> - ➤ `http://cs.simons-rock.edu/python/pythonpath.html`
> - ➤ `https://docs.djangoproject.com/en/1.6/ref/django-admin/`

2.4   Use a Version Control System

Version control systems are also known as revision control or source control. Whenever you work on any Django project, you should use a version control system to keep track of your code changes.

Wikipedia has a detailed comparison of different version control systems:

- ➤ `http://en.wikipedia.org/wiki/Comparison_of_revision_control_software`

Of all the options, **Git** and **Mercurial** seem to be the most popular among Django developers. Both Git and Mercurial make it easy to create branches and merge changes.

When using a version control system, it's important to not only have a local copy of your code repository, but also to use a code hosting service for backups. For this, we recommend that you use GitHub (`https://github.com/`) or Bitbucket (`https://bitbucket.org/`).

2.5   Consider Using Vagrant for Development Setup

Vagrant is a popular tool for creating, configuring, and managing reproducible development environments. The benefit of using it is that it makes working with virtualizations of operating systems via tools like **VirtualBox** much easier. For example, if our development laptops run OS X but a project's configuration is Ubuntu-specific, we can use Vagrant and the project's Vagrantfile to quickly get a virtual Ubuntu development environment set up locally, complete with all the packages and setup configurations needed for the project.

We go a little more into Vagrant in chapter 29, *Identical Environments: The Holy Grail.*

2.6 Summary

This chapter covered using the same database in development as in production, pip, virtualenv, and version control systems. These are good to have in your tool chest, since they are commonly used not just in Django, but in the majority of Python software development.

3 | How to Lay Out Django Projects

Project layout is one of those areas where core Django developers have differing opinions about what they consider best practice. In this chapter, we present our approach, which is one of the most commonly-used ones.

PACKAGE TIP: Django Project Templates

There are a number of project templates that really kickstart a Django project and follow the patterns described in this chapter. Two packages that closely match the patterns are listed below:

- ➤ https://github.com/twoscoops/django-twoscoops-project
  Featured in this chapter.
- ➤ https://github.com/rdegges/django-skel
  More features but more challenging to set up.

3.1 Django 1.6's Default Project Layout

Let's examine the default project layout that gets created when you run startproject and startapp:

```
EXAMPLE 3.1

$ django-admin.py startproject mysite
$ cd mysite
$ django-admin.py startapp my_app
```

Here's the resulting project layout:

```
EXAMPLE 3.2
mysite/
    manage.py
    my_app/
        __init__.py
        admin.py
        models.py
        tests.py
        views.py
    mysite/
        __init__.py
        settings.py
        urls.py
        wsgi.py
```

There are a number of problems with Django's default project layout. While useful for the tutorial, it's not quite as useful once you are trying to put together a real project. The rest of this chapter will explain why.

3.2   Our Preferred Project Layout

We rely on a three-tiered approach that builds on what is generated by the `django-admin.py` `startproject` management command. We place that inside another directory which serves as the git repository root. Our layouts at the highest level are:

```
EXAMPLE 3.3
<repository_root>/
    <django_project_root>/
        <configuration_root>/
```

Let's go over each level in detail:

3.2.1   Top Level: Repository Root

The top-level *<repository_root>/* directory is the absolute root directory of the project. In addition to the *<django_project_root>* we also place other critical components like the *README.rst*, *docs/* directory, *design/* directory, *.gitignore*, *requirements.txt* files, and other high-level files that are required for deployment.

Figure 3.1: Yet another reason why repositories are important.

3.2.2   Second Level: Django Project Root

Generated by the `django-admin.py startproject` command, this is what is traditionally considered the Django project root.

This directory contains the *<configuration_root>*, media and static directories, a site-wide templates directory, as well as Django apps specific to your particular project.

TIP: Common Practice Varies Here

Some developers like to make the *<django_project_root>* the *<repository_root>* of the project.

3.2.3   Third Level: Configuration Root

Also generated by the `django-admin.py startproject` command, the *<configuration_root>* directory is where the settings module and base URLConf (*urls.py*) are placed. This must be a valid Python package (containing an *__init__.py* module).

① ② ③

Figure 3.2: Three-tiered scoop layout.

3.3   Sample Project Layout

Let's take a common example: a simple rating site. Imagine that we are creating Ice Cream Ratings, a web application for rating different brands and flavors of ice cream.

This is how we would lay out such a project:

```
EXAMPLE 3.4
icecreamratings_project/
    .gitignore
    Makefile
    docs/
    README.rst
    requirements.txt
    icecreamratings/
        manage.py
        media/  # Development ONLY!
        products/
```

```
profiles/
ratings/
static/
templates/
icecreamratings/
    __init__.py
    settings/
    urls.py
    wsgi.py
```

Let's do an in-depth review of this layout. As you can see, in the *icecreamratings_project/* directory, which is the *<repository_root>* , we have the following files and directories. We describe them in the table below:

File or Directory	Purpose
.gitignore	Lists the files and directories that Git should ignore. (This file is different for other version control systems. For example, if you are using Mercurial instead, you'd have an *.hgignore* file.)
README.rst and docs/	Developer-facing project documentation. You'll read more about this in chapter 21, *Documentation*.
Makefile	Contains simple deployment tasks and macros. For more complex deployments you may want to rely on tools like `Fabric`.
requirements.txt	A list of Python packages required by your project, including the Django 1.6 package. You'll read more about this in chapter 19, *Django's Secret Sauce: Third-Party Packages*.
icecreamratings/	The <django_project_root> of the project.

Table 3.1: Repository Root Files and Directories

When anyone visits this project, they are provided with a high-level view of the project. We've found that this allows us to work easily with other developers and even non-developers. For example, it's not uncommon for designer-focused directories to be created in the root directory.

Many developers like to make this at the same level as our *<repository_root>*, and that's perfectly alright with us. We just like to see our projects a little more separated.

Inside the *icecreamratings_project/icecreamratings* directory, at the *<django_project_root>*, we place the following files/directories:

File or Directory	Purpose
manage.py	If you leave this in, don't modify its contents. Refer to chapter 5, *Settings and Requirements Files* for more details.
media/	For use in development only: user-generated static media assets such as photos uploaded by users. For larger projects, this will be hosted on separate static media server(s).
products/	App for managing and displaying ice cream brands.
profiles/	App for managing and displaying user profiles.
ratings/	App for managing user ratings.
static/	Non-user-generated static media assets including CSS, JavaScript, and images. For larger projects, this will be hosted on separate static media server(s).
templates/	Where you put your site-wide Django templates.
icecreamratings/	The *<configuration_root>* of the project, where project-wide *settings*, *urls.py*, and *wsgi.py* modules are placed (We'll cover settings layout later in chapter 5, *Settings and Requirements Files*).

Table 3.2: Django Project Files and Directories

TIP: Conventions For Static Media Directory Names

In the example above, we follow the official Django documentation's convention of using *static/* for the (non-user-generated) static media directory.

If you find this confusing, there's no harm in calling it *assets/* or *site_assets/* instead. Just remember to update your STATICFILES_DIRS setting appropriately.

3.4   What About the Virtualenv?

Notice how there is no virtualenv directory anywhere in the project directory or its subdirectories? That is completely intentional.

A good place to create the virtualenv for this project would be a separate directory where you keep all of your virtualenvs for all of your Python projects. We like to put all our environments in one directory and all our projects in another.

Figure 3.3: An isolated environment, allowing your ice cream to swim freely.

For example, on Mac OS X or Linux:

EXAMPLE 3.5

```
~/projects/icecreamratings_project/
~/.envs/icecreamratings/
```

On Windows:

EXAMPLE 3.6

```
c:\projects\icecreamratings_project\
c:\envs\icecreamratings\
```

If you're using virtualenvwrapper (only for Mac OS X or Linux), that directory defaults to *~/.virtualenvs/* and the virtualenv would be located at:

EXAMPLE 3.7

```
~/.virtualenvs/icecreamratings/
```

TIP: Listing Current Dependencies

If you have trouble determining which versions of dependencies you are using in your virtualenv, at the command-line you can list your dependencies by typing:

EXAMPLE 3.8

```
$ pip freeze --local
```

Also, remember, there's no need to keep the contents of your virtualenv in version control since it already has all the dependencies captured in *requirements.txt*, and since you won't be editing any of the source code files in your virtualenv directly. Just remember that *requirements.txt* does need to remain in version control!

3.5 Using a Startproject Template to Generate Our Layout

Want to use our layout with a minimum of fuss? If you have Django 1.6 (or even Django 1.5 or 1.4), you can use the `startproject` command as follows, all on one line:

EXAMPLE 3.9

```
$ django-admin.py startproject --template=https://github.com/
          twoscoops/django-twoscoops-project/zipball/master
          --extension=py,rst,html icecreamratings_project
```

This will create an *icecreamratings_project* directory where you run the command, which will be a project following the layout example we provided. It also will build settings, requirements, and templates in the same pattern as those items are described later in the book.

3.6   Other Alternatives

As we mentioned, there's no one right way when it comes to project layout. It's okay if a project differs from our layout, just so long as things are either done in a hierarchical fashion or the locations of elements of the project (docs, templates, apps, settings, etc) are documented in the root *README.rst* .

Figure 3.4: Project layout differences of opinion can cause ice cream fights.

3.7   Summary

In this chapter, we covered our approach to basic Django project layout. We provided a detailed example to give you as much insight as possible into our practices.

Project layout is one of those areas of Django where practices differ widely from developer to developer and group to group. What works for a small team may not work for a large team with distributed resources. Whatever layout is chosen should be documented clearly.

4 | Fundamentals of Django App Design

It's not uncommon for new Django developers to become understandably confused by Django's usage of the word "app." So before we get into Django app design, it's very important that we go over some definitions.

A Django project is a web application powered by the Django web framework.

Django apps are small libraries designed to represent a single aspect of a project. A Django project is made up of many Django apps. Some of those apps are internal to the project and will never be reused; others are third-party Django packages.

INSTALLED_APPS is the list of Django apps used by a given project in available in its IN-STALLED_APPS setting.

Third-party Django packages are simply pluggable, reusable Django apps that have been packaged with the Python packaging tools. We'll begin coverage of them in chapter 19, *Django's Secret Sauce: Third-Party Packages*.

Figure 4.1: It'll make more sense when you turn the page.

APPS ARE CONTAINERS IN THE FREEZER.

PACKAGES ARE CONTAINERS STILL AT THE STORE, WAITING TO BE INSTALLED AS APPS.

Figure 4.2: Did that make sense? If not, read it again.

4.1 The Golden Rule of Django App Design

James Bennett volunteers as both a Django core developer and as its release manager. He taught us everything that we know about good Django app design. We quote him:

> "The art of creating and maintaining a good Django app is that it should follow the truncated Unix philosophy according to Douglas McIlroy: 'Write programs that do one thing and do it well.'"

In essence, **each app should be tightly focused on its task**. If an app can't be explained in a single sentence of moderate length, or you need to say 'and' more than once, it probably means the app is too big and should be broken up.

4.1.1 A Practical Example of Apps in a Project

Imagine that we're creating a web application for our fictional ice cream shop called "Two Scoops." Picture us getting ready to open the shop: polishing the countertops, making the first batches of ice cream, and building the website for our shop.

We'd call the Django project for our shop's website *twoscoops_project*. The apps within our Django project might be something like:

> ➤ A *flavors* app to track all of our ice cream flavors and list them on our website.
> ➤ A *blog* app for the official Two Scoops blog.
> ➤ An *events* app to display listings of our shop's events on our website: events such as Strawberry Sundae Sundays and Fudgy First Fridays.

Each one of these apps does one particular thing. Yes, the apps relate to each other, and you could imagine *events* or *blog* posts that are centered around certain ice cream flavors, but it's much better to have three specialized apps than one app that does everything.

In the future, we might extend the site with apps like:

> ➤ A *shop* app to allow us to sell pints by mail order.
> ➤ A *tickets* app, which would handle ticket sales for premium all-you-can-eat ice cream fests.

Notice how events are kept separate from ticket sales. Rather than expanding the *events* app to sell tickets, we create a separate *tickets* app because most events don't require tickets, and because event calendars and ticket sales have the potential to contain complex logic as the site grows.

Eventually, we hope to use the *tickets* app to sell tickets to Icecreamlandia, the ice cream theme park filled with thrill rides that we've always wanted to open.

Did we say that this was a fictional example? Ahem...well, here's an early concept map of what we envision for Icecreamlandia:

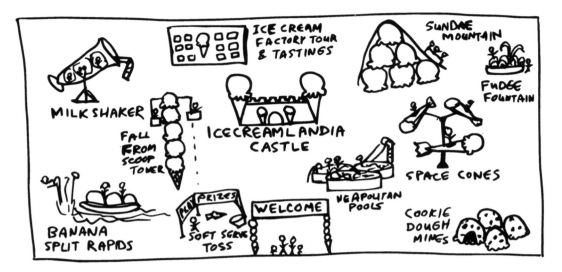

Figure 4.3: Our vision for Icecreamlandia.

4.2   What to Name Your Django Apps

Everyone has their own conventions, and some people like to use really colorful names. We like to use naming systems that are dull, boring, and obvious. In fact, we advocate doing the following:

When possible keep to single word names like *flavors*, *animals*, *blog*, *polls*, *dreams*, *estimates*, and *finances*. A good, obvious app name makes the project easier to maintain.

As a general rule, the app's name should be a plural version of the app's main model, but there are many good exceptions to this rule, blog being one of the most common ones.

Don't just consider the app's main model, though. You should also consider how you want your URLs to appear when choosing a name. If you want your site's blog to appear at http://www.example.com/weblog/, then consider naming your app weblog rather than *blog*, *posts*, or *blogposts*, even if the main model is Post, to make it easier for you to see which app corresponds with which part of the site.

Use valid, PEP 8-compliant, importable Python package names: short, all-lowercase names without numbers, dashes, periods, spaces, or special characters. If needed for readability, you can use underscores to separate words, although the use of underscores is discouraged.

4.3   When in Doubt, Keep Apps Small

Don't worry too hard about getting app design perfect. It's an art, not a science. Sometimes you have to rewrite them or break them up. That's okay.

Try and keep your apps small. Remember, it's better to have many small apps than to have a few giant apps.

Figure 4.4: Two small, single-flavor pints are better than a giant, 100-flavor container.

4.4   Summary

This chapter covered the art of Django app design. Specifically, each Django app should be tightly-focused on its own task, possess a simple, easy-to-remember name. If an app seems too complex, it should be broken up into smaller apps. Getting app design right takes practice and effort, but it's well worth the effort.

5 | Settings and Requirements Files

Django 1.6 has over 130 settings that can be controlled in the settings module, most of which come with default values. Settings are loaded when your server starts up, and experienced Django developers stay away from trying to change settings in production since they require a server restart.

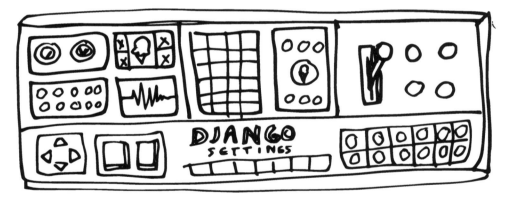

Figure 5.1: As your project grows, your Django settings can get pretty complex.

Some best practices we like to follow:

> **All settings files need to be version-controlled**. This is especially true in production environments, where dates, times, and explanations for settings changes absolutely must be tracked.
> **Don't Repeat Yourself**. You should inherit from a base settings file rather than cutting-and-pasting from one file to another.
> **Keep secret keys safe**. They should be kept out of version control.

5.1 Avoid Non-Versioned Local Settings

We used to advocate the non-versioned **local_settings anti-pattern**. Now we know better.

As developers, we have our own necessary settings for development, such as settings for debug tools which should be disabled (and often not installed to) staging or production servers.

Furthermore, there are often good reasons to keep specific settings out of public or private code repositories. The SECRET_KEY setting is the first thing that comes to mind, but API key settings to services like Amazon, Stripe, and other password-type variables need to be protected.

> ## WARNING: Protect Your Secrets!
>
> The SECRET_KEY setting is used in Django's cryptographic signing functionality, and needs to be set to a unique, unpredictable setting best kept out of version control. Running Django with a known SECRET_KEY defeats many of Django's security protections, which can lead to serious security vulnerabilities. For more details, read
> `https://docs.djangoproject.com/en/1.6/topics/signing/`.
>
> The same warning for SECRET_KEY also applies to production database passwords, AWS keys, OAuth tokens, or any other sensitive data that your project needs in order to operate.
>
> Later in this chapter we'll show how to handle the SECRET_KEY issue in the "Keep Secret Keys Out With Environment Settings" section.

A common solution is to create *local_settings.py* modules that are created locally per server or development machine, and are purposefully kept out of version control. Developers now make development-specific settings changes, including the incorporation of business logic without the code being tracked in version control. Staging and deployment servers can have location specific settings and logic without them being tracked in version control.

What could possibly go wrong?!?

Ahem...

> ➤ Every machine has untracked code.

➤ How much hair will you pull out, when after hours of failing to duplicate a production bug locally, you discover that the problem was custom logic in a production-only setting?

➤ How fast will you run from everyone when the 'bug' you discovered locally, fixed and pushed to production was actually caused by customizations you made in your own *local_settings.py* module and is now crashing the site?

➤ Everyone copy/pastes the same *local_settings.py* module everywhere. Isn't this a violation of Don't Repeat Yourself but on a larger scale?

Let's take a different approach. Let's break up development, staging, test, and production settings into separate components that inherit from a common base object in a settings file tracked by version control. Plus, we'll make sure we do it in such a way that server secrets will remain secret.

Read on and see how it's done!

5.2   Using Multiple Settings Files

TIP: History of This Setup Pattern

The setup described here is based on the so-called "The One True Way", from Jacob Kaplan-Moss' The Best (and Worst) of Django talk at OSCON 2011. See http://2scoops.co/the-best-and-worst-of-django.

Instead of having one *settings.py* file, with this setup you have a *settings/* directory containing your settings files. This directory will typically contain something like the following:

```
Example 5.1

settings/
    __init__.py
    base.py
    local.py
    staging.py
    test.py
    production.py
```

WARNING: Requirements + Settings

Each settings module should have its own corresponding requirements file. We'll cover this at the end of this chapter in section 5.5, 'Using Multiple Requirements Files.'

Settings file	Purpose
base.py	Settings common to all instances of the project.
local.py	This is the settings file that you use when you're working on the project locally. Local development-specific settings include DEBUG mode, log level, and activation of developer tools like django-debug-toolbar. Developers sometimes name this file *dev.py*.
staging.py	Staging version for running a semi-private version of the site on a production server. This is where managers and clients should be looking before your work is moved to production.
test.py	Settings for running tests including test runners, in-memory database definitions, and log settings.
production.py	This is the settings file used by your live production server(s). That is, the server(s) that host the real live website. This file contains production-level settings only. It is sometimes called *prod.py*.

Table 5.1: Settings files and their purpose

TIP: Multiple Files with Continuous Integration Servers

You'll also want to have a *ci.py* module containing that server's settings. Similarly, if it's a large project and you have other special-purpose servers, you might have custom settings files for each of them.

Let's take a look at how to use the shell and runserver management commands with this setup. You'll have to use the --settings command line option, so you'll be entering the following at the command-line.

To start the Python interactive interpreter with Django, using your *settings/local.py* settings file:

EXAMPLE 5.2

```
python manage.py shell --settings=twoscoops.settings.local
```

To run the local development server with your *settings/local.py* settings file:

EXAMPLE 5.3

```
python manage.py runserver --settings=twoscoops.settings.local
```

TIP: DJANGO_SETTINGS_MODULE and PYTHONPATH

A great alternative to using the `--settings` command line option everywhere is to set the `DJANGO_SETTINGS_MODULE` and `PYTHONPATH` environment variable to your desired settings module path. You'd have to set `DJANGO_SETTINGS_MODULE` to the corresponding settings module for each environment, of course.

For those with a more comprehensive understanding of virtualenv, another alternative is to set `DJANGO_SETTINGS_MODULE` and `PYTHONPATH` in the postactivate script. Then, once the virtualenv is activated, you can just type `python` from anywhere and import those values into your project. This also means that typing `django-admin.py` at the command-line works without the `--settings` option.

For the settings setup that we just described, here are the values to use with the `--settings` command line option or the `DJANGO_SETTINGS_MODULE` environment variable:

Environment	Option To Use With `--settings` (or `DJANGO_SETTINGS_MODULE` **value**)
Your local development server	`twoscoops.settings.local`
Your staging server	`twoscoops.settings.staging`
Your test server	`twoscoops.settings.test`
Your production server	`twoscoops.settings.production`

Environment	Option To Use With `--settings` (or `DJANGO_SETTINGS_MODULE` **value**)

Table 5.2: Setting DJANGO_SETTINGS_MODULE per location

5.2.1 A Development Settings Example

As mentioned earlier, we need settings configured for development, such as selecting the console email backend, setting the project to run in DEBUG mode, and setting other configuration options that are used solely for development purposes. We place development settings like the following into *settings/local.py*:

```
EXAMPLE 5.4
# settings/local.py
from .base import *

DEBUG = True
TEMPLATE_DEBUG = DEBUG

EMAIL_BACKEND = 'django.core.mail.backends.console.EmailBackend'

DATABASES = {
    "default": {
        "ENGINE": "django.db.backends.postgresql_psycopg2",
        "NAME": "twoscoops",
        "USER": "",
        "PASSWORD": "",
        "HOST": "localhost",
        "PORT": "",
    }
}

INSTALLED_APPS += ("debug_toolbar", )
```

Now try it out at the command line with:

EXAMPLE 5.5

```
python manage.py runserver --settings=twoscoops.settings.local
```

Open `http://127.0.0.1:8000` and enjoy your development settings, ready to go into version control! You and other developers will be sharing the same development settings files, which for shared projects, is awesome.

Yet there's another advantage: No more 'if DEBUG' or 'if not DEBUG' logic to copy/paste around between projects. Settings just got a whole lot simpler!

At this point we want to take a moment to note that Django settings files are the single, solitary place we advocate using `import *`. The reason is that *for the singular case of Django setting modules we want to override all the namespace.*

5.2.2 Multiple Development Settings

Sometime we're working on a large project where different developers need different settings, and sharing the same *dev.py* settings module with teammates won't do.

Well, it's still better tracking these settings in version control than relying on everyone customizing the same *dev.py* or *local_settings.py* module to their own tastes. A nice way to do this is with multiple dev settings files, e.g. *dev_audrey.py* and *dev_pydanny.py*:

EXAMPLE 5.6

```
# settings/dev_pydanny.py
from .local import *

# Set short cache timeout
CACHE_TIMEOUT = 30
```

Why? It's not only good to keep all your own settings files in version control, but it's also good to be able to see your teammates' dev settings files. That way, you can tell if someone's missing a vital or helpful setting in their local development setup, and you can make sure that everyone's local settings files are synchronized. Here is what our projects frequently use for settings layout:

```
EXAMPLE 5.7
settings/
    __init__.py
    base.py
    dev_audreyr.py
    dev_pydanny.py
    local.py
    staging.py
    test.py
    production.py
```

5.3   Separate Configuration from Code

One of the causes of the local_settings anti-pattern is that putting SECRET_KEY, AWS keys, API keys, or server-specific values into settings files has problems:

➤ Config varies substantially across deploys, code does not.

➤ Secret keys are configuration values, not code.

➤ Secrets often should be just that: secret! Keeping them in version control means that everyone with repository access has access to them.

➤ Platforms-as-a-service usually don't give you the ability to edit code on individual servers. Even if they allow it, it's a terribly dangerous practice.

To resolve this, our answer is to use **environment variables** in a pattern we like to call, well, **The Environment Variables Pattern**.

Every operating system supported by Django (and Python) provides the easy capability to create environment variables.

Here are the benefits of using environment variables for secret keys:

➤ Keeping secrets out of settings allows you to store every settings file in version control without hesitation. All of your Python code really should be stored in version control, including your settings.

➤ Instead of each developer maintaining an easily-outdated, copy-and-pasted version of the *local_settings.py.example* file for their own development purposes, everyone shares the same version-controlled *settings/local.py* .

➤ System administrators can rapidly deploy the project without having to modify files containing Python code.

➤ Most platforms-as-a-service recommend the use of environment variables for configuration and have built-in features for setting and managing them.

TIP: 12 Factor App: Store Config in the Environment

If you've read the 12 Factor App's article on configuration you'll recognize this pattern. For reference, see `http://12factor.net/config`. Some developers even advocate combining the use of environment variables with a single settings modules. We cover this practice in section 32, '12 Factor-Style Settings.'

5.3.1 A Caution Before Using Environment Variables for Secrets

Before you begin setting environment variables, you should have the following:

➤ A way to manage the secret information you are going to store.

➤ A good understanding of how bash works with environment variables on servers, or a willingness to have your project hosted by a platform-as-a-service.

For more information, see `http://2scoops.co/wikipedia-env-variable`.

WARNING: Environment Variables Do Not Work with Apache

If your target production environment uses Apache, then you will discover that setting operating system environment variables as described below doesn't work. Confusing the issue is that Apache has its own environment variable system, which is almost but not quite what you'll need.

If you are using Apache and want to avoid the local_settings anti-pattern, we recommend reading section 5.4, 'When You Can't Use Environment Variables,' later in this chapter.

5.3.2   How to Set Environment Variables Locally

On Mac and many Linux distributions that use **bash** for the shell, one can add lines like the following to the end of a *.bashrc*, *.bash_profile*, or *.profile*. When dealing with multiple projects using the same API but with different keys, you can also place these at the end of your virtualenv's *bin/activate* script:

```
EXAMPLE 5.8
$ export SOME_SECRET_KEY=1c3-cr3am-15-yummy
$ export AUDREY_FREEZER_KEY=y34h-r1ght-d0nt-t0uch-my-1c3-cr34m
```

On Windows systems, it's a bit trickier. You can set them one-by-one at the command line (**cmd.exe**) in a persistent way with the setx command, but you'll have to close and reopen your command prompt for them to go into effect. A better way is to place these commands at the end of the virtualenv's *bin/activate.bat* script so they are available upon activation:

```
EXAMPLE 5.9
> setx SOME_SECRET_KEY 1c3-cr3am-15-yummy
```

PowerShell is much more powerful than the default Windows shell and comes with Windows Vista and above. Setting environment variables while using PowerShell:

For the current Windows user only:

```
EXAMPLE 5.10
[Environment]::SetEnvironmentVariable("SOME_SECRET_KEY",
                                      "1c3-cr3am-15-yummy", "User")
[Environment]::SetEnvironmentVariable("AUDREY_FREEZER_KEY",
                    "y34h-r1ght-d0nt-t0uch-my-1c3-cr34m", "User")
```

Machine-wide:

```
EXAMPLE 5.11
[Environment]::SetEnvironmentVariable("SOME_SECRET_KEY",
                                      "1c3-cr3am-15-yummy", "Machine")
```

```
[Environment]::SetEnvironmentVariable("AUDREY_FREEZER_KEY",
                "y34h-r1ght-d0nt-t0uch-my-1c3-cr34m", "Machine")
```

For more information on Powershell, see http://2scoops.co/powershell

---

TIP: virtualenvwrapper Makes This Easier

Mentioned earlier in this book, **virtualenvwrapper**, simplifies per-virtualenv environment variables. It's a great tool. Of course, it requires an understanding of the shell and either Mac OS X or Linux.

5.3.3   How to Set Environment Variables in Production

If you're using your own servers, your exact practices will differ depending on the tools you're using and the complexity of your setup. For the simplest 1-server setup for test projects, you can set the environment variables manually. But if you're using scripts or tools for automated server provisioning and deployment, your approach may be more complex. Check the documentation for your deployment tools for more information.

If your Django project is deployed via a platform-as-a-service, check the documentation for specific instructions. We've included Heroku instructions here so that you can see that it's similar for platform-as-a-service options.

On Heroku, you set environment variables with the following command, executed from your development machine:

EXAMPLE 5.12

```
$ heroku config:set SOME_SECRET_KEY=1c3-cr3am-15-yummy
```

To see how you access environment variables from the Python side, open up a new Python prompt and type:

```
EXAMPLE 5.13
>>> import os
>>> os.environ["SOME_SECRET_KEY"]
"1c3-cr3am-15-yummy"
```

To access environment variables from one of your settings files, you can do something like this:

```
EXAMPLE 5.14
# Top of settings/production.py
import os
SOME_SECRET_KEY = os.environ["SOME_SECRET_KEY"]
```

This snippet simply gets the value of the SOME_SECRET_KEY environment variable from the operating system and saves it to a Python variable called SOME_SECRET_KEY.

Following this pattern means all code can remain in version control, and all secrets remain safe.

5.3.4   Handling Missing Secret Key Exceptions

In the above implementation, if the SECRET_KEY isn't available, it will throw a KeyError, making it impossible to start the project. That's great, but a KeyError doesn't tell you that much about what's actually wrong. Without a more helpful error message, this can be hard to debug, especially under the pressure of deploying to servers while users are waiting and your ice cream is melting.

Here's a useful code snippet that makes it easier to troubleshoot those missing environment variables. If you're using our recommended environment variable secrets approach, you'll want to add this to your *settings/base.py* file:

```
EXAMPLE 5.15
# settings/base.py
import os


# Normally you should not import ANYTHING from Django directly
```

```
# into your settings, but ImproperlyConfigured is an exception.
from django.core.exceptions import ImproperlyConfigured


def get_env_variable(var_name):
    """Get the environment variable or return exception."""
    try:
        return os.environ[var_name]
    except KeyError:
        error_msg = "Set the %s environment variable" % var_name
        raise ImproperlyConfigured(error_msg)
```

Then, in any of your settings files, you can load secret keys from environment variables as follows:

```
EXAMPLE 5.16
SOME_SECRET_KEY = get_env_variable("SOME_SECRET_KEY")
```

Now, if you don't have SOME_SECRET_KEY set as an environment variable, you get a traceback that ends with a useful error message like this:

```
EXAMPLE 5.17
django.core.exceptions.ImproperlyConfigured: Set the SOME_SECRET_KEY
environment variable.
```

WARNING: Don't Import Django Components Into Settings Modules

This can have many unpredictable side effects, so avoid any sort of import of Django components into your settings. ImproperlyConfigured is the exception because it's the official Django exception for...well...improperly configured projects. And just to be helpful we add the name of the problem setting to the error message.

> ## TIP: Using django-admin.py Instead of manage.py
>
> The official Django documentation says that you should use *django-admin.py* rather than *manage.py* when working with multiple settings files:
>
> `https://docs.djangoproject.com/en/1.6/ref/django-admin/`
>
> That being said, if you're struggling with *django-admin.py*, it's perfectly okay to develop and launch your site running it with *manage.py*.

5.4   When You Can't Use Environment Variables

The problem with using environment variables to store secrets is that it doesn't always work. The most common scenario for this is when using Apache for serving HTTP, but this also happens even in Nginx-based environments where operations wants to do things in a particular way. When this occurs, rather than going back to the **local_settings anti-pattern**, we advocate using non-executable files kept out of version control in a method we like to call the **secrets file pattern**.

To implement the **secrets file pattern**, follow these three steps:

❶ Create a secrets file using the configuration format of choice, be it JSON, Config, YAML, or even XML.

❷ Add a secrets loader (JSON-powered example below) to manage the secrets in a cohesive, explicit manner.

❸ Add the secrets file name to the *.gitignore* or *.hgignore*.

5.4.1   Using JSON Files

Our preference is to use shallow JSON files. The JSON format has the advantage of being the format of choice for various Python and non-Python tools. To use the JSON format, first create a *secrets.json* file:

EXAMPLE 5.18

```
{
    "FILENAME": "secrets.json",
    "SECRET_KEY": "I've got a secret!",
    "DATABASES_HOST": "127.0.0.1",
    "PORT": "5432"
}
```

To use the *secrets.json* file, add the following code to your base settings module.

EXAMPLE 5.19

```python
# settings/base.py

import json

# Normally you should not import ANYTHING from Django directly
# into your settings, but ImproperlyConfigured is an exception.
from django.core.exceptions import ImproperlyConfigured

# JSON-based secrets module
with open("secrets.json") as f:
    secrets = json.loads(f.read())

def get_secret(setting, secrets=secrets):
    """Get the secret variable or return explicit exception."""
    try:
        return secrets[setting]
    except KeyError:
        error_msg = "Set the {0} environment variable".format(setting)
        raise ImproperlyConfigured(error_msg)

SECRET_KEY = get_secret("SECRET_KEY")
```

Now we are loading secrets from non-executable JSON files instead of from unversioned executable code. Hooray!

5.4.2 Using Config, YAML, and XML File Formats

While we prefer the forced simplicity of shallow JSON, others might prefer other file formats. We'll leave it up to the reader to create additional `get_secret()` alternatives that work with these formats. Just remember to be familiar with things like `yaml.safe_load()` and XML bombs. See section 23.9, 'Defend Against Python Code Injection Attacks.'

5.5 Using Multiple Requirements Files

Finally, there's one more thing you need to know about multiple settings files setup. It's good practice for each settings file to have its own corresponding requirements file. This means we're only installing what is required on each server.

To follow this pattern, recommended to us by Jeff Triplett, first create a *requirements/* directory in the **<repository_root>**. Then create '.*txt*' files that match the contents of your settings directory. The results should look something like:

```
EXAMPLE 5.20
requirements/
    base.txt
    local.txt
    staging.txt
    production.txt
```

In the *base.txt* file, place the dependencies used in all environments. For example, you might have something like the following in there:

```
EXAMPLE 5.21
Django==1.6.0
psycopg2==2.5.1
South==0.8.4
```

Your *local.txt* file should have dependencies used for local development, such as:

EXAMPLE 5.22

```
-r base.txt # includes the base.txt requirements file

coverage==3.7
django-debug-toolbar==0.11
```

The needs of a continuous integration server might prompt the following for a *ci.txt* file:

EXAMPLE 5.23

```
-r base.txt # includes the base.txt requirements file

coverage==3.7
django-jenkins==0.14.1
```

Production installations should be close to what is used in other locations, so *production.txt* commonly just calls *base.txt*:

EXAMPLE 5.24

```
-r base.txt # includes the base.txt requirements file
```

5.5.1   Installing From Multiple Requirements Files

For local development:

EXAMPLE 5.25

```
$ pip install -r requirements/local.txt
```

For production:

EXAMPLE 5.26

```
$ pip install -r requirements/production.txt
```

5.5.2 Using Multiple Requirements Files With Platforms as a Service (PaaS)

See chapter 27, *Deployment:Platforms as a Service.*

TIP: Pin Requirements Exactly

All the pip requirements.txt examples in this chapter are explicitly set to a package version. This ensures a more stable project. We cover this at length in subsection 19.7.2, 'Add Package and Version Number to Your Requirements.'

5.6 Handling File Paths in Settings

If you switch to the multiple settings setup and get new file path errors to things like templates and media, don't be alarmed. This section will help you resolve these errors.

We humbly beseech the reader to never hardcode file paths in Django settings files. This is *really* bad:

```
BAD EXAMPLE 5.1
# settings/base.py

# Configuring MEDIA_ROOT
# 'DONT DO THIS! Hardcoded to just one user's preferences
MEDIA_ROOT = "/Users/pydanny/twoscoops_project/media"

# Configuring STATIC_ROOT
# 'DONT DO THIS! Hardcoded to just one user's preferences
STATIC_ROOT = "/Users/pydanny/twoscoops_project/collected_static"

# Configuring TEMPLATE_DIRS
# 'DONT DO THIS! Hardcoded to just one user's preferences
TEMPLATE_DIRS = (
    "/Users/pydanny/twoscoops_project/templates",
)
```

The above code represents a common pitfall called **hardcoding**. The above code, called a **fixed path**, is bad because as far as you know, **pydanny** (Daniel Greenfeld) is the only person who has set up their computer to match this path structure. Anyone else trying to use this example will see their project break, forcing them to either change their directory structure (unlikely) or change the settings module to match their preference (causing problems for everyone else including pydanny).

Don't hardcode your paths!

To fix the path issue, we dynamically set a project root variable intuitively named BASE_DIR at the top of the base settings module. Since BASE_DIR is determined in relation to the location of base.py, your project can be run from any location on any development computer or server.

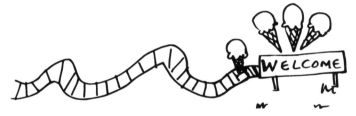

Figure 5.2: While we're at it, let's go down this path.

We find the cleanest way to set a BASE_DIR-like setting is with **Unipath** (http://pypi.python.org/pypi/Unipath/), a Python package that does elegant, clean path calculations:

```
EXAMPLE 5.27
# At the top of settings/base.py
from unipath import Path

BASE_DIR = Path(__file__).ancestor(3)
MEDIA_ROOT = BASE_DIR.child("media")
STATIC_ROOT = BASE_DIR.child("static")
STATICFILES_DIRS = (
    BASE_DIR.child("assets"),
)
TEMPLATE_DIRS = (
```

```
        BASE_DIR.child("templates"),
)
```

If you really want to set your BASE_DIR with the Python standard library's os.path library, though, this is one way to do it in a way that will account for paths:

```
EXAMPLE 5.28
# At the top of settings/base.py
from os.path import join, abspath, dirname

here = lambda *dirs: join(abspath(dirname(__file__)), *dirs)
BASE_DIR = here("..", "..")
root = lambda *dirs: join(abspath(BASE_DIR), *dirs)

# Configuring MEDIA_ROOT
MEDIA_ROOT = root("media")

# Configuring STATIC_ROOT
STATIC_ROOT = root("collected_static")

# Additional locations of static files
STATICFILES_DIRS = (
    root("assets"),
)

# Configuring TEMPLATE_DIRS
TEMPLATE_DIRS = (
    root("templates"),
)
```

With your various path settings dependent on BASE_DIR, your file path settings should work, which means your templates and media should be loading without error.

> **TIP: How different are your settings from the Django defaults?**
>
> If you want to know how things in your project differ from Django's defaults, use the `diffsettings` management command.

5.7 Summary

Remember, everything except for critical security related values ought to be tracked in version control.

Any project that's destined for a real live production server is bound to need multiple settings and requirements files. Even beginners to Django need this kind of settings/requirements file setup once their projects are ready to leave the original development machine. We provide our solution, as well as an Apache-friendly solution since it works well for both beginning and advanced developers.

Also, if you prefer a different shell than the ones provided, environment variables still work. You'll just need to know the syntax for defining them.

The same thing applies to requirements files. Working with untracked dependency differences increases risk as much as untracked settings.

6 | Database/Model Best Practices

Models are the foundation of most Django projects. Racing to write Django models without thinking things through can lead to problems down the road.

All too frequently we developers rush into adding or modifying models without considering the ramifications of what we are doing. The quick fix or sloppy "temporary" design decision that we toss into our code base now can hurt us in the months or years to come, forcing crazy workarounds or corrupting existing data.

So keep this in mind when adding new models in Django or modifying existing ones. Take your time to think things through, and design your foundation to be as strong and sound as possible.

PACKAGE TIP: Our Picks For Working With Models

Here's a quick list of the model-related Django packages that we use in practically every project.

> **South** for database migrations. For future reference, in Django 1.7 the need for South will be mitigated by the new `django.db.migrations` module.
> **django-model-utils** to handle common patterns like **TimeStampedModel**.
> **django-extensions** has a powerful management command called `shell_plus` which autoloads the model classes for all installed apps. The downside of this library is that it includes a lot of other functionality which breaks from our preference for small, focused apps.

6.1 Basics

6.1.1 Break Up Apps With Too Many Models

If there are 20+ models in a single app, think about ways to break it down into smaller apps, as it probably means your app is doing too much. In practice, we like to lower this number to no more than five models per app.

6.1.2 Don't Drop Down to Raw SQL Until It's Necessary

Most of the queries we write are simple. The **Object-Relational Model** or **ORM** provides a great productivity shortcut: not only generating decent SQL queries for common use cases, but providing model access/update functionality that comes complete with validation and security. If you can write your query easily with the ORM, then take advantage of it!

It's also good to keep in mind that if you ever release one of your Django apps as a third-party package, using raw SQL will decrease the portability of the work.

Finally, in the rare event that the data has to be migrated from one database to another, any database-specific features that you use in your SQL queries will complicate the migration.

So when should you actually write raw SQL? If expressing your query as raw SQL would drastically simplify your Python code or the SQL generated by the ORM, then go ahead and do it. For example, if you're chaining a number of QuerySet operations that each operate on a large data set, there may be a more efficient way to write it as raw SQL.

TIP: Malcolm Tredinnick's Advice On Writing SQL in Django

Django core developer Malcolm Tredinnick said (paraphrased):

> "The ORM can do many wonderful things, but sometimes SQL is the right answer. The rough policy for the Django ORM is that it's a storage layer that happens to use SQL to implement functionality. If you need to write advanced SQL you should write it. I would balance that by cautioning against overuse of the raw() and extra() methods."

TIP: Jacob Kaplan-Moss' Advice On Writing SQL in Django

Django project co-leader Jacob Kaplan-Moss says (paraphrased):

> "If it's easier to write a query using SQL than Django, then do it. extra()
> is nasty and should be avoided; raw() is great and should be used where
> appropriate."

Figure 6.1: This flavor of ice cream contains raw SQL. It's a bit chewy.

6.1.3   Add Indexes as Needed

While adding db_index=True to any model field is easy, understanding when it should be done takes a bit of judgment. Our preference is to start without indexes and add them as needed.

When to consider adding indexes:

➤ The index is used frequently, as in 10-25% of all queries.

➤ There is real data, or something that approximates real data, so we can analyze the results of indexing.

➤ We can run tests to determine if indexing generates an improvement in results.

When using PostgreSQL, `pg_stat_activity` tells us what indexes are actually being used.

Once a project goes live, chapter 22, *Finding and Reducing Bottlenecks*, has information on index analysis.

6.1.4   Be Careful With Model Inheritance

Model inheritance in Django is a tricky subject. Django provides three ways to do model inheritance: **abstract base classes**, **multi-table inheritance**, and **proxy models**.

WARNING: Django Abstract Base Classes <> Python Abstract Base Classes
Don't confuse Django abstract base classes with the abstract base classes in the Python standard library's abc module, as they have very different purposes and behaviors.

Here are the pros and cons of the three model inheritance styles. To give a complete comparison, we also include the option of using no model inheritance to begin with:

Model Inheritance Style	Pros	Cons
No model inheritance: if models have a common field, give both models that field.	Makes it easiest to understand at a glance how Django models map to database tables.	If there are a lot of fields duplicated across models, this can be hard to maintain.
Abstract base classes: tables are only created for derived models.	Having the common fields in an abstract parent class saves us from typing them more than once. We don't get the overhead of extra tables and joins that are incurred from multi-table inheritance.	We cannot use the parent class in isolation.

Multi-table inheritance: tables are created for both parent and child. An implied `OneToOneField` links parent and child.	Gives each model its own table, so that we can query either parent or child model. Also gives us the ability to get to a child object from a parent object: `parent.child`	Adds substantial overhead since each query on a child table requires joins with all parent tables. We strongly recommend against using multi-table inheritance. See the warning below.
Proxy models: a table is only created for the original model.	Allows us to have an alias of a model with different Python behavior.	We cannot change the model's fields.

Table 6.1: Pros and Cons of the Model Inheritance Styles

WARNING: Avoid Multi-Table Inheritance

Multi-table inheritance, sometimes called "concrete inheritance," is considered by the authors and many other developers to be a bad thing. We strongly recommend against using it. We'll go into more detail about this shortly.

Here are some simple rules of thumb for knowing which type of inheritance to use and when:

> ➤ If the overlap between models is minimal (e.g. you only have a couple of models that share one or two obvious fields), there might not be a need for model inheritance. Just add the fields to both models.
> ➤ If there is enough overlap between models that maintenance of models' repeated fields causes confusion and inadvertent mistakes, then in most cases the code should be refactored so that the common fields are in an abstract base class.
> ➤ Proxy models are an occasionally-useful convenience feature, but they're very different from the other two model inheritance styles.
> ➤ At all costs, everyone should avoid multi-table inheritance (see warning above) since it adds both confusion and substantial overhead. Instead of multi-table inheritance, use explicit `OneToOneFields` and `ForeignKeys` between models so you can control when joins are traversed.

6.1.5 Model Inheritance in Practice: The TimeStampedModel

It's very common in Django projects to include a `created` and `modified` timestamp field on all your models. We could manually add those fields to each and every model, but that's a lot of work and adds the risk of human error. A better solution is to write a `TimeStampedModel` to do the work for us:

EXAMPLE 6.1

```python
# core/models.py
from django.db import models


class TimeStampedModel(models.Model):
    """
    An abstract base class model that provides self-
    updating ``created`` and ``modified`` fields.
    """
    created = models.DateTimeField(auto_now_add=True)
    modified = models.DateTimeField(auto_now=True)

    class Meta:
        abstract = True
```

Take careful note of the very last two lines in the example, which turn our example into an abstract base class:

EXAMPLE 6.2

```python
class Meta:
    abstract = True
```

By defining `TimeStampedModel` as an abstract base class when we define a new class that inherits from it, Django doesn't create a `core_timestampedmodel` table when syncdb is run.

Let's put it to the test:

EXAMPLE 6.3

```python
# flavors/models.py
```

```
from django.db import models

from core.models import TimeStampedModel

class Flavor(TimeStampedModel):
    title = models.CharField(max_length=200)
```

This only creates one table: the flavors_flavor database table. That's exactly the behavior we wanted.

On the other hand, if TimeStampedModel was not an abstract base class (i.e. a concrete base class via multi-table inheritance), it would also create a core_timestampedmodel table. Not only that, but all of its subclasses including Flavor would lack the fields and have implicit foreign keys back to TimeStampedModel just to handle created/modified timestamps. Any reference to Flavor that reads or writes to the TimeStampedModel would impact two tables. (Thank goodness it's abstract!)

Remember, concrete inheritance has the potential to become a nasty performance bottleneck. This is even more true when you subclass a concrete model class multiple times.

Further reading:

➤ http://2scoops.co/1.6-model-inheritance

6.1.6   Use South for Migrations

South is the predominant Django tool for managing data and schema migrations. South is being rewritten and included in Django itself as django.db.migrations in the forthcoming 1.7 release. For either case, get to know their features well.

A few South tips:

➤ As soon as a new app or model is created, take that extra minute to create the initial South migrations for that new app or model.

➤ Write reverse migrations and test them! You can't always write perfect round-trips, but not being able to back up to an earlier state really hurts bug tracking and sometimes deployment in larger projects.

➤ While working on a Django app, flatten migration(s) to just one before pushing the new code to production. In other words, commit **"just enough migrations"** to get the job done.

➤ Never remove migration code that's already in production.

➤ If a project has tables with millions of rows in them, do extensive tests against data of that size on staging servers before running a South migration on a production server. Migrations on real data can take much, much, much more time than anticipated.

WARNING: A Caution About Removing Migrations From Existing Projects In Production

We're reiterating the bullet on removing migrations from existing projects in production. Removing migrations is analogous to deleting an audit trail, and any problems that may be caused by deletion of migrations might not be detectable for some time. If you do take this route, it's a good idea to document in the README of a project the precise commits where migration removals occurred.

Figure 6.2: Cones flying south for the winter.

6.2 Django Model Design

One of the most difficult topics that receives the least amount of attention is how to design good Django models.

How do you design for performance without optimizing prematurely? Let's explore some strategies here.

6.2.1 Start Normalized

We suggest that readers of this book need to be familiar with **database normalization**. If you are unfamiliar with database normalization, make it your responsibility to gain an understanding, as working with models in Django effectively requires a working knowledge of this. Since a detailed explanation of the subject is outside the scope of this book, we recommend the following resources:

➤ http://en.wikipedia.org/wiki/Database_normalization
➤ http://en.wikibooks.org/wiki/Relational_Database_Design/Normalization

When you're designing your Django models, always start off normalized. Take the time to make sure that no model should contain data already stored in another model.

At this stage, use relationship fields liberally. Don't denormalize prematurely. You want to have a good sense of the shape of your data.

6.2.2 Cache Before Denormalizing

Often, setting up caching in the right places can save you the trouble of denormalizing your models. We'll cover caching in much more detail in chapter 22, *Finding and Reducing Bottlenecks*, so don't worry too much about this right now.

6.2.3   Denormalize Only if Absolutely Needed

It can be tempting, especially for those new to the concepts of data normalization, to denormalize prematurely. Don't do it! Denormalization may seem like a panacea for what causes problems in a project. However it's a tricky process that risks adding complexity to your project and dramatically raises the risk of losing data.

Please, please, please explore caching before denormalization.

When a project has reached the limits of what the techniques described in chapter 22, *Finding and Reducing Bottlenecks* can address, that's when research into the concepts and patterns of database denormalization should begin.

6.2.4   When to Use Null and Blank

When defining a model field, you have the ability to set the null=True and the blank=True options. By default, they are False.

Knowing when to use these options is a common source of confusion for developers.

We've put this guide together to serve as a guide for standard usage of these model field arguments.

Field Type	Setting null=True	Setting blank=True
CharField, TextField, SlugField, EmailField, CommaSeparatedInteger-Field, etc.	*Don't do this.* Django's convention is to store empty values as the empty string, and to always retrieve NULL or empty values as the empty string for consistency.	*Okay.* Do this if you want the corresponding form widget to accept empty values. If you set this, empty values get stored as empty strings in the database.

Field Type	Setting null=True	Setting blank=True
FileField, ImageField	*Don't do this.* Django stores the path from MEDIA_ROOT to the file to the image in a CharField, so the same pattern applies to FileFields.	*Okay.* The same pattern for CharField applies here.
BooleanField	*Don't do this.* Use NullBooleanField instead.	*Don't do this.*
IntegerField, FloatField, DecimalField, etc	*Okay* if you want to be able to set the value to NULL in the database.	*Okay* if you want the corresponding form widget to accept empty values. If so, you will also want to set null=True.
DateTimeField, DateField, TimeField, etc.	*Okay* if you want to be able to set the value to NULL in the database.	*Okay* if you want the corresponding form widget to accept empty values, or if you are using auto_now or auto_now_add. If so, you will also want to set null=True.
ForeignKey, ManyToManyField, OneToOneField	*Okay* if you want to be able to set the value to NULL in the database.	*Okay* if you want the corresponding form widget (e.g. the select box) to accept empty values.
GenericIPAddressField	*Okay* if you want to be able to set the value to NULL in the database.	*Okay* if you want to make the corresponding field widget accept empty values.
IPAddressField	*Not recommended for use.* See warning below.	*Not recommended for use.* See warning below.

Table 6.2: When to Use Null and Blank by Field

TIP: Use GenericIPAddressField Instead of IPAddressField

For a variety of reasons including support for both IPv4 and IPv6, GenericIPAddress-Field is a much better field to use than IPAddressField. Furthermore, using Generic-IPAddressField future-proofs your project because IPAddressField is scheduled to be deprecated in Django 1.7.

Figure 6.3: A common source of confusion.

6.2.5   When to Use BinaryField

Added in Django 1.6, this field allows for the storage of raw binary data, or **bytes**. We can't perform filters, excludes, or other SQL actions on the field, but there are use cases for it. For example we could store:

➤ MessagePack-formatted content.
➤ Raw sensor data.
➤ Compressed data e.g. the type of data Sentry stores as a BLOB, but is required to base64–encode due to legacy issues.

The possibilities are endless, but remember that binary data can come in huge chunks, which can slow down databases. If this occurs and becomes a bottleneck, the solution might be to save the binary data in a file and reference it with a `FileField`.

> ## WARNING: Don't Serve Files from BinaryField!
>
> Storing files in a database field should never happen. If it's being considered as a solution to a problem, find a certified database expert and ask for a second opinion.
>
> To summarize PostgreSQL expert Frank Wiles on the problems with using a database as a file store:
>
> ➤ 'read/write to a DB is always slower than a filesystem'
> ➤ 'your DB backups grow to be huge and more time consuming'
> ➤ 'access to the files now requires going through your app (Django) and DB layers'
> See `http://2scoops.co/three-things-not-to-put-in-database`
>
> When someone thinks there is a good use case for serving files from a database, and quotes a success like `https://npmjs.org` (stored files in CouchDB), it's time to do your research. The truth is that `https://npmjs.org`, as of this writing, is trying to migrate it's database-as-file-store system to a more traditional file serving method (see `https://scalenpm.org`).

6.3   Model Managers

Every time we use the Django ORM to query a model, we are using an interface called a **model manager** to interact with the database. Model managers are said to act on the full set of all possible instances of this model class (all the data in the table) to restrict the ones you want to work with. Django provides a default model manager for each model class, but we can define our own.

Here's a simple example of a custom model manager:

```
EXAMPLE 6.4
from django.db import models
from django.utils import timezone


class PublishedManager(models.Manager):

    use_for_related_fields = True
```

```
    def published(self, **kwargs):
        return self.filter(pub_date__lte=timezone.now(), **kwargs)


class FlavorReview(models.Model):
    review = models.CharField(max_length=255)
    pub_date = models.DateTimeField()


    # add our custom model manager
    objects = PublishedManager()
```

Now, if we first want to display a count of all of the ice cream flavor reviews, and then a count of just the published ones, we can do the following:

```
EXAMPLE 6.5

>>> from reviews.models import FlavorReview
>>> FlavorReview.objects.count()
35
>>> FlavorReview.objects.published().count()
31
```

Easy, right? Yet wouldn't it make more sense if you just added a second model manager? That way you could have something like:

```
BAD EXAMPLE 6.1

>>> from reviews.models import FlavorReview
>>> FlavorReview.objects.filter().count()
35
>>> FlavorReview.published.filter().count()
31
```

On the surface, replacing the default model manager seems like the obvious thing to do. Unfortunately, our experiences in real project development makes us very careful when we use this method. Why?

First, when using model inheritance, children of abstract base classes receive their parent's model manager, and children of concrete base classes do not.

Second, the first manager applied to a model class is the one that Django treats as the default. This breaks significantly with the normal Python pattern, causing what can appear to be unpredictable results from QuerySets.

With this knowledge in mind, in your model class, `objects = models.Manager()` should be defined manually above any custom model manager.

WARNING: Know the Model Manager Order of Operations

Always set `objects = models.Manager()` above any custom model manager that has a new name.

Additional reading:

➤ https://docs.djangoproject.com/en/1.6/topics/db/managers/

6.4 Transactions

As of Django 1.6, the default behavior of the ORM is to autocommit every query when it is called. In the case of data modification, this means that every time a `.create()` or `.update()` is called, it immediately modifies data in the SQL database. The advantage of this is that it makes it easier for beginning developers to understand the ORM. The disadvantage is that if a view (or some other operation) requires two or more database modifications to occur, if one modification succeeds and the other fails, the database is at risk of corruption.

The way to resolve the risk of database corruption is through the use of database transactions. A database transaction is where two or more database updates are contained in a single **unit of work**. If a single update fails, all the updates in the transaction are rolled back. To make this work, a database transaction, by definition, must be **atomic, consistent, isolated** and **durable**. Database practitioners often refer to these properties of database transactions using the acronym **ACID**.

Django has a powerful and relatively easy-to-use transaction mechanism that was overhauled and modernized with the release of 1.6. This makes it much easier to lock down database integrity on a project, using decorators and context managers in a rather intuitive pattern.

6.4.1   Wrapping Each HTTP Request In a Transaction

EXAMPLE 6.6

```
# settings/base.py

DATABASES = {
    'default': {
        # ...
        'ATOMIC_REQUESTS': True,
    },
}
```

Django makes it easy to handle all web requests inside of a transaction with the ATOMIC_REQUESTS setting. By setting it to True as show above, all requests are wrapped in transactions, including those that only read data. The advantage of this approach is safety: all database queries in views are protected, the disadvantage is performance can suffer. We can't tell you just how much this will affect performance, as it depends on individual database design and how well various database engines handle locking.

When using Django 1.6, we've found that this is a great way to ensure at the start that a write-heavy project's database maintains integrity. With lots of traffic, however, we've had to go back and change things to a more focused approach. Depending on the size this can be a small or monumental task.

Another to remember when using ATOMIC_REQUESTS, is that only the database state is rolled back on errors. It's quite embarrassing to send out a confirmation email and then have the transaction that wraps a request rolled back. This problem may crop up with any "write" to anything other than the database: sending email or SMS, calling a third-party API, writing to the filesystem, etc. Therefore, when writing views that create/update/delete records but interact with non-database items, you may choose to decorate the view with transaction.non_atomic_requests().

WARNING: Aymeric Augustin on `non_atomic_requests()`

Core Django developer and main implementer of the new transaction system, Aymeric Augustin says, "This decorator requires tight coupling between views and models, which will make a code base harder to maintain. We might have come up with a better design if we hadn't had to provide it for backwards-compatibility."

Then you can use the more explicit declaration as described below in this super-simple API-style function-based view:

EXAMPLE 6.7

```python
# flavors/views.py

from django.db import transaction
from django.http import HttpResponse
from django.shortcuts import get_object_or_404
from django.utils import timezone

from .models import Flavor

@transaction.non_atomic_requests
def posting_flavor_status(request, pk, status):
    flavor = get_object_or_404(Flavor, pk=pk)

    # This will execute in autocommit mode (Django's default).
    flavor.latest_status_change_attempt = timezone.now()
    flavor.save()

    with transaction.atomic():
        # This code executes inside a transaction.
        flavor.status = status
        flavor.latest_status_change_success = timezone.now()
        flavor.save()
        return HttpResponse("Hooray")

    # If the transaction fails, return the appropriate status
    return HttpResponse("Sadness", status_code=400)
```

If you are using `ATOMIC_REQUESTS=True` and want to switch to a more focused approach described in the following section, we recommend an understanding of *bottleneck analysis* (chapter 22), *good test coverage* (chapter 20), and *continuous integration* (chapter 30) before you undertake this effort.

TIP: Projects Touching Medical or Financial Data

For these kinds of projects, engineer systems for eventual consistency rather than for transactional integrity. In other words, be prepared for transactions to fail and rollbacks to occur. Fortunately, because of transactions, even with a rollback, the data will remain accurate and clean.

6.4.2   Explicit Transaction Declaration

Explicit transaction declaration is one way to increase site performance. In other words, specifying which views and business logic are wrapped in transactions and which are not. The downside to this approach is that it increases development time.

TIP: Aymeric Augustin on ATOMIC_REQUESTS vs Explicit Transaction Declaration

Aymeric Augustin says, 'Use ATOMIC_REQUESTS as long as the performance overhead is bearable. That means "forever" on most sites.'

When it comes to transactions, here are some good guidelines to live by:

➤ Database operations that do not modify the database *should not be* wrapped in transactions.
➤ Database operations that modify the database *should be* wrapped in a transactions.
➤ Special cases including database modifications that require database reads and performance considerations can affect the previous two guidelines.

If that's not clear enough, here is a table explaining when different Django ORM calls should be wrapped in transactions.

Purpose	ORM method	Generally Use Transactions?
Create Data	.create(), .bulk_create(), .get_or_create(),	✓
Retrieve Data	.get(), .filter(), .count(), .iterate(), .exists(), .exclude(), .in_bulk, etc.	
Modify Data	.update()	✓
Delete Data	.delete()	✓

Table 6.3: When to Use Transactions

We also cover this in chapter 22, *Finding and Reducing Bottlenecks*, specifically subsection subsection 22.2.4, 'Switch ATOMIC_REQUESTS to False.'

> ## TIP: Never Wrap Individual ORM Method Calls
>
> Django's ORM actually relies on transactions internally to ensure consistency of data. For instance, if an update affects multiple tables because of concrete inheritance, Django has that wrapped up in transactions.
>
> Therefore, it is never useful to wrap an individual ORM method [`.create()`, `.update()`, `.delete()`] call in a transaction. Instead, use transactions when you are calling several ORM methods in a view, function, or method.

6.4.3 django.http.StreamingHttpResponse and Transactions

If a view is returning `django.http.StreamingHttpResponse`, it's impossible to handle transaction errors once the response has begun. If your project uses this response method then `ATOMIC_REQUESTS` should do one of the following:

1. Set `ATOMIC_REQUESTS` to Django's default, which is `False`. Then you can use the techniques explored in subsection 6.4.2. Or...
2. Wrap the view in the `django.db.transaction.non_atomic_requests` decorator.

Keep in mind that you can use `ATOMIC_REQUESTS` with a streaming response, but the transaction will only apply to the view itself. If the generation of the response stream triggers additional SQL queries, they will be made in autocommit mode. Hopefully generating a response doesn't trigger database writes...

6.4.4   Transactions in MySQL

If the database being used is **MySQL**, transactions may not be supported depending on your choice of table type such as **InnoDB** or **MyISAM**. If transactions are not supported, Django will always function in autocommit mode, regardless of ATOMIC_REQUESTS or code written to support transactions. For more information, we recommend reading the following articles:

- ► http://2scoops.co/1.6-transactions-in-mysql
- ► http://dev.mysql.com/doc/refman/5.0/en/sql-syntax-transactions.html

6.4.5   Django ORM Transaction Resources

- ► https://docs.djangoproject.com/en/1.6/topics/db/transactions/
  Django's documentation on transactions.
- ► http://2scoops.co/1.5-transaction-recipe Blog post by Christophe Pettus that might prove useful for projects still on Django 1.5 or earlier.
- ► https://github.com/Xof/xact Christophe's packaging of the recipe described in his blog post, providing better PostgreSQL support for legacy Django 1.5 projects.

6.5   Summary

Models are the foundation for most Django projects, so take the time to design them thoughtfully.

Start normalized, and only denormalize if you've already explored other options thoroughly. You may be able to simplify slow, complex queries by dropping down to raw SQL, or you may be able to address your performance issues with caching in the right places.

Don't forget to use indexes. Add indexes when you have a better feel for how you're using data throughout your project.

If you decide to use model inheritance, inherit from abstract base classes rather than concrete models. You'll save yourself from the confusion of dealing with implicit, unneeded joins.

Watch out for the "gotchas" when using the `null=True` and `blank=True` model field options. Refer to our handy table for guidance.

Until Django 1.7 is released, use South to manage your data and schema migrations. It's a fantastic tool. You may also find django-model-utils and django-extensions pretty handy.

Finally, database transaction are a powerful tool for protecting the integrity of your data.

Our next chapter is where we begin talking about views.

7 | Function- and Class-Based Views

Both function-based views (FBVs) and class-based views (CBVs) are in Django 1.6. We recommend that you understand how to use both types of views.

TIP: Function-Based Views Are Not Deprecated

During the release of Django 1.5, there was a bit of confusion about FBVs due to the wording of the release notes and incorrect information on some blog posts. To clarify:

❶ **Function-based views are still in Django**. No plans exist for removing function-based views from Django. They are in active use, and they are great to have when you need them.

❷ Function-based generic views such as `direct_to_template` and `object_list` were deprecated in Django 1.3 and removed in 1.5.

7.1 When to Use FBVs or CBVs

Whenever you implement a view, think about whether it would make more sense to implement as a FBV or as a CBV. Some views are best implemented as CBVs, and others are best implemented as FBVs.

If you aren't sure which method to choose, on the next page we've included a flow chart that might be of assistance.

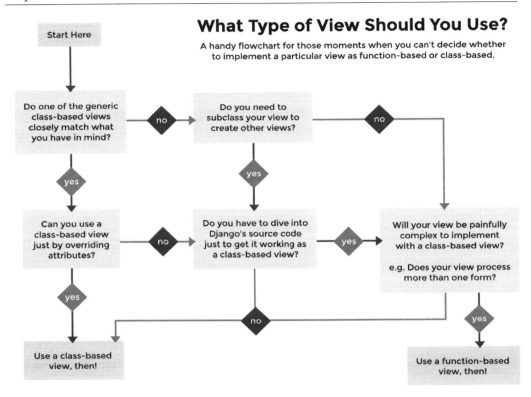

Figure 7.1: Should you use a FBV or a CBV? flow chart.

This flowchart follows our preference for using CBVs over FBVs. We prefer to use CBVs for most views, using FBVs to implement only the custom error views or complicated ones that would be a pain to implement with CBVs.

> ## TIP: Alternative Approach - Staying With FBVs
>
> Some developers prefer to err on the side of using FBVs for most views and CBVs only for views that need to be subclassed. That strategy is fine as well.

7.2 Keep View Logic Out of URLConfs

Requests are routed to views via **URLConfs**, in a module that is normally named *urls.py*. Per Django's URL design philosophy (http://2scoops.co/1.6-url-design), the coupling of views with urls is loose, allows for infinite flexibility, and encourages best practices.

And yet, this is what Daniel feels like yelling every time he sees complex *urls.py* files:

> *"I didn't write J2EE XML and Zope ZCML configuration files back in the day just so you darn kids could stick logic into Django url modules!"*

Remember that Django has a wonderfully simple way of defining URL routes. Like everything else we bring up in this book, that simplicity is to be honored and respected. The rules of thumb are obvious:

1. The views modules should contain view logic.
2. The URL modules should contain URL logic.

Ever see code like this? Perhaps in the official Django tutorial?

```
BAD EXAMPLE 7.1
from django.conf.urls import patterns, url
from django.views.generic import DetailView

from tastings.models import Tasting

urlpatterns = patterns("",
    url(r"^(?P<pk>\d+)/$",
        DetailView.as_view(
            model=Tasting,
            template_name="tastings/detail.html"),
        name="detail"),
    url(r"^(?P<pk>\d+)/results/$",
        DetailView.as_view(
            model=Tasting,
            template_name="tastings/results.html"),
        name="results"),
)
```

At a glance this code might seem okay, but we argue that it violates the Django design philosophies:

➤ **Loose coupling** between views, urls, and models has been replaced with tight coupling, meaning you can never reuse the view definitions.

➤ **Don't Repeat Yourself** is violated by using the same/similar arguments repeatedly between CBVs.

➤ Infinite flexibility (for URLs) is destroyed. Class inheritance, the primary advantage of Class Based Views, is impossible using this anti-pattern.

➤ Lots of other issues: What happens when you have to add in authentication? And what about authorization? Are you going to wrap each URLConf view with two or more decorators? Putting your view code into your URLConfs quickly turns your URLConfs into an unmaintainable mess.

In fact, we've heard from developers that seeing CBVs defined in URLConfs this way was part of why they steered clear of using them.

Alright, enough griping. We'll show our preferences in the next section.

7.3 Stick to Loose Coupling in URLConfs

Figure 7.2: Loose coupling of chocolate chip cookie dough ice cream.

Here is how to create URLconfs that avoid the problems we mentioned on the previous page. First, we write the views:

EXAMPLE 7.1

```
# tastings/views.py
from django.views.generic import ListView, DetailView, UpdateView
```

```
from django.core.urlresolvers import reverse

from .models import Tasting

class TasteListView(DetailView):
    model = Tasting

class TasteDetailView(ListView):
    model = Tasting

class TasteResultsView(TasteDetailView):
    template_name = "tastings/results.html"

class TasteUpdateView(UpdateView):
    model = Tasting

    def get_success_url(self):
        return reverse("tastes:detail",
            kwargs={"pk": self.object.pk})
```

Then we define the urls:

```
EXAMPLE 7.2
# tastings/urls.py
from django.conf.urls import patterns
from django.conf.urls import url

from . import views

urlpatterns = patterns("",
    url(
        regex=r"^$",
        view=views.TasteListView.as_view(),
        name="list"
    ),
    url(
```

```
            regex=r"^(?P<pk>\d+)/$",
            view=views.TasteDetailView.as_view(),
            name="detail"
    ),
    url(
            regex=r"^(?P<pk>\d+)/results/$",
            view=views.TasteResultsView.as_view(),
            name="results"
    ),
    url(
            regex=r"^(?P<pk>\d+)/update/$",
            view=views.TasteUpdateView.as_view(),
            name="update"
    )
)
```

Your first response to our version of this should go something like, *"Are you sure this is a good idea? You changed things to use two files AND more lines of code! How is this better?"*

Well, this is the way we do it. Here are some of the reasons we find it so useful:

> **Don't Repeat Yourself**: No argument or attribute is repeated between views.
> **Loose coupling**: We've removed the model and template names from the URLConf because views should be views and URLConfs should be URLConfs. We should be able to call our views from one or more URLConfs, and our approach lets us do just that.
> **URLConfs should do one thing and do it well**: Related to our previous bullet, our URLConf is now focused primarily on just one thing: URL routing. We aren't tracking down view logic across both views and URLConfs, we just look in our views.
> **Our views benefit from being class-based**: Our views, by having a formal definition in the views module, can inherit from other classes. This means adding authentication, authorization, new content formats, or any other business requirement tossed our way is much easier to handle.
> **Infinite flexibility**: Our views, by having a formal definition in the views module, can implement their own custom logic.

7.3.1 What If We Aren't Using CBVs?

The same rules apply.

We've encountered debugging nightmares of projects using FBVs with extensive URLConf hackery, such as elaborate tricks with the __file__ attribute of Python modules combined with directory walking and regular expressions to automagically create URLConfs. If that sounds painful, it was.

Keep logic out of URLConfs!

7.4 Use URL Namespaces

What URL namespaces do is provide an identifier for app-level and instance level namespaces. URL namespaces are one of those things where on the surface they seem like they might not help much, but once a developer begins using them they wonder why they didn't use them already. We'll sum up using URL namespaces as follows:

Instead of writing URL names like `tastings_detail` write them like `tastings:detail`.

Before we explain why this is so useful, we'll provide an example of usage based on the app-level URLConf code from example 7.2. In the root URLConf we would add:

```
EXAMPLE 7.3
# urls.py at root of project
urlpatterns += patterns('',
    url(r'^tastings/', include('tastings.urls', namespace='tastings'),
)
```

To see this in action in a view, let's take a look at a snippet of code from example 7.1:

```
EXAMPLE 7.4
# tastings/views.py snippet
class TasteUpdateView(UpdateView):
    model = Tasting
```

```
    def get_success_url(self):
        return reverse("tastes:detail",
            kwargs={"pk": self.object.pk})
```

See this in action in an HTML template:

EXAMPLE 7.5

```
{% extends "base.html" %}

{% block title %}Tastings{% endblock title %}

{% block content %}
<ul>
  {% for tasting in tastings %}
    <li>
      <a href="{% url "tastings:detail" taste.pk %}">{{ taste.title }}</a>
      <small>
        (<a href="{% url "tastings:update" taste.pk %}">update</a>)
      </small>
    </li>


  {% endfor %}
</ul>
{% endblock content %}
```

Now that we've understand how to implement URL namespaces, let's cover why they are useful.

7.4.1 Makes for Shorter, More Obvious and Don't Repeat Yourself URL names

In example 7.2 what we don't see are URL names like "tastings_detail" and "tastings_results" that copy the model or app name. Instead there are simple, obvious names like "*detail*" and "*results*". This greatly increases the legibility of apps, especially to newer Django developers.

Also, who wants to type "tastings" or whatever an app is called so many extra times?

7.4.2   Increases Interoperability with Third-Party Libraries

One of the problems of writing URL names things like <myapp>_detail is when app names collide. While this might not be a problem with things like our *tastings* app, it's certainly happened to the authors with blog and contact applications. Fortunately, URL namespaces makes this easy to resolve. Assuming that we have an existing contact app, but needed to add a second one, using URL namespaces we could integrate them to our root URLConf like so:

EXAMPLE 7.6

```
# urls.py at root of project
urlpatterns += patterns('',
    url(r'^contact/', include('contactmonger.urls',
                                    namespace='contactmonger')),
    url(r'^report-problem/', include('contactapp.urls',
                                    namespace='contactapp')),
)
```

Then work them into our templates doing the following:

EXAMPLE 7.7

```
{% extends "base.html" %}
{% block title %}Contact{% endblock title %}
{% block content %}
<p>
  <a href="{% url "contactmonger:create" %}">Contact Us</a>
</p>
<p>
  <a href="{% url "contactapp:report" %}">Report a Problem</a>
</p>
{% endblock content %}
```

7.4.3 Easier Searches, Upgrades, and Refactors

Considering the prevalence of underscores in names for PEP 8-friendly frameworks like Django, searching code or names like "tastings_detail" can be challenging. When a result comes up, is that for a view name, a URL name, or something else?

On the other hand, searching for "tastings:detail" makes for obvious search result responses. Which can and has made upgrades and refactoring of apps and projects easier, including when interacting with new third-party libraries.

7.4.4 Allows for More App and Template Reverse Tricks

We're not going to cover any tricks here, because we feel such things are almost never justified. In fact, usually they just add to the complexity of a project without adding any tangible benefit. However, there are a couple use cases worth mentioning:

- ➤ Development tools like django-debug-toolbar that perform debug-level introspection.
- ➤ Projects that allow end-users to add "modules" to change or alter the behavior of their account.

While developers can use either of these to justify the use of creative URL namespaces tricks, as always, we recommend trying the simplest approach first.

7.5 Try to Keep Business Logic Out of Views

In the past, we've placed an amazing amount of sophisticated business logic into our views. Unfortunately, when it became time to generate PDFs, add a REST API, or serve out other formats, placing so much logic in our views made it much harder to deliver new formats.

This is where our preferred approach of model methods, manager methods, or general utility helper function come into play. When business logic is placed into easily reusable components, and called from within views, it makes extending components of the project to do more things much easier.

Since it's not always possible to do this at the beginning of a project, our rule of thumb has become whenever we find ourselves duplicating business logic instead of Django boilerplate between views, it's time to move code out of the view.

7.6 Django Views are Functions

When it comes down to it, every Django view is a function. This function takes an HTTP request object and turns it into a HTTP response object. If you know anything about basic mathematical functions, this process of change should look very familiar.

EXAMPLE 7.8

```
# Django FBV as a function
HttpResponse = view(HttpRequest)


# Deciphered into basic math (remember functions from algebra?)
y = f(x)


# ... and then translated into a CBV example
HttpResponse = View.as_view()(HttpRequest)
```

This concept of change serves as a foundation for all sorts of things you can do with Django views, be they function- or class-based.

TIP: Class-Based Views Are Actually Called as Functions

Django's CBVs appear to be very different than FBVs. However, the `View.as_view()` classmethod called in URLConfs is actually returning a callable instance of the view. In other words, a callback function that handles the request/response cycle exactly the same manner as a function-based view!

7.6.1 The Simplest Views

With this in mind, it's good to remember the simplest possible views that can be created with Django:

EXAMPLE 7.9

```
# simplest_views.py
from django.http import HttpResponse
```

```
from django.views.generic import View

# The simplest FBV
def simplest_view(request):
    # Business logic goes here
    return HttpResponse("FBV")

# The simplest CBV
class SimplestView(View):
    def get(self, request, *args, **kwargs):
        # Business logic goes here
        return HttpResponse("CBV")
```

Why is this useful to know?

> ➤ Sometimes we need a one-off views that do tiny things.
> ➤ Understanding the simplest Django views means we better understand what they are really doing.
> ➤ Illustrates how Django FBVs are HTTP method neutral, but Django CBVs require specific HTTP method declaration.

7.7 Summary

This chapter started with discussing when to use either FBVs or CBVs, and matched our own preference for the latter. In fact, in the next chapter we'll start to dig deep into the functionality that can be exploited when using FBVs, followed up by a chapter on CBVs.

We also discussed keeping view logic out of the URLConfs. We feel view code belongs in the apps' *views.py* modules, and URLConf code belongs in the apps' *urls.py* modules. Adhering to this practice allows for object inheritance when used with class-based views, easier code reuse, and greater flexibility of design.

8 | Best Practices for Function-Based Views

In Django since the beginning of the project, **function-based views** are in frequent use by developers around the world. While class-based views have risen in usage, the simplicity of using a function is appealing to both new and experienced developers alike. While the authors are in the camp of preferring CBVs, we work on projects that use FBVs and here are some patterns we've grown to enjoy.

8.1 Advantages of FBVs

The simplicity of FBVs comes at the expense of code reuse: FBVs don't have the same ability to inherit from superclasses the way that CBVs do. They do have the advantage of being more obviously functional in nature, which lends itself to a number of interesting strategies.

We follow these guidelines when writing FBVs:

- Less view code is better.
- Never repeat code in views.
- Views should handle presentation logic. Try to keep business logic in models when possible, or in forms if you must.
- Keep your views simple.
- Use them to write custom 403, 404, and 500 error handlers.
- Complex nested-if blocks are to be avoided.

8.2 Passing the HttpRequest Object

There are times where we want to reuse code in views, but not tie it into global actions such as **middleware** or **context processors**. Starting in the introduction of this book, we advised creating utility functions that can be used across the project.

For many utility functions, we are taking an attribute or attributes from the `django.http.HttpRequest` (or `HttpRequest` for short) object and gathering data or performing operations. What we've found, is by having the request object itself as a primary argument, we have simpler arguments on more methods. This means less cognitive overload of managing function/method arguments: just pass in the `HttpRequest` object!

EXAMPLE 8.1

```python
# sprinkles/utils.py

from django.core.exceptions import PermissionDenied


def check_sprinkle_rights(request):
    if request.user.can_sprinkle or request.user.is_staff:
        return request

    # Return a HTTP 403 back to the user
    raise PermissionDenied
```

The `check_sprinkle_rights()` function does a quick check against the rights of the user, raising a `django.core.exceptions.PermissionDenied` exception, which triggers a custom HTTP 403 view as we describe in subsection 26.3.3.

You'll note that we return back a `HttpRequest` object rather than an arbitrary value or even a `None` object. We do this because as Python is a dynamically typed language, we can attach additional attributes to the `HttpRequest`. For example:

EXAMPLE 8.2

```python
# sprinkles/utils.py

from django.core.exceptions import PermissionDenied
```

```
def check_sprinkles(request):
    if request.user.can_sprinkle or request.user.is_staff:
        # By adding this value here it means our display templates
        #   can be more generic. We don't need to have
        #   {% if request.user.can_sprinkle or request.user.is_staff %}
        #   instead just using
        #   {% if request.can_sprinkle %}
        request.can_sprinkle = True
        return request


    # Return a HTTP 403 back to the user
    raise PermissionDenied
```

There's another reason, which we'll cover shortly. In the meantime, let's demonstrate this code in action:

EXAMPLE 8.3

```
# sprinkles/views.py

from django.shortcuts import get_object_or_404
from django.shortcuts import render

from .utils import check_sprinkles
from .models import Sprinkle

def sprinkle_list(request):
    """Standard list view"""

    request = check_sprinkles(request)

    return render(request,
        "sprinkles/sprinkle_list.html",
        {"sprinkles": Sprinkle.objects.all()})

def sprinkle_detail(request, pk):
    """Standard detail view"""
```

```python
    sprinkle = get_object_or_404(Sprinkle, pk=pk)

    request = check_sprinkles(request)

    return render(request, "sprinkles/sprinkle_detail.html",
        {"sprinkle": sprinkle})

def sprinkle_preview(request):
    """"preview of new sprinkle, but without the
            check_sprinkles function being used.
    """
    sprinkle = Sprinkle.objects.all()
    return render(request,
        "sprinkles/sprinkle_preview.html",
        {"sprinkle": sprinkle})
```

Another good feature about this approach is that it's trivial to integrate into class-based views:

EXAMPLE 8.4

```python
# sprinkles/views.py
from django.views.generic import DetailView

from .utils import check_sprinkles
from .models import Sprinkle

class SprinkleDetail(DetailView):
    """Standard detail view"""

    model = Sprinkle

    def dispatch(self, request, *args, **kwargs):
        request = check_sprinkles(request)
        return super(SprinkleDetail, self).dispatch(
                                request, *args, **kwargs)
```

> ## TIP: Specific Function Arguments Have Their Place
>
> The downside to single argument functions is that specific function arguments like 'pk', 'flavor' or 'text' make it easier to understand the purpose of a function at a glance. In other words, try to use this technique for actions that are as generic as possible.

Since we're repeatedly reusing functions inside functions, wouldn't it be nice to easily recognize when this is being done? This is when we bring decorators into play.

8.3   Decorators are Sweet

For once, this isn't about ice cream, it's about code! In computer science parlance, **syntactic sugar** is a syntax added to a programming language in order to make things easier to read or to express. In Python, decorators are a feature added not out of necessity, but in order to make code cleaner and *sweeter* for humans to read. So yes, decorators are sweet.

When we combine the power of simple functions with the syntactic sugar of decorators, we get handy, reusable tools like the extremely useful to the point of being ubiquitous `django.contrib.auth.decorators.login_required` decorator.

Here's a sample decorator template for use in function-based views:

```
EXAMPLE 8.5
# simple decorator template
import functools


def decorator(view_func):
    @functools.wraps(view_func)
    def new_view_func(request, *args, **kwargs):
        # You can modify the request (HttpRequest) object here.
        response = view_func(request, *args, **kwargs)
        # You can modify the response (HttpResponse) object here.
        return response
    return new_view_func
```

That might not make too much sense, so we'll go through it step-by-step, using in-line code comments to clarify what we are doing. First, let's modify the decorator template from the previous example to match our needs:

EXAMPLE 8.6

```python
# sprinkles/decorators.py
from functools import wraps


from . import utils


# based off the decorator template from Example 8.5
def check_sprinkles(view_func):
    """Check if a user can add sprinkles"""
    @wraps(view_func)
    def new_view_func(request, *args, **kwargs):
        # Act on the request object with utils.can_sprinkle()
        request = utils.can_sprinkle(request)

        # Call the view function
        response = view_func(request, *args, **kwargs)

        # Return the HttpResponse object
        return response
    return wraps(view_func)(new_view_func)
```

Then we attach it to the function thus:

EXAMPLE 8.7

```python
# views.py
from django.shortcuts import get_object_or_404, render

from .decorators import check_sprinkles
from .models import Sprinkle

# Attach the decorator to the view
@check_sprinkles
def sprinkle_detail(request, pk):
```

```
"""Standard detail view"""

sprinkle = get_object_or_404(Sprinkle, pk=pk)

return render(request, "sprinkles/sprinkle_detail.html",
    {"sprinkle": sprinkle})
```

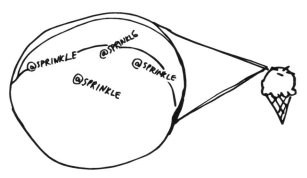

Figure 8.1: If you look at sprinkles closely, you'll see that they're Python decorators.

TIP: What About functools.wraps()?

Astute readers may have noticed that our decorator examples used the `functools.wraps()` decorator function from the Python standard library. This is a convenience tool that copies over metadata including critical data like docstrings to the newly decorated function. It's not necessary, but it makes project maintenance much easier.

8.3.1 Be Conservative with Decorators

As with any powerful tool, decorators can be used the wrong way. Too many decorators can create their own form of obfuscation, making even complex class-based view hierarchies seem simple in comparison. When using decorators, establish a limit of how many decorators can be set on a view and stick with it.

Video on the subject: http://www.2scoops.co/how-to-write-obfuscated-python/

8.3.2   Additional Resources on Decorators

➤ Decorators Explained: `http://2scoops.co/decorators-explained`
➤ Decorators and Functional Python: `http://2scoops.co/decorators-functional-python`
➤ "Appendix C: Useful Resources", specifically the section on "Useful Python Material"

8.4   Passing the HttpResponse object

Just as with the `HttpRequest` object, we can also pass around the `HttpResponse` object from function to function. Think of this as a selective `Middleware.process_request()` method (see `http://2scoops.co/1.6-process-response`).

Yes, this technique can be leveraged with decorators. See Example 8.5 which gives a hint as to how this can be accomplished.

8.5   Summary

Function-based views are still alive and well in the Django world. If we remember that every function accepts a `HttpRequest` object and returns an `HttpResponse` object, we can use that to our advantage. We can leverage in generic `HttpRequest` and `HttpResponse` altering functions, which can also be used to construct decorator functions.

We'll close this chapter by acknowledging that every lesson we've learned about function-based views can be applied to what we begin to discuss next chapter, class-based views.

9 | Best Practices for Class-Based Views

Django provides a standard way to write class-based views (CBVs). In fact, as we mentioned in previous chapters, a Django view is just a callable that accept a request object and returns a response. For function-based views (FBVs), the view function is that callable. For CBVs, the view class provides an as_view() class method that returns the callable. This mechanism is implemented in django.views.generic.View. All CBVs should inherit from that class, directly or indirectly.

Django also provides a series of generic class-based views (GCBVs) that implement common patterns found in most web projects and illustrate the power of CBVs.

Shortly after the release of Django 1.3, due to the placement of all views, there was some confusion between the general concept of CBVs because of the placement of all CBVs, including non-generic views in django.views.generic. These early problems have been addressed almost entirely, thanks to improvements in the documentation, resources such as Marc Tamlyn and Charles Denton's ccbv.co.uk code inspector, and the advent of third party packages designed to expedite CBV development.

PACKAGE TIP: Filling the Missing Parts of Django GCBVs

Out of the box, Django does not provide critically important mixins for GCBVs, including authentication. The **django-braces** library addresses most of these issues. It provides a set of clearly coded mixins that make Django GCBVs much easier and faster to implement. The next few chapters will demonstrate its mixins in various code examples.

9.1 Guidelines When Working With CBVs

- ➤ Less view code is better.
- ➤ Never repeat code in views.
- ➤ Views should handle presentation logic. Try to keep business logic in models when possible, or in forms if you must.
- ➤ Keep your views simple.
- ➤ Don't use CBVs to write custom 403, 404, and 500 error handlers. Use FBVs instead.
- ➤ Keep your **mixins** simpler.

9.2 Using Mixins With CBVs

Think of mixins in programming along the lines of mixins in ice cream: you can enhance any ice cream flavor by mixing in crunchy candy bits, sliced fruit, or even bacon.

Figure 9.1: Popular and unpopular mixins used in ice cream.

Soft serve ice cream greatly benefits from mixins: ordinary vanilla soft serve turns into birthday cake ice cream when sprinkles, blue buttercream icing, and chunks of yellow cake are mixed in.

In programming, a mixin is a class that provides functionality to be inherited, but isn't meant for instantiation on its own. In programming languages with multiple inheritance, mixins can be used to add enhanced functionality and behavior to classes.

You can use the power of mixins to composite useful and interesting new view classes for your Django apps.

When using mixins to composite your own view classes, we recommend these rules of inheritance provided by Kenneth Love. The rules follow Python's **method resolution order**, which in the most simplistic definition possible, proceeds from left to right:

❶ The base view classes provided by Django *always* go to the right.
❷ Mixins go to the left of the base view.
❸ Mixins should inherit from Python's built-in object type.

Example of the rules in action:

```
EXAMPLE 9.1

from django.views.generic import TemplateView


class FreshFruitMixin(object):

    def get_context_data(self, **kwargs):
        context = super(FreshFruitMixin,
                    self).get_context_data(**kwargs)
        context["has_fresh_fruit"] = True
        return context


class FruityFlavorView(FreshFruitMixin, TemplateView):
    template_name = "fruity_flavor.html"
```

In our rather silly example, the FruityFlavorView class inherits from both FreshFruit-Mixin and TemplateView.

Since TemplateView is the base view class provided by Django, it goes on the far right (rule 1), and to its left we place the FreshFruitMixin (rule 2). This way we know that our methods and properties will execute correctly.

Finally, FreshFruitMixin inherits from object (rule 3).

9.3 Which Django GCBV Should Be Used for What Task?

The power of generic class-based views comes at the expense of simplicity: GCBVs come with a complex inheritance chain that can have up to eight superclasses on import. Trying to work out exactly which view to use or which method to customize can be very challenging at times.

To mitigate this challenge, here's a handy chart listing the name and purpose of each Django CBV. All views listed here are assumed to be prefixed with `django.views.generic`.

Name	Purpose	Two Scoops Example
`View`	Base view or handy view that can be used for anything.	See section 9.6, `Using Just django.views.generic.View`.
`RedirectView`	Redirect user to another URL	Send users who visit `/log-in/` to `/login/`.
`TemplateView`	Display a Django HTML template.	The `/about/` page of our site.
`ListView`	List objects	List of ice cream flavors.
`DetailView`	Display an object	Details on an ice cream flavor.
`FormView`	Submit a form	The site's contact or email form.
`CreateView`	Create an object	Create a new ice cream flavor.
`UpdateView`	Update an object	Update an existing ice cream flavor.
`DeleteView`	Delete an object	Delete an unpleasant ice cream flavor like Vanilla Steak.
Generic date views	For display of objects that occur over a range of time.	Blogs are a common reason to use them. For Two Scoops, we could create a public history of when flavors have been added to the database.

Table 9.1: Django CBV Usage Table

> ## TIP: The Three Schools of Django CBV/GCBV Usage
>
> We've found that there are three major schools of thought around CBV and GCBV usage. They are:
>
> ### The School of "Use all the generic views"!
> This school of thought is based on the idea that since Django provides functionality to reduce your workload, why not use that functionality? We tend to belong to this school of thought, and have used it to great success, rapidly building and then maintaining a number of projects.
>
> ### The School of "Just use django.views.generic.View"
> This school of thought is based on the idea that the base Django CBV does just enough and is 'the True CBV, everything else is a Generic CBV'. In the past year, we've found this can be a really useful approach for tricky tasks for which the resource-based approach of "Use all the views" breaks down. We'll cover some use cases for it in this chapter.
>
> ### The School of "Avoid them unless you're actually subclassing views"
> Jacob Kaplan-Moss says, "My general advice is to start with function views since they're easier to read and understand, and only use CBVs where you need them. Where do you need them? Any place where you need a fair chunk of code to be reused among multiple views."
>
> We generally belong to the first school, but it's good for you to know that there's no real consensus on best practices here.

9.4 General Tips for Django CBVs

This section covers useful tips for all or many Django CBV and GCBV implementations.

9.4.1   Constraining Django CBV/GCBV Access to Authenticated Users

While the Django CBV documentation gives a helpful working example of using the `django.contrib.auth.decorators.login_required` decorator with a CBV, the example contains a lot of boilerplate cruft: http://2scoops.co/1.6-login-required-cbv

Fortunately, django-braces provides a ready implementation of a `LoginRequiredMixin` that you can attach in moments. For example, we could do the following in all of the Django GCBVs that we've written so far:

```
EXAMPLE 9.2
# flavors/views.py
from django.views.generic import DetailView

from braces.views import LoginRequiredMixin

from .models import Flavor

class FlavorDetailView(LoginRequiredMixin, DetailView):
    model = Flavor
```

TIP: Don't Forget the GCBV Mixin Order!

Remember that:

➤ `LoginRequiredMixin` must always go on the far left side.
➤ The base view class must always go on the far right side.

If you forget and switch the order, you will get broken or unpredictable results.

9.4.2   Performing Custom Actions on Views With Valid Forms

When you need to perform a custom action on a view with a **valid** form, the `form_valid()` method is where the GCBV workflow sends the request.

EXAMPLE 9.3

```python
from django.views.generic import CreateView

from braces.views import LoginRequiredMixin

from .models import Flavor

class FlavorCreateView(LoginRequiredMixin, CreateView):
    model = Flavor
    fields = ('title', 'slug', 'scoops_remaining')

    def form_valid(self, form):
        # Do custom logic here
        return super(FlavorCreateView, self).form_valid(form)
```

To perform custom logic on form data that has already been validated, simply add the logic to form_valid(). The return value of form_valid() should be a django.http.HttpResponseRedirect.

9.4.3   Performing Custom Actions on Views With Invalid Forms

When you need to perform a custom action on a view with an **invalid** form, the form_invalid() method is where the Django GCBV workflow sends the request. This method should return a django.http.HttpResponse.

EXAMPLE 9.4

```python
from django.views.generic import CreateView

from braces.views import LoginRequiredMixin

from .models import Flavor

class FlavorCreateView(LoginRequiredMixin, CreateView):
    model = Flavor
```

```
def form_invalid(self, form):
    # Do custom logic here
    return super(FlavorCreateView, self).form_invalid(form)
```

Just as you can add logic to form_valid(), you can also add logic to form_invalid().

You'll see an example of overriding both of these methods in chapter 11, *More Things To Know About Forms*, subsection 11.2.1, 'Form Data Is Saved to the Form, Then the Model Instance.'

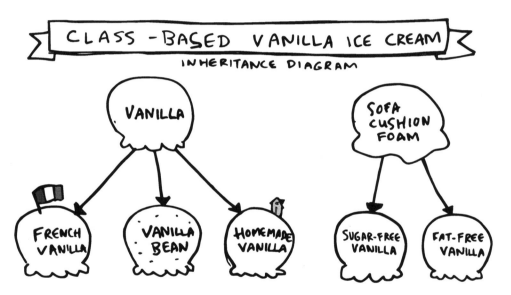

Figure 9.2: The other CBV: class-based vanilla ice cream.

9.4.4 Using the View Object

If you are using class-based views for rendering content, consider using the view object itself to provide access to properties and methods that can be called by other method and properties. They can also be called from templates. For example:

EXAMPLE 9.5

```python
from django.utils.functional import cached_property
from django.views.generic import UpdateView, TemplateView

from braces.views import LoginRequiredMixin

from .models import Flavor
from .tasks import update_users_who_favorited

class FavoriteMixin(object):

    @cached_property
    def likes_and_favorites(self):
        """Returns a dictionary numbers of likes"""
        likes = self.object.likes()
        favorites = self.object.favorites()
        return {
            "likes": likes,
            "favorites": favorites,
            "favorites_count": favorites.count(),

        }

class FlavorUpdateView(LoginRequiredMixin, FavoriteMixin, UpdateView):
    model = Flavor
    fields = ('title', 'slug', 'scoops_remaining')

    def form_valid(self, form):
        update_users_who_favorited(
            instance=self.object,
            favorites=self.likes_and_favorites['favorites']
        )
        return super(FlavorCreateView, self).form_valid(form)

class FlavorDetailView(LoginRequiredMixin, FavoriteMixin, TemplateView):
    model = Flavor
```

The nice thing about this is the various *flavors/* app templates can now access this property:

EXAMPLE 9.6

```
{# flavors/base.html #}
{% extends "base.html" %}


{% block likes_and_favorites %}
<ul>
  <li>Likes: {{ view.likes_and_favorites.likes }}</li>
  <li>Favorites: {{ view.likes_and_favorites.favorites_count }}</li>
</ul>
{% endblock likes_and_favorites %}
```

9.5   How GCBVs and Forms Fit Together

A common source of confusion with GCBVs is their usage with Django forms.

Using our favorite example of the ice cream flavor tracking app, let's chart out a couple of examples of how form-related views might fit together.

First, let's define a flavor model to use in this section's view examples:

EXAMPLE 9.7

```
# flavors/models.py
from django.core.urlresolvers import reverse
from django.db import models

STATUS = (
    (0, "zero"),
    (1, "one"),
)


class Flavor(models.Model):
    title = models.CharField(max_length=255)
    slug = models.SlugField()
    scoops_remaining = models.IntegerField(default=0, choices=STATUS)
```

```
def get_absolute_url(self):
    return reverse("flavor_detail", kwargs={"slug": self.slug})
```

Now, let's explore some common Django form scenarios that most Django users run into at one point or another.

9.5.1   Views + ModelForm Example

This is the simplest and most common Django form scenario. Typically when you create a model, you want to be able to add new records and update existing records that correspond to the model.

In this example, we'll show you how to construct a set of views that will create, update and display Flavor records. We'll also demonstrate how to provide confirmation of changes.

Here we have the following views:

❶ **FlavorCreateView** corresponds to a form for adding new flavors.
❷ **FlavorUpdateView** corresponds to a form for editing existing flavors.
❸ **FlavorDetailView** corresponds to the confirmation page for both flavor creation and flavor updates.

To visualize our views:

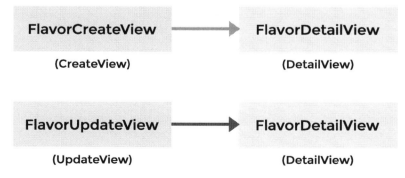

Figure 9.3: Views + ModelForm Flow

Note that we stick as closely as possible to Django naming conventions. FlavorCreateView subclasses Django's CreateView, FlavorUpdateView subclasses Django's UpdateView, and FlavorDetailView subclasses Django's DetailView.

Writing these views is easy, since it's mostly a matter of using what Django gives us:

```
EXAMPLE 9.8
# flavors/views.py
from django.views.generic import CreateView, UpdateView, DetailView

from braces.views import LoginRequiredMixin

from .models import Flavor

class FlavorCreateView(LoginRequiredMixin, CreateView):
    model = Flavor
    fields = ('title', 'slug', 'scoops_remaining')

class FlavorUpdateView(LoginRequiredMixin, UpdateView):
    model = Flavor
    fields = ('title', 'slug', 'scoops_remaining')

class FlavorDetailView(DetailView):
    model = Flavor
```

Simple at first glance, right? We accomplish so much with just a little bit of code!

But wait, there's a catch. If we wire these views into a *urls.py* module and create the necessary templates, we'll uncover a problem:

The FlavorDetailView is not a confirmation page.

For now, that statement is correct. Fortunately, we can fix it quickly with a few modifications to existing views and templates.

The first step in the fix is to use django.contrib.messages to inform the user visiting the FlavorDetailView that they just added or updated the flavor.

We'll need to override the `FlavorCreateView.form_valid()` and `FlavorUpdate-View.form_valid()` methods. We can do this conveniently for both views with a `FlavorActionMixin`.

For the confirmation page fix, we change *flavors/views.py* to contain the following:

```
EXAMPLE 9.9
# flavors/views.py

from django.contrib import messages
from django.views.generic import CreateView, UpdateView, DetailView

from braces.views import LoginRequiredMixin

from .models import Flavor

class FlavorActionMixin(object):

    fields = ('title', 'slug', 'scoops_remaining')

    @property
    def success_msg(self):
        return NotImplemented

    def form_valid(self, form):
        messages.info(self.request, self.success_msg)
        return super(FlavorActionMixin, self).form_valid(form)

class FlavorCreateView(LoginRequiredMixin, FlavorActionMixin,
                        CreateView):
    model = Flavor
    success_msg = "Flavor created!"

class FlavorUpdateView(LoginRequiredMixin, FlavorActionMixin,
                        UpdateView):
    model = Flavor
    success_msg = "Flavor updated!"
```

```
class FlavorDetailView(DetailView):
    model = Flavor
```

Earlier in this chapter, we covered a simpler example of how to override form_valid() within a GCBV. Here, we reuse a similar form_valid() override method by creating a mixin to inherit from in multiple views.

Now we're using Django's **messages** framework to display confirmation messages to the user upon every successful add or edit. We define a FlavorActionMixin whose job is to queue up a confirmation message corresponding to the action performed in a view.

TIP: Mixins Should Inherit From Object

Please take notice that the FlavorActionMixin inherits from Python's object type rather than a pre-existing mixin or view. It's important that mixins have as shallow inheritance chain as possible. Simplicity is a virtue!

After a flavor is created or updated, a list of messages is passed to the context of the FlavorDetailView. We can see these messages if we add the following code to the views' template and then create or update a flavor:

```
EXAMPLE 9.10
{# templates/flavors/flavor_detail.html #}
{% if messages %}
    <ul class="messages">
        {% for message in messages %}
        <li id="message_{{ forloop.counter }}"
            {% if message.tags %} class="{{ message.tags }}"
                {% endif %}>
            {{ message }}
        </li>
        {% endfor %}
    </ul>
{% endif %}
```

TIP: Reuse the Messages Template Code!

It is common practice to put the above code into your project's base HTML template. Doing this allows message support for templates in your project.

To recap, this example demonstrated yet again how to override the `form_valid()` method, incorporate this into a mixin, how to incorporate multiple mixins into a view, and gave a quick introduction to the very useful `django.contrib.messages` framework.

9.5.2 Views + Form Example

Sometimes you want to use a Django `Form` rather than a `ModelForm`. Search forms are a particularly good use case for this, but you'll run into other scenarios where this is true as well.

In this example, we'll create a simple flavor search form. This involves creating a HTML form that doesn't modify any flavor data. The form's action will query the ORM, and the records found will be listed on a search results page.

Our intention is that when using our flavor search page, if users do a flavor search for "Dough", they should be sent to a page listing ice cream flavors like "Chocolate Chip Cookie Dough," "Fudge Brownie Dough," "Peanut Butter Cookie Dough," and other flavors containing the string "Dough" in their title. Mmm, we definitely want this feature in our web application.

There are more complex ways to implement this, but for our simple use case, all we need is a single view. We'll use a `FlavorListView` for both the search page and the search results page.

Here's an overview of our implementation:

Figure 9.4: Views + Form Flow

In this scenario, we want to follow the standard internet convention for search pages, where 'q' is used for the search query parameter. We also want to accept a GET request rather than a POST request, which is unusual for forms but perfectly fine for this use case. Remember, this form doesn't add, edit, or delete objects, so we don't need a POST request here.

To return matching search results based on the search query, we need to modify the standard queryset supplied by the ListView. To do this, we override the ListView's get_queryset() method. We add the following code to *flavors/views.py*:

EXAMPLE 9.11

```python
from django.views.generic import ListView

from .models import Flavor

class FlavorListView(ListView):
    model = Flavor

    def get_queryset(self):
        # Fetch the queryset from the parent get_queryset
        queryset = super(FlavorListView, self).get_queryset()

        # Get the q GET parameter
        q = self.request.GET.get("q")
        if q:
            # Return a filtered queryset
            return queryset.filter(title__icontains=q)
        # Return the base queryset
        return queryset
```

Now, instead of listing all of the flavors, we list only the flavors whose titles contain the search string.

As we mentioned, search forms are unusual in that unlike nearly every other HTML form they specify a GET request in the HTML form. This is because search forms are not changing data, but simply retrieving information from the server. The search form should look something like this:

EXAMPLE 9.12
```
{# templates/flavors/_flavor_search.html #}
{% comment %}
    Usage: {% include "flavors/_flavor_search.html" %}
{% endcomment %}
<form action="{% url "flavor_list" %}" method="GET">
    <input type="text" name="q" />
    <button type="submit">search</button>
</form>
```

> ## TIP: Specify the Form Target in Search Forms
>
> We also take care to specify the URL in the form action, because we've found that search forms are often included in several pages. This is why we prefix them with '_' and create them in such a way as to be included in other templates.

Once we get past overriding the `ListView`'s `get_queryset()` method, the rest of this example is just a simple HTML form. We like this kind of simplicity.

9.6   Using Just django.views.generic.View

It's entirely possible to build a project just using `django.views.generic.View` for all the views. It's not as extreme as one might think. For example, if we look at the official Django documentation's introduction to class-based views (http://2scoops.co/1.6-using-cbvs), we can see the approach is very close to how function-based views are written. In fact, we highlighted this two chapters ago in subsection 7.6.1 'The Simplest Views' because it's important.

Imagine instead of writing function-based views with nested-ifs representing different HTTP methods or class-based views where the HTTP methods are hidden behind `get_context_data()` and `form_valid()` methods, they are readily accessible to developers. Imagine something like:

EXAMPLE 9.13
```
from django.shortcuts import get_object_or_404
```

```python
from django.shortcuts import render, redirect
from django.views.generic import View

from braces.views import LoginRequiredMixin

from .forms import FlavorForm
from .models import Flavor

class FlavorView(LoginRequiredMixin, View):

    def get(self, request, *args, **kwargs):
        # Handles display of the Flavor object
        flavor = get_object_or_404(Flavor, pk=kwargs['slug'])
        return render(request,
            "flavors/flavor_detail.html",
                {"flavor": flavor}
            )

    def post(self, request, *args, **kwargs):
        # Handles updates of the Flavor object
        flavor = get_object_or_404(Flavor, pk=kwargs['slug'])
        form = FlavorForm(request.POST)
        if form.is_valid():
            form.save()
        return redirect("flavors:detail", flavor.slug)
```

While we can do this in a function-based view, it can be argued that the GET/POST method declarations within the FlavorView are more easier to read than the traditional "if request.method == ..." conditions. In addition, since the inheritance chain is so shallow, it means using mixins doesn't threaten us with cognitive overload.

What we find really useful, even on projects which use a lot of generic class-based views, is using the django.views.generic.View class with a GET method for displaying JSON, PDF or other non-HTML content. All the tricks that we've used for rendering CSV, Excel, and PDF files in function-based views apply when using the GET method. For example:

EXAMPLE 9.14

```python
from django.http import HttpResponse
from django.shortcuts import get_object_or_404
from django.views.generic import View

from braces.views import LoginRequiredMixin

from .models import Flavor
from .reports import make_flavor_pdf


class PDFFlavorView(LoginRequiredMixin, View):

    def get(self, request, *args, **kwargs):
        # Get the flavor
        flavor = get_object_or_404(Flavor, pk=kwargs['slug'])

        # create the response
        response = HttpResponse(mimetype='application/pdf')

        # generate the PDF stream and attach to the response
        response = make_flavor_pdf(response, flavor)

        return response
```

This is a pretty straight-forward example, but if we have to leverage more mixins and deal with more custom logic, the simplicity of `django.views.generic.View` makes it much easier than the more heavyweight views. In essence, we get all the advantages of function-based views combined with the object-oriented power that CBVs gave us starting with Django 1.3.

9.7 Additional Resources

➤ http://2scoops.co/1.6-topics-class-based-views
➤ http://2scoops.co/1.6-cbv-generic-display
➤ http://2scoops.co/1.6-cbv-generic-editing
➤ http://2scoops.co/1.6-cbv-mixins
➤ http://2scoops.co/1.6-ref-class-based-views

- ➤ The GCBV inspector at `http://ccbv.co.uk`
- ➤ `www.python.org/download/releases/2.3/mro/`
- ➤ `http://pydanny.com/tag/class-based-views.html`

PACKAGE TIP: Other Useful CBV Libraries

- ➤ **django-extra-views** Another great CBV library, django-extra-views covers the cases that django-braces does not.
- ➤ **django-vanilla-views** A very interesting library that provides all the power of classic Django GCBVs in a vastly simplified, easier-to-use package. Works great in combination with django-braces, but there are a few places where things won't work.

9.8 Summary

This chapter covered:

- ➤ Using mixins with CBVs
- ➤ Which Django CBV should be used for which task
- ➤ General tips for CBV usage
- ➤ Connecting CBVs to forms
- ➤ Using the base `django.views.generic.View`

The next chapter explores common CBV/form patterns. Knowledge of these are helpful to have in your developer toolbox.

10 | Common Patterns for Forms

Django forms are powerful, flexible, extensible, and robust. For this reason, the Django admin and CBVs use them extensively. In fact, all the major Django API frameworks use ModelForms as part of their validation because of their powerful validation features.

Combining forms, models, and views allows us to get a lot of work done for little effort. The learning curve is worth it: once you learn to work fluently with these components, you'll find that Django provides the ability to create an amazing amount of useful, stable functionality at an amazing pace.

PACKAGE TIP: Useful Form-Related Packages

➤ **django-floppyforms** for rendering Django inputs in HTML5.
➤ **django-crispy-forms** for advanced form layout controls. By default, forms are rendered with Twitter Bootstrap form elements and styles. This package plays well with django-floppyforms, so they are often used together.
➤ **django-forms-bootstrap** is a simple tool for rendering Django forms using Twitter Bootstrap styles. This package plays well with django-floppyforms but conflicts with django-crispy-forms.

10.1 The Power of Django Forms

You might not be aware of the fact that even if your Django project uses an API framework and doesn't serve HTML, you are probably still using Django forms. Django forms are not just for web pages; their powerful validation features are useful on their own.

Interestingly enough, the design that Django's API frameworks use is some form of class-based view. They might have their own implementation of CBVs (i.e. django-tastypie) or run off of Django's own CBVs (django-rest-framework), but the use of inheritance and composition is a constant. We would like to think this is proof of the soundness of both Django forms and the concept of CBVs.

With that in mind, this chapter goes explicitly into one of the best parts of Django: forms, models, and CBVs working in concert. This chapter covers five common form patterns that should be in every Django developer's toolbox.

10.2 Pattern 1: Simple ModelForm With Default Validators

The simplest data-changing form that we can make is a ModelForm using several default validators as-is, without modification. In fact, we already relied on default validators in chapter 9, *Best Practices for Class-Based Views*, subsection 9.5.1, "Views + ModelForm Example."

If you recall, using ModelForms with CBVs to implement add/edit forms can be done in just a few lines of code:

```
EXAMPLE 10.1
# flavors/views.py
from django.views.generic import CreateView, UpdateView

from braces.views import LoginRequiredMixin

from .models import Flavor

class FlavorCreateView(LoginRequiredMixin, CreateView):
    model = Flavor
    fields = ('title', 'slug', 'scoops_remaining')

class FlavorUpdateView(LoginRequiredMixin, UpdateView):
    model = Flavor
    fields = ('title', 'slug', 'scoops_remaining')
```

To summarize how we use default validation as-is here:

> ➤ `FlavorCreateView` and `FlavorUpdateView` are assigned `Flavor` as their model.
> ➤ Both views auto-generate a `ModelForm` based on the Flavor model.
> ➤ Those `ModelForms` rely on the default field validation rules of the Flavor model.

Yes, Django gives us a lot of great defaults for data validation, but in practice, the defaults are never enough. We recognize this, so as a first step, the next pattern will demonstrate how to create a custom field validator.

10.3 Pattern 2: Custom Form Field Validators in ModelForms

What if we wanted to be certain that every use of the `title` field across our project's dessert apps started with the word 'Tasty'?

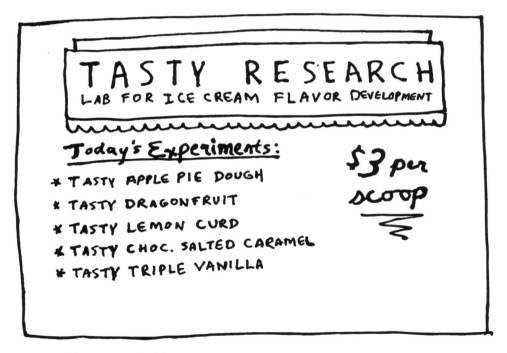

Figure 10.1: At Tasty Research, every flavor must begin with "Tasty".

This is a string validation problem that can be solved with a simple **custom field validator**.

In this pattern, we cover how to create custom single-field validators and demonstrate how to add them to both abstract models and forms.

Imagine for the purpose of this example that we have a project with two different dessert-related models: a Flavor model for ice cream flavors, and a Milkshake model for different types of milkshakes. Assume that both of our example models have title fields.

To validate all editable model titles, we start by creating a *validators.py* module:

```
EXAMPLE 10.2
# core/validators.py
from django.core.exceptions import ValidationError


def validate_tasty(value):
    """Raise a ValidationError if the value doesn't start with the
        word 'Tasty
    """
    if not value.startswith(u"Tasty"):
        msg = u"Must start with Tasty"
        raise ValidationError(msg)
```

In Django, a custom field validator is simply a function that raises an error if the submitted argument doesn't pass its test.

Of course, while our validate_tasty() validator function just does a simple string check for the sake of example, it's good to keep in mind that form field validators can become quite complex in practice.

TIP: Test Your Validators Carefully

Since validators are critical in keeping corruption out of Django project databases, it's especially important to write detailed tests for them.

These tests should include thoughtful edge case tests for every condition related to your validators' custom logic.

In order to use our `validate_tasty()` validator function across different dessert models, we're going to first add it to an abstract model called `TastyTitleAbstractModel`, which we plan to use across our project.

Assuming that our `Flavor` and `Milkshake` models are in separate apps, it doesn't make sense to put our validator in one app or the other. Instead, we create a *core/models.py* module and place the `TastyTitleAbstractModel` there.

EXAMPLE 10.3

```
# core/models.py
from django.db import models

from .validators import validate_tasty


class TastyTitleAbstractModel(models.Model):

    title = models.CharField(max_length=255, validators=[validate_tasty])

    class Meta:
        abstract = True
```

The last two lines of the above example code for *core/models.py* make `TastyTitleAbstract-Model` an abstract model, which is what we want.

Let's alter the original *flavors/models.py* `Flavor` code to use `TastyTitleAbstractModel` as the parent class:

EXAMPLE 10.4

```
# flavors/models.py
from django.core.urlresolvers import reverse
from django.db import models

from core.models import TastyTitleAbstractModel


class Flavor(TastyTitleAbstractModel):
    slug = models.SlugField()
    scoops_remaining = models.IntegerField(default=0)
```

```
    def get_absolute_url(self):
        return reverse("flavor_detail", kwargs={"slug": self.slug})
```

This works with the `Flavor` model, and it will work with any other tasty food-based model such as a `WaffleCone` or `Cake` model. Any model that inherits from the `TastyTitleAbstract-Model` class will throw a validation error if anyone attempts to save a model with a title that doesn't start with 'Tasty'.

Now, let's explore a couple of questions that might be forming in your head:

➤ What if we wanted to use `validate_tasty()` in just forms?
➤ What if we wanted to assign it to other fields besides the title?

To support these behaviors, we need to create a custom `FlavorForm` that utilizes our custom field validator:

```
EXAMPLE 10.5
# flavors/forms.py
from django import forms

from core.validators import validate_tasty
from .models import Flavor

class FlavorForm(forms.ModelForm):
    def __init__(self, *args, **kwargs):
        super(FlavorForm, self).__init__(*args, **kwargs)
        self.fields["title"].validators.append(validate_tasty)
        self.fields["slug"].validators.append(validate_tasty)

    class Meta:
        model = Flavor
```

A nice thing about both examples of validator usage in this pattern is that we haven't had to change the `validate_tasty()` code at all. Instead, we just import and use it in new places.

Attaching the custom form to the views is our next step. The default behavior of Django model-based edit views is to auto-generate the ModelForm based on the view's model attribute. We are going to override that default and pass in our custom *FlavorForm*. This occurs in the *flavors/views.py* module, where we alter the create and update forms as demonstrated below:

```python
EXAMPLE 10.6

# flavors/views.py
from django.contrib import messages
from django.views.generic import CreateView, UpdateView, DetailView

from braces.views import LoginRequiredMixin

from .models import Flavor
from .forms import FlavorForm

class FlavorActionMixin(object):

    model = Flavor
    fields = ('title', 'slug', 'scoops_remaining')

    @property
    def success_msg(self):
        return NotImplemented

    def form_valid(self, form):
        messages.info(self.request, self.success_msg)
        return super(FlavorActionMixin, self).form_valid(form)

class FlavorCreateView(LoginRequiredMixin, FlavorActionMixin,
                            CreateView):
    success_msg = "created"
    # Explicitly attach the FlavorForm class
    form_class = FlavorForm

class FlavorUpdateView(LoginRequiredMixin, FlavorActionMixin,
                            UpdateView):
    success_msg = "updated"
    # Explicitly attach the FlavorForm class
```

```
    form_class = FlavorForm

class FlavorDetailView(DetailView):
    model = Flavor
```

The `FlavorCreateView` and `FlavorUpdateView` views now use the new `FlavorForm` to validate incoming data.

Note that with these modifications, the `Flavor` model can either be identical to the one at the start of this chapter, or it can be an altered one that inherits from `TastyTitleAbstractModel`.

10.4 Pattern 3: Overriding the Clean Stage of Validation

Let's discuss some interesting validation use cases:

- ➤ Multi-field validation
- ➤ Validation involving existing data from the database that has already been validated

Both of these are great scenarios for overriding the `clean()` and `clean_<field_name>()` methods with custom validation logic.

After the default and custom field validators are run, Django provides a second stage and process for validating incoming data, this time via the `clean()` method and `clean_<field_name>()` methods. You might wonder why Django provides more hooks for validation, so here are our two favorite arguments:

❶ The `clean()` method is the place to validate two or more fields against each other, since it's not specific to any one particular field.

❷ The clean validation stage is a better place to attach validation against persistent data. Since the data already has some validation, you won't waste as many database cycles on needless queries.

Let's explore this with another validation example. Perhaps we want to implement an ice cream ordering form, where users could specify the flavor desired, add toppings, and then come to our store and pick them up.

Since we want to prevent users from ordering flavors that are out of stock, we'll put in a clean_slug() method. With our flavor validation, our form might look like:

EXAMPLE 10.7

```python
# flavors/forms.py
from django import forms
from flavors.models import Flavor


class IceCreamOrderForm(forms.Form):
    """Normally done with forms.ModelForm. But we use forms.Form here
        to demonstrate that these sorts of techniques work on every
        type of form.
    """

    slug = forms.ChoiceField("Flavor")
    toppings = forms.CharField()

    def __init__(self, *args, **kwargs):
        super(IceCreamOrderForm, self).__init__(*args,
                    **kwargs)
        # We dynamically set the choices here rather than
        # in the flavor field definition. Setting them in
        # the field definition means status updates won't
        # be reflected in the form without server restarts.
        self.fields["slug"].choices = [
            (x.slug, x.title) for x in Flavor.objects.all()
        ]
        # NOTE: We could filter by whether or not a flavor
        #       has any scoops, but this is an example of
        #       how to use clean_slug, not filter().

    def clean_slug(self):
        slug = self.cleaned_data["slug"]
        if Flavor.objects.get(slug=slug).scoops_remaining <= 0:
            msg = u"Sorry, we are out of that flavor."
            raise forms.ValidationError(msg)
        return slug
```

For HTML-powered views, the `clean_slug()` method in our example, upon throwing an error, will attach a "Sorry, we are out of that flavor" message to the flavor HTML input field. This is a great shortcut for writing HTML forms!

Now imagine if we get common customer complaints about orders with too much chocolate. Yes, it's silly and quite impossible, but we're just using 'too much chocolate' as a completely mythical example for the sake of making a point.

In any case, let's use the `clean()` method to validate the flavor and toppings fields against each other.

EXAMPLE 10.8

```
# attach this code to the previous example (9.7)
def clean(self):
    cleaned_data = super(IceCreamOrderForm, self).clean()
    slug = cleaned_data.get("slug", "")
    toppings = cleaned_data.get("toppings", "")


    # Silly "too much chocolate" validation example
    if u"chocolate" in slug.lower() and \
            u"chocolate" in toppings.lower():
        msg = u"Your order has too much chocolate."
        raise forms.ValidationError(msg)
    return cleaned_data
```

There we go, an implementation against the impossible condition of too much chocolate!

TIP: Common Fields Used In Multi-Field Validation

It is common practice for user account forms involved with email and password entry to force the user to enter the same data twice. Other things to check for against those fields include:

> ➤ Strength of the submitted password.
> ➤ If the email model field isn't set to `unique=True`, whether or not the email is unique.

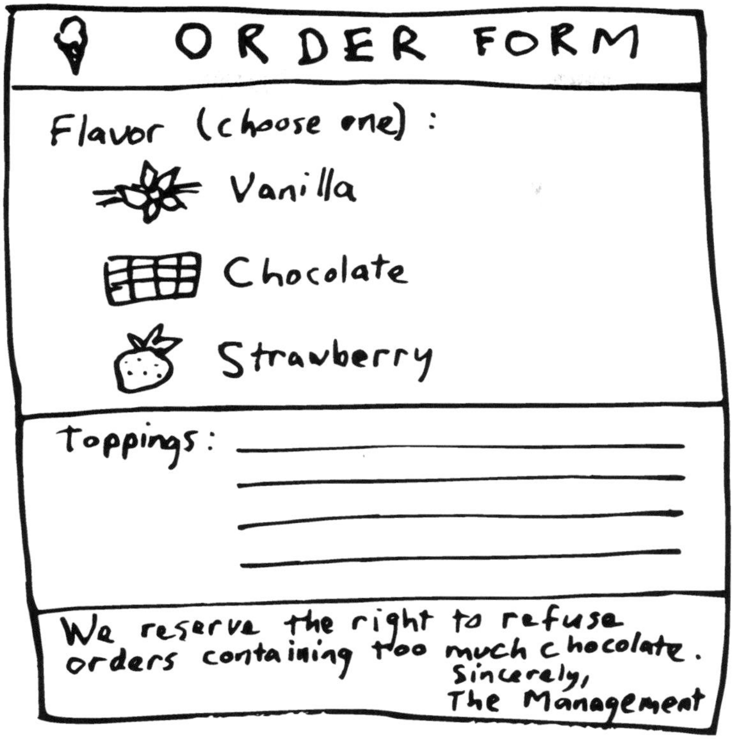

Figure 10.2: Why would they do this to us?

10.5 Pattern 4: Hacking Form Fields (2 CBVs, 2 Forms, 1 Model)

This is where we start to get fancy. We're going to cover a situation where two views/forms correspond to one model. We'll hack Django forms to produce a form with custom behavior.

It's not uncommon to have users create a record that contains a few empty fields which need additional data later. An example might be a list of stores, where we want each store entered into the system as fast as possible, but want to add more data such as phone number and description later. Here's our `IceCreamStore` model:

EXAMPLE 10.9

```
# stores/models.py
```

```
from django.core.urlresolvers import reverse
from django.db import models


class IceCreamStore(models.Model):
    title = models.CharField(max_length=100)
    block_address = models.TextField()
    phone = models.CharField(max_length=20, blank=True)
    description = models.TextField(blank=True)


    def get_absolute_url(self):
        return reverse("store_detail", kwargs={"pk": self.pk})
```

The default ModelForm for this model forces the user to enter the title and block_address
field but allows the user to skip the phone and description fields. That's great for initial data
entry, but as mentioned earlier, we want to have future updates of the data to require the phone
and description fields.

The way we implemented this in the past before we began to delve into their construction was
to override the phone and description fields in the edit form. This resulted in heavily-duplicated
code that looked like this:

```
BAD EXAMPLE 10.1
# stores/forms.py
from django import forms


from .models import IceCreamStore


class IceCreamStoreUpdateForm(forms.ModelForm):
    # Don't do this! Duplication of the model field!
    phone = forms.CharField(required=True)
    # Don't do this! Duplication of the model field!
    description = forms.TextField(required=True)

    class Meta:
        model = IceCreamStore
```

This form should look very familiar. Why is that?

Well, we're nearly copying the IceCreamStore model!

This is just a simple example, but when dealing with a lot of fields on a model, the duplication becomes extremely challenging to manage. In fact, what tends to happen is copy-pasting of code from models right into forms, which is a gross violation of **Don't Repeat Yourself**.

Want to know how gross? Using the above approach, if we add a simple help_text attribute to the description field in the model, it will not show up in the template until we also modify the description field definition in the form. If that sounds confusing, that's because it is.

A better way is to rely on a useful little detail that's good to remember about Django forms: instantiated form objects store fields in a dict-like attribute called fields.

Instead of copy-pasting field definitions from models to forms, we can simply apply new attributes to each field in the __init__() method of the ModelForm:

EXAMPLE 10.10

```python
# stores/forms.py
# Call phone and description from the self.fields dict-like object
from django import forms

from .models import IceCreamStore

class IceCreamStoreUpdateForm(forms.ModelForm):

    class Meta:
        model = IceCreamStore

    def __init__(self, *args, **kwargs):
        # Call the original __init__ method before assigning
        # field overloads
        super(IceCreamStoreUpdateForm, self).__init__(*args,
                    **kwargs)
        self.fields["phone"].required = True
        self.fields["description"].required = True
```

This improved approach allows us to stop copy-pasting code and instead focus on just the field-specific settings.

An important point to remember is that when it comes down to it, Django forms are just Python classes. They get instantiated as objects, they can inherit from other classes, and they can act as superclasses.

Therefore, we can rely on inheritance to trim the line count in our ice cream store forms:

```
EXAMPLE 10.11
# stores/forms.py
from django import forms

from .models import IceCreamStore

class IceCreamStoreCreateForm(forms.ModelForm):

    class Meta:
        model = IceCreamStore
        fields = ("title", "block_address", )

class IceCreamStoreUpdateForm(IceCreamStoreCreateForm):

    def __init__(self, *args, **kwargs):
        super(IceCreamStoreUpdateForm,
                self).__init__(*args, **kwargs)
        self.fields["phone"].required = True
        self.fields["description"].required = True

    class Meta(IceCreamStoreCreateForm.Meta):
        # show all the fields!
        fields = ("title", "block_address", "phone",
                "description", )
```

WARNING: Use Meta.fields and Never Use Meta.exclude

We use `Meta.fields` instead of `Meta.exclude` so that we know exactly what fields we are exposing. See chapter 23, *Security Best Practices*, section 23.13, 'Don't use ModelForms.Meta.exclude'.

Finally, now we have what we need to define the corresponding CBVs. We've got our form classes, so let's use them in the `IceCreamStore` create and update views:

```
EXAMPLE 10.12

# stores/views
from django.views.generic import CreateView, UpdateView

from .forms import IceCreamStoreCreateForm
from .forms import IceCreamStoreUpdateForm
from .models import IceCreamStore

class IceCreamCreateView(CreateView):
    model = IceCreamStore
    form_class = IceCreamStoreCreateForm

class IceCreamUpdateView(UpdateView):
    model = IceCreamStore
    form_class = IceCreamStoreUpdateForm
```

We now have two views and two forms that work with one model.

10.6   Pattern 5: Reusable Search Mixin View

In this example, we're going to cover how to reuse a search form in two views that correspond to two different models.

Assume that both models have a field called `title` (this pattern also demonstrates why naming standards in projects is a good thing). This example will demonstrate how a single CBV can be used to provide simple search functionality on both the `Flavor` and `IceCreamStore` models.

We'll start by creating a simple search mixin for our view:

EXAMPLE 10.13

```python
# core/views.py
class TitleSearchMixin(object):

    def get_queryset(self):
        # Fetch the queryset from the parent's get_queryset
        queryset = super(TitleSearchMixin, self).get_queryset()

        # Get the q GET parameter
        q = self.request.GET.get("q")
        if q:
            # return a filtered queryset
            return queryset.filter(title__icontains=q)
        # No q is specified so we return queryset
        return queryset
```

The above code should look very familiar as we used it almost verbatim in the Forms + View example. Here's how you make it work with both the `Flavor` and `IceCreamStore` views. First the flavor views:

EXAMPLE 10.14

```python
# add to flavors/views.py
from django.views.generic import ListView

from core.views import TitleSearchMixin
from .models import Flavor

class FlavorListView(TitleSearchMixin, ListView):
    model = Flavor
```

And we'll add it to the ice cream store views:

EXAMPLE 10.15

```python
# add to stores/views.py
from django.views.generic import ListView
```

```
from core.views import TitleSearchMixin
from .models import Store


class IceCreamStoreListView(TitleSearchMixin, ListView):
    model = Store
```

As for the form? We just define it in HTML for each `ListView`:

EXAMPLE 10.16

```
{# form to go into stores/store_list.html template #}
<form action="" method="GET">
    <input type="text" name="q" />
    <button type="submit">search</button>
</form>
```

and

EXAMPLE 10.17

```
{# form to go into flavors/flavor_list.html template #}
<form action="" method="GET">
    <input type="text" name="q" />
    <button type="submit">search</button>
</form>
```

Now we have the same mixin in both views. Mixins are a good way to reuse code, but using too many mixins in a single class makes for very hard-to-maintain code. As always, try to keep your code as simple as possible.

10.7 Summary

We began this chapter with the simplest form pattern, using a `ModelForm`, CBV, and default validators. We iterated on that with an example of a custom validator.

Next, we explored more complex validation. We covered an example overriding the clean methods. We also closely examined a scenario involving two views and their corresponding forms that were tied to a single model.

Finally, we covered an example of creating a reusable search mixin to add the same form to two different apps.

11 | More Things to Know About Forms

95% of Django projects should use ModelForms.

91% of all Django projects use ModelForms.

80% of ModelForms require trivial logic.

20% of ModelForms require complicated logic.

– pydanny made-up statistics™

Django's forms are really powerful, but there are edge cases that can cause a bit of anguish.

If you understand the structure of how forms are composed and how to call them, most edge cases can be readily overcome.

11.1 Use the POST Method in HTML Forms

Every HTML form that alters data must submit its data via the POST method:

EXAMPLE 11.1

```
<form action="{% url "flavor_add" %}" method="POST">
```

The only exception you'll ever see to using POST in forms is with search forms, which typically submit queries that don't result in any alteration of data. Search forms that are idempotent should use the GET method.

11.1.1   Don't Disable Django's CSRF Protection

This is covered in chapter 23, *Security Best Practices*, section 23.7, 'Always Use CSRF Protection With Forms That Modify Data.' Also, please familiarize yourself with Django's documentation on the subject: `https://docs.djangoproject.com/en/1.6/ref/contrib/csrf/`

11.2   Know How Form Validation Works

Form validation is one of those areas of Django where knowing the inner workings will drastically improve your code. Let's take a moment to dig into form validation and cover some of the key points.

When you call `form.is_valid()`, a lot of things happen behind the scenes. The following things occur according to this workflow:

① If the form has bound data, `form.is_valid()` calls the `form.full_clean()` method.
② `form.full_clean()` iterates through the form fields and each field validates itself:
  ⓐ Data coming into the field is coerced into Python via the `to_python()` method or raises a `ValidationError`.
  ⓑ Data is validated against field-specific rules, including custom validators. Failure raises a `ValidationError`.
  ⓒ If there are any custom `clean_<field>()` methods in the form, they are called at this time.
③ `form.full_clean()` executes the `form.clean()` method.
④ If it's a `ModelForm` instance, `form._post_clean()` does the following:
  ⓐ Sets `ModelForm` data to the Model instance, regardless of whether `form.is_valid()` is `True` or `False`.
  ⓑ Calls the model's `clean()` method. For reference, saving a model instance through the ORM does not call the model's `clean()` method.

If this seems complicated, just remember that it gets simpler in practice, and that all of this functionality lets us really understand what's going on with incoming data. The example in the next section should help to explain this further.

Figure 11.1: When ice cream validation fails.

11.2.1 Form Data Is Saved to the Form, Then the Model Instance

We like to call this the *WHAT?!?* of form validation. At first glance, form data being set to the form instance might seem like a bug. But it's not a bug. It's intended behavior.

In a ModelForm, form data is saved in two distinct steps:

❶ First, form data is saved to the form instance.
❷ Later, form data is saved to the model instance.

Since ModelForms don't save to the model instance until they are activated by the form.save() method, we can take advantage of this separation as a useful feature.

For example, perhaps you need to catch the details of failed submission attempts for a form, saving both the user-supplied form data as well as the intended model instance changes.

A simple, perhaps simplistic, way of capturing that data is as follows. First, we create a form failure history model in *core/models.py*:

EXAMPLE 11.2

```
# core/models.py
from django.db import models
```

```python
class ModelFormFailureHistory(models.Model):
    form_data = models.TextField()
    model_data = models.TextField()
```

Second, we add the following to the FlavorActionMixin in *flavors/views.py*:

EXAMPLE 11.3

```python
# flavors/models.py
import json

from django.contrib import messages
from django.core import serializers

from core.models import ModelFormFailureHistory

class FlavorActionMixin(object):

    @property
    def success_msg(self):
        return NotImplemented

    def form_valid(self, form):
        messages.info(self.request, self.success_msg)
        return super(FlavorActionMixin, self).form_valid(form)

    def form_invalid(self, form):
        """Save invalid form and model data for later reference."""
        form_data = json.dumps(form.cleaned_data)
        model_data = serializers.serialize("json",
                    [form.instance])[1:-1]
        ModelFormFailureHistory.objects.create(
            form_data=form_data,
            model_data=model_data
        )
        return super(FlavorActionMixin,
                    self).form_invalid(form)
```

If you recall, `form_invalid()` is called after failed validation of a form with bad data. When it is called here in this example, both the cleaned form data and the final data saved to the database are saved as a `ModelFormFailureHistory` record.

11.3 Summary

Once you dig into forms, keep yourself focused on clarity of code and testability. Forms are one of the primary validation tools in your Django project, an important defense against attacks and accidental data corruption.

12 | Templates: Best Practices

One of Django's early design decisions was to limit the functionality of the template language. This heavily constrains what can be done with Django templates, which is actually a very good thing since it forces us to keep business logic in the Python side of things.

Think about it: the limitations of Django templates force us to put the most critical, complex and detailed parts of our project into .py files rather than into template files. Python happens to be one of the most clear, concise, elegant programming languages of the planet, so why would we want things any other way?

12.1 Follow a Minimalist Approach

We recommend taking a minimalist approach to your template code. Treat the so-called limitations of Django templates as a blessing in disguise. Use those constraints as inspiration to find simple, elegant ways to put more of your business logic into Python code rather than into templates.

Taking a minimalist approach to templates also makes it much easier to adapt your Django apps to changing format types. When your templates are bulky and full of nested looping, complex conditionals, and data processing, it becomes harder to reuse business logic code in templates, not to mention impossible to use the same business logic in template-less views such as API views. Structuring your Django apps for code reuse is especially important as we move forward into the era of increased API development, since APIs and web pages often need to expose identical data with different formatting.

To this day, HTML remains a standard expression of content, and therein lies the practices and patterns for this chapter.

12.2 Template Architecture Patterns

We've found that for our purposes, simple 2-tier or 3-tier template architectures are ideal. The difference in tiers is how many levels of template extending needs to occur before content in apps is displayed. See the examples below:

12.2.1 2-Tier Template Architecture Example

With a 2-tier template architecture, all templates inherit from a single root *base.html* file.

```
EXAMPLE 12.1

templates/
    base.html
    dashboard.html # extends base.html
    profiles/
        profile_detail.html # extends base.html
        profile_form.html # extends base.html
```

This is best for sites with a consistent overall layout from app to app.

12.2.2 3-Tier Template Architecture Example

With a 3-tier template architecture:

➤ Each app has a *base_<app_name>.html* template. App-level base templates share a common parent *base.html* template.
➤ Templates within apps share a common parent *base_<app_name>.html* template.
➤ Any template at the same level as *base.html* inherits *base.html*.

```
EXAMPLE 12.2

templates/
    base.html
    dashboard.html # extends base.html
    profiles/
```

```
base_profiles.html # extends base.html
profile_detail.html # extends base_profiles.html
profile_form.html # extends base_profiles.html
```

The 3-tier architecture is best for websites where each section requires a distinctive layout. For example, a news site might have a local news section, a classified ads section, and an events section. Each of these sections requires its own custom layout.

This is extremely useful when we want HTML to look or behave differently for a particular section of the site that groups functionality.

12.2.3   Flat Is Better Than Nested

Figure 12.1: An excerpt from the Zen of Ice Cream.

Complex template hierarchies make it exceedingly difficult to debug, modify, and extend HTML pages and tie in CSS styles. When template block layouts become unnecessarily nested, you end up digging through file after file just to change, say, the width of a box.

Giving your template blocks as shallow an inheritance structure as possible will make your templates easier to work with and more maintainable. If you're working with a designer, your designer will thank you.

That being said, there's a difference between excessively-complex template block hierarchies and templates that use blocks wisely for code reuse. When you have large, multi-line chunks of the same or very similar code in separate templates, refactoring that code into reusable blocks will make your code more maintainable.

The *Zen of Python* includes the aphorism "*Flat is better than nested*" for good reason. Each level of nesting adds mental overhead. Keep that in mind when architecting your Django templates.

TIP: The Zen of Python

At the command line, do the following:

```
python -c 'import this'
```

What you'll see is the *Zen of Python*, an eloquently-expressed set of guiding principles for the design of the Python programming language.

12.3   Limit Processing in Templates

The less processing you try to do in your templates, the better. This is particularly a problem when it comes to queries and iteration performed in the template layer.

Whenever you iterate over a queryset in a template, ask yourself the following questions:

1. How large is the queryset? Looping over gigantic querysets in your templates is almost always a bad idea.
2. How large are the objects being retrieved? Are all the fields needed in this template?
3. During each iteration of the loop, how much processing occurs?

If any warning bells go off in your head, then there's probably a better way to rewrite your template code.

> **WARNING: Why Not Just Cache?**
>
> Sometimes you can just cache away your template inefficiencies. That's fine, but before you cache, you should first try to attack the root of the problem.
>
> You can save yourself a lot of work by mentally tracing through your template code, doing some quick run time analysis, and refactoring.

Let's now explore some examples of template code that can be rewritten more efficiently.

Suspend your disbelief for a moment and pretend that the nutty duo behind Two Scoops ran a 30-second commercial during the Super Bowl. "Free pints of ice cream for the first million developers who request them! All you have to do is fill out a form to get a voucher redeemable in stores!"

Figure 12.2: Two Scoops, official halftime sponsor of the Super Bowl.

Naturally, we have a "vouchers" app to track the names and email addresses of everyone who requested a free pint voucher. Here's what the model for this app looks like:

EXAMPLE 12.3

```
# vouchers/models.py
from django.core.urlresolvers import reverse
from django.db import models
from .managers import VoucherManager


class Voucher(models.Model):
    """Vouchers for free pints of ice cream."""
    name = models.CharField(max_length=100)
    email = models.EmailField()
    address = models.TextField()
    birth_date = models.DateField(blank=True)
    sent = models.BooleanField(default=False)
    redeemed = models.BooleanField(default=False)

    objects = VoucherManager()
```

This model will be used in the following examples to illustrate a few "gotchas" that you should avoid.

12.3.1   Gotcha 1: Aggregation in Templates

Since we have birth date information, it would be interesting to display a rough breakdown by age range of voucher requests and redemptions.

A very bad way to implement this would be to do all the processing at the template level. To be more specific in the context of this example:

➤ Don't iterate over the entire voucher list in your template's JavaScript section, using JavaScript variables to hold age range counts.
➤ Don't use the add template filter to sum up the voucher counts.

Those implementations are ways of getting around Django's limitations of logic in templates, but they'll slow down your pages drastically.

The better way is to move this processing out of your template and into your Python code. Sticking to our minimal approach of using templates only to *display* data that has already been processed, our template looks like this:

EXAMPLE 12.4

```
{# templates/vouchers/ages.html #}
{% extends "base.html" %}

{% block content %}
<table>
    <thead>
        <tr>
            <th>Age Bracket</th>
            <th>Number of Vouchers Issued</th>
        </tr>
    </thead>
    <tbody>
        {% for age_bracket in age_brackets %}
        <tr>
            <td>{{ age_bracket.title }}</td>
            <td>{{ age_bracket.count }}</td>
        </tr>
        {% endfor %}
    </tbody>
</table>
{% endblock content %}
```

In this example, we can do the processing with a model manager, using the Django ORM's aggregation methods and the handy *dateutil* library described in Appendix A: *Packages Mentioned In This Book*:

EXAMPLE 12.5

```
# vouchers/managers.py
from django.utils import timezone

from dateutil.relativedelta import relativedelta
```

```
from django.db import models

class VoucherManager(models.Manager):
    def age_breakdown(self):
        """Returns a dict of age brackets/counts."""
        age_brackets = []
        now = timezone.now()

        delta = now - relativedelta(years=18)
        count = self.model.objects.filter(birth_date__gt=delta).count()
        age_brackets.append(
            {"title": "0-17", "count": count}
        )
        count = self.model.objects.filter(birth_date__lte=delta).count()
        age_brackets.append(
            {"title": "18+", "count": count}
        )
        return age_brackets
```

This method would be called from a view, and the results would be passed to the template as a context variable.

12.3.2   Gotcha 2: Filtering With Conditionals in Templates

Suppose we want to display a list of all the Greenfelds and the Roys who requested free pint vouchers, so that we could invite them to our family reunion. We want to filter our records on the name field.

A very bad way to implement this would be with giant loops and if statements at the template level.

```
BAD EXAMPLE 12.1
<h2>Greenfelds Who Want Ice Cream</h2>
<ul>
```

```
{% for voucher in voucher_list %}
    {# Don't do this: conditional filtering in templates #}
    {% if "greenfeld" in voucher.name.lower %}
        <li>{{ voucher.name }}</li>
    {% endif %}
{% endfor %}
</ul>


<h2>Roys Who Want Ice Cream</h2>
<ul>
{% for voucher in voucher_list %}
    {# Don't do this: conditional filtering in templates #}
    {% if "roy" in voucher.name.lower %}
        <li>{{ voucher.name }}</li>
    {% endif %}
{% endfor %}
</ul>
```

In this bad snippet, we're looping and checking for various "if" conditions. That's filtering a potentially gigantic list of records in templates, which is not designed for this kind of work, and will cause performance bottlenecks. On the other hand, databases like PostgreSQL and MySQL are great at filtering records, so this should be done at the database layer. The Django ORM can help us with this as demonstrated in the next example.

EXAMPLE 12.6

```
# vouchers/views.py
from django.views.generic import TemplateView

from .models import Voucher


class GreenfeldRoyView(TemplateView):
    template_name = "vouchers/views_conditional.html"

    def get_context_data(self, **kwargs):
        context = super(GreenfeldRoyView, self).get_context_data(**kwargs)
        context["greenfelds"] = \
```

```
                Voucher.objects.filter(name__icontains="greenfeld")
        context["roys"] = Voucher.objects.filter(name__icontains="roy")
        return context
```

Then to call the results, we use the following, simpler template:

```
EXAMPLE 12.7

<h2>Greenfelds Who Want Ice Cream</h2>
<ul>
{% for voucher in greenfelds %}
    <li>{{ voucher.name }}</li>
{% endfor %}
</ul>


<h2>Roys Who Want Ice Cream</h2>
<ul>
{% for voucher in roys %}
    <li>{{ voucher.name }}</li>
{% endfor %}
</ul>
```

It's easy to speed up this template by moving the filtering to a model manager. With this change, we now simply use the template to display the already-filtered data.

The above template now follows our preferred minimalist approach.

12.3.3   Gotcha 3: Complex Implied Queries in Templates

Despite the limitations on logic allowed in Django templates, it's all too easy to find ourselves calling unnecessary queries repeatedly in a view. For example, if we list users of our site and all their flavors this way:

```
BAD EXAMPLE 12.2
{# list generated via User.object.all() #}
<h1>Ice Cream Fans and their favorite flavors.</h1>
<ul>
{% for user in user_list %}
    <li>
        {{ user.name }}:
        {# DON'T DO THIS: Generated implicit query per user #}
        {{ user.flavor.title }}
        {# DON'T DO THIS: Second implicit query per user!!! #}
        {{ user.flavor.scoops_remaining }}
    </li>
{% endfor %}
</ul>
```

Then calling each user generates a second query. While that might not seem like much, we are certain that if we had enough users and made this mistake frequently enough, our site would have a lot of trouble.

One quick correction is to use the Django ORM's `select_related()` method:

```
EXAMPLE 12.8
{% comment %}
List generated via User.object.all().select_related("flavors")
{% endcomment %}
<h1>Ice Cream Fans and their favorite flavors.</h1>
<ul>
{% for user in user_list %}
    <li>
        {{ user.name }}:
        {{ user.flavor.title }}
        {{ user.flavor.scoops_remaining }}
    </li>
{% endfor %}
</ul>
```

One more thing: If you've embraced using model methods, the same applies. Be cautious putting too much query logic in the model methods called from templates.

12.3.4   Gotcha 4: Hidden CPU Load in Templates

Watch out for innocent-looking calls in templates that result in intensive CPU processing. Although a template might look simple and contain very little code, a single line could be invoking an object method that does a lot of processing.

Figure 12.3: Bubble gum ice cream looks easy to eat but requires a lot of processing.

Common examples are template tags that manipulate images, such as the template tags provided by libraries like **sorl-thumbnail**. In many cases tools like this work great, but we've had some issues. Specifically, the manipulation and the saving of image data to file systems (often across networks) inside a template means there is a choke point within templates.

This is why projects that handle a lot of image or data processing increase the performance of their site by taking the image processing out of templates and into views, models, helper methods, or asynchronous messages queues like Celery.

12.3.5   Gotcha 5: Hidden REST API Calls in Templates

You saw in the previous gotcha how easy it is to introduce template loading delays by accessing object method calls. This is true not just with high-load methods, but also with methods that contain REST API calls. A good example is querying an unfortunately slow maps API hosted by a third-party service that your project absolutely requires. Don't do this in the template code by calling a method attached to an object passed into the view's context.

Where should actual REST API consumption occur? We recommend doing this in:

> ➤ JavaScript code so after your project serves out its content, the client's browser handles the work. This way you can entertain or distract the client while they wait for data to load.
> ➤ The view's Python code where slow processes might be handled in a variety of ways including message queues, additional threads, multiprocesses, or more.

12.4 Don't Bother Making Your Generated HTML Pretty

Bluntly put, no one cares if the HTML generated by your Django project is attractive. In fact, if someone were to look at your rendered HTML, they'd do so through the lens of a browser inspector, which would realign the HTML spacing anyway. Therefore, if you shuffle up the code in your Django templates to render pretty HTML, you are wasting time obfuscating your code for an audience of yourself.

And yet, we've seen code like the following. This evil code snippet generates nicely formatted HTML but itself is an illegible, unmaintainable template mess:

```
BAD EXAMPLE 12.3

{% comment %}Don't do this! This code bunches everything
together to generate pretty HTML.
{% endcomment %}
{% if list_type=="unordered" %}<ul>{% else %}<ol>{% endif %}{% for
syrup in syrup_list %}<li class="{{ syrup.temperature_type|roomtemp
}}"><a href="{% url 'syrup_detail' syrup.slug %}">{% syrup.title %}
</a></li>{% endfor %}{% if list_type=="unordered" %}</ul>{% else %}
</ol>{% endif %}
```

A better way of writing the above snippet is to use indentation and one operation per line to create a readable, maintainable template:

```
EXAMPLE 12.9

{# Use indentation/comments to ensure code quality #}
```

```
{# start of list elements #}
{% if list_type=="unordered" %}
    <ul>
{% else %}
    <ol>
{% endif %}


{% for syrup in syrup_list %}
    <li class="{{ syrup.temperature_type|roomtemp }}">
        <a href="{% url 'syrup_detail' syrup.slug %}">
            {% syrup.title %}
        </a>
    </li>
{% endfor %}

{# end of list elements #}
{% if list_type=="unordered" %}
    </ul>
{% else %}
    </ol>
{% endif %}
```

Are you worried about the volume of whitespace generated? Don't be. First of all, experienced developers favor readability of code over obfuscation for the sake of optimization. Second, there are compression and minification tools that can help more than anything you can do manually here. See chapter 22, *Finding and Reducing Bottlenecks*, for more details.

12.5   Exploring Template Inheritance

Let's begin with a simple *base.html* file that we'll inherit from another template:

```
EXAMPLE 12.10
{# simple base.html #}
{% load staticfiles %}
<html>
```

```
<head>
    <title>
        {% block title %}Two Scoops of Django{% endblock title %}
    </title>
    {% block stylesheets %}
        <link rel="stylesheet" type="text/css"
                href="{% static "css/project.css" %}">
    {% endblock stylesheets %}
</head>
<body>
    <div class="content">
        {% block content %}
            <h1>Two Scoops</h1>
        {% endblock content %}
    </div>
</body>
</html>
```

The *base.html* file contains the following features:

➤ A title block containing: "Two Scoops of Django".

➤ A stylesheets block containing a link to a *project.css* file used across our site.

➤ A content block containing "<h1>Two Scoops</h1>".

Our example relies on just three template tags, which are summarized below:

Template Tag	Purpose
{% load %}	Loads the staticfiles built-in template tag library
{% block %}	Since *base.html* is a parent template, these define which child blocks can be filled in by child templates. We place links and scripts inside them so we can override if necessary.
{% static %}	Resolves the named static media argument to the static media server.

Table 12.1: Template Tags in base.html

To demonstrate *base.html* in use, we'll have a simple *about.html* inherit the following from it:

- ➤ A custom title.
- ➤ The original stylesheet and an additional stylesheet.
- ➤ The original header, a sub header, and paragraph content.
- ➤ The use of child blocks.
- ➤ The use of the {{ block.super }} template variable.

EXAMPLE 12.11

```
{% extends "base.html" %}
{% load staticfiles %}
{% block title %}About Audrey and Daniel{% endblock title %}
{% block stylesheets %}
    {{ block.super }}
    <link rel="stylesheet" type="text/css"
            href="{% static "css/about.css" %}">
{% endblock stylesheets %}
{% block content %}
    {{ block.super }}
    <h2>About Audrey and Daniel</h2>
    <p>They enjoy eating ice cream</p>
{% endblock content %}
```

When we render this template in a view, it generates the following HTML:

EXAMPLE 12.12

```
<html>
<head>
    <title>
        About Audrey and Daniel
    </title>
        <link rel="stylesheet" type="text/css"
                href="/static/css/project.css">
        <link rel="stylesheet" type="text/css"
                href="/static/css/about.css">
</head>
<body>
```

```
    <div class="content">
            <h1>Two Scoops</h1>
            <h2>About Audrey and Daniel</h2>
            <p>They enjoy eating ice cream</p>
    </div>
</body>
</html>
```

Notice how the rendered HTML has our custom title, the additional stylesheet link, and more material in the body?

We'll use the table below to review the template tags and variables in the *about.html* template.

Template Object	Purpose
{% extends %}	Informs Django that about.html is inheriting or extending from base.html
{% block %}	Since about.html is a child template, block overrides the content provided by base.html. For example, this means our title will render as <title>Audrey and Daniel</title>.
{{ block.super }}	When placed in a child template's block, it ensures that the parent's content is also included in the block. For example, in the content block of the about.html template, this will render <h1>Two Scoops</h1>.

Table 12.2: Template Objects in about.html

Note that the {% block %} tag is used differently in *about.html* than in *base.html*, serving to override content. In blocks where we want to preserve the *base.html* content, we use {{ block.super }} variable to display the content from the parent block. This brings us to the next topic, {{ block.super }}.

12.6   block.super Gives the Power of Control

Let's imagine that we have a template which inherits everything from the *base.html* but replaces the projects' link to the *project.css* file with a link to *dashboard.css*. This use case might occur when you have a project with one design for normal users, and a dashboard with a different design for staff.

If we aren't using {{ block.super }}, this often involves writing a whole new base file, often named something like *base_dashboard.html*. For better or for worse, we now have two template architectures to maintain.

If we are using {{ block.super }}, we don't need a second (or third or fourth) base template. Assuming all templates extend from base.html we use {{ block.super }} to assume control of our templates. Here are three examples:

Template using both *project.css* and a custom link:

```
EXAMPLE 12.13
{% extends "base.html" %}
{% block stylesheets %}
    {{ block.super }} {# this brings in project.css #}
    <link rel="stylesheet" type="text/css"
        href="{% static "css/custom.css" %}" />
{% endblock %}
```

Dashboard template that excludes the *project.css* link:

```
EXAMPLE 12.14
{% extends "base.html" %}
{% block stylesheets %}
    <link rel="stylesheet" type="text/css"
        href="{% static "css/dashboard.css" %}" />
    {% comment %}
        By not using {{ block.super }}, this block overrides the
        stylesheet block of base.html
    {% endcomment %}
{% endblock %}
```

Template just linking the *project.css* file:

EXAMPLE 12.15

```
{% extends "base.html" %}
{% comment %}
    By not using {% block stylesheets %}, this template inherits the
    stylesheets block from the base.html parent, in this case the
    default project.css link.
{% endcomment %}
```

These three examples demonstrate the amount of control that {{ block.super }} provides. The variable serves a good way to reduce template complexity, but can take a little bit of effort to fully comprehend.

TIP: block.super Is Similar But Not the Same as super()

For those coming from an object oriented programming background, it might help to think of the behavior of the {{ block.super }} variable to be like a very limited version of the Python built-in function, super(). In essence, the {{ block.super }} variable and the super() function both provide access to the parent.

Just remember that they aren't the same. For example, the {{ block.super }} variable doesn't accept arguments. It's just a nice mnemonic that some developers might find useful.

12.7   Useful Things to Consider

The following are a series of smaller things we keep in mind during template development.

12.7.1   Avoid Coupling Styles Too Tightly to Python Code

Aim to control the styling of all rendered templates entirely via CSS and JS.

Use CSS for styling whenever possible. Never hardcode things like menu bar widths and color choices into your Python code. Avoid even putting that type of styling into your Django templates.

Here are some tips:

> ➤ If you have magic constants in your Python code that are entirely related to visual design layout, you should probably move them to a CSS file.
> ➤ The same applies to JavaScript.

12.7.2   Common Conventions

Here are some naming and style conventions that we recommend:

> ➤ We prefer underscores over dashes in template names, block names, and other names in templates. Most Django users seem to follow this convention. Why? Well, because underscores are allowed in names of Python objects but dashes are forbidden.
> ➤ We rely on clear, intuitive names for blocks. `{% block javascript %}` is good.
> ➤ We include the name of the block tag in the endblock. Never write just `{% endblock %}`, include the whole `{% endblock javascript %}`.
> ➤ Templates called by other templates are prefixed with '_'. This applies to templates called via `{% include %}` or custom template tags. It does not apply to templates inheritance controls such as `{% extends %}` or `{% block %}`.

12.7.3   Location, Location, Location!

Templates should usually go into the root of the Django project, at the same level as the apps. This is the most common convention, and it's an intuitive, easy pattern to follow.

The only exception is when you bundle up an app into a third-party package. That packages template directory should go into app directly. We'll explore this in section 19.9, 'How to Release Your Own Django Packages.'

12.7.4   Use Named Context Objects

When you use generic display CBVs, you have the option of using the generic `{{ object_list }}` and `{{ object }}` in your template. Another option is to use the ones that are named after your model.

For example, if you have a Topping model, you can use {{ topping_list }} and {{ topping }} in your templates, instead of {{ object_list }} and {{ object }}. This means both of the following template examples will work:

EXAMPLE 12.16

```
{# toppings/topping_list.html #}
{# Using implicit names #}
<ol>
{% for object in object_list %}
    <li>{{ object }} </li>
{% endfor %}
</ol>


{# Using explicit names #}
<ol>
{% for topping in topping_list %}
    <li>{{ topping }} </li>
{% endfor %}
</ol>
```

12.7.5   Use URL Names Instead of Hardcoded Paths

A common developer mistake is to hardcode URLs in templates like this:

BAD EXAMPLE 12.4

```
<a href="/flavors/">
```

The problem with this is that if the URL patterns of the site need to change, all the URLs across the site need to be addressed. This impacts HTML, JavaScript, and even RESTful APIs.

Instead, we use the {% url %} tag and references the names in our **URLConf** files:

EXAMPLE 12.17

```
<a href="{% url 'flavors_list' %}">
```

12.7.6   Debugging Complex Templates

A trick recommended by Lennart Regebro is that when templates are complex and it becomes difficult to determine where a variable is failing, you can force more verbose errors through the use of the TEMPLATE_STRING_IF_INVALID setting:

```
EXAMPLE 12.18

# settings/local.py
TEMPLATE_STRING_IF_INVALID = "INVALID EXPRESSION: %s"
```

12.7.7   Don't Replace the Django Template Engine

If you need **Jinja2** or any other templating engine for certain views, then it's easy enough to use it for just those views without having to replace Django templates entirely.

For more details, see chapter 16, *Tradeoffs of Replacing Core Components*, for a case study about replacing the Django template engine with Jinja2.

12.8   Error Page Templates

Even the most tested and analyzed site will have a few problems now and then, and that's okay. The problem lies in how you handle those errors. The last thing that you want to do is show an ugly response or a blank web server page back to the end user.

It's standard practice to create at least *404.html* and *500.html* templates. See the GitHub HTML Styleguide link at the end of this section for other types of error pages that you may want to consider.

We suggest serving your error pages from a static file server (e.g. Nginx or Apache) as entirely self-contained static HTML files. That way, if your entire Django site goes down but your static file server is still up, then your error pages can still be served.

If you're on a PaaS, check the documentation on error pages. For example, Heroku allows users to upload a custom static HTML page to be used for 500 errors.

> **WARNING: Resist the Temptation to Overcomplicate Your Error Pages**
>
> Interesting or amusing error pages can be a draw to your site, but don't get carried away. It's embarrassing when your 404 page has a broken layout or your 500 page can't load the CSS and JavaScript. Worse yet is dynamic 500 error pages that break in the event of a database failure.

GitHub's 404 and 500 error pages are great examples of fancy but entirely static, self-contained error pages:

> ➤ https://github.com/404
> ➤ https://github.com/500

View the source of either of them and you'll notice that:

> ➤ All CSS styles are inline in the head of the same HTML page, eliminating the need for a separate stylesheet.
> ➤ All images are entirely contained as data within the HTML page. There are no `<img>` links to external URLs.
> ➤ All JavaScript needed for the page is contained within the HTML page. There are no external links to JavaScript assets.

For more information, see the Github HTML Styleguide:

> ➤ https://github.com/styleguide/templates/2.0

12.9   Summary

In this chapter, we covered the following:

> ➤ Template inheritance, including the use of `{{ block.super }}`.
> ➤ Writing legible, maintainable templates.
> ➤ Easy methods to optimize template performance.
> ➤ Issues with limitations of template processing.
> ➤ Error page templates.

➤ Many other helpful little details about templates.

In the next chapter we'll examine template tags and filters.

13 | Template Tags and Filters

Django provides dozens of default template tags and filters, all of which share the following common traits:

➤ All of the defaults have clear, obvious names.
➤ All of the defaults do just one thing.
➤ None of the defaults alter any sort of persistent data.

These traits serve as very good best practices when you have to write your own template tags. Let's now dive a bit deeper into practices and recommendations when writing custom filters and template tags.

13.1 Filters Are Functions

Filters are functions that accept just one or two arguments, and that don't give developers the ability to add behavior controls in Django templates.

We feel that this simplicity makes filters less prone to abuse, since they are essentially just functions with decorators that make Python usable inside of Django templates. This means that they can be called as normal functions (although we prefer to have our filters call functions imported from helper modules).

In fact, a quick scan of the source code of Django's default filters at http://2scoops.co/1.6-slugify-source shows that the slugify() template filter simply calls the django.utils.text.slugify function.

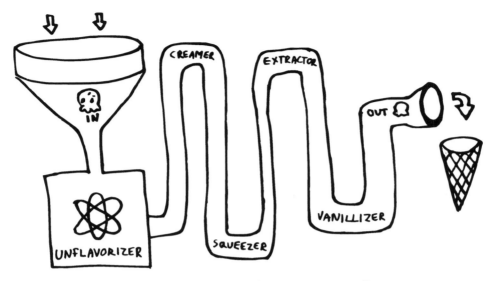

Figure 13.1: This filter transforms 1-2 flavors of ice cream into vanilla, outputting to a cone.

13.1.1 Filters Are Easy to Test

Testing a filter is just a matter of testing a function, which we cover in chapter 20, *Testing Stinks and Is a Waste of Money!*

13.1.2 Filters, Code Reuse, and Performance

It's not necessary to import `django.template.defaultfilters.slugify`. Instead use `django.utils.text.slugify`. While it might seem to be perfectly acceptable, until Django 1.7 is released, `django.template.defaultfilters.slugify` performs an import each time it's used, it can turn into a performance bottleneck.

Similarly, `remove_tags` is available at `django.utils.html.remove_tags()`.

Since filters are just functions, we advocate that anything but the simplest logic for them be moved to more reusable utility functions, perhaps stored in a *utils.py* module. Doing this makes it easier to introspect code bases and test, and can mean dramatically fewer imports.

13.1.3   When to Write Filters

Filters are good for modifying the presentation of data, and they can be readily reused in REST APIs and other output formats. Being constrained to two arguments limits the functionality so it's harder (but not impossible) to make them unbearably complex.

13.2   Custom Template Tags

"Please stop writing so many template tags. They are a pain to debug."

– Audrey Roy, while debugging Daniel Greenfeld's code.

While template tags are great tools when developers have the discipline to keep them in check, in practice they tend to get abused. This section covers the problems that you run into when you put too much of your logic into template tags and filters.

13.2.1   Template Tags Are Harder To Debug

Template tags of any complexity can be challenging to debug. When they include opening and closing elements, they become even harder to handle. We've found liberal use of log statements and tests are very helpful when they become hard to inspect and correct.

13.2.2   Template Tags Make Code Reuse Harder

It can be difficult to consistently apply the same effect as a template tag on alternative output formats used by REST APIs, RSS feeds, or in PDF/CSV generation. If you do need to generate alternate formats, it's worth considering putting all logic for template tags into *utils.py*, for easy access from other views.

13.2.3   The Performance Cost of Template Tags

Template tags can have a significant performance cost, especially when they load other templates. While templates run much faster than they did in previous versions of Django, it's easy to lose those performance benefits if you don't have a deep understanding of how templates are loaded in Django.

If your custom template tags are loading a lot of templates, you might want to consider caching the loaded templates. See `http://2scoops.co/1.6-template-cached-loader` for more details.

13.2.4   When to Write Template Tags

These days, we're very cautious about adding new template tags. We consider two things before writing them:

➤ Anything that causes a read/write of data might be better placed in a model or object method.

➤ Since we implement a consistent naming standard across our projects, we can add an abstract base class model to our `core.models` module. Can a method or property in our project's abstract base class model do the same work as a custom template tag?

When should you write new template tags? We recommend writing them in situations where they are only responsible for rendering of HTML. For example, Projects with very complex HTML layouts with many different models or data types might use them to create a more flexible, understandable template architecture.

PACKAGE TIP: We Do Use Custom Template Tags

It sounds like we stay away from custom template tags, but that's not the case. We're just cautious. Interestingly enough, Daniel has been involved with at least three prominent libraries that make extensive use of template tags.

➤ django-crispy-forms

➤ django-wysiwyg

➤ django-uni-form (deprecated, use django-crispy-forms instead)

13.3   Naming Your Template Tag Libraries

The convention we follow is *<app_name>_tags.py*. Using the twoscoops example, we would have files named thus:

> ➤ *flavors_tags.py*
> ➤ *blog_tags.py*
> ➤ *events_tags.py*
> ➤ *tickets_tags.py*

This makes determining the source of a template tag library trivial to discover.

WARNING: Don't Name Your Template Tag Libraries with the Same Name as Your App

For example, naming the *events* app's templatetag library *events.py* is problematic.
This will cause all sorts of problems because of the way that Django loads template tags.
If you do this, expect things to break.

WARNING: Don't Use Your IDE's Features as an Excuse to Obfuscate Your Code

Do not rely on your text editor or IDE's powers of introspection to determine the name of your templatetag library.

13.4   Loading Your Template Tag Modules

In your template, right after {% extends "base.html" %} (or any other parent template besides *base.html*) is where you load your template tags:

```
EXAMPLE 13.1

{% extends "base.html" %}


{% load flavors_tags %}
```

Simplicity itself! Explicit loading of functionality! Hooray!

13.4.1 Watch Out for This Crazy Anti-Pattern

Unfortunately, there is an obscure anti-pattern that will drive you mad with fury each and every time you encounter it:

```
BAD EXAMPLE 13.1
# Don't use this code!
# It's an evil anti-pattern!
from django import template
template.add_to_builtins(
    "flavors.templatetags.flavors_tags"
)
```

The anti-pattern replaces the explicit load method described above with an implicit behavior which supposedly fixes a "Don't Repeat Yourself" (DRY) issue. However, any DRY "improvements" it creates are destroyed by the following:

➤ It will add some overhead due to the fact this literally loads the template tag library into each and every template loaded by `django.template.Template`. This means every inherited template, template {% `include` %}, `inclusion_tag`, and more will be impacted. While we have cautioned against premature optimization, we are also not in favor of adding this much unneeded extra computational work into our code when better alternatives exist.

➤ Because the template tag library is implicitly loaded, it immensely adds to the difficulty in introspection and debugging. Per the **Zen of Python**, "Explicit is better than Implicit."

➤ The `add_to_builtins` method has no convention for placement. To our chagrin, we often find it placed in an `__init__` module or the template tag library itself, either of which can cause unexpected problems.

Fortunately, this is obscure because beginning Django developers don't know enough to make this mistake and experienced Django developers get really angry when they have to deal with it.

13.5 Summary

It is our contention that template tags and filters should concern themselves only with the manipulation of presentable data. So long as we remember this when we write or use them, our projects run faster and are easier to maintain.

Starting in the next chapter we leave templates behind and explore the world of REST from both the server and client sides.

14 | Building REST APIs

Today's internet is much more than HTML-powered websites. Developers need to support AJAX and the mobile web. Having tools that support easy creation of **JSON, YAML, XML**, and other formats is important. By design, a **Representational State Transfer (REST) Application Programming Interface (API)** exposes application data to other concerns.

We'll go over the other side of REST APIs in chapter 15, *Consuming REST APIs in Templates*.

PACKAGE TIP: Packages For Crafting APIs

- ➤ **django-rest-framework** builds off of Django CBVs, adding a wonderful browsable API feature. It has a lot of features, follows elegant patterns, and is great to work with. In 2013 this library leaped forward in functionality, providing even more powerful tools for building CBV or FBV powered REST APIs.
- ➤ **django-tastypie** is a mature API framework that implements its own class-based view system. It's a feature-rich, mature, powerful, stable tool for creating APIs from Django models. It was created by Daniel Lindsley, the developer also behind django-haystack, the most commonly used Django search library.
- ➤ **django-braces** *can* be used in direct conjunction with Django CBVs to create super-quick, super-simple one-off REST API views. The downside is that when you get into the full range of HTTP methods such as PUT, it rapidly becomes a hindrance due to how Django presents raw data to the developer.

Figure 14.1: A tasty pie is one filled with ice cream.

14.1 Fundamentals of Basic REST API Design

The Hypertext Transfer Protocol (HTTP) is a protocol for distributing content that provides a set of methods to declare actions. By convention, REST APIs rely on these methods, so use the appropriate HTTP method for each type of action:

Purpose of Request	HTTP Method	Rough SQL equivalent
Create a new resource	POST	INSERT
Read an existing resource	GET	SELECT
Request the metadata of an existing resource	HEAD	
Update an existing resource	PUT	UPDATE
Update part of an existing resource	PATCH	UPDATE
Delete an existing resource	DELETE	DELETE
Return the supported HTTP methods for the given URL	OPTIONS	
Echo back the request	TRACE	
Tunneling over TCP/IP (usually not implemented)	CONNECT	

Table 14.1: HTTP Methods

A couple of notes on the above:

➤ If you're implementing a read-only API, you might only need to implement GET methods.

➤ If you're implementing a read-write API you must at least also use POST, but should also consider using PUT and DELETE.

➤ By definition, GET, PUT, and DELETE are idempotent. POST and PATCH are not.

➤ PATCH is often not implemented, but it's a good idea to implement it if your API supports PUT requests.

➤ django-rest-framework and django-tastypie handle all of this for you.

Here are some common HTTP status codes that you should consider supporting when implementing your REST API. Note that this is a partial list; a much longer list of status codes can be found at `http://en.wikipedia.org/wiki/List_of_HTTP_status_codes`.

HTTP Status Code	Success/Failure	Meaning
200 OK	Success	GET - Return resource
		PUT - Provide status message or return resource
201 Created	Success	POST - Provide status message or return newly created resource
204 No Content	Success	DELETE
304 Unchanged	Redirect	ANY - Indicates no changes since the last request. Used for checking Last-Modified and Etag headers to improve performance.
400 Bad Request	Failure	PUT, POST - Return error messages, including form validation errors.
401 Unauthorized	Failure	ALL - Authentication required but user did not provide credentials.
403 Forbidden	Failure	ALL - User attempted to access restricted content
404 Not Found	Failure	ALL - Resource is not found
405 Method Not Allowed	Failure	ALL - An invalid HTTP method was attempted.
410 Gone	Failure	ALL - A method was attempted that is no longer supported. Mobile applications can test for this condition, and if it occurs, tell the user to upgrade.

Table 14.2: HTTP Status Codes

14.2   Implementing a Simple JSON API

Let's use the *flavors* app example from previous chapters as our base, providing the capability to create, read, update, and delete flavors via HTTP requests using AJAX, python-requests, or some other library. We'll also use **django-rest-framework**, as it provides us with the capability to build a REST API quickly using patterns similar to the class-based views that we describe in previous chapters. We'll begin by listing the Flavor model again:

EXAMPLE 14.1

```
# flavors/models.py
from django.core.urlresolvers import reverse
from django.db import models


class Flavor(models.Model):
    title = models.CharField(max_length=255)
    slug = models.SlugField()
    scoops_remaining = models.IntegerField(default=0)


    def get_absolute_url(self):
        return reverse("flavor_detail", kwargs={"slug": self.slug})
```

Now let's add in some views:

EXAMPLE 14.2

```
# flavors/views
from rest_framework.generics import ListCreateAPIView
from rest_framework.generics import RetrieveUpdateDestroyAPIView

from .models import Flavor


class FlavorCreateReadView(ListCreateAPIView):
    model = Flavor


class FlavorReadUpdateDeleteView(RetrieveUpdateDestroyAPIView):
    model = Flavor
```

We're done! Wow, that was fast!

WARNING: Our Simple API Does Not Use Permissions

If you implement an API using our example, don't forget to authenticate users and assign them permissions appropriately!

Now we'll wire this into our *flavors/urls.py* module:

```
EXAMPLE 14.3
# flavors/urls.py
from django.conf.urls.defaults import patterns, url

from flavors import views

urlpatterns = patterns("",
    url(
        regex=r"^api/$",
        view=views.FlavorCreateReadView.as_view(),
        name="flavor_rest_api"
    ),
    url(
        regex=r"^api/(?P<slug>[-\w]+)/$",
        view=views.FlavorReadUpdateDeleteView.as_view(),
        name="flavor_rest_api"
    )
)
```

What we are doing is reusing the same view and URLConf name, making it easier to manage when you have a need for a JavaScript-heavy front-end. All you need to do is access the Flavor resource via the {% url %} template tag.

In case it's not clear exactly what our URLConf is doing, let's review it with a table:

Url	View	Url Name (same)
/api/flavors/	FlavorCreateReadView	flavor_rest_api
/api/flavors/:slug/	FlavorReadUpdateDeleteView	flavor_rest_api

Table 14.3: URLConf for the Flavor REST APIs

The end result is the traditional REST-style API definition:

EXAMPLE 14.4

```
flavors/api/
flavors/api/:slug/
```

TIP: Common Syntax for Describing REST APIs

It's not uncommon to see syntax like what is described in Example 14.4. In this particular case, /flavors/api/:slug/ includes a :slug value. This represents a variable, but in a manner suited for documentation across frameworks and languages, and you'll see it used in many third-party REST API descriptions.

We've shown you (if you didn't know already) how it's very easy to build REST APIs in Django, now let's go over some advice on maintaining and extending them.

14.3   REST API Architecture

Building quick APIs is easy with tools like django-rest-framework and django-tastypie, but extending and maintaining them to match your project's needs takes a bit more thought.

14.3.1   Code for an App Should Remain in the App

When it comes down to it, REST APIs are just views. In our opinion, REST API views should go into *views.py* modules and follow the same guidelines we endorse when it comes to any other view. The same goes for app or model specific serializers and renderers. If you do have app specific serializers or renderers the same applies.

14.3.2   Try to Keep Business Logic Out of API Views

It's a good idea to try to keep as much logic as possible out of API views. If this sounds familiar, it should. We covered this in 'Try to Keep Business Logic out of Views,' chapter 7 *Function- and Class-Based Views*, and remember, API views are just another type of view, after all.

Figure 14.2: An Ice Cream as a Service API.

14.3.3 Grouping API URLs

If you have REST API views in multiple Django apps, how do you build a project-wide API that looks like this?

```
EXAMPLE 14.5
api/flavors/ # GET, POST
api/flavors/:slug/ # GET, PUT, DELETE
api/users/ # GET, POST
api/users/:slug/ # GET, PUT, DELETE
```

In the past, we placed all API view code into a dedicated Django app called *api* or *apiv1*, with custom logic in some of the REST views, serializers, and more. In theory it's a pretty good approach, but in practice it means we have logic for a particular app in more than just one location.

Our current approach is to lean on URL configuration. When building a project-wide API we write the REST views in the *views.py* modules, wire them into a URLConf called something like *core/api.py* or *core/apiv1.py* and include that from the project root's *urls.py* module. This means that we might have something like the following code:

EXAMPLE 14.6

```python
# core/api.py
"""Called from the project root's urls.py URLConf thus:
        url(r"^api/", include("core.api"), namespace="api"),
"""
from django.conf.urls.defaults import patterns, url

from flavors import views as flavor_views
from users import views as user_views

urlpatterns = patterns("",
    # {% url "api:flavors" %}
    url(
        regex=r"^flavors/$",
        view=flavor_views.FlavorCreateReadView.as_view(),
        name="flavors"
    ),
    # {% url "api:flavors" flavor.slug %}
    url(
        regex=r"^flavors/(?P<slug>[-\w]+)/$",
        view=flavor_views.FlavorReadUpdateDeleteView.as_view(),
        name="flavors"
    ),
    # {% url "api:users" %}
    url(
        regex=r"^users/$",
        view=user_views.UserCreateReadView.as_view(),
        name="users"
    ),
    # {% url "api:users" user.slug %}
```

```
url(
    regex=r"^users/(?P<slug>[-\w]+)/$",
    view=user_views.UserReadUpdateDeleteView.as_view(),
    name="users"
),
)
```

14.3.4   Test Your API

We find that Django's test suite makes it really easy to test API implementations. It's certainly much easier than staring at curl results! Testing is covered at length in chapter 20, *Testing Stinks and Is a Waste of Money!*, and we even include in that chapter the tests we wrote for our simple JSON API (see subsection 20.3.1).

14.3.5   Version Your API

It's a good practice to abbreviate the urls of your with the version number e.g. /api/v1/flavors or /api/v1/users and then as the API changes, /api/v2/flavors or /api/v2/users. When the version number changes, existing customers can continue to use the previous version without unknowingly breaking their calls to the API.

Also, in order to avoid angering API consumers, it's critical to maintain both the existing API and the predecessor API during and after upgrades. It's not uncommon for the deprecated API to remain in use for several months.

When you do implement an API, provide customers/users with a deprecation warning along with ample time so they can perform necessary upgrades and not break their own applications. From personal experience, the ability to send a deprecation warning to end users is an excellent reason to request email addresses from users of even free and open-source API services.

14.4   Evaluating REST Frameworks

When you begin considering REST frameworks, it's worthwhile to consider the following:

14.4.1   How Much Boilerplate Do You Want to Write?

These days, most frameworks make an effort to reduce boilerplate when dealing with resources. In fact, usually when we hear grumbling on the lines of '*X framework has too much boilerplate!!!*' it is actually a matter of trying to figure out how to implement **Remote Procedure Calls** in a resource-driven system.

Speaking of Remote Procedure calls, let's move on to the next sub-section...

14.4.2   Are Remote Procedure Calls Easy to Implement?

The resource model used by REST frameworks to expose data is very powerful, but it doesn't cover every case. Specifically, resources don't always match the reality of application design. For example, it is easy to represent syrup and a sundae as two resources, but what about the action of pouring syrup? Using this analogy, we change the state of the sundae and decrease the syrup inventory by one. While we could have the API user change things individually, that can generate issues with database integrity. Therefore *in some cases it can be good idea to present a method* like `sundae.pour_syrup(syrup)` to the client as part of the RESTful API.

In computer science terms, `sundae.pour_syrup(syrup)` could be classified as a **Remote Procedure Call** or **RPC**.

Depending on the REST framework or system you chose, RPC calls can be easy or challenging to implement. This is an area that needs to be investigated early on, as it's painful to discover in the middle of a project that a framework of choice makes this a pain point.

Additional Reading:

- ➤ `https://en.wikipedia.org/wiki/Remote_Procedure_Call`
- ➤ `https://en.wikipedia.org/wiki/Resource-oriented_architecture`

14.4.3   CBVs or FBVs?

As mentioned in the previous chapters, the authors prefer CBVs, but other developers prefer FBVs. If this is a sticking point, then consider exploring options that support FBV-based implementations such as django-rest-framework.

14.5   Additional Reading

We highly recommend reading the following:

- http://en.wikipedia.org/wiki/REST
- http://en.wikipedia.org/wiki/List_of_HTTP_status_codes
- http://jacobian.org/writing/rest-worst-practices/

14.6   Summary

In this chapter we covered:

- API creation libraries.
- Grouping strategies.
- Fundamentals of basic REST API design.
- Implementing a simple JSON API.

Coming up next, we'll go over the other side of REST APIs in chapter 15, *Consuming REST APIs in Templates*.

15 | Consuming REST APIs in Templates

Now that we've covered both creating REST APIs and template best practices, let's combine them. In other words, these are best practices for using Django-powered tools to display content to the end user in the browser using content managed by REST APIs and presented by modern JavaScript frameworks.

WARNING: This Chapter Will Be Brief

Our challenge in writing this chapter is twofold:

➤ Django is a backend framework.
➤ The modern JavaScript/HTML5 landscape is rapidly evolving.

Therefore, we're going to cover best practices at a very high level.

With the advent of faster JavaScript engines and a maturation of the associated community, there has been a rise in new JavaScript frameworks that make integration of RESTful APIs easy. In the Django world as of the release of this book, things seem to have settled down to one of four options:

Angular.js `http://angularjs.org`

An open-source JavaScript framework, maintained by Google, that assists with running single-page applications. It's also capable of creating easy-to-implement improvements to existing multi-page applications. We readily admit it's our preferred JavaScript library and seems to have hit critical mass in the Django community.

Backbone.js `http://backbonejs.org`

> The first of the modern JavaScript libraries to really hit critical mass in popularity. It's built on top of the really useful underscore.js library.

Ember.js `http://emberjs.com`

> A well-regarded framework with its roots in the pioneering SproutCore framework.

jQuery `http://jquery.com/`

> While it's no longer the cool kid on the block, 75 percent of the web can't be wrong.

These libraries can really improve what we like to call the 'immediate user experience'. However, with every good thing there are always things to consider and things to do.

15.1 Learn How to Debug the Client

Debugging client-side JavaScript is a lot more than simply writing `console.log()` and `console.dir()` statements. There are a number of tools for debugging and finding errors, and some of them are specifically written for particular JavaScript frameworks. Once a tool of choice is chosen, it's an excellent idea to take a day to learn how to write client-side tests.

Reference material:

- ➤ `http://2scoops.co/chrome-developer-tools`
- ➤ `https://developer.mozilla.org/en-US/docs/Debugging_JavaScript`

15.2 Consider Using JavaScript-Powered Static Asset Preprocessors

We like to use Python everywhere, including JavaScript and CSS minification. However, as of the publication of this book, it can be argued that the JavaScript community is maintaining their version of these tools better than the Python community. That's perfectly okay, because since they've done the work on this part of the toolchain, we can focus on the rest of our work.

The most commonly used tool for this kind of work is **Grunt**, found at `gruntjs.com`. Think of it as an automation tool like python's Fabric or Invoke, but for JavaScript. Grunt.js requires **node.js** to be installed, but since that works everywhere Python does (including Windows), it won't be a problem.

15.3   Making Content Indexable by Search Engines

Single-page applications or content served by REST APIs are increasingly popular. However, without care this content won't be indexed by search engines such as Google or Bing. If all the content is only available to authenticated users this isn't a big deal, but if reaching search engines is important, then here are some steps that can be used to address the problem.

15.3.1   Hand-Craft the sitemap.xml

Write a custom view instead of Django's built-in sitemap app:

```
EXAMPLE 15.1
# core/views.py
from __future__ import absolute_import

from django.views.generic import TemplateView

from .flavors.models import Flavor

class SiteMapView(TemplateView):
    template_name = "sitemap.xml"

    def flavors(self):
        return Flavor.objects.all()
```

Then hand-craft the sitemap.xml (note: this is a *simple* example):

```
EXAMPLE 15.2
<?xml version="1.0" encoding="UTF-8"?>
<urlset xmlns="http://www.sitemaps.org/schemas/sitemap/0.9">
    {# Snip the home page, contact, etc #}
    {% for flavor in view.flavors %}
        <url>
            <loc>{{ site.domain }}/app/#{{ flavor.slug }}</loc>
            <lastmod>{{ flavor.modified }}</lastmod>
```

```
            <changefreq>monthly</changefreq>
            <priority>0.8</priority>
        </url>
    {% endfor %}
</urlset>
```

There are a lot of other things you can do, making Google's web crawling specification an important resource for anyone creating single page apps:

`https://developers.google.com/webmasters/ajax-crawling/`.

15.3.2   Use a Service to Make Your Site Crawlable

Rather than do the work of generating a sitemap yourself, consider using a service to do the work for you. For example, for a fee, `brombone.com` crawls your Angular.js, Ember.js, or Backbone.js site and shows Google pre-rendered HTML representing the data that you want to display.

15.3.3   Wait for Search Engines to Figure It Out

The teams behind Google Search and other search engines are very well aware of the growing use of single page apps.In theory some of them are already searching through content rendered by client-side JavaScript. Over time, their ability to weed the chaff from real content is only going to grow. If SEO isn't important to you right now but will be in the future, consider waiting until they figure it out.

15.4   Real-Time Woes a.k.a. Latency

Let's say we've put together a well-designed, well-indexed, well-cached real-time project with the widest bandwidth piping content to the world. We can handle any load, and our test users applaud the speed and functionality of the project. Things look great, and we look forward to bonuses and raises.

Then the complaints from the other side of the planet start coming in about the slow speed of the application. Our effort isn't 'real-time' to any of a potentially large block of users and our client/boss is really unhappy.

Congratulations, we've just hit the speed of light!

This isn't a joke, it's a very real problem. Here, Django isn't the problem. Instead, it's physics. The time it takes for HTTP requests to transmit back and forth across half the circumference of the planet is noticeable to human beings. Add in server-side and client-side processing, and we risk alienating potential or existing users.

Also, keep in mind that even the fastest local connections have hiccups and slow-downs. So it's not uncommon for 'real-time' applications to have ways to handle this sort of behavior.

15.4.1 Solution: Mask the Latency with Animations

One of the more common fixes is to have JavaScript-powered animation distract the user from latency issues. We encounter this every time we use a single page app with an attractive interface, including all modern web-based email clients.

15.4.2 Solution: Fake Successful Transactions

Another solution involves processing the request on the client-side as if the request successfully made it to the server. We'll need to include client-side logic to handle failures, but Javascript frameworks handling HTTP requests are asynchronous, making this feasible, albeit possibly complicated.

If you've ever suddenly discovered that your cloud-based spreadsheet hadn't save the data entered for the past 30 seconds, you've uncovered this kind of JavaScript powered trickery in action.

15.4.3 Solution: Geographically Based Servers

Geographically-based servers across all seven continents is an option. However, for Django this is not trivial to implement, not at the programming or database level. It requires a significant volume of skills and expertise that's outside the scope of this book.

If you have the time and budget, this can be an exciting avenue to explore and we encourage it. However, unless you've done this before there is a good chance you are going to underestimate the effort involved.

15.4.4   Solution: Restrict Users Geographically

Sometimes we just don't have a choice. Perhaps our application is too reliant on 'real-time' performance and geolocating servers might be outside the budget. We might make some people unhappy, but that can be mitigated to some degree by saying things like, 'Support in your country is coming soon!'

15.5   Avoid the Anti-Patterns

Here are a number of anti-patterns that we've discovered when it comes to projects consuming REST APIs for content.

15.5.1   Building Single Page Apps When Multi-Page Apps Suffice

Single-page apps are challenging and fun to build, but does a traditional CMS-site need to be one? Certainly the content pages can include API-powered editing controls, but when building this kind of site, there is something to be said for traditional HTML pages.

However, when working with legacy projects, it's often easier to add new features as single-page apps. This allows for the maintainers of the project to deliver improved experiences with new features, while preserving the stability of the existing code base. A good example of this might be adding a calendar application to an existing project.

15.5.2   Not Writing Tests

When you first begin working in a new language or framework, including client-side JavaScript, it's tempting to skip the tests. In a word, don't. Working in the client is getting more complicated and sophisticated every year. Between evolving client-side standards, things are simply not as readable there as on the server side.

We cover Django/Python testing in chapter 20. A good reference for JavaScript testing is `http://2scoops.co/stack-overflow-javascript-unit-test-tools-for-tdd`

15.5.3   Not Understanding JavaScript Memory Management

Single-page apps are great, but the complex implementations where users keep them open constantly will hold objects in the browser for a very long time. Eventually, if not managed, this can cause browser slowdowns and crashes. Each JavaScript framework comes with tools or advice on how to handle this potential problem, and it's a good idea to know the recommended approach.

15.5.4   Storing Data in the DOM When It's Not jQuery

After years of using jQuery, some of us have grown used to using DOM elements to store data (especially Daniel). However, when using other JavaScript frameworks this isn't ideal. They have their own mechanisms for handling client data, and by not following them we risk losing out on some of the features promised by these frameworks.

We recommend looking up the data management methods for your chosen JavaScript framework and embracing them as deeply as possible.

15.6   AJAX and the CSRF Token

If you use AJAX with Django, you may discover that triggering the CSRF token validation blocks your ability to use your API.

Django's CSRF protection seems like an inconvenience when writing AJAX. However, if you're using **jQuery** then you can just create a *csrf.js* and use the following on any page with AJAX that is updating data.

```
EXAMPLE 15.3

// Place at /static/js/csrf.js
// using jQuery
function csrfSafeMethod(method) {
    // These HTTP methods do not require CSRF protection
```

```
        return (/^(GET|HEAD|OPTIONS|TRACE)$/.test(method));
    }
    $.ajaxSetup({
        crossDomain: false, // Obviates need for sameOrigin test
        beforeSend: function(xhr, settings) {
            if (!csrfSafeMethod(settings.type)) {
                xhr.setRequestHeader("X-CSRFToken", csrftoken);
            }
        }
    });
```

WARNING: This Works Only for jQuery 1.5+

This JavaScript will not work with versions of jQuery before 1.5. Please read the CSRF documentation specific to other versions of Django.

Now let's include the JavaScript on a page which has a shopping cart form for ordering ice cream:

```
EXAMPLE 15.4
{% extends "base.html" %}
{% load static %}

{% block title %}Ice Cream Shopping Cart{% endblock %}

{% block content %}
    <h1>Ice Cream Shopping Cart</h1>
    <div class="shopping-cart"></div>
{% endblock %}

{% block javascript %}
    {{ block.super }}
    <script type="text/javascript"
        src="{% static "js/csrf.js" %}"></script>
    <script type="text/javascript"
        src="{% static "js/shopping_cart.js" %}"></script>
{% endblock %}
```

15.6.1   Additional reading

➤ https://docs.djangoproject.com/en/1.6/ref/contrib/csrf/

15.7   Improving JavaScript Skills

One of the best things we can do when implementing the consumption of REST APIs in templates is to ensure our JavaScript skills are up to par. While Python developers sometimes like to grumble about JavaScript, it is a very capable language in its own right. Any responsible web developer will take the time to ramp up their skills so they can reap the benefits of modern JavaScript frameworks.

15.7.1   Assessing Skill Levels

Noted JavaScript developer Rebecca Murphey created a JavaScript assessment tool. We found it a wonderful way to determine how much JavaScript we actually knew, and what we needed to improve.

See https://github.com/rmurphey/js-assessment

15.7.2   Learn More JavaScript!

There are a plethora of JavaScript resources for taking basic skills and making them better. We list our favorites at the end of Appendix C, 'Additional Resources.'

15.8   Follow Javascript Coding Standards

In the case of JavaScript, we advocate the following guides for both front- and back-end work:

> *Felix's Node.js Style Guide*
> http://nodeguide.com/style.html
> *idiomatic.js*
> https://github.com/rwaldron/idiomatic.js/

15.9 Django and Javascript Tutorials

> http://2scoops.co/kevin-stone-django-angular-tutorial
> http://paltman.com/2012/04/30/integration-backbonejs-tastypie/

15.10 Summary

Material covered in this chapter included:

> Debugging the client.
> Javascript static asset preprocessors.
> Making content indexable by search engines.
> Real-time woes.
> Client-side anti-patterns.
> AJAX and CSRF tokens.
> Improving JavaScript skills.

16 | Tradeoffs of Replacing Core Components

There's a lot of hype around swapping out core parts of Django's stack for other pieces. Should you do it?

Short Answer: Don't do it. These days, even Instagram says on Forbes.com that it's completely unnecessary: http://2scoops.co/instagram-insights

Long Answer: It's certainly possible, since Django modules are simply just Python modules. Is it worth it? Well, it's worth it only if:

> ➤ You are okay with sacrificing your ability to use third-party Django packages.
> ➤ You have no problem giving up the powerful Django admin.
> ➤ You have already made a determined effort to build your project with core Django components, but you are running into walls that are major blockers.
> ➤ You have already analyzed your own code to find and fix the root causes of your problems. For example, you've done all the work you can to reduce the numbers of queries made in your templates.
> ➤ You've explored all other options including caching, denormalization, etc.
> ➤ Your project is a real, live production site with tons of users. In other words, you're certain that you're not just optimizing prematurely.
> ➤ You're willing to accept the fact that upgrading Django will be extremely painful or impossible going forward.

That doesn't sound so great anymore, does it?

16.1   The Temptation to Build FrankenDjango

Every year, a new fad leads waves of developers to replace some particular core Django component. Here's a summary of some of the fads we've seen come and go.

Fad	Reasons
For performance reasons, replacing the database/ORM with a NoSQL database and corresponding ORM replacement.	Not okay: ``I have an idea for a social network for ice cream haters. I just started building it last month. I need it to be web-scale!!!1!''    Okay: ``Our site has 50M users and I'm hitting the limits of what I can do with indexes, query optimization, caching, etc. We're also pushing the limits of our Postgres cluster. I've done a lot of research on this and am going to try storing a simple denormalized view of our activity feed data in Redis to see if it helps.''
For design reasons, replacing the database/ORM with a NoSQL database and corresponding ORM replacement.	Not okay: ``SQL Sucks! We're going with a document-oriented database like CouchDB or MongoDB.''    Okay: ``We've done our homework and PostgreSQL's HSTORE datatype perfectly suits our needs. We get the advantage of a document store combined with the stability of a relational database!''
Replacing Django's template engine with Jinja2, Mako, or something else.	Not okay: ``I read on Hacker News that Jinja2 is faster. I don't know anything about caching or optimization, but I need Jinja2!''    Not okay: ``I hate having logic in Python modules. I just want logic in my templates!'' Sometimes okay: ``I have a small number of views which generate 1MB+ HTML pages designed for Google to index!''

Table 16.1: Fad-based Reasons to Replace Components of Django

Figure 16.1: Replacing more core components of cake with ice cream seems like a good idea. Which cake would win? The one on the right, of course.

16.2 Case Study: Replacing the Django Template Engine

Let's take a closer look at one of the most common examples of replacing core Django components: replacing the Django template engine with **Jinja2**.

16.2.1 Excuses, Excuses

The excuse for doing this used to be performance. That excuse is no longer quite as valid. A lot of work has gone into improving the performance of Django's templating system, and newer benchmarks indicate that performance is greatly improved.

A common excuse for replacing the Django template engine is to give you more flexibility. This is a poor excuse because your template layer should be as thin as possible. Case in point, adding 'flexibility' to templates also means adding complexity.

16.2.2 What if I'm Hitting the Limits of Templates?

Are you really? You might just be putting your logic in the wrong places:

➤ If you are putting tons of logic into templates, template tags, and filters, consider moving that logic into model methods or helper utilities.

➤ Whatever can't be placed into model methods might go into views.

➤ Template tags and filters should be a last resort. We covered this in more detail in chapter 13, *Template Tags and Filters*.

16.2.3 What About My Unusual Use Case?

Okay, but what if I need to generate a 1 MB+ HTML page for Google to index?

Interestingly enough, this is the only use case that we know of for replacing Django 1.6 templates. The size of these pages can and will crash browsers, so it's really meant for machines to read from each other. These giant pages require tens of thousands of loops to render the final HTML, and this is a place where Jinja2 (or other template engines) might provide a noticeable performance benefit.

However, besides these exceptions, we've found we don't need Jinja2. So rather than replace Django templates across the site, we use Jinja2 in only the affected view:

EXAMPLE 16.1

```python
# flavors/views.py
import os
from django.conf import settings
from django.http import HttpResponse

from jinja2 import Environment, FileSystemLoader

from syrup.models import Syrup

JINJA2_TEMPLATES_DIR = os.path.join(
        settings.PROJECT_ROOT,
        "templates",
        "jinja2"
)
JINJA2_LOADER = FileSystemLoader(JINJA2_TEMPLATES_DIR)
JINJA2_ENV = Environment(loader=JINJA2_LOADER)
```

```
TEMPLATE = JINJA2_ENV.get_template("big_syrup_list.html")


def big_syrup_list(request):
    object_list = Syrup.objects.filter()
    content = TEMPLATE.render(object_list=object_list)
    return HttpResponse(content)
```

As we demonstrate, it's pretty easy to bring in the additional performance of Jinja2 without removing Django templates from a project.

16.3   Non-Relational Databases vs. Relational Databases

Even Django projects that use relational databases for persistent data storage rely on non-relational databases. If a project relies on tools like Memcached for caching and Redis for queueing, then it's using non-relational databases.

The problem occurs when NoSQL solutions are used to completely replace Django's relational database functionality without considering in-depth the long-term implications.

16.3.1   Understand ACID

ACID is an acronym for:

Atomicity means that all parts of a transaction work or it all fails. Without this, you risk data corruption.

Consistency means that any transaction will keep data in a valid state. Strings remain strings and integers remain integers. Without this, you risk data corruption.

Isolation means that concurrent execution of data within a transaction will not collide or leak into another transaction. Without this, you risk data corruption.

Durability means that once a transaction is committed, it will remain so even if the database server is shut down. Without this, you risk data corruption.

Did you notice how each of those descriptions ended with *'Without this, you risk data corruption.'*? This is because in the case of most NoSQL engines, there is little-to-no mechanism for *ACID* compliance. It's much easier to corrupt the data, which is mostly a non-issue for things like caching but another thing altogether for projects handling processing of persistent medical or e-commerce data.

16.3.2   Don't Use Non-Relational Databases for Relational Tasks

Imagine if we were to use a non-relational database to track the sale of properties, property owners, and how property laws worked for them in 50 US states. There a lot of unpredictable details, so wouldn't a schemaless datastore be perfect for this task?

Perhaps...

We would need to track the *relationship* between properties, property owners, and laws of 50 states. Our Python code would have to maintain the referential integrity between all the components. We would also need to ensure that the right data goes into the right place.

For a task like this, stick with a relational database.

16.3.3   Ignore the Hype and Do Your Own Research

It's often said that non-relational databases are faster and scale better than relational databases. Whether or not this is true true, don't blindly swallow the marketing hype of the companies behind any particular alternative database solution.

Instead, do as we do: search for benchmarks, read case studies describing when things went right or wrong, and form opinions as independently as possible.

Also, experiment with unfamiliar NoSQL databases on small hobby side projects before you make major changes to your main project infrastructure. Your main codebase is not a playground.

16.3.4   How We Use Non-Relational Databases With Django

This is how we prefer to do things:

➤ If we use a *non-relational data store*, limit usage to short-term things like caches, queues, and sometimes denormalized data. But avoid it if possible, to reduce the number of moving parts.

➤ Use *relational data stores* for long-term, relational data and sometimes denormalized data

For us, this is the sweet spot that makes our Django projects shine.

16.4 Summary

Always use the right tool for the right job. We prefer to go with stock Django components, just like we prefer using a scoop when serving ice cream. However, there are times when other tools make sense.

Just don't follow the fad of mixing vegetables into your ice cream. You simply can't replace the classic strawberry, chocolate, and vanilla with supposedly "high-performance" flavors such as broccoli, corn, and spinach. That's taking it too far.

17 | Working With the Django Admin

When people ask, *"What are the benefits of Django over other web frameworks?"* the admin is what usually comes to mind.

Imagine if every gallon of ice cream came with an admin interface. You'd be able to not just see the list of ingredients, but also add/edit/delete ingredients. If someone was messing around with your ice cream in a way that you didn't like, you could limit or revoke their access.

Figure 17.1: Chocolate chip ice cream with an admin interface.

Pretty surreal, isn't it? Well, that's what web developers coming from another background feel like when they first use the Django admin interface. It gives you so much power over your web application automatically, with little work required.

17.1 It's Not for End Users

The Django admin interface is designed for site administrators, not end users. It's a place for your site administrators to add/edit/delete data and perform site management tasks.

Although it's possible to stretch it into something that your end users could use, you really shouldn't. It's just not designed for use by every site visitor.

17.2 Admin Customization vs. New Views

It's usually not worth it to heavily customize the Django admin. Sometimes, creating a simple view or form from scratch results in the same desired functionality with a lot less work.

We've always had better results with creating custom management dashboards for client projects than we have with modifying the admin to fit the need of the client.

17.3 Viewing String Representations of Objects

The default admin page for a Django app looks something like this:

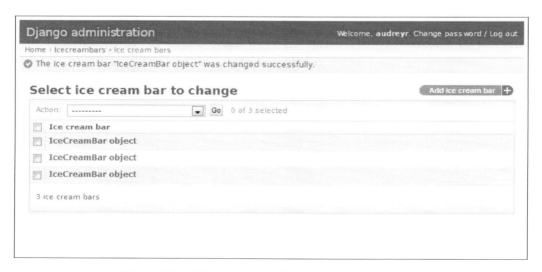

Figure 17.2: Admin list page for an ice cream bar app.

That's because the default string representation of an `IceCreamBar` object is "IceCreamBar object".

It would be helpful to display something better here. We recommend that you do the following as standard practice:

❶ Always implement the `__str__()` method for each of your Django models. If you are using Python 2.7, decorate the `__str__()` method with `django.utils.encoding.python_2_unicode_compatible`. This will give you a better default string representation in the admin and everywhere else.

❷ If you want to change the admin list display in a way that isn't quite a string representation of the object, then use `list_display`.

Implementing `__str__()` is simple:

```
EXAMPLE 17.1
from django.db import models
from django.utils.encoding import python_2_unicode_compatible


class IceCreamBar(models.Model):
    name = models.CharField(max_length=100)
    shell = models.CharField(max_length=100)
    filling = models.CharField(max_length=100)
    has_stick = models.BooleanField(default=True)


    @python_2_unicode_compatible  # For Python 3.3 and 2.7
    def __str__(self):
        return self.name
```

The result:

Django administration   Welcome, **audreyr**. Change password / Log out

Home › Icecreambars › Ice cream bars

Select ice cream bar to change

Add ice cream bar ➕

Action: |---------| Go   0 of 3 selected

- ☐ **Ice cream bar**
- ☐ **Strawberry Pie**
- ☐ **Mint Cookie Crunch**
- ☐ **Vanilla Crisp**

3 ice cream bars

Figure 17.3: Improved admin list page with better string representation of our objects.

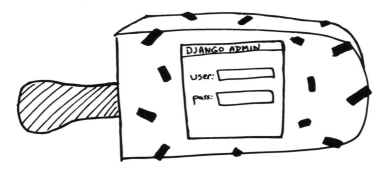

Figure 17.4: What? An admin interface for ice cream bars?

It's more than that. When you're in the shell, you see the better string representation:

```
Example 17.2

>>> IceCreamBar.objects.all()
[<IceCreamBar: Vanilla Crisp>, <IceCreamBar: Mint Cookie Crunch>,
<IceCreamBar: Strawberry Pie>]
```

The __str__() method is called whenever you call unicode() on an object. This occurs in the Django shell, templates, and by extension the Django admin. Therefore, try to make the results of _str_() nice, readable representation of Django model instances.

For working in Python 2.7, Django also provides the _unicode_() method as a default if we don't add a _str_() method. In fact, in all our years working with Django and Python 2.7, neither author has ever bothered writing a _str_() method.

If you still want to show data for additional fields on the app's admin list page, you can then use list_display:

```
EXAMPLE 17.3

from django.contrib import admin


from .models import IceCreamBar


class IceCreamBarAdmin(admin.ModelAdmin):
    list_display = ("name", "shell", "filling",)


admin.site.register(IceCreamBar, IceCreamBarAdmin)
```

The result with the specified fields:

Figure 17.5: Further improvements to the admin list page.

17.4   Adding Callables to ModelAdmin Classes

You can use callables such as methods and functions to add functionality to the Django `django.contrib.admin.ModelAdmin` class. This allows you to really modify the list and display screens to suit your ice cream project needs.

For example, it's not uncommon to want to see the exact URL of a model instance in the Django admin. If you define a `get_absolute_url()` method for your model, what Django provides in the admin is a link to a redirect view whose URL is very different from the actual object URL. Also, there are cases where the `get_absolute_url()` method is meaningless (REST APIs come to mind).

In the example below, we demonstrate how to use a simple callable to provide a link to our target URL:

```
EXAMPLE 17.4
from django.contrib import admin
from django.core.urlresolvers import reverse
from django.utils.html import format_html

from icecreambars.models import IceCreamBar

class IceCreamBarAdmin(admin.ModelAdmin):

    list_display = ("name", "shell", "filling",)
    readonly_fields = ("show_url",)

    def show_url(self, instance):
        url = reverse("ice_cream_bar_detail",
                   kwargs={"pk": instance.pk})
        response = format_html("""<a href="{0}">{1}</a>""", url, url)
        return response

    show_url.short_description = "Ice Cream Bar URL"
    # Displays HTML tags
    # Never set allow_tags to True against user submitted data!!!
    show_url.allow_tags = True
```

```
admin.site.register(IceCreamBar, IceCreamBarAdmin)
```

Since a picture is worth a thousand words, here is what our callable does for us:

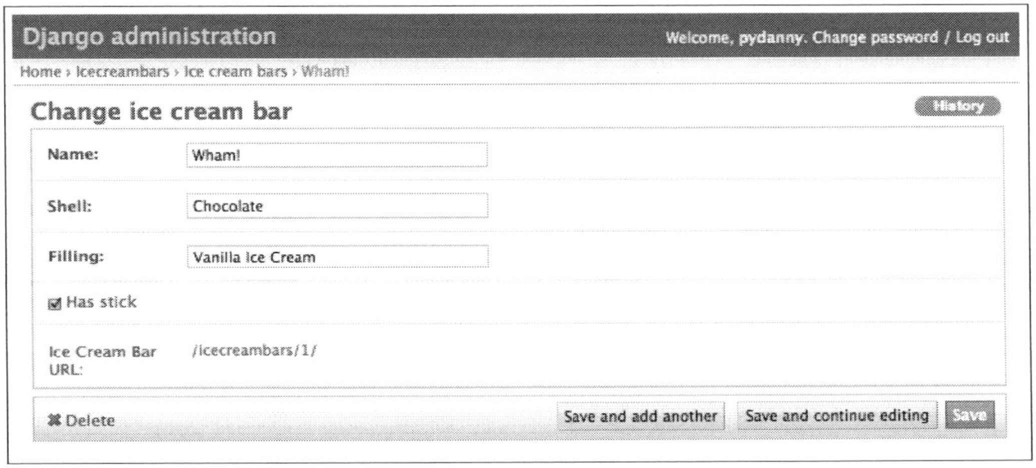

Figure 17.6: Displaying URL in the Django Admin.

WARNING: Use the allow_tags attribute With Caution

The allow_tags attribute, which is set to False by default, can be a security issue. When allow_tags is set to True, HTML tags are allowed to be displayed in the admin. Our hard rule is allow_tags can only be used on system generated data like primary keys, dates, and calculated values. Data such as character and text fields are completely out, as is any other user entered data.

17.5 Don't Use list_editable in Multiuser Environments

This is a feature of django.contrib.admin that replaces the normal admin list view with a form, allowing for a user to edit multiple records at the same time. Unfortunately, records are identified not by primary keys, but by their ordered position. While this is fine for a project with a single person with admin-level access, on a multi-user project it's very serious problem. Here is what happens:

❶ Ice cream bars are in descending `created` order.

❷ Daniel brings up the list field for ice cream bars and begins making changes.

❸ Audrey decides to add a "Peppermint Sundae" ice cream bar. Since it's the last item added, it's now the first IceCreamBar object returned.

❹ Daniel finally saves his changes, but the records he saw all receive the data from the next record, corrupting at least 50 records (Django's default admin display number).

Pointed out to us originally by Tomasz Paczkowski, our good friend and co-organizer of Django Circus 2013, this is a known bug in Django. It will hopefully be correcting in a future release of the project. In the meantime, if there is a need for this kind of display, it's best to generate your own list update view.

Related Django tickets:

➤ `https://code.djangoproject.com/ticket/11313`
➤ `https://code.djangoproject.com/ticket/17118`

17.6   Django's Admin Documentation Generator

One of the more interesting developer tools that Django provides is the `django.contrib.admindocs` package. Created in an era before the advent of the documentation tools that we cover in chapter 21, *Documentation: Be Obsessed*, it remains a useful tool.

It's useful because it introspects the Django framework to display docstrings for project components like models, views, custom template tags, and custom filters. Even if a project's components don't contain any docstrings, simply seeing a list of harder-to-introspect items like oddly named custom template tags and custom filters can be really useful in exploring the architecture of a complicated, existing application.

Using `django.contrib.admindocs` is easy, but we like to to reorder the steps described in the formal documentation:

❶ `pip install docutils` into your project's **virtualenv**.

❷ Add `django.contrib.admindocs` to your `INSTALLED_APPS`.

❸ Add `(r'^admin/doc/', include('django.contrib.admindocs.urls'))` to your root URLConf. Make sure it's included before the `r'^admin/'` entry, so that requests to `/admin/doc/` don't get handled by the latter entry.

❹ *Optional*: Linking to templates requires the `ADMIN_FOR` setting to be configured.

❺ *Optional*: Using the admindocs bookmarklets requires the `XViewMiddleware` to be installed.

Once you have this in place, go to `/admin/doc/` and explore. You may notice a lot of your project's code lacks any sort of documentation. This is addressed in the formal documentation on `django.contrib.admindocs`: <u>http://2scoops.co/1.6-admindocs</u> and our own chapter on chapter 21, *Documentation: Be Obsessed*.

17.7 Securing the Django Admin and Django Admin Docs

It's worth the effort to take the few extra steps to prevent hackers from accessing the admin, since the admin gives you so much power over your site. See chapter 23, *Security Best Practices* for details, specifically section 23.17, 'Securing the Django Admin,' and section 23.18, 'Securing Admin Docs.'

17.8 Using Custom Skins with the Django Admin

Over the years there have been a number of efforts to reskin or theme the Django Admin. These range from the venerable, stable, and very popular django-grappelli to more recent up-and-comers. They turn Django's 2005-era admin design into lovely styles more friendly to the modern eye.

PACKAGE TIP: Custom django.contrib.admin skins

Here are some of the more popular custom skins that work for both Python 3.3 and 2.7:

> ➤ **django-grappelli** is the grand-daddy of all custom Django skins. Stable, robust, and with a unique but friendly style.
> ➤ **django-suit** is a relatively recent project and like many modern custom Django skins, is built using the familiar Twitter Bootstrap front-end framework.
> ➤ **django-admin-bootstrapped** is another port of the Django admin to Twitter Bootstrap.

A more complete list can be found at
<u>https://www.djangopackages.com/grids/g/admin-styling/</u>.

Django has a gigantic community, so why aren't there more skins?

It turns out that besides the most basic CSS-based modifications, creating custom Django themes is very challenging. For anyone who has delved into the source code for these projects, it's clear that custom admin skins require arcane code to account for some of the idiosyncrasies of `django.contrib.admin`.

Patrick Kranzlmueller, maintainer of django-grappelli, goes into great detail in his article on the subject, 'A Frontend Framework for the Django Admin Interface', which you can read at the link below:

➤ http://sehmaschine.net/blog/django-admin-frontend-framework.

Here are some tips when working with custom `django.contrib.admin` skins:

17.8.1   Evaluation Point: Documentation is Everything

As mentioned earlier, writing a custom skin for `django.contrib.admin` is hard. While the successful skins are relatively easy to add to a project, it's the edge cases (invariably involved in extending the `ModelAdmin` object) that can hurt.

Therefore, when evaluating one of these projects for use on a project, check to see how far the documentation goes beyond installation instructions.

17.8.2   Write Tests for Any Admin Extensions You Create

For our purposes, we've found that while clients enjoy the more modern themes, you have to be careful of how far you extend these admin skins. What works great in vanilla `django.contrib.admin` can break in a custom skin. Since the custom skins have to wrap portions of `django.contrib.admin` abstractions in curious ways, debugging these problems can prove to be a mind-numbing nightmare.

Therefore, if you use a custom skin, the best practice is to write tests of the admin, especially for any customization. Yes, it is a bit of work up front, but it means catching these bugs much, much earlier.

For more on testing, see chapter 20.

17.9   Summary

In this chapter we covered the following:

- ➤ Who should be using the Django admin.
- ➤ When to use the Django admin and when to roll a new dashboard.
- ➤ String representation of objects.
- ➤ Adding callables to Django admin classes.
- ➤ Warned about using `django.contrib.admin.ModelAdmin.list_editable`.
- ➤ Using Django's admin docs.
- ➤ Encouraging you to secure the Django admin.
- ➤ Advised on working with custom Django skins.

18 | Dealing With the User Model

The best practices for this changed significantly in Django 1.5. The "right way" before Django 1.5 was a bit confusing, and there's still confusion around pre-1.5, so it's especially important that what we describe here is only applied to Django 1.5 or higher.

So let's go over best practices for Django 1.6.

18.1   Use Django's Tools for Finding the User Model

The advised way to get to the user class is as follows:

```
EXAMPLE 18.1

# Stock user model definition
>>> from django.contrib.auth import get_user_model
>>> get_user_model()
<class 'django.contrib.auth.models.User'>


# When the project has a custom user model definition
>>> from django.contrib.auth import get_user_model
>>> get_user_model()
<class 'profiles.models.UserProfile'>
```

It is now possible to get two different User model definitions depending on the project configuration. This doesn't mean that a project can have two different User models; it means that every project can customize its own User model. This was introduced in Django 1.5 and a radical departure from earlier versions of Django.

18.1.1   Use settings.AUTH_USER_MODEL for Foreign Keys to User

In Django 1.6, the official preferred way to attach ForeignKey, OneToOneField, or Many-ToManyField to User is as follows:

```
EXAMPLE 18.2

from django.conf import settings
from django.db import models


class IceCreamStore(models.Model):

    owner = models.OneToOneField(settings.AUTH_USER_MODEL)
    title = models.CharField(max_length=255)
```

Yes, it looks a bit strange, but that's what the official Django docs advise.

Figure 18.1: This looks strange too.

WARNING: Don't Change settings.AUTH_USER_MODEL!

Once set in a project, changing settings.AUTH_USER_MODEL requires changing your database schema accordingly. It's one thing to add or modify User model fields, it's another thing to create a whole new User object.

18.1.2   Don't Use get_user_model() for Foreign Keys to User

This is bad, as it tends to create import loops.

The other thing you have to do is set this in your settings:

EXAMPLE 18.4

```
AUTH_USER_MODEL = "profiles.KarmaUser"
```

18.3.2   Option 2: Subclass AbstractBaseUser

AbstractBaseUser is the bare-bones option with only 3 fields: password, last_login, and is_active.

Choose this option if:

➤ You're unhappy with the fields that the User model provides by default, such as first_name and last_name.
➤ You prefer to subclass from an extremely bare-bones clean slate but want to take advantage of the AbstractBaseUser sane default approach to storing passwords.

If you want to go down this path, we recommend the following reading:

Official Django Documentation Example
> http://2scoops.co/1.6-custom-user-model-example

Source code of django-authtools (Especially admin.py, forms.py, and models.py)
> https://github.com/fusionbox/django-authtools

18.3.3   Option 3: Linking Back From a Related Model

This code is very similar to the pre-Django 1.5 project technique of creating 'Profile' models. Before discarding this approach as legacy, consider the following use cases:

Use Case: Creating a Third Party Package

➤ We are creating a third-party package for publication on PyPI.
➤ The package needs to store additional information per user, perhaps a Stripe ID or another payment gateway identifier.

➤ We want to be as unobtrusive to the existing project code as possible. Loose coupling!

Use Case: Internal Project Needs

➤ We are working on our own Django project.
➤ We want different types of users to have different fields.
➤ We might have some users with a combination of different user types.
➤ We want to handle this at the model level, instead of at other levels.
➤ We want this to be used in conjunction with a custom user model from options #1 or #2.

Either of these use cases provide motive for the continued use of this technique.

To make this technique work, we continue to use `django.contrib.models.User` (called preferably via `django.contrib.auth.get_user_model()`) and keep your related fields in separate models (e.g. `Profiles`). Here's an example:

EXAMPLE 18.5
```python
# profiles/models.py

from django.conf import settings
from django.db import models

from flavors.models import Flavor

class EaterProfile(models.Model):

    # Default user profile
    # If you do this you need to either have a post_save signal or
    #     redirect to a profile_edit view on initial login.
    user = models.OneToOneField(settings.AUTH_USER_MODEL)
    favorite_ice_cream = models.ForeignKey(Flavor, null=True, blank=True)

class ScooperProfile(models.Model):

    user = models.OneToOneField(settings.AUTH_USER_MODEL)
    scoops_scooped = models.IntegerField(default=0)

class InventorProfile(models.Model):
```

```
user = models.OneToOneField(settings.AUTH_USER_MODEL)
flavors_invented = models.ManyToManyField(Flavor, null=True, blank=True)
```

Using this approach, we can query for any user's favorite ice cream trivially with the ORM: `user.eaterprofile.favorite_ice_cream`. In addition, `Scooper` and `Inventor` profiles provide individual data that only applies to those users. Since that data is isolated into dedicated models, it's much harder for accidents between user types to occur.

The only downside to this approach is that it's possible to take it too far in complexity of profiles or in the supporting code. As always, keep your code as simple and clean as possible.

TIP: Stop Using the user.get_profile() Method

The `user.get_profile()` method is deprecated in Django 1.6 and will be removed in Django 1.7.

18.4 Summary

The new `User` model makes this an exciting time to be involved in Django. We are getting to participate in a major infrastructure change with wide-ranging implications. We are the ones who get to pioneer the best practices.

In this chapter we covered the new method to find the `User` model and define our own custom ones. Depending on the needs of a project, they can either continue with the current way of doing things or customize the actual user model.

The next chapter is a dive into the world of third-party packages.

19 | Django's Secret Sauce: Third-Party Packages

The real power of Django is more than just the framework and documentation available at https://djangoproject.com. It's the vast, growing selection of third-party Django and Python packages provided by the open source community. There are many, many third-party packages available for your Django projects which can do an incredible amount of work for you. These packages have been written by people from all walks of life, and they power much of the world today.

Figure 19.1: A jar of Django's mysterious secret sauce. Most don't have a clue what this is.

Much of professional Django and Python development is about the incorporation of third-party packages into Django projects. If you try to write every single tool that you need from scratch, you'll have a hard time getting things done.

This is especially true for us in the consulting world, where client projects consist of many of the same or similar building blocks.

Figure 19.2: The secret is out. It's just hot fudge.

19.1   Examples of Third-Party Packages

Appendix A: *Packages Mentioned In This Book* covers all of the packages mentioned throughout Two Scoops of Django. This list is a great starting point if you're looking for highly-useful packages to consider adding to your projects.

Note that not all of those packages are Django-specific, which means that you can use some of them in other Python projects. (Generally, Django-specific packages generally have names prefixed with "django-", but there are many exceptions.)

19.2   Know About the Python Package Index

The **Python Package Index (PyPI)**, located at `https://pypi.python.org/pypi`, is a repository of software for the Python programming language. As of the start of 2014, it lists over 37,000 packages, including Django itself.

For the vast majority of Python community, no open-source project release is considered official until it occurs on the Python Package Index.

The Python Package Index is much more than just a directory. Think of it as the world's largest center for Python package information and files. Whenever you use **pip** to install a particular release of Django, pip downloads the files from the Python Package Index. Most Python and Django packages are downloadable from the Python Package Index in addition to pip.

19.3   Know About DjangoPackages.com

Django Packages (https://www.djangopackages.com/) is a directory of reusable apps, sites, tools and more for your Django projects. Unlike PyPI, it doesn't store the packages themselves, instead providing a mix of hard metrics gathered from the Python Package Index, GitHub, Bitbucket, ReadTheDocs, and "soft" data entered by users.

Django Packages is best known as a comparison site for evaluating package features. On Django Packages, packages are organized into handy grids so they can be compared against each other.

Django Packages also happens to have been created by the authors of this book, with contributions from many, many people in the Python community. We continue to maintain and improve it as a helpful resource for Django users.

19.4   Know Your Resources

Django developers unaware of the critical resources of Django Packages and the Python Package Index are denying themselves one of the most important advantages of using Django and Python. If you are not aware of these tools, it's well worth the time you spend educating yourself.

As a Django (and Python) developer, make it your mission to use third-party libraries instead of reinventing the wheel whenever possible. The best libraries have been written, documented, and tested by amazingly competent developers working around the world. Standing on the shoulders of these giants is the difference between amazing success and tragic downfall.

As you use various packages, study and learn from their code. You'll learn patterns and tricks that will make you a better developer.

On the other hand, it's very important to be able to identify the good packages from the bad. It's well worth taking the time to evaluate packages written by others the same way we evaluate our own work. We cover this later in this chapter in section 19.10, 'What Makes a Good Package.'

19.5   Tools for Installing and Managing Packages

To take full advantage of all the packages available for your projects, having **virtualenv** and **pip** installed isn't something you can skip over. It's mandatory.

Refer to chapter 2, *The Optimal Django Environment Setup*, for more details.

19.6 Package Requirements

As we mentioned earlier in chapter 5, *Settings and Requirements Files*, we manage our Django/Python dependencies with requirements files. These files go into the ***requirements/*** directory that exists in the root of our projects.

> ## TIP: Researching Third-Party Packages To Use
>
> If you want to learn more about the dependencies we list in this and other chapters, please refer to Appendix A: *Packages Mentioned In This Book*.

19.7 Wiring Up Django Packages: The Basics

When you find a third-party package that you want to use, follow these steps:

19.7.1 Step 1: Read the Documentation for the Package

Are you sure you want to use it? Make sure you know what you're getting into before you install any package.

19.7.2 Step 2: Add Package and Version Number to Your Requirements

If you recall from chapter 5, *Settings and Requirements Files*, a ***requirements/base.txt*** file looks something like this (but probably longer):

```
EXAMPLE 19.1
Django==1.6
coverage==3.7
django-extensions==1.2.5
django-floppyforms==1.1
```

Note that each package is pinned to a specific version number. *Always* pin your package dependencies to version numbers.

What happens if you don't pin your dependencies? You are almost guaranteed to run into problems at some point when you try to reinstall or change your Django project. When new versions of packages are released, you can't expect them to be backwards-compatible.

Our sad example: Once we followed a software-as-a-service platform's instructions for using their library. As they didn't have their own Python client, but an early adopter had a working implementation on GitHub, those instructions told us to put the following into our *requirements/base.txt*:

```
BAD EXAMPLE 19.1
-e git+https://github.com/erly-adptr/py-junk.git#egg=py-jnk
```

Our mistake. We should have known better and pinned it to a particular git revision number.

Not the early adopter's fault at all, but they pushed up a broken commit to their repo. Once we had to fix a problem on a site very quickly, so we wrote a bugfix and tested it locally in development. It passed the tests. Then we deployed it to production in a process that grabs all dependency changes; of course the broken commit was interpreted as a valid change. Which meant, while fixing one bug, we crashed the site.

Not a fun day.

The purpose of using pinned releases is to add a little formality and process to our published work. Especially in Python, GitHub and other repos are a place for developers to publish their work-in-progress, not the final, stable work upon which our production-quality projects depend.

One more thing, when pinning dependencies, try to pin the dependencies of dependencies. It just makes deployment and testing that much more predictable.

19.7.3   Step 3: Install the Requirements Into Your Virtualenv

Assuming you are already in a working virtualenv and are at the **<repo_root>** of your project, you `pip install` the appropriate requirements file for your setup, e.g. *requirements/dev.txt*.

If this is the first time you've done this for a particular virtualenv, it's going to take a while for it to grab all the dependencies and install them.

19.7.4   Step 4: Follow the Package's Installation Instructions Exactly

Resist the temptation to skip steps unless you're very familiar with the package. Since open-source Django package developers tend to take pride in their documentation and love to get people to use their packages, most of the time the installation instructions they've authored make it easy to get things running.

19.8   Troubleshooting Third-Party Packages

Sometimes you run into problems setting up a package. What should you do?

First, make a serious effort to determine and solve the problem yourself. Pore over the documentation and make sure you didn't miss a step. Search online to see if others have run into the same issue. Be willing to roll up your sleeves and look at the package source code, as you may have found a bug.

If it appears to be a bug, see if someone has already reported it in the package repository's issue tracker. Sometimes you'll find workarounds and fixes there. If it's a bug that no one has reported, go ahead and file it.

If you still get stuck, try asking for help in all the usual places: StackOverflow, IRC #django, the project's IRC channel if it has its own one, and your local Python user group. Be as descriptive and provide as much context as possible about your issue.

19.9   Releasing Your Own Django Packages

Whenever you write a particularly useful Django app, consider packaging it up for reuse in other projects.

The best way to get started is to follow Django's *Advanced Tutorial: How to Write Reusable Apps*, for the basics: https://docs.djangoproject.com/en/1.6/intro/reusable-apps/

In addition to what is described in that tutorial, we recommend that you also:

➤ Create a public repo containing the code. Most Django packages are hosted on GitHub these days, so it's easiest to attract contributors there, but various alternatives exist (Gitlab, Sourceforge, Bitbucket, Launchpad, Gitorious, Assembla, etc.).

➤ Release the package on the Python Package Index (`http://pypi.python.org`). Follow the submission instructions at `http://2scoops.co/submit-to-pypi`.

➤ Add the package to Django Packages (`https://www.djangopackages.com`).

➤ Use Read the Docs (`https://readthedocs.org/`) to host your **Sphinx** documentation.

TIP: Where Should I Create A Public Repo?

There are websites that offer free source code hosting and version control for open-source projects. As mentioned in chapter 2, "The Optimal Django Environment Setup", GitHub or Bitbucket are two popular options.

When choosing a hosted version control service, keep in mind that pip only supports Git, Mercurial, Bazaar, and Subversion.

19.10 What Makes a Good Package?

Here's a checklist for you to use when releasing a new open-source Django or Python package. Much of this applies to Python packages that are not Django-specific. This checklist is also helpful for when you're evaluating a Django/Python package to use in any of your projects.

This section is adapted from our DjangoCon 2011 talk, *"Django Package Thunderdome: Is Your Package Worthy?"*: `http://2scoops.co/django-thunderdome-slides`

19.10.1 Purpose

Your package should do something useful and do it well. The name should be descriptive. The package repo's root folder should be prefixed with 'django-' to help make it easier to find.

If part of the package's purpose can be accomplished with a related Python package that doesn't depend on Django, then create a separate Python package and use it as a dependency.

19.10.2   Scope

Your package's scope should be tightly focused on one small task. This means that your application logic will be tighter, and users will have an easier time patching or replacing the package.

19.10.3   Documentation

A package without documentation is a pre-alpha package. Docstrings don't suffice as documentation.

As described in chapter 21, *Documentation: Be Obsessed*, your docs should be written in **ReStructuredText**. A nicely-formatted version of your docs should be generated with Sphinx and hosted publicly. We encourage you to use `https://readthedocs.org/` with webhooks so that your formatted documentation automatically updates whenever you make a change.

If your package has dependencies, they should be documented. Your package's installation instructions should also be documented. The installation steps should be bulletproof.

19.10.4   Tests

Your package should have tests. Tests improve reliability, make it easier to advance Python/Django versions, and make it easier for others to contribute effectively. Write up instructions on how to run your package's test suite. If you or any contributor can run your tests easily before submitting a pull request, then you're more likely to get better quality contributions.

19.10.5   Activity

Your package should receive regular updates from you or contributors if/when needed. When you update the code in your repo, you should consider uploading a minor or major release to the Python Package Index.

19.10.6   Community

Great open-source packages, including those for Django, often end up receiving contributions from other developers in the open source community. All contributors should receive attribution in a *CONTRIBUTORS.rst* or *AUTHORS.rst* file.

Be an active community leader if you have contributors or forks of your package. If your package is forked by other developers, pay attention to their work. Consider if there are ways that parts or all of their work can be merged into your fork. If the package's functionality diverges a lot from your package's purpose, be humble and consider asking the other developer to give their fork a new name.

19.10.7   Modularity

Your package should be as easily pluggable into any Django project that doesn't replace core components (templates, ORM, etc) with alternatives. Installation should be minimally invasive. Be careful not to confuse modularity with over-engineering, though.

19.10.8   Availability on PyPI

All major and minor releases of your package should be available for download from the Python Package Index. Developers who wish to use your package should not have to go to your repo to get a working version of it. Use proper version numbers per the next section.

19.10.9   Uses the Broadest Requirements Specifiers Possible

Your third-party package should specify in *setup.py* in the `install_requires` argument what other libraries your package requires in the broadest terms possible:

```
EXAMPLE 19.2

# requirements for django-blarg

Django>=1.5,<1.7
requests>=1.2.3,<2.0
```

On the other hand, this is bad:

```
BAD EXAMPLE 19.2

# DON'T DO THIS!
# requirements for django-blarg

Django==1.5.2
requests==1.2.3
```

The reason is dependency graphs. Every so often something that you absolutely pin to a specific version of Django or another library will break on someone else's site project. For example, what if this was a deployed project's requirements.txt file?

```
EXAMPLE 19.3

# requirements.txt for the mythical web site 'icecreamratings.com'
Django==1.6
requests==2.2.1-
djangoblarg==1.0

# Note that unlike the -djangoblarg library , we explicitly pin
# the requirements so we have total control over the environment
```

What would happen if applied to Example 19.3 is that the Django 1.5.2 requirement would overwrite the Django 1.6 specification during installation of requirements. As there are several backwards incompatibilities between Django 1.5.2 and 1.6, django-blarg could make our site simply throw HTTP 500 errors.

Additional Reading:

➤ http://www.pip-installer.org/en/latest/logic.html#requirement-specifiers

➤ http://nvie.com/posts/pin-your-packages/

19.10.10   Proper Version Numbers

Like Django and Python, we prefer to adhere to the strict version of **PEP 386** naming schema. In fact we follow the '**A.B.C**' pattern. Let's go through each element:

'**A**'   represents the major version number. Increments should only happen with large changes that break backwards compatibility from the previous major version. It's not uncommon to see large API changes between versions.

'**B**'   is the minor version number. Increments include less breaking changes, or deprecation notices about forthcoming changes.

'**C**'   represents bugfix releases, and purists call this the 'micro' release. It's not uncommon for developers to wait until a project has its first release at this level before trying the latest major or minor release of an existing project.

For alpha, beta, or release-candidates for a project, the convention is to place this information as a suffix to the upcoming version number. So you might have:

➤ Django 1.6
➤ django-crispy-forms 1.1b1

> ### WARNING: Don't Upload Unfinished Code To PyPI
>
> PyPI, the Python Package Index, is meant to be the place where dependable, stable packages can be harnessed to build Python projects. *PyPI is not the place for Alpha, Beta, or Release Candidate code*, especially as pip and other tools will fetch the latest release by default.
>
> Be nice to other developers and follow the convention of only placing proper releases on PyPI.
>
> *Note:* While recent versions of pip no longer install pre-releases by default, it's dangerous to expect users of code to have the latest pip version installed.

Additional Reading:

➤ http://www.python.org/dev/peps/pep-0386
➤ http://semver.org/

19.10.11   Name

The name of the project is absolutely critical. A well-named project makes it easy to discover and remember, a poor name hides it from potential users, can scare off its use from some developer shops, and even block it from being listed on PyPI, Django Packages, and other resources.

We did cover the basics in section 4.2, 'What to Name Your Django Apps,' but here are tips that apply to open-source Django packages:

➤ *Check to see that the name isn't already registered on PyPI.* Otherwise, it won't be trivial to install with **pip**.
➤ *Check to see that the name isn't on Django Packages.* This applies only to packages designed for use with Django.
➤ *Don't use names that include obscenity.* While you might find them funny, it's unfortunate for others. For example a noted developer once created a library that couldn't be used at NASA until he agreed to change the name.

19.10.12   License

Your package needs a license. Preferably, it should be licensed under the **BSD** or **MIT** licenses, which are generally accepted for being permissive enough for most commercial or noncommercial uses.

Create a *LICENSE.rst* file in your repo root, mention the license name at the top, and paste in the appropriate text from the approved list at the **Open Source Initiative** (OSI) http://opensource.org/licenses/category for the license that you choose.

> ### TIP: Licenses Protect You and the World
>
> In this era of casual litigation and patent trolls adding a software license isn't just a matter of protecting your ownership of the code. It's much, much more. If you don't license your code, or use an unapproved license not vetted by real lawyers, you run the risk of your work being used as a weapon by a patent troll, or in the case of financial or medical disaster, you could be held liable.
>
> OSI-approved licenses all include a couple critical statements on **copyright, redistribution, disclaimer of warranty**, and **limitation of liability**.

19.10.13   Clarity of Code

The code in your Django package should be as clear and simple as possible, of course. Don't use weird, unusual Python/Django hacks without explaining what you are doing.

19.10.14   Use URL Namespaces

Described in section 7.4, URL namespaces allow for greater Interoperability. Using means it's easier to manage collisions between projects, or even prepare for it ahead of time.

If there is concern about future collisions, settings-based URL namespace systems can be implemented. This is where the project defines its URL namespace as a setting, then provides a Django context processor and detailed instructions on use. While it's not hard to implement, it does create a level of abstraction that can make a project a little bit harder to maintain.

19.11   Creating Your Own Packages the Easy Way

Releasing your own bit of code can be a wonderfully rewarding experience. Everyone should do it!

That said, putting all the pieces together in order to make a reusable Django package is a lot of work, and it's common to get things wrong. Fortunately, **Cookiecutter** makes this easy.

PACKAGE TIP: Cookiecutter: Project Templates Make Easy

Audrey has created a popular utility for generating project templates. It's easy to use and very powerful. Numerous templates exist for Python and Django packages.

- ➤ https://github.com/audreyr/cookiecutter
- ➤ http://cookiecutter.readthedocs.org/

In the Cookiecutter templates referenced below, we have vetted them by aggressively asking for them to be reviewed by leaders in both the Django and Python communities. Just use the following bash example at the command-line:

```
EXAMPLE 19.4

# Only if you installed cookiecutter yet
$ pip install cookiecutter


# Creating a Django Package from scratch
$ cookiecutter https://github.com/pydanny/cookiecutter-djangopackage.git


# Creating a Python Package from scratch
$ cookiecutter https://github.com/audreyr/cookiecutter-pypackage.git
```

You'll be prompted to provide information. The generated result will be an implementation of a base Django/Python/etc package template that includes code, documentation, tests, license, and much more.

19.12   Maintaining Your Open-Source Package

WARNING: Open-Source Burnout and Giving Too Much

Unless you are getting paid professionally to do open-source work, remember that this is volunteer work done for pleasure. Do what you can at your own pace, and just try your best.

The open-source packages that you create have a life of their own. They mature over time, changing as their needs and the development standards grow over time. Here are some things we should do when maintaining open-source projects:

19.12.1   Give Credit for Pull Requests

When someone submits a pull request that's accepted, treat them right. Make sure to add the contributor to a project's author document called something like *CONTRIBUTORS.txt* or *AU-THORS.txt*.

19.12.2   Handling Bad Pull Requests

Sometimes you get pull requests that you just have to reject. Be nice and positive about it, since a well-handled rejected pull request can make a friend for life.

Here are problematic pull requests that should be considered for rejection:

➤ *Any pull request that fails the tests.* Ask for fixes. See chapter 20.
➤ *Any added code that reduces test coverage.* Again, see chapter 20.
➤ *Pull requests should change/fix as little as possible.* Large, wide-sweeping changes in a pull request should be rejected, with comments to isolate changes in smaller, atomic pull requests.
➤ *Overly complex code submissions should be carefully considered.* There is nothing wrong with asking for simplification, better comments, or even rejecting an overly complex pull request.
➤ *Code that breaks PEP-8 needs to be resubmitted.* The Django world follows PEP-8 very closely, and so should your project. Submissions that violate PEP 8 can be requested to be improved.
➤ *Code changes combined with major whitespace cleanup.* If someone submits a change of two lines of code and corrects 200 lines of whitespace issues, the diff on that pull request is functionally unreadable and should be rejected. Whitespace cleanups need to be in their own pull request.

> ## WARNING: Code Changes Combined With Major Whitespace Cleanup
>
> We're adding a warning because this is arguably a form of code obfuscation by a third party. One could argue it's potentially a security risk. What better way to inject malignant code than through a pull request?

19.12.3   Do Formal PyPI Releases

In the Python community, it's considered irresponsible to force developers to rely on a 'stable' master or trunk branch of critical open source projects because the PyPI version is out of date. This can cause problems as open source code repositories are not considered to be good sources of production quality code. For example, which particular commit or tag should be used? On the other hand, PyPI, is a known resource designed to securely provide valid installable packages.

In the Python world, the accepted best practice is to release when significant (or even minor) changes or bugfixes happen on trunk or master. In fact, minor bug fix releases are a part of every ongoing software project and no one faults anyone for these kinds of things (except in US government IT contracts, but that's outside the scope of this book).

If you aren't sure how this works, please look at python-request's change history, it being one of Python's most popular projects: http://2scoops.co/requests-history

To create and upload your distribution, use the following steps:

```
EXAMPLE 19.5
$ pip install twine
$ python setup.py sdist
$ twine upload dist/*
```

PACKAGE TIP: What is Twine?

Twine is the preferred library for uploading packages to PyPI. The problem with `python setup.py` is that it sends files over a non-SSH connection, exposing your library to a man-in-the-middle attack. In contrast, twine uses only verified TLS to upload your package.

That's not all! Twine works better at uploading Wheels (see the next subsection), doesn't require executing the setup.py, and even pre-signs your releases. If you are seriously security minded, it's the tool of choice.

19.12.4   Create and Deploy Wheels to PyPI

According to PEP 427, Wheels are the new standard of python distribution. They are intended to replace eggs and provide a number of advantages including faster installation and allow secure digital signing. Support is offered in pip >= 1.4 and setuptools >= 0.8.

EXAMPLE 19.6

```
$ pip install wheel
$ pip install twine
```

Then, after you've deployed your package to PyPI, run the following commands:

EXAMPLE 19.7

```
$ python setup.py bdist_wheel
$ twine upload dist/*
```

For supporting Python 2.7 and 3.3+, Twine makes universal wheels when the optional *setup.cfg* file is at the same level as *setup.py* and includes this snippet:

EXAMPLE 19.8
```
# setup.cfg
[wheel]
universal = 1
```

Wheel Resources:

Specification: PEP 427 http://www.python.org/dev/peps/pep-0427/
Wheel Package on PyPI https://pypi.python.org/pypi/wheel
Documentation http://wheel.readthedocs.org/
Advocacy http://pythonwheels.com/

19.12.5   Upgrade the Package to New Versions of Django

Every once in awhile, Django is updated with a minor release. Approximately once a year there is a major Django release. When this happens, it's very important to run our package's test suite in a **virtualenv** that contain Django's latest release.

If for no other reason, this is an excellent reason to include tests in your project.

19.12.6   Follow Good Security Practices

We discuss security in-depth in chapter 23, *Security Best Practices*. However, core Django, Python, and PyPy developer Alex Gaynor has an incredibly useful article for maintainers of any open source project:

http://alexgaynor.net/2013/oct/19/security-process-open-source-projects/

> ### TIP: Alex Gaynor on Security for Open Source Projects
>
> 'Security vulnerabilities put your users, and often, in turn, their users at risk. As an author and distributor of software, you have a responsibility to your users to handle security releases in a way most likely to help them avoid being exploited.'

19.12.7   Provide Sample Base Templates

Always include some basic templates for views using your project. We prefer to write either incredibly simple HTML or use a common front-end frameworks such as Twitter Bootstrap. This makes 'test-driving' the project much easier for developers who are considering using it to solve their problems. Invariably they'll modify the templates inside their own *templates/* directory, but this just makes everything so much easier.

In addition, include a *templates/myapp/base.html* to increase interoperability. You can see a description and example of this in cookiecutter-djangopackage:

`http://2scoops.co/cookiecutter-djangopackage-base.html`

19.12.8   Give the Package Away

Sometimes, life takes you away from maintaining a package. It might be family or a new job, but sometimes you just have no need for a particular open-source project. Time considerations might mean that you don't have the ability to review pull requests or explore ideas for new features. If you're the creator of a project it can be extremely challenging to let it go.

However, by giving a project away to an active maintainer, it can be reborn and prove more useful. It also earns the respect of the developer community at large.

Some notable giveaways in the Django and Python communities include:

> ➤ Ian Bicking and pip/virtualenv.
> ➤ Jesper Nøhr and django-piston.
> ➤ Daniel Greenfeld and django-uni-form.
> ➤ Rob Hudson and django-debug-toolbar.

19.13   Additional Reading

The following are links to useful articles for anyone contributing to, creating, or maintaining open source libraries:

> ➤ `http://alexgaynor.net/2013/sep/26/effective-code-review/`

➤ http://2scoops.co/sharing-your-labor-of-love-pypi-quick-and-dirty

➤ http://2scoops.co/jeff-knupp-open-sourcing-a-python-project

19.14 Summary

Django's real power is in the vast selection of third-party packages available to you for use in your Django projects.

Make sure that you have pip and virtualenv installed and know how to use them, since they're your best tools for installing packages on your system in a manageable way.

Get to know the packages that exist. The Python Package Index and Django Packages are a great starting point for finding information about packages.

Package maturity, documentation, tests, and code quality are good starting criteria when evaluating a Django package.

Installation of stable packages is the foundation of Django projects big and small. Being able to use packages means sticking to specific releases, not just the trunk or master of a project. Barring a specific release, you can rely on a particular commit. Fixing problems that a package has with your project takes diligence and time, but remember to ask for help if you get stuck.

We also covered how to create your own third-party package, and provided basic instruction on how to use cookiecutter to jump-start you on your way to releasing something on the Python Package Index. We also included instructions on using the new Wheel format.

Finally, we provided guidance on how to maintain a package.

20 | Testing Stinks and Is a Waste of Money!

There, got you to this chapter.

Now you have to read it.

We'll try and make this chapter interesting.

20.1 Testing Saves Money, Jobs, and Lives

Daniel's Story: Ever hear the term "smoke test"?

Gretchen Davidian, a Management and Program Analyst at **NASA**, told me that when she was still an engineer, her job as a tester was to put equipment intended to get into space through such rigorous conditions that they would begin emitting smoke and eventually catch on fire.

That sounds exciting! Employment, money, and lives were on the line, and knowing Gretchen's attention to detail, I'm sure she set a lot of hardware on fire.

Keep in mind that for a lot of us, as software engineers, the same risks are on the line as NASA. I recall in 2004 while working for a private company how a single miles-vs-kilometers mistake cost a company hundreds of thousands of dollars in a matter of hours. Quality Assurance (QA) staff lost their jobs, which meant that money and health benefits were gone. In other words, employment, money, and possibly lives can be lost without adequate tests. While the QA staff were very dedicated, everything was done via manually clicking through projects, and human error simply crept into the testing process.

Today, as Django moves into a wider and wider set of applications, the need for automated testing is just as important as it was for Gretchen at NASA and for the poor QA staff in 2004. Here are some cases where Django is used today that have similar quality requirements:

- ➤ Your application handles medical information.
- ➤ Your application provides life-critical resources to people in need.
- ➤ Your application works with other people's money now or will at some point in the future.

PACKAGE TIP: Useful Library For Testing Django Projects

We like to use **coverage.py**.

This tool provides clear insight into what parts of your code base are covered by tests, and what lines haven't been touched by tests. You also get a handy percentage of how much of your code is covered by tests. Even 100% test coverage doesn't guarantee a bug-free application, but it helps.

We want to thank Ned Batchelder for his incredible work in maintaining coverage.py. It's a superb project and is useful for any Python related project.

20.2 How to Structure Tests

Let's say we've just created a new Django app. The first thing we do is delete the default but useless *tests.py* module that `django-admin.py startapp` creates.

In its place, because most apps need them, we create *test_forms.py*, *test_models.py*, *test_views.py* modules. Tests that apply to forms go into *test_forms.py*, model tests go into *test_models.py*, and so on.

Here's what it looks like:

```
EXAMPLE 20.1
popsicles/
    __init__.py
    admin.py
    forms.py
```

```
models.py
test_forms.py
test_models.py
test_views.py
views.py
```

Also, if we have other files besides *forms.py*, *models.py* and *views.py* that need testing, we create corresponding test files.

We like this approach because per the *Zen of Python*'s statement that "*Flat is better than nested,*" this makes it easier to navigate a Django app.

TIP: Prefix Test Modules With test_

It's critically important that we always prefix test modules with *test_*, otherwise Django's test runner can't discover our test files.

20.3   How to Write Unit Tests

It's not uncommon for programmers to feel at the top of their game at the moment they are writing code. When they revisit that same code in months, weeks, days, or even hours and it's not uncommon for programmers to feel as if that same code is of poor quality.

The same applies to writing unit tests.

Over the years, we've evolved a number of practices we like to follow when writing tests, including **unit tests**. Our goal is always to write the most meaningful tests in the shortest amount of time. Hence the following:

20.3.1   Each Test Method Tests One Thing

A test method must be extremely narrow in what it tests. A single test *should never* assert the behavior of multiple views, models, forms, or even multiple methods within a class. Instead, a single test should assert the behavior of a single view, model, form, method or function.

Of course, therein lies a conundrum. How does one run a test for a view, when views often require the use of models, forms, methods, and functions?

The trick is to be absolutely minimalistic when constructing the environment for a particular test, as shown in the example below:

EXAMPLE 20.2

```
# flavors/test_api.py
import json

from django.core.urlresolvers import reverse
from django.test import TestCase

from flavors.models import Flavor

class FlavorAPITests(TestCase):

    def setUp(self):
        Flavor.objects.get_or_create(title="A Title", slug="a-slug")

    def test_list(self):
        url = reverse("flavor_object_api")
        response = self.client.get(url)
        self.assertEquals(response.status_code, 200)
        data = json.loads(response.content)
        self.assertEquals(len(data), 1)
```

In this test, taken from code testing the API we presented in section 14.2, 'Implementing a Simple JSON API,' chapter 14, *Building REST APIs*, we use the setUp() method to create the minimum possible number of records needed to run the test.

Here's a much larger example, one based off of the REST API example that we provided in chapter 14.

EXAMPLE 20.3

```
# flavors/test_api.py
import json
```

```
from django.core.urlresolvers import reverse
from django.test import TestCase
from django.utils.http import urlencode

from flavors.models import Flavor

class DjangoRestFrameworkTests(TestCase):

    def setUp(self):
        Flavor.objects.get_or_create(title="title1", slug="slug1")
        Flavor.objects.get_or_create(title="title2", slug="slug2")

        self.create_read_url = reverse("flavor_rest_api")
        self.read_update_delete_url = \
            reverse("flavor_rest_api", kwargs={"slug": "slug1"})

    def test_list(self):
        response = self.client.get(self.create_read_url)

        # Are both titles in the content?
        self.assertContains(response, "title1")
        self.assertContains(response, "title2")

    def test_detail(self):
        response = self.client.get(self.read_update_delete_url)
        data = json.loads(response.content)
        content = {"id": 1, "title": "title1", "slug": "slug1",
                                        "scoops_remaining": 0}
        self.assertEquals(data, content)

    def test_create(self):
        post = {"title": "title3", "slug": "slug3"}
        response = self.client.post(self.create_read_url, post)
        data = json.loads(response.content)
        self.assertEquals(response.status_code, 201)
        content = {"id": 3, "title": "title3", "slug": "slug3",
```

```
                                              "scoops_remaining": 0}
        self.assertEquals(data, content)
        self.assertEquals(Flavor.objects.count(), 3)

    def test_delete(self):
        response = self.client.delete(self.read_update_delete_url)
        self.assertEquals(response.status_code, 204)
        self.assertEquals(Flavor.objects.count(), 1)
```

20.3.2   For Views, When Possible Use the Request Factory

The `django.test.client.RequestFactory` provides a way to generate a request instance that can be used as the first argument to any view. This provides a greater amount of isolation then the standard Django test client, but it does require a little bit of extra work on the part of the test writer. This is because the request factory doesn't support middleware, including session and authentication.

See `http://2scoops.co/1.6-request-factory`

20.3.3   Don't Write Tests That Have to Be Tested

Tests should be written as simply as possible. If the code in a test (or the code called to help run a test) feels complicated or abstracted, then you have a problem. In fact, we ourselves are guilty of writing overly complicated utility test functions that required their own tests in the past. As you can imagine, this made debugging the actual tests a nightmare.

20.3.4   Don't Repeat Yourself Doesn't Apply to Writing Tests

The `setUp()` method is really useful for generating reusable data across all test methods in a test class. However, sometimes we need similar but different data between test methods, which is where we often fall into the trap of writing fancy test utilities. Or worse, we decide that rather than write 20 similar tests, we can write a single method that when passed certain arguments will handle all the work for us.

Our favorite method of handling these actions is to just dig in and write the same or similar code multiple times. In fact, we'll quietly admit to copy/pasting code between tests to expedite our work.

20.3.5   Don't Rely on Fixtures

We've learned over time that using fixtures is problematic. The problem is that fixtures are hard to maintain as a project's data changes over time. Modifying JSON-formatted files to match your last migration is hard, especially as it can be difficult to identify during the JSON load process where your JSON file(s) is either broken or a subtly inaccurate representation of the database.

Rather than wrestle with fixtures, we've found it's easier to write code that relies on the ORM. Other people like to use third-party packages.

PACKAGE TIP: Tools to Generate Test Data

The following are popular tools for test data generation:

- ➤ **factory boy** A package that generates model test data.
- ➤ **model mommy** Another package that generates model test data.
- ➤ **mock** Not explicitly for Django, this allows you to replace parts of your system with mock objects. This project made its way into the standard library as of Python 3.3.

20.3.6   Things That Should Be Tested

Everything! Seriously, you should test whatever you can, including:

Views: Viewing of data, changing of data, and custom class-based view methods.
Models: Creating/updating/deleting of models, model methods, model manager methods.
Forms: Form methods, clean() methods, and custom fields.

Validators: Really dig in and write multiple test methods against each custom validator you write. Pretend you are a malignant intruder attempting to damage the data in the site.

Signals: Since they act at a distance, signals can cause grief especially if you lack tests on them.

Filters: Since filters are essentially just functions accepting one or two arguments, writing tests for them should be easy.

Template Tags: Since template tags can do anything and can even accept template context, writing tests often becomes much more challenging. This means you really need to test them, since otherwise you may run into edge cases.

Miscellany: Context processors, middleware, email, and anything else not covered in this list.

The only things that shouldn't be tested are parts of your project that are already covered by tests in core Django and third-party packages. For example, a model's fields don't have to be tested if you're using Django's standard fields as-is. However, if you're creating a new type of field (e.g. by subclassing FileField), then you should write detailed tests for anything that could go wrong with your new field type.

Figure 20.1: Test as much of your project as you can, as if it were free ice cream.

20.3.7   Document the Purpose of Each Test

Just as it is a good idea to document the purpose of a class, method, or function with docstrings, it is also a good idea to document the purpose the test analogs of these items. If undocumented code makes a project somewhat harder to maintain, undocumented test code can make a project impossible to test. To remedy this, a little bit of docstring can go a long way.

If you think this is boring, well, we've found that a good way to deal with an impossible-to-debug problem is to document the related tests. By the time the tests are documented, you have either figured out the problem or you have documented tests. Either case is a win!

20.4   Continuous Integration

For projects of any size, we recommend setting up a continuous integration (CI) server to run the project's test suite whenever code is committed and pushed to the project repo. See chapter 30, *Continuous Integration* for more details.

20.5   Who Cares? We Don't Have Time for Tests!

> *"Tests are the Programmer's stone, transmuting fear into boredom."* –Kent Beck

Let's say you are confident of your coding skill and decide to skip testing to increase your speed of development. Or maybe you feel lazy. It's easy to argue that even with test generators and using tests instead of the shell, they can increase the time to get stuff done.

Oh, really?

What about when it's time to upgrade?

That's when the small amount of work you did up front to add tests saves you a lot of work.

For example, in the summer of 2010, Django 1.2 was the standard when we started Django Packages (http://www.djangopackages.com). Since then we've stayed current with new Django versions, which has been really useful. Because of our pretty good test coverage, moving up a version of Django (or the various dependencies) has been easy. Our path to upgrade:

➤ Upgrade the version in a local instance of Django Packages.

➤ Run the tests.

➤ Fix any errors that are thrown by the tests.

➤ Do some manual checking.

If Django Packages didn't have tests, any time we upgraded *anything* we would have to click through dozens and dozens of scenarios manually, which is error-prone. Having tests means we can make changes and dependency upgrades with the confidence that our users (i.e. the Django community) won't have to deal with a buggy experience.

This is the benefit of having tests.

20.6   The Game of Test Coverage

A great, fun game to play is trying get **test coverage** as high as possible. Every day that we increase our test coverage is a victory, and every day that the coverage goes down is a loss.

20.7   Setting Up the Test Coverage Game

Yes, we call test coverage a game. It's a good tool for developers to push themselves. It's also a nice metric that both developers and their clients/employers/investors can use to help evaluate the status of a project.

We advocate following these steps because most of the time we want to only test our own projects' apps, not all of Django and the myriad of third-party libraries that are the building blocks of our project. Testing those 'building blocks' takes an enormous amount of time, which is a waste because most are already tested or require additional setup of resources.

20.7.1   Step 1: Start Writing Tests

We've done that already, right?

20.7.2   Step 2: Run Tests and Generate Coverage Report

Let's try it out! In the command-line, at the *<project_root>*, type:

EXAMPLE 20.4

```
$ coverage run manage.py test --settings=twoscoops.settings.test
```

If we have nothing except for the default tests for two apps, we should get a response that looks like:

EXAMPLE 20.5

```
Creating test database for alias "default"...

..

-----------------------------------------------

Ran 2 tests in 0.008s

OK

Destroying test database for alias "default"...
```

This doesn't look like much, but what it means is that we've constrained our application to only run the tests that you want. Now it's time to go and look at and analyze our embarrassingly low test coverage numbers.

20.7.3   Step 3: Generate the report!

coverage.py provides a very useful method for generating HTML reports that don't just provide percentage numbers of what's been covered by tests, it also shows us the places where code is not tested. In the command-line, at the *<project_root>*:

EXAMPLE 20.6

```
$ coverage html --omit="admin.py"
```

Ahem...don't forget to change *<project-root>* to match the development machine's structure! For example, depending on where one does things, the *<path-to-project-root>* could be:

➤ */Users/audreyr/code/twoscoops/twoscoops/*

➤ */Users/pydanny/projects/twoscoops/twoscoops/*

➤ *c:\ twoscoops*

After this runs, in the *<project_root>* directory there is a new directory called *htmlcov/*. In the *htmlcov/* directory, open the *index.html* file using any browser.

What is seen in the browser is the test results for our test run. Unless we already wrote some tests, the total on the front page will be in the single digits, if not at 0%. Click into the various modules listed and we'll should see lots of code that's red-colored. *Red is bad.*

Let's go ahead and admit that our project has a low coverage total. If your project has a low coverage total, you need to admit it as well. It's okay just so long as we also resolve to improve the coverage total.

In fact, there is nothing wrong in saying publicly that you are working to improve a project's test coverage. Then, other developers (including ourselves) will cheer you on!

20.8   Playing the Game of Test Coverage

The game has a single rule:

> *Mandate that no commit can lower test coverage.*

If we add a feature or bugfix and coverage is 65% when we start, we can't merge our code in until coverage is at least 65% again. At the end of each day, if test coverage goes up by any amount, it means we're winning.

Keep in mind that the gradual increase of test coverage can be a very good thing over huge jumps. Gradual increases can mean that we developers aren't putting in bogus tests to bump up coverage numbers; instead, we are improving the quality of the project.

20.9   Summary

All of this might seem silly, but testing can be very serious business. In a lot of developer groups this subject, while gamified, is taken very seriously. Lack of stability in a project can mean the loss of clients, contracts, and even employment.

In the next chapter we cover a common obsession of Python developers: documentation.

21 | Documentation: Be Obsessed

Given a choice between ice cream and writing great documentation, most Python developers would probably choose to write the documentation. That being said, writing documentation while eating ice cream is even better.

When you have great documentation tools like **reStructuredText** and **Sphinx**, you actually can't help but want to add docs to your projects.

> ### PACKAGE TIP: Install Sphinx Systemwide
>
> We've found that simply installing *Sphinx* fetches for us all the pieces you need to document our Django (or Python) project. We recommend **pip** installing Sphinx systemwide, as you'll want to have it handy for every Django project.

21.1 Use reStructuredText for Python Docs

You'll want to learn and follow the standard Python best practices for documentation. These days, reStructuredText (**RST**) is the most common *markup* language used for documenting Python projects.

What follows are links to the formal reStructuredText specification and a couple sample projects which benefit from using it:

- ➤ http://2scoops.co/restructured-text-specification
- ➤ https://docs.djangoproject.com/en/1.6/

➤ http://docs.python.org

While it's possible to study the formal documentation for reStructuredText and learn at least the basics, here is a quick primer of some very useful commands you should learn.

```
EXAMPLE 21.1

Section Header
==============

**emphasis (bold/strong)**

*italics*

Simple link: http://django.2scoops.org
Fancier Link: `Two Scoops of Django`_

.. _Two Scoops of Django: https://django.2scoops.org

Subsection Header
-----------------

#) An enumerated list item

#) Second item

* First bullet

* Second bullet

  * Indented Bullet

  * Note carriage return and indents

Literal code block::

    def like():
        print("I like Ice Cream")
```

```
    for i in range(10):
        like()

Python colored code block (requires pygments):

code-block:: python

    # You need to "pip install pygments" to make this work.

    for i in range(10):
        like()

JavaScript colored code block:

code-block:: javascript

    console.log("Don't use alert()");
```

21.2 Use Sphinx to Generate Documentation From reStructuredText

Sphinx is a tool for generating nice-looking docs from your *.rst* files. Output formats include **HTML**, **LaTeX**, manual pages, and plain text.

Follow the instructions to generate Sphinx docs: `http://sphinx-doc.org/`.

TIP: Build Your Sphinx Documentation at Least Weekly

You never know when bad cross-references or invalid formatting can break the Sphinx build. Rather than discover that the documentation is unbuildable at an awkward moment, just make a habit of creating it on a regular basis.

21.3 What Docs Should Django Projects Contain?

Developer-facing documentation refers to notes and guides that developers need in order to set up and maintain a project. This includes notes on installation, deployment, architecture, how to run tests or submit pull requests, and more. We've found that it really helps to place this documentation in all our projects, private or public. Here we provide a table that describes what we consider the absolute minimum documentation:

Filename or Directory	Reason	Notes
README.rst	Every Python project you begin should have a README.rst file in the repository root.	Provide at least a short paragraph describing what the project does. Also, link to the installation instructions in the docs/ directory.
docs/	Your project documentation should go in one, consistent location. This is the Python community standard.	A simple directory.
docs/deployment.rst	This file lets you take a day off.	A point-by-point set of instructions on how to install/update the project into production, even if it's done via something powered by Ruby, Chef, Fabric, or a Makefile.
docs/installation.rst	This is really nice for new people coming into a project or when you get a new laptop and need to set up the project.	A point-by-point set of instructions on how to onboard yourself or another developer with the software setup for a project.
docs/architecture.rst	A guide for understanding what things evolved from as a project ages and grows in scope.	This is how you imagine a project to be in simple text and it can be as long or short as you want. Good for keeping focused at the beginning of an effort.

Table 21.1: Documentation Django Projects Should Contain

Figure 21.1: Even ice cream could benefit from documentation.

21.4   Additional Documentation Resources

➤ http://www.python.org/dev/peps/pep-0257 Official specification on docstrings.

➤ https://readthedocs.org/ Read the Docs is a free service that can host your Sphinx documentation.

➤ http://pythonhosted.org/ Python Hosted is another free service for documentation hosting.

21.5   The Markdown Alternative

Markdown is a plain text formatting syntax not too dissimilar to reStructuredText. While it doesn't have all the built-in features of reStructuredText, it does have the advantage of being easier to learn. While used infrequently in the Python and Django communities, it's very popular in tangential places including the JavaScript and technical book-writing community.

When using Markdown instead of reStructuredText for open-source projects, keep the following in mind:

➤ **PyPI** will not format the `long_description` if it's written in anything except reStructuredText.

➤ Many Python and Django developers will search reStructuredText-powered documentation sources before Markdown-powered ones.

Markdown resources:

➤ https://en.wikipedia.org/wiki/Markdown

➤ http://documentup.com will host README documents written in Markdown format.

➤ http://progrium.viewdocs.io/ allows for Markdown documents to be organized and displayed in a Sphinx-like format. Also provides free hosting.

➤ http://johnmacfarlane.net/pandoc/ is a great tool for converting between Markdown to other formats, but it's not perfect. It's better for small efforts than anything substantial.

21.6 Wikis and Other Documentation Methods

For whatever reason, if you can't place developer-facing documentation in the project itself, you should have other options. While wikis, online document stores, and word processing documents don't have the feature of being placed in version control, they are better than no documentation.

Please consider creating documents within these other methods with the same names as the ones we suggested in the table on the previous page.

21.7 Summary

In this chapter we went over the following:

➤ The use of reStructuredText to write documentation in plaintext format.
➤ The use Sphinx to render your documentation in HTML and EPUB formats. If you know how to install LaTeX you can even render it as PDF. For reference, installing LaTeX is easy to do on Linux and Windows and a bit harder on Mac OS X.
➤ Advice on the documentation requirements for any Django project.

Next, we'll take a look at common bottlenecks in Django projects and ways to deal with them.

22 | Finding and Reducing Bottlenecks

This chapter covers a few basic strategies for identifying bottlenecks and speeding up your Django projects.

22.1 Should You Even Care?

Remember, premature optimization is bad. If your site is small- or medium-sized and the pages are loading fine, then it's okay to skip this chapter.

On the other hand, if your site's user base is growing steadily or you're about to land a strategic partnership with a popular brand, then read on.

22.2 Speed Up Query-Heavy Pages

This section describes how to reduce bottlenecks caused by having too many queries, as well as those caused by queries that aren't as snappy as they could be.

We also urge you to read up on database access optimization in the official Django docs: http://2scoops.co/1.6-db-optimization

22.2.1 Find Excessive Queries With Django Debug Toolbar

You can use **django-debug-toolbar** to help you determine where most of your queries are coming from. You'll find bottlenecks such as:

➤ Duplicate queries in a page.

➤ ORM calls that resolve to many more queries than you expected.

➤ Slow queries.

You probably have a rough idea of some of the URLs to start with. For example, which pages don't feel snappy when they load?

Install django-debug-toolbar locally if you don't have it yet. Look at your project in a web browser, and expand the SQL panel. It'll show you how many queries the current page contains.

PACKAGE TIP: Packages for Profiling and Performance Analysis

django-debug-toolbar is a critical development tool and an invaluable aid in page-by-page analysis. We also recommend adding **django-cache-panel** to your project, but only configured to run when *settings/dev.py* module is called. This will increase visibility into what your cache is doing.

django-extensions comes with a tool called `RunProfileServer` that starts Django's runserver command with hotshot/profiling tools enabled.

newrelic (`http://newrelic.com`) is a commercial service. In addition to their paid service, they provide a free service that can really help in performance analysis of staging or production sites.

22.2.2   Reduce the Number of Queries

Once you know which pages contain an undesirable number of queries, figure out ways to reduce that number. Some of the things you can attempt:

➤ Try using `select_related()` in your ORM calls to combine queries. It follows `ForeignKey` relations and combines more data into a larger query. If using CBVs, django-braces makes doing this trivial with the `SelectRelatedMixin`. Beware of queries that get too large by explicitly passing the related field names you are interested in. Only the specified relations will be followed. Combine that with careful testing!

➤ If the same query is being generated more than once per template, move the query into the Python view, add it to the context as a variable, and point the template ORM calls at this new context variable.

➤ Implement caching using a key/value store such as **Memcached**. Then write tests to assert the number of queries run in a view. See `http://2scoops.co/1.6-test-num-queries` for instructions.

➤ Use the `django.utils.functional.cached_property` decorator to cache in memory the result of method call for the life of an object instance. This is incredibly useful, so please see subsection 26.2.3, '`django.utils.functional.cached_property`' in chapter 26.

WARNING: Don't Use the Depth Argument with select_related

Previously, developers would use the '`depth`' argument to constrain the number of joins performed by `select_related()`. However, because its behavior was somewhat unpredictable, this approach has been deprecated.

22.2.3   Speed Up Common Queries

The length of time it takes for individual queries can also be a bottleneck. Here are some tips, but consider them just starting points:

➤ Make sure your indexes are helping speed up your most common slow queries. Look at the raw SQL generated by those queries, and index on the fields that you filter/sort on most frequently. Look at the generated WHERE and ORDER_BY clauses.

➤ Understand what your indexes are actually doing in production. Development machines will never perfectly replicate what happens in production, so learn how to analyze and understand what's really happening with your database.

➤ Look at the query plans generated by common queries.

➤ Turn on your database's slow query logging feature and see if any slow queries occur frequently.

➤ Use django-debug-toolbar in development to identify potentially-slow queries defensively, before they hit production.

Once you have good indexes, and once you've done enough analysis to know which queries to rewrite, here are some starting tips on how to go about rewriting them:

❶ Rewrite your logic to return smaller result sets when possible.

❷ Re-model your data in a way that allows indexes to work more effectively.

❸ Drop down to raw SQL in places where it would be more efficient than the generated query.

TIP: Use EXPLAIN ANALYZE / EXPLAIN

If you're using PostgreSQL, you can use EXPLAIN ANALYZE to get an extremely detailed query plan and analysis of any raw SQL query. For more information, see:

➤ `http://www.revsys.com/writings/postgresql-performance.html`

➤ `http://2scoops.co/craig-postgresql-perf2`

The MySQL equivalent is the EXPLAIN command, which isn't as detailed but is still helpful. For more information, see:

➤ `http://dev.mysql.com/doc/refman/5.6/en/explain.html`

A nice feature of django-debug-toolbar is that the SQL pane has an EXPLAIN feature.

22.2.4 Switch ATOMIC_REQUESTS to False

The clear, vast majority of Django projects will run just fine with the setting of ATOMIC_REQUESTS to True. Generally, the penalty of running all database queries in a transaction isn't noticeable. However, if your bottleneck analysis points to transactions causing too much delay, it's time to change the project run as ATOMIC_REQUESTS to True. See subsection 6.4.2, 'Explicit Transaction Declaration,' for guidelines on this setting.

22.3 Get the Most Out of Your Database

You can go a bit deeper beyond optimizing database access. Optimize the database itself! Much of this is database-specific and already covered in other books, so we won't go into too much detail here.

22.3.1 Know What Doesn't Belong in the Database

Frank Wiles of Revolution Systems taught us that there are two things that should never go into any large site's relational database:

Logs. Don't add logs to the database. Logs may seem OK on the surface, especially in development. Yet adding this many writes to a production database will slow their performance. When the ability to easily perform complex queries against your logs is necessary, we recommend third-party services such as Splunk or Loggly, or use of document-based NoSQL databases.

Ephemeral data. Don't store ephemeral data in the database. What this means is data that requires constant rewrites is not ideal for use in relational databases. This includes examples such as django.contrib.sessions, django.contrib.messages, and metrics. Instead, move this data to things like Memcached, Redis, Riak, and other non-relational stores.

TIP: Frank Wiles on Binary Data in Databases

Actually, Frank says that there are three things to never store in a database, the third item being binary data. Storage of binary data in databases is addressed by `django.db.models.FileField`, which does the work of storing files on file servers like AWS CloudFront or S3 for you. Exceptions to this are detailed in subsection 6.2.5.

22.3.2 Getting the Most Out of PostgreSQL

If using **PostgreSQL**, be certain that it is set up correctly in production. As this is outside the scope of the book, we recommend the following articles:

- ► `http://wiki.postgresql.org/wiki/Detailed_installation_guides`
- ► `http://wiki.postgresql.org/wiki/Tuning_Your_PostgreSQL_Server`
- ► `http://www.revsys.com/writings/postgresql-performance.html`
- ► `http://2scoops.co/craig-postgresql-perf`
- ► `http://2scoops.co/craig-postgresql-perf2`

For further information, you may want to read the book "*PostgreSQL 9.0 High Performance*":
`http://amzn.to/1fWctM2`

22.3.3   Getting the Most Out of MySQL

It's easy to get **MySQL** running, but optimizing production installations requires experience and understanding. As this is outside the scope of this book, we recommend the following books by MySQL experts to help you:

➤ *"High Performance MySQL"* `http://amzn.to/188VPcL`

22.4   Cache Queries With Memcached or Redis

You can get a lot of mileage out of simply setting up Django's built-in caching system with Memcached or Redis. You will have to install one of these tools, install a package that provides Python bindings for them, and configure your project.

You can easily set up the per-site cache, or you can cache the output of individual views or template fragments. You can also use Django's low-level cache API to cache Python objects.

Reference material:

➤ `https://docs.djangoproject.com/en/1.6/topics/cache/`
➤ `https://github.com/sebleier/django-redis-cache/`

22.5   Identify Specific Places to Cache

Deciding where to cache is like being first in a long line of impatient customers at Ben and Jerry's on free scoop day. You are under pressure to make a quick decision without being able to see what any of the flavors actually look like.

Here are things to think about:

➤ Which views/templates contain the most queries?
➤ Which URLs are being requested the most?
➤ When should a cache for a page be invalidated?

Let's go over the tools that will help you with these scenarios.

22.6   Consider Third-Party Caching Packages

Third-party packages will give you additional features such as:

➤ Caching of QuerySets.
➤ Cache invalidation settings/mechanisms.
➤ Different caching backends.
➤ Alternative or experimental approaches to caching.

A couple of the popular Django packages for caching are:

➤ **django-cache-machine**
➤ **johnny-cache**

See `http://www.djangopackages.com/grids/g/caching/` for more options.

> **WARNING: Third-Party Caching Libraries Aren't Always the Answer**
>
> Having tried many of the third-party Django cache libraries, we have to ask our readers to test them very carefully and be prepared to drop them. They are cheap, quick wins, but can lead to some hair-raising debugging efforts at the worst possible times.
>
> Cache invalidation is hard, and in our experience, magical cache libraries are better for projects with more static content. By-hand caching is a lot more work, but leads to better performance in the long run and doesn't risk those terrifying moments.

22.7   Compression and Minification of HTML, CSS, and JavaScript

When a browser renders a web page, it usually has to load HTML, CSS, JavaScript, and image files. Each of these files consumes the user's bandwidth, slowing down page loads. One way to reduce bandwidth consumption is via compression and minification. Django even provides tools for you: `GZipMiddleware` and the `{% spaceless %}` template tag. Through the at-large Python community, we can even use **WSGI** middleware that performs the same task.

The problem with making Django and Python do the work is that compression and minification take up system resources, which can create bottlenecks of their own. A better approach is to use **Apache** and **Nginx** web servers configured to compress the outgoing content. If you are maintaining your own web servers, this is absolutely the way to go.

A very common middle approach that we endorse is to use a third-party Django library to compress and minify the CSS and JavaScript in advance. Our preference is django-pipeline which comes recommended by Django core developer Jannis Leidel.

Tools and libraries to reference:

- ➤ Apache and Nginx compression modules
- ➤ **django-pipeline**
- ➤ **django-compressor**
- ➤ **django-htmlmin**
- ➤ Django's built-in spaceless tag: `http://2scoops.co/1.6-spaceless-tag`
- ➤ Django's included GZip middleware: `http://2scoops.co/1.6-gzip-middleware`
- ➤ `http://www.djangopackages.com/grids/g/asset-managers/`

22.8 Use Upstream Caching or a Content Delivery Network

Upstream caches such as **Varnish** are very useful. They run in front of your web server and speed up web page or content serving significantly. See `http://varnish-cache.org/`.

Content Delivery Networks (CDNs) like Akamai and Amazon Cloudfront serve static media such as images, video, CSS, and JavaScript files. They usually have servers all over the world, which serve out your static content from the nearest location. Using a CDN rather than serving static content from your application servers can speed up your projects.

22.9 Other Resources

Advanced techniques on scaling, performance, tuning, and optimization are beyond the scope of this book, but here are some starting points.

On general best practices for web performance:

➤ YSlow's *Web Performance Best Practices and Rules*:
  `http://developer.yahoo.com/yslow/`
➤ Google's Web *Performance Best Practices*:
  `https://developers.google.com/speed/docs/best-practices/rules_intro`

On scaling large Django sites:

➤ "Django Performance Tips" article by Jacob Kaplan-Moss:
  `http://jacobian.org/writing/django-performance-tips/`
➤ David Cramer often writes and speaks about scaling Django at Disqus. Read his blog and keep an eye out for his talks, Quora posts, comments, etc. `http://justcramer.com/`
➤ Watch videos and slides from past DjangoCons and PyCons about different developers' experiences. Scaling practices vary from year to year and from company to company:
  `http://lanyrd.com/search/?q=django+scaling`

Figure 22.1: With your site running smoothly, you'll be feeling as cool as a cone.

22.10 Summary

In this chapter we explored a number of bottleneck reduction strategies including:

➤ Whether you should even care about bottlenecks in the first place.
➤ Profiling your pages and queries.
➤ Optimizing queries.
➤ Using your database wisely.
➤ Caching queries.
➤ Identifying what needs to be cached.

➤ Compression of HTML, CSS, and JavaScript.

➤ Exploring other resources.

In the next chapter, we'll go over the basics of securing Django projects.

23 | Security Best Practices

When it comes to security, Django has a pretty good record. This is due to security tools provided by Django, solid documentation on the subject of security, and a thoughtful team of core developers who are extremely responsive to security issues. However, it's up to individual Django developers such as ourselves to understand how to properly secure Django-powered applications.

This chapter contains a list of things helpful for securing your Django application. This list is by no means complete. Consider it a starting point.

23.1 Harden Your Servers

Search online for instructions and checklists for server hardening. Server hardening measures include but are not limited to things like changing your SSH port and disabling/removing unnecessary services.

23.2 Know Django's Security Features

Django 1.6's security features include:

- ➤ Cross-site scripting (XSS) protection.
- ➤ Cross-site request forgery (CSRF) protection.
- ➤ SQL injection protection.
- ➤ Clickjacking protection.
- ➤ Support for SSL/HTTPS, including secure cookies.
- ➤ Secure password storage, using the PBKDF2 algorithm with a SHA256 hash by default.
- ➤ Automatic HTML escaping.

➤ An expat parser hardened against XML bomb attacks.

➤ Hardened JSON, YAML, and XML serialization/deserialization tools.

Most of Django's security features "just work" out of the box without additional configuration, but there are certain things that you'll need to configure. We've highlighted some of these details in this chapter, but please make sure that you read the official Django documentation on security as well: `https://docs.djangoproject.com/en/1.6/topics/security/`

23.3 Turn Off DEBUG Mode in Production

Your production site should not be running in **DEBUG** mode. Attackers can find out more than they need to know about your production setup from a helpful DEBUG mode stack trace page. For more information, see

`https://docs.djangoproject.com/en/1.6/ref/settings/#debug`.

Keep in mind that when you turn off DEBUG mode, you will need to set **ALLOWED_HOSTS** or risk raising a SuspiciousOperation error. For more information on setting AL-LOWED_HOSTS see section 23.6, 'Use Django 1.6's Allowed Hosts Validation.'

23.4 Keep Your Secret Keys Secret

If your SECRET_KEY setting is not secret, this means you risk everything from remote code execution to password hacking. Your API keys and other secrets should be carefully guarded as well. These keys should not even be kept in version control.

We cover the mechanics of how to keep your SECRET_KEY out of version control in chapter 5, *Settings and Requirements Files*, section 5.3, 'Keep Secret Keys Out With Environment Variables,' and section 5.4, 'Loading Secrets from Files Instead of From Environment Variables.'

23.5 HTTPS Everywhere

It is always better to deploy a site behind HTTPS. Not having HTTPS means that malicious network users can sniff authentication credentials between your site and end users. In fact, all data sent between your site and end users is up for grabs.

Your entire site should be behind HTTPS. Your site's static resources should also be served via HTTPS, otherwise visitors will get warnings about "insecure resources" which should rightly scare them away from your site. For reference, these warnings exist because they are a potential man-in-the-middle vector.

TIP: Jacob Kaplan-Moss on HTTPS vs HTTP

Django co-leader Jacob Kaplan-Moss says, "Your whole site should only be available via HTTPS, not HTTP at all. This prevents getting "firesheeped" (having a session cookie stolen when served over HTTP). The cost is usually minimal."

If visitors try to access your site via HTTP, they should be redirected to HTTPS. This can be done either through configuration of your web server or with Django middleware. Performance-wise, it's better to do this at the web server level, but if you don't have control over your web server settings for this, then redirecting via Django middleware is fine.

PACKAGE TIP: Django Middleware Packages That Force HTTPS

Two packages that force HTTPS/SSL across your entire site through Django middleware:

➤ **django-sslify** https://github.com/rdegges/django-sslify
➤ **django-secure** https://github.com/carljm/django-secure

The difference is that django-sslify is more minimalist and does nothing but force HTTPS, whereas django-secure also helps you configure and check other security settings.

You should purchase an SSL certificate from a reputable source rather than creating a self-signed certificate. To set it up, follow the instructions for your particular web server or platform-as-a-service.

23.5.1   Use Secure Cookies

Your site should inform the target browser to never send cookies unless via HTTPS. You'll need to set the following in your settings:

EXAMPLE 23.1

```
SESSION_COOKIE_SECURE = True
CSRF_COOKIE_SECURE = True
```

Read   https://docs.djangoproject.com/en/1.6/topics/security/#ssl-https for more details.

23.5.2   Use HTTP Strict Transport Security (HSTS)

HSTS is usually configured at the web server level. Follow the instructions for your web server or platform-as-a-service.

If you have set up your own web servers, Wikipedia has sample HSTS configuration snippets that you can use: https://en.wikipedia.org/wiki/HTTP_Strict_Transport_Security

When you enable HSTS, your site's web pages include a HTTP header that tells HSTS-compliant browsers to only connect to the site via secure connections:

➤ HSTS-compliant browsers will redirect HTTP links to HTTPS.

➤ If a secure connection isn't possible (e.g. the certificate is self-signed or expired), an error message will be shown and access will be disallowed.

To give you a better idea of how this works, here's an example of what a HTTP Strict Transport Security response header might look like:

EXAMPLE 23.2

```
Strict-Transport-Security: max-age=31536000; includeSubDomains
```

Some HSTS configuration advice:

❶ You should use HSTS' `includeSubDomains` mode if you can. This prevents attacks involving using non-secured subdomains to write cookies for the parent domain.

❷ Set `max-age` to a small value like 3600 (1 hour) during initial deployment of a secured site to make sure you haven't screwed something up or forgotten to make some portion of the site available via HTTPS. We suggest this small value because once you set `max-age`, you can't unset it for users; their browsers control expiration, not you.

❸ Once you've confirmed that your site is properly secured, set `max-age` to a large value like 31536000 (12 months) or 63072000 (24 months) if you can.

> ### WARNING: Choose Your HSTS Policy Duration Carefully
>
> Remember that HSTS is a one-way switch. It's a declaration that for the next N seconds, your site will be HTTPS-only. Don't set a HSTS policy with a `max-age` longer than you are able to maintain. Browsers do not offer an easy way to unset it.

Note that HSTS should be enabled *in addition* to redirecting all pages to HTTPS as described earlier.

23.6 Use Django 1.6's Allowed Hosts Validation

In production you must set `ALLOWED_HOSTS` in your settings to a list of allowed host/domain names in order to avoid raising `SuspiciousOperation` exceptions. This is a security measure to prevent use of fake HTTP host headers to submit requests.

We recommend that you avoid setting wildcard values here. For more information, read the Django documentation on `ALLOWED_HOSTS` and the `get_host()` method:

➤ http://2scoops.co/1.6-allowed-hosts
➤ http://2scoops.co/1.6-get_host

23.7 Always Use CSRF Protection With HTTP Forms That Modify Data

Django comes with cross-site request forgery protection (CSRF) built in, and usage of it is actually introduced in Part 4 of the Django introductory tutorial. It's easy to use, and Django even throws a friendly warning during development when you forget to use it.

In our experience, the only use case for turning off CSRF protection across a site is for creating machine-accessible APIs. API frameworks such as django-tastypie and django-rest-framework do this for you. Since API requests should be signed/authenticated on a per-request basis, these two frameworks don't normally rely on HTTP cookies for authentication. Therefore, CSRF isn't always a problem when using these frameworks.

If you are writing an API from scratch that accepts data changes, it's a good idea to become familiar with Django's CSRF documentation at
`https://docs.djangoproject.com/en/1.6/ref/contrib/csrf/`.

TIP: HTML Search Forms

Since HTML search forms don't change data, they use the HTTP GET method and do not trigger Django's CSRF protection.

You should use Django's `CsrfViewMiddleware` as blanket protection across your site rather than manually decorating views with `csrf_protect`.

23.7.1 Posting Data via AJAX

You should use Django's CSRF protection even when posting data via AJAX. Do not make your AJAX views CSRF-exempt.

Instead, when posting via AJAX, you'll need to set an HTTP header called **X-CSRFToken**.

The official Django documentation includes a snippet that shows how to set this header for only POST requests, in conjunction with jQuery 1.5 or higher's cross-domain checking:
`https://docs.djangoproject.com/en/1.6/ref/contrib/csrf/#ajax`

See our complete example of how to use this snippet in practice in section 15.6, AJAX and the CSRF Token, in chapter 14, *Building REST APIs*.

Recommended reading:

➤ `https://docs.djangoproject.com/en/1.6/ref/contrib/csrf/`

23.8 Prevent Against Cross-Site Scripting (XSS) Attacks

XSS attacks usually occur when users enter malignant JavaScript that is then rendered into a template directly. This isn't the only method, but it is the most common. Fortunately for us, Django by default escapes <, >, ', ", and &, which is all that is needed for proper HTML escaping.

The following are recommended by the Django security team:

23.8.1 Use Django Templates Over mark_safe

Django gives developers the ability to mark content strings as safe, meaning that Django's own safeguards are taken away. Even for small snippets of HTML, try to use the template rendering system, rather than mark_safe.

23.8.2 Don't Allow Users to Set Individual HTML Tag Attributes

If you allow users to set individual attributes of HTML tags, that gives them a venue for injecting malignant JavaScript.

23.8.3 Use JSON Encoding for Data Consumed by JavaScript

Rely on JSON encoding rather than finding ways to dump Python structures directly to templates. It's not just easier to integrate into client-side JavaScript, it's also safer.

23.8.4 Additional Reading

There are other avenues of attack that can occur, so educating yourself is important.

- ➤ http://2scoops.co/1.6-docs-on-html-scraping
- ➤ http://en.wikipedia.org/wiki/Cross-site_scripting

23.9   Defend Against Python Code Injection Attacks

We once were hired to help with a project that had some security issues. The requests coming into the site were being converted from `django.http.HttpRequest` objects directly into strings via creative use of the `str()` function, then saved to a database table. Periodically, these archived Django requests would be taken from the database and converted into Python dicts via the `eval()` function. This meant that arbitrary Python code could be run on the site at any time.

Needless to say, upon discovery the critical security flaw was quickly removed. This just goes to show that no matter how secure Python and Django might be, we always need to be aware that certain practices are incredibly dangerous.

23.9.1   Python Built-ins That Execute Code

Beware of the `eval()`, `exec()`, and `execfile()` built-ins. If your project allows arbitrary strings or files to be passed into any of these functions, you are leaving your system open to attack.

For more information, read "Eval Really Is Dangerous" by Ned Batchelder:
`http://nedbatchelder.com/blog/201206/eval_really_is_dangerous.html`

23.9.2   Python Standard Library Modules That Can Execute Code

> *"Never unpickle data received from an untrusted or unauthenticated source."*

> – `http://docs.python.org/2/library/pickle.html`

You should not use the Python standard library's `pickle` module to deserialize anything which could have been modified by the user. As a general rule, avoid accepting pickled values from user for any reason. For more information, read "Why Python Pickle Is Insecure" by Nadia Alramli: `http://nadiana.com/python-pickle-insecure`.

23.9.3   Third-Party Libraries That Can Execute Code

When using PyYAML, only use `safe_load()`. While the use of **YAML** in the Python and Django communities is rare, it's not uncommon to receive this format from other services. Therefore, if you are accepting YAML documents, only load them with the `yaml.safe_load()` method.

For reference, the `yaml.load()` method will let you create Python objects, *which is really bad*. As Ned Batchelder says, `yaml.load()` should be renamed to `yaml.dangerous_load()`:
`http://nedbatchelder.com/blog/201302/war_is_peace.html`

23.9.4   Be Careful with Cookie-Based Sessions

Typically most Django sites use either database- or cache-based sessions. These function by storing a hashed random value in a cookie which is used as a key to the real session value, which is stored in the database or cache. The advantage of this is that only the key to the session data is sent to the client, making it very challenging for malignant coders to penetrate Django's session mechanism.

However, Django sites can also be built using cookie-based sessions, which place the session data entirely on the client's machine. While this means slightly less storage needs for the server, it comes with security issues that justify caution. Specifically:

❶ It is possible for users to read the contents of cookie-based sessions.
❷ If an attacker gains access to a project's SECRET_KEY and your session serializer is JSON-based, they gain the ability to falsify session data.
❸ If an attacker gains access to a project's SECRET_KEY and your session serializer is pickle-based, they gain the ability to not only falsify session data and also execute arbitrary code. In other words, not only can they assume new rights and privileges, they can also upload working Python code. If you are using pickle-based sessions or are considering using them, please read the tip below.

TIP: Use JSON for Cookie-Based Sessions

As of Django 1.6, the default serializer is JSON-based, meaning that even if an attacker discovers a project's SECRET_KEY, they can't execute arbitrary code. If you are running Django 1.5.3 or higher, please set the SESSION_SERIALIZER setting to 'django.contrib.sessions.serializers.JSONSerializer'.

Resources on the subject:

➤ http://2scoops.co/1.6-http-session-serialization
➤ http://2scoops.co/1.6-settings-session-serializer

Another thing to consider is that cookie-based sessions are a potential client-side performance bottleneck. Transmitting the session data server-to-client is generally not an issue, but client-to-server transmissions are much, much slower. This is literally the difference between download and upload speeds all internet users encounter.

In general, we try to avoid cookie-based sessions.

Additional reading:

➤ http://2scoops.co/1.6-cookie-based-sessions
➤ http://2scoops.co/django-session-based-cookies-alert
➤ http://yuiblog.com/blog/2007/03/01/performance-research-part-3/

23.10 Validate All Incoming Data With Django Forms

Django's forms are a wonderful framework designed to validate Python dictionaries. While most of the time we use them to validate incoming HTTP requests containing POST, there is nothing limiting them to be used just in this manner.

For example, let's say we have a Django app that updates its model via CSV files fetched from another project. To handle this sort of thing, it's not uncommon to see code like this (albeit in not as simplistic an example):

```
BAD EXAMPLE 23.1

import csv
import StringIO

from .models import Purchase

def add_csv_purchases(rows):

    rows = StringIO.StringIO(rows)
    records_added = 0

    # Generate a dict per row, with the first CSV row being the keys
    for row in csv.DictReader(rows, delimiter=","):
        # DON'T DO THIS: Tossing unvalidated data into your model.
        Purchase.objects.create(**row)
        records_added += 1
    return records_added
```

In fact, what you don't see is that we're not checking to see if sellers, stored as a string in the Purchase model, are actually valid sellers. We could add validation code to our add_csv_purchases() function, but let's face it, keeping complex validation code understandable as requirements and data changes over time is hard.

A better approach is to validate the incoming data with a Django Form like so:

```
EXAMPLE 23.3

import csv
import StringIO

from django import forms

from .models import Purchase, Seller

class PurchaseForm(forms.ModelForm):

    class Meta:
```

```
            model = Purchase

    def clean_seller(self):
        seller = self.cleaned_data["seller"]
        try:
            Seller.objects.get(name=seller)
        except Seller.DoesNotExist:
            msg = "{0} does not exist in purchase #{1}.".format(
                seller,
                self.cleaned_data["purchase_number"]
            )
            raise forms.ValidationError(msg)
        return seller


def add_csv_purchases(rows):

    rows = StringIO.StringIO(rows)

    records_added = 0
    errors = []
    # Generate a dict per row, with the first CSV row being the keys.
    for row in csv.DictReader(rows, delimiter=","):

        # Bind the row data to the PurchaseForm.
        form = PurchaseForm(row)
        # Check to see if the row data is valid.
        if form.is_valid():
            # Row data is valid so save the record.
            form.save()
            records_added += 1
        else:
            errors.append(form.errors)

    return records_added, errors
```

What's really nice about this practice is that rather than cooking up our own validation system for incoming data, we're using the well-proven data testing framework built into Django.

23.11   Disable the Autocomplete On Payment Fields

You should disable the HTML field autocomplete browser feature on fields that are gateways to payment. This includes credit card numbers, CVVs, PINs, credit card dates, etc. The reason is that a lot of people use public computers or their personal computers in public venues.

For reference, Django forms make this easy:

```
EXAMPLE 23.4

from django import forms


class SpecialForm(forms.Form):
    my_secret = forms.CharField(
            widget=forms.TextInput(attrs={'autocomplete': 'off'}))
```

23.12   Handle User-Uploaded Files Carefully

The only way to completely safely serve user-provided content is from a completely separate domain. For better or worse, there are an infinite number of ways to bypass file type validators. This is why security experts recommend the use of **content delivery networks** (CDNs): they serve as a place to store potentially dangerous files.

If you must allow upload and download of arbitrary file types, make sure that the server uses the "Content-Disposition: attachment" header so that browsers won't display the content inline.

23.12.1   When a CDN Is Not An Option

When this occurs, uploaded files must be saved to a directory that does not allow them to be executed. In addition, at the very least make sure the HTTP server is configured to serve images with image content type headers, and that uploads are restricted to a whitelisted subset of file extensions.

Take extra care with your web server's configuration here, because a malicious user can try to attack your site by uploading an executable file like a CGI or PHP script and then accessing the URL. This won't solve every problem, but it's better than the defaults.

Consult your web server's documentation for instructions on how to configure this, or consult the documentation for your platform-as-a-service for details about how static assets and user-uploaded files should be stored.

23.12.2   Django and User-Uploaded Files

Django has two model fields that allow for user uploads: `FileField` and `ImageField`. They come with some built-in validation, but the Django docs also strongly advise you to "pay close attention to where you're uploading them and what type of files they are, to avoid security holes."

If you are only accepting uploads of certain file types, do whatever you can do to ensure that the user is only uploading files of those types. For example, you can:

> ➤ Use the **python-magic** library to check the uploaded file's headers:
> `https://github.com/ahupp/python-magic`
> ➤ Validate the file with a Python library that specifically works with that file type. Unfortunately this isn't documented, but if you dig through Django's `ImageField` source code, you can see how Django uses PIL to validate that uploaded image files are in fact images.
> ➤ Use **defusedxml** instead of native Python XML libraries or lxml. See section 23.22.

WARNING: Custom Validators Aren't the Answer Here

Don't just write a custom validator and expect it to validate your uploaded files before dangerous things happen. Custom validators are run against field content after they've already been coerced to Python by the field's `to_python()` method.

If the contents of an uploaded file are malicious, any validation happening after `to_python()` is executed may be too late.

Further reading:

> ➤ `https://docs.djangoproject.com/en/1.6/ref/models/fields/#filefield`

23.13   Don't Use ModelForms.Meta.exclude

When using ModelForms, always use Meta.fields. Never use Meta.exclude. The use of Meta.exclude is considered a grave security risk, specifically a **Mass Assignment Vulnerability**. *We can't stress this strongly enough. Don't do it.*

One common reason we want to avoid the Meta.exclude attribute is that its behavior implicitly allows all model fields to be changed except for those that we specify. When using the excludes attribute, if the model changes after the form is written, we have to remember to change the form. If we forget to change the form to match the model changes, we risk catastrophe.

Let's use an example to show how this mistake could be made. We'll start with a simple ice cream store model:

```python
EXAMPLE 23.5
# stores/models.py
from django.conf import settings
from django.db import models


class Store(models.Model):
    title = models.CharField(max_length=255)
    slug = models.SlugField()
    owner = models.ForeignKey(settings.AUTH_USER_MODEL)
    # Assume 10 more fields that cover address and contact info.
```

Here is the *wrong way* to define the ModelForm fields for this model:

```python
BAD EXAMPLE 23.2
# DON'T DO THIS!
from django import forms

from .models import Store


class StoreForm(forms.ModelForm):

    class Meta:
        model = Store
```

```
# DON'T DO THIS: Implicit definition of fields.
#                Too easy to make mistakes!
excludes = ("pk", "slug", "modified", "created", "owner")
```

In contrast, this is the *right way* to define the same ModelForm's fields:

EXAMPLE 23.6

```
from django import forms

from .models import Store

class StoreForm(forms.ModelForm):

    class Meta:
        model = Store
        # Explicitly specifying the fields we want
        fields = (
            "title", "address_1", "address_2", "email",
            "usstate", "postal_code", "city",
        )
```

The first code example, as it involves less typing, appears to be the better choice. It's not, as when you add a new model field you now you need to track the field in multiple locations (one model and one or more forms).

Let's demonstrate this in action. Perhaps after launch we decide we need to have a way of tracking store co-owners, who have all the same rights as the owner. They can access account information, change passwords, place orders, and specify banking information. The store model receives a new field as shown on the next page:

EXAMPLE 23.7

```
# stores/models.py
from django.conf import settings
from django.db import models
```

```
class Store(models.Model):
    title = models.CharField(max_length=255)
    slug = models.SlugField()
    owner = models.ForeignKey(settings.AUTH_USER_MODEL)
    co_owners = models.ManyToManyField(settings.AUTH_USER_MODEL)
    # Assume 10 more fields that cover address and contact info.
```

The first form code example which we warned against using relies on us to remember to alter it to include the new co_owners field. If we forget, then anyone accessing that store's HTML form can add or remove co-owners. While we might remember a single form, what if we have more than one ModelForm for a model? In complex applications this is not uncommon.

On the other hard, in the second example, where we used Meta.fields we know exactly what fields each form is designed to handle. Changing the model doesn't alter what the form exposes, and we can sleep soundly knowing that our ice cream store data is more secure.

23.13.1 Mass Assignment Vulnerabilities

The problem we describe in this section is a **Mass Assignment Vulnerability**.

These occur when the patterns such as Active Record, designed to empower developers, create security risks for web applications. The solution is the approach we advocate in this section, which is explicit definition of fields that can be modified.

See https://en.wikipedia.org/wiki/Mass_assignment_vulnerability for more detail.

23.14 Don't Use ModelForms.Meta.fields = "__all__"

This includes every model field in your model form. It's a shortcut, and a dangerous one. It's very similar to what we describe in section 23.13, and even with custom validation code, exposes projects to form-based Mass Assignment Vulnerabilities. We advocate avoiding this technique as much as possible, as we feel that it's simply impossible to catch all variations of input.

23.15   Beware of SQL Injection Attacks

The Django ORM generates properly-escaped SQL which will protect your site from users attempting to execute malignant, arbitrary SQL code.

Django allows you to bypass its ORM and access the database more directly through raw SQL. When using this feature, be especially careful to escape your SQL code properly.

23.16   Never Store Credit Card Data

Unless you have a strong understanding of the PCI-DSS security standards (https://www.pcisecuritystandards.org/) and adequate time/resources/funds to validate your PCI compliance, storing credit card data is too much of a liability and should be avoided.

Instead, we recommend using third-party services like Stripe, Balanced Payments, PayPal, and others that handle storing this information for you, and allow you to reference the data via special tokens. Most of these services have great tutorials, are very Python and Django friendly, and are well worth the time and effort to incorporate into your project.

TIP: Educate Yourself on PCI compliance

Ken Cochrane has written an excellent blog post on PCI compliance. Please read http://2scoops.co/guide-to-pci-compliant-web-apps

---

TIP: Read the Source Code of Open Source E-Commerce Solutions

If you are planning to use any of the existing open-source Django e-commerce solutions, examine how the solution handles payments. If credit card data is being stored in the database, even encrypted, then please consider using another solution.

23.17   Secure the Django Admin

Since the Django admin gives your site admins special powers that ordinary users don't have, it's good practice to make it extra secure.

23.17.1   Change the Default Admin URL

By default, the admin URL is *yoursite.com/admin/*. Change it to something that's long and difficult to guess.

TIP: Jacob Kaplan-Moss Talks About Changing the Admin URL

Django project co-leader Jacob Kaplan-Moss says (paraphrased) that it's an easy additional layer of security to come up with a different name (or even different domain) for the admin.

It also prevents attackers from easily profiling your site. For example, attackers can tell which version of Django you're using, sometimes down to the point-release level, by examining the content of *admin/* on a project.

23.17.2   Use django-admin-honeypot

If you're particularly concerned about people trying to break into your Django site, **django-admin-honeypot** is a package that puts a fake Django admin login screen at *admin/* and logs information about anyone who attempts to log in.

See `https://github.com/dmpayton/django-admin-honeypot` for more information.

23.17.3   Only Allow Admin Access via HTTPS

This is already implied in the "Use SSL/HTTPS in Production" section, but we want to especially emphasize here that your admin needs to be SSL-secured. If your site allows straight HTTP access, you will need to run the admin on a properly-secured domain, adding to the complexity of your deployment. Not only will you need a second deployment procedure, but you'll need to include logic in your URLConf in order to remove the admin from HTTP access. In the experience of the authors, it's much easier to put the whole site on SSL/HTTPS.

Without SSL, if you log into your Django admin on an open WiFi network, it's trivial for someone to sniff your admin username/password.

23.17.4   Limit Admin Access Based on IP

Configure your web server to only allow access to the Django admin to certain IP addresses. Look up the instructions for your particular web server.

An acceptable alternative is to put this logic into middleware. It's better to do it at the web server level because every middleware component adds an extra layer of logic wrapping your views, but in some cases this can be your only option. For example, your platform-as-a-service might not give you fine-grain control over web server configuration.

23.17.5   Use the allow_tags Attribute With Caution

The `allow_tags` attribute, which is set to `False` by default, can be a security issue. When `allow_tags` is set to `True`, in conjunction with `django.utils.html.format_html`, HTML tags are allowed to be displayed in the admin.

Our hard rule is `allow_tags` can only be used on system-generated data like primary keys, dates, and calculated values. Data such as character and text fields are completely out, as is any other user-entered data.

23.18   Secure the Admin Docs

Since the Django admin docs give your site admins a view into how the project is constructed, it's good practice to keep them extra-secure just like the Django admin. Borrowing from the previous section on the Django admin, we advocate the following:

➤ Changing the admin docs URL to something besides *yoursite.com/admin/doc/*.

➤ Only allowing admin docs access via HTTPS.

➤ Limiting admin docs access based on IP.

23.19   Monitor Your Sites

Check your web servers' access and error logs regularly. Install monitoring tools and check on them frequently. Keep an eye out for suspicious activity.

23.20   Keep Your Dependencies Up-to-Date

You should always update your projects to work with the latest stable release of Django. This is particularly important when a release includes security fixes. Subscribe to:

➤ The official Django weblog at `https://www.djangoproject.com/weblog/`

➤ The official django-announce mailing list at `http://2scoops.co/django-announce`

It's also good to keep your third-party dependencies up-to-date, and to watch for important security announcements relating to them.

23.21   Prevent Clickjacking

Clickjacking is when a malicious site tricks users to click on a concealed element of another site that they have loaded in a hidden frame or iframe. An example is a site with a false social media 'login' button that is really a purchase button on another site.

Django has instructions and components to prevent this from happening:

➤ `https://docs.djangoproject.com/en/1.6/ref/clickjacking/`

23.22   Guard against XML Bombing With defusedxml

Attacks against XML libraries are nothing new. For example, the amusingly titled but devastating 'Billion Laughs' attack (`http://en.wikipedia.org/wiki/Billion_laughs`) was discovered in 2003.

Unfortunately, Python, like many other programming languages, doesn't account for this or other venues of attack via XML. Furthermore, third-party Python libraries such as *lxml* are vulnerable to at least 4 well-known XML-based attacks. For a list of Python and Python library vulnerabilities see http://2scoops.co/python-xml-vulnerabilities.

Fortunately for us, Christian Heimes created **defusedxml**, a Python library designed to patch Python's core XML libraries and some of the third-party libraries (including lxml).

For more information, please read:

➤ https://pypi.python.org/pypi/defusedxml

23.23 Give Your Site a Security Checkup

Erik Romijn has created Pony Checkup, an automated security checkup tool for Django websites. There are several security practices that can easily be probed from the outside, and this is what his site checks for. It's not a security audit, but it's a great, free way to make certain that your production deployment doesn't have any gaping security holes.

If you have a Django site in production, we recommend that you go and try out:

➤ http://ponycheckup.com

23.24 Put Up a Vulnerability Reporting Page

It's a good idea to publish information on your site about how users can report security vulnerabilities to you.

GitHub's "Responsible Disclosure of Security Vulnerabilities" page is a good example of this and rewards reporters of issues by publishing their names:
http://2scoops.co/responsible-disclosure-of-security-vulnerabilities

23.25 Have a Plan Ready For When Things Go Wrong

Handling security failures is incredibly stressful. There is a sense of urgency and panic that can overwhelm our better judgement, leading to snap decisions that can involve ill-advised 'bugfixes' and public statements that worsen the problem.

Therefore, it's critical that a point-by-point plan be written and made available to maintainers and even non-technical participants of a project. Here is a sample plan:

1. Shut everything down or put it in read-only mode.
2. Put up a static HTML page.
3. Back everything up.
4. Email security@djangoproject.com, even if it's your fault.
5. Start looking into the problem.

Let's go over these steps:

23.25.1 Shut Everything Down or Put It in Read-Only Mode

The first thing to do is remove the ability for the security problem to continue. That way, further damage is hopefully prevented.

On Heroku:

```
EXAMPLE 23.8

$ heroku maintenance:on
Enabling maintenance mode for myapp... done
```

For projects you deploy yourself or with automated tools, you're going to have create this capability yourself. Fortunately, other people have faced this before so we come prepared with reference material:

- http://2scoops.co/nginx-http503-page for putting up maintenance 503 pages.
- **django-db-tools** is is great for flipping a project's database in and out of read-only mode.
- Other tools can be found at http://2scoops.co/emergency-management

23.25.2 Put Up a Static HTML Page

You should have a maintenance page formatted and ready to go when you launch your project. This way, when things go wrong and you've shut everything down, you can display that to the end user. If done well, the users might understand and give you the breathing room to work out the problem.

23.25.3 Back Everything Up

Get a copy of the code and then the data off the servers and keep it on a local hard drive or SSD. You might also consider a bonded, professional storage company.

Why? First, when you back things up at this stage, you are protecting your audit trail. This might provide you with the capability to determine where and when things went wrong.

Second, and this might be unpleasant to hear, but malignant staff can as many problems as any bug or penetration staff. What that means is that the best software-based security is useless against a developer who creates a backdoor or a non-technical staff level user who decides to cause trouble.

23.25.4 Email security@djangoproject.com, Even if It's Your Fault

Actually, don't worry about whose fault it is, just send a quick email summarizing the problem. Ask for help while you are at it.

There are a number of reasons why this is important:

> ➤ Writing up a quick summary will help you focus and gather your thoughts. You're going to be under an amazing amount of stress. The stress and urgency of the situation can make you attempt stupid things that can aggravate the problem.
> ➤ You never know, the Django security team might have good advice or even an answer for you.
> ➤ It might be a Django problem! If that is the case, the Django security team needs to know so they can mitigate the problem for everyone else before it becomes public.

TIP: Jacob Kaplan-Moss on Reporting to the Django Project

Django co-leader and Director of Security for Heroku Jacob Kaplan-Moss says, "I'd much rather have people send things that aren't actual problems in Django to security@djangoproject.com than accidentally disclose security issues publicly because they don't know better."

23.25.5   Start Looking Into the Problem

You've shut things down, backed everything up, are displaying a static HTML page, emailed security@djangoproject.com, and are looking at the problem. By following the above steps, you've given yourself (and possibly your team) time to breathe and figure out what really happened.

This will be a stressful time and people will be on the edge of panic. Start doing research, perhaps in this book, ask questions as per chapter 31, *Where and How to Ask Django Questions*, and find a resolution.

Before you implement a correction, it's often better to make sure you have a real, proper fix for the problem then do a rushed emergency patch that destroys everything. Yes, this is where tests and continuous integration shine.

Stay positive: now is the time for everyone to come together and fix the problem. Start taking notes, ask for help from the best people you know, remind yourself (or the team) that you have the will and the smarts to fix things, and make things right!

> ### WARNING: The Nightmare of the Zero-Day Attack
>
> A **Zero-Day Attack** is when there is an attack or communicated threat of an attack that occurs on the first day (or hour) of a project launch or upgrade. This means that there is no time to address and patch the vulnerability, making the compromise especially difficult to manage. If there was ever a reason to have a battle plan for handling security issues, this is it.
>
> See https://en.wikipedia.org/wiki/0day

23.26   Keep Up-to-Date on General Security Practices

We end this chapter with some common-sense advice.

First, keep in mind that security practices are constantly evolving, both in the Django community and beyond. Subscribe to http://2scoops.co/django-announce and check Twitter, Hacker News, and various security blogs regularly.

Second, remember that security best practices extend well beyond those practices specific to Django. You should research the security issues of every part of your web application stack, and you should follow the corresponding sources to stay up to date.

TIP: Good Books and Articles on Security

Paul McMillan, Django core developer, security expert, and Two Scoops reviewer, recommends the following books:

- ➤ *"The Tangled Web: A Guide to Securing Modern Web Applications"*:
  `http://amzn.to/1hXAAyx`
- ➤ *"The Web Application Hacker's Handbook"*:
  `http://amzn.to/1dZ7xEY`

In addition, we recommend the following reference sites:

- ➤ `https://code.google.com/p/browsersec/wiki/Main`
- ➤ `https://wiki.mozilla.org/WebAppSec/Secure_Coding_Guidelines`

23.27 Summary

Please use this chapter as a starting point for Django security, not the ultimate reference guide. See the Django documentation's list for additional security topics:

`http://2scoops.co/1.6-additional-security-topics`

Django comes with a good security record due to the diligence of its community and attention to detail. Security is one of those areas where it's a particularly good idea to ask for help. If you find yourself confused about anything, ask questions and turn to others in the Django community for help.

24 | Logging: What's It For, Anyway?

Logging is like rocky road ice cream. Either you can't live without it, or you forget about it and wonder once in awhile why it exists.

Anyone who's ever worked on a large production project with intense demands understands the importance of using the different log levels appropriately, creating module-specific loggers, meticulously logging information about important events, and including extra detail about the application's state when those events are logged.

While logging might not seem glamorous, remember that it is one of the secrets to building extremely stable, robust web applications that scale and handle unusual loads gracefully. Logging can be used not only to debug application errors, but also to track interesting performance metrics.

Logging unusual activity and checking logs regularly is also important for ensuring the security of your server. In the previous chapter, we covered the importance of checking your server access and error logs regularly. Keep in mind that application logs can be used in similar ways, whether to track failed login attempts or unusual application-level activity.

24.1 Application Logs vs. Other Logs

This chapter focuses on application logs. Any log file containing data logged from your Python web application is considered an application log.

In addition to your application logs, you should be aware that there are other types of logs, and that using and checking all of your server logs is necessary. Your server logs, database logs, network logs, etc. all provide vital insight into your production system, so consider them all equally important.

24.2   Why Bother With Logging?

Logging is your go-to tool in situations where a stack trace and existing debugging tools aren't enough. Whenever you have different moving parts interacting with each other or the possibility of unpredictable situations, logging gives you insight into what's going on.

The different log levels available to you are DEBUG, INFO, WARNING, ERROR, and CRITICAL. Let's now explore when it's appropriate to use each logging level.

24.3   When to Use Each Log Level

In places other than your production environment, you might as well use all the log levels. Log levels are controlled in your project's settings modules, so we can fine tune this recommendation as needed to account for load testing and large scale user tests.

In your production environment, we recommend using every log level except for DEBUG.

Figure 24.1: Appropriate usage of CRITICAL/ERROR/WARNING/INFO logging in ice cream.

Since the same CRITICAL, ERROR, WARNING, and INFO logs are captured whether in production or development, introspection of buggy code requires less modification of code. This is important to remember, as debug code added by developers working to fix one problem can create new ones.

The rest of this section covers how each log level is used.

24.3.1   Log Catastrophes With CRITICAL

Use the CRITICAL log level only when something catastrophic occurs that requires urgent attention.

For example, if your code relies on an internal web service being available, and if that web service is part of your site's core functionality, then you might log at the CRITICAL level anytime that the web service is inaccessible.

This log level is never used in core Django code, but you should certainly use it in your code anywhere that an extremely serious problem can occur.

24.3.2   Log Production Errors With ERROR

Let's look at core Django for an example of when ERROR level logging is appropriate. In core Django, the ERROR log level is used very sparingly. There is one very important place where it is used: whenever code raises an exception that is not caught, the event gets logged by Django using the following code:

```
EXAMPLE 24.1
# Taken directly from core Django code.
# Used here to illustrate an example only, so don't
# copy this into your project.
logger.error("Internal Server Error: %s", request.path,
    exc_info=exc_info,
    extra={
        "status_code": 500,
        "request": request
    }
)
```

How does Django put this to good use? Well, when DEBUG=False is in your settings, everyone listed in ADMINS immediately gets emailed the following:

➤ A description of the error

> ➤ A complete Python traceback from where the error occurred
> ➤ Information about the HTTP request that caused the error

If you've ever received one of those email notifications, you know how useful ERROR logs are when you need them most.

Similarly, we recommend that you use the ERROR log level whenever you need to log an error that is worthy of being emailed to you or your site admins. When your code catches the exception, log as much information as you can to be able to resolve the problem.

For example, an exception may be thrown when one of your views cannot access a needed third-party API. When the exception is caught, you can log a helpful message and the API's failure response, if any.

24.3.3 Log Lower-Priority Problems With WARNING

This level is good for logging events that are unusual and potentially bad, but not as bad as ERROR-level events.

For example, if you are using **django-admin-honeypot** to set up a fake *admin/* login form, you might want to log intruders' login attempts to this level.

Django uses the log level in several parts of CsrfViewMiddleware, to log events that result in a **403 Forbidden** error. For example, when an incoming POST request is missing its csrf_token, the event gets logged as follows:

EXAMPLE 24.2

```
# Taken directly from core Django code.
# Used here to illustrate an example only, so don't
# copy this into your project.
logger.warning("Forbidden (%s): %s",
               REASON_NO_CSRF_COOKIE, request.path,
    extra={
        "status_code": 403,
        "request": request,
    }
)
```

24.3.4   Log Useful State Information With INFO

We recommend using this level to log any details that may be particularly important when analysis is needed. These include:

> ➤ Startup and shutdown of important components not logged elsewhere
> ➤ State changes that occur in response to important events
> ➤ Changes to permissions, e.g. when users are granted admin access

In addition to this, the INFO level is great for logging any general information that may help in performance analysis. It's a good level to use while hunting down problematic bottlenecks in your application and doing profiling.

24.3.5   Log Debug-Related Messages to DEBUG

In development, we recommend using DEBUG and occasionally INFO level logging wherever you'd consider throwing a print statement into your code for debugging purposes.

Getting used to logging this way isn't hard. Instead of this:

```
BAD EXAMPLE 24.1
from django.views.generic import TemplateView

from .helpers import pint_counter

class PintView(TemplateView):

    def get_context_data(self, *args, **kwargs):
        context = super(PintView, self).get_context_data(**kwargs)
        pints_remaining = pint_counter()
        print("Only %d pints of ice cream left." % (pints_remaining))
        return context
```

We do this:

```
EXAMPLE 24.3
import logging

from django.views.generic import TemplateView

from .helpers import pint_counter

logger = logging.getLogger(__name__)

class PintView(TemplateView):

    def get_context_data(self, *args, **kwargs):
        context = super(PintView, self).get_context_data(**kwargs)
        pints_remaining = pint_counter()
        logger.debug("Only %d pints of ice cream left." % pints_remaining)
        return context
```

Sprinkling `print` statements across your projects results in problems and technical debt:

➤ Depending on the web server, a forgotten print statement can bring your site down.

➤ *Print statements are not recorded.* If you don't see them, then you miss what they were trying to say.

➤ As the Django world migrates more and more to Python 3, old-style print statements like `print IceCream.objects.flavor()` will break your code.

Unlike `print` statements, logging allows different report levels and different response methods. This means that:

➤ We can write `DEBUG` level statements, leave them in our code, and never have to worry about them doing anything when we move code to production.

➤ The response method can provide the response as email, log files, console and `stdout`. It can even report as pushed HTTP requests to applications such as *Sentry*!

Note that there's no need to go overboard with debug-level logging. It's great to add `logging.debug()` statements while you're debugging, but there's no need to clutter your code with logging every single line.

Figure 24.2: Appropriate usage of DEBUG logging in ice cream.

24.4 Log Tracebacks When Catching Exceptions

Whenever you log an exception, it's usually helpful to log the stack trace of the exception. Python's logging module supports this:

- ❶ `Logger.exception()` automatically includes the traceback and logs at ERROR level.
- ❷ For other log levels, use the optional `exc_info` keyword argument.

Here's an example of adding a traceback to a WARNING level log message:

```
EXAMPLE 24.4

import logging
import requests


logger = logging.getLogger(__name__)


def get_additional_data():
    try:
        r = requests.get("http://example.com/something-optional/")
    except requests.HTTPError as e:
```

```
        logger.exception(e)
        logger.debug("Could not get additional data", exc_info=True)
        return None
    return r
```

24.5   One Logger Per Module That Uses Logging

Whenever you use logging in another module, don't import and reuse a logger from elsewhere. Instead, define a new logger specific to the module like this:

EXAMPLE 24.5

```
# You can place this snippet at the top
# of models.py, views.py, or any other
# file where you need to log.
import logging

logger = logging.getLogger(__name__)
```

What this gives you is the ability to turn on and off only the specific loggers that you currently need. If you're running into a strange issue in production that you can't replicate locally, you can temporarily turn on DEBUG logging for just the module related to the issue. Then, when you identify the problem, you can turn that logger back off in production.

24.6   Log Locally to Rotating Files

When you create a new Django project with startproject, your default settings file is configured to email ERROR and higher log messages to whomever you list in ADMINS. This occurs via a handler called AdminEmailHandler that comes with Django.

In addition to this, we recommend also writing logs of level INFO and higher to rotating log files on disk. On-disk log files are helpful in case the network goes down or emails can't be sent to your admins for some reason. Log rotation keeps your logs from growing to fill your available disk space.

A common way to set up log rotation is to use the UNIX **logrotate** utility with `logging.handlers.WatchedFileHandler`.

Note that if you are using a platform-as-a-service, you might not be able to set up rotating log files. In this case, you may need to use an external logging service such as Loggly: `http://loggly.com/`.

24.7 Other Logging Tips

> ➤ Control the logging in settings files per the Django documentation on logging: `https://docs.djangoproject.com/en/1.6/topics/logging/`
> ➤ While debugging, use the Python logger at `DEBUG` level.
> ➤ After running tests at `DEBUG` level, try running them at `INFO` and `WARNING` levels. The reduction in information you see may help you identify upcoming deprecations for third-party libraries.
> ➤ Don't wait until it's too late to add logging. You'll be grateful for your logs if and when your site fails.
> ➤ You can do useful things with the emails you receive when `ERROR` or higher level events occur. For example, you can configure a PagerDuty (`http://www.pagerduty.com/`) account to alert you and your team repeatedly until you've taken action.

PACKAGE TIP: Logutils Provides Useful Handlers

The **logutils** package by Vinay Sajip comes with a number of very interesting logging handlers. Features include:
> ➤ Colorizing of console streams under Windows, Linux and Mac OS X.
> ➤ The ability to log to queues. Useful in situations where you want to queue up log messages to a slow handler like `SMTPHandler`.
> ➤ Classes that allow you to write unit tests for log messages.
> ➤ An enhanced `HTTPHandler` that supports secure connections over HTTPS.

Some of the more basic features of logutils are so useful that they have been absorbed into the Python standard library!

24.8   Necessary Reading Material

- https://docs.djangoproject.com/en/1.6/topics/logging/
- http://docs.python.org/2/library/logging.html
- http://docs.python.org/2/library/logging.config.html
- http://docs.python.org/2/library/logging.handlers.html
- http://docs.python.org/2/howto/logging-cookbook.html

24.9   Useful Third-Party Tools

- Sentry (https://www.getsentry.com/) aggregates errors for you.
- App Enlight (https://appenlight.com/) tracks errors and performance issues in your app.
- loggly.com (http://loggly.com/) simplifies log management and provides excellent query tools.

24.10   Summary

Django projects can easily take advantage of the rich logging functionality that comes with Python. Combine logging with handlers and analysis tools, and suddenly you have real power. You can use logging to help you improve the stability and performance of your projects.

In the next chapter we'll discuss signals, which become much easier to follow, debug, and understand with the help of logging.

25 | Signals: Use Cases and Avoidance Techniques

The Short Answer: Use signals as a last resort.

The Long Answer: Often when new Djangonauts first discover signals, they get signal-happy. They start sprinkling signals everywhere they can and feeling like real experts at Django.

After coding this way for a while, projects start to turn into confusing, knotted hairballs that can't be untangled. Signals are being dispatched everywhere and hopefully getting received somewhere, but at that point it's hard to tell what exactly is going on.

Many developers also confuse signals with asynchronous message queues such as what Celery (`http://www.celeryproject.org/`) provides. Make no mistake, *signals are synchronous and blocking*, and calling performance-heavy processes via signals provides absolutely no benefit from a performance or scaling perspective. In fact, moving such processes unnecessarily to signals is considered code obfuscation.

Signals can be useful, but they should be used as a last resort, only when there's no good way to avoid using them.

25.1 When to Use and Avoid Signals

Do not use signals when:

> ➤ The signal relates to one particular model and can be moved into one of that model's methods, possibly called by `save()`.

➤ The signal can be replaced with a custom model manager method.

➤ The signal relates to a particular view and can be moved into that view.

It might be okay to use signals when:

➤ Your signal receiver needs to make changes to more than one model.

➤ You want to dispatch the same signal from multiple apps and have them handled the same way by a common receiver.

➤ You want to invalidate a cache after a model save.

➤ You have an unusual scenario that needs a callback, and there's no other way to handle it besides using a signal. For example, you want to trigger something based on the save() or init() of a third-party app's model. You can't modify the third-party code and extending it might be impossible, so a signal provides a trigger for a callback.

> ### TIP: Aymeric Augustin Thoughts on Signals
>
> Django core developer Aymeric Augustin says: "I advise not to use signals as soon as a regular function call will do. Signals obfuscate control flow through inversion of control. They make it difficult to discover what code will actually run. Besides, Django doesn't provide a canonical location to register signals at application start-up; this is a long standing problem and the core team hopes to resolve this as part of the "app-loading" project.
>
> Use a signal only if the piece of code sending it has positively no way to determine what its receivers will be."

25.2   Signal Avoidance Techniques

Let's go over some scenarios where you can simplify your code and remove some of the signals that you don't need.

25.2.1   Using Custom Model Manager Methods Instead of Signals

Let's imagine that our site handles user-submitted ice cream-themed events, and each ice cream event goes through an approval process. These events are set with a status of "Unreviewed" upon creation. The problem is that we want our site administrators to get an email for each event submission so they know to review and post things quickly.

We could have done this with a signal, but unless we put in extra logic in the post_save() code, even administrator created events would generate emails.

An easier way to handle this use case is to create a custom model manager method and use that in your views. This way, if an event is created by an administrator, they don't have to go through the review process.

Since a code example is worth a thousand words, here is how we would create such a method:

EXAMPLE 25.1

```
# events/managers.py
from django.db import models


class EventManager(models.Manager):

    def create_event(self, title, start, end, creator):
        event = self.model(title=title,
                           start=start,
                           end=end,
                           creator=creator)
        event.save()
        event.notify_admins()
        return event
```

Now that we have our custom manager with its custom manager method in place, let's attach it to our model (which comes with a notify_admins() method:

EXAMPLE 25.2

```
# events/models.py
from django.conf import settings
from django.core.mail import mail_admins
from django.db import models


from model_utils.models import TimeStampedModel
```

```python
from .managers import EventManager

class Event(TimeStampedModel):

    STATUS_UNREVIEWED, STATUS_REVIEWED = (0, 1)
    STATUS_CHOICES = (
        (STATUS_UNREVIEWED, "Unreviewed"),
        (STATUS_REVIEWED, "Reviewed"),
    )

    title = models.CharField(max_length=100)
    start = models.DateTimeField()
    end = models.DateTimeField()
    status = models.IntegerField(choices=STATUS_CHOICES,
                                 default=STATUS_UNREVIEWED)
    creator = models.ForeignKey(settings.AUTH_USER_MODEL)

    objects = EventManager()

    def notify_admins(self):
        # create the subject and message
        subject = "{user} submitted a new event!".format(
                    user=self.creator.get_full_name())
        message = """TITLE: {title}
START: {start}
END: {end}""".format(title=self.title, start=self.start,
                     end=self.end)

        # Send to the admins!
        mail_admins(subject=subject,
            message=message,
            fail_silently=False)
```

Using this follows a similar pattern to using the User model. To generate an event, instead of calling create(), we call a create_event() method.

```
EXAMPLE 25.3
>>> from django.contrib.auth import get_user_model
>>> from django.utils import timezone
>>> from events.models import Event
>>> user = get_user_model().get(username="audreyr")
>>> now = timezone.now()
>>> event = Event.objects.create_event(
...     title="International Ice Cream Tasting Competition",
...     start=now,
...     end=now,
...     user=user
...     )
```

25.2.2   Validate Your Model Elsewhere

If you're using a pre_save signal to trigger input cleanup for a specific model, try writing a custom validator for your field(s) instead.

If validating through a ModelForm, try overriding your model's clean() method instead.

25.2.3   Override Your Model's Save or Delete Method Instead

If you're using pre_save and post_save signals to trigger logic that only applies to one particular model, you might not need those signals. You can often simply move the signal logic into your model's save() method.

The same applies to overriding delete() instead of using pre_delete and post_delete signals.

25.2.4   Use a Helper Function Instead of Signals

We find this approach useful under two conditions:

❶ *Refactoring*: Once we realize that certain bits of code no longer need to be obfuscated as signals and want to refactor, the question of 'Where do we put the code that was in a signal?' arises. If it doesn't belong in a model manager, custom validator, or overloaded model method, where does it belong?

❷ *Architecture*: Sometimes developers use signals because we feel the model has become too heavyweight and we need a place for code. While Fat Models are a nice approach, we admit it's not much fun to have to parse through a 500 or 2000 line chunk of code.

This solution, suggested to us by Django core developer Aymeric Augustin, is to place the code in helper functions. If done right, this helps us write cleaner, more reusable code.

One interesting thing about this approach is to test the transition out of signals. Simply follow these steps:

❶ Write a test for the existing signal call.

❷ Write a test for the business logic of the existing signal call as if it were in a separate function.

❸ Write a helper function that duplicates the business logic of the signal, matching the assertions of the test your wrote in the second step.

❹ Run the tests.

❺ Call the helper function from the signal.

❻ Run the tests again.

❼ Remove the signal and call the helper function from the appropriate location.

❽ Run the tests again.

❾ Rinse and repeat until done.

This approach allows us to carefully remove the signal without breaking things. It also helps us identify when an existing signal is required for a specific process.

25.3 Summary

Signals are a powerful tool in any Django developer's toolbox. However, they are easy to misuse and it's good practice to delve into why and when to use them.

26 | What About Those Random Utilities?

26.1 Create a Core App for Your Utilities

Sometimes we end up writing shared classes or little general-purpose utilities that are useful everywhere. These bits and pieces don't belong in any particular app. We don't just stick them into a sort-of-related random app, because we have a hard time finding them when we need them. We also don't like placing them as "random" modules in the root of the project.

Our way of handling our utilities is to place them into a Django app called *core* that contains modules which contains functions and objects for use across a project. (Other developers follow a similar pattern and call this sort of app *common*, *generic*, *util*, or *utils*.)

For example, perhaps our project has both a custom model manager and a custom view mixin used by several different apps. Our *core* app would therefore look like:

```
EXAMPLE 26.1

core/
    __init__.py
    managers.py  # contains the custom model manager(s)
    models.py
    views.py  # Contains the custom view mixin(s)
```

> ## TIP: Django App Boilerplate: The models.py Module
>
> Don't forget that in order to make a Python module be considered a Django app, a `models.py` module is required! However, we only make the core module a Django app if we need to do one or more of the following:
>
> ➤ Have non-abstract models in *core*.
>
> ➤ Have admin auto-discovery working in *core*.
>
> ➤ Have template tags and filters.

Now, if we want to import our custom model manager and/or view mixin , we import using the same pattern of imports we use for everything else:

EXAMPLE 26.2

```
from core.managers import PublishedManager
from core.views import IceCreamMixin
```

26.2   Django's Own Swiss Army Knife

The Swiss army knife is a multi-purpose tool that is compact and useful. Django has a number of useful helper functions that don't have a better home than the `django.utils` package. It's tempting to dig into the code in `django.utils` and start using things, but don't. Most of those modules are designed for internal use and their behavior or inclusion can change between Django version.

Instead, read `https://docs.djangoproject.com/en/1.6/ref/utils/` to see which modules in there are stable.

> ## TIP: Malcolm Tredinnick On Django's Utils Package.
>
> Django core developer Malcolm Tredinnick liked to think of `django.utils` as being in the same theme as Batman's utility belt: indispensable tools that are used everywhere internally.

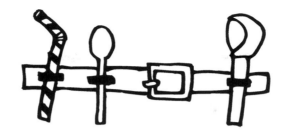

Figure 26.1: A utility belt for serious ice cream eaters.

There are some gems in there that have turned into best practices:

26.2.1 django.contrib.humanize

This is a set of localized template filters designed to give user presented data a more 'human' touch. For example it includes a filter called 'intcomma' that converts integers to strings containing commas (or periods depending on locale) every three digits.

While django.contrib.humanize's filters are useful for making template output more attractive, we can also import each filter individually as a function. This is quite handy when processing any sort of text, especially when used in conjunction with REST APIs.

26.2.2 django.utils.encoding.force_text(value)

This forces Django to take anything and turn it into a plain str representation on Python 3 and unicode on Python 2. It avoids the display of a django.utils.functional.__proxy__ object. For more details, see Appendix D.

26.2.3 django.utils.functional.cached_property

Reinout van Rees educated us about this incredibly useful method decorator introduced in Django 1.5. What it does is cache in memory the result of a method with a single self argument as a property. This has wonderful implications in regards to performance optimization of a project. We use it in every project, enjoying how it allows us to cache the results of expensive computations trivially.

For a description on how to use the cached_property decorator, the official Django documentation on the subject is excellent: http://2scoops.co/1.6-cached_property

In addition to the potential performance benefits, we've used this decorator to make sure that values fetched by methods remain static over the lifetime of their object. This has proven very useful when dealing with third-party APIs or dealing with database transactions.

26.2.4 django.utils.html.format_html(format_str, *args, **kwargs)

This is similar to Python's str.format() method, except designed for building up HTML fragments. All args and kwargs are escaped before being passed to str.format() which then combines the elements.

See http://2scoops.co/1.6-format_html for details on use.

26.2.5 django.utils.html.remove_tags(value, tags)

When we need to accept content from users and want to strip out a list of tags, this function removes those tags for we while keeping all other content untouched.

26.2.6 django.utils.html.strip_tags(value)

When we need to accept content from users and have to strip out anything that could be HTML, this function removes those tags for we while keeping all the existing text between tags.

26.2.7 django.utils.six

Six is a Python 2 and 3 compatibility library by Benjamin Peterson. It's bundled directly into Django (hence it's placement in Django's utils library), but we can also find it as an independent package for other projects.

- ➤ Six on PyPI: https://pypi.python.org/pypi/six
- ➤ Six documentation: http://pythonhosted.org/six/
- ➤ Six repo on BitBucket: https://bitbucket.org/gutworth/six
- ➤ Six in Django: https://github.com/django/django/blob/master/django/utils/six.py

> **WARNING: Having Problems With Using django.utils.six With Django 1.5?**
>
> Upgrade to at least Django 1.5.5 and these problems should go away. This release updated Django's packaged version of six to match the latest PyPI release.

26.2.8   django.utils.text.slugify(value)

We recommend that whatever you do, don't write your own version of the slugify() function, as any inconsistency from what Django does with this function will cause subtle yet nasty problems in our data. Instead, we use the same function that Django uses and slugify() consistently.

It is possible to use django.templates.defaultfilters.slugify() in our Python code, as this calls the function described here. Nevertheless, we like to use the function directly from Django's utils directory, as it is a more appropriate import path.

However we decide to import this function, we try to keep it consistent across a project as there is a use case for when it has to be replaced, as described in the package tip on the next page.

PACKAGE TIP: slugify and languages besides English

Tomasz Paczkowski points out that we should note that slugify() can cause problems
with localization:

> EXAMPLE 26.3
>
> ```
> >>> from django.utils.text import slugify
> >>> slugify(u"straße") # German
> u"strae"
> ```

Fortunately, **unicode-slugify**, is a Mozilla foundation-supported project that addresses
the issue:

> EXAMPLE 26.4
>
> ```
> >>> from slugify import slugify
> >>> slugify(u"straße") # Again with German
> u"straße"
> ```

26.2.9 django.utils.timezone

It's good practice for us to have time zone support enabled. Chances are that our users live in
more than one time zone.

When we use Django's time zone support, date and time information is stored in the database
uniformly in UTC format and converted to local time zones as needed.

26.2.10 django.utils.translation

Much of the non-English speaking world appreciates use of this tool, as it provides Django's
i18n support. See Appendix D for a more in-depth reference.

26.3   Exceptions

Django comes with a lot of exceptions. Most of them are used internally, but a few of them stand out because the way they interact with Django can be leveraged in fun and creative ways. These, and other built-in Django exceptions, are documented at https://docs.djangoproject.com/en/dev/ref/exceptions.

26.3.1   django.core.exceptions.ImproperlyConfigured

The purpose of this module is to inform anyone attempting to run Django that there is a configuration issue. It serves as the single Django code component considered acceptable to import into Django settings modules. We discuss it in both chapter 5 and Appendix E.

26.3.2   django.core.exceptions.ObjectDoesNotExist

This is the base Exception from which all DoesNotExist exceptions inherit from. We've found this is a really nice tool for working with utility functions that fetch generic model instances and do something with them. Here is a simple example:

```
EXAMPLE 26.5
# core/utils.py
from django.core.exceptions import ObjectDoesNotExist

class BorkedObject(object):
    loaded = False


def generic_load_tool(model, pk):
    try:
        instance = model.objects.get(pk=pk)
    except ObjectDoesNotExist:
        return BorkedObject()
    instance.loaded = True
    return instance
```

Also using this exception, we can create our own variant of Django's `django.shortcuts.get_object_or_404` function, perhaps raising a HTTP 403 exception instead of a 404:

EXAMPLE 26.6

```python
# core/utils.py
from django.core.exceptions import MultipleObjectsReturned
from django.core.exceptions import ObjectDoesNotExist
from django.core.exceptions import PermissionDenied


def get_object_or_403(model, **kwargs):
    try:
        return model.objects.get(**kwargs)
    except ObjectDoesNotExist:
        raise PermissionDenied
    except MultipleObjectsReturned:
        raise PermissionDenied
```

26.3.3 django.core.exceptions.PermissionDenied

This exception is used when users, authenticated or not, attempt to get responses from places they are not meant to be. Raising it in a view will trigger the view to return a `django.http.HttpResponseForbidden`.

This exception can prove useful to use in functions that are touching the sensitive data and components of a high-security project. It means that if something bad happens, instead of just returning a 500 exception, which may rightly alarm users, we simply provide a "Permission Denied" screen.

EXAMPLE 26.7

```python
# stores/calc.py


def finance_data_adjudication(store, sales, issues):

    if store.something_not_right:
```

```
        msg = "Something is not right. Please contact the support team."
        raise PermissionDenied(msg)

    # Continue on to perform other logic.
```

In this case, if this function were called by a view and something was 'not right,' then the Per-missionDenied exception would force the view to display the project's 403 error page. Speak-ing of 403 error pages, we can set this to any view we want. In the root URLConf of a project, just add:

```
EXAMPLE 26.8
# urls.py

handler403 = 'core.views.permission_denied_view'
```

As always, with exception-handling views, because they handle all HTTP methods equally, we prefer to use function-based views.

26.4   Serializers and Deserializers

Whether it's for creating data files or generating one-off simple REST APIs, Django has some great tools for working with serialization and deserialization of data of JSON, Python, YAML and XML data. They include the capability to turn model instances into serialized data and then return it back to model instances.

Here is how we serialize data:

```
EXAMPLE 26.9
# serializer_example.py
from django.core.serializers import get_serializer

from favorites.models import Favorite

# Get and instantiate the serializer class
```

```
# The 'json' can be replaced with 'python' or 'xml'.
# If you have pyyaml installed, you can replace it with
#   'pyyaml'
JSONSerializer = get_serializer("json")
serializer = JSONSerializer()


favs = Favorite.objects.filter()[:5]


# Serialize model data
serialized_data = serializer.serialize(favs)


# save the serialized data for use in the next example
with open("data.json", "w") as f:
    f.write(serialized_data)
```

Here is how we deserialize data:

EXAMPLE 26.10

```
# deserializer_example.py
from django.core.serializers import get_serializer

from favorites.models import Favorite

favs = Favorite.objects.filter()[:5]

# Get and instantiate the serializer class
# The 'json' can be replaced with 'python' or 'xml'.
# If you have pyyaml installed, you can replace it with
#   'pyyaml'
JSONSerializer = get_serializer("json")
serializer = JSONSerializer()

# open the serialized data file
with open("data.txt") as f:
    serialized_data = f.read()
```

```python
# deserialize model data into a generator object
#   we'll call 'python data'
python_data = serializer.deserialize(serialized_data)


# iterate through the python_data
for element in python_data:
    # Prints 'django.core.serializers.base.DeserializedObject'
    print(type(element))

    # Elements have an 'object' that are literally instantiated
    #   model instances (in this case, favorites.models.Favorite)
    print(
        element.object.pk,
        element.object.created
    )
```

Django already provides a command-line tool for using these serializers and deserializers: the dumpdata and loaddata management commands. While we can use them, they don't grant us the same amount of control that direct code access to the serializers provides.

This brings us to something that we always need to keep in mind when using Django's built-in serializers and deserializers: they can cause problems. From painful experience, we know that they don't handle complex data structures well.

Consider these guidelines that we follow in our projects:

- ➤ Serialize data at the simplest level.
- ➤ Any database schema change may invalidate the serialized data.
- ➤ Don't just import serialized data. Consider using Django's form libraries to validate incoming data before saving to the database.

Let's go over some of the features provided by Django when working with specific formats:

26.4.1   django.core.serializers.json.DjangoJSONEncoder

Out of the box, Python's built-in JSON module can't handle encoding of date/time or decimal types. Anyone who has done Django for a while has run into this problem. Fortunately for all of us, Django provides a very useful JSONEncoder class. See the code example below:

```
EXAMPLE 26.11

# json_encoding_example.py
import json

from django.core.serializers.json import DjangoJSONEncoder
from django.utils import timezone

data = {"date": timezone.now()}

# If you don't add the DjangoJSONEncoder class then
# the json library will throw a TypeError.
json_data = json.dumps(data, cls=DjangoJSONEncoder)

print(json_data)
```

26.4.2   django.core.serializers.pyyaml

While powered by the third-party library, pyyaml, Django's YAML serializer tools handles the time conversion from Python-to-YAML that pyyaml doesn't.

For deserialization, it also uses the yaml.safe_load() function under the hood, which means that we don't have to worry about code injection. See subsection 23.9.3 *Third-Party Libraries That Can Execute Code* for more details.

26.4.3   django.core.serializers.xml_serializer

By default Django's XML serializer uses Python's built-in XML handlers. It also incorporates elements of Christian Heimes' **defusedxml** library, protecting usage of it from XML bomb attacks. For more information, please read section 23.22, 'Guard against XML bombing with defusedxml.'

26.5 Summary

We follow the practice of putting often reused files into utility packages. We enjoy being able to remember where we placed our often reused code. Projects that contain a mix of core, common, util, and utils directories are just that much harder to navigate.

Django's own 'utility belt' includes a plethora of useful tools, including useful functions, exceptions, and serializers. Leveraging them is on of the ways experienced Django developers accelerate development and avoid some of the tangles that can be caused by some of the very features of Django.

Now that we've covered tools to make things work, in the next chapter we'll cover what to do when a production site has problems.

27 | Deployment: Platforms as a Service

If you're working on a small side project or are a founder of a small startup, you'll definitely save time by using a **Platform as a Service (PaaS)** instead of setting up your own servers. Even large projects can benefit from the advantages of using them.

First, a public service message:

TIP: Never Get Locked Into a Platform as a Service

There are amazing services which will host your code, databases, media assets, and also provide a lot of wonderful accessories services. These services, however, can go through changes that can destroy your project. These changes include crippling price increases, performance degradation, unacceptable terms of service changes, untenable service license agreements, sudden decreases in availability, or can simply go out of business.

This means that it's in your best interest to do your best to avoid being forced into architectural decisions based on the needs of your hosting provider. Be ready to be able to move from one provider to another without major restructuring of your project.

We try to make sure that our projects are not intrinsically tied to any hosting solution, meaning that we are not locked into a single vendor's pricing, policies, and functionality.

As a WSGI-compliant framework, Django is supported on many PaaS providers. The most commonly-used Django-friendly PaaS companies as of this writing are:

➤ Heroku (http://heroku.com) is a popular option in the Python community well known for it's documentation and add-ons system. If you choose this option, please read http://www.theherokuhackersguide.com/ by Randall Degges.

➤ PythonAnywhere (https://www.pythonanywhere.com) is a Python-powered PaaS that is incredibly beginner friendly.

Why do we like these services? We've evaluated them carefully for our needs. Your needs may be different, so read on about how to choose a PaaS.

27.1   Evaluating a PaaS

When a PaaS is chosen to host a project, that project forces architecture concessions in order for the application to work in their system. Therefore, even if we heed our warning at the top of this chapter, extracting ourselves from the PaaS takes effort and time.

Therefore, when a PaaS is chosen for a project, or while we are using a PaaS, we constantly consider the following:

27.1.1   Compliance

Before you begin evaluating any other aspect, it's critical to check to see if the PaaS meets local or federal mandates. Examples:

➤ Many medical-based projects in the United States require meeting HIPAA standards. If the PaaS doesn't meet HIPAA standards, and the project contains user medical data and a project is deployed there, *everyone involved is at risk for civil and criminal prosecution under Title II of HIPAA*. See https://en.wikipedia.org/wiki/HIPAA#Security_Rule

➤ Most e-commerce projects require at least SSL, and anything dealing with credit cards needs to adhere to PCI. While services like Stripe often make this moot, many projects require internal integration of credit card processing. Make sure the PaaS complies with the PCI specification. See http://2scoops.co/wikipedia-PCI-standard.

27.1.2   Pricing

Most PaaS options provide a free tier for beginner and toy projects, and Heroku and PythonAnywhere are good examples of this trend. We've gotten a lot of mileage out of this, and it's been great. You can even add extra services for a reasonable monthly fee. However, if one loses track of projects and services, then this 'reasonable fee' can quickly add up to a hefty monthly service bill. Therefore, it's a good idea to keep up on service costs and your monthly provider bills.

At the other end of things, if high traffic is anticipated, it's a good idea to see how much a site will cost with all the settings dialed up. For example, Heroku maxed out on dynos and enterprise PostgreSQL will cost over $40,000 a month. While the chances of a project needing this much horsepower is slim, the fact that Heroku offers this means that it can and does happen.

While all of this is going on, keep in mind that PaaS companies are under no legal or moral obligation to keep their prices or pricing methods static. In fact, developers we know of have built architecture for projects to take advantage of how billing is done by a PaaS, only to face crippling bills when the said PaaS changes its terms. To make matters worse, because they had tied their internal infrastructure tightly to the billing structure of the PaaS, they lacked the option of quickly moving off.

27.1.3   Uptime

For PaaS this is a very tricky issue. They would really like to provide 99.999999% uptime (sometimes referred to as the 'nines'), but even with the best engineering, it's not entirely under their control:

> ➤ Most of them, including Heroku and PythonAnywhere, rent space from vendors such as AWS and Rackspace. If those services go down, then they go down.
> ➤ All of them are reliant on the physical infrastructure of the internet. Natural disasters or industrial accidents can bring everything to a halt.

Even if we ignore these factors, providing a PaaS infrastructure is a hard business. It's more than standing up servers or Linux containers, it's maintaining a billing system, customer-facing tools, customer contact systems, and a host of other systems. This volume of work, challenging in its own right, can conflict with the business of making sure our projects work and scale as we need them.

That said, because it is integral to their business to provide consistent service, they aim for as high a stability number as they can. In general most PaaS companies have pretty good uptime, slowly increasing over time as they make continual system improvements. Furthermore, the good companies provide status pages and publish formal reports about any outages or issues. Therefore, we don't bother with reading outage reports that are over a few months old, as they are not indicative of the current engineering status of a company.

However, if there are recent, multiple reports of outages, or a recent outage of an unacceptable duration, we consider other PaaS options.

WARNING: If You Need Very High Uptime

It's worth mentioning that for projects that are life-critical, i.e. people could die if they lack immediate access, then a PaaS is not the right solution. Instead, please use a infrastructure service that provides a formal Service License Agreement.

27.1.4   Staffing

Yes, it's important to know about the staffing level of a PaaS:

- ➤ If a PaaS lacks staff, then they can't provide 24x7 engineering support, especially across holidays. No matter how enthusiastic a small shop is, and the deals they offer, they can't fix problems when their engineer is sleeping.
- ➤ Do they have the staff to answer emails and problem tickets? If their engineering staff is managing all of these requests, when do they have time to maintain the system?

We recommend testing out their level of support and responsiveness by filing a support ticket early on. Use this opportunity to ask a thoughtful question about something that's unclear in their documentation, or get needed help from their staff.

27.1.5   Scaling

How easy is it to scale up? If an e-commerce site is mentioned on CNN or on national television, can the site be dialed up quickly?

On the flip side, how easy it is to scale back down? Sometimes a traffic spike is followed by slow periods and it should be easy to dial things back.

Finally, can we automate this process?

27.1.6   Documentation

In chapter 21, *Documentation: Be Obsessed* we make it pretty clear that we really care about documentation. While we readily admit to exploiting every channel we know to ask questions (see chapter 31, *Where and How to Ask Django Questions*), we want the services that we use to have good, maintained documentation. It's important to have this as readily-found reference material, and it demonstrates that the PaaS in question is serious about what they do.

TIP: Why We Don't Document How each PaaS works

Every PaaS changes their API and documentation over time, some more rapidly than others. Since the Django PaaS space is still evolving rapidly, specific PaaS commands and instructions are not listed here. We ask the reader to follow the documentation listed on the PaaS provider site.

27.1.7   Performance Degradation

Sometimes a project that has been running for a while under consistent load starts to slow down. When this occurs, it could be caused by one or more problems. We use the following workflow:

❶ Check the project's commit history for changes could have caused a performance degradation. There may even be a major bug hiding.

❷ Examine the project for undiscovered performance bottlenecks. See chapter 22, *Finding and Reducing Bottlenecks.*

❸ Ask the PaaS support team to look into the problem. They might have a quick answer for you.

❹ The physical hardware that the project is running on might have a problem. The 'cloud' is actually hardware and hardware breaks or gets old. Start up a new project instance, port the data, and update the DNS records to match if that resolves the issue.

❺ Ask the PaaS support team for further assistance. It doesn't hurt to ask for help, especially as a paying customer.

If none of this works, consider running the project on another PaaS or your own servers. If it runs well in another environment, it might be time to move it off.

TIP: Free/Beginner Tiers will Run Slowly

The free tier of any PaaS is not going to run fast or handle any significant load. That takes resources that cost the PaaS money. Even with the hefty angel or VC funding in the tech industry, it's just not going to happen. If the PaaS provides a free or inexpensive tier that handles very high loads, see the next section on 'Company Stability.'

27.1.8   Geography

Consider the location of primary usage compared to the location of the PaaS. For example, if the majority of users are in China, then a PaaS that only serves from US-based data centers isn't a good option. Latency issues can cause clients and users to become quickly unhappy with a project.

27.1.9   Company Stability

A PaaS is an enormous undertaking. When done well, it requires a lot of overhead. Engineers, servers, customer support, account, and marketing are all expensive business. Since the advent of PaaS solutions, we've seen a number of them fail because of lack of sales, over expenditure of funds, and sheer exhaustion by overworked staff. Fortunately, they've all provided a grace period during which projects were given time to move off, but it's not realistic to count on that.

Therefore, it behooves us to look at the pricing plans carefully. Once a PaaS is out of its beta or initial launch period, if there isn't a way to capture profitability, then using the PaaS is risky.

27.2 Best Practices for Deploying to PaaS

27.2.1 Aim For Identical Environments

The holy grail of deployment is identical environments between development and production. However, as soon as you decide to use a PaaS, this is no longer possible as the production system configuration is beyond your control. Nevertheless, the closer your can keep things identical between development and production the more maintainable your project will be.

Some PaaS platforms provide tools like Heroku's Foreman to provide a very loosely similar operating process. However, there is nothing like using Linux locally to replicate production. We cover this in chapter 29, *Identical Environments: The Holy Grail.*

27.2.2 Automate All the Things!

When it comes time to push an update to a production instance, it's never a good idea to do all the steps manually. It's simply too easy to make a mistake. Our solution is to use simple automation using one of the following tools:

> ➤ **Makefiles** are useful for simple projects. Their limited capability means we won't be tempted to make things too fancy. As soon as you need more power, it's time to use something else. Something like Invoke as described in the next bullet.
> ➤ **Invoke** is the direct descendant of the venerable **Fabric** library. It is similar to Fabric, but is designed for running tasks locally rather than on a remote server. Tasks are defined in Python code, which allows for a bit more complexity in task definitions (although it's easy to take things too far). It has full support for Python 3.3.

27.2.3   Maintain a Staging Instance

With automation often comes the ability to run staging instances of projects at a lower cost tier. This is a great place to test production deployments, not to mention a place to demo feature changes.

27.2.4   Prepare for Disaster With Backups And Rollbacks

Even with all the precautions we take, sometimes deployments just blow up. Therefore, before any change is pushed a live site, we make certain for a particular PaaS we know how to:

➤ Restore databases and user-uploaded files from backups.

➤ Roll back to a previous code push.

27.2.5   Keep External Backups

The great virtue of PaaS is that they abstract away many deployment and operational issues, allowing us to focus on writing our project. With that comes the risk that the PaaS might encounter their own problems. While some PaaS (including Heroku) provide the capability to generate backups, it's a good idea to periodically run backups to external services. This includes the databases and uploaded user files.

Suggestions for storing the data include Dropbox, Crashplan, Amazon S3, and Rackspace Cloud Files, but there are many more. Which service to choose should be based on architectural decisions such as the location of the PaaS (For example, Heroku-based projects would use Amazon services).

27.3   Summary

Platforms as a Service are a great way to expedite delivery of deployable projects. They allow for developers to quickly harness significant resources that are maintained by specialized operations teams. On the other hand, they do come with a price tag and various limitations. Therefore, deciding to use a PaaS should be based per the project and skill set at hand, not out of personal preference.

In addition, it's a good idea to honor the practices we provide in this chapter, or to listen carefully to peers to determine what they do to best utilize these services.

In the next chapter, we cover the nuts and bolts of deployment at a high level.

28 | Deploying Django Projects

Deployment of Django projects is an in-depth topic that could fill an entire book on its own. Here, we touch upon deployment at a high level.

28.1 Single-Server For Small Projects

If our Django project is small and we're not expecting a large number of users, then a single-server setup should be sufficient.

A single-server setup might have all of this on a single server, with options listed below in descending order of author preference:

- ➤ Relational database
    1. PostgreSQL
    2. MySQL
- ➤ Production-quality HTTP server
    1. Nginx + uWSGI
    2. Nginx + gunicorn
    3. Apache + mod_wsgi
- ➤ Process manager
    1. **Supervisord**
    2. **init scripts**
- ➤ NoSQL store for handling ephemeral data
    1. Redis for caching and asynchronous message queues
    2. Memcached for caching
    3. RabbitMQ for asynchronous message queues

28.2   Multi-Server For Medium to Large Projects

Companies and growing startups who opt not to use a PaaS typically use a multi-server setup.

28.2.1   Basic Multi-Server Setup

Here is what a basic multi-server setup might look like:

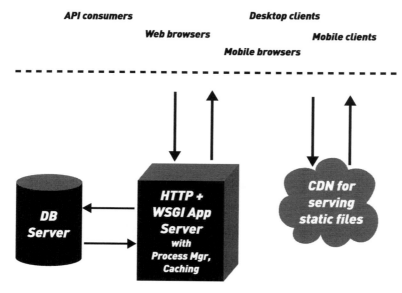

Figure 28.1: Example of a basic multi-server setup.

This is what you need at the most basic level:

➤ **Database server**. Typically PostgreSQL in our projects.
➤ **WSGI application server**. Typically uWSGI or Gunicorn behind Nginx, or Apache with mod_wsgi.

We'll also need to be able to manage processes. For larger scale efforts we recommend in descending order of preference:

❶ **Supervisord**

❷ **init scripts**

Additionally, we may also want one or more of the following:

> **Static file server**. If we want to do it ourselves, Nginx or Apache are fast at serving static files. However, CDNs such as Amazon CloudFront are relatively inexpensive at the basic level.
> **Caching server**, running Redis, Memcached or Varnish.
> **Miscellaneous server**. If our site performs any CPU-intensive tasks, or if tasks involve waiting for an external service (e.g. the Twitter API) it can be convenient to offload them onto a server separate from your WSGI app server.

By having specialized servers that each focus on one thing, they can be switched out, optimized, or changed in quantity to serve a project's needs.

TIP: Using Redis for All Ephemeral Data

Redis has similar features to Memcached, but adds in the following:
> Authentication, which Memcached doesn't have out of the box.
> State is saved, if a server is restarted the data doesn't go away.
> Additional data types means it can be used as an asynchronous message queue, in conjunction with tools like **celery** and **rq**.

28.2.2   Advanced Multi-Server Setup

Here is an example of a much larger multi-server setup, complete with multiple servers of each type and load balancing:

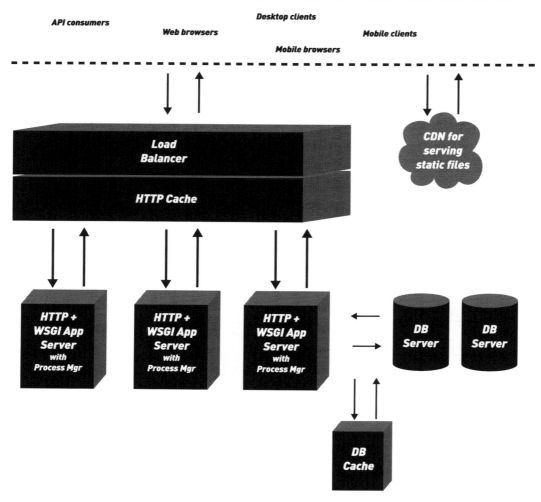

Figure 28.2: Example of an advanced multi-server setup.

Load balancers can be hardware- or software-based. Commonly-used examples include:

> ➤ **Software-based**: HAProxy, Varnish, Nginx
> ➤ **Hardware-based**: Foundry, Juniper, DNS load balancer
> ➤ **Cloud-based**: Amazon Elastic Load Balancer, Rackspace Cloud Load Balancer

---

TIP: Horizontal vs. Vertical Scaling

The above is an example of horizontal scaling, where more servers are added to handle load. Before scaling horizontally, it's good to scale vertically by upgrading your servers' hardware and maxing out the RAM on each server. Vertical scaling is relatively easy, since it's just a matter of throwing money at the problem.

TIP: Scaling Horizontally and Sessions

When scaling horizontally, make sure that users don't need sticky sessions. For example, if someone uploads a file to server 1, and then comes back thru the load balancer and lands on server 2, that shouldn't cause problems. Ways around this are storing uploaded media in a common shared drive or more commonly on cloud-based systems such as Amazon S3.

28.3   WSGI Application Servers

Always deploy your Django projects with **WSGI**.

Django 1.6's `startproject` command, sets up a *wsgi.py* file for us. This file contains the default configuration for deploying our Django project to any WSGI server. For what it's worth, the sample project templates we recommend in chapter 3, *How to Lay Out Django Projects* also includes a *wsgi.py* in it's *config/* directory.

The most commonly-used WSGI deployment setups are:

❶ **uWSGI** behind a **Nginx** proxy.
❷ **Gunicorn** behind a **Nginx** proxy.
❸ **Apache** with **mod_wsgi**.

Here's a quick summary comparing the three setups.

Setup	Advantages	Disadvantages
uWSGI behind Nginx	Written in pure C. Lots of great features and options. Said to be better performing than the other setup options.	Documentation still growing. Not as time-tested as Apache.
Gunicorn (sometimes with Nginx)	Gunicorn is written in pure Python. Supposedly this option has slightly better memory usage, but your mileage may vary.	Documentation is brief for nginx (but growing). Not as time-tested as Apache.
Apache with mod_wsgi	Has been around for a long time and is tried and tested. Very stable. Works on Windows. Lots of great documentation, to the point of being kind of overwhelming.	Doesn't work with environment variables. Apache configuration can be overly complex and painful for some. Lots of crazy conf files.

Table 28.1: Gunicorn vs Apache vs uWSGI

WARNING: Do Not Use mod_python

In 2013 the mod_python project, dead since 2010, was relaunched independently of the Apache Software Foundation by its founder, Grisha Trubetskoy. There is even WSGI compatibility in this new version. However, *relaunched doesn't mean ready for production.*

For the moment, the official Django documentation explicitly warns against using mod_python and we concur. Even if the project is reborn, the lack of evidence of production releases causes us to be extremely cautious about using it for real projects. Until there are a substantial number of positive usage reports, we suggest that you only use the new mod_python HTTP server for experimental purposes.

Nevertheless, we salute and encourage Grisha's efforts.

There's a lot of debate over which option is faster. Don't trust benchmarks blindly, as many of them are based on serving out tiny "Hello World" pages, which of course will have different performance from real web applications.

Ultimately, though, all three choices are in use in various high volume Django sites around the world. Configuration of any high volume production server can be very difficult, and if a site is busy enough it's worth investing time in learning one of these options very well.

The disadvantage of setting up our own web servers is the added overhead of extra sysadmin work. It's like making ice cream from scratch rather than just buying and eating it. Sometimes we just want to buy ice cream so we can focus on the enjoyment of eating it.

Each server has its own quirks, and we'll cover a few of them below:

28.3.1   uWSGI and Django

uWSGI is quickly growing in popularity amongst Django developers who enjoy playing around with system engineering. As it's still relatively new, articles and resources on the subject can be hard to find.

Useful reading:

- ➤ http://uwsgi-docs.readthedocs.org
- ➤ https://docs.djangoproject.com/en/1.6/howto/deployment/wsgi/uwsgi/
- ➤ http://justcramer.com/2013/06/27/serving-python-web-applications/
  David Cramer's blog article arguing for using Nginx + UWSGI

28.3.2   Apache and Environment Variables

Apache doesn't work with environment variables as described in chapter 5. You'll need to do something like load a local configuration file for secret values into your settings module written in .ini, .cfg, .json, or .xml formats. Please read section 5.4, 'When You Can't Use Environment Variables'.

28.3.3   Apache and Virtualenv

Thanks to the hard work of Graham Dumpleton, getting Apache to work with virtualenv is a task that's pretty straightforward:

- ➤ If using mod_wsgi 3.4 or newer and daemon mode, just add the following option to the `WSGIDaemonProcess` directive:

  `python-home=/some/path/to/root/of/virtualenv`
- ➤ If using embedded mode: `WSGIPythonHome /some/path/to/root/of/virtualenv`
- ➤ If using mod_wsgi 3.3 or older and daemon mode, instead use the following option to `WSGIDaemonProcess` where X.Y is the Python version: `python-path=/some/path/to/root/of/virtualenv/lib/pythonX.Y`

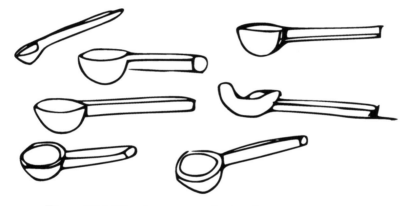

Figure 28.3: How ice cream is deployed to cones and bowls.

28.4   Automated, Repeatable Deployments

When we configure our servers, we really shouldn't be SSHing into our servers and typing in configuration commands from memory. It's too easy to forget what we've done. If servers configured this way go down and need to be recreated in an emergency, it's almost impossible to set them up identically to what we had before.

Instead, our server setup should be automated and documented in a way that makes it trivial to recreate everything from scratch. In the reader's case, you or your sysadmin should be able to set up everything without having to log into a single server manually.

Specifically, this means:

➤ We should be able to spin up and configure our entire server setup from scratch by running a command, then sitting back and watching as everything happens automatically.

➤ Even if it's just a single command, it should be documented precisely. Imagine that someone just got hired by our company. On their first day of work, without knowledge of our web application or servers, he or she should be able to open your ***deployment.rst*** document and set up our production servers.

➤ Each time we run the command, there should be no dependency on pre-existing server state.

➤ Any scripts should be idempotent, producing the same results no matter whether they are run for the first time or the hundredth time.

In order to achieve all of the above, we typically use one or more infrastructure automation and management tools.

Figure 28.4: Infrastructure automation can be very powerful.

28.4.1 Infrastructure Automation Tools

Among Django users, Ansible, SaltStack, Puppet, and Chef are the most popular tools for automating deployments.

All of these automation tools tend to be complex to set up and use, with a steep learning curve. That's because they're designed to manage not just one server, but thousands or more.

Here is what these tools can perform at large scale:

Remote execution:

➤ Installing packages via apt-get or other system package management tools on remote servers
➤ Running commands on remote servers. For example, running the virtualenv command with the –no-site-packages option on staging/production servers.
➤ Starting services, and restarting them under certain conditions. For example, restarting an Nginx web server when the site's Nginx configuration file changes.
➤ When a command is executed remotely, logging and returning the response from the server.

Configuration management:

➤ Creating or updating conf files for services. For example, creating a pg_hba.conf file for a freshly installed PostgreSQL instance.
➤ Populating configuration values differently for different servers, based on variables like each server's particular IP address or OS-specific information.

Orchestration and targeting:

➤ Controlling which servers a job is sent to, and when it should be sent.
➤ Managing various components at a high level, creating pipelines to handle different workflows.
➤ Pushing jobs to servers from a master server, in push mode.
➤ Asking the master server what needs to occur, in pull mode.

Ansible, SaltStack, Puppet, and Chef are pretty similar and can perform all of the above. Let's explore what differentiates them:

Tool	Pros	Cons
SaltStack	Primarily push mode. Blazing fast transport via 0mq. YAML config. Lots of Salt states and examples online. Large community. Open source. Written in Python.	Complexity can be a bit overwhelming at first.
Ansible	Primarily push mode. Slower transport over SSH, but can use Fireball Mode which sets up a temporary 0mq daemon. Doesn't require daemons running on remote servers aside from OpenSSH. YAML config. Open source. Written in Python.	Newer and still evolving, so there are less examples available. No official WSGI or Django example.
Chef	Lots of recipes available. Large community. Open source.	Extremely steep learning curve. Written in Ruby, and recipes are written in Ruby.
Puppet	Large community. Open source.	Steep learning curve. Written in Ruby. Config is written in a custom DSL which can be difficult to work with.

Table 28.2: Infrastructure Automation Tool Comparison

TIP: What about Fabric and Invoke?

Fabric and it's Python 3-friendly successor Invoke are tools that allow you to execute remote commands. Smaller in scope than the above, it focuses on doing one thing well. It is frequently used in conjunction with all of the above tools.

A few years ago, the hot topic of every Python meetup seemed to be deployment configuration with Puppet, Chef, and Fabric. This combination is still in heavy use today by many companies.

The trend now seems to be SaltStack or Ansible. Since they're written in Python, as a Python user it's easy to dig into their source code. The reality of development is that whenever you rely on a tool for long enough at large scale, you end up hitting bugs or interesting edge cases. When this happens, you'll be grateful that you can search the issue tracker, find others with the same problem, and look at or even modify source code if you need to.

Keep in mind that things are evolving quickly. If you spend a lot of your time on devops, you need to read blogs, follow other operations engineers on Twitter, attend infrastructure-related meetups, and keep the pulse of new developments.

Figure 28.5: Hopefully, one day someone will invent a one-button machine that deploys Django projects and makes ice cream.

28.4.2 SaltStack

A typical SaltStack setup for Django project server provisioning consists of a master server and multiple minion servers.

The master server is where all of the Salt states reside. These tell Salt what installation, configuration, and other setup steps need to occur on the minion servers. Installation of Salt is easy since salt-master and salt-minion are available in all major distro package managers. It's good practice to keep your project's Salt states in a directory that is version-controlled with its own separate repo.

The minions are all the servers that are needed to run your Django project. Your web application servers (WSGI servers), database servers, caching servers, and any other servers all start out as blank servers with a fresh operating system install (e.g. Ubuntu 12.04 LTS). During provisioning, your Salt master server tells the minions what software needs to be installed and what config steps need to be performed.

To create those fresh virtual servers in the first place, typically you either use salt-cloud (part of core Salt) or you write Fabric scripts that hit your cloud server provider's API to set up as many server instances as your project needs.

SaltStack officially maintains a number of pre-written Salt states, which they call **formulas**. We recommend starting out with their Django formula and adapting it to fit your project setup's needs: https://github.com/saltstack-formulas/django-formula

In addition to setting up your staging and production servers, Salt is also great for setting up your development team's local dev environments. See chapter 29, *Identical Environments: The Holy Grail*, for more details.

TIP: Alternate Configurations: Masterless and Local Master

For smaller projects, you can either:

➤ Use Salt in masterless mode, setting up your staging and production servers as minions.
➤ Install Salt locally and use your local development machine as the master.

TIP: Advice From the SaltStack Team

➤ Salt-ssh allows you to run salt commands and states without installing the Salt agent on servers you wish to control.
➤ You can run the salt-master and salt-minion on the same machine, if desired.

Barry Morrison maintains a SaltStack setup that includes Django, PostgreSQL, and many other tools. It includes a Vagrant setup, something we cover in the next chapter. See https://github.com/esacteksab/Salted-Django

28.4.3   Ansible

While the Ansible community is smaller than the SaltStack community, it is growing very rapidly due to Ansible's simplicity, elegant design, and small learning curve.

A very good start-to-finish example of using Ansible for single-server provisioning of a Django project can be found in Test-Driven Web Development with Python, at
`http://chimera.labs.oreilly.com/books/1234000000754/`

28.5   Summary

In this chapter we provided a very high level overview for deploying Django projects, including basic descriptions of single and multi-server setups. We also covered different WSGI application servers and different methods to automate infrastructure tasks.

In the next chapter we'll cover an offshoot of automated deployment: identical environments.

29 | Identical Environments: The Holy Grail

Taking things a step further, consider this: what if our development environment was identical to our project's staging, test, and production environments?

Of course, that might not be possible. If our production infrastructure consists of 10,000 servers, it's completely unrealistic to have another 10,000 local servers for development purposes.

But there are environment differences that you can eliminate:

➤ Choice of operating system. If we're developing on a Mac or on Windows, and if our site is deployed on Ubuntu Linux, then there are huge differences between how our Django project works locally and how it works in production.

➤ Python setup differences. Let's face it, many developers and sysadmins don't even know which version of Python they have running locally, although no one will admit it. Why? Because setting up Python properly and understanding your setup completely is hard.

Okay, so how do we eliminate these differences?

You could give up that silvery new MacBook Pro and get yourself hardware that's identical to your production site's hardware. Install the same production operating system, and configure your dev setup identically. Re-install the OS and re-configure everything every time you make a change.

Oh wait, that's not practical at all! That's like going to the supermarket every time you want to eat a spoonful of ice cream. It's just going to be annoying.

Here are the actual realistic options as of this writing:

➤ Develop inside of a virtual machine. This used to be a lot more impractical than it is today: you'd have to start up a VM and either SSH in manually (pretty slow) or use the VM's desktop GUI (unbearably slow). But now things are different. With Vagrant and advances in computing power, this is easy enough to do.

➤ Develop inside of a Docker-managed LxC container. This option is sort of like developing inside of a VM, except more lightweight. An LxC container shares the host OS but has its own isolated process and memory space. With Docker, for development purposes an LxC container behaves as if it were a VM.

29.1   The Present: Vagrant

Vagrant (`http://www.vagrantup.com`) is a wrapper around VirtualBox and other virtualization platforms. It allows you to spin up a virtual machine (VM) at the command line with just one command. VM instances created with Vagrant are headless and accessible via command line, without the overhead of the desktop GUI.

29.1.1   Advantages of Vagrant

One of the best things about Vagrant is that our VM can automatically be provisioned via shell scripts, Salt, Ansible, Chef, or Puppet. This allows us to:

➤ Set up identical local development environments for everyone on our project's dev team.
➤ Configure these local development environments in a way similar to our staging, test, and production servers.
➤ Strongly encourages us to learn and use an automated provisioning system like SaltStack, Ansible, Chef, or Puppet.
➤ Has great integration with VirtualBox.

With our team's local dev environments all created and provisioned automatically in the same way, we know that no one's setup only works with some unknown custom configuration. With the isolation of a VM, we eliminate problems caused by different developers having different operating systems. Overall, we save hours and hours of troubleshooting.

29.1.2   Disadvantages of Vagrant

The potential downsides of Vagrant are:

- ➤ Automatic configuration should not replace understanding of the underlying architecture of a project.
- ➤ On older development machines, running virtual instances can slow performance to a crawl.

29.1.3   Vagrant Resources

- ➤ `http://www.vagrantup.com` Vagrant home page.
- ➤ `https://www.virtualbox.org` VirtualBox home page.
- ➤ `http://2scoops.co/gswd-introduction-and-launch` The 'Getting Started with Django' introduction includes Vagrant instructions.

29.2   Experimental: Docker

Docker (`http://www.docker.io`) is an open-source project that allows us to easily create lightweight, portable, self-sufficient Linux containers (LXC) from any application. These are the same kind of containers used by many Platforms as a Service to host applications.

29.2.1   Advantages of Docker

Docker containers are individual units, but run in the same kernel as their host, allowing for extremely fast post-setup deployments. By leveraging Docker, we can:

- ➤ Automate the packaging and deployment of applications.
- ➤ Create lightweight, private Platform as a Service environments.
- ➤ Automate testing and **continuous integration** and deployment.
- ➤ Deploy and scale applications, databases, and backend services.
- ➤ Work in conjunction with Vagrant.

29.2.2   Warning: Docker Is Under Heavy Development

As useful as Docker promises to be, it's still in the early stages of development. As of January, 2013, `docker.io` still warns that it is under heavy development, and not for production. However, it does power the `dotCloud.com` PaaS that originated it, and many people have found Docker to be incredibly useful in production efforts.

Our contention is that Docker has a lot of promise, but being an early adopter requires good operations experience and the ability to assume some amount of risk during deployments.

29.2.3   Docker Resources

- `http://www.docker.io` Docker home page.
- `http://www.slideshare.net/fullscreen/dotCloud/why-docker/1`   Slide deck explaining Docker. Great first read!
- `http://www.docker.io/gettingstarted/#1` Interactive command line tutorial.
- `http://docs.docker.io/en/latest/` Docker Formal Documentation

29.3   Summary

Mirroring environments between development and other places means everything installs and performs almost identically. Every year, thanks to the growing capabilities of tools like Vagrant and VirtualBox, it becomes easier and easier to replicate environments between systems. Using these tools can make the life of a developer much easier and less stressful.

30 | Continuous Integration

Continuous integration (CI) is one of those things where, to explain the concept, we quote one of its originators:

> Continuous integration is a software development practice where members of a team integrate their work frequently, usually each person integrates at least daily — leading to multiple integrations per day. Each integration is verified by an automated build (including test) to detect integration errors as quickly as possible. Many teams find that this approach leads to significantly reduced integration problems and allows a team to develop cohesive software more rapidly.

> — Martin Fowler, `http://2scoops.co/martin-fowler-continuous-integration`

Here's a typical development workflow when using continuous integration:

❶ Developer writes code, runs local tests against it, then pushes the code to an instance of a code repository such as Git or Mercurial. This should happen at least once per day.

❷ The code repository informs an automation tool that code has not been submitted for integration.

❸ Automation integrates the code into the project, building out the project. Any failures during the build process and the commit is rejected.

❹ Automation runs developer-authored tests against the new build. Any failures of the tests and the commit is rejected.

❺ The developer is notified of success or the details of failure. Based on the report, the developer can mitigate the failures. If there are no failures, the developer celebrates and moves to the next task.

The advantages of this process are immediately clear. Thanks to continuous integration, we have the following:

➤ Earlier warnings of bugs and breakdowns.

➤ Deployment-breaking issues in the code are more frequently caught.

➤ Daily merges to the main trunk mean that no one's code dramatically changes the code base.

➤ Immediate positive and negative feedback is readily available about the project.

➤ Automation tools that make this possible include a lot of metrics that make both developers and managers happy.

30.1 Principles of Continuous Integration

Now that we've gone over why continuous integration is great, let's go over some key components when using this work process. This is our interpretation of principles explored Martin Fowler's discussion of the topic at http://2scoops.co/ci-practices

30.1.1 Write Lots of Tests!

One of the nice things about continuous integration is that it ties so well with everything we discuss in chapter 20. Without comprehensive tests, continuous integration simply lacks that killer punch. Sure, some people would argue that without tests, continuous integration is useful for checking if a deployment would succeed and keeps everyone on the same branch, but we think they are thinking from the perspective of statically-typed languages, where a successful compilation already provides significant guarantees regarding the functionality of the software.

30.1.2 Keeping the Build Fast

This is a tricky one. Your tests should arguably be running against the same database engine as your production machine. However, under certain circumstances, tests can take a minute or ten. Once a test suite takes that long, Continuous Integration stops being advantageous, and starts becoming a burden.

It's at this point that developers (including the authors) begin considering using Sqlite3 in-memory for tests. We'll admit that we've done it ourselves. Unfortunately, because SQLite3's behaves significantly differently than **PostgreSQL** or **MySQL**, this can be a mistake. For example, field types are not constrained the same way.

Here are a few tips for speeding up testing on large projects:

- ➤ Avoid fixtures. This is yet another reason why we advise against their use.
- ➤ Avoid `TransactionTestCase` except when absolutely necessary.
- ➤ Avoid heavyweight `setUp()` methods.
- ➤ Write small, focused tests that run at lightning speed, plus a few larger integration-style tests.
- ➤ Learn how to optimize your database for testing. This is discussed in public forums like Stack Overflow: `http://stackoverflow.com/a/9407940/93270`

30.2 Tools for Continuously Integrating your Project

Use the following tools:

30.2.1 Tox

`http://tox.readthedocs.org/`

This is a generic virtualenv management and testing command-line tool that allows us to test our projects against multiple Python and Django versions with a single command at the shell. You can also test against multiple database engines. It's how the authors and oodles of developers around the world check the compatibility of their code against different versions of Python.

If that isn't enough to convince you:

- ➤ Tox checks that packages install correctly with different Python versions *and interpreters*. Check on Python 2.7, 3.3, and PyPy all in one go!
- ➤ Tox runs tests in each of the environments, configuring your test tool of choice.
- ➤ Tox can act "as a frontend to continuous integration servers, reducing boilerplate and merging CI and shell-based testing."

30.2.2   Jenkins

http://jenkins-ci.org/

Jenkins is a extensible continuous integration engine used in private and open source efforts around the world. It is the standard for automating the components of Continuous Integration, with a huge community and ecosystem around the tool. If an alternative to Jenkins is considered, it should be done so after careful consideration.

30.3   Continuous Integration as a Service

Jenkins is an awesome tool, but sometimes you want to have someone else do the work in regards to setting it up and serving it. There are various services that provide automation tools powered by Jenkins or analogues. Some of these plug right into popular repo hosting sites like GitHub and BitBucket, and most provide free repos for open source projects. Some of our favorites include:

Service	Python Versions Supported	Link
Travis-CI	3.3, 3.2, 2.7, 2.6, PyPy	https://travis-ci.org
CircleCI	3.4, 3.3, 2.7, 2.6, PyPy, many more	https://circleci.com
Drone.io	2.7, 3.3	https://drone.io/

Table 30.1: Continuous Integration Services

30.4   Additional Resources

➤ http://en.wikipedia.org/wiki/Continuous_Integration
➤ http://jenkins-ci.org/
➤ http://www.caktusgroup.com/blog/2010/03/08/django-and-hudson-ci-day-1/
➤ http://bartek.im/showoff-jenkins/
➤ http://ci.djangoproject.com/
➤ http://docs.python-guide.org/en/latest/scenarios/ci.html

30.5 Summary

Continuous integration has become a standard for open-source and private projects around the world. While there is the cost of doing work up front, the benefits of safer deployments and more robust projects easily outweigh the investment. Furthermore, there are enough resources and recipes that setting up continuous integration is faster than ever.

One final note: even if tests are not written for a project, the practice of continual project building makes continuous integration worth the setup.

31 | Where and How to Ask Django Questions

All developers get stuck at one point or another on something that's impossible to figure out alone. When you get stuck, don't give up!

31.1 What to Do When You're Stuck

Follow these steps to increase your chances of success:

1. Troubleshoot on your own as much as possible. For example, if you're having issues with a package that you just installed, make sure the package has been installed into your virtualenv properly, and that your virtualenv is active.
2. Read through the documentation in detail, to make sure you didn't miss something.
3. See if someone else has had the same issue. Check Google, mailing lists, and StackOverflow.
4. Can't find anything? Now ask on StackOverflow. Construct a tiny example that illustrates the problem. Be as descriptive as possible about your environment, the package version that you installed, and the steps that you took.
5. Still don't get an answer after a couple of days? Try asking on the django-users mailing list or in IRC.

31.2 How to Ask Great Django Questions in IRC

IRC stands for **Internet Relay Chat**. There are channels like #python and #django on the Freenode IRC network, where you can meet other developers and get help.

A warning to those who are new to IRC: sometimes when you ask a question in a busy IRC channel, you get ignored. Sometimes you even get trolled by cranky developers. Don't get discouraged or take it personally!

The IRC #python and #django channels are run entirely by volunteers. You can and should help out and answer questions there too, whenever you have a few free minutes.

❶ When you ask something in IRC, be sure that you've already done your homework. Use it as a last resort for when StackOverflow doesn't suffice.

❷ Paste a relevant code snippet and traceback into `https://gist.github.com/` (or another pastebin).

❸ Ask your question with as much detail and context as possible. *Paste the link to your code snippet/traceback.* Be friendly and honest.

> ### TIP: Use a Pastebin!
>
> Don't ever paste code longer than a few characters into IRC. Seriously, don't do it. You'll annoy people. Use a pastebin!

❹ When others offer advice or help, thank them graciously and make them feel appreciated. A little gratitude goes a long way. A lot of gratitude could make someone's day. Think about how you would feel if you were volunteering to help for free.

31.3 Insider Tip: Be Active in the Community

The biggest secret to getting help when you need it is simple: be an active participant in the Python and Django communities.

The more you help others, the more you get to know people in the community. The more you put in, the more you get back.

31.3.1 10 Easy Ways to Participate

❶ Attend Python and Django user group meetings. Join all the local groups that you can find on `http://wiki.python.org/moin/LocalUserGroups`. Search meetup.com for Python and join all the groups near you.

❷ Attend Python and Django conferences in your region and country. Learn from the experts. Stay for the entire duration of the sprints and contribute to open-source projects. You'll meet other developers and learn a lot.

❸ Contribute to open source Django packages and to Django itself. Find issues and volunteer to help with them. File issues if you find bugs.

❹ Join #python and #django on IRC Freenode and help out.

❺ Find and join other smaller niche Python IRC channels. There's #pyladies, and there are also foreign-language Python IRC channels listed on `http://www.python.org/community/irc/`.

❻ Answer Django questions on StackOverflow.

❼ Meet other fellow Djangonauts on Twitter. Be friendly and get to know everyone.

❽ Join the Django group on LinkedIn, comment on posts, and occasionally post things that are useful to others.

❾ Volunteer for diversity efforts. Get involved with PyLadies and help make the Python community more welcoming to women. Remember that there are many angles to diversity: something as small as helping with a PyCon in an underrepresented country can make a major difference.

❿ Subscribe to Planet Django, an aggregated feed of blog posts about Django. Comment on blogs and get to know the community. `http://www.planetdjango.org/`

Figure 31.1: The ice cream eating help desk.

31.4   Summary

One of the strengths of Django is the human factor of the community behind the framework. Assume a friendly, open stance when you need guidance and odds are the community will rise to the task of helping you. They won't do your job for you, but in general they will reach out and attempt to answer questions or point you in the right direction.

32 | Closing Thoughts

While we've covered a lot of ground here in this second edition of the book. Yet this is just the tip of the ice cream cone. We plan to add more material and revise the existing material as time goes on, with a new edition released about once per year.

We'd genuinely love to hear from you, and so would the rest of the Django community. For specific book content-related feedback, this time around we're using GitHub issues to track submissions and commentary from readers. Report any of the following at `https://github.com/twoscoops/two-scoops-of-django-1.6/issues`:

- ➤ Did you find any of the topics unclear or confusing?
- ➤ Any errors or omissions that we should know about?
- ➤ What additional topics would you like us to cover in a future edition of this book?

We hope that this has been a useful and worthwhile read for you. If you enjoyed reading this book, please tell others by writing a positive review on Amazon. We need and appreciate your support.

This link will take you straight to the review page: `http://2scoops.co/1.6-review`

Cheers to your success with your Django projects!

Daniel Greenfeld and Audrey Roy

- ➤ `pydanny.com` / `audreyr.com` / `twoscoopspress.org`
- ➤ GitHub: @pydanny and @audreyr
- ➤ Twitter: @pydanny, @audreyr, and @twoscoopspress
- ➤ Facebook: twoscoopspress

Appendix A: Packages Mentioned In This Book

This is a list of the third-party Python and Django packages that we've described or mentioned in this book. We've also snuck in a few really useful packages that we don't mention in the book but that we feel are extremely useful.

As for the packages that we're currently using in our own projects: the list has some overlap with this list but is always changing. Please don't use this as the definitive list of what you should and should not be using.

Core

Django https://djangoproject.com
> The web framework for perfectionists with deadlines.

django-debug-toolbar http://django-debug-toolbar.readthedocs.org/
> Display panels used for debugging Django HTML views.

django-model-utils https://pypi.python.org/pypi/django-model-utils
> Useful model utilities including a time stamped model.

Pillow https://pypi.python.org/pypi/Pillow
> Friendly installer for the Python Imaging Library.

pip http://www.pip-installer.org
> Package installer for Python. Comes built-in with Python 3.4 or higher.

South http://south.readthedocs.org
> Easy database migrations for Django.

Sphinx http://sphinx-doc.org/
> Documentation tool for Python projects.

virtualenv http://virtualenv.org
> Virtual environments for Python.

virtualenvwrapper http://www.doughellmann.com/projects/virtualenvwrapper/
> Makes virtualenv better for Mac OS X and Linux!

Asynchronous

celery http://www.celeryproject.org/
> Distributed task queue.

django-celery http://docs.celeryproject.org/en/latest/django/
> Celery integration for Django.

rq https://pypi.python.org/pypi/rq
> A simple, lightweight, library for creating background jobs, and processing them.

Database

django-db-tools https://pypi.python.org/pypi/django-db-tools
> Great for flipping a site in and out of read-only mode.

psycopg2 https://pypi.python.org/pypi/psycopg2
> PostgreSQL database adapter.

South http://south.readthedocs.org
> Easy database migrations for Django.

Deployment

circus https://pypi.python.org/pypi/circus
> Program that lets you run and watch multiple processes and sockets. Used at Mozilla, complicated, and not for small projects.

dj-database-url https://pypi.python.org/pypi/dj-database-url
> This simple Django utility allows you to easily use Heroku for database access.

django-heroku-memcacheify https://pypi.python.org/pypi/django-heroku-memcacheify
> Easy Memcached settings configuration for Heroku.

Fabric https://pypi.python.org/pypi/Fabric

> Simple tool for remote execution and deployment.

Invoke https://pypi.python.org/pypi/invoke

> Like Fabric, but for creating and executing local tasks.

Supervisor http://supervisord.org/

> Supervisord is a client/server system that allows its users to monitor and control a number of processes on UNIX-like operating systems.

Forms

django-crispy-forms http://django-crispy-forms.readthedocs.org/

> Rendering controls for Django forms. Uses Twitter Bootstrap widgets by default, but skinnable.

django-floppyforms http://django-floppyforms.readthedocs.org/

> Form field, widget, and layout that can work with django-crispy-forms.

django-forms-bootstrap https://pypi.python.org/pypi/django-forms-bootstrap

> A simple form filter for using Django forms with Twitter Bootstrap.

Logging

logutils https://pypi.python.org/pypi/logutils

> Adds useful handlers for logging.

Sentry http://getsentry.com

> Exceptional error aggregation, with an open-source code base.

App Enlight https://appenlight.com/ Track errors and performance issues in your project.

Newrelic http://newrelic.com

> Realtime logging and aggregation platform.

Project Templates

Cookiecutter http://cookiecutter.readthedocs.org

> Not explicitly for Django, a command-line utility for creating project and app templates. It's focused, heavily tested and well documented. By one of the authors of this book.

django-twoscoops-project https://github.com/twoscoops/django-twoscoops-project
The sample project layout detailed in chapter 3 of this book.

django-skel https://github.com/rdegges/django-skel
Django project template optimized for Heroku deployments.

cookiecutter-django https://github.com/pydanny/cookiecutter-django
An alternative project layout by one of the authors of this book.

REST APIs

django-rest-framework http://django-rest-framework.org/
Expose model and non-model resources as a RESTful API.

django-tastypie http://django-tastypie.readthedocs.org
Expose model and non-model resources as a RESTful API.

Security

defusedxml https://pypi.python.org/pypi/defusedxml
Must-have Python library if you are accepting XML from any foreign source.

django-admin-honeypot https://pypi.python.org/pypi/django-admin-honeypot
A fake Django admin login screen to notify admins of attempted unauthorized access.

django-ratelimit-backend https://pypi.python.org/pypi/django-ratelimit-backend
Login rate-limiting at the auth backend level.

django-secure https://pypi.python.org/pypi/django-secure
Helps you lock down your site's security using practices advocated by security specialists.

django-sslify https://github.com/rdegges/django-sslify
Forcing HTTPs across your Django site.

Twine https://pypi.python.org/pypi/twine
Uses only verified TLS to upload to PyPI protecting your credentials from theft. Has other useful features worth looking at.

Testing

coverage http://coverage.readthedocs.org/
Checks how much of your code is covered with tests.

factory boy https://pypi.python.org/pypi/factory_boy

A package that generates model test data.

model mommy https://pypi.python.org/pypi/model_mommy

Another package that generates model test data.

mock https://pypi.python.org/pypi/mock

Not explicitly for Django, this allows you to replace parts of your system with mock objects. This project made its way into the standard library as of Python 3.3.

pytest http://pytest.org/

A mature full-featured Python testing tool that is very useful for Python and Django projects.

pytest-django http://pytest-django.readthedocs.org/

pytest-django is a plugin for py.test that provides a set of useful tools for testing Django applications and projects.

tox http://tox.readthedocs.org/

A generic virtualenv management and test command line tool that allows testing of projects against multiple Python version with a single command at the shell.

User Registration

django-allauth http://django-allauth.readthedocs.org/

General-purpose registration and authentication. Includes Email, Twitter, Facebook, GitHub, Google, and lots more.

python-social-auth http://django-social-auth.readthedocs.org/

Easy social authentication and registration for Twitter, Facebook, GitHub, Google, and lots more.

Views

django-braces http://django-braces.readthedocs.org

Drop-in mixins that really empower Django's class-based views.

django-extra-views http://django-extra-views.readthedocs.org/

Provides a number of additional generic class-based views to complement those provide by Django itself.

django-vanilla-views http://django-vanilla-views.org/

Simplifies Django's generic class-based views by simplifying the inheritance chain.

Miscellaneous

dj-stripe `https://pypi.python.org/pypi/dj-stripe`
    Django + Stripe made easy.

django-compressor `http://django-compressor.readthedocs.org/`
    Compresses linked and inline JavaScript or CSS into a single cached file.

django-extensions `http://django-extensions.readthedocs.org/`
    Provides `shell_plus` management command and a lot of other utilities.

django-haystack `http://django-haystack.readthedocs.org/`
    Full-text search that works with SOLR, Elasticsearch, and more.

django-pipeline `http://django-pipeline.readthedocs.org/`
    Compression of CSS and JS. Use with cssmin and jsmin packages.

django-htmlmin `https://pypi.python.org/pypi/django-htmlmin`
    HTML minifier for django.

envdir `http://envdir.readthedocs.org/` A Python port of daemontools' envdir.

flake8 `https://pypi.python.org/pypi/flake8`
    Checks code quality by using PyFlakes, pep8, and other tools.

pathlib `https://pypi.python.org/pypi/pathlib` Object-oriented filesystem paths being merged into Python as of release 3.4.

pip-tools `https://github.com/nvie/pip-tools`
    A set of tools to keep your pinned Python dependencies fresh.

python-dateutil `https://pypi.python.org/pypi/python-dateutil`
    Provides powerful extensions to Python's datetime module.

pyyaml `https://pypi.python.org/pypi/PyYAML`
    YAML parser and emitter for Python.

requests `http://docs.python-requests.org`
    Easy-to-use HTTP library that replaces Python's urllib2 library.

unicode-slugify `https://github.com/mozilla/unicode-slugify`
    A Mozilla-supported slugifier that supports unicode characters.

Unipath `https://pypi.python.org/pypi/Unipath`
    Object-oriented alternative to os/os.path/shutil.

Appendix B: Troubleshooting

This appendix contains tips for troubleshooting common Django installation issues.

Identifying the Issue

Often, the issue is one of:

- ➤ That Django isn't on your system path, or
- ➤ That you're running the wrong version of Django

Run this at the command line:

```
EXAMPLE 32.1
python -c "import django; print django.get_version()"
```

If you're running Django 1.6, you should see the following output:

```
EXAMPLE 32.2
1.6
```

Don't see the same output? Well, at least you now know your problem. Read on to find a solution.

Our Recommended Solutions

There are all sorts of different ways to resolve Django installation issues (e.g. manually editing your PATH environment variable), but the following tips will help you fix your setup in a way that is consistent with what we describe in chapter on The Optimal Django Environment Setup.

Check Your Virtualenv Installation

Is **virtualenv** installed properly on your computer? At the command line, try creating a test virtual environment and activating it.

If you're on a Mac or Linux system, verify that this works:

```
EXAMPLE 32.3
$ virtualenv testenv
$ source testenv/bin/activate
```

If you're on Windows, verify that this works:

```
EXAMPLE 32.4
C:\code\> virtualenv testenv
C:\code\> testenv\Scripts\activate
```

Your virtualenv should have been activated, and your command line prompt should now have the name of the virtualenv prepended to it.

On Mac or Linux, this will look something like:

```
EXAMPLE 32.5
(testenv) $
```

On Windows, this will look something like:

```
EXAMPLE 32.6
(testenv) >
```

Did you run into any problems? If so, study the Virtualenv documentation (http://virtualenv.org) and fix your installation of Virtualenv.

If not, then continue on.

Check if Your Virtualenv Has Django 1.6 Installed

With your virtualenv activated, check your version of Django again:

```
EXAMPLE 32.7

python -c "import django; print django.get_version()"
```

If you still don't see 1.6, then try using pip to install Django 1.6 into testenv:

```
EXAMPLE 32.8

(testenv) $ pip install Django==1.6
```

Did it work? Check your version of Django again. If not, check that you have **pip** installed correctly as per the official documentation (http://pip-installer.org).

Check for Other Problems

Follow the instructions in the official Django docs for troubleshooting problems related to running django-admin.py:
https://docs.djangoproject.com/en/1.6/faq/troubleshooting/

Appendix C: Additional Resources

This appendix lists additional resources that are applicable to modern Django and Python. While there is more content available then what is listed here, much of it is out of date. Therefore, we will only list content that is current and applicable to Django 1.6, Python 2.7.x, or Python 3.4.x.

Beginner Python Material

Learn Python the Hard Way

http://learnpythonthehardway.org/

If you don't know Python, this free for HTML, paid for lessons resources is one of the best places to start. The author takes you through Python the same way he learned guitar, through rote and repetition. Don't worry about the title, this is a good way to get started with Python.

Beginner Django Material

Official Django 1.6 Documentation

https://docs.djangoproject.com/en/1.6/

The official Django documentation has seen a significant amount of improvement with the release of versions 1.6 and 1.5. If you've used a previous version of Django, make sure that you are reading the correct edition of the documentation.

Tango with Django

http://www.tangowithdjango.com/

A free online book designed to get you going fast and to learn by example using Django 1.5.4.

Test-Driven Web Development with Python

http://chimera.labs.oreilly.com/books/1234000000754/ Harry Percieval's book is a great way to revisit the Django tutorial and learn agile/TDD processes at the same time. The HTML edition is even free!

Getting Started with Django

http://gettingstartedwithdjango.com/

Partially funded by the Django Software Foundation this is a free video lesson series for Django 1.5. The creator, Kenneth Love, was a technical reviewer for this book, and many of the practices advocated in the video series match those presented in this book.

More Advanced Django Material

Pro Django, 2rd Edition

http://amzn.to/1c3sOfj

A wonderful deep-dive into Django, this book has been updated for Python 3 and Django 1.5. We're friends and fans of the author, Marty Alchin, and readily admit that it helped us ramp up our Django skills.

ccbv.co.uk

http://ccbv.co.uk/

A website that has provides detailed descriptions, with full methods and attributes, for each of Django's class-based generic views.

pydanny's blog

http://pydanny.com/tag/django.html

A good amount of this blog is about modern Django. As the author of this blog is also one of this book's authors, the style of the blog loosely resembles the content of this book.

GoDjango

https://godjango.com

A series of short videos that each focus on something challenging to do with Django. The more recent episodes are for Django 1.5 and you can access more material by "going pro".

Getting Started with Django Rest Framework and AngularJS

http://www.2scoops.co/kevin-stone-django-angular-tutorial/ Kevin Stone's amazing Django + Angular tutorial is an epic piece of work. It's 25 pages long when printed out, and great for kickstarting yourself into understanding Django, Django Rest Framework, and Angular.js.

Django Model Behaviors

http://blog.kevinastone.com/django-model-behaviors.html

Kevin Stone explores how to structure models and associated code in large Django projects.

Two Scoops of Django: Best Practices for Django 1.5 (electronic version)

`http://2scoops.co/two-scoops-1.5`

The first edition of this book in electronic format.

Two Scoops of Django: Best Practices for Django 1.5 (print version)

`http://amzn.to/188W07W`

The first printed edition of this book, which you can still order from Amazon.

Useful Python Material

Python Cookbook, 3rd Edition

`http://amzn.to/I3Sv6q`

An incredible book by Python luminaries David Beazley and Brian Jones, it's filled with delicious ice cream recipes... err... incredibly useful Python recipes for any developer using Python 3.3 or greater.

Treading on Python Volume 2

`http://amzn.to/1kVWi2a`

Covers more advanced Python structures.

Writing Idiomatic Python 3.3

`http://amzn.to/1aS5df4`

Jeff Knupp's book has a lot of great tips for optimizing your code and increasing the legibility of your work. There are a few places where his work differs from our practices (imports being the largest area of difference), but overall we concur with his practices.

Writing Idiomatic Python 2.7

`http://amzn.to/1fj9j7z`

Jeff Knupp's Idiomatic Python, but for Python 2.7.3.

Lincoln Loop's Django Best Practices

`http://lincolnloop.com/django-best-practices/`

This free website resource is a really good reference of practices similar to those espoused in this book.

Effective Django

`http://effectivedjango.com`

Nathan Yergler's free website is an excellent combination of notes and examples developed for talks prepared for PyCon 2012, PyOhio 2012, PyCon 2013, and Eventbrite web engineering.

JavaScript Resources

Books:

Secrets of a JavaScript Ninja   (Print and Kindle)
> `http://amzn.to/18QzT0r`

Definitive Guide to JavaScript   (Print and Kindle)
> `http://amzn.to/1cGVkDD`

JavaScript: The Good Parts   (Print and Kindle)
> `http://amzn.to/1auwJ6x`

JavaScript Patterns   (Print and Kindle)
> `http://amzn.to/1dii9Th`

Web Resources:

Mozilla Developer Network
> `https://developer.mozilla.org/en-US/docs/Web/JavaScript`

Learning JavaScript Design Patterns
> `http://addyosmani.com/resources/essentialjsdesignpatterns/book/`

Stack Overflow
> `http://stackoverflow.com/questions/tagged/javascript`

WARNING: Stay Away From W3C Schools

One problem about JavaScript (and CSS) research on the web is that W3C Schools will turn up at the top of search engine results. This is unfortunate, because much of the data there is outdated enough to be incorrect. Be smart and avoid this resource.

We scan the results page for the Mozilla Developer Network (MDN) link, usually around the third position, and click on that one.

Appendix D: Internationalization and Localization

Django and Python provides a lot of very useful tools for dealing with **internationalization**, **localization**, and of course, **Unicode**.

This appendix, added as of the second edition, contains a list of things helpful for preparing your Django application for non-English readers and non-USA users. This list is by no means complete, and we invite the reader to provide additional feedback.

Start Early

It is always easier to start with and grow an internationalized, localized project than to convert an existing project.

Define Python Source Code Encodings

In PEP 263 we are given a formal specification for defining how encoding of Python modules is to occur. Amongst other things, this affects how Python handles unicode literals. To define this encoding in internationalized projects, at the top each module add:

EXAMPLE 32.9

```
# -*- coding: utf-8 -*-
```

Or as shown in the next code example:

EXAMPLE 32.10

```
#!/usr/bin/python
# -*- coding: utf-8 -*-
```

More information can be found at http://www.python.org/dev/peps/pep-0263/

Wrap Content Strings with Translation Functions

Every string presented to end users should be wrapped in a translation function. This is described in-depth in the official Django documentation on django.utils.translation at http://2scoops.co/1.6-translation. Since that is a lot of text to swallow, the table on the following page is a reference guide for knowing when and where to use what translation function for what tasks.

Function	Purpose	Link
ugettext()	For content executed at runtime, e.g. form validation errors.	http://2scoops.co/33
ugettext_lazy()	For content executed at compile time, e.g. verbose_name in models.	http://2scoops.co/32
string_concat()	Replaces the standard str.join() method for joining strings. Rarely used.	http://2scoops.co/37

Table 32.1: django.utils.translation Function Reference

Convention: Use the Underscore Alias to Save Typing

As you know, normally we aren't fans of abbreviations or shortcuts. However, in the case of internationalizing Python code, the existing convention is to use a _, or underscore, to save on letters.

EXAMPLE 32.11

```
# -*- coding: utf-8 -*-
```

```
from django.utils.translation import ugettext as _

print(_("We like gelato."))
```

Don't Interpolate Words in Sentences

We used to do this all the time, even in the previous (Django 1.5) edition of the book. This is when you use slightly-clever code to construct sentences out of various Python objects. For reference, this was part of Example 8.7:

```
BAD EXAMPLE 32.1
# DON'T DO THIS!

# Skipping the rest of imports for the sake of brevity
class FlavorActionMixin(object):

    @property
    def action(self):
        msg = "{0} is missing action.".format(self.__class__)
        raise NotImplementedError(msg)

    def form_valid(self, form):
        msg = "Flavor {0}!".format(self.action)
        messages.info(self.request, msg)
        return super(FlavorActionMixin, self).form_valid(form)

# Snipping the rest of this module for the sake of brevity
```

While seemingly handy in that it makes for a self-maintaining mixin, it is overly clever in we can't internationalize the result of calling self.__class__. In other words, you can't just add django.utils.translation the following and expect it to produce anything meaningful for translators to work from:

```
BAD EXAMPLE 32.2

# DON'T DO THIS!
from django.utils.translations import ugettext as _

# Skipping the rest of this module for the sake of brevity


    def form_valid(self, form):


        # This generates a useless translation object.
        msg = _("Flavor {0}!".format(self.action))
        messages.info(self.request, msg)
        return super(FlavorActionMixin, self).form_valid(form)


# Skipping the rest of this module for the sake of brevity
```

Rather than writing code that constructs sentences out of various Python constructs, now we write more meaningful dialogues that can be readily translated. This means a little more work, but the result is a more easily translatable project. Hence why we now follow this pattern:

```
EXAMPLE 32.12

# -*- coding: utf-8 -*-
# Skipping the rest of imports for the sake of brevity
from django.utils.translation import ugettext as _

class FlavorActionMixin(object):

    @property
    def success_msg(self):
        return NotImplemented


class FlavorCreateView(LoginRequiredMixin, FlavorActionMixin,
                        CreateView):
    model = Flavor


    # Slightly longer but more meaningful dialogue
    success_msg = _("Flavor created!")
```

```
# Skipping the rest of this module for the sake of brevity
```

For reference, you can combine individual strings representing meaningful sentences and dialogues into larger values. However, you shouldn't build sentences by concatenating pieces, because other languages may require a different order. For the same reason, you should always include punctuation in translated strings. See as follows:

```
EXAMPLE 32.13
# -*- coding: utf-8 -*-
from django.utils.translation import ugettext as _


class FlavorActionMixin(object):

    @property
    def success_msg(self):
        return NotImplemented


class FlavorCreateView(LoginRequiredMixin, FlavorActionMixin,
                       CreateView):
    model = Flavor

    # Example combining strings
    part_one = _("Flavor created! ")
    part_two = _("Let's go try it!")
    success_msg = part_one + part_two


# Skipping the rest of this module for the sake of brevity
```

Unicode Tricks

Here are some things we've learned when dealing with unicode-related issues.

Python 3 Can Make Unicode Easier

In our experience Python 3 makes unicode handling much, much easier. While in theory things can and are back-ported to Python 2.7, we've found that when using Python 3 we just don't have the same kinds of problems. If working on a new project, this is as good a reason as any to consider switching to Python 3.

Use django.utils.encoding.force_text() Instead of unicode()

When you are working with Python 2.7.x or Python 3.3+ and need to ensure that a useful string-type value is returned, don't use the unicode() or str() built-ins. What can happen is that under certain circumstances, instead of returning a unicode or str object, Django will return a nigh-meaningless django.utils.functional.__proxy__ object, which is a lazy instance of the data requested.

Instead, do as our friend Douglas Miranda suggested to us, and use django.utils.encoding.force_text. In the case that you are dealing with a proxy object or lazy instance, it resolves them as strings.

> ### TIP: Django is Lazy
>
> One of the ways that Django does optimizations is via lazy loading, a design pattern which defers initialization of an object until it is needed. The place where this is most obviously used is Django's ORM, as described at http://2scoops.co/1.6-querysets-are-lazy. This use of lazy objects can cause problems with display of content, hence the need for django.utils.encoding.force_text().

Browser Page Layout

Assuming you've got your content and Django templates internationalized and localized, you can discover that your layouts are broken.

A good Django-based example is Mozilla and their add-on site for Firefox at `https://add-ons.firefox.org`. On this site they handle translations for over 80 languages. Unfortunately, a title that fits the page in English breaks the site in more verbose languages such as German.

Mozilla's answer is to determine the width of a title container, then use JavaScript adjust the font size of the title text downwards until the text fits into the container with wrapping.

A simpler way of handling this issue is to assume that other languages can take up twice as much space as English. English is a pretty concise language that, because of its short words, handles text wrapping very well.

Appendix E: Settings Alternatives

Here a couple of alternative patterns for managing settings that we feel can be recommended. They avoid the **local_settings anti-pattern** and allow for management of configuration that will work with either the **Environment Variables Pattern** or the **Secrets File Pattern**.

> ## WARNING: Converting Existing Settings is Hard
>
> If you have an existing project using multiple settings modules and you want to convert it to the single settings style, you might want to reconsider. Migrating settings approaches is always a tricky process, and requires deep and wide test coverage. Even with the best test coverage, there is a chance it's not going to be worth it.
>
> For these reasons, we suggest being conservative about switching to new settings approaches. Only do it when the current settings management approach has become a pain point, not when a new method becomes popular.

Twelve Factor-Style Settings

If we're relying on environment variables, why not use the simplest *settings.py* system possible? Bruno Renié, creator of django-floppyforms and FeedHQ (https://feedhq.org), advocates an alternate approach to Django settings files, in which all environments use the same single settings file.

The argument for this approach is that when using the multiple settings files approach, you end up with environment-specific code. For instance, when doing local development, you're not running the code with production settings. This increases the chance of running into production-specific bugs when you update some code without updating the production settings accordingly.

This style involves using sensible default settings and as few environment specific values as possible. When combined with tools like **Vagrant** and **Docker**, it means that mirroring production is trivial.

It results in a much simpler settings file, and for Twelve Factor App fans, it's right in line with that approach.

If you want to see an example of the approach in action, check out FeedHQ's settings module:
`https://github.com/feedhq/feedhq/blob/master/feedhq/settings.py`

We've enjoyed this approach for new and smaller projects. When done right, it makes things elegantly simple.

However, it's not a perfect solution for all problems:

➤ It doesn't provide much benefit for simplification when development environments are drastically different than production.
➤ It doesn't work as well with projects being deployed to more than one operating system.
➤ Complex settings on large projects are not really simplified or shortened by this approach. It can be challenging to use on large or complex projects.

If you would like to know more about this approach, we recommend the following articles:

➤ `http://bruno.im/2013/may/18/django-stop-writing-settings-files/`
➤ `http://12factor.net/config`

Multiple Settings with Configuration Objects

One of the criticisms of the 'One True Way' approach to settings is that it relies on the use of `import *`. For some developers, this creates a case of *bad code smell*, and is one of the arguments for the **Twelve Factor-Style Settings** approach explored in the previous section. However, many developers like the multiple settings file approach as it works well on projects being deployed to multiple operating systems and environments, and it also breaks up overly large settings modules.

Fortunately, there is a version of the multiple settings approach that does explicit imports invented by Brandon Konkle that explores turning it on its head to implement explicit settings.

If you want to see how it's done, see `http://2scoops.co/bkonkle-inverted-one-true-way`.

> ### PACKAGE TIP: django-configurations
>
> This approach uses the noted django-configurations library to ease project configuration.

Appendix F: Working with Python 3

Django's official documentation has a well-written page that covers much of what's involved with working with Python 3. Here are some specific sections you should pay careful attention to:

Django Official Docs on Python 3 http://2scoops.co/1.6-python3
Coding Guidelines http://2scoops.co/1.6-python3-coding-guidelines
Writing Compatible Code with Six http://2scoops.co/1.6-python3-six

Here are some other things you should know.

Most Critical Packages Work with Python 3

As of the time of this writing, Django Packages lists over 205 packages that support Python 3. This includes such critical libraries as:

- ➤ Django itself
- ➤ South
- ➤ Pillow
- ➤ django-braces
- ➤ django-crispy-forms
- ➤ django-debug-toolbar
- ➤ django-floppyforms
- ➤ django-rest-framework
- ➤ python-requests

You can see a list of Django specific libraries at https://www.djangopackages.com/python3/.

Checking for Python 3 Compatibility

Here are the steps we follow in rough order when determining if a third-party library actually works with Python 3:

- ➤ Check on `https://www.djangopackages.com/python3/`.
- ➤ Look up the package on **PyPI** and see if any of its trove classifiers mention Python 3 status.
- ➤ See if a pull request for Python 3 support is outstanding.
- ➤ Run the test suite using Python 3.3.
- ➤ If a Django project, check the models for `__str__()` methods. If it has them, it's a pretty good indicator that it's Python 3.3 friendly.

Converting a Library to Work with Python 3.3

How we convert Python 2 code to Python 3:

- ➤ Get the test harness working with Python 3.
- ➤ Lean on `django.contrib.six` as much as possible. Add a *compat.py* module only if absolutely needed.
- ➤ Fix any problems you find in the code. Try to keep solutions as simple as possible.
- ➤ Submit the pull request.
- ➤ Politely poke the package owner to accept the pull request.
- ➤ Once the owner accepts the pull request, gently poke the package owner to push the update to PyPI.

TIP: Dealing with Slow Maintainers

Ranting to or complaining about slow-moving maintainers is absolutely counter-productive. People have lives and jobs that sometimes get in the way of open source. It's more productive to be patient, be polite, and if necessary do an absolutely minimal fork or find a working alternative.

Use Python 3.3.3 or Later

Django is a large, complicated system. While it's heavily tested for multiple versions of Python 3, we've found that it just works better with more recent versions of the language. For example, syncdb fails in curious ways with Python 3.3.0.

Working With Python 2 and 3

We usually encounter this scenario when we are writing a third-party package for use in Django or even just vanilla Python. However, there are use cases where an entire Django project might be deployed to Python 2.7 as well as Python 3.3. Fortunately, most of the following suggestions apply no matter the scale of the project.

Tests and Continuous Integration

If there isn't a working test harness and functioning continuous integration, now is the time to set it up. Testing compatibility across major Python versions simply requires automation.

Keep Compatibility Minimally Invasive

The last thing that a project needs is complex branches to deal with different versions of Python. Therefore, use the following imports at the top of a Python module to keep code identical:

EXAMPLE 32.14

```
# The __future__ imports in this module means that all code
# in this example will work identically in Python 2.7 and
# Python 3 or higher.


# Multi-Line and Absolute/Relative imports will work identically across
# Python versions.
from __future__ import absolute_import


# Any division will return float objects. Example 3 / 2 = 1.5
from __future__ import division
```

```
# All strings defined in Python 2 and 3 can use Python 3's name = 'django'
# syntax for defining unicode-friendly strings.
from __future__ import unicode_literals
```

When we do need more complexity or any sort of logic, that's when it's time to create a *compat.py* module.

Use django.utils.encoding.python_2_unicode_compatible in Models

Rather than write both __str__() and __unicode__() methods, use django.utils.encoding.python_2_unicode_compatible so it only has to be written once. See section 17.3, 'Viewing String Representations of Objects.'

Resources

The following are useful resources for Python 3 topics:

Porting Django apps to Python 3
http://youtu.be/cJMGvAYYUyY
This is Jacob Kaplan-Moss' PyCon US 2013 video on the subject.

Porting to Python 3
http://python3porting.com/
Lennart Regebro's free HTML or paid e-book bundle on the subject of moving from Python 2 to 3.

Python Cookbook, 3rd Edition
http://amzn.to/I3Sv6q
David Beazley and Brian Jones' book of handy recipes for Python 3.

Writing Idiomatic Python 3.3
http://amzn.to/1aS5df4
Jeff Knupp's guide to writing Python 3 code the 'right' way.

Acknowledgments

This book was not written in a vacuum. We would like to express our thanks to everyone who had a part in putting it together.

The Python and Django Community

The Python and Django communities are an amazing family of friends and mentors. Thanks to the combined community we met each other, fell in love, and were inspired to write this book.

Technical Reviewers for 1.6

We can't begin to express our gratitude to our technical reviewers. Without them this book would have been littered with inaccuracies and broken code.

Aymeric Augustin is a software engineer with a background in mathematics and computer science. He's a proud member of the Django community and an active committer since 2011. Most recently, he led the software team behind Autolib', a car sharing service. He lives in Paris, France.

Barry Morrison is a self-proclaimed geek, lover of all technology. He is a multidiscipline systems administrator with more than 10 years experience with Windows, Linux, and storage in both the public and private sectors. He is also a Python and Django aficionado and Arduino tinkerer. He lives in California.

Ken Cochrane is a senior member of the technical team at Docker Inc., the commercial entity behind the Docker project. Ken has been involved with Docker from the outset, and is responsible for a number of key aspects of the project, including the Docker Index and

Registry. He is a graduate of the University of Maine, and has led development projects for LL Bean, CashStar, Fairchild Semiconductor, and Wright Express.

Security Chapter Reviewer for 1.6

Paul McMillan found Django in 2008 while looking for a more structured approach to web programming. He stuck around after figuring out that the developers of Django had already invented many of the wheels he needed. His passion for breaking (and then fixing) things led to his current role working to maintain and improve the security of Django. Paul works in Berkeley, California as a web developer and security consultant.

Technical Reviewers for 1.5

The following individuals gave us their invaluable help, aid and encouragement for the initial release of this book. We give special recognition here to Malcolm for his contributions to this book and the world.

Malcolm Tredinnick lived in Sydney, Australia and spent much of his time travelling internationally. He was a Python user for over 15 years and Django user since just after it was released to the public in mid-2005, becoming a Django core developer in 2006. A user of many programming languages, he felt that Django was one of the better web libraries/frameworks that he used professionally and was glad to see its incredibly broad adoption over the years. In 2012 when he found out that we were co-hosting the first PyCon Philippines, he immediately volunteered to fly out, give two talks, and co-run the sprints. Sadly, he passed away in March of 2013, just two months after this book was released. His leadership and generosity in the Python and Django community will always be remembered.

The following were also critical in supporting the first edition of this book.

Kenneth Love
Lynn Root
Barry Morrison
Jacob Kaplan-Moss
Jeff Triplett
Lennart Regebro

Randall Degges
Sean Bradley

Chapter Reviewers for 1.5

The following are people who gave us an amazing amount of help and support with specific chapters during the writing of this book. We would like to thank Preston Holmes for his contributions to the User model chapter, Tom Christie for his sage observations to the REST API chapter, and Donald Stufft for his support on the Security chapter.

Alpha Reviewers for 1.5

During the Alpha period an amazing number of people sent us corrections and cleanups. This list includes: Brian Shumate, Myles Braithwaite, Robert Węglarek, Lee Hinde, Gabe Jackson, Jax, Baptiste Mispelon, Matt Johnson, Kevin Londo, Esteban Gaviota, Kelly Nicholes, Jamie Norrish, Amar Šahinović, Patti Chen, Jason Novinger, Dominik Aumayr, Hrayr Artunyan, Simon Charettes, Joe Golton, Nicola Marangon, Farhan Syed, Florian Apolloner, Rohit Aggarwa, Vinod Kurup, Mickey Cheong, Martin Bächtold, Phil Davis, Michael Reczek, Prahlad Nrsimha Das, Peter Heise, Russ Ferriday, Carlos Cardoso, David Sauve, Maik Hoepfel, Timothy Goshinski, Francisco Barros, João Oliveira, Zed Shaw, and Jannis Leidel.

Beta Reviewers for 1.5

During the Beta period an awesome number of people sent us corrections, cleanups, bug fixes, and suggestions. This includes: Francisco Barros, Florian Apolloner, David Beazley, Alex Gaynor, Jonathan Hartley, Stefane Fermigier, Deric Crago, Nicola Marangon, Bernardo Brik, Zed Shaw, Zoltán Árokszállási, Charles Denton, Marc Tamlyn, Martin Bächtold, Carlos Cardoso, William Adams, Kelly Nichols, Nick August, Tim Baxter, Joe Golton, Branko Vukelic, John Goodleaf, Graham Dumpleton, Richard Cochrane, Mike Dewhirst, Jonas Obrist, Anthony Burke, Timothy Goshinski, Felix Ingram, Steve Klass, Vinay Sajip, Olav Andreas Lindekleiv, Kal Sze, John Jensen, Jonathan Miller, Richard Corden, Dan Poirier, Patrick Jacobs, R. Michael Herberge, and Dan Loewenherz.

Final Reviewers for 1.5

During the Final period the following individuals sent us corrections, cleanups, bug fixes, and suggestions. This includes: Chris Jones, Davide Rizzo, Tiberiu Ana, Dave Castillo, Jason Bittel, Erik Romijn, Darren Ma, Dolugen Buuraldaa, Anthony Burke, Hamish Downer, Wee Liat, Álex González, Wee Liat, Jim Kalafut, Harold Ekstrom, Felipe Coelho, Andrew Jordan, Karol Breguła, Charl Botha, Fabio Natali, Tayfun Sen, Garry Cairns, Dave Murphy, Chris Foresman, Josh Schreuder, Marcin Pietranik, Vraj Mohan, Yan Kalchevskiy, Jason Best, Richard Donkin, Peter Valdez, Jacinda Shelly, Jamie Norrish, Daryl Yu, Xianyi Lin, Tyler Perkins, Andrew Halloran, Tobias G. Waaler, Robbie Totten, Gabriel Duman, Nick Smith, Lachlan Musicman, Eric Woudenberg, Jim Munro, Larry Prince, Hamid Hoorzad, Matt Harrison, Aymeric Augustin, Khee Chin, Douglas Miranda, Saul Shanabrook.

If your name is not on this list but should be, please send us an email so that we can make corrections!

Typesetting

We thank Laura Gelsomino for helping us with all of our LaTeX issues and for improving upon the book layout.

Laura Gelsomino is an economist keen about art and writing, and with a soft spot for computers, who found the meeting point between her interests the day she discovered LaTeX. Since that day, she habitually finds any excuse to vent her aesthetic sense on any text she can lay her hands on, beginning with her economic models.

We originally typeset the alpha version of the first editions with iWork Pages. Later editions of the book were written using LaTeX. All editions have been written on the Macbook Air.

Index

Made in the USA
Lexington, KY
23 February 2014